DEDICATION.

TO THE WIDOWS, CHILDREN, FATHERS, MOTHERS,

BROTHERS AND SISTERS

OF THE

CONFEDERATE DEAD,

WHO NOW SLEEP BENEATH THE SHADOWS OF

NORTHERN PRISONS,

THIS VOLUME IS MOST RESPECTFULLY DEDICATED

BY THE AUTHOR.

NEW MARKET BATTLEFIELD MILITARY MUSEUM

The New Market Battlefield Military Museum is internationally known as the largest collection of historically important memorabilia pertaining to the Civil War, the Battle of New Market, and American Military History from 1750 to date.

PREFACE.

The task of writing this, the darkest page in the history of the struggle between the States, is certainly not as grateful nor as inspiriting as that of recording deeds of valor done on blood-stained fields of battle; yet I feel that in compiling this work I am performing a sacred duty, in vindicating the memory of fallen heroes, as well as erasing a dark stain most unjustly cast upon the character of the Southern people.

It may be said that enough has been written upon this painful theme; and this would be true if only one side of the question were entitled to a hearing. But unless a people are to be condemned unheard, upon the *ex parte* statements of their adversaries, the friends of justice and humanity everywhere will hail with satisfaction the proofs herein contained of the rectitude of the Confederate Government in its policy toward prisoners of war.

The future historian who shall undertake to write an unbiassed story of the War between the States, will be compelled to weigh in the scales of justice all its parts and features; and if the revolting crimes against prisoners which have formed the burden of recrimination between the South and the North have been indeed committed, the perpetrators must be held accountable. Be they of the South or of the North, they can not escape history. Neither will they *then* have the privilege of "making" it.

The Southern actors in the great struggle would be recreant to the duty which they owe to their posterity, were they to permit the false allegations of the Northern historian to be accepted as true without attempting a refutation and vindication. My official position giving me peculiar opportunities for discharging one part of this task, I have undertaken it as my share of the duty all owe to those who fell in defence of their country, their homes and their firesides; to those whose graves are scattered from the great Lakes to the Gulf of Mexico—from the shores of the Atlantic to the border-lands of the Far West.

> "They never fail who die
> In a great cause. The block may soak their gore;
> Their heads may sodden in the sun; their limbs
> Be strung to city gates and castle walls—
> But still their spirit walks abroad. Though years
> Elapse, and others share as dark a doom,
> They but augment the deep and sweeping thoughts
> Which o'erpower all others, and conduct
> The world at last to freedom."

I propose in the following pages to show, from official Confederate and Federal documents, 1st. That the sufferings at Andersonville were the results of a malignant pestilence, coupled with the uncontrollable events of a fierce and bitter war; 2d. That Captain Wirz expiated his alleged crimes under the form of a trial that can reflect no credit on the Government that tried him, and that his life was taken away by suborned testimony; 3d. That his alleged co-conspirators were entirely innocent of the crimes charged; 4th. That the Federal authorities at Washington prevented the exchange of prisoners of war; and that by exchanging the prisoners, three-fourths of all the lives lost in prisons North and South could have been saved.

I do not seek, at this late date, to stir up strife, or rekindle the dormant fires that lie smouldering in the land that gave me birth; but believing that *all* should be known, I offer this compilation to every honest lover of truth and justice, as an humble tribute in the shape of material for the use of the future historian of the late Confederate States.

While I am conscious of its imperfections, I trust that this my first attempt at authorship will be received by a generous public in the same spirit that has urged me to undertake the task of vindicating my misrepresented countrymen; and that the truths I record, however inadequately set forth, may have the effect to remove some of those deep-seated prejudices that have so long rendered the people of the North incapable of judging fairly their former adversaries of the South.

Justice to the living, the memory of the dead, and a desire that the truth may prevail over error and falsehood, have prompted me to give to the world this impartial account, which, however imperfect, is at least written fearlessly and honestly.

One disadvantage I have had in common with all other Southern historians of the War, in being debarred access to that considerable portion of the archives of the Confederacy now locked up in Washington; and though I have in my possession numerous official documents relating to Andersonville and other prisons, yet various links were wanting for a complete narrative. These I have, to a great extent, been enabled to supply by the kindness of gentlemen formerly in official positions, and of my old comrades in arms. Among others, I am indebted to Ex-President Jefferson Davis, Gen. G. W. C. Lee, Gen. S. Cooper, Col. Robt. Ould, Col. R. E. Withers, Surgeon J. H. White, Major John H. Gee, and Capt. W. S. Winder, for valuable papers. I also acknowledge obligations to the *Southern Review*, to the Hon. A. H. Stephens' *War between the States*, and to Professor Joseph Jones's papers on Andersonville.

To Mr. W. H. Kemper, of Virginia, an old friend and comrade, my thanks are also due for valuable assistance in the arrangement of the work.

R. R. S.

CONTENTS.

THE SOUTHERN SIDE;

OR

ANDERSONVILLE PRISON.

CHAPTER I.

Andersonville, before the war, was an insignificant station on the Southwestern Railroad, in Sumter County, Georgia. It is about sixty miles from Macon, and ten miles from Americus, the shire town of the county. Its latitude is 32° 10′ N.; longitude 85° W. from Washington. The climate is mild, and subject to no great extremes of heat and cold; the mean annual range of the thermometer being about 60° Fahrenheit. The following scientific report of this place, made to the author by Prof. Jones, will more fully explain the general character of the country, soil, water, &c.

CAMP SUMTER, ANDERSONVILLE, GA.,
September 23*d*, 1864.

Surgeon R. R. STEVENSON,
In charge of Confederate States Military Prison Hospitals, Andersonville, Ga.

SIR:—In accordance with your request that I should furnish you with the general results of my observations upon the medical topography of Andersonville, the following facts are presented. The surgeon in charge of the Confederate States

Military Prison Hospitals will please excuse the brevity and imperfections of this communication, as my duties and labors have been such that I have had but an hour or two to devote to its preparation.

General View of the Medical Topography of Andersonville and the Country in the Immediate Vicinity.

Elevation of the Country.— The country is rolling, and is elevated between three and four hundred feet above the level of the sea. The hills vary in height from forty to one hundred and twenty feet above the level of the water-courses. The summit of the hill upon which the Confederate States General Hospital is situated is elevated one hundred and eight feet above the branch of Sweet Water Creek, which flows at its base. The railroad station is elevated about sixty-six feet above the level of this branch of Sweet Water Creek.

Character of the Soil.—The surface soil is sandy, with but little vegetable mould. For agricultural purposes the soil of this immediate locality may be characterized as light sandy soil; many of the hills which have been cleared and washed by the rains present a red appearance, from the presence of oxide of iron. The hills are composed of alternate layers of sand and pipe-clay, commonly called soap-stone. Both the sand and clay present various colors, from pure white to deep red.

Geological Position.— I have as yet discovered no fossils by which the geological position of this region may with certainty be determined. As far, however, as my knowledge of the country lying above and below extends, this region should be referred to the Tertiary; or more exactly, to the upper or burrh stone strata of the Eocene formation.

Character of Water.— I have carefully analysed the waters from various localities, and find them all remarkably pure; the waters of the wells and of the small streams do not differ to any great extent in specific gravity from that of distilled water, and they contain only mere traces of the chlorides and sulphates, and of the salts of lime, magnesia and iron. The well upon the summit of the hill near your headquarters is of remarkable purity, and in fact it may be considered as equal in purity to the purest well-water in the world. The temperature, 18° C., is sufficiently cool in this climate to render it refreshing. The waters of the branches of Sweet Water Creek are equally pure, with the exception of the presence of minute quantities of vegetable matter; these do not however exist in sufficient quantity to be of the slightest moment in a medical point of view. The waters of these creeks are not so pleasant as the well-water, because their temperature is several degrees higher, and subject to considerable variations according to the volume and rapidity of the current and the degree of external heat. I think that we are justified, from this examination of the water of Andersonville, in the conclusion that little or no lime exists in the soil.

I have also carefully examined the waters within the stockade and hospital, and find them to be of remarkable purity. The water of the stream that enters the stockade, as well as of the bold spring which mingles its waters with the stream just after its entrance into the stockade, and which are extensively used by the prisoners for drinking and cooking, is of great purity, containing only traces of the sulphates, chlorides, and salts of lime, iron and magnesia. The same is true of the water of the stream which enters the hospital enclosure, as well as of the deep wells within the hospital grounds.

Vegetation.— The forest-trees covering the high grounds consist chiefly of the long-leaf pine (*Pinus Australis*), yellow or two-leaved pine (*P. Mitis*), barren scrub oak (*Quercus Catesbæi*), red oak (*Q. Rubra*), Spanish oak, black oak, post oak (*Q. Obtusiloba*), upland willow oak (*Q. Phellos*), wild plum, persimmon (*Diospyros Virginiana*), chinquapin, and other small shrubs, as the whortleberry, haw, sweet leaf, &c.

The swamps are clothed chiefly with black gum (*Nyssa Grandidentata*), tupelo (*N. Aquatica, N Sylvatica*), sweet gum (*Liquidambar Styraciflua*), red flowery maple (*Acer Rubrum*), small magnolia (*Magnolia Glauca*), red bay (*Laurus Cerasus*), and numerous shrubs characteristic of this region.

From this examination we conclude that there is no recognizable source of disease in the waters and soil of Andersonville.

I hope to be able in future to communicate my views more fully upon the soil and climate, when I shall have more time at my command. In conclusion, allow me to return my thanks for the prompt and efficient assistance which you have so cheerfully and courteously rendered me in my "pathological investigations," ordered by the Surgeon-general.

Very respectfully, your obedient servant,

JOSEPH JONES,
Surgeon P. A. C. S.

After repeated efforts by the Confederate States Government to effect a general exchange of prisoners, it was determined to locate a large prison in Southwest Georgia. Andersonville was the site selected, for various humane considerations: first, its superiority over Richmond, Va., in obtaining supplies of food, water and timber, "in the immediate neighborhood of saw and grist mills," and the advantage of a warmer climate. These important considerations, connected with the fact that Richmond was constantly exposed to raiding parties by the enemy, were the principal causes of the removal of the prisoners to Andersonville. Captain W. S. Winder, a son of General John H. Winder, who was afterwards made chief in command of all the prisons and prisoners east of the Mississippi River was dispatched from Richmond with orders to secure the location of a prison in this portion of Georgia. Andersonville was the site selected, and in due course of time a stockade was built here for the accommodation of ten thousand prisoners.

It was constructed by planting large pickets five feet in the ground, and projecting above the surface some twenty feet in height. This enclosure contained at first about twenty acres; afterwards, to meet the daily increasing number of prisoners, it was enlarged to thirty acres. Surrounding this were two outer lines of pickets, the outer one at a distance of one hundred and eighty feet from the main line. These lines were not so high as the inner or first line, being twelve and sixteen feet respectively. These lines were intended as a means of defence and offence, while they also prevented the prisoners from tunnelling out.

A work of the size of this prison was completed by no ordinary means. General Howell Cobb, who was at this time commanding the militia districts of Georgia and Florida, ordered the impressment of some five or six hundred negroes to assist in the work, thereby greatly facilitating its progress.

The shape of the prison was that of a parallelogram. A bold stream of water ran westward through the enclosure, and from the edge of the stream to the brow of the hill on each side was a gradual inclined plane. The camp inside of the prison presented two hill-sides, one facing the north and the other the south. A strong dam was erected at the upper side of the stockade, in order to give the water below an increased velocity. This stream along the entire course of the stockade was a boxed canal, the upper part being used for bathing purposes and the lower portion as a privy. This was an admirable arrangement; and if it had not been that the fortunes of war crowded the prisoners to this post, producing the direful effects of an unforeseen pestilence, a better selection could not have been made in this part of the South for the health and comfort of the captives. At each angle of the prison was a small fort, only one of which had mounted guns; these, with the outer lines of pickets and rifle-pits in échelon, completed the works of offence and defence. Along the inner line of pickets, sentry-boxes were placed at regular intervals for the guards. Large fires were kept up on dark nights, to aid the sentries in detecting those who might attempt to escape.

On the inside of the prison, about twenty feet from the picket-lines, was the "dead line"; this was a barrier employed in the discipline of prisons both North and South to prevent the prisoners from escaping; it was made by driving stakes securely into the ground, with pieces of timber nailed along the top of the stakes, the whole being about five feet high.*

The camp on each side of the stream was laid off in regular streets running at right angles, experience having taught those in charge of prisoners that close barracks in a warm climate would breed disease. A number of sheds were erected to protect the prisoners from the inclemency of the weather. As the prisoners were constantly arriving by thousands before the interior arrangements were complete, they were instructed to improvise temporary coverings from the timber already in the stockade, until suitable winter-quarters could be provided for them. These were made in various ways; some were of plank, some tents, some thatched cottages, some adobe huts, some brush arbors, presenting a miniature city, grotesque in appearance and singular in its construction. It was amusing to observe in this camp of from ten to thirty thousand prisoners, the alacrity with which thousands of them would enter into speculation, or "dickering" as they called it. There were groceries, restaurants, sutlers, merchants, brokers, bakers, wood-dealers, and even land-jobbers engaged in buying and selling ten or twenty feet square of land. The ground occupied by the prison was at first almost covered with pine-stumps, the timber having been used for the construction of the prison and temporary shelters. These stumps were all dug up by the

* The arrangement as described was perhaps peculiar to Andersonville or other Southern prisons. It would appear, indeed, that in many of the prisons of the North (notably Fort Delaware and Point Lookout) the "dead line" was almost as imaginary as a line of latitude or longitude, and the unfortunate captives not expert in prison geography were liable to be shot down at any moment at the whim of the sentry, while entirely unconscious of having trespassed upon a "line" which they could not see.

EXECUTION BY PRISONERS.

prisoners for lightwood, and the vivid light derived from this "fat pine," as it is termed in the South, enlivened many a game of "euchre" and "seven-up." All classes of men were represented here, the honest ploughboy and the city ruffian: Jew and Christian, men of every tongue, race and nativity, were enclosed in this one prison. The men became apparently reckless, I might say thoroughly brutalized by long confinement and deferred hopes of exchange; they seemed to become indifferent to the ordinary decencies of life, and many of them grew as filthy and disgusting in their habits as are the insane or idiotic with whom there is no sense of shame or moral restraint. Here too moral restraints generally lost their force, and the worst passions of the worst men began to assert themselves unchecked; murders and robberies were of frequent occurrence, and so reckless had a portion of the prisoners become, that the more humane among them petitioned General Winder for leave to try the offenders by a court-martial chosen from their own number. This being granted, they proceeded to try the offenders, and the result was that six of their number were found guilty by their comrades of murder, and were hung on a gallows inside the stockade, in the presence of the assembled prisoners. This checked the evil to some extent.

On the north side of the prison, good and substantial barrack accommodations were begun, and the sheds were nearly completed when the work was stopped on account of prison gangrene and scurvy attacking the prisoners, resulting in such great mortality that the post was afterwards abandoned, that is, for the regular reception of prisoners. The prison had two gates, one for egress and the other for ingress. Several bold springs of pure water emerged from the north bank of the stream, and numerous wells of pure water existed inside of the prison. Many of the prisoners lost their lives in attempting to tunnel out of the prison from secret passages that led from these wells. In consequence of the outer line of pickets, tunnelling was in most instances a failure. I remember one poor fellow was permitted to make his tunnel, as he thought, a success. The reader can imagine his chagrin when he came to the top of the ground and found himself confronted by another line of pickets.

On the outer side of the prison, and near the place of ingress, was the baking and cook house. In this place a part of the rations was cooked; the rest was done inside of the stockade by the prisoners. The rations were issued to the prisoners, guards and attendants, regularly once a day; occasionally some of the prisoners would be put on half-rations for some misdemeanor. The rations furnished to the prisoners and Confederate troops on duty there were the same in quantity and quality: all fared alike. The first prisoners that were brought to this post, March 1, 1864, were a motley crew of eight hundred and fifty foreigners, under the name of Federal troops from the New England States. Their petitions for exchange to the Government that had entrapped them into its service had fallen upon deaf ears. Their long prison-life told fearfully upon them; home-sickness and hopes deferred had borne them down altogether. They were marched off to their new prison, and soon made themselves tolerably comfortable. Colonel A. W. Persons, of Fort Valley, Ga., had temporary command of the post at this time, a small detachment of Confederate troops being under him for guard duty. Gen. Joseph E. Johnston, in his movement toward Atlanta, engaging the enemy almost every day for three months, was adding thousands of prisoners to the already crowded post of Andersonville. The prisoners from this source — the Army of the Tennessee — were usually received when no provision had been made for them; the results of the battle-field being, of course, beyond the prevision of man. Thousands of them would at times arrive shortly after the telegrams announcing their capture. Under these circumstances it was impossible to be fully prepared to receive them. It will also be observed that by the first of May, 1864, the prison was taxed to its fullest extent, viz. for the reception of 10,000 men. The enlargement of the prison from its original dimensions was thought to be of sufficient capacity to receive all the prisoners that would possibly be sent here. It may be asked, why were the prisoners sent from Richmond to this post when it was in a crowded condition? The fact is that General Lee's army at this time were living on short rations; not so much in consequence of a scarcity of provisions in the Confederacy, as the difficulty in transporting the supplies. At this time there was only one line of communication from the southern portion of the Confederate States to Richmond, and that was over the North Carolina Railroad, *via* Danville, Va. Under these circumstances the relief consequent upon the removal of ten or twenty thousand men from the scene of General Lee's operations can be readily understood. Self-preservation is the first law of nature, for communities as well as individuals, and the removal of the prisoners to Andersonville was the only alternative, particularly as the Confederate Commissioner of Exchange (Colonel Ould) could not, through the obstinacy of the Federal Government, effect an exchange, as will be shown by official documents in another part of this work. The object in the removal of the prisoners was in the interest of humanity, however disastrous the results may have afterwards proved.

About the middle of May gangrene and scurvy began to make their appearance, and by the 20th of June these diseases had reached to such a point that General Winder (who did not arrive there until the 17th day of June, 1864) deemed it expedient to remove the prisoners to other points immediately, thereby seeking to abate the pestilence by dividing them into smaller posts. It must not be imagined that suitable provisions could be made for twenty or thirty thousand prisoners in a few days. It must be remembered that even at this late date many unforeseen difficulties had to be overcome. The few remaining railroads of the South were taxed to their utmost extent, and there was great difficulty in obtaining transportation. Barrack accommodations had to be built; supplies were to be collected; all these things had to be done before the prisoners could be removed. As soon as all the preliminaries were arranged, General Winder received orders to remove the prisoners to Millen and other points, as he might deem most suitable for their health, comfort and safety. About this time the Federal Government, knowing the straitened circumstances of the South, would occasionally make the semblance of an offer to exchange prisoners. This was done, as circumstances afterwards proved, with no idea of carrying out the provisions of the cartel, but simply to balk and frustrate the designs of the Confederate Government in making suitable provisions to take care of the captives for any length of time.

About the 25th of July, 1864, General Winder made a report to the War Department at Richmond, stating fully the condition of the prisoners, and recommending, first, the removal of at least 20,000 to other points remote from Andersonville; second, that the barracks or sheds already commenced should be completed, as they could be used for hospital purposes; third, that a number of disabled soldiers be detailed to raise vegetables for the prisoners, since they needed these as well as medicines; that until this could be done, a suitable number of agents be permitted to travel through the country by railroad to procure vegetables, &c.; fourth, that hospital accommodations should be erected outside the prison. This report was sent to the War Department at Richmond, and the suggestions were sanctioned. They were carried out almost to the letter in some instances, as will be shown by official documents in another part of this work. By the last of September 1864 all the prisoners, except 5000 not able to bear transportation, were removed from Andersonville, and it virtually ceased to be a post for the reception of prisoners. Still, inasmuch as the Government had expended a large amount of money and devoted much time to render it a suitable place for a prison, it was not deemed advisable to abandon it altogether, and the place was therefore put in process of renovation. By the carelessness of the prisoners in the use of the sinks over the boxed canal, this had become a nuisance. To remedy this it was covered with sand and lime and the channel enlarged; the dam was improved, and the passage for the water at the lower side of the prison widened, so as to give the water free exit. The barracks and cook-house were enlarged, and the hospital buildings outside the prison were begun. General Jno. H. Winder, with his staff, composed of Capt. W. S. Winder, A. A. G., Capt. R. B. Winder, A. Q. M., and Surgeon J. H. White, proceeded with the prisoners to Millen, Georgia. They remained there, however, but a short time, the approach of Gen. Sherman's army forcing them to remove their prisoners to Florence, S. C.

As before mentioned, none but the sick and wounded, together with the attendants, nurses and medical officers, and a small guard, were left at Andersonville. The post was now placed in command of Colonel Gibbs, with R. B. Thomas, A. A. G., Major G. M. Proctor, and Capt. J. W. Armstrong had charge of the commissary department. Capt. Henry Wirz had the same control over the discipline of the hospital that he had formerly held over the prison; Surgeon R. R. Stevenson was placed in chief control of the medical department, with some thirty assistant-surgeons and contract-doctors. The process of renovating the post was now pushed on with vigor and rapidity, considering the small force and limited means at the command of Captain Wirz. In a short time the whole premises were in a much improved condition, and the chances of the sick were growing more hopeful. At one time it had been thought by the medical officers of the post that nearly all the infected would die, but by the use of vegetables in such quantities as could be procured, and an acid beer made from corn-meal and sorghum molasses, the death-rate fell from about 3000 in August to 1C0 for the month of December.

A temporary hospital had been improvised by Surgeon J.

H. White, and established outside of the prison enclosure. This was done when gangrene and scurvy appeared in the stockade; but it was still inadequate to receive all the infected sick, and four hundred and fifty-one of these died in the prison. This temporary hospital was similar to the ordinary field-hospital improvised after a great battle. It covered about five acres of ground, was well shaded and watered, and stood between two water-courses, upon a promontory of land sloping in two different directions. It was enclosed by a plank fence, and supplied with tents and tent-flies. Sometimes as many as 2500 prisoners would be in this enclosure. Of this number 2000 would be on the sick-list, and the remainder, convalescents, cooks, nurses, &c., were paroled to a certain limit around the hospital grounds, in order to give them the advantage of looking after the comfort of their sick comrades, in the way of getting wood, pine-boughs, straw, &c. A great many of these men violated their paroles and left their dying comrades, afterwards to appear on the witness-stand to give evidence against those who had befriended them whilst they were in prison.

The rules and regulations of the hospital were posted up in conspicuous places; the roll was called twice a day; the men were divided into squads of ninety and messes of fifteen men, in the same manner that had been practised in the prison. The squads were under the charge of a sergeant, who was held responsible for the good conduct of his company. The hospital was divided into four divisions, each under the charge of a medical officer, who was responsible to the chief surgeon—at first Surgeon J. H. White, after him Surgeon R. R. Stevenson, and lastly Surgeon Clayton. The rations and medicines issued to the prisoners in both the prison and hospital were of the same kind and quantity that were issued to the Confederate troops.

Strenuous efforts were made by the writer to have the hospital-sheds built as suggested by him in his report to the

Surgeon-general. It was proposed to erect forty sheds, twenty feet wide by one hundred feet in length, eight feet high at the eaves, with a space of thirty feet between them, each shed capable of containing from twenty to forty patients. The sides of the sheds were covered with awnings, to be raised or lowered at pleasure for ventilation, which the sick in a warm climate so much need. These buildings were nearly all completed, and were standing at the end of the war as a monument to the intentions of their builders.

The dead were buried about a half-mile to the northwest of the prison. They were placed side by side in long trenches, and well covered up. Each grave was carefully marked by a stake bearing a number corresponding with that on the hospital register, which gave the name, rank, regiment, company, and disease of the patient. Among the Confederate surgeons there were some who remained by their dying patients when even their own countrymen had deserted them, and who carefully preserved the long death-rolls for the benefit of those who at some future day might wish to know the last resting-place of their comrades and friends. Some of these devoted men died at their posts; and perhaps a day may come when in this city of the dead a memorial shall be raised to commemorate their fidelity to their calling and to humanity.

Every comfort was provided for the sick and wounded that could be obtained within the limited means of the Confederate Government. Nothing more strikingly shows the great resources of the Southern country than the fact that it fed its own soldiers in the field, its citizens, the prisoners, and almost fed the hosts of Grant and Sherman; and notwithstanding the destruction of railroads, supplies, mills, factories, farming implements, &c., by Federal raiders, cases of actual suffering for food on the part of soldiers, citizens, and prisoners, were seldom witnessed until near the close of the war.

It is useless at this point for me to go into a minute detail of the remote cause of the miseries and sufferings that occurred here, as this will be sufficiently shown by various official records in another part of this work. I may, however, mention that diarrhœa, dysentery, scurvy, and gangrene were the principal diseases of which the prisoners died. These maladies arose mainly from a want of that diet to which the Northern soldiers had been accustomed. The quantity was quite sufficient to sustain life, but the bread was made from corn-meal, and not from wheaten flour. This produced diarrhœa, and hence laid the foundation of all those symptoms resulting from defective nutrition. To this may be added the moral degradation of the prisoners themselves, as was shown by their filthy habits and defective hygienic regulations. Almost every prisoner that paid a strict regard to personal cleanliness escaped the pestilence. Disappointment and despondency in regard to exchanges seem to have been the most potent cause in lowering the vitality of mind and body and predisposing the men to disease. In corroboration of this fact I will mention that Dr. Joseph Jones, who was ordered to Andersonville by the Surgeon-general for the purpose of making certain "pathological investigations on the cadaver," says in his report to the Surgeon-general:—"Surrounded by these depressing agencies, the postponement of the general exchange of prisoners, and the constantly receding hopes of deliverance, through the action of their own Government, depressed the already desponding spirits, and destroyed those mental and moral energies so necessary for a successful struggle against disease and its agents. Home-sickness and disappointment, mental depression and distress, attending the daily longings for an apparently hopeless release, appeared to be as potent agencies in the destruction of these prisoners as the physical causes of actual diseases."

At one time there were nearly 8000 sick prisoners in the prison and hospital, and the mortality was very great during the months of July, August, and September, 1864, notwithstanding all possible efforts were made by the surgeons as well as the officers of the post to check its ravages. The greatest difficulty was experienced in procuring medicines and anti-scorbutics. These were made contraband of war by an order of the Federal Government, and the most rigid discipline failed to make the prisoners pay that attention to cleanliness which was absolutely necessary. The medical corps was altogether insufficient in numbers to attend to the vast amount of patients, and it was impossible to procure medical assistance. The cooks, nurses, and attendants were drawn from paroled prisoners, and many of these abandoned their trust and made their escape on the first opportunity that presented, leaving their sick and dying comrades to perish. The guards on duty here were similarly affected with gangrene and scurvy. Captain Wirz had gangrene in an old wound which he had received in the battle of Manassas in 1861, and was absent from the post some four weeks on surgeon's certificate.* General Winder had gangrene of the face, and was forbidden by his surgeon, J. H. White, to go inside the stockade. Colonel G. C. Gibbs, commandant of the post, had gangrene of the face, and was furloughed under the medical certificate of surgeons Wible and Gore, of Americus, Ga. The writer of these pages can fully attest the effects of gangrene and scurvy, contracted while on duty there; their marks will follow him to his grave. The Confederate graveyard at Andersonville will fully prove that the mortality among the guards was almost as great in proportion to the number of men as among the Federals. For a period of some three months (July, August, and Spetember, 1864), Captain Wirz and the few faithful medical officers of the post were engaged night and day in ministering to the wants of the sick and dying, and caring for the dead. So arduous were their duties that many of the medical officers were taken sick and had to abandon their post. In

*In his trial, certain Federal witnesses swore to his killing certain prisoners in August 1864, when he (Wirz) was actually absent on sick leave in Augusta, Ga., at the time.

fact, the pestilence assumed such fearful proportions, that Medical Director S. H. Stout could scarcely induce such medical men as could be spared from the pressing wants of the service (Georgia was at this time one vast hospital) to go to Andersonville.

It was this horrible condition of affairs at Andersonville and other prison-posts that prompted Colonel Ould, the Confederate Commissioner of Exchange, to make his repeated efforts in the interest of humanity to get the Federal Government (as they had refused all further exchanges) to send medicines, supplies of clothing, &c. (offering to pay for them in gold or cotton), for the exclusive use of the Federal prisoners, to be dispensed, if desired, by Federal surgeons sent for that purpose. The same motives prompted the President and Vice-president of the Confederate States to make the proposal to parole and send them home, although they were the only hostages held for a like number of suffering Confederate prisoners held at the North. These facts cannot be denied or explained away. Writers for effect may descant on "rebel barbarity," and present to a horrified world the photographs of diseased and emaciated wretches as proof of their charges; but the fact remains that the authorities at Washington, by obstinately refusing to listen to the liberal and repeated proposals of the Confederate Government, were the real authors of most of this misery and death.

Thirteen thousand men lie buried in the graveyard at Andersonville. When the web of falsehood, concealment and perjury called "the Wirz trial" shall be rent, and the truth known, it will be seen that the real responsibility lies with the men who sacrificed these poor wretches to their own ambition.

CHAPTER II.

The difficulties experienced by the Confederate authorities can perhaps be more fully illustrated and explained by a few pertinent quotations from the elaborate report of Prof. Joseph Jones, M. D. This report was made since the close of the war, and embodies also the suppressed reports of Surgeons White and Stevenson in the Wirz trial. The extracts read as follows:

"The facts recorded in the following pages are of such a nature that justice to my distressed and afflicted countrymen, as well as to myself, demands a correct history of these investigations upon the diseases of the Federal prisoners confined at Andersonville, Ga. Hearing of the unusual mortality amongst the Federal prisoners confined at Andersonville, I expressed, during an official visit to Richmond, Va., in the month of August, 1864, to the Surgeon-general, S. P. Moore, C. S. A., a desire to vist Camp Sumter, with the design of instituting a series of inquiries upon the nature and cause of the prevailing diseases. The Surgeon-general furnished me with the following letter to the surgeon in charge of the Confederate States Military Prison-hospital at Andersonville:

CONFEDERATE STATES OF AMERICA,
SURGEON-GENERAL'S OFFICE, RICHMOND, VA., *August 6th*, 1864.

Surgeon J. H. WHITE,
In charge of Hospital for Federal Prisoners, Andersonville, Ga.

SIR:—The field for pathological investigations afforded by the large collection of Federal prisoners in Georgia is of great extent and importance, and it is believed that results of value to the profession may be obtained by a careful investigation of the effects of diseases upon this large body of men, subjected to a decided change of climate and to the circumstances peculiar to prison life. The surgeon in charge of the hospital for the Federal prisoners, together with his assistants, will afford every facility to Surgeon Joseph Jones in the prosecution of the labors ordered by the Surgeon-general.

Efficient assistance must be rendered Surgeon Jones by the medical officers, not only in his examinations into the causes and symptoms of the various diseases, but especially in the arduous labors of *post-mortem* examinations. The medical officers will assist in the performance of such post-mortems as Surgeon Jones may indicate, in order that this great field for pathological investigation may be explored for the benefit of the medical department of the Confederate army.

S. P. MOORE, *Surg.-Gen. C. S. A.*

"As soon as the necessary preparations could be made, I repaired to Andersonville and examined carefully the condition and diseases of the sick and wounded Federal prisoners in the Confederate States military hospital, and instituted a series of post-mortem examinations with the design of elucidating the pathology of the prevailing diseases. . . . .

"In consequence of the refusal on the part of the commandant of the interior of the prison to admit me into the stockade on the order of the Surgeon-general C. S. A., the following communication was addressed to the commandant of the post:

CAMP SUMTER, ANDERSONVILLE, GA.,
September 16th, 1864.

Brig.-general JOHN H. WINDER,
Commandant Post Andersonville.

GENERAL:—I respectfully request the Commandant of the post of Andersonville to grant me permission, and to furnish the necessary pass, to visit the sick and medical officers within the stockade of the Confederate States prison; I desire to institute certain inquiries ordered by the Surgeon-general.

Surgeon Isaiah H. White, chief surgeon of the post, and Surgeon R. R. Stevenson, in charge of prison-hospital, have afforded me every facility for the prosecution of my labors amongst the sick outside of the stockade.

My secretary, Mr. Manigault, will exhibit to you the originals of the orders under which I am now acting, and in accordance with which the present request is respectfully made.

Respectfully your ob't serv't,
JOSEPH JONES, *Surgeon P. A. C. S.*

"The following reply was received through Captain W. S. Winder, A. A. G.:—

CAMP SUMTER, ANDERSONVILLE, GA.,
September 17th, 1864.

CAPTAIN:—You will permit Surgeon Joseph Jones, who has orders from the Surgeon-general, to visit the sick within the stockade that are under medical treatment. Surgeon Jones is ordered to make certain investigations which may prove useful to his profession.

Very respectfully, by direction of General Winder,
W. S. WINDER, *A. A. G.*

Capt. H. WIRZ, *Commanding Prison.*

. . . .

"The following communication was addressed to the Surgeon-general, from Macon, the centre of my labors:

MACON, GA., 19*th October*, 1864.

Surgeon-general S. P. MOORE, C. S. A., War Department, Richmond, Va.

SIR:—I have the honor to give the following brief outline of my labors, conducted in accordance with the orders of the Surgeon-general:

Immediately after the brief report upon hospital gangrene had been forwarded to the Surgeon-general, I repaired to Camp Sumter, Andersonville, Georgia, and instituted a series of investigations upon the diseases of the Federal prisoners. The field was of great extent and of extraordinary interest. There were more than five thousand (5000) seriously sick in the hospital and stockade, and the deaths ranged from ninety to one hundred and thirty each day. Since the establishment of this prison, on the 24th of February 1864, to the present time, over ten thousand Federal prisoners have died; that is, near one-third of the entire number have perished in less than seven months. I instituted careful investigations into the condition of the sick and well, and performed numerous *post-mortem* examinations, and executed drawings of the diseased structures. The medical topography of Andersonville and the surrounding country was examined, and the waters of the streams, springs and wells around and within the stockade and hospital carefully analysed. Diarrhœa, scurvy and hospital gangrene were the diseases which have been the main causes of the extraordinary mortality. . . .

Very respectfully your obedient servant,

JOSEPH JONES, *Surgeon P. A. C. S.*

In the preface to his report, Dr. Jones, defending his position when he was taken to Washington City after the surrender, to testify in the "Wirz Trial," says:

"After the disastrous close of a struggle which had enlisted all my sympathies and engaged all my energies, broken in health, fortune and spirits, I desired only peace and rest; and filing away the investigations amongst the Confederate sick and wounded, turned my attention wholly to the pressing necessities of the time. I desired especially that the report on the Federal prisoners at Andersonville should never see the light of day, because it was prepared solely for the eye of the Surgeon-general of the Confederate States Army; and the frank manner in which all the subjects had been discussed would only engender angry feelings, and place weapons in the hands of the victors; and also because one of the chief reasons which stimulated the preparation of this report was no longer active, namely, the rectification of such abuses in the conduct of military prison-hospitals as would deprive the United States Government of all excuse in continuing retaliatory measures upon the gallant soldiers of the Confederacy who have been or who might be so unfortunate as to become prisoners of war. By a deliberate and well-calculated policy, thousands of the Southern troops were confined for months, and even years, in Northern prisons, without any possibility of exchange; and I felt it to be the duty of all their fellow-soldiers and countrymen to avoid all unnecessary abuses in military prisons, and to advocate that line of policy in the treatment of prisoners of war which would tend to insure the most humane treatment of Confederate prisoners during their distressing and painful captivity. Without any warning, I was suddenly summoned to Washington by the United States authorities, and ordered to deliver up 'all papers, reports, records, &c., of every kind in my possession pertaining to the Andersonville prison.' To a paroled prisoner of war there was neither option nor appeal in the matter. The following letter was addressed to the Judge-advocate immediately upon my arrival in Washington:

WASHINGTON, D. C., *Oct. 3d*, 1865.

COL. CHIPMAN, Judge-advocate U. S. Army, Washington, D. C.

SIR:—On the 23d of September I received the following order:

OFFICE PROV. MAR. GEN., DEP'T GA.
AUGUSTA, GA., *Sept. 22d*, 1865.

Prof. Joseph Jones will report forthwith to Col. Chipman, Judge-advocate at Washington, D. C., as a witness in the Wirz case, now on trial in that city, and will take with him all papers, reports, records, &c., of every kind in his possession pertaining to the Andersonville prison. Quartermaster will furnish transportation.

By command of Major-General Steedman,
HENRY W. SNOW, *Lt.-Col. and Act. Pro.-mar.-gen. Dist. Ga.*

Immediately upon the receipt of this order, I reported to General Steedman, and informed him that I had in my possession *none* of the *original* records of Andersonville, but only the materials of a report (including copies of some of the records of the Confederate States Military Prison Hospital) which I had prepared in compliance with the orders of the Surgeon-general Confederate States Army, but which had never been presented on account of the destruction of all railroad communication with Richmond, Virginia, before the completion of the report. I asked for information whether this order related to matters which had never been formally and officially presented to the Medical Department of the Confederate States. General Steedman informed me that the order was absolute, admitting of but one construction, and related to all matter in my possession connected with the Andersonville prison; and that my report, although incomplete and never officially presented or recognised, was nevertheless included, and must be immediately surrendered to the Judge-advocate.

In complying with the preceding order, I respectfully submit the following:

My inspection of the Confederate States military prison-hospital of Camp Sumter, Andersonville, Ga., together with the accompanying pathological investigations, designed to determine the causes of the great mortality amongst the Federal prisoners, were instituted in compliance with the following order:

CONFEDERATE STATES OF AMERICA, SURGEON-GENERAL'S OFFICE,
WAR DEPARTMENT, RICHMOND, VA., *August 6th*, 1864.

Surgeon Joseph Jones is directed to institute an extended investigation upon the causes, pathology and treatment of fevers and the relations of climate and soil to disease.

Surgeon Joseph Jones will visit those parts of the Confederate States, and prosecute his investigations in those cities, armies, and regimental and general hospitals, which he may deem necessary as suitable fields for the establishment of the results indicated in this order.

Medical directors of the field and hospital, and the chief surgeons of corps, divisions, districts and brigades, and surgeons and assistant surgeons of regiments and general hospitals, will afford every facility to Surgeon Jones to carry out these instructions, and will respond as far as possible to his inquiries by letter and circular; and will furnish him with copies of all field and hospital reports which he may deem necessary for the illustration of the subjects of inquiry indicated in this order. Surgeon Jones will embody the results of his labors, relating to the diseases of the Confederate army, in substantial volumes; and will deposit them in the Surgeon-general's office, for the use of the medical department of the Confederate army.

S. P. MOORE, *Surgeon-general C. S. A.*

After the completion (about the end of September 1864) of these labors at Andersonville, I instituted a series of researches upon hospital gangrene, pyaemia, and small-pox, which were prevailing extensively amongst the sick and wounded of the Confederate troops of the Army of Tennessee, then under the command of General Hood. My active labors in the field did not cease until the middle of November, when I returned to Augusta, and commenced the elaboration of the results of my investigations into a report to the Surgeon-general. Before the completion of this report, all communication by railroad was cut off by the armies of Generals Sherman and Grant between Augusta and Richmond, the seat of the Confederate Government. It was my design to make a similar inspection of all the Confederate military prisons, and to draw up an extended report upon the causes of disease and death, together with observations upon the best methods of remedying existing evils. In justice to myself, as well as to those most nearly connected with this investigation, I would respectfully call the attention of Col. Chipman, Judge-advocate U. S. Army, to the fact, that the matter I now place in his hands, in obedience to the demands of a power from which there is no appeal, was prepared solely for the consideration of the Surgeon-general of the Confederate army, and was designed to promote the cause of humanity and to advance the interests of the medical profession. This being granted, I feel assured that the

Judge-advocate will appreciate the deep pain which the anticipation gives me, that these labors may be diverted from their original mission, to be applied to the prosecution of criminal cases. The same principle which led me to endeavor to deal humanely and justly by these suffering prisoners, and to make a truthful representation of their condition to the medical department of the Confederate army, now actuates me in recording my belief that, as far as my knowledge extends, there was no deliberate or wilful design on the part of the Chief Executive, Jefferson Davis, and the highest authorities of the Confederate Government, to injure the health and destroy the lives of these Federal prisoners. On the 21st of May, 1861, it was enacted by the Congress of the Confederate States of America, "That all prisoners of war taken, whether on land or at sea, during the pending hostilities with the United States, shall be transferred by the captors from time to time, and as often as convenient, to the Department of War; and it shall be the duty of the Secretary of War, with the approval of the President, to issue such instructions for the Quartermaster-general and his subordinates, as shall provide for the safe custody and sustenance of prisoners of war; and the rations furnished prisoners of war shall be the same in quantity and quality as those furnished to enlisted men in the army of the Confederacy." By an act of February 1864, the Quartermaster-general was relieved of this duty, and the Commissary-general of Subsistence was ordered to provide for the sustenance of prisoners of war. According to General Orders No. 159, Adjutant and Inspector-general's office, C. S. A.:—"Hospitals for prisoners of war are placed on the same footing as other Confederate States hospitals in all respects, and will be managed accordingly."

The Federal prisoners were removed to southwestern Georgia in the early part of 1864, not only to secure a place of confinement more remote than Richmond and other large towns from the operations of the United States forces, *but also to secure a more abundant and easy supply of food.* As far as my experience extends, no prisoner who had been reared upon wheat bread, and who was held in captivity for any length of time, could retain his health and escape either scurvy or diarrhœa if confined to the Confederate ration issued to the soldiers in the field, of unbolted corn-meal and bacon. The large armies of the Confederacy suffered more than once from scurvy, and as the war progressed, secondary hemorrhage and hospital gangrene increased to a great extent from the deteriorated condition of the blood dependent upon the prolonged use of salt meat; and but for the extra supplies received from home and from various benevolent state institutions, scurvy, diarrhœa and dysentery would have committed still greater ravages. It is believed by the citizens of the Southern States that the Confederate authorities earnestly desired to effect a continuous and speedy exchange of prisoners of war in their hands, on the ground that the retention of these soldiers in captivity was a great calamity, not only entailing a heavy expenditure of the scant means of subsistence, already insufficient to support their suffering, half-starved, half-clad and unpaid armies, struggling in the field with overwhelming numbers, and embarrassing their imperfect and dilapidated lines of communication, but also as depriving them of the services of a veteran army fully equal to one-third the numbers actively engaged in the field; and the history of subsequent events has shown that the retention in captivity of the Confederate prisoners was one of the efficient causes of the final and complete overthrow of the Confederate Government.

Without at all attempting to justify the abuses which have been alleged against those directly engaged in keeping the Federal prisoners, it is my honest belief that if the exhausted condition of the Confederate Government, with its bankrupt currency, with its retreating and constantly diminishing armies, with the apparent impossibility of filling up the vacancies by death, desertion and sickness, of gathering a guard of reserves of sufficient strength to allow of the proper enlargement of the military prisons, and with a country torn and bleeding along all its borders, with its starving women and children and old men fleeing from the desolating march of contending armies, crowding the dilapidated and overburdened railroad lines, and adding to the distress and consuming the poor charities of those in the interior, who were harassed by the loss of sons and brothers and husbands and by the fearful visions of starvation and undefined misery, could be fully realized, much of the suffering of the Federal prisoners would be attributed to causes connected with the distressed condition of the Southern States.

Very respectfully your obedient servant,

JOSEPH JONES.

"In the trial of the Commandant of the interior of the Confederate States military prison of Andersonville, by the United States military in the Capitol at Washington, only those portions of my report were used in the prosecution by the Judge-advocate which related to the diseases and sufferings of the Federal prisoners. In the extracts read before the court whilst I occupied the witness-stand, everything relating to the distressed condition of the Southern States and to the difficulties under which the medical officers labored in the discharge of their duties, *as well as the inspection reports appended*, were suppressed. When upon the witness-stand, after hearing the 'extracts' read from my report, I was compelled by a sense of justice to my suffering fellow-countrymen to state, that I had appeared before that military tribunal in obedience to the demands of a power from which there was no appeal, and that my report contained other matter relating to the straitened condition of the Confederate Government, as well as inspection reports, which demonstrated clearly that the medical officers in charge of the sick and wounded Federal prisoners had made efforts to alleviate their sufferings.

"These reasons have led me to desire to place all the facts before the public, who have already had access to certain *selected facts*. . . .

"JOSEPH JONES.

"AUGUSTA, GEORGIA, *November*, 1865."

Thus run the "extracts" copied from the preface of Prof. Jones's report on Andersonville. They show that Judge-advocate Chipman purposely suppressed all the extenuating circumstances in favor of Captain Wirz and his alleged co-conspirators. Nothing, it appears, was admitted in this mock trial but garbled "extracts," together with tortured and suborned testimony. I will give the reader a few more of these "extracts" from the same papers, and close this chapter with the *inspection reports, &c.*, which were made by Surgeons White and Stevenson to the Surgeon-general, and were suppressed in the trial which declared them co-conspirators with Captain Wirz.

In concluding his report on the medical topography of Andersonville, Prof. Jones makes use of the following language:

"After a careful examination, I was impressed with the belief that the highlands of Andersonville and of this region of country were as healthy as any region of the world situated in the same latitude and at the same elevation above the sea; and that this locality, chosen by the Confederate States for the confinement of the Federal prisoners, was much more salubrious than most of the region of Georgia lying to the south and southeast. . . .

"In conclusion, as far as my physical and pathological investigations extended, I was compelled to believe that the diseases which proved so fatal to the Federal prisoners confined at Andersonville, Georgia, were due to causes other than those connected with the soil, waters and climate. The heat of this climate may have promoted the rapid decomposition of the filth which, in violation of all hygienic laws, was allowed to accumulate in the stockade and hospital grounds; and also in itself the heat may have proved a cause of debility; but still the fearful mortality could not properly be referred to this condition of climate, or to all the other elements of climate combined. No blame can be attached to the Confederate authorities

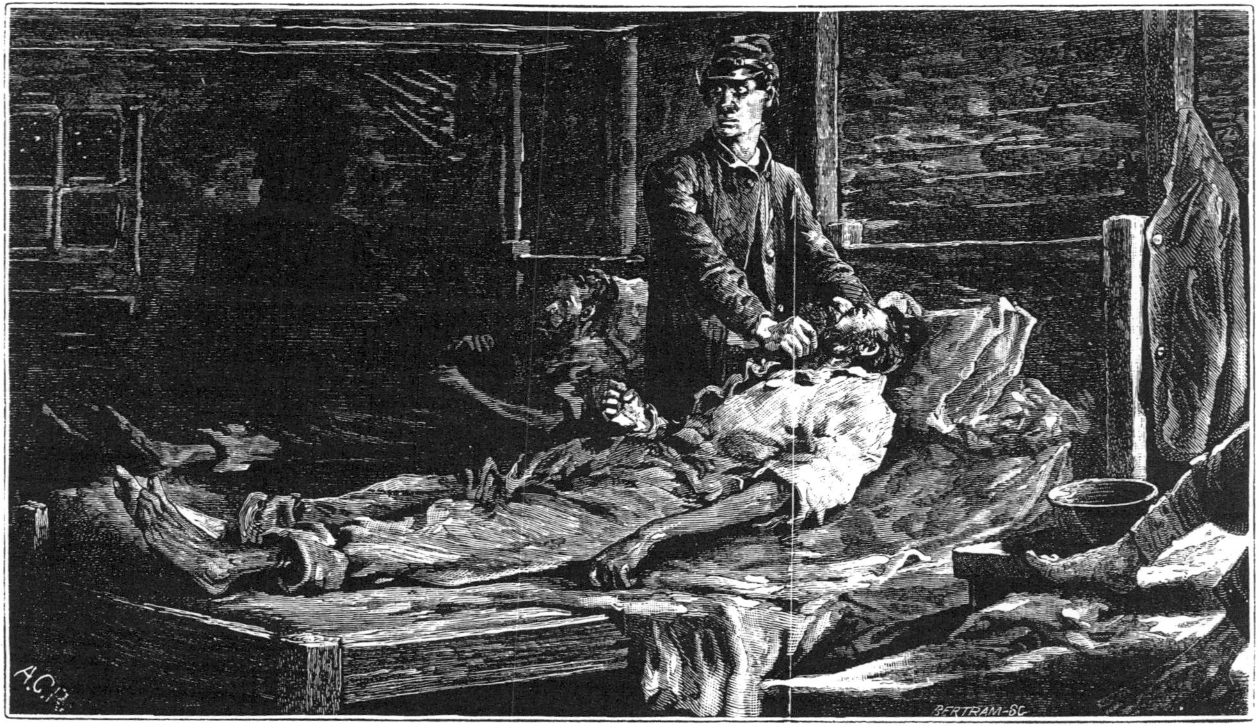

MURDER IN THE HOSPITAL.

for the collection of the Federal prisoners at this elevated and healthy locality, which was more salubrious than one-half the territory of South Carolina, Georgia, Alabama, Mississippi and Louisiana. . . .

"In this collection of men from all parts of the civilised world, every phase of human character was represented; the stronger preyed upon the weaker, and even the sick who were unable to defend themselves, were robbed of their scanty supplies of food and clothing. Dark stories were afloat of men, both sick and well, who were murdered at night—strangled to death by their comrades for scant supplies of clothing or money. I heard a sick and wounded Federal prisoner accuse his nurse, a fellow-prisoner, of the United States army, of having stealthily, during his sleep, inoculated his wounded arm with gangrene, that he might destroy his life and fall heir to his clothing. The excuse given for the absence of Confederate guards and police within the inclosure of the stockade, was the insufficiency of men capable of performing military duty. At the time of the establishment, and during the existence, of the military prison at Andersonville, the Confederate Government was sorely pressed on every side; the best States were being overrun and desolated, and, with all the forces that could be gathered from all quarters, the main armies are largely outnumbered, and are being steadily pressed back, leaving a desolated and ruined country. It is with difficulty that the Confederate Government can spare at the present time of reserves, composed of old men and boys (many of whom are wholly unfit to perform even guard duty), to guard this large number of prisoners, which they have ever been anxious to exchange, and which the Confederate authorities believed to be forced upon their hands by the persistent action of the United States Government. Similar excuses are given for the crowded condition of the stockade. Thus it is affirmed that the operations, as well as the sudden and formidable raids, of the United States forces in Virginia, around Richmond, and in northwestern Georgia, have compelled the sudden and continuous removal of prisoners of war to a place of safety. The military operations of the United States have reduced the railroad system of the Confederate States east of the Mississippi, practically, to one long and uncertain line. The utmost capacity of the railroads of the Southern Confederacy, which are now in a most deplorable condition, is taxed with the transportation of troops, sick and wounded soldiers, prisoners of war, munitions of war, and provisions for the armies in the field. Notwithstanding the utmost exertions of the Confederate authorities, the armies in the field are, as is well known to the Surgeon-general, but poorly fed and clothed at the best, and ofttimes are upon less than *one-quarter rations.* And were it not for supplies received in foraging and through private sources, it would appear almost impossible that the Confederate army should be able to keep the field with anything like its present numbers. The Surgeon-general is also well acquainted with the fact that, at the present time, large numbers, and it might almost be said entire armies, of Confederate troops are suffering with symptoms of scurvy; and hospital gangrene and pyaemia are making fearful ravages amongst the poorly fed, badly clothed, and imperfectly treated wounded of the Army of Tennessee, now contending for the possession of Georgia. Again, the Confederate currency has depreciated almost to a nominal value, and large numbers of the citizens are refusing to take it in the purchase of provisions or lumber. In this section of Georgia, the means of cutting and hauling lumber are scarce, not only from the original absence of machinery and scarcity of surplus horses and mules, but also from the extensive destruction of the saw-mills by the contending armies in the northern parts of the State, and from the natural decay of machinery during three years of war in a country cut off from all intercourse with the surrounding world, and possessing at its best estate but few workshops for the manufacture of machinery. Axes, spades, tools, and implements of all kinds are exceedingly scarce in this section of country; and the State has been so often under the hands of the impressing officer that it is difficult to obtain teams for hauling lumber.

"Notwithstanding that my labors relate to the investigation of the causes and nature of diseases, I do not deem it improper thus to make a simple statement to the Surgeon-general of these facts, in connection with those results of my labors which appear to reflect upon the action of certain officers. . . .

"I visited two thousand sick within the stockade, lying under four long sheds, which had been built at the northern portion for barracks. At this time only one medical officer was in attendance, whereas at least twenty medical officers should have been employed. I was informed that several of the medical officers appointed to attend the sick within the stockade were sick, and that the duty was so arduous, and the exhalations from the sick and filth of the prison were so deleterious, that it was impossible for the medical officers to stand the service for any length of time. Great difficulty was experienced by the surgeon in charge of the post to induce medical officers and physicians to accept positions in the stockade or hospital, on account of the absence of many of the facilities for the treatment of the sick, and the great and numerous depressing agencies, and the consequent unsatisfactory results of practice. So distressing was the service, and so great were the obstacles to successful and satisfactory practice amongst these men, whose constitutions had been sapped by the loss of all hope of exchange on the part of their own Government, and by long confinement upon unvarying diet, that the more energetic Confederate surgeons and assistant surgeons endeavored to get transfers to other fields of labor, preferring the hardships and exposures of service at the front. It is also to be considered, that not only is there a scarcity of physicians in the Confederacy, but it is especially difficult to command the services of competent physicians in this sparsely settled country. Added to all this, the gigantic military operations in Georgia, attended with the utter destruction of her territory in the rear of the Federal forces, and with the serious wounding of thousands of Confederate troops, have absorbed the sympathies and attention, and commanded the abilities of almost every available physician in the State. The hospitals of the Army of Tennessee have been in constant motion for months, following the continuous series of disasters and evacuations in Northern Georgia, and are crowded with seriously wounded, suffering in many cases with the most extensive hospital gangrene, and with fatal pyaemia. Every town and village in Georgia is filled with the sick and wounded of the Army of Tennessee, and the privations and sufferings of the Confederate troops, even amongst their own countrymen, are great beyond description, and equal to those of any armies in ancient or modern times. With the whole energies of this people engaged in such a terrible and unequal struggle, it is not singular that medical talent of the highest order should be scarce, and difficult of access and control at the interior posts. The very condition and results of the contest also, without doubt, tend to excite such prejudice as would disincline medical officers from voluntarily seeking service amongst the captive enemies, who are the representatives of those who are seeking to conquer and desolate their native land.

"A feeling of disappointment, and even of resentment, on account of the action of the United States Government upon the subject of the exchange of prisoners, appeared to be a cause of universal regret and of deep and injurious despondency. I heard some of the prisoners go so far as to exonerate the Confederate Government from any charge of intentionally subjecting them to protracted confinement, with its necessary and unavoidable suffering, in a country cut off from all intercourse with foreign nations, and sorely pressed on all sides; whilst on the other hand, they charged their prolonged captivity upon their own Government, which was attempting to make the negro equal to the white man. That I have not misrepresented the sentiments of these prisoners is shown by the following resolutions, passed a short time after my examination of the stockade, by these same Andersonville prisoners who had been transferred to Savannah. These resolutions were published in the Savannah papers:—

At a mass meeting held September 28th, 1864, by the Federal prisoners confined at Savannah, Ga., it was unanimously agreed that the following resolutions be sent to the President of the United States, in the hope that he might thereby take such steps as in his wisdom he may think necessary for our speedy exchange or parole.

Resolved, That while we would declare our unbounded love for the Union, for the home of our fathers, and for the graves of those we venerate, we would beg most respectfully that our situation as prisoners be diligently inquired into, and every obstacle consistent with the honor and dignity of the Government at once removed.

Resolved, That while allowing the Confederate authorities all due praise for the attention paid to prisoners, numbers of our men are daily consigned to early graves, in the prime of manhood, far from home and kindred, and this is not caused intentionally by the Confederate Government, but by force of circumstances; the prisoners are obliged to go without shelter, and, in a great portion of cases, without medicine.

Resolved, That, whereas, ten thousand of our brave comrades have descended into an untimely grave within the last six months, and as we believe their death was caused by the difference of climate, the peculiar kind and insufficiency of food, and lack of proper medical treatment; and whereas those difficulties still remain, we would declare as our firm belief, that unless we are speedily exchanged, we have no other alternative but to share the lamentable fate of our comrades. Must this thing still go on? Is there no hope?

Resolved, That, whereas, the cold and inclement season of the year is fast approaching, we hold it to be our duty as soldiers and citizens of the United States, to inform our Government that the majority of our prisoners are without proper clothing, in some cases being almost naked, and are without blankets to protect us from the scorching sun by day or the heavy dews by night, and we would most respectfully request the Government to make some arrangement whereby we can be supplied with these, to us, necessary articles.

Resolved, That, whereas, the term of service of many of our comrades having expired, they, having served truly and faithfully for the term of their several enlistments, would most respectfully ask their Government, are they to be forgotten? Are past services to be ignored? Not having seen their wives and little ones for over three years, they would most respectfully, but firmly request the Government to make some arrangements whereby they can be exchanged or paroled.

Resolved, That, whereas, in the fortune of war, it was our lot to become prisoners, we have suffered patiently, and are still willing to suffer, if by so doing we can benefit the country; but we must most respectfully beg to say, that we are not willing to suffer to further the ends of any party or clique to the detriment of our honor, our families, and our country, and we beg that this affair be explained to us, that we may continue to hold the Government in that respect which is necessary to make a good citizen and soldier.

P. Bradley,
Chairman of Committee in behalf of Prisoners.

" . . . In presuming to step aside for one moment from the line of labor indicated in the Surgeon-general's order, and to volunteer suggestions with reference to the amelioration of suffering, and the rectification of abuses, I am well aware that the same principles of enlarged humanity which the Surgeon-general has ever displayed in the management of the medical department in its varied and difficult relations, as well to the Federal prisoners as to the Confederate armies, actuates the Chief Executive, as well as the high officers of the Government charged with the general direction of such matters; and that no effort has been spared by the Confederate authorities, through Colonel Robert Ould, Agent of Exchange, to effect a complete and speedy exchange of Federal prisoners in their hands. As long as the Confederate Government is compelled to hold these prisoners as hostages for the safe return and exchange of the captive men of its own armies, it is difficult to devise efficient measures for the mitigation of much of the suffering of such an immense army of prisoners (equal at least to one-fourth of the Confederate forces actively engaged in the field east of the Mississippi), in a purely agricultural and sparsely settled country, with imperfect lines of communication, with but few manufactories, without commerce, cut off from all communication with the surrounding world, deprived of even the necessary medicines, which have been declared by its enemies 'contraband of war'; with torn and bleeding borders, with progressively diminishing powers of subsistence and resistance, with its entire fighting population in arms, and yet steadily driven back and overpowered by the hosts of the enemy, with a constant driving in of the population from the constantly contracting borders upon the overcrowded and distressed centre, and with a corresponding increase of travel upon the dilapidated railroads, already taxed far beyond their capacity with the transportation of troops, the munitions of war, and the sick and wounded. In Georgia especially, the very State in which these prisoners are confined, is the pressure of the Confederate disasters felt with daily increasing force. The disastrous campaign in Northern Georgia has been attended with the desolation of the fairest portions of the State. Thousands of families from the devastated regions, and from all the towns and villages from Chattanooga to Atlanta, and beyond, have fled to the regions considered more safe from invasion, and are occupying old cars, depots, sheds and tents, along the entire railroad system of Georgia. Thousands of old men, delicate women, and defenceless children have not only lost all their earthly possessions, but are without a roof to cover their heads, and are dependent for their daily bread upon the charities of the State government. The hospitals attached to the Army of Tennessee are in a constant state of motion, and the poorly fed and imperfectly treated wounded are suffering with the worst forms of hospital gangrene and pyaemia. Every available building, including churches and colleges and schoolhouses, suitable for hospital purposes, in all the towns and villages, are crowded with the sick and wounded, and Georgia may, with truth, be said to be one vast hospital. It is, therefore, with a sincere appreciation of the great difficulties of the situation, that I respectfully present for the consideration of the Surgeon-general the conditions which I believe to be essential to the relief of these suffering prisoners.

"1st. Such an increase of the Confederate guard as will allow of the enlargement and proper police of the military prison and hospital. The average area to each prisoner should be increased at least five-fold. The guard should be sufficiently strong within the prison to compel the prisoners to observe strict hygienic rules, not only with reference to the deposition and removal of fecal matters and filth of all kinds, but also with reference to personal cleanliness by frequent ablutions. The experience at this place demonstrates that the enforcement of proper hygienic rules must depend upon a regularly appointed and accountable guard, and not upon the prisoners. The removal of large numbers of the Federal prisoners to Millen, Savannah, Charleston, and other points, will without doubt tend to better the hygienic condition of the prisoners, for a time at least; but it is evident that if no system of police be established within the new prisons, then matters will gradually assume the same deplorable condition as at this place.

"2d. The construction of suitable barracks and hospital buildings. These have been projected and commenced, but the work should be hurried to a completion before cold weather.

"3d. The increase of the medical staff, and the appointment of one or more chaplains.

"4th. The appointment of disabled Confederate soldiers as nurses, ward-masters, and apothecaries; many of these men who are incapable of performing active service in the field, possess the necessary intelligence and physical ability to act as hospital attendants, and also to enforce the necessary sanitary regulations.

"5th. The great prevalence of scurvy demands that a liberal supply of fresh vegetables, sweet potatoes and fresh milk, should be issued. If the sour oranges of Florida and of the Southern seacoast could be obtained, they would produce the best results in the treatment of scurvy. I consider an abundant and regular supply of fresh milk as also essential to the treatment of chronic diarrhœa and dysentery, which are prevailing to so great an extent, and which appear to be entirely beyond control under the present mode of treatment and diet. I suggested to the surgeon in charge of the prison hospital the propriety of purchasing a number of cows for the use of the sick."

CHAPTER III.

The difficulties under which the medical officers labored in the treatment of the sick and wounded prisoners at Andersonville, are shown in the following "Reports," copied from the hospital records, which were embodied, and fortunately preserved in Surgeon Joseph Jones's able, elaborate, and unbiassed investigations upon the diseases of the Federal prisoners at Andersonville:

C. S. MILITARY PRISON, ANDERSONVILLE, GA.,
CHIEF SURGEON'S OFFICE, *April 25th*, 1864.

GENERAL:—I have the honor to report that the total number of patients treated up to date is two thousand six hundred and ninety-seven, with seven hundred and eighteen deaths. The large ratio of mortality is due to the debilitated condition in which many of the prisoners were when admitted into the prison — having been confined for a long time in other prisons — and to the absence of proper hospital accommodation, the construction of which has been prevented by the difficulty experienced in obtaining lumber; and small-pox was introduced into the prison by prisoners sent from Richmond, Va. Vaccination has been resorted to; the disease has not spread to any extent, and is now on the decline.

The sick are treated in tents, of which there is an inadequate supply. The present location of the hospital is objectionable, for the following reasons:—The drainage of the sinks of the prison passes through the hospital grounds. The contiguity to the prisoners will disseminate disease amongst them. The hospital being within the stockade, hospital bedding, diet, and other supplies for the comfort of the sick and wounded, are stolen by the prisoners, and the impossibility of keeping them out of the hospital is a source of annoyance to the sick. I therefore most respectfully suggest that the hospital be placed outside of the stockade, and erected on a site adjacent, and admirably adapted to the purpose.

Respectfully submitted,

ISAIAH H. WHITE, *Chief Surgeon.*

To Brigadier-general MARCUS J. WRIGHT, C. S. Army.

C. S. MILITARY PRISON, ANDERSONVILLE, GA.,
April 26th, 1864.

S. P. MOORE, *Surgeon-general C. S. A.*

SIR:—Your communication of the 15th inst., acknowledging receipt of sanitary report, and asking if the attention of the commanding officer had been called to the police of the camp, is at hand. In reply, I have the honor to state that the evil has been remedied, and the condition of the camp at the time of the report was no fault of the commanding officer, but was due to the great difficulty experienced in obtaining shovels and other tools requisite. Your honor should be informed that the prison is located in a section barren of resources, and great difficulty is experienced in obtaining the necessary appliances for its proper organisation, and a large number of prisoners arrived before its completion. I take pleasure in stating that the commanding officer, and the chief of each staff department, are using every effort to effect a thorough organisation.

Very respectfully, your obedient servant,

ISAIAH H. WHITE, *Chief Surgeon.*

SANITARY REPORT.

In compliance with regulations, I have the honor to make the following report of the sanitary condition of the C. S. Military Prison at Andersonville:

There is nothing in the topography of the country that can be said to have influenced the health of the command. The location is elevated and well drained. The soil is sandy, without vegetable mould or other cryptogamous growth likely to engender malaria. The large ratio of diseases of the digestive system has been due to long confinement in prison, with the diet. I am convinced from observation that a majority of the cases of diarrhœa and dysentery have, more or less, scorbutic connection. The bakery and other culinary arrangements have just been completed, up to which time there had been an inadequate supply of cooking utensils, and in consequence thereof the articles of diet have been insufficiently cooked. The ration is the same as that issued to the Confederate soldiers in the field, namely, beef, one pound, or in lieu, one-third pound of bacon; corn-meal, one and a quarter pounds, with an occasional issue of rice, beans, molasses and vinegar. The arrangements for a thorough policing of the prison are not yet finished. Through the centre of stockade passes a stream, affording an ample supply of good water. At the upper end of the prison it is designed to construct two dams of different heights; the upper to be used for drinking, the lower for bathing; over the remainder of the stream are to be arranged the sinks. The stream has sufficient volume and velocity to carry off all ordure. Once a day the flood-gates of the dams mentioned above are to be opened, thereby driving off all deposits that may have collected during the day. At present the police of the camp is defective, but the commander of the interior, Captain Wirz, is using every effort to effect the arrangement mentioned above, which has been retarded up to the present time by an inadequate supply of the necessary tools. The habits of the men, as a rule, are filthy in the extreme, and as soon as the arrangements for bathing have been completed it will be necessary to compel them to bathe at stated periods. The dimensions of the prison will not admit of exercise, the absence of which, with the depressing influences, produced by disappointed hopes of exchange, is a prolific source of disease.

The large ratio of mortality is due to the debilitated condition of the prisoners, produced by long confinement in prison, and to the absence of proper hospital accommodations. The worst cases are treated in tents, of which there is an inadequate supply. The present location of the hospital is objectionable, for the following reasons:— The prisoners with their camp-fires are densely crowded around the hospital, preventing a free circulation of air, so necessary to the treatment of the class of diseases prevailing. The mistaken kindness of their comrades who visit them, and furnish them improper diet, produces deleterious consequences. It is to be admitted, however, that such instances are rare, and in many instances assistance is refused to dying comrades in the same tent. In consequence of the predatory forays upon the hospital, by which the sick are robbed of their blankets, clothes, and diet, it will be impossible to furnish the hospital with proper bedding and diet while the hospital remains within the stockade. The drainage from the prison passing through the hospital grounds is another great objection to its location; I therefore most respectfully suggest that authority be granted to place the hospital outside the stockade, and that an adequate supply of tents be furnished until proper hospitals can be constructed.

ISAIAH H. WHITE, *Chief Surgeon.*

May 6th, 1864.

CAPTAIN:—I have the honor to submit the following report of the sanitary condition of the C. S. Military Prison at Andersonville, Ga.:

The prison is situated on two opposing banks of a stream, which furnishes an ample supply of good water for drinking and bathing purposes. The location is elevated and well drained. The soil is sandy, without vegetable mould or other cryptogamous growth likely to engender malaria. The prisoners are not supplied with barracks or tents, but most of them have provided themselves with little huts, made of boughs, thus making themselves comparatively comfortable. This, however, will be insufficient during the extremely hot weather of the summer months. There being no trees, or other protection from the rays of the sun, and crowded together as they are, it will be necessary to furnish them with tents, or other more capacious quarters than those now occupied, in order that they may be divided off into proper streets, admitting free circulation of air and the enforcing of the necessary police regulation. At the upper end of the stream it is designed to construct two dams, of different altitudes, the upper for drinking, and the lower for bathing purposes; over the remainder of the stream it is designed to construct the sinks. The stream is of sufficient volume and velocity to carry off all ordure.

The number of cases treated from the foundation of the prison, up to date, has been 4588, with 1026 deaths. The number reported sick and wounded for the month of April exhibits a ratio of 316.1 cases and 57.6 deaths per 1000 of mean strength.

Amongst the first prisoners admitted there was a large ratio of diseases of the respiratory system, contracted in transit from Richmond during very cold weather, and the majority of which resulted fatally, in consequence of the absence of barracks and hospital accommodations, and the emaciated condition of the subjects, due to long confinement in prison. The diseases now prevailing are those of the digestive system, diarrhœa and dysentery, which have in most instances a scorbutic connection. The rations of the prisoners are the same as those issued to Confederate soldiers in the field, namely, one pound of beef, or in lieu, three-quarters of a pound of bacon, one and a quarter pounds meal, with an occasional issue of beans, rice, molasses and vinegar. The bakery and other culinary arrangements have just been completed, and rations are now issued cooked. Up to this time there has been an inadequate supply of cooking utensils, in consequence of which the food was improperly prepared, and increased the number of cases of diarrhœa and dysentery.

The ratio of mortality is due to the lack of vitality in the subjects, produced by long confinement in prison, with its depressing influences on the mind. The remedies employed are unassisted by the *vis medicatrix naturæ,* without which remedial agencies are powerless. It is also impossible to treat diseases with success with the present hospital accommodations. The patients are now treated in tent-flies, of which there is an inadequate supply. The location of the hospital is also objectionable. The prisoners, with their camp-fires, are densely crowded around the hospital, producing contaminating effluvia, and preventing the free circulation of air, so necessary to the treatment of disease. In consequence of the forays upon the hospital by the prisoners, it is impossible to supply the sick with proper comforts. The drainage from the sinks of the prison passing through the hospital grounds, is another objection to its location. I therefore respectfully suggest that authority be granted to place the hospital outside of the stockade, and that an adequate supply of tents to accommodate one thousand sick be immediately furnished.

Respectfully submitted,

ISAIAH H. WHITE, *Chief Surgeon.*

Captain BOWIE, ***May,*** **1864.**

CHIEF SURGEON'S OFFICE, ANDERSONVILLE, GA.,
June 20th, 1864.

SIR:—I have the honor to submit the following report of the sanitary condition of the C. S. Military Prison, Andersonville, Ga.:

Your inspection of the prison has no doubt convinced you of the too crowded condition of the prisoners within the stockade, which, combined with the absence of barrack accommodation, is a prolific source of disease. The arrangements for the enforcing of proper regulations for cleanliness of the camp are in progress. The hospital up to the 22d ultimo was located within the stockade, where it was impossible to provide the sick with the necessary comforts. The supply of tents has never been adequate to accommodate the number of sick. The

CROWDED HOSPITAL AT ANDERSONVILLE.

present site of the hospital affords a fine shade, and a good supply of water for drinking and cleanliness. The area is a parallelogram, whose sides are two hundred and sixty and three hundred and forty feet. There are two hundred and more tents of all kinds, the majority of which are small picket-tents, and tent-flies, ill adapted to hospital purposes. The capacity consistent with comfort does not exceed eight hundred men ; but in consequence of an inadequate supply, they have been compelled to accommodate one thousand and twenty of the worst cases. They are now so crowded as to render it necessary to refuse admission to many cases which cannot be treated with success in the kind of quarters occupied by the inmates of the prison. Two hundred hospital-tents are required to accommodate the present and daily increasing number of sick. Delay in obtaining medical supplies frequently arises, in consequence of the requisitions being required to be sent to Medical Director of Hospitals at Atlanta for approval, whilst the supplies are drawn from Macon, Ga., only sixty miles distant. I would suggest, for the consideration of the proper authority, the propriety of permitting the medical purveyor at Macon to issue on requisition of the chief surgeon of the post, approved by the commanding officer. The supply of medicines is not at all times equal to the demand, being issued in quantities much less than is allowed by the supply table. The deficiencies which occur cannot be properly met, in consequence of the delay which arises from sending requisitions to Atlanta for approval, and awaiting their return.

The report of sick and wounded for the month of April exhibits a ratio per one thousand (1000) of mean strength, three hundred and six and one-tenth cases treated, and fifty-seven and six-tenths deaths. May, six hundred and forty and thirty-three one-hundredths cases treated, and forty-seven and three-tenths deaths. The daily ratio per one thousand of mean strength for the twenty days of the present month, has been one and five-sevenths deaths, which, taken as an average for the thirty days, would make fifty-one and four-tenths deaths per one thousand of mean strength for the month of June. The morning report of C. S. M. Prison shows remaining in hospital one thousand and twenty-two; in quarters, two thousand six hundred and sixty-five; deaths, forty; strength of command, twenty-three thousand nine hundred and eleven.

The number of medical officers on duty at the prison is inadequate to perform the duties required of them. There are in all twelve, seven of whom attend sick-call, and five on duty at hospital; of the entire number, five are employed by contract. I would suggest that the medical force be increased by ten additional officers.

Respectfully submitted,

ISAIAH H. WHITE, *Chief Surgeon.*

Captain HAMMOND.

SANITARY REPORT OF C. S. MILITARY PRISON HOSPITAL, ANDERSONVILLE, GEORGIA.

There is nothing in the topography of the country that can be said to have influenced the health of the command, except, perhaps, in the immediate camp, through which passes a stream of water, the margins of which are low and swampy, and have been recently drained with a view of reclaiming them for camping purposes; the result of which has been to expose to the rays of the summer's sun a large surface covered with decaying vegetable matter, a condition favorable to the production of malarious diseases. This surface in now being covered with dry sand. With this exception, the land is high and well drained, and the soil light and sandy.

The prisoners being from the United States, have been as much influenced, perhaps, by the climate as any other agency. The prison was built to accommodate ten thousand (10,000) prisoners, in which have unavoidably been placed over twenty-six thousand (26,000), causing them to become so crowded as to prevent a proper circulation and due allowance of pure air.

With this crowded condition there is an absence of barracks or tents; the only protection from the weather being little huts made of boughs, blankets, and small picket-tents, used in the U. S. Army, which, being irregularly arranged, obstruct the free circulation of air. Within the last few days the stockade has been increased ten acres, relieving the crowded condition heretofore existing. Barracks are also being constructed; it, however, is an immense task, and will not soon be completed.

The diet of the prisoners is the same as that issued to Confederate soldiers in the field, namely, one pound of beef, or one-third pound bacon, and one and a quarter pounds of meal, with an occasional issue of beans and rice.

There is great lack of cleanliness on the part of the prisoners. The chief cause of disease and mortality is long confinement in prison, which, in connection with the diet (having produced scurvy among them), has so lowered their vitality as to render them unable to resist disease.

The hospital in the early part of the quarter being situated within the stockade, it was impossible to supply the sick with the necessary comforts; hospital bedding, diet, &c., being stolen from the hospital by the prisoners. In the latter part of May, authority was granted to move the hospital without the stockade. The condition of the sick has been much improved by the change. They are now treated in a hospital camp, well supplied with shade and water. The tents are for the most part small and ill-adapted to hospital purposes, and insufficient in number to accommodate the large number of sick to be treated. The tents are filled to excess, and many men are refused admission to hospital for want of room.

During the quarter, the prison has been on several occasions without any medicines whatever. Requisitions are made for one month's supply, which are filled in such diminished quantity as to create the necessity for other requisitions during the month. These have to go to Atlanta for approval; in consequence of the irregularity of the mail, they do not return frequently under eight or ten days; they have then to be sent to the medical purveyor at Macon, where they are usually filled with promptness; but before they are received, one-half the period drawn for has elapsed, and the former supply is exhausted.

The number of medical officers on duty at the prison is inadequate to perform the required duties. There are over twenty-six thousand (26,000) prisoners, with only thirteen (13) medical officers; of this number, five attend the hospital, where there are eleven hundred and thirty-four (1134) sick.

Respectfully submitted,

ISAIAH H. WHITE, *Chief Surgeon Post.*

Quarter ending June 30th, 1864.

HEADQUARTERS POST, ANDERSONVILLE, GA.,
MED. DEPARTMENT, *June 26th*, 1864.

SIR:—I have just established a hospital for the troops on duty at this post, to accommodate one hundred sick, and have assigned Assistant-surgeon W. B. Harrison in charge. Be pleased to instruct me through what channel medical officers serving with the troops doing duty at this post are to report.

On the removal of the hospital from the stockade, I informed you what accommodation I had made for the sick. The strength of the command having increased to twenty-five thousand men, more than double that for which hospital accommodations were prepared, the hospital is now filled far beyond its healthy capacity. I have tents of all kinds to accommodate eight hundred men, in which I have been compelled to crowd over twelve hundred, being unable to procure others. General Winder, commanding post, has telegraphed to Richmond, to see if we can obtain the tents that were occupied by the prisoners on Belle Isle, at Richmond, Virginia. If successful, it will take some weeks for them to reach here. For humanity's sake, please assist me in obtaining two hundred tents at once. There are nearly three thousand (3000) sick in the prison, many of whom require hospital treatment, which cannot be furnished because of the already crowded condition of the hospital. It is impossible to get tents from the quartermaster in this department.

The number of medical officers on duty here is utterly inadequate to perform the duties required of them. There are one thousand and thirty-five patients in hospital, with only five medical officers; only eight to attend sick call at the prison, with a command of twenty-five thousand men, and the number increasing each day. Please assign one or more good surgeons that I can place in charge of the different divisions of the prison hospital.

The direct contact into which the surgeon in charge of the prison hospital is brought with the commandant of the interior of the prison, would produce incalculable discord and confusion, if he were not willing to coöperate, and forego many things that would be desired for the proper arrangement of a hospital. I hope you will consider these things in making the assignment. Send a man of sufficient intelligence and zeal for the cause, to duly appreciate all the disadvantages to be encountered.

Surgeon Stout's communication of the 7th inst., in relation to recommending competent private physicians for contract, has been received. Being an entire stranger here, I have no one to recommend. It seems impossible to obtain any one exempt from military service, almost any employment being more lucrative. I am aware that the recent operations of the army have created a great demand for medical officers in your department, and it is with great reluctance that I urge the necessity of assigning at least ten additional officers.

Very respectfully your obedient servant,

ISAIAH H. WHITE, *Chief Surgeon of Post.*

S. M. BEMIS, *Surgeon P. A. C. A., Acting Med. Direct. Hospitals.*

CHIEF SURGEON'S OFFICE, ANDERSONVILLE, GA.,
July 1st, 1864.

S. P. MOORE, *Surgeon-general C. S. A.*

SIR:—I am instructed by the General Commanding to represent that inconvenience and delay arise in obtaining medical and hospital supplies, in consequence of requisitions being required to be sent to Surgeon Stout, Medical Director of Hospitals at Atlanta, Ga., for approval. In consequence of the mails, eight or ten days frequently elapse before the requisition with approval returns to this office, which has then to be sent to the medical purveyer at Macon. Before the medicines arrive here, two weeks (or one-half the period for which the requisition is made) have elapsed, creating a scarcity, and in some instances an entire lack of medicines. In addition to prisoners, of which there are twenty-six thousand three hundred and sixty-seven (26,367), the command consists of five regiments and one company of artillery as guard. I am informed by Surgeon Stout, that medical officers on duty with these regiments do not report through him. Brigadier-general John H. Winder, commanding post, reports directly to Secretary of War, this not being considered a part of any military department in this State. If compatible with the interests of the service, I most respectfully request that I be permitted to report directly to the Surgeon-general, and that the medical purveyor at Macon, Ga., be instructed to issue to this post on requisition with my approval.

Very respectfully your obedient servant,

ISAIAH H. WHITE, *Chief Surgeon Post.*

CHIEF SURGEON'S OFFICE, ANDERSONVILLE, GA.,
August 2d, 1864.

COLONEL:—I have the honor to submit the following report of the sanitary condition of the C. S. Military Prison:

The number of sick on morning report is one thousand three hundred and five (1305) in hospital, and five thousand and ten (5010) in quarters.

The total number of deaths from the organisation of the prison (February 24, 1864) up to date, is four thousand five hundred and eighty-five.

The following table exhibits the ratio per one thousand (1000) of mean strength during the different months:

Months.	Mean Strength.	Deaths.	Ratio per 100 of Mean Strength.
March	7,500	283	37.4
April	10,000	576	57.6
May	15,000	708	47.2
June	22,291	1201	53.87
July	29,030	1817	62.7

Owing to insufficient hospital accommodations, many are treated in quarters who should be in hospital. The present capacity of the hospital is for one thousand four hundred sick. The hospital is situated in an oak grove, affording good shade. Through the prison passes a stream of water, furnishing an ample supply of water for cleanliness. Drinking water is obtained, of good quality, from wells and springs on the banks of the stream. The tents are insufficient in number, and not of proper size for the treatment of sick. Most of them are the small fly-tent and tent-flies. There should be at least two hundred hospital- or five hundred wall-tents to properly accommodate the sick. It has been impossible, up to this time, to obtain straw for bedding, this not being a grain-growing district. Small crops of wheat have been raised this year, and efforts are being made to collect a sufficient quantity as soon as the present crop is threshed. But there is lack of transportation at the post, and farmers are unwilling to hire their own teams for the purpose. The attendants are paroled prisoners, who, as a rule, are faithful in the performance of their duty, being actuated by the improvement of their own condition on removal from the stockade, and a fear of return if negligent in the performance of duty, apart from the desire to serve their own sick comrades.

The number of medical officers, until the recent call of the militia by the Governor of Georgia, was utterly inadequate; since that time, a number of physicians have been employed by contract, and others have been detailed by the Governor to serve in the medical department. These having been but recently assigned, it is impossible to decide upon their proficiency. The other medical officers, with a few exceptions, are capable and attentive. The physicians who have been recently employed will no doubt cancel their contracts as soon as the militia is disbanded, and the services of the detailed physicians will also be lost. With this view, I would suggest that a sufficient number of competent medical officers be assigned.

There is a deficiency of medical supplies issued by the medical purveyor. Supplies of medicines have been occasionally entirely exhausted, and we have been left several days at a time without any whatever. This has arisen from the delay experienced in sending requisitions to the medical director at Atlanta for approval. The hospital ration is commuted as for other general hospitals, and supplies for the subsistence and comfort of sick are purchased with the hospital fund. Heretofore we have been able to supply the sick with vegetables, but during the entire month of July the commissary has been without funds, and difficulty has been experienced in purchasing on time. The rations issued to the prisoners is the same as that issued to Confederate soldiers in the field, namely, one-third pound pork, one and a quarter pounds meal, with an occasional issue of beans, rice and molasses. The meal is issued unbolted, and when baked is coarse and unwholesome. Amongst the old prisoners, scurvy prevails to a great extent, which is usually accompanied by diseases of the digestive organs. This, in connection with the mental depression produced by long imprisonment, is the chief cause of the mortality. There is nothing in the topography of the country that can be said to influence the health of the prison. The land is high and well drained, the soil light and sandy, with no marshes or other source of malaria in the vicinity. The densely crowded condition of the prisoners, with the innumerable little shelters irregularly arranged, precludes the enforcement of proper police, and prevents free circulation of air.

The lack of barrack accommodation exposes the men to tne heat of the sun during the day, and to the dews at night, and is a prolific source of disease. The margins of the stream passing through the stockade are low and boggy, and having been recently drained, has exposed a large surface covered with vegetable mould to the rays of the sun, a condition favorable to the development of malarious diseases. It is the design of the commandant of the prison to cover the surface with dry sand, but the work has been unavoidably delayed. . . . Captain Wirz, the commandant of the prison, has doubtless explained to you the difficulties which have prevented these, with other projected improvements in the way of bathing and other arrangements for cleanliness.

Very respectfully your ooeaient servant,

ISAIAH H. WHITE, *Chief Surgeon of Post.*

To Colonel CHANDLER.

REPORT OF CHIEF SURGEON WHITE TO GENERAL WINDER ON THE SANITARY CONDITION OF THE MILITARY PRISON AT ANDERSONVILLE.

CHIEF SURGEON'S OFFICE, ANDERSONVILLE, GA.,
August 6th, 1864.

GENERAL:—I have the honor to submit the following report of the sanitary condition of the C. S. Military Prison:

I. *Medical Topography of the Station.*—The location is high and well drained; the soil light and sandy. Near the stockade, in a southward direction, is a creek whose margins are muddy and boggy. Through the centre of the stockade passes a smaller stream of similar character. The condition is favorable to the development of malarious diseases, but the report of the sick and wounded for the month of July exhibits a small ratio of this class of diseases. Out of ten thousand six hundred and twenty-one cases treated, only five hundred and five are of a malarious character. This cause appears to have acted more on the garrison than on the prisoners; out of sixteen hundred and three cases treated, one hundred and forty-five malarious cases are reported.

II. *The Climate.*—The climate is hot, and the prisoners coming from a much higher latitude, have been influenced greatly by this agency.

III. *Nature of Barracks and Hospital Accommodations.*—The prisoners are without barracks or tents. Thirty thousand men aer densely crowded together, sheltered only by blankets and low hovels, densely and irregularly arranged, preventing free circulation, engendering foul and noxious vapors, and precluding any system of police: the men are exposed during the day to the rays of the sun, and the dews at night, and many are unprotected during the rains.

IV. The hospital accommodations are utterly inadequate to accommodate the large number of sick. The hospital is located in a grove, on the banks of the creek, southeast of the stockade. The site is the most eligible in the vicinity, with the present appliances. There is a great deficiency in the number of tents in which the sick are treated; they are also too small for hospital purposes. A constant increase in the number of prisoners, and hence of the sick, has called for a continued expansion of hospital accommodations. The hospital camp was first designed to accommodate one thousand sick, and was fitted up as best could be with the means at hand. Since that time the number of sick in hospital has increased to two thousand two hundred and eight, and three hundred and seventeen attendants; total, two thousand five hundred and twenty-five; the result of which has been to place the hospital in a constant state of organisation, and the efforts to make some provision for all have resulted in leaving all portions of the hospital in an unfinished state. All the tents of the original camp have been filled with bunks; at present, the quartermaster cannot furnish plank to complete the others. It has been impossible to obtain straw for bedding, there being none in the country until the present crop. The Chief Surgeon has made every effort to have it supplied. Until the number of sick became so large, pine-straw was used for the purpose; but it being necessary to renew the supply once in two weeks (in consequence of vermin), it is impossible to obtain a sufficient quantity. It would require five wagons constantly employed to furnish an adequate supply. The Chief Surgeon has instructed the agent for the purchase of supplies, after subsistence or comfort of sick, to purchase wheat-straw and ship by railroad, the quartermaster having failed to supply us.

V. *Diet.*—The ration consists of one-third pound of bacon, one and a quarter pounds meal. The meal is unbolted, and when baked the bread is coarse and irritating, producing diseases of the organs of the digestive system (diarrhœa and dysentery). The absence of vegetable diet has produced scurvy to an alarming extent, especially amongst the old prisoners.

VI. *Water.*—The drinking water is obtained from springs settled on the banks of the stream, and from wells, and to some extent from the stream. The water obtained from the stream is unfit for use, containing many impurities from the bakery and cook-house. Some of the camps of the garrison are situated on this stream, the surface drainage from which empties into this stream before passing through the stockade. The supply from the springs near the stream is a little brackish, but better than the stream. A large number of wells have been dug in the prison, affording water of an excellent quality.

VII. *Clothing.*—Those who have been prisoners for a long time are badly supplied with clothing, and but few of them have a change, in consequence of which they are for the most part very filthy.

VIII. *General Habits of the Men as to Cleanliness.*—With but few exceptions, they are filthy as regards their persons and clothing, and do not seem to appreciate the great necessity for bathing.

IX. *Police System of the Camp.*—This is sadly defective. . . The bottom land through which the stream passes is filthy beyond description. The character of the land is low and swampy; a large surface covered with vegetable mould is exposed to the rays of the sun, a condition favorable to the development of malarious diseases. . . The place of exit of the stream beyond the stockade is not sufficiently bold to permit a free efflux, and the fall of the stream beyond the stockade is not great enough. . .

X. *Crowded Condition of the Prison.*—The prison is filled far beyond its healthy capacity. The number of prisoners should be reduced sufficiently to admit of their camps being regularly laid out, with streets of sufficient width to admit free circulation of air, and the enforcement of stringent police regulations. An area of sufficient size should be left for exercise.

XI. *Mental Depression.*—Long confinement and hope deferred have produced, with many of the prisoners, a state of mental depression, dreaded by the physician even in civil practice, which, combined with the existing state of physical debility, renders them unable to resist disease.

The Evils within the Power of the Proper Authority to Correct.

I. *The Crowded Condition of the Prisoners.*—The number within the stockade should not exceed fifteen thousand. This would allow ample room for the remainder to be camped in order, with streets of sufficient width to allow free circulation of air, and enforcement of police regulations. All that portion of the camp on the north side of the stream could then be used for exercise, where roll-calls could also be held, thereby materially aiding the commandant of the interior.

II. *Construction of Barracks and Hospital Accommodations.*—There should be no delay in the construction of barracks; with the greatest amount of energy, it will be difficult to complete them before cold weather comes on, when they will be required more than at present. Too great stress cannot be placed on the necessity for the construction of proper accommodations for the sick. There are at present two thousand two hundred and eight in hospital, all poorly provided for, and some three hundred without any shelter whatever. There are, also, at least one thousand men now in stockade who are helpless, and should be at once removed to hospital. Their removal is prevented by the absence of accommodations. The construction of hospitals should be at once begun, and in the meantime the sick should be at once transferred to some points where they can be properly provided for. An officer should be employed to arrange the stream passing through the stockade. The bottom land should be covered over with sand, the stream be made deeper and wider, the walls and bottom covered with plank; the same arrangements to continue outside, conducting the drainage freely to the creek beyond, and, if necessary, build a dam to prevent the overflow of the banks. The stream from the stockade to the railroad should also be improved, and the use of it by the troops or others outside should be prohibited. At the upper part of the stream, proper bathing arrangements should be constructed.

III. *Enforce Stringent Police Regulations.*—Some stringent rules of police should be established, and scavenger wagons should be sent in every day to remove the collections of filth. A large quantity of mouldy bread and other decomposing matter scattered through the camp and beyond the dead-line should be removed at once. If necessary, sentinels should be instructed to fire on any one committing a nuisance in any other place than the sinks.

IV. *Establishment of Regulations in regard to Cleanliness.*—

It should be the duty of Confederate sergeants attending roll-calls, or others, to see that all men of their command bathe at stated intervals, and that their clothes are washed at least once a week. For this purpose, soap should be issued to the prisoners.

V. *Improvement in Rations.*—The meal should be bolted or sifted before being issued. Arrangements should be speedily made by which rice, beans and other anti-scorbutics should be issued during the present season; green corn might be issued in lieu of bread ration, if not regularly, at least three times a week. If possible, the prisoners should be supplied with vinegar, and with an occasional issue of molasses in lieu of the meat ration, which would tend greatly to correct the scurvy which prevails to a great extent.

Very respectfully your obedient servant,

ISAIAH H. WHITE, *Chief Surgeon of Post.*

Brigadier-general JOHN H. WINDER.

OFFICE OF SURGEON IN CHARGE C. S. MILITARY PRISON HOSPITAL,
ANDERSONVILLE, GA., *September 1st*, 1864.

SIR:—Having been assigned to duty in charge of C. S. Military Prison Hospital at this place, and finding no building of any character whatever for the accommodation of the sick and wounded, I respectfully submit to your consideration the accompanying plan of a series of sheds for the accommodation of the sick and wounded, covering a space of ground four hundred and fifty by nine hundred feet. These sheds can be erected very rapidly, and with but little expense to the Government.

I propose to make these sheds one hundred feet long, twenty-two feet wide, and eight feet high at the eaves. Posts set in the ground, with a streamer running the entire length of the building, twelve inches from the eaves, to which is attached an awning made from old tents (of which any quantity can be procured). This at once gives a ward that will contain fifty patients (the awning to be raised or lowered at pleasure) in a well-ventilated room. I propose to erect forty of these sheds, giving ten to the division, with a capacity of five hundred patients to the division, or two thousand to the hospital.

I also propose a cooking, baking, and convalescent dining-room to each division, with one special diet kitchen and laundry to the whole hospital, the whole to be enclosed with a stockade. Outside the stockade I propose to erect a suitable depot building for the reception of commissary stores, medicines, &c. A hospital of this description can be erected at this post or any other, where lumber and material are so easily procured, with much less cost to the Government than by any other means. While tents may answer for temporary purposes, I am opposed to using them for permanent hospitals, it being a matter of impossibility to keep them properly policed. Hoping that this plan may meet with your favorable consideration, and that I will receive your coöperation on this subject, I have the honor to be,

Very respectfully your obedient servant,

R. R. STEVENSON, *Surgeon in Charge.*

TO S. P. MOORE, *Surgeon-general C. S. A , Richmond, Va.*

OFFICE OF SURGEON IN CHARGE C. S. MILITARY PRISON HOSPITAL,
ANDERSONVILLE, GA., *September 16th,* 1864.

SIR:—I have the honor to report to you that I have been assigned to duty by Surgeon I. H. White, Chief Surgeon of Post, in charge of Confederate States Military Hospital. In assuming the responsibilities of so important a position, and before entering upon my duties, I deem it necessary to make the following statement of the sanitary condition of the hospital, and appliances for the comfort of the sick and wounded. The topography, climate and prevalent diseases of the country have been given you in former reports by my predecessor. I shall confine myself principally to the following:

I. *Nature of Barrack Accommodations.*—The stockade (in

the shape of a parallelogram) includes twenty-seven acres of ground. A considerable stream of water passes through it, running in a westward direction. In this space of ground from thirty to forty thousand prisoners have been crowded, with no protection whatever from the burning rays of the sun, except such as could be made from blankets or dirt hovels. Along the banks of the stream the ground is quite boggy, and water is constantly oozing from the low banks. Recently four sheds have been built inside the stockade; these were the beginning of a series of barracks capable of accommodating two hundred and seventy men each. . . . From three to four thousand sick and wounded men are inside the stockade. The number of medical officers is entirely inadequate to the demands of the sick. At present writing only four medical officers are on duty; whereas, to take the proper care of the sick and wounded, there should be not less than twenty-five efficient medical officers constantly on duty in the stockade, in order to meet the wants of the sick, and keep the proper register and reports. Under the present régime, hundreds die in the stockade, and are buried, whose names and diseases are unknown. This can be remedied by no other means than by a sufficient corps of medical officers. All the medical officers who have been on duty here are detailed men from the militia and contract physicians, and as a matter of course are very inefficient.

II. *Nature of Hospital Accommodations.*—The hospital is situated near the southwest corner of the stockade, covering about five acres of ground, inclosed by a frail board fence. A sluggish stream of water flows through the southern part of the lot. The ground is sloping, and facing the southeast. On the southwest side of the enclosure is a swamp, about three hundred yards in width, and on the northwest side is the stream which flows through the stockade. The banks being very low, and subject to overflow, from these swamps arise putrid exhalations, at times almost insupportable. It will be seen by the accompanying drawing that the hospital is but a short distance from the confluence of the branch and creek; and although on rolling table-land, it is much lower than the surrounding country, and very near where the branch disembogues from the stockade, occupying such a position that all the surrounding depressing agencies would seem to centre in the hospital. As well as in the stockade, the number of medical officers is deficient, being composed (with a few exceptions) of men either detailed or under contract. On examining the roster, I find that twenty-four medical officers are charged to the hospital, and yet but twelve are on duty. The rest (either by order of Governor Brown or their own request) are off on sick leave or leave of indulgence. In order to attend to the wants of the sick and wounded, not less than thirty efficient medical officers should be on duty in the hospital. Confusion will necessarily occur without this number.

From eighteen hundred to twenty-five hundred patients are crowded into this space. Tents of a very inferior quality are the only means of protection, a majority of them being in the small "A" tents. Temporary bunks are erected in most of them by driving forks into the ground, and placing small poles or boards to lie on; a great number of patients are compelled to lie on the ground, in consequence of the smallness of the tents. The cooking arrangements are very deficient; two large kettles, erected on a furnace, are nearly all the utensils that are used. The bread is of the most unhealthy character, being made of coarse unbolted corn-meal. This of itself, under the most favorable circumstances, must prove a source of great irritation to the bowels. Scurvy, gangrene, and bowel affections are prevailing at present to an alarming extent. Frequent issues of green corn, peas, molasses, vinegar, rice, flour and sweet potatoes are being made; and under suitable hospital accommodations, the condition of the sick would be greatly ameliorated. The purveyor's department has been able to supply nearly all the necessary medicines. The indigenous remedies are being extensively used with much good effect. The medical officers in charge of the different wards and divisions are all diligent, and seem willing to discharge their duties, although laboring under many and great disadvantages.

Great efforts have been made to make the stockade secure in preventing the escape of the prisoners; but little attention is paid to the hygienic and sanitary condition of the sick. Surgeon I. H. White, Chief Surgeon of Post, informs me that timely requisitions have been made on the quartermaster's department for the necessary materials to make the sick and wounded comfortable, but thus far he has been able to procure scarcely anything. The means of transportation being very limited, both by railroad and teams, have proved a source of great annoyance. I would respectfully suggest that the necessary steps be taken to secure transportation for hospital material over all other stores, except ammunition. This would at once remedy a great evil.

The greatest amount of confusion seems to have prevailed in consequence of soliciting attachés for the hospital from Federal prisoners, in place of disabled Confederate soldiers. Great waste in property, medicines and provisions has been the result. This I shall endeavor to correct as speedily as possible.

I would respectfully request that an efficient quartermaster and commissary be ordered to report to me for special hospital duty, with full power from the War Department to provide for the comfort of the sick and wounded Federal prisoners. Without an arrangement of this kind, I very much fear the hospital department in C. S. Military Prison will continue to be neglected. Hoping that this communication may meet with favorable consideration, I have the honor to be,

Very respectfully your obedient servant,

R. R. STEVENSON, *Surgeon in Charge.*

To S. P. MOORE, *Surgeon-general C. S. A., Richmond, Va.*

CHAPTER IV.

In giving the causes that led to the great mortality of Federal prisoners at Andersonville, in addition to thosé already enumerated, I must not neglect Professor Jones's opinions as furnished in his "Report on the Pathological Investigations," before referred to. They embody the most correct and trustworthy data that have been furnished on the subject; and while they are of special interest to the medical profession, for which they were, strictly speaking, intended, yet they embody information likely to be of interest to the general reader. They read as follows:

I. *The great mortality among the Federal prisoners confined in the military prison at Andersonville, was not referable to climatic causes, or to the nature of the soil and waters.*

The Confederate States military prison at Camp Sumter was located by the Confederate authorities in an elevated, dry and healthy region, supplied with pure and wholesome water. The effects of malaria, which acts with greater or less intensity according to the character of the soil, the elevation of the country, and the presence or absence of marshes and swamps, and according to the season and temperature, and the amount of rain and of moisture in the atmosphere, throughout the entire belt of the Southern Atlantic and Gulf States, appear in the case of these prisoners to have been neutralized to a great extent by the artificial atmosphere generated within the crowded stockade and hospital.

II. *Not only were malarial fevers of infrequent occurrence amongst the Federal prisoners, but typhoid fever was rare and typhus fever was unknown.*

The Confederate guard camped around the military prison and hospital, suffered much more heavily both from malarial and typhoid fevers. I observed a number of severe cases of genuine typhoid fever among the Confederate reserves, composed almost entirely of recruits—boys and old men; while on the other hand I did not observe a single case of either typhoid or typhus fever among the Federal prisoners.

Among the Confederate troops in all parts of the Southern Confederacy, typhoid fever prevailed to the greatest extent in the earliest periods of the war, and among the recruits who had never before seen service, and especially among the recruits from the country. As the war progressed, this disease gradually disappeared from among the veterans, and its prolonged existence in the army appeared to be due to the constant addition of fresh recruits.

The infrequent occurrence of typhoid fever among those Federal prisoners, notwithstanding the existence of all the causes which are so dogmatically affirmed by a host of writers to be sufficient and essential to the development and rapid spread of this disease, may be explained by the fact that these prisoners had been long in confinement, and had probably passed through the diseases incident to camps and prisons, and the majority had had typhoid fever (which, as a general rule, attacks but once during a lifetime) before coming to Andersonville.

Here we have, in the dirty tents and mud-hovels, and crowded, filthy condition of the prisoners, in an atmosphere loaded with the foul exhalations of human excrements, fermentation of bread, and all other imaginable kinds of filth, all the apparent conditions for the generation of typhus fever, and of all the various contagious fevers. But still typhus fever was absent; and this disease had prevailed neither in the Confederate, nor in the Federal armies and military prisons.

The absence of typhus fever, notwithstanding the existence of every circumstance—as filth, bad diet, crowding, mental depression, bad and scant food, which has been declared as sufficient to cause its generation, would seem to show that the conditions for the origin of this disease are not so defined and well known as many writers would make them to appear by dogmatic assertions and superficial reasoning. This great experiment of Andersonville, perhaps the greatest and most remarkable of modern times, strongly sustains the view that typhus and typhoid fevers are dependent upon the action of special poisons, the conditions for the origin and action of which are as definite and as limited as in the case of the poisons of small-pox and measles. It would appear from the results of the experiment of Andersonville, as well as from the large number of well established facts presented during the course of the present inquiry, that neither typhoid nor typhus fevers can be generated by animal exhalations from putrefying excrements or bodies; but that these diseases are propagated by a special poison emitted by the living body, either directly, or through the excretions or secretions. Thus, if the excrements from a person suffering with typhoid fever are capable of communicating the disease, they do so in virtue of any decomposition set up in them after their removal from the living body. According to this view, the excrements from the diseased bowels of the typhoid patient resemble in their contagious power the poisonous secretions and scabs of the skin of the small-pox patient. However, while admitting that there is nothing unreasonable in the supposition that typhoid fever may be propagated through the matters thrown off from the diseased bowels, at the same time we are constrained to acknowledge that there are no experiments to prove that the excrements of typhoid fever will generate the disease if transported to a perfectly healthy locality, and allowed to contaminate a certain definite confined portion of air inhabited by healthy individuals, not otherwise exposed to the poison of typhoid fever.

The absence of typhoid fever from the Confederate armies and prisoners would seem to sustain the view that this disease does not arise *de novo*, but must be imported from some existing source of infection, as from those great places of its permanent abode, the mud-hovels and crowded cities of

Europe, and especially of Ireland and Hungary. While certain circumstances favor the rapid spread of typhus and typhoid fevers, when once introduced, it is illogical and erroneous to assign those conditions, without absolute experimental proof, as the causes for the origin of these diseases *de novo.*

III. *The chief causes of death among the Federal prisoners of Andersonville were scurvy and its results, and bowel affections, chronic and acute diarrhœa, and dysentery.*

Notwithstanding the exposure of these prisoners without shelter, the diseases referable more directly to this cause, as pneumonia, bronchitis, catarrh, and rheumatism, did not prevail to a greater extent among the Federal prisoners than among the Confederate soldiers in the field, who were in like manner exposed to the cold of winter and the heat of summer, without tents, and without any other shelter than that which they were able to construct with their hands.

IV. *The effects of salt meat and of farinaceous food without fresh vegetables were manifested in the great prevalence of scurvy.*

The scorbutic condition thus induced modified the course of every disease, poisoned every wound, however slight, and lay at the foundation of those obstinate and exhausting diarrhœas and dysenteries which swept off thousands of these unfortunate men. The Federal prisoners received the same rations in kind, quality and amount issued to the Confederate soldiers in the field. These rations were insufficient, and without that variety of fresh meat and vegetables which would ward off scurvy from soldiers as well as prisoners. As far as my experience extended, no body of troops could be confined exclusively to the Confederate ration without suffering materially in their health, and without manifesting symptoms of the scurvy. The Confederate ration grew worse and worse as the war progressed, and as portion after portion of the most fertile regions of the Confederate States were overrun and devastated by the Federal armies. In the straitened condition of the Confederate States, the support of an army of fifty thousand prisoners, forced upon their hands by a relentless policy, was a great and distressing burden, which consumed their scant resources and exhausted their over-taxed energies. It was the belief of the army as well as of the people, that the Confederate Government not only earnestly desired the exchange of all prisoners of war in their hands, but also that the Confederate authorities charged with the exchange of prisoners had used every effort in their power, consistent with their views of national honor and rectitude, to effect an exchange of all prisoners in their hands, and to establish definite rules by which all prisoners of war might be continuously exchanged as soon as possible after capture. Whatever the feelings of resentment on the part of the Confederates may have been against those who were invading and desolating their native land, which had been purchased by the blood of their ancestors from the Indians and English, the desire for the speedy exchange and return of the great army of veterans held captive in Northern prisons, was earnest and universal; and this desire for speedy and continuous exchange on the part of the Government, as well as on the part of the people, sprang not merely from motives of compassion for their unfortunate kindred and fellow-soldiers, but also from the dictates of that policy which would exchange, on the part of a weak and struggling people, a large army of prisoners (consumers and non-combatants, requiring an army for their guard) for an army of tried veterans. Apart from the real facts of the case, it is impossible to conceive that any Government, in the distressed and struggling state of the Confederate States, could deliberately advocate any policy which would deprive it of a large army of veterans, and compel it to waste its scant supplies, already insufficient for the support of its struggling and retreating armies, upon an immense number of prisoners. And, as the result has shown, the destruction of the Confederate Government was accomplished as much by the persistent retention in captivity of the Confederate soldiers, as by the emancipation and arming of the slaves.

V. *From the sameness of the food, and from the action of the poisonous gases in the densely crowded and filthy stockade and hospital, the blood was altered in its constitution, even before the manifestation of actual disease.*

In both the well and the sick, the red corpuscles were diminished; and in all diseases uncomplicated with inflammation, the fibrinous element was deficient. In cases of ulceration of the mucous membrane of the intestinal canal, the fibrinous element of the blood appeared to be increased; while in simple diarrhœa, uncomplicated with ulceration, and dependent upon the character of the food and the existence of scurvy, it was either diminished or remained stationary. Heart-clots were very common, if not universally present, in the cases of ulceration of the intestinal mucous membrane; while in the uncomplicated cases of diarrhœa and scurvy, the blood was fluid and did not coagulate readily, and the heart-clots and fibrinous concretions were almost universally absent. From the watery condition of the blood, there resulted various serous effusions into the pericardium, into the ventricles of the brain, and into the abdominal cavity.

In almost all the cases which I examined after death, even in the most emaciated, there was more or less serous effusion into the abdominal cavity. In cases of hospital gangrene of the extremities, and in cases of gangrene of the intestines, heart-clots and firm coagula were universally present. The presence of these clots in the cases of hospital gangrene, whilst they were absent in the cases in which there were no inflammatory symptoms, appears to sustain the conclusion that hospital gangrene is a species of inflammation (imperfect and irregular though it may be in its progress), in which the fibrinous element and coagulability of the blood are increased, even in those who are suffering from such a condition of the blood and from such diseases as are naturally accompanied with a decrease in the fibrinous constituent.

VI. *The impoverished condition of the blood, which led to serous effusions within the ventricles of the brain, and around the brain and spinal cord, and into the pericardial and abdominal cavities, was gradually induced by the action of several causes, but chiefly by the character of the food.*

The Federal prisoners, as a general rule, had been reared upon wheat bread and Irish potatoes; and the Indian corn, so extensively used at the South, was almost unknown to them as an article of diet previous to their capture. Owing to the impossibility of obtaining the necessary sieves in the Confederacy for the separation of the husk from the corn-meal, the rations of the Confederate soldiers, as well as of the Federal prisoners, consisted of unbolted corn-flour, and meal and grist; this circumstance rendered the corn-bread still more disagreeable and distasteful to the Federal prisoners. While Indian meal, even when prepared with the husk, is one of the most wholesome and nutritious forms of food, as has been already shown by the health and rapid increase of the Southern population, and especially of the negroes, previous to the present war, and by the strength, endurance and activity of the Confederate soldiers, who were throughout the war confined to a great extent to unbolted corn-meal; it is nevertheless true that those who have not been reared upon corn-meal, or who have not accustomed themselves to its use gradually, become excessively tired of this kind of diet when suddenly confined to it without a due proportion of wheat bread. Large numbers of the Federal prisoners appeared to be utterly disgusted with Indian corn, and immense piles of corn-bread could be seen in the stockade and hospital inclosures. Those who were so disgusted with this form of food that they had no appetite to partake of it, except in quantities insufficient to supply the waste of the tissues, were, of course, in the condition of men slowly starving, notwithstanding that the only farinaceous form of food which the Confederate States produced in sufficient abundance for the maintenance of armies was not withheld from them. In such cases, an urgent feeling of hunger was not a prominent symptom; and even when it existed at first, it soon disappeared, and was succeeded by an actual loathing of food. In this state the muscular strength was rapidly diminished, the tissues wasted, and the thin skeleton-like forms moved about with the appearance of utter exhaustion and dejection. The mental condition connected with long confinement, with the most miserable surroundings, and with no hope for the future, also depressed all the nervous and vital actions, and was especially active in destroying the appetite. The effects of mental depression, and of defective nutrition, were manifested not only in the slow, feeble motions of the wasted, skeleton-like forms, but also in such lethargy, listlessness, and torpor of the mental faculties as rendered these unfortunate men oblivious and indifferent to their afflicted condition. In many cases, even of the greatest apparent suffering and distress, instead of showing any anxiety to communicate the causes of their distress, or to relate their privations, and their longings for their homes and their friends and relatives, they lay in a listless, lethargic, uncomplaining state, taking no notice either of their own distressed condition, or of the gigantic mass of human misery by which they were surrounded. Nothing appalled and depressed me so much as this silent, uncomplaining misery. It is a fact of great interest, that notwithstanding this defective nutrition in men subjected to crowding and filth, contagious fevers were rare; and typhus fever, which is supposed to be generated in just such a state of things as existed at Andersonville, was unknown. These facts, established by my investigations, stand in striking contrast with such a statement as the following by a recent English writer:

"A deficiency of food, especially of the nitrogenous part, quickly leads to the breaking up of the animal frame. Plague, pestilence and famine are associated with each other in the public mind, and the records of every country show how closely they are related. The medical history of Ireland is remarkable for the illustrations of how much mischief may be occasioned by a general deficiency of food. Always the habitat of fever, it every now and then becomes the very hot-bed of its propagation and development. Let there be but a small failure in the usual imperfect supply of food, and the lurking seeds of pestilence are ready to burst into frightful activity. The famine of the present century is but too forcible and illustrative of this. It fostered epidemics which have not been witnessed in this generation, and gave rise to scenes of devastation and misery which are not surpassed by the most appalling epidemics of the Middle Ages. The principal form of the scourge was known as the contagious famine fever (typhus), and it spread, not merely from end to end of the country in which it had originated, but, breaking through all boundaries, it crossed the broad ocean, and made itself painfully manifest in localities where it was previously unknown. Thousands fell under the virulence of its action, for wherever it came it struck down a seventh of the people, and of those whom it attacked one out of nine perished. Even those who escaped the fatal influence of it, were left the miserable victims of scurvy and low fever."

While we readily admit that famine induces that state of the system which is the most susceptible to the action of fever poisons, and thus induces the state of the entire population which is most favorable for the rapid and destructive spread of all contagious fevers, at the same time we are forced by the facts established by the present war, as well as by a host of others, both old and new, to admit that we are still ignorant of the causes necessary for the origin of typhus fever. Added to the imperfect nature of the rations issued to the Federal prisoners, the difficulties of their situation were at times greatly increased by the sudden and desolating Federal raids in Virginia, Georgia, and other States, which necessitated the sudden transportation from Richmond and other points threatened of large bodies of prisoners, without the possibility of much previous preparation; and not only did these men suffer in transition upon the dilapidated and overburdened line of railroad communication, but after arriving at Andersonville, the rations were frequently insufficient to supply the sudden addition of several thousand men. And as the Confederacy became more and more pressed, and when powerful hostile armies were plunging through her bosom, the Federal prisoners of Andersonville suffered incredibly during the hasty removal to Millen, Savannah, Charleston, and other points, supposed at the time to be secure from the enemy. Each one of these causes must be weighed when an attempt is made to estimate the unusual mortality among these prisoners of war.

VII. *Scurvy, arising from sameness of food and imperfect nutrition, caused, either directly or indirectly, nine-tenths of the deaths among the Federal prisoners at Andersonville.*

Not only were the deaths referred to unknown causes, to apoplexy, to anasarca, and to debility, traceable to scurvy and its effects; and not only was the mortality in small-pox, pneumonia, and typhoid fever, and in all acute diseases, more than doubled by the scorbutic taint, but even those all but universal and deadly bowel affections arose from the same causes, and derived their fatal character from the same conditions which produced the scurvy. In truth, these men at Andersonville were in the condition of a crew at sea, confined in a foul ship upon salt meat and unvarying food, and without fresh vegetables. Not only so, but these unfortunate prisoners were like men forcibly confined and crowded upon a ship tossed about on a stormy ocean, without a rudder, without a compass, without a guiding-star, and without any apparent boundary or end to their voyage; and they reflected in their steadily increasing miseries the distressed condition and waning fortunes of a devastated and bleeding country, which was compelled, in justice to her own unfortunate sons, to hold these men in this most distressing captivity.

I saw nothing in the scurvy which prevailed so universally at Andersonville, at all different from this disease as described by various standard writers. The mortality was no greater than that which has afflicted a hundred ships upon long voyages, and it did not exceed the mortality which has, upon more than one occasion, and in a much shorter period of time, annihilated large armies and desolated beleaguered cities . . . The general results of my investigations upon the chronic diarrhœa and dysentery of the Federal prisoners of Andersonville were similar to those of the English surgeons during the war against Russia.

IX. *Drugs exercised but little influence over the progress and fatal termination of chronic diarrhœa and dysentery in the military prison and hospital at Andersonville, chiefly because the proper form of nourishment (milk, rice, vegetables, anti-scorbutics, and nourishing animal and vegetable soups) was not issued, and could not be procured in sufficient quantities for these sick prisoners.*

Opium allayed pain and checked the bowels temporarily, but the frail dam was soon swept away, and the patient appeared to be but little better, if not the worse, for this merely palliative treatment. The root of the difficulty could not be reached by drugs; nothing short of the wanting elements of nutrition would have tended in any manner to restore the tone of the digestive system, and of all the wasted and degenerated organs and tissues. My opinion to this effect was expressed most decidedly to the medical officers in charge of these unfortunate men. The correctness of this view was sustained by the healthy and robust condition of the paroled prisoners, who received an extra ration, and who were able to make considerable sums by trading, and who supplied themselves with a liberal and varied diet . . .

X. *The fact that hospital gangrene appeared in the stockade first, and originated spontaneously, without any previous contagion, and occurred sporadically all over the stockade and prison hospital, was proof positive that this disease will arise whenever the conditions of crowding, filth, foul air, and bad diet are present.*

The exhalations from the hospital and stockade appeared to exert their effects to a considerable distance outside of these localities. The origin of gangrene among these prisoners appeared clearly to depend in great measure upon the state of the general system, induced by diet, exposure, neglect of personal cleanliness, and by various external noxious influences. The rapidity of the appearance and action of the gangrene depended upon the powers and state of the constitution, as well as upon the intensity of the poison in the atmosphere, or upon the direct application of poisonous matter to the wounded surface. This was further illustrated by the important fact, that hospital gangrene, or a disease resembling this form of gangrene, attacked the intestinal canal of patients laboring under ulceration of the bowels, although there were no local manifestations of gangrene upon the surface of the body. This mode of termination in cases of dysentery was quite common in the foul atmosphere of the Confederate States Military Prison Hospital; and in the depressed, depraved condition of the system of these Federal prisoners, death ensued very rapidly after the gangrenous state of the intestines was established.

XI. *A scorbutic condition of the system appeared to favor the origin of foul ulcers, which frequently took on true hospital gangrene.*

Scurvy and gangrene frequently existed in the same individual. In such cases, vegetable diet with vegetable acids would remove the scorbutic condition without curing the hospital gangrene. . . Scurvy consists not only in an alteration in the constitution of the blood, which leads to passive hemorrhages from the bowels, and the effusion into the various tissues of a deeply-colored fibrinous exudation; but, as we have conclusively shown by *post-mortem* examination, this state is also attended with consistence of the muscles of the heart, and of

CHAPTER V.

In making as brief an analysis as may be consistent with a correct understanding and appreciation of some of the most important testimony reported by the Commission in the "Wirz Trial," some degree of apparent prolixity is unavoidable. In some instances I shall have to give *verbatim* copies of official documents; yet in doing this, I shall be enabled to show conclusively that many of the witnesses testified falsely; that many whose testimony would have been of great value to the prisoner, were not permitted to testify at all, and that numbers, through fear of sharing the same fate as Wirz, were deterred from telling the truth. This latter consideration must account in a great measure for the peculiar character of the testimony of a *few* of the Confederate officers, who were either traitors disguised in Confederate uniforms, or were influenced by the fear of conviction and imprisonment by the court-martial. Such was the case with more than one of the witnesses summoned for the defence.

The parties that testified in the trial may be divided into several classes. The first included such men as Dr. A. S. James, Dr. J. S. Dillard, Dr. R. E. Mudd, Capt. J. W. Armstrong, Col. Robert Ould, and others. These men were summoned for the defence. Colonel Ould's subpœna was revoked by Judge-advocate Chipman, and he was not permitted to testify at all. (The truth of this appears in his published statement to the *National Intelligencer*, under date of August 17th, 1868.) The testimony of the rest of this class was passed over by the court, the prisoner not being allowed any of the advantages that their evidence might have afforded him before an impartial tribunal. General R. E Lee, whose name had been stricken out in "the revised indictment" as a co-conspirator with Captain Wirz, would certainly appear to have been a competent witness; yet his subpœna for the defence was suppressed by the Judge-advocate. And why? It is difficult to refrain from denunciation in the face of such palpable, shameless wrong. Revenge, not justice, was what the military court and the Northern people craved. They sought not to elicit the truth concerning their hapless victims, but to hang them. If the facts did not warrant the execution of the prisoners, so much the worse for the facts! Hence, of all possible witnesses in the case, it was clear that they had least use for one like Lee; a man whose character lifted him far beyond the reach of the chicanery, bribery, threats, and trickery, by which the facile witnesses in this mockery of justice were moulded to the requirements of an unscrupulous and vindictive persecution. Hence, too, the revocation of Col. Ould's subpœna and suppression of his testimony.

The second class of witnesses includes such men as Drs. Thornburg, Barnes, Bates, and perhaps a few others. The value of their testimony (if it be correctly given in the report of the Commission) may be judged by a few extracts. Dr. Barnes testified that:—"Green corn, which was an anti-scorbutic, was taken away from the patients and prisoners, the latter of whom were arrested and severely punished for buying it." Again:—"That stimulants to support the system for the month of September (1864) were 36 barrels, all of which were drunk by the medical directors Drs. White and Stevenson, and their friends." Again:—"That the greatest number of deaths in one day was 207, or 8½ each hour in the day. This was in August, 1864." Such absurd and extravagantly malicious falsehoods might well be met by simple denial; yet, in order to show that this testimony is false, I will give the reader a statement of the kind and amount of vegetables and provisions that were furnished the sick and wounded prisoners, in such quantities as could be procured by the officers in charge. These articles were allowed the captives in addition to the regular rations drawn from the commissary; and were procured by agents, as suggested by General Winder in his report to the Confederate Government. The following extract from the vouchers (B) will show for itself, viz:

"Purchased by W. H. H. Phelps, purchasing agent for Confederate States Military Prison Hospitals, as per duplicate vouchers for the months of *September*, October, November, and December, the following supplies, vegetables, &c.:—Vinegar, 1910 gallons; soap, 11,696 pounds; dried beans, 13 bushels; hard soap, 564 pounds; coffee, 354 pounds; lard, 300 pounds; Irish potatoes, 112 bushels; bicarb soda, 112 pounds; sweet potatoes, 2125 bushels; dried fruit, 63 bushels; brown sugar, 1300 pounds; milk, 77 gallons; green tea, 20 pounds; hops, 30 pounds." In addition to this there were expended, as appears by these vouchers, some $10,638 Confederate currency for cabbages, turnips, beans, GREEN CORN, potatoes, salads, &c., exclusively for the sick and wounded prisoners. It must be borne in mind that the demand made at this time by the hospitals belonging to the Army of the Tennessee for "anti-scorbutics," made it somewhat difficult at times to procure them; but for all this, the Federal captives fared as well as the Confederate troops. In the semi-annual return (C) to the Surgeon-general, for medicines, hospital stores, instruments, bedding, &c., for the year ending December 31st, 1864, we find that the amount of whiskey received and issued was 285 gallons—about *seven barrels.* The greatest number of deaths (127) occurred on the 23d day of August, 1864, when gangrene and scurvy were at their height.

Let us now inspect a sample of Dr. Thornburg's testimony. On the witness-stand he stated that Dr. R. R. Stevenson was charged, before he left Andersonville, with embezzling about eighty thousand dollars of the "Hospital Fund," for which he was court-martialed and relieved of duty there. This is too grave a charge to be slighted, even when preferred by an accuser so disreputable. I must therefore ask the reader's attention to the following *verbatim* copies of documents, which furnish in themselves a sufficient refutation:—

[Special Order No. 8] HEADQUARTERS C. S MILITARY PRISONS, (East of the Mississippi,) COLUMBIA, S. C., *December* 20*th*, 1864.

. . . .

VI. Surgeon R. R. Stevenson is hereby relieved from duty at Andersonville, Ga., and will report, without delay, to these headquarters for assignment to duty. J. H. WINDER, *Brigadier-general.*

Surgeon R. R STEVENSON, *Andersonville, Ga.*

Before leaving Andersonville, Surgeon R. R. Stevenson was presented with the following copy of resolutions, passed at a meeting held by the medical and other officers of the post:

ANDERSONVILLE, GA.. *December* 27*th*, 1864.

At a meeting of the medical and other officers of this post, the following preamble and resolutions were adopted:—

WHEREAS, Our Government has found it for the good of the service to relieve Surgeon R. R. Stevenson, in charge of General Hospitals at this post, and to order him to a point where his services as a medical officer can be more advantageously used; therefore be it

Resolved, 1st. That in our associations with Surgeon Stevenson, we have found him a most efficient and faithful officer, ever watchful of the condition of the sick under his charge, promptly using every effort in his power to ameliorate their sufferings. He has always been kind and courteous to the officers under his command, whilst at the same time exacting from them their every duty.

2d. That whilst we recognise the wisdom of our Government in transferring Surgeon Stevenson to a field where his diversified talents may find a more congenial sphere in which to develop themselves, we part with him with feelings of heartfelt regret.

3d. That a copy of these resolutions be handed to Surgeon Stevenson, as a testimonial of appreciation of his arduous labors, day and night, in trying to arrest and modify the fearful maladies that have surrounded this post for the past five months.

4th. That a copy of these resolutions be sent to the *Telegraph and Confederate*, *Atlanta Intelligencer*, and *Memphis Appeal*, for publication.

G. G. ROY, Assist. Surgeon, *Chairman.* A. S. JAMES, Assist. Surgeon, *Secretary.*

OFFICERS OF THE POST:

G. C. GIBBS, Col. Comd'g Post.
H. WIRZ, Capt. Comd'g Prison.
I H. WRIGHT, Capt. and A. Q. M.
I. W. ARMSTRONG, Jr., Capt. & A.C.S.
R. B. THOMAS, A. A. G. Post.
J. ORMAND, A. A. G. Prison.
A. THORNBURG, Assist. Surgeon.
G. L. D. RICE, A. Assist. Surgeon.
F. A. MCVEIGH, A. Ass't Surgeon.
W. R. D. THOMPSON, A. Ass't Sur.
J. CREWS PELAT, Ass't Surgeon.
J. S. DILLARD, Ass't Surgeon.
T. A. WARREN, Sur. 4th Ga. Res.
R. E. MUDD, Ass't Surgeon.
J. H. WILEY, Sec'y Med. Board.

Amount of funds transferred to Surgeon R. R. Stevenson, medical officer in charge of C. S. Military Hospitals, Andersonville, Ga., for the purchase of supplies for the comfort of the sick and wounded:

1864.		1864.	
September 3d, ...	$ 6,000.00	October 31st, ...	$12,500.00
" 21st, ...	1,000.00	November 22d, . . .	4,000.00
October 25th, ...	3,000.00	" 28th, ...	500.00
" 30th, ...	3,900.00	" 30th, . . .	7,000 00
" 30th, ...	25,000.00		
		Total, ...	$32,900.00

I certify that the above is a correct copy from my books.

G. M. PROCTOR, *Major and C. S.*

ANDERSONVILLE, GA., *December 2d*, 1864.

Thus, in the first place, we find Dr. Thornburg voluntarily giving his unqualified endorsement and approval of the conduct and integrity of Surgeon Stevenson in a public meeting, and afterwards charging him on the witness-stand, according to the reported testimony before the commission in the Wirz trial, with embezzling prison-funds to the amount of eighty thousand dollars, when in reality all the money he (Stevenson) ever received during his charge at Andersonville was sixty-two thousand nine hundred dollars, and this was expended as per duplicate vouchers annexed (D):

Received of Surgeon R. R. Stevenson, Andersonville, Georgia, December 31st, 1864, sixty-two thousand nine hundred dollars, being the amount of the hospital fund for the purchase of supplies and comforts for the sick and wounded Federal prisoners, for the months of September, October, November, and December 1864.

A. F. PHARR, G. M. PROCTOR,
J. L. DANSE, WM. M. FEDDEMAN,
D. W. MASSEY, I. H. WHITE.
W. J. W. KERR,

We will now notice some of the testimony of one Dr. Bates, who was flatteringly designated on the trial by the Judge-advocate (Chipman), as a "Rebel surgeon," one on whose testimony the court could rely. The reader will bear in mind that this "Rebel surgeon" of such strong secession proclivities, had to be conscripted and taken to Richmond under a guard before he could be induced to do anything for his country's good. He stated on the trial:—"The men (in October 1864) would gather around me and ask me for a bone. I would give them whatever I could find at my disposition without robbing others. I well knew that the appropriation of one ration took it from the general issue; that when I appropriated an extra ration to one man, some one else would fall minus. I then fell back upon the distribution of bones; they (the prisoners) did not presume to ask me for meat at all." Again he says, "all the rations of meat they (the prisoners) received was two ounces of boiled beef per day." To prove the incorrectness of this statement, I insert an extract from duplicate vouchers of the quantity of rations due and issued to the sick and attendants of Confederate States Military Prison Hospital for the months of September, October, November and December, 1864, viz:

Number of rations due Confederate States Military Prison Hospital for the year and months above given, 224,221.

Number of rations issued on the above return, viz: Of bacon and beef, 133,931 pounds; of meal and flour, 240,136 pounds; of rice and peas, 57,323 pounds; of syrup, 5465 gallons; besides soap, candles, salt, &c. This would give an average of 9½ ounces of meat and 17 ounces of bread to each man *per diem*. In addition to this, the sum of $62,900 was expended for other supplies for the comfort and subsistence of the prisoners.

The annexed order will show the status of the Confederate Government on the subject of hospital rations for prisoners of war:

[General Orders, No. 159.] ADJUTANT AND INSPECTOR'S OFFICE, RICHMOND, VA., *December 4th*, 1863.

I. Hospitals for prisoners of war are placed on the same footing as other Confederate States Hospitals in all respects, and will be managed accordingly.

II. The hospital ration is fixed, until further orders, at the same rates of issues now made to soldiers in the field. If a greater allowance is required of any particular article, special requisitions must be made therefor.

By order,

S. COOPER, *Adj't and Inspector-general.*

Perhaps the best illustration of the kind and quantity of

rations issued to the Confederate troops in camp, field and hospital, is given by the "depositions" of Confederate soldiers before the "United States Sanitary Commission" in New York, in 1864. Extracts from this Commission read as follows, viz:

Testimony taken at De Camp Hospital, U. S. A., New York, June 17th, 1864. Commissioner present, Mr. Wilkins.

A. B. Bannon, Co. K, 24th Ga. Inf., Army Va., sworn. "I have been in Confederate hospitals in the field. We had straw to lie on, a few had sheets." Again: "Our rations consisted of bacon half a pound, or one pound of beef; rice, coffee, and sugar occasionally; of bread we had six hard biscuits a day, or half a pound of meal or flour a day."

ALBERT B. BANNON.

Sworn to before me, Warren Webster, Assistant Surgeon U. S. A., in charge of hospital.

"Deposition" of William M. Farmer, Co. H., 24th Georgia Infantry, Army Va.:—Have been in Confederate States service since August 1861. I was taken prisoner at Cool Arbor. Rations in our service were bacon half a pound, or the same amount of beef; rice, coffee, and sugar occasionally; bread, six hard biscuits a day, or half a pound of meal or flour per day. W. M. FARMER.

Sworn to before me, Warren Webster, Assistant Surgeon U. S. A., in charge of hospital.

"Deposition" of D. F. Prince, Co. H., 51st regiment North Carolina Infantry, Army Va.:—Have been in the service since March 1862. In my command we always got one pound of beef, or half pound of bacon, *per diem*. We had one pound of flour, or one and a quarter pounds of corn-meal, a day; we had no tea or coffee; had salt, and occasionally a gill of peas or rice a day. D. F. PRINCE.

Sworn to before me, Warren Webster, Assistant Surgeon U. S. A., in charge of hospital.

"Deposition" of Joseph Whichard, Co. G., 8th regiment N. Vol. Inf.: "Have been in the Confederate service since September 1861. Was wounded and taken prisoner at Cool Arbor. Rations in our service consisted of bacon half a pound, and ten hard biscuits, daily; on a march we generally fared pretty well, as we then had an opportunity of foraging through the country. J. WHICHARD.

Sworn to before me, Warren Webster, Assistant Surgeon U. S. A., in charge of hospital.

The condition of the Confederate commissariat at this late date, may be ascertained more fully by the annexed communication of Major French to Colonel Northrop. It so fully explains the situation that I refrain from any comments whatever:

BUREAU OF SUBSISTENCE, RICHMOND, *October* 18*th*, 1864.
Colonel L. B. NORTHROP, *Commissary-general of Subsistence.*

COLONEL:—I have the honor to submit for your consideration the enclosed memorandum of meats on hand at the various depots and posts in the Confederate States, from which you will see at a glance the alarming condition of the commissariat. Georgia, Alabama, and Mississippi are the only States where we have an accumulation, and from these all the armies of the Confederacy are now subsisting, *to say nothing of the prisoners.* The chief commissary of Georgia telegraphs that he cannot send forward another pound. Alabama, under the most urgent call, has recently shipped 125,000 pounds, but canno ship more. Mississippi is rendering all the aid possible to the command o General Beauregard in supplying beef. She is without bacon. Florida is exhausted, and can only respond to the local demand. South Carolina is scarcely able to subsist the troops at Charleston and *the prisoners* in the interior of the State. During my late trip to North Carolina, I visited every section of the State, for the purpose of ascertaining the true condition of affairs, and under your orders to send forward every pound of meat possible to the Army of Northern Virginia, and to supply the forts at Wilmington. After a thorough and careful examination, I was unable (taking into consideration the local daily issues) to ship to either Virginia or Wilmington; and but for the timely arrival of the steamer Banshee at Wilmington, General Lee's order for thirty days' reserve at the forts could not have been furnished. From the enclosed memorandum you will notice that we have only on hand in the Confederate States 4,105,048 rations of fresh meat, and 3,426,519 rations of bacon and pork, which subsist three hundred thousand men twenty-five days. We are now compelled to subsist, independent of the armies of the Confederacy, *the prisoners of war*, the Navy Department, and the different bureaus of the War Department.

Very respectfully your obedient servant,
S. B. FRENCH, *Major and C. S.*

On the 5th of December the Commissary-general placed the condition of the commissariat before the Secretary of War, in connection with a statement of the amount of subsistence then on hand, showing only nine days' rations for General Lee's army, and quoting also from a letter that day received, stating that his (Lee's) men were deserting on account of short rations. From a telegram from General Lee to President Davis, it appears that the Army of Northern Virginia was entirely destitute of meat, and but for the timely arrival of several ship-loads of supplies at Wilmington, starvation or surrender would have been inevitable.

In a secret session of the Confederate Congress at Richmond, we find the following points enumerated in regard to the question of subsistence:

I. That there was not meat enough in the Southern Confederacy for the armies it had in the field.

II. That there was not in Virginia, either bread or meat enough for the armies within her limits.

III. That the bread supply from other places depended absolutely upon the keeping open the railroad connections of the South.

IV. That the meat must be obtained from abroad through a seaport, and by a different system from that which prevailed.

V. That the bread could not be had by impressment, but must be paid for in market rates.

VI. That the payment must be made in cash, (which, so far, had not been furnished, and from present indications could not be,) and, if possible, in a better medium than at present circulating.

VII. That the transportation was not now adequate, from whatever cause, to meet the demands of the service.

VIII. That the supply of fresh meat to General Lee's army was precarious; and if the army fell back from Richmond and Petersburg, there was every probability that it would cease altogether.

On more than one occasion General Lee urged the importance of having at least thirty days' reserves of provisions at Lynchburg and Richmond in the winter of 1863–4. As has been shown, this was an impossibility. The prisoners had to be fed; and though the great bulk of them were in Danville, Salisbury, or *in transitu* to the post at Andersonville, yet a sufficient number were in Richmond, and long enough, to consume some thirty thousand barrels of flour. Here we see the Federal prisoner consuming that which justly belonged to the Confederate soldier. This, however, was an integral part of the Federal war-policy, like the refusal to exchange prisoners. It certainly succeeded; though whether the success justified the atrocious sufferings and death it inflicted, not merely on their enemies, but on their own men, who vainly appealed for mercy and justice, is a question which, happily, we of the South are not called upon to answer. And the tribunal before which it must be answered is one where all endeavors to shift the responsibility and the odium, all falsehood, evasion and perjury, will be unavailing.

CHAPTER VI.

Under orders from the War Department, Col. D. F. Chandler, as inspecting officer, made a report on the condition of the prisoners at Andersonville, which reached the department on the 17th day of August, 1864. This report, with an enclosure from Surgeon I. H. White, (requesting, among other matters, that an additional force of commissioned medical officers be ordered to report to him for duty) set forth a full description of the difficulties and sufferings at Andersonville. It also embodied some suggestions as to their comfort and safe-keeping. In this report of Col. Chandler was plainly manifested a spirit of prejudice against General Winder. The paper was dwelt on with great emphasis and pertinacity by Judge-advocate Chipman in the trial of Wirz, as affording conclusive evidence of intentional and deliberate cruelty on the part of the authorities at Richmond toward Federal prisoners of war. Let us, then, examine this report in all its phases and bearings, to discover such evidences of cruelty, if they are herein to be found. We find it endorsed by the authorities at Richmond, as follows, viz:

ADJUTANT AND INSPECTOR-GENERAL'S OFFICE,
RICHMOND, VA., *August 18th*, 1864.

Respectfully submitted to the Secretary of War. The condition of the prison at Andersonville is a reproach to us as a nation. The Engineer and Ordnance Departments were applied to, and they authorised their issue, and I so telegraphed General Winder. Col. Chandler's recommendations are coincided with. By order of General Cooper.

R. H. CHILTON, *A. A. and I. G.*

These reports show a condition of things at Andersonville which calls very loudly for the interposition of the department, in order that a change be made. J. A. CAMPBELL, *Assistant Secretary of War.*

It is impossible to order medical officers in place of the contract physicians. They are not to be had at present.

S. P. MOORE, *Surgeon-general.*

It must be borne in mind that the important subject of the removal of the prisoners from Andersonville was under consideration by the Confederate authorities, even before Col. Chandler made his report to the War Department. This is proven by the following telegrams, letters, &c., from General Winder to the War Department:

To S. COOPER, *A. G. C. S. A.*, *Richmond, Va.* [*Telegram.*]

The stockade is already taxed to its utmost extent. The mortality is already considerable. I shall require additional guards, and an additional force in the engineer and medical departments.

J. H. WINDER, *Brigadier-general.*

ANDERSONVILLE, *June 25th*, 1864.

[*Telegram.*] RICHMOND, VA., *June 30th*, 1864.

To Brigadier-general WINDER, *Andersonville, Ga.*

Enlarge the stockade—place the prisoners properly. The assistance you desire in the different departments will be furnished as soon as possible. By order of General Cooper.

R. H. CHILTON, *A. A. and I. G.*

The following extract from a letter from General Winder to General Cooper, under date of July 21st, 1864, shows that Generals Winder and Cooper were conferring on the subject of the condition of the prisoners prior to Colonel Chandler's visit and report on Andersonville. The extract reads as follows:

"You speak of placing the prisoners properly. I do not comprehend what is intended by it. I know of but one way to place them, and that is to put them in the stockade, where they have between four and five square yards to the man. This includes streets, and two acres of ground about the stream."

General Cooper would certainly not have indorsed on Chandler's report that he (Cooper) had telegraphed to General

Winder in regard to issues, &c., if General Winder had never applied to him for assistance in the engineer and medical departments.

General Winder did enlarge the stockade; but for all this, the daily increasing difficulties of disease, and the unforeseen events of the battle-field in adding continually large numbers of prisoners to this post, made it necessary to attempt to abandon the post as a military prison; and we find the following telegrams, letters, &c., relative to the removal of the prisoners:

[*Telegram.*] RICHMOND, VA., *August 19th*, 1864.

To Brigadier-general WINDER, *Andersonville, Ga.*

Your communication on the subject of removal of prisoners received—write letter. By order of the President.

J. A. SEDDON, *Secretary of War.*

To Surgeon I. H. WHITE, *Andersonville, Ga.* [*Telegram.*]

Divide the hospital funds among the prison hospitals now being established at other points—write letter.

S. P. MOORE, *Surgeon-general.*

RICHMOND, VA., *September 1st*, 1864.

[*Letter.*] CONFEDERATE STATES OF AMERICA,
SURGEON-GENERAL'S OFFICE,
RICHMOND, VA., *September 12th*, 1864.

SIR:—You are instructed to assign the medical officers now on duty with sick prisoners at Andersonville, Ga., to the points that have been selected for the accommodation of the prisoners. All the sick whose lives will not be endangered by transportation, will be removed. The medical officers selected will be required to accompany the sick.

You will visit each station and see that such arrangements are made for the sick as their wants may require, and use all the means for their comfort that the Government can possibly furnish.

Very respectfully, your obedient servant,

S. P. MOORE, *Surgeon-General C. S. A.*

To Surgeon I. H. WHITE, *C. S. Military Prison Hospital, Andersonville, Ga.*

As mentioned in a previous chapter, the bulk of the prisoners were removed to Millen, (Camp Lawton) Georgia.

To give the reader an idea of the difficulties attending the proper care and attention of the sick, I will insert an extract from a letter from Surgeon I. H. White, bearing on the subject:

OFFICE CHIEF SURGEON C. S. M. PRISONS, GEORGIA AND ALABAMA,
CAMP LAWTON, GA., *Nov. 9th*, 1864.

SIR:—Dr. Pharr has arrived and furnished me with $3500 "Hospital Fund," which is a mere drop in the bucket. We are building hospitals, and your experience has taught you that we cannot rely on the Quartermaster's department to furnish us with anything. I start with the experience of six months to purchase everything that we require. The Commissary department renders null the law of Congress creating a "hospital fund" to provide for the comfort of the sick and wounded, by failing to meet requisitions for funds. This fact has been represented to the Surgeon-general without palliation. I have also made verbal statement of the fact to General Winder, who directed me to address him a communication on the subject. I have delayed doing so, hoping that Major Proctor would eventually supply our wants. I am determined that these facts shall be properly represented to the War Department, if your requisitions are not filled. I require for immediate use at this post at least ten thousand dollars . . .

We have been quite busy for the last two days in selecting the sick to be exchanged. After getting them all ready at the depot, we were notified by telegraph not to send them, and had to take them, together with those sent from your post, back to the stockade. Many of these poor fellows, already broken down, will succumb through despair . . .

I am respectfully, your obedient servant,

I. H. WHITE.

Surgeon R. R. STEVENSON, *in charge of Post, Andersonville.*

OFFICE SURGEON IN CHARGE C. S. M. PRISON HOSPITALS,
ANDERSONVILLE, GA., *November 4th*, 1864.

COLONEL:—Under orders from Brigadier-general J. H. Winder, I respectfully request that W. H. H. Phelps of your post, a disabled conscript, be redetailed and ordered to report to me for assignment to duty as purchasing agent of vegetables and antiscorbutics for the sick and wounded prisoners now under my charge at this place.

Yours truly,

R. R. STEVENSON, *Surgeon in Charge.*

LEON VON ZINKEN, *Col. Commanding Post, Columbus, Ga.*

[*Endorsement.*] OFFICE MEDICAL DIRECTOR HOSPITALS,
COLUMBUS, GA., *Nov. 7th*, 1864.

COLONEL:—If this conscript is pronounced unable for field service, I have no objection to his acting as purchasing agent for Surgeon Stevenson's hospitals. He will of course be under the restrictions of your communication on this subject.

S. M. BEMISS, *Acting Medical Director.*

[*Endorsement.*] W. H. H. Phelps is hereby ordered to report to Surgeon R. R. Stevenson for duty as purchasing agent for his hospitals.

LEON VON ZINKEN, *Col. Commanding.*

In summing up the evidence in the trial of Captain Wirz and his alleged co-conspirators, Chipman, the Judge-advocate, makes use of the following language:—"Let us see what the evidences are of a common design to murder by starvation these hapless, helpless wretches. First, then, who are the officers, high and low, civil and military, whom the evidence implicates in this great crime? As I shall show you by this conspiracy, as directly implicated and as perpetrators, the prisoner at the bar, Brigadier-general John H. Winder, Surgeon Isaiah H. White, Surgeon R. R. Stevenson, Dr. Kerr, Captain R. B. Winder, Captain W. S. Winder. Remote from the scene, but no less responsible than those named — nay, rather with a greater weight of guilt resting upon them, are the leader of the rebellion, his war-minister, his surgeon-general, his commissary and quartermaster-general, his commissioner of exchange, and all others sufficiently high in authority to have prevented these atrocities, and to whom the knowledge of them was brought. Chief among the conspirators and actual participators in the crime, the immediate tool first and last of the rebel government, we shall see was General Winder."

After descanting at some length in the style of the genuine special pleader, and with a tirade of abuse, in support of the charges of cruelty, he says :—" Do I do injustice to the leaders of the rebellion? Have I drawn inferences that are unwarrantable? Is it indeed true that these men, high in authority, are not responsible? I think not. Motives are presumed from actions, and actions speak louder than words. What was the action of Mr. Davis and his war-minister upon these reports? The papers were pigeon-holed in the Secretary's office, not even being dignified by being placed upon the regular files in the proper offices."

Again :—" The closest scrutiny of the immense record of this trial will show that, up to the close of that prison, there were no steps taken by the rebel government, by General Winder, or by any of the officers of his staff, clothed with proper authority, to alleviate in any material particular the great sufferings of that place." And in his letter to Ambrose

Spencer after the trial, he writes as follows:—"While the evidence adduced convicts Wirz of contributing directly to the death of over TEN THOUSAND UNION SOLDIERS, and with his own hand, and by his direct order, committing THIRTEEN individual murders; the evidence also presents the horrible fact, that he was but an instrument in the hands of Jefferson Davis, James A. Seddon, and other prominent rebels; and while Wirz suffered deservedly, there are those yet unpunished richly worthy an ignominious death."

It must appear evident to the candid reader that the facts and data that have been given in regard to the policy of the officials at Richmond, prove conclusively that the prisoners were all cared for by the Confederates to the full extent of their means. Certainly, no act of intentional cruelty has been proven. It must also appear that a great portion of the evidence sought against Wirz by the Judge-advocate of the court was false. Not a single charge was sustained by a competent witness.

The organs of the Federal Government boasted that the "South" was on its trial before this court; when in reality the trial itself was a desperate subterfuge, an expedient to draw the eyes of the civilised world from the cruel acts of Stanton, Butler, and others, who were the true actors in the great tragedy, and upon whose heads the responsibility of the sufferings at Andersonville must rest. Whatever may have been the errors of the South, and however sore her trials, no one can say with truth that her leaders or people ever stooped to acts of wholesale cruelty to her unfortunate captives. Victorious or defeated, she never added retaliation and vandalism to the unavoidable horrors of war.

The Judge-advocate (Chipman) dwelt with special emphasis on the cruelty of General Winder towards the Federal prisoners, basing his charges principally upon the report which Colonel Chandler had made to the War Department. His command of the vernacular seemed inadequate to supply him with invectives of sufficient force to show the chief in control of the prison department in the proper light. He was described as the "Alva" of a preconcerted system of torture and cruelty —the concentration of all that was bad. To use the language of one of his fanatical defamers since the trial, "he (Winder) was the tool of Davis, who was the modern Caligula of the rebellion — the very incarnation of the brutalising effects of the system of slavery." This aged and gallant officer (General John H. Winder) died some time before the close of the war. His silent slumber was not disturbed by the slanders and revilings of those who sought in this trial to blacken his memory, and make his name a byword and a reproach. Duty impels me, as well as justice to his memory, to say, that during my long and pleasant intercourse with him in the management of the Federal prisoners, his conduct was always marked with humanity and kindness, and on no occasion did he wantonly or maliciously misuse any of the captives under his control. This assertion is corroborated by the following extract from a letter written to me since the close of the war by General S. Cooper, formerly Adjutant-general of the Army of the Confederate States of America. It explains itself, and needs no comments:*

ALEXANDRIA, VA., *July 9th*, 1871.

DR. R. R. STEVENSON.

DEAR SIR:—I have received your letter of the 24th ultimo, and will cheerfully comply with your wishes, as far as my memory will serve, in respect to your work entitled "The Southern Side; or, Andersonville Prison," &c. I shall labor under some difficulties, for want of official records of my office pertaining to the subject, all of which were captured by the enemy at the close of the war, and are now in the hands of the Government at Washington. I can, however, with perfect truth, declare as my conviction, that General Winder, who had the control of the Northern prisoners, was an honest, upright, humane gentleman, and as such I had known him for many years. He had the reputation in the Confederacy of treating the prisoners confided to his general supervision with great kindness and consideration, and fully possessed the confidence of the Government, which would not have been the case had he adopted a different course of action towards them; and this was exemplified by his assignment to Andersonville by the special direction of the President. Both

* See also letters of Hon. R. G. H. Kean, and Hon. James A. Seddon, in Appendix.

the President and Secretary of War always manifested great anxiety that the prisoners should be kindly treated, and amply provided with food to the extent of our means, and they both used their best means and exertions to these ends. . . .

S. COOPER.

It is well known that a large number of the prisoners that testified against Capt. Wirz were among those who had been paroled by the authorities in charge of the prisoners, to the end that they might assist their suffering comrades in the hospital department. In nearly every instance these men would attempt to escape, but by the vigilance of Capt. Wirz and the guards they were generally caught, and were put back in prison, with no prospect of being again paroled for duty outside. As a matter of course, they were incensed against Wirz, and their testimony was against him. The value of testimony of this character would certainly not be great. Men that would violate their paroles, and leave their dying comrades to suffer as they did, at Andersonville, would certainly not be competent witnesses in a court of justice. We find that Captain Henry Wirz was placed by General Winder in charge as superintendent of the interior of the prison at Andersonville, on the 12th day of April, 1864; by his orders he was held to strict accountability for the escape of the prisoners. Supplies for prisoners were issued upon his requisitions, and under his orders all passes to visit the prison were granted. All the details of management connected with the discipline of the prison were under his immediate control. He reported directly to General Winder. This task (herculean as it afterwards proved to be) was not one of any ordinary character, even then, when we take into consideration the rapidity with which the prisoners were sent to this place from the Army of the Tennessee, and from the prisons in and around Richmond. At one time some 33,000 men were here. The maladies that scourged the place, the difficulties in procuring subsistence and comforts, must all be taken into consideration. It must be recollected that there was great difficulty, at this time, in getting supplies, in consequence of raiding parties breaking up railroad communications. The guards that were furnished Captain Wirz were very inefficient. They were composed of boys under eighteen years of age, and men over forty-five. These raw troops knew but little of the duties of a soldier. The only troops on which he could depend were a fragment of the 55th Georgia Infantry, and Captain Gamble's battery of light artillery. Sentinels were stationed at regular intervals around the prison. In many instances the guards, being bribed, were detected in conniving at the escape of prisoners. The regulations of the prison were necessarily strict. All military men understand that no large body of men can be controlled without strict discipline. A dead-line was established along the inside of the prison, as before described, and the sentinels were instructed to let no one cross it under any pretence whatever, but to fire upon any prisoner if he tried to cross it after being halted three distinct times. The rules and regulations of the post and prison were posted up in conspicuous places, and all the orders pertaining to the prison were read and explained to the prisoners at the proper time. Occasionally these orders were violated, and the prescribed penalties inflicted.

The following statements, taken from the reports of the United States Sanitary Commission, New York, 1864, will show the character of the discipline as practised in Northern prisons that contained Confederate captives:

" . . . There have been five men shot, three killed and two wounded, here since this has been a prison: one killed in the river making his escape, about one hundred yards from the shore, at night; one killed for attempting to climb over the fence towards the river, and one man was wounded (died since) for committing a nuisance on the bank contrary to orders, and was ordered by the sentry to stop. He called the sentry a Yankee son of a ——, and would not stop; the ball wounded two men, the other said he deserved all he got.

Another was killed accidentally by the sentry shooting at another prisoner, who was committing a nuisance and who would not obey the 'order.' The orders are to prevent nuisances occurring in the barracks, which were detrimental to health and cleanliness. Even with these rules, nuisances are not unfrequently committed. Special orders No. 157 are the same as those I refer to, and are as follows:

[Special orders No. 157.]

HEADQUARTERS FORT DELAWARE, *June 1st*, 1864.

The officer of the guard must read and explain these orders to each relief of his guard regularly before having it posted.

I. No sentinel must communicate with, nor allow any person to communicate with, any of the prisoners, nor permit any of the prisoners to go outside of the limits (dead-line) of their barracks, without permission of the Commanding General or the officers in charge of the prisoners.

II. It is the duty of the sentinels to prevent the prisoners from escaping, or cutting, defacing, or in any way damaging the Government property, or from committing any nuisance in or about the barracks, or from using any abusive or insolent language towards them, and from any violation of good order. Should the sentinel detect any prisoner in violating these instructions, he must order him three distinct times to halt; and if the prisoner obeys the order, the sentinel must call the corporal of the guard and have the prisoner placed in arrest; but should the prisoner fail to halt when so ordered, the sentinel must enforce his order by bayonet or ball.

By command of Brig. Genl. SCHOEPF.

G. W. AHL, *Captain and A. A. A. G.*

They exist in all the prisons.

A. G. WOLF, *Lieutenant and Commissary of Prisoners.*

Sworn and subscribed to before me.

D. B. BROWN, *U. S. Sanitary Commissioner.*

June 21, 1864.

It affords me great pleasure to step aside from the line of my defence, to acknowledge, in behalf of the Confederate prisoners, the many kind deeds done for them while in Northern prisons by some noble men and women (not members of the "Sanitary Commission") of the North. They spared neither pains nor expense in trying to ameliorate the "dreary void of prison life"; and many a poor, famishing soldier who was living on the miserable, scanty fare of the prison, as well as receiving curses for being a "traitor," "secessionist," "rebel,"

&c., had occasion to rejoice in the contents of some of the well laden boxes of provisions sent them by these angels of mercy. These acts of kindness were prompted by the spontaneous outpouring of the nobler and better feelings of our nature, as well as a recognition that the cause in which the Confederate soldier was engaged was just. These kind favors will always be remembered by the Southern people with gratitude. The Federal authorities, however, after a time forbade the express companies from carrying even these articles to them; or if they did, it was managed so that the parties to whom they were destined did not receive them.

CHAPTER VII.

Henry Wirz was a physician by profession, and was born at Zurich, Switzerland, in 1822. He emigrated to America in 1849. He first settled in Louisville, Kentucky, and subsequently removed to Louisiana, where he practised his profession. When the war broke out, he was among the first to enlist in the Southern cause. He served as a private in the memorable battles of Manassas and Bull Run, where he received a wound in the arm, injuring the bone, from which he never recovered, to the day of his execution. He was detailed from the hospital department at Richmond, and placed as a clerk in the Libby Prison. Afterwards he was commissioned as a captain in the Confederate army, and was appointed Deputy Provost Marshal, and visited all the prisons of the South in 1862–3, as an inspecting officer.

In the latter part of 1863 he was sent by President Davis to carry secret dispatches to the Confederate Commissioners, Mr. Mason in England, and Mr. Slidell in France, and to all the financial agents of the Confederate Government in Europe. On his return in January, 1864, he was assigned to duty under Brigadier-general John H. Winder, who placed him as superintendent of the Confederate States Military Prison at Andersonville, where he was still on duty at the close of the war.

In direct violation of the terms of the surrender made between Generals Johnston and Sherman, he was arrested by Captain Noyes, under orders from General Wilson, and sent to Macon, Ga. From here he was shortly afterwards sent to Washington City, and there confined in the Old Capitol Prison. After several months spent in getting the witnesses ready, making up the charges, and arranging all the machinery of a grand tribunal, whose duty it seemed was to sit in judgment over the fallen South, the following orders were issued, in place of the first, which included as co-conspirators, General Robert E. Lee, ex-President Jefferson Davis, James A. Seddon, and others, whose names were stricken off the list in the second indictment. All the names, however, except that of General Lee, were replaced in the "findings" by the court. I insert the charges and specifications in full, so as to give the reader a chance to note the spirit that prevailed at the time.

[Special Orders No. 453.]

WAR DEPARTMENT, ADJUTANT-GENERAL'S OFFICE,
WASHINGTON, *August 23d*, 1865.

. . . .

III. A Special Military Commission is hereby appointed to meet in this city, at 11 o'clock A. M. on the 23d day of August, 1865, or as soon thereafter as practicable, for the trial of Henry Wirz, and such other prisoners as may be brought before it.

Detail for the Commission:—Major-general L. Wallace, U. S. Volunteers; Brevet Major-general G. Mott, U. S. Volunteers; Brevet Major-general J. W. Geary, U. S. Volunteers; Brevet Major-general L. Thomas, Adjutant-general U. S.

Army; Brigadier-general Francis Fessenden, U. S. Volunteers; Brigadier-general E. S. Bragg, U. S. Volunteers; Brevet Brigadier-general John T. Ballier, Colonel 98th Pennsylvania Volunteers; Brevet Colonel T. Allcock, Lieutenant-colonel 4th New York Artillery; Lieutenant-colonel I. H. Stibbs, 12th Iowa Volunteers. Colonel N. P. Chipman, additional aide-de-camp, Judge-advocate of the Commission, with such assistants as he may select, with the approval of the Judge-advocate General.

The Commission will sit without regard to hours.

By order of the President of the United States.

E. D. TOWNSEND, *Assistant Adjutant-General.*

The charges and specifications read as follows:

CHARGE I.

Maliciously, wilfully, and traitorously, and in aid of the then existing armed rebellion against the United States of America, on or before the first day of March, 1864, and on divers other days between that day and the tenth day of April, 1865, combining, confederating and conspiring together with John H. Winder, Richard B. Winder, Isaiah H. White, W. S. Winder, R. R. Stevenson, and others unknown, to injure the health and destroy the lives of soldiers in the military service of the United States, then held, and being prisoners of war within the lines of the so-called Confederate States, and in the military prisons thereof, to the end that the armies of the United States might be weakened and impaired, in violation of the laws and customs of war.

Specification.—In this, that he, the said Henry Wirz, did combine, confederate and conspire with them, the said John H. Winder, Richard B. Winder, Isaiah H. White, W. S. Winder, R. R. Stevenson, and others whose names are unknown, citizens of the United States aforesaid, and who were then engaged in armed rebellion against the United States, maliciously, traitorously, and in violation of the laws of war, to impair and injure the health and to destroy the lives—by subjecting to torture and great suffering, by confining in unhealthy and unwholesome quarters, by exposing to the inclemency of winter and to the dews and burning sun of summer, by compelling the use of impure water, and by furnishing insufficient and unwholesome food—of large numbers of Federal prisoners, to wit: the number of thirty thousand, soldiers in the military service of the United States of America, held as prisoners of war at Andersonville, in the State of Georgia, within the lines of the so-called Confederate States, on or before the first day of March, A. D. 1864, and at divers times between that day and the tenth day of April, A. D. 1865, to the end that the armies of the United States might be weakened and impaired, and the insurgents engaged in armed rebellion against the United States might be aided and comforted. And he, the said Henry Wirz, an officer in the military service of the so-called Confederate States, being then and there commandant of a military prison at Andersonville, in the State of Georgia, located by authority of the so-called Confederate States, for the confinement of prisoners of war, and as such commandant fully clothed with authority, and in duty bound to treat, care and provide for such prisoners held as aforesaid, as were or might be placed in his custody, according to the law of war, did, in furtherance of such combination, confederation and conspiracy, and incited thereunto by them, the said John H. Winder, Richard B. Winder, Isaiah H. White, W. S. Winder, R. R. Stevenson, and others whose names are unknown, maliciously, wickedly and traitorously confine a large number of such prisoners of war, soldiers in the military service of the United States, to the amount of thirty thousand men, in unhealthy and unwholesome quarters, in a close and small area of ground wholly inadequate to their wants and destructive to their health, which he well knew and intended; and while there so confined, during the time aforesaid, did, in furtherance of his evil design, and in aid of the said conspiracy, wilfully and maliciously neglect to furnish tents, barracks or other shelter sufficient for their protection from the inclemency of winter and the dews and burning sun of summer; and with such evil intent did take, or cause to be taken from them, their clothing, blankets, camp equipage, and other property at the time of being placed in his custody; and with like malice and evil intent, did refuse to furnish, or cause to be furnished, food either of a quality or quantity sufficient to preserve health and sustain life; and did refuse and neglect to furnish wood sufficient for cooking in summer and to keep said prisoners warm in winter, and did compel the said prisoners to subsist upon unwholesome food, and that in limited quantities entirely inadequate to sustain health, which he well knew; and did compel the said prisoners to use unwholesome water, reeking with the filth and garbage of the prison and prison-guard, and the offal and drainage of the cook-house of said prison. Whereby the prisoners became greatly reduced in their bodily strength, and emaciated and injured in their bodily health, their minds impaired, and their intellects broken; and many of them, to wit: the number of ten thousand, whose names are unknown, sickened and died by reason thereof, which he, the said Henry Wirz, then and there well knew and intended; and so knowing and evilly intending, did refuse and neglect to provide proper lodgings, food, or nourishment for the sick, and necessary medicine and medical attendance for the restoration of their health; and did knowingly, wilfully, and maliciously, in furtherance of his evil designs, permit them to languish and die from want of care and proper treatment.

And the said Henry Wirz, still pursuing his evil purposes, did permit to remain in the said prison, among the emaciated sick and languishing living, the bodies of the dead, until they became corrupt and loathsome, and filled the air with fœtid and noxious exhalations, and thereby greatly increased the unwholesomeness of the prison, insomuch that great numbers of said prisoners, to wit, the number of one thousand, whose names are unknown, sickened and died by reason thereof.

And the said Henry Wirz, still pursuing his wicked and cruel purpose, wholly disregarding the usages of civilised warfare, did, at the time and place aforesaid, maliciously and wilfully subject the prisoners aforesaid to cruel, unusual, and infamous punishment, upon slight, trivial, and fictitious pretences, by fastening large balls of iron to their feet, and binding large numbers of the prisoners aforesaid closely together with large chains around their necks and feet, so that they walked with the greatest difficulty; and being so confined, were subjected to the burning rays of the sun, often without food or drink for hours and even days, from which said cruel treatment large numbers, to wit: the number of one hundred, whose names are unknown, sickened, fainted, and died. And he, the said Wirz, did further cruelly treat and injure said prisoners by maliciously confining them within an instrument of torture, called "the stocks," thus depriving them of the use of their limbs, and forcing them to lie, sit, and stand for many hours without the power of changing position, and being without food or drink, in consequence of which many, to wit: the number of thirty, whose names are unknown, sickened and died.

And he, the said Wirz, still wickedly pursuing his evil purpose, did establish and cause to be designated within the prison enclosure containing said prisoners a "dead line," being a line around the inner face of the stockade or wall inclosing said prison, and about twenty feet distant from and within said stockade; and having so established said dead-line, which was in many places an imaginary line, and in many other places marked by insecure and shifting strips of boards nailed upon the top of small and insecure stakes or posts, he, the said Wirz, instructed the prison-guard stationed around the top of said stockade to fire upon and kill any of the prisoners aforesaid who might touch, fall upon, pass over, or under, or across the said dead-line; pursuant to which said instructions, maliciously and needlessly given by said Wirz, the said prison guard did fire upon and kill a large number of said prisoners, to wit: the number of about three hundred.

And the said Wirz, still pursuing his evil purpose, did keep and use ferocious and bloodthirsty beasts, dangerous to human life, called bloodhounds, to hunt down prisoners of war aforesaid who made their escape from his custody, and did then and there wilfully and maliciously suffer, incite, and encourage the said beasts to seize, tear, mangle, and maim the bodies and limbs of said fugitive prisoners of war, which the said beasts, incited as aforesaid, then and there did, whereby a large number of said prisoners of war, who during the time aforesaid made their escape and were recaptured, and were by the said beasts then and there cruelly and inhumanly injured, insomuch that many of said prisoners, to wit: the number of about fifty, died.

And the said Wirz, still pursuing his wicked purpose, and still aiding in carrying out said conspiracy, did use and cause to be used, for the pretended purpose of vaccination, impure and poisonous vaccine-matter, which said impure and poisonous vaccine-matter was then and there, by the direction and order of said Wirz, maliciously, cruelly, and wickedly deposited in the arms of many of said prisoners, by reason of which large numbers of them, to wit: one hundred, lost the use of their arms, and many of them, to wit: about the number of two hundred, were so injured that they soon after died.

All of which he, the said Henry Wirz, well knew and maliciously intended, and in aid of the then existing rebellion against the United States, with the view to assist in weakening and impairing the armies of the United States, and in furtherance of the said conspiracy, and with the full knowledge, consent and connivance of his co-conspirators aforesaid, he the said Wirz then and there did.

Charge II.

Murder in Violation of the Laws and Customs of War.

Specification 1.—In this, that the said Henry Wirz, an officer in the military service of the so-called Confederate States of America, at Andersonville, in the State of Georgia, on or about the eighth day of July A. D. 1864, then and there being commandant of a prison there located by the authority of the said so-called Confederate States, for the confinement of prisoners of war, taken and held as such from the armies of the United States of America, while acting as said commandant, feloniously, wilfully, of his malice aforethought, did make an assault; and he, the said Henry Wirz, a certain pistol, called a revolver, then and there loaded and charged with gunpowder and bullets, which said pistol, the said Henry Wirz, in his hand then and there held to, against and upon a soldier belonging to the army of the United States, in his, the said Henry Wirz's, custody, as a prisoner of war, whose name is unknown, then and there feloniously and of his malice aforethought, did shoot and discharge, inflicting upon the body of the soldier aforesaid a mortal wound with the pistol aforesaid, in consequence of which said mortal wound, murderously inflicted by the said Henry Wirz, the said soldier thereafter, to wit: on the ninth day of July A. D. 1864, died.

Specification 2.—In this, that the said Henry Wirz, an officer in the military service of the so-called Confederate States of America, at Andersonville, in the State of Georgia, on or about the twentieth day of September A. D. 1864, then and there being commandant of a prison there located by the authority of the said so-called Confederate States, for the confinement of prisoners of war, taken and held as such from the armies of the United States of America, while acting as said commandant, feloniously, wilfully, and of his malice aforethought, did jump upon, stamp, kick, bruise, and otherwise injure, with the heels of his boots, a soldier belonging to the army of the United

States, in his, the said Henry Wirz's, custody, as a prisoner of war, whose name is unknown, of which said stamping, kicking, and bruising, maliciously done and inflicted by the said Wirz, the said soldier soon thereafter, to wit: on the twentieth day of September A. D. 1864, died.

Specification 3.—In this, that the said Henry Wirz, an officer in the military service of the so-called Confederate States of America, at Andersonville, in the State of Georgia, on or about the thirteenth day of June A. D. 1864, then and there being commandant of a prison there located by the authority of the said so-called Confederate States, for the confinement of prisoners of war, taken and held as such from the armies of the United States of America, while acting as said commandant, feloniously and of his malice aforethought, did make an assault, and he, the said Henry Wirz, a certain pistol called a revolver, then and there loaded and charged with gunpowder and bullets, which said pistol the said Henry Wirz in his hand then and there had and held to, against and upon a soldier belonging to the army of the United States, in his, the said Henry Wirz's, custody as a prisoner of war, whose name is unknown, then and there feloniously, and of his malice aforethought, did shoot and discharge, inflicting upon the body of the soldier aforesaid, a mortal wound with the pistol aforesaid, in consequence of which said mortal wound, murderously inflicted by the said Henry Wirz, the said soldier immediately, to wit: on the day aforesaid, died.

Specification 4.—In this, that the said Henry Wirz, an officer in the military service of the so-called Confederate States of America, at Andersonville, in the State of Georgia, on or about the thirtieth of May A. D. 1864, then and there being commandant of a prison there located by the authority of the said so-called Confederate States, for the confinement of prisoners of war taken and held as such, from the armies of the United States of America, while acting as said commandant, feloniously and of his malice aforethought, did make an assault, and he, the said Henry Wirz, a certain pistol called a revolver, then and there loaded and charged with gunpowder and bullets, which said pistol the said Henry Wirz in his hand then and there had and held to, against and upon a soldier belonging to the army of the United States, in his, the said Henry Wirz's, custody as a prisoner of war, whose name is unknown, then and there feloniously and of his malice aforethought, did shoot and discharge, inflicting upon the body of the soldier aforesaid a mortal wound with the pistol aforesaid, in consequence of which said mortal wound, murderously inflicted by the said Henry Wirz, the said soldier, on the thirtieth day of May A. D. 1864, died.

Specification 5.—In this, the said Henry Wirz, an officer in the military service of the so-called Confederate States of America, at Andersonville, in the State of Georgia, on or about the twentieth day of August A. D. 1864, then and there being commandant of a prison there located by the authority of the said so-called Confederate States, for the confinement of prisoners of war taken and held as such from the armies of the United States of America, while acting as said commandant, feloniously and of his malice aforethought, did confine and bind with an instrument of torture called "the stocks," a soldier belonging to the army of the United States, in his, the said Henry Wirz's, custody as a prisoner of war, whose name is unknown, in consequence of which said cruel treatment, maliciously and murderously inflicted as aforesaid, he, the said soldier, soon thereafter, to wit: on the thirtieth day of August A. D. 1864, died.

Specification 6.—In this, that the said Henry Wirz, an officer in the military service of the so-called Confederate States of America, at Andersonville, in the State of Georgia, on or about the first day of February A. D. 1865, then and there being commandant of a prison there located by the authority of the said so-called Confederate States, for the confinement of prisoners of war, taken and held as such from the armies of the United States of America, while acting as said commandant, feloniously and of his malice aforethought, did confine and bind within an instrument of torture called "the stocks," a soldier belonging to the army of the United States, in his, the said Henry Wirz's, custody as a prisoner of war, whose name is unknown, in consequence of which said cruel treatment, maliciously and murderously inflicted as aforesaid, he, the said soldier, soon thereafter, to wit: on the sixth day of February A. D. 1864, died.

Specification 7.—In this, the said Henry Wirz, an officer in the military service of the so-called Confederate States of America, at Andersonville, in the State of Georgia, on or about the twentieth day of July A. D. 1864, then and there being commandant of a prison there located by the authority of the said so-called Confederate States, for the confinement of prisoners of war taken and held as such from the armies of the United States of America, while acting as said commandant, feloniously and of his malice aforethought, did fasten and chain together several persons, soldiers belonging to the army of the United States, in his, the said Henry Wirz's, custody as prisoners of war, whose names are unknown, binding the necks and feet of said prisoners closely together, and compelling them to carry great burdens, to wit, large iron balls chained to their feet, so that in consequence of the said cruel treatment inflicted upon them by the said Henry Wirz as aforesaid, one of the said soldiers, a prisoner of war as aforesaid, whose name is unknown, on the twenty-fifth day of July A. D. 1864, died.

Specification 8.—In this, that the said Henry Wirz, an officer in the military service of the so-called Confederate States of America, at Andersonville, in the State of Georgia, on or about the fifteenth day of May A. D. 1864, then and there being commandant of a prison there located by the authority of the said so-called Confederate States, for the confinement of prisoners of war taken and held as such from the armies of the United States of America, while acting as said commandant, feloniously, wilfully and of his malice aforethought, did order a rebel soldier, whose name is unknown, then on duty as a sentinel or guard to the prison of which said Henry Wirz was commandant as aforesaid, to fire upon a soldier belonging to the army of the United States in his, the said Henry Wirz's, custody as a prisoner of war, whose name is unknown; and in pursuance of said order so as aforesaid, maliciously and murderously given as aforesaid, he, the said rebel soldier, did with a musket loaded with gunpowder and bullet, then and there fire at the said soldier so as aforesaid held as a prisoner of war, inflicting upon him a mortal wound with the musket aforesaid, of which he, the said prisoner, soon thereafter, to wit, on the day aforesaid, died.

Specification 9.—In this, that the said Henry Wirz, an officer in the military service of the so-called Confederate States of America, at Andersonville, in the State of Georgia, on or about the first day of July A. D. 1864, then and there being commandant of a prison there located by the authority of the said so-called Confederate States, for the confinement of prisoners of war taken and held as such from the armies of the United States of America, while acting as said commandant, feloniously and in his malice aforethought, did order a rebel soldier, whose name is unknown, then on duty as a sentinel or guard to the prison of which said Wirz was commandant as aforesaid, to fire upon a soldier belonging to the army of the United States, in his, the said Henry Wirz's, custody as a prisoner of war, whose name is unknown; and in pursuance of said order so as aforesaid, maliciously and murderously given as aforesaid, he, the said rebel soldier, did with a musket loaded with gunpowder and bullet, then and there fire at the said soldier so as aforesaid held as a prisoner of war, inflicting upon him a mortal wound with the said musket, of which he, the said prisoner, soon thereafter, to wit, on the day aforesaid, died.

Specification 10.—In this, the said Henry Wirz, an officer in the military service of the so-called Confederate States of America, at Andersonville, in the State of Georgia, on or about the twentieth day of August A. D. 1864, then and there being commandant of a prison there located by the authority of the said so-called Confederate States, for the confinement of prisoners of war taken and held as such from the armies of the United States of America, while acting as said commandant, feloniously and of his malice aforethought, did order a rebel soldier, whose name is unknown, then on duty as a sentinel or guard to the prison of which said Wirz was commandant as aforesaid, to fire upon a soldier belonging to the army of the United States, in his, the said Henry Wirz's, custody as a prisoner of war, whose name is unknown; and in pursuance of said order so as aforesaid, maliciously and murderously given as aforesaid, he, the said rebel soldier, did with a musket loaded with gunpowder and bullet, then and there fire at the said soldier so as aforesaid held as a prisoner of war, inflicting upon him a mortal wound with the said musket, of which he, the said prisoner, soon thereafter, to wit, on the day aforesaid, died.

Specification 11.—In this, that the said Henry Wirz, an officer in the military service of the so-called Confederate States of America, at Andersonville, in the State of Georgia, on or about the first day of July A. D. 1864, then and there being commandant of a prison there located by the authority of the said so-called Confederate States, for the confinement of prisoners of war taken and held as such from the armies of the United States of America, while acting as said commandant, feloniously and of his malice aforethought, did cause, incite, and urge certain ferocious, bloodthirsty animals, called bloodhounds, to pursue, attack, wound, tear in pieces a soldier belonging to the army of the United States, in his, the said Henry Wirz's, custody as a prisoner of war, whose name is unknown, and in consequence thereof the said bloodhounds did, then and there, with the knowledge, encouragement, and instigation of him, the said Wirz, maliciously and murderously given by him, attack and mortally wound the said soldier, in consequence of which said mortal wound he, the said prisoner, soon thereafter, to wit: on the sixth day of July A. D. 1864, died.

Specification 12.—In this, that the said Henry Wirz, an officer in the military service of the so-called Confederate States of America, at Andersonville, in the State of Georgia, on or about the twenty-seventh day of July A. D. 1864, then and there being commandant of a prison there located by the authority of the said so-called Confederate States, for the confinement of prisoners of war taken and held as such from the armies of the United States of America, while acting as said commandant, feloniously and of his malice aforethought, did order a rebel soldier, whose name is unknown, then on duty as a sentinel or guard to the prison of which said Wirz was commandant as aforesaid, to fire upon a soldier belonging to the army of the United States, in his, the said Henry Wirz's, custody as a prisoner of war, whose name is unknown; and in pursuance of said order so as aforesaid, maliciously and murderously given as aforesaid, he, the said rebel soldier, did, with a musket loaded with gunpowder and bullet, then and there fire at the said soldier so as aforesaid held as a prisoner of war, inflicting upon him a mortal wound with the said musket, of which said mortal wound he, the said prisoner soon thereafter, to wit: on the day aforesaid, died.

Specification 13.—In this, that the said Henry Wirz, an officer in the military service of the so-called Confederate States of America, at Andersonville, in the State of Georgia, on or about the third day of August A. D. 1864, then and there being commandant of a prison there located by the authority of the said so-called Confederate States of America, for the confinement of prisoners of war taken and held as such from the armies of the United States of America, while acting as said commandant, feloniously and of his malice aforethought, did make an assault upon a soldier belonging to the army of the United States, in his, the said Wirz's, custody as a prisoner of war, whose name is unknown, and with a pistol called a revolver, then and there held in the hands of the said Wirz, did beat and bruise said soldier upon the head, shoulders, and breast, inflicting thereby mortal wounds, from which said beating and bruising aforesaid, and mortal wounds caused thereby, the said soldier soon thereafter, to wit: on the fourth day of August A. D. 1864, died.

By order of the President of the United States.

N. P. CHIPMAN, *Colonel and A. A. D. C.,*
Judge Advocate.

We witness in this extraordinary proceeding a man arrested in time of peace, and placed before a court which under the Constitution of the United States had no legal right to try him. The Constitution of the United States expressly declares that "No person shall be held to answer for a capital or otherwise infamous crime, unless on presentment or indictment of a grand jury," &c. "In all criminal prosecutions the accused shall enjoy the right of a speedy and public trial by an impartial jury," &c. (See Articles V. and VI. Amendments to the Constitution). "The trial of *all crimes,* except in cases of impeachment, shall be by jury," &c. (Art. II. Section 2, Constitution). The last remnant of the Confederate forces surrendered in April 1865, and peace was declared; yet we find, nearly four months afterwards, a military court is convened to try Captain Henry Wirz. Here we see a direct violation of the "charter of liberty"—the President usurping his power, a court without a legal existence, and its proceedings such as in any court of justice would have been pronounced a nullity.

Without pursuing this line of argument further, we find that the prisoner put in pleas in bar to the effect:

1st. That he had been paroled by General J. H. Wilson, and that he should not be held a prisoner.

2d. He denied the jurisdiction of the court to try him.

3d. That the war being ended and civil law restored, there is no military law under which he could be tried.

4th. He moved to quash the charges, for vagueness as to time, place, and manner of offences.

5th. That he had been on the 21st of August put upon trial to these charges, and that the court had been broken up without his agency or consent. Having once been put in jeopardy, he cannot now be arraigned as before, but is entitled to an acquittal.

6th. He claimed a discharge, because as an officer in the Confederate army he was entitled to the terms agreed to between Generals Sherman and Johnston, upon the surrender of the latter.

All these were overruled except as to the jurisdiction of the court, and the prisoner then put in the plea of not guilty.

The trial dragged along for nearly three months, the Northern press heralding forth to the civilised world the horrible scenes alleged to have been committed by Captain Wirz and his co-conspirators. *Harper's Weekly* was filled each week with some new cut or scene of the "Monster Wirz," or the "Brute Winder." The reporters of the *New York Herald* and *Tribune* were busy in picturing the Southern people as brutal barbarians. So great was the excitement, that a portion of the Canadian and English press were led to believe that the Southern people were not fit for the freedom to which they had aspired, and so expressed themselves. After the trial had continued for several days, Messrs. Hughes, Denver, and Peck, counsel for Captain Wirz, withdrew from the trial, satisfied that they could do their client no good, as his doom was fixed on the day that he was arrested. Lewis Schade, Esq., at the earnest request of the prisoner, remained until the close of the trial. The trial was concluded on the 4th of November 1865, after the examination of something over one hundred witnesses; and shortly afterwards we find the following:

[*General Court Martial—Orders No.* 607.]

WAR DEPARTMENT, ADJUTANT-GENERAL'S OFFICE,
WASHINGTON, *November 6th*, 1865.

Before a military commission which convened at Washington, D. C., August 23d, 1865, pursuant to paragraph 3, special orders No. 453, dated August 23d, 1865, and paragraph 13, special orders No. 524, dated October 2d, 1865, War Department, Adjutant-general's Office, Washington, and of which Major-general Lewis Wallace, United States Volunteers, is president, was arraigned and tried Henry Wirz.

FINDING.—The Commission having maturely considered the evidence adduced, find the accused, Henry Wirz, as follows:

Of specification to Charge I. *guilty*, after amending said specification to read as follows:—"In this, that he, the said Henry Wirz, did combine, confederate and conspire with them, the said Jefferson Davis, James A. Seddon, Howell Cobb, John H. Winder, Richard B. Winder, Isaiah H. White, W. S. Winder, W. Shelby Reed, R. R. Stevenson, S. P. Moore, —— Keer, late hospital-steward at Andersonville; James Duncan, Wesley W. Turner, Benjamin Harris, and others whose names are unknown, citizens of the United States aforesaid, and who were then engaged in armed rebellion against the United States, maliciously, traitorously, and in violation of the laws of war, to impair and injure the health and to destroy the lives—by subjecting to torture and great suffering, by confining in unhealthy and unwholesome quarters, by exposing to the inclemency of winter and to the dews and burning sun of summer, by compelling the use of impure water, and by furnishing insufficient and unwholesome food—of large numbers of Federal prisoners, to wit, the number of about forty-five thousand, soldiers in the military service of the United States of America, held as prisoners of war at Andersonville, in the State of Georgia, within the line of the so-called Confederate States, on or before the 27th day of March A. D. 1864, and at divers times between that day and the 10th day of April A. D. 1865, to the end that the armies of the United States might be weakened and impaired, and the insurgents engaged in armed rebellion against the United States might be aided and comforted.

Of charge I. "guilty."

Of specification first to charge II. "guilty."

Of specification second to charge II. "guilty."

Of specification third to charge II. "guilty."

Of specification fourth to charge II. "not guilty."

Of specification five to charge II. "guilty."

Of specification six to charge II. "guilty."

Of specification seven to charge II. "guilty."

Of specifications eight and nine to charge II. "guilty."

Of specification ten to charge II. "not guilty."

Of specification eleven to charge II. "guilty."

Of specification twelve to charge II. "guilty."

Of specification thirteen to charge II. "not guilty."

Of charge II. "guilty."

SENTENCE.—And the Commission does, therefore, sentence him, the said Henry Wirz, to be hanged by the neck till he be dead, at such time and place as the President of the United States may direct, two-thirds of the court concurring therein.

II.—The proceedings, findings and sentence in the foregoing case having been submitted to the President of the United States, the following are his orders:

The proceedings, findings and sentence of the court in the within case are approved, and it is ordered that the sentence be carried into execution by the officer commanding the Department of Washington, on Friday the 10th day of November, 1865, between the hours of 6 o'clock A. M. and 12 o'clock noon. ANDREW JOHNSON, *President.*

III.—Major-General C. C. Augur, commanding the Department of Washington, is commanded to cause the foregoing sentence in the case of Henry Wirz to be duly executed in accordance with the President's order.

IV.—The Military Commission, of which Major-General Lewis Wallace, United States Volunteers, is president, is hereby dissolved. By command of the President of the United States.

E. D. TOWNSEND, *Assistant Adjutant-general.*

Thus was Captain Wirz "tried," and the iniquitous proceedings were consummated by his execution, on the 10th day of November, 1865.

Captain Henry Wirz, though compelled to suffer an ignominious death, died as a brave man should die — fully conscious of having striven to discharge his duty to his country. He had been taken by treachery; cast into a dungeon without the opportunity of consulting with his friends, or seeing his wife and little children; his counsel had forsaken him; a mob, aroused and incensed by a venal press, was crying for his blood; but his courage and fortitude never forsook him. Just before his execution he was promised his life if he would implicate certain leading men in the South in the crimes with which he was charged. He answered, "I would not become a traitor, even if I knew anything, to save my own life."

The helpless condition of this unfortunate man is fully illustrated by the following letter sent by him to the editor of the *News* during the trial. As a matter of course, the appeal was unheeded:

OLD CAPITOL PRISON,
WASHINGTON CITY, D. C., *August 27th*, 1865.

To the Editor of the *New York News*:

Although a perfect stranger to you, I take, in my unfortunate and helpless condition, the liberty to address you this letter, knowing that, as a friend to the downtrodden South, you cannot but have some sympathy for a man who, as he believes, is innocently about to be sacrificed—a sympathy which I hope will prompt you to interest yourself in his behalf. I am a native of Switzerland, and, having been for years before the war a resident of Louisiana, could not do otherwise than take up arms to defend the State and country of my adoption when it was invaded. I joined the Confederate army in 1861, and served faithfully the cause I considered to be a rightful one. In 1862, the United States troops destroyed my home, and my wife and three children had to seek shelter among friends. I lost all I possessed, but a few negroes who still remained faithful. In 1864 I was ordered to report to the officer of the military prison at Andersonville, Georgia. By this officer I was put in command of the prison, and remained in that position from April 1864 until 1865. When the South ceased the struggle, I was still in Andersonville with my family, believing myself fully protected by the terms of the agreement between Generals Sherman and Johnston, and never dreaming that I, a poor captain and subaltern officer, would be made to answer with my life for what is now alleged to have been done at Andersonville. I was, in violation of a safe-conduct which was given me by a staff-officer of General Wilson, arrested in Macon, Georgia, was kept there in confinement for two weeks, and then sent on to Washington, and am now, by order of the President of the United States, brought before a court to be tried under the most atrocious charges. I have no friends here. I am helpless; and unless I can get help, will have to lose the last thing which I possess in this world—my good name and my life. My conscience is clear. I have never dealt cruelly with a prisoner under my charge. If they suffered for want of shelter, food, clothing and necessaries, I could not help it, having no control over these things—things which the Confederate Government could give only in very limited quantity, even to our own men, as everybody knows who will be just and impartial. My legal advisers (Messrs. Schade and Baker) seeing my helplessness, have undertaken to conduct my defence. They are both doing it from generosity and compassion, knowing full well that I have not the means to remunerate them for their trouble. But I cannot expect them to furnish the means which it absolutely requires in the conducting of a case of such importance. Copies of depositions have to be made, messengers have to be sent here and there to get up testimony; and how can this be done without money? I have none to give; and, no doubt, my case will be lost—my life sacrificed—for want of the money to defray the expenses of such a trial. But my counsel believe, from the evidence already in their possession, that if the necessary means can be obtained, my acquittal must be the result. On this condition, I take the liberty to appeal to you to assist me, and let me not be the victim of injustice. Your influence is such that it will not require very great efforts to collect the necessary means for a vigorous carrying on of the defence. I am myself without clothes, without any means to alleviate the hardships of a close confinement. My health is bad, and the prison fare is not calculated to benefit a sick, or at least a suffering man. Still, these things I have borne without murmuring, and hope, with the help of God, to bear yet for a while longer.

Hoping that this petition will receive a favorable reception on your part, and assuring you again that nothing but the direst necessity could induce me to address you, I remain, sir, with the greatest respect, your obedient servant,

H. Wirz,
Late Capt. and A. A. G. C. S. A.

During the trial Capt. Wirz appealed to Col. Chipman for permission to consult some of the clergy in regard to his spiritual welfare. This request was granted, and they visited him under the surveillance of a guard. The following is his appeal to Col. Chipman:

"You will, I hope, excuse my liberty to address you these lines, but not knowing to whom to appeal, I refer the matter to you. I am now a prisoner since the 7th of May, 1865. I have been deprived of all the chances to receive the consolations of religion even necessary to anybody, and truly more so to a man charged with crimes so heinous, so terrible, that the mere thought of them makes me shudder. Although I know myself full well that I am wrongfully accused, that an all-seeing, all-knowing God knows my innocence, still I need some encouragement from others, not to sink under the heavy burden which is placed upon me. Under these circumstances I respectfully ask that permission be granted to Rev. Fathers Whelan and Hamilton to visit me, and administer such spiritual comforts as my unfortunate position requires. They are both men of integrity, and will not profit by the occasion to see or do anything but what their duties as ministers of the Gospel will permit. Hoping that this, my humble request, may be favorably received, and the permission be granted, I remain, Colonel, most respectfully,

"Your obedient servant,

"H. WIRZ."

These reverend gentlemen, seeing that his mind and body were breaking down under his hopeless and forlorn condition, besought the authorities to grant him a respite for a few days, thus relieving him from the harassing details of the trial that had dragged its slow length along for nearly three months. This was, however, denied him, and he was forced to proceed with the trial.

At the close of this "mockery of justice," Captain Wirz stated in his own behalf substantially as follows:—"He appeared to put on record his answer to the charges on which he was arraigned, and to protest and vindicate his innocence. He was there to answer for all his official and personal acts at Andersonville, and, if he could, convince the court that they had been void of offence before God and man. He trusted that he would not be held responsible for the official or personal misdeeds of others. He would be judged by his own acts; and if they had been such as to warrant his conviction on any of the charges, let him be visited with punishment commensurate with his offence. He did not ask for mercy, but he demanded justice. In analysing the evidence he would endeavor to be simple and concise, and, above all things, frank and truthful." After reviewing the charges and specifications, confuting them, and denying all knowledge whatever of conspiracy with Jefferson Davis, R. E. Lee, and others, of "wilfully and maliciously" destroying the lives of Federal prisoners, he concluded his argument in the following mournful strain:—"The statement which I now close will probably survive me and you alike; it will stand as a complete answer to all the mass of misrepresentation heaped against me. May God so direct and enlighten you in your deliberations, that your character for impartiality and justice may be protected, my character defended, and the few days of my natural life spared to my helpless family."

The following letter from Captain Wirz was addressed to President Johnson four days before his execution:

"With a trembling hand, with a heart filled with the most conflicting emotions, and with a spirit hopeful one moment and despairing the next, I have taken the liberty of addressing you. When I consider your exalted position; when I think for a moment that in your hand rests the weal or woe of millions — yea, the peace of the world — well may I pause to call to my aid courage enough to lay before you my humble petition. I have heard you spoken of as a man willing and ready at all times and under all circumstances to do justice, and that no man, however humble he may be, need fear to approach you; and therefore I have come to the conclusion that you will allow me the same privilege as extended to hundreds and thousands of others. It is not my desire nor intention to enter into an argument as to the merits of my case. In your hands, if I am rightfully informed, are all the records and evidences bearing upon this point, and it would be presumption on my part to say one word about it. There is only one thing that I ask, and it is expressed in few words:—Pass your sentence. For six weary months I have been a prisoner; for six months my name has been in the mouth of every one; by thousands I am considered a monster of cruelty, a wretch that ought not to pollute the earth any longer. Truly, when I pass in my mind over the testimony given, I sometimes almost doubt my own existence. I doubt that I am the Captain Wirz spoken of. I doubt that such a man ever lived, such as he is said to be; and I am inclined to call on the mountains to fall upon and bury me and my shame. But oh, sir, while I wring my hands in mute and hopeless despair, there speaks a small but unmistakable voice within me, that says:—'Console thyself, thou knowest thy innocence, fear not; if men hold thee guilty, God does not, and a new life will pervade your being.' Such has been the state of my mind for weeks and months, and no punishment that human ingenuity can inflict could increase my distress. The pangs of death are short, and therefore I humbly pray that you will pass your sentence without delay. Give me death or liberty. The one I do not fear; the other I crave. If you believe me guilty of the terrible charges that have been heaped upon me, deliver me to the executioner. If not guilty, in your estimation, restore me to liberty and life. A life such as I am now living is no life. I breathe, sleep, eat, but it is only the mechanical functions I perform, and nothing more. Whatever you decide I shall accept. If condemned to death, I shall suffer without a murmur. If restored to liberty, I will thank and bless you for it.

"I would not convey the idea to your mind, Mr. President, that I court death. Life is sweet; however lowly or humble man's station may be, he clings to life. His soul is filled with awe when he contemplates the future, the unknown land where the judgment is, before which he will have to give an account of his words, thoughts, and deeds. Well may I remember, too, that I have erred like all other human beings. But of those things for which I may perhaps suffer a violent death, I am not guilty; and God judge me. I have said all that I wished to say. Excuse my boldness in addressing you, but I could

9

not help it. I cannot bear this suspense much longer. May God bless you, and be with you. Your task is a great and fearful one. In life or death I shall pray for you, and for the prosperity of the country in which I have passed some of my happiest as well as darkest days."

CHAPTER VIII.

It will be remembered that Messrs. Hughes, Denver, and Peck were retained as counsel for Captain Wirz; but upon ascertaining the biased nature of the court, and perceiving that they could be of no benefit whatever to their client, they withdrew from the defence. Lewis Schade, Esq., of Washington City, at the earnest appeal of the unfortunate man, kindly consented to appear for the defence. His published statement afterwards to the "American people," shows that he was prompted by those humane instincts that should pervade the breast of every advocate of justice and truth. His statement is as follows:

"Intending to leave the United States for some time, I feel it my duty before I start, to fulfill in part a promise which, a few hours before his death, I gave to my unfortunate client, Captain Wirz, who was executed at Washington on the 10th day of November, 1865. Protesting up to the last moment his innocence of those monstrous crimes with which he was charged, he received my word that, having failed to save him from a felon's doom, I would, as long as I lived, do everything in my power to clear his memory. I did that the more readily, as I was then already perfectly convinced that he suffered wrongfully. Since that time his unfortunate children, both here and in Europe, have constantly implored me to wipe out the terrible stains which now cover the name of their father. Though the times do not seem propitious for obtaining full justice; yet, considering that man is mortal, I will, before entering upon a perilous voyage, perform my duty to those innocent orphans, and also to myself. I will now give a brief statement of the causes which led to the arrest and execution of Captain Wirz. In April 1865, President Johnson issued a proclamation, stating that from evidence in the possession of the 'Bureau of Military Justice,' it appeared that Jefferson Davis was implicated in the assassination of Abraham Lincoln, and for that reason the President offered a reward of $100,000 on the capture of the then fugitive ex-President of the Southern Confederacy. That testimony has since been found to be entirely false and a mere fabrication, and the suborner Conover is now under sentence in the jail of this city; the two perjurers whom he suborned having turned State's evidence against him, whilst the individual by whom Conover was suborned has not yet been brought to justice.

"Certain high and influential enemies of Jefferson Davis, either then already aware of the character of the testimony of those witnesses, or not thinking their testimony quite sufficient to hang Mr. Davis, expected to find the wanting material in the terrible mortality of Union prisoners at Andersonville. Orders were issued accordingly to arrest a subaltern officer, Captain Wirz, a poor, friendless and wounded prisoner of war, (he being included in the surrender of General Johnston) and, besides, a foreigner by birth. On the 7th day of May he was placed in the Old Capitol Prison at Washington, and from that time the greater part of the Northern press was busily engaged in forming the unfortunate man, in the eyes of the Northern people, into such a monster that it became almost impossible for him to obtain counsel. Even his countryman, the Swiss Consul-general, publicly refused to accept money to defray the expenses of the trial. He was doomed before he was heard, and even the permission to be heard according to law was denied him. To increase the excitement and give eclat to the proceeding, and to influence still more the public mind, the trial took place under the very dome of the Capitol of the nation. A military commission, presided over by one of the most arbitrary and despotic generals in the country, was formed; and the paroled prisoner of war, his wounds still open, and so feeble that he had to recline during the trial on a sofa. How that trial was conducted the whole world knows. The enemies of generosity and humanity believed it to be a sure thing to get at Jefferson Davis. Therefore, the first charge was that of conspiracy between Wirz, Jefferson Davis, Seddon, Howell Cobb, R. B. Winder, R. R. Stevenson, and a number of others, to kill the Union prisoners. The trial lasted for three months; but, unfortunately for the bloodthirsty instigators, not a particle of evidence was produced showing the existence of such a conspiracy, yet Captain Wirz was found guilty of that charge. Having thus failed, another effort was made. On the night before the execution of the prisoner, a telegram was sent to the Northern press from this city, stating that Wirz had made important disclosures to General L. C. Baker, the well-known detective, implicating Jefferson Davis, and that the confession would probably be given to the public. On the same evening some parties came to the confessor of Wirz, Rev. Father Boyle, and also to me, one of them informing me that a high Cabinet officer wished to assure Wirz, that if he would implicate Jefferson Davis with the atrocities committed at Andersonville, his sentence would be commuted. He, the messenger, or whoever he was, requested me to inform Wirz of this. In presence of Father Boyle I told Wirz, next morning, what had happened. The Captain simply and quietly replied: 'Mr. Schade, you know that I have always told you that I do not know anything about Jefferson Davis, he had no connection with me as to what was done at Andersonville. If I knew anything of him I would not become a traitor against him, or anybody else, even to save my life.' He likewise denied that he had ever made any statement whatever to General Baker. Thus ended the attempt to suborn Captain Wirz against Jefferson Davis. That alone shows what a man he was. How many of his defamers would have done the same? With his wounded arm in a sling, the poor paroled prisoner mounted, two hours later, the scaffold. His last words were that he died innocent; and so he did. The 10th day of November, 1865, will indeed be a black stain upon the pages of American history. To weaken the effect of his declaration of innocence, and of the noble manner in which Wirz died, a telegram was manufactured here and sent North, stating that on the 27th day of October, Mrs. Wirz, (who actually was 900 miles, on that day, away from Washington) had been prevented by that Stantonian *deus ex machina*, General L. C. Baker, *from poisoning her husband.* Thus, on the same day when the unfortunate family lost their husband and father, a cowardly and atrocious attempt was made to blacken their character also. On the next day I branded the whole as an infamous lie, and since then I have never heard of it again, though it emanated from a Brigadier-general of the United States army.

"All those who were charged with having conspired with Captain Wirz have since been released, except Jefferson Davis, the prisoner of the American 'Castle Chillon.' Captain Winder was let off without trial; and if any of the others have been tried, which I do not know, certainly none of them have been hung. As Captain Wirz could not conspire alone, nobody will now, in view of that important fact, consider him guilty of that charge. So much then for charge No. I.

"As to charge No. II., to wit: Murder, in violation of the laws and customs of war,—I do not hesitate to declare what about 145 out of 160 witnesses on both sides declared during the trial, that Captain Wirz never murdered or killed any Union prisoners with his own hands or otherwise. All those witnesses (about twelve to fifteen) who testified that they saw Captain Wirz kill a prisoner, have sworn falsely; abundant proofs of that assertion being in existence. The hands of Captain Wirz are clear of the blood of prisoners of war. He would certainly have at least intimated to me a knowledge of the alleged murders with which he was charged. In almost all cases, no names of the alleged murdered men could be given; and where it was done, no such persons could be identified. The terrible scene in court when he was confronted with one of the witnesses, and the latter insisting that Wirz was the man who killed a certain Union prisoner, which irritated the prisoner so much that he almost fainted, will still be remembered. That man (Grey) swore falsely; and God alone knows what the poor, innocent prisoner must have suffered at that moment. That scene was depicted and illustrated in the Northern newspapers as if Wirz had broken down on account of his guilt. Seldom has a mortal suffered more than that friendless and forsaken man. Fearing lest this communication should be too long, I will merely speak of the principal and most intelligent of those false witnesses, who testified to individual murder on the part of Captain Wirz. Upon his testimony the Judge-advocate, in his final argument, laid particular stress, on account of his intelligence. This witness prepared also pictures of the alleged cruelties of Wirz, which were handed to the Commission, and are now on record, copies of which appeared at the time in Northern illustrated papers. He swore that his name was Felix de-la-Baume, and represented himself as a Frenchman and grand-nephew of Marquis Lafayette. After having so well testified and shown so much zeal, he received a recommendation signed by the members of the Commission. On the 11th day of October, before the taking of the testimony was concluded, he was appointed to a clerkship in the Department of the Interior. This occurred whilst one of the witnesses for the defence (Duncan) was arrested in open court and placed in prison before he had testified. After the execution of Captain Wirz, some of the Germans of Washington recognised in de-la-Baume a deserter from the Seventh New York (Steuben's)

Regiment, whose name was not de-la-Baume, but Felix Oeser, a native of Saxony. They went to Secretary Harlan, and he dismissed the impostor, and the important witness in the Wirz trial, on the 21st day of November, eleven days after the execution. Nobody who is acquainted with the Conover testimony, in consequence of which the President of the United States was falsely induced to place a reward of $100,000 upon the head of an innocent man, will be astonished at the above disclosures of the character of testimony before military commissions. So much for charge II. If from twelve to fifteen witnesses could be found who were willing to testify to so many acts of murder on the part of Wirz, there must certainly have been no lack of such who were willing to swear to minor offences. Such was the unnatural state of the public mind against the prisoner at that time, that such men regarded themselves, and were regarded, as heroes, after having testified in the manner above described; whilst, on the other hand, the witnesses for the defence were intimidated, particularly after one of them had been arrested. But who is responsible for the many lives that were lost at Andersonville and in the Southern prisons? That question has not fully been settled; but history will tell on whose heads the guilt for those sacrificed hecatombs of human beings is to be placed. It was certainly not the fault of poor Captain Wirz when, in consequence of medicines having been declared contraband of war by the North, the Union prisoners died for the want of the same. How often have we read during the war that ladies going South had been arrested and placed in the Old Capitol Prison by the Union authorities, because some quinine or other medicine had been found concealed in their clothing? Our navy prevented the ingress of medical stores from the seaside, and our troops repeatedly destroyed drug-stores, and even the supplies of private physicians in the South. Thus the scarcity of medicines became general all over the South. . . .

"That provisions in the South were scarce will astonish

nobody, when it is remembered how the war was carried on. General Sheridan boasted in his report that, in the Shenandoah Valley alone, he burnt over two thousand barns filled with wheat and corn, and all the mills in the whole tract of country; that he destroyed all factories of cloth, or killed and drove off every animal — even the poultry—that could contribute to human sustenance. And these desolations were repeated in different parts of the South, and so thoroughly, that last month, two years after the end of the war, Congress had to appropriate a million of dollars to save the people of those regions from actual starvation. The destruction of railroads and other means of transportation by which food could be supplied by abundant districts to those without it, increased the difficulties in giving sufficient food to our prisoners. The Confederate authorities, aware of their inability to maintain their prisoners, informed the Northern agents of the great mortality, and urgently requested that the prisoners should be exchanged, even without regard to the surplus which the Confederates had on the exchange-roll from former exchanges — that is, man for man. But our War Department did not consent to an exchange. They did not want to 'exchange skeletons for healthy men.' Finally, when all hopes of exchange were gone, Colonel Ould, the Confederate Commissioner of Exchange, offered, early in August, 1864, to deliver up all the Federal sick and wounded, without requiring an equivalent in return, and pledged that the number would amount to ten or fifteen thousand; and if it did not, he would make up that number with well men. Although this offer was made in August, the transportation was not sent for them (to Savannah) until December, although he urged and implored (to use his own words) that haste should be made. During that very period the most of the deaths at Andersonville occurred. Congressman Covode, who lost two sons in Southern prisons, will do well if he inquires who those 'skeletons' were which the Hon. Secretary of War (Stanton) did not want to exchange for healthy men. If he does, he will hereafter be perhaps less bitter against the people of the South. . . .

"We used justly to proclaim in former times that ours was the 'land of the free and the home of the brave.' But when one half of the country is shrouded in a despotism which now only finds a parallel in Russian Poland; and when our generals and soldiers quietly permit that their former adversaries shall be treated worse than the Helots of old, brave soldiers though they may be, who, when the forces and resources of both sections were more equal, have not seldom seen the backs of our best generals, not to speak of such men as Butler and consorts; then we may well question whether the Star-spangled Banner still waves 'over the land of the free and the home of the brave.' A noble and brave soldier never permits his antagonist to be calumniated and trampled upon after an honorable surrender. Besides, notwithstanding the decision of the highest legal tribunal in the land that military commissions are unconstitutional, the earnest and able protestations of President Johnson, and the sad results of military commissions, yet such military commissions are again established by recent legislation of Congress all over the suffering and starving South. History is just, and, as Mr. Lincoln used to say, 'we cannot escape history.' Puritanical hypocrisy, self-adulation and self-glorification, will not save those enemies of liberty from their just punishment. Not even a Christian burial of the remains of Captain Wirz has been allowed by Secretary Stanton. They still lie side by side with those of another and acknowledged victim of military commissions, the unfortunate Mrs. Surratt, in the yard of the former jail of this city. If anybody should desire to reply to this, I politely beg that it may be done before the 1st of May next, as I shall then leave the country, to return in the fall. After that day, letters will reach me in care of the American Legation, or Mr. Benedetto Bolzani, Leipzig street No. 38, Berlin, Prussia.

"LOUIS SCHADE, *Attorney at Law.*

"WASHINGTON, D. C., *April 4th*, 1867."

In corroboration of this statement of Mr. Schade in regard to the trial of Captain Wirz, made some two years after the close of the war, I will insert some extracts from a letter written to the editor of the *New York Daily News* some months (August 9th, 1865) before the trial commenced. It is from the pen of an officer on General Sheridan's staff, who was himself a prisoner at Andersonville, at a period when the most frightful mortality prevailed there. It is plain and pointed, and contains facts that cannot be controverted. It reads as follows:

To the Editor of the *New York News:*

SIR:—I learn by various telegrams from Washington, that Captain Wirz, late commandant of the prison at Andersonville, Ga., is now confined in the Old Capitol Prison, and that numerous witnesses have been summoned, whose testimony it is supposed will completely unveil the horrors of that place. Captain Wirz, it is affirmed, is charged with having been the principal cause of the death of many thousands of Union soldiers who now sleep there forever. Having been for several months an inmate of the stockade at Andersonville, I propose herein to consider, in the first place, the causes of the excessive mortality there, and secondly, how much of its frightful suffering is justly chargeable to Captain Wirz. In doing this I am convinced that (although possibly opposed by some) I shall be supported by all those who have had opportunities of learning the truth in the case, and whose love of truth and magnanimity will impel them not to join in the hue and cry against one whose offence seems to be, that in doing his duty he did it well. Forbearance toward a conquered foe having ever been the attribute of the truly great, I cannot conceive how justice will be vindicated, the Union perpetuated, or the character of our country elevated, by the trial and execution of this man. The horror of the public has been excited, and a desire for vengeance stimulated, by one-sided narrations and pictorial illustrations of suffering, until, not content with having supped on horrors for four years, the vitiated appetite of unappeasable men still calls for more. I am not aware that Capt. Wirz was selected for the position he filled from any inherent cruelty of disposition, or for any peculiar fitness for the task. His duty was simply that of jailor. Prisoners of war were committed to his charge, and he was held responsible for their safe custody, *i. e.* their retention. The mortality at Andersonville resulted mainly from the following causes: 1st. Want of food; 2d. Want of shelter; 3d. Want of medical attendance and hospital diet; 4th. Causes of a purely local nature, coupled with the moral degradation exhibited by the prisoners themselves. By the want of proper food I mean, the dietary scale was neither of the kind nor quality to which most of the prisoners had been accustomed. Still, it was the ordinary diet of the Confederate army, and they had nothing else to give us. Thousands of the prisoners had never eaten bread made of corn meal, or any preparation of it whatever; and with those, its use commonly resulted in diarrhœa, which, aggravated by the excessive use of water, generally in a few days became chronic. Every one knows the difficulty of treating this disease, even under the most favorable circumstances. At first the meal was issued uncooked, and the prisoners allowed to go out of the stockade in squads under guard to collect fuel. This privilege was accorded with the understanding that an escape would not be attempted. In a short time, however, Captain Wirz was compelled to withdraw the favor, for it was evident that no reliance could be placed in the promises of our men. This want of good faith resulted lamentably for all. Fuel became scarce, as only a few wagon-loads were distributed *per diem* to the prisoners, and the share of each man for three or four days would not surpass in size an ordinary cane. It was impossible to be otherwise, for the limited number of wagons and teams of the post were incessantly employed in hauling rations and carrying the dead to their graves. The corn-meal was, therefore, eaten in a semi-cooked state, and sickness commonly followed. Beans (or peas as they are called South) were not on the bill of fare. They were cooked in large kettles, with bacon or beef, as might happen, and would have been palatable and nutritious had even the most ordinary care been exercised in their preparation. *But the cooks were our own men,* liberated from the stockade for this special duty, on parole, and receiving therefor an extra ration and the liberty of the entire post, besides other privileges. Their own wants were bountifully supplied. The choicest of everything was theirs; but this secured, nothing involving either trouble or extra labor was wasted upon their unfortunate comrades. The beans were cooked as received from the commissary, mingled with pods, stones, and sand. The beef or bacon, covered with the filth of the cook-house, was flung into the sickening mess, and a compound was produced which even Macbeth's witches would have pronounced "*slab and good.*" When all was ready, it was dipped into barrels and hauled into the stockade for distribution. A brawny prisoner (whose nationality I shall not mention), detailed to superintend the issue of the rations, mounted each wagon as it entered, and indulged to the utmost his proclivities for murder. This he actually effected in one instance at least, beside inflicting innumerable serious injuries upon his fellow-prisoners; but, as he was forwarded for exchange long ago, I suppose ere this he has received an *honorable* discharge from the United States service in consideration *of his sufferings.*

As for the quantity of food, I know that until Generals Sherman and Kilpatrick destroyed the railroad communications of the South, the ration as issued by the post commissary was nearly, if not equal to that of our guards. The issues were based upon the morning reports of the prison; but as many hundred men inside and out of the stockade drew double rations or more, there would necessarily be a deficiency among those not so fortunate. The numerous instances of starvation which have been cited, occurred, not from the lack, but from the nature of the food. Many such cases I have noticed where men have wasted away to skeletons with abundance of provisions in their tents. To eat were death, and it was death to abstain. The avidity with which our poor fellows devoured the delicacies offered them on arriving within our lines, was owing no more to their hunger than to the tempting nature of the viands. Could it have been possible for the Confederates to have bettered the diet of their prisoners, it is too much to expect of humanity that they would content themselves with their simple fare while we feasted.

The want of shelter exercised a marked influence. Had the men observed good faith when allowed to go out for wood, it is certain that in time all those unprovided with blankets or shelter-tents would have found shelter enough to protect them from the sun and dew. It was not until last September, however, that barracks were commenced. Had not the prisoners been removed to Millen, Florence, Savannah, Blackshears, and other posts, for their health, all would have been sheltered before winter set in. Last August there were probably thirty-five thousand men at Andersonville. More than half of these either bought or were provided with shelter of some kind. The rest lived as they best might, crouching by day in the shadows of the tents, and at night sleeping where they could find room. I mentioned a few weeks since, in the columns of a Brooklyn paper, some of the causes of this destitution. Many of our men were taken in battle, their baggage generally at the rear. Others, too feeble or indolent to carry their blankets or knapsacks, threw them away; and very many *sold* their effects by piecemeal, until they had stripped themselves as far as decency would permit, and farther, to gratify every impulse of appetite whenever an opportunity offered. Fruits and tempting edibles were displayed at every railroad station, and purchased with the blankets, clothing, and shoes of our infatuated men. Hundreds of them, I dare-say thousands, have bartered away their lives for a momentary gratification. When asked, however, how they lost their clothing and blankets, they almost invariably replied, "*The rebs stripped me.*" All of these houseless and naked men were blistered by the sun and chilled by the dews. These were the men who waited for the dead at the gates, and stripped every corpse to positive nudity, whenever the immediate friends or comrades of the deceased rejected the loathsome rags. These are they whose portraitures have filled our pictorials, and upon whose testimony of suffering and starvation the conviction of Captain Wirz will be sought; and whose vindictiveness, now in the hour of the triumph to which they contributed little or nothing, is only equalled by their total want of magnanimity, manhood and self-control while prisoners.

For some time after the organisation of the post, and before the extension of the original stockade, the sick received hospital treatment inside the enclosure. The great number of prisoners captured in the struggle against Grant and Sherman, necessitated the removal of the hospital, which was accordingly located a short distance outside. The accommodations were limited; so much so, in fact, that, without artifice or favor, it was almost impossible to gain admittance. The medical staff was quite numerous, and I suppose of the average ability. The stewards, ward-masters, nurses, cooks, &c., *were all our own men.* The principle ailments were chronic diarrhœa, dropsy, gangrene, and scurvy; of the first three, probably four-fifths of the patients died. The treatment for scurvy was somewhat more successful; and would have been still more so, had not these same *hospital attendants* exhibited all the demoniacal cruelty which is now so eagerly attributed to Captain Wirz. Anti-scorbutics were procured when possible. Wheat-flour and whiskey were also issued *for*, but not *to*, the sick; for these good *Samaritans of ours* would make the flour into tempting little biscuits, which retailed for twenty-five cents apiece in the stockade; and the whiskey, when diluted, would net them five dollars per canteen. Poultry, eggs, and fruit were disposed of in like manner; only enough being issued to the sick to make a semblance of hospital treatment. When the sick were brought out every morning to fill the places of those whose death had made room for them, a general scramble would ensue among the nurses to secure those who would probably give the least trouble. Very expert judges, too, were these nurses of the probable amount of plunder a patient would yield, either before or after death. There were no coroner's inquests at Andersonville; and for the credit of humanity, and our national character, it is well there were none. Many a dismal horror is locked up forever in the breasts of men, who could tell of some patient sufferer musing at midnight on his home and loved ones, and hoping, with reason perhaps, for his recovery, who felt the fierce clutch at his throat, and yielded his life that the few dollars he had secreted about his person might accrue to his murderer! Many of these *hospital attendants* came into our lines at Vicksburg with abundance of money, obtained either by downright robbery or by swindling the sick of their rations. An admittance to the hospital was generally a passport to the grave; yet such were the delusions of hope, that our poor fellows, knowing their almost inevitable fate, went there and died. The medical treatment was faulty, of course. All that the physician could do, was merely an approximation to the proper treatment. The stringency of the blockade (medicines and hospital supplies being contraband of war) was such that drugs were not procurable. Our men by this means were the principal sufferers; for the Confederates, not being so subject to the diseases which swept off so many of ours, were successfully treated with the herbs and indigenous remedies furnished by the laboratory at Macon.

The local peculiarities of Andersonville were not of themselves of a character to induce any excessive mortality. The spot was selected mainly with a view to its salubrity, and such is abundantly proved by the fact that very few of our men who were out on parole died . . .

I have thus, as briefly as possible, endeavored to show why thirteen thousand of our men lie buried at Andersonville. It is frightful to contemplate this vast charnel-house, and think that one man should now stand accused of being the author of it. The Hon. Henry S. Foote recently, in a letter, avowed his disbelief of the participation of the Confederate Government in a plot to starve or otherwise murder our prisoners. Starvation did undoubtedly occur, but from causes I have already enumerated. Many men were shot at Andersonville for crossing the limits assigned them. Every man in the stockade knew that to cross, or even touch the "dead line," was to court death. The prisoners were soldiers, and knew the arbitrary requirements of military discipline; and yet the guard is blamed for doing that which, if undone, would have subjected them to trial and punishment. Some of our men were shot accidentally. I remember, too, that some of our military prisons at the North had the like regulations. Small favor was shown a rebel soldier at Point Lookout, and the negro guard there only asked the shadow of an excuse to fire. All war is cruel, but I saw no more cruelty exercised at Andersonville than, in my opinion, was necessary to keep the prisoners within bounds . . . I have known our own men to volunteer to accompany the hounds and bring back our fugitives. Should these men receive an honorable discharge, and Captain Wirz be convicted and sentenced to an infamous punishment? Is he to be held responsible for the deaths in hospital, when our own men, deputed and paid to nurse the sick, more than neglected their duty? And because our own men, scoffing at every prudential consideration of cleanliness, wilfully neglected every precaution which would conduce to their health, is he to be held up to the world as a murderer of hitherto unknown magnitude? I trust not. In our national heraldry I see an olive-branch for the conquered, not a hangman's noose.

Believe me, sir, I have no personal interest or object in making this statement or appeal. I never spoke to Captain

Wirz, nor he to me. Not a single favor, directly or otherwise, have I ever received from him. Love of justice, and an utter disbelief in the complete depravity of man, alone impel me. And above all, for the credit of our common country, let it never be said that an American soldier, whether Northern or Southern, could deliberately assassinate thirteen thousand defenceless men, trusting to him alone for protection.

Respectfully yours,

M. S. H.

CHAPTER IX.

In giving an account of Andersonville, the most important prison-post of the South, and resisting the attempts of the North to fasten the odium of cruelty and barbarity to prisoners of war on the Southern people, I should neglect a manifest duty were I to pass unnoticed the well-attested sufferings of Southern men in Northern prisons. Yet, in so doing, I heartily disclaim any intention or desire to generate further strife between the lately opposing sections of the Republic. If any be offended by truth plainly told, the misfortune is theirs, the fault not mine.

In the first place, then, to show that the *theory* of war, as held—or, at any rate, publicly declared—by the North was like that of the civilised world in general, it may be well to quote a few paragraphs from the "General Orders No. 100," issued April 24th, 1863, for the government of the armies of the United States; after which it will be in order to consider Mr. Wade's "Retaliatory Resolutions," by way of contrast and illustration.

EXTRACTS FROM "GENERAL ORDERS NO. 100."

XI. The law of war not only disclaims all cruelty and bad faith concerning engagements concluded with the enemy during the war, but also the breaking of stipulations solemnly contracted by belligerents, in the time of peace, avowedly intended to remain in force in case of war between the contracting parties. . . .

XVI. Military necessity does not admit of cruelty—that is, the infliction of suffering for the sake of suffering or revenge—nor in maiming or wounding, except in fight, nor of torture to extort confessions. . . .

XLVI. A prisoner of war is subject to no punishment for being a public enemy, nor is any revenge wreaked upon him by the intentional infliction of suffering or disgrace, by cruel punishment, want of food, by mutilation, death, or other barbarity. . . .

LXXII. Money and other valuables on the person of a prisoner, such as watches or jewelry, as well as extra clothing, are regarded by the American army as the private property of the prisoners, and the appropriation of such valuables or money is considered dishonorable, and is prohibited. . . .

LXXV. Prisoners of war are subject to confinement or imprisonment, such as may be deemed necessary on account of safety, but they are to be subjected to no other intentional suffering or indignity. . . .

LXXVI. Prisoners of war shall be fed upon plain and wholesome food whenever practicable, and treated with humanity. . . .

CXIX. Prisoners of war may be released from captivity by exchange, and, under certain circumstances, also by parole. . . .

These orders would seem to have been sufficiently explicit on the subject of humanity towards prisoners, to have restrained the officers in charge of Southern prisoners from acts of cruelty; but, unfortunately, they seem to have been promulgated only for effect. If those in charge of prisoners in Northern forts were ever furnished with these instructions, they were as a dead letter; certainly they were not carried out in good faith. In proof of this position, I avail myself again of "extracts" from the *Southern Review*, an ably conducted journal, one that must be taken by all candid men as good authority. It says:

"There were a dozen prisons in the North, in either one of which the treatment of prisoners was utterly disgraceful and barbarous, exceeding in tyrannical cruelty anything that was developed in the 'Wirz trial,' even upon the testimony of Government witnesses. No tribunal will ever arraign the officers who committed these atrocities; no judicial sentence will ever condemn the functionaries who countenanced and approved them, and indeed directed their perpetration. Of most of them no record will be kept. It is difficult now to get the brave men who suffered in silence to speak of the treatment which they were forced to undergo, as it deserves to be spoken of. The accounts from all these prisons are much the same. The same systematic torture prevailed in every one of them; and the sufferings of the Southern prisoners were intensely aggravated by the inhumanity of the negro guards, who were in most instances detailed for prison police-duty. As yet but little has been published on the subject. We propose now to give a few experiences, which were written when they were fresh in the memory of those who had themselves suffered, and who had witnessed the privations and cruelties to which others were subjected. The first extracts are taken from the journal of a resident of Baltimore, who at one time had his own share of prison life. The number of Federal prisoners became so great, and the war became so protracted, that the Federal administration was finally forced to yield to the clamor of the friends of the captured men, and to make arrangements for obtaining their release. The exchange of prisoners was accordingly recommenced early in 1865. Most of the Southern prisoners, some of whom had been confined for eighteen months, were brought through Pennsylvania to Baltimore, to be shipped to Fortress Monroe. On reaching Baltimore they were taken from the cars on the outskirts of the town, and marched through the streets about one and a half miles to the point of embarkation. Speaking of the condition of those Southern prisoners of war, the writer says:

"*February* 21*st.*—Prisoners for exchange continue to pass through. They are in a most wretched condition. Pale and emaciated, they look as if they had hardly strength to stand. Some of them had silver sixpences, which they had evidently managed to retain secreted on their persons, which they held up, begging for bread. Miss B., who saw them pass by, could not stand the sight. They looked, she said, as if they hardly had strength to hold up the little coin. One man came down the street a few days ago, clad in a pair of drawers and a blanket. Blood marked the track of his feet. Miss W. appealed to one of the officers in charge for permission to give him some clothing, but was rudely refused. On the boat that is to take them to Fortress Monroe, they are huddled together in a distressing manner, with very little protection against the cold and driving rain. The day is as bad as a winter day can be.

"*February* 23*d.*—F. B. showed me a letter to-day he had lately received from Colonel St. Leger Grenfell, an Englishman, who was formerly on General John H. Morgan's staff. He left the Southern service, and was allowed to come to New York from Nassau. Afterwards he went to Canada. He was accused of complicity in the attempt to release the prisoners from Johnson's Island, made a few months since, of which Grenfell declares that he was perfectly innocent. He was confined in McLean Barracks, Chicago. He writes:—'They have tried hard to kill me. I have suffered much from long-continued confinement in a cell 6 feet by $3\frac{1}{2}$, ill-ventilated, and bad food. I had the dysentery when they shut me up. Yesterday the manacles were knocked off for the first time.' The treatment of the officers and men under General Morgan's command in Ohio was infamous. They were not allowed to converse with each other, even while sitting side by side at their meals. For the slightest infraction of any of the very stringent regulations to which they were subjected, they were confined in dark and narrow cells for days. So severe were the sufferings of some of those who were punished, that when they were taken from the cells the blood gushed from their ears.

"*February 26th.*—The petty malignity and dirty trickery of Federal jailors is hardly to be believed. We have just received news of the disposition of the Christmas dinner which was provided for the prisoners in the hospital known as West's building. Mrs. G., Mrs. H., and other ladies, knowing how meagre was the fare of these poor fellows, applied to General Lew. Wallace for permission to send them something to eat on Christmas day. Wallace refused to allow them to communicate with the prisoners, but gave them permission to furnish what food they liked for this occasion. Several loads of provisions, such as beef, turkeys, and even expensive luxuries, were accordingly procured, and delivered at the hospital door. It was supposed that they had been handed over to the prisoners. To-day, one of them who is out brings information that on the day they were sent, two or three of the prisoners who were strong enough to crawl to the windows saw the yard lined with boxes and baskets, which they felt sure were for them. This was all they saw of them. Not an ounce of anything reached its destination.

"*March 1st.*—James W. Washington, 12th Virginia Cavalry, died a few days ago at Fort McHenry; he was captured in the Shenandoah Valley. Sheridan, who has committed terrible devastation there, treats most of the men he captures as guerillas. Some of them are sent to Fort McHenry, where Brigadier-general Morris confines them in cells. These cells are of the most horrid character. They cannot be 6 feet long, or more than 2½ feet wide. They are not high enough to stand in. They are side by side, and have each an iron-grated door, which opens in a narrow gangway. At one end of this gangway is a heavy door opening into the guard-room. There are window-panes in the top of this door, through which a dim light is thrown a few hours each day. It is inhuman to confine a felon in such cells. Washington was stripped of his clothing when captured, and clad in a summer suit. His treatment was so bad and his sufferings so great that he lost his senses and died.

"*March 3d.*—The condition of many of the prisoners who now go through here daily for exchange is heartrending. From Elmira down, no provision is made for food. Some of them are very weak and require sustenance. When the trains are not detained it is bad enough; but when they are delayed, as they often are more than a day, it is much worse. On several occasions, five and six or more have died in the cars, of prostration.

"*March 5th.*—Mr. T. H. has been here from New York. He was very kind to the prisoners in Fort Lafayette, and is now attending to the distribution of money and clothes from the English fund raised at the Liverpool Bazaar. He had no conception whatever of the severity and brutality of the military authorities in this State; so little is known even in New York of what passes here. Any paper which attempted to publish the truth would not be allowed a second issue. Yesterday Mr. H. went to see the prisoners, as they were being marched through the streets. He was not allowed to approach them, and was driven back several times with the bayonet, although he told the guard he was from the North and had no friends nor acquaintances among the prisoners. One of the men wrote on a piece of paper which he contrived to throw out, 'For God's sake get us something to eat, we are starving.' Another message of the same kind was thrown to

CONFEDERATE PRISONERS PASSING THROUGH BALTIMORE.

a little boy from one of the ambulances, and was brought to Mr. H. There were twenty-five ambulances of sick. They were closed in. Several prisoners, who were too weak to stand the fatigue of the journey and so long a fast, were already dead. No one was allowed to give a cup of cold water to the rest. It is evident that it is the aim of the administration to land these men at the exchanging point with the minimum amount of life in them, and so broken down by starvation and ill-treatment that they must be for a long time unfit for duty. Few of the prisoners suffer from wounds; the weaker ones have been killed off long ago. S. S., in passing through here from Camp Douglas, gives a description of prison-life that is heart-rending; he says that 1200 men died there, not one of whom would have lost his life with ordinarily decent care.

"*March* 11*th.*—More prisoners. These poor fellows are not provided with food on the cars. They remain sometimes as long as two days without anything to eat. Mrs. E. G. saw one of them, as they passed down the street, stoop to pick up some garbage, which he literally devoured. She had in her pocket a small bottle of mint-cordial. She stepped forward to the guard and asked him to give it to the famished man, who seemed scarcely able to drag himself along. The guard struck her in the breast with his hand, and told her to stand off. 'That is all you are fit for,' said she, 'to make war against women.' A few days ago the guard charged with fixed bayonets among some ladies who attempted to relieve the wants of starving fellow-creatures.

"*March* 12*th.*—Miss W., who saw the prisoners that passed through yesterday, was horrified at the inhuman treatment they received. One man begged the guard for a morsel of bread. He was brutally refused. He lay down and died in a short time. One who was in a car which had not been opened, attempted to raise a window. 'Faugh!' said the guard, 'what a smell of small-pox!' 'Well there may be a smell,' was the reply; 'there are four dead bodies in here, and we are stifling with the heat and smell. The windows are all down; give us air or we shall suffocate.' The guard closed the window by force. A man wounded in both legs was being supported by two Confederate surgeons, who carried him toward an ambulance. The guard struck him twice with the bayonet, ordering him to move on, in spite of the remonstrances of the surgeons. His conduct was so revolting that a Federal surgeon finally noticed it, and commanded him to desist. He received, however, no reprimand.

"*March 29th.*—Heard to-day of the death of young Arthur Gilmor. He passed through here a few days ago for exchange. He had then chronic dysentery, and was exceedingly ill. His sister saw him, and every effort was made to obtain permission from the military authorities to have him placed in a hospital until he was able to stand the journey. This was positively refused, unless he would consent to take the oath of allegiance, although he was then known to be in a dying condition. He did not live to reach the Southern soil. The process of exhaustion, as practised by the administration, has been terribly inhuman. The stoppage of the exchange of prisoners cut like a two-edged sword; for at Andersonville, where the Federal prisoners were sent, partly for safety and partly that they might be near food-supplies, the Northern constitution has given way and the men have died rapidly."

Says the writer:—"These few extracts, it must be borne in mind, tell only a portion of the truth. We add to them several statements obtained from prisoners soon after their release from the different Northern prisons and forts. They are all original communications, none of which have ever been made public. It will be seen from their tone and style that they are from the hands of educated gentlemen.

CAMP DOUGLAS.

S. S. writes:—"We arrived at Camp Douglas, near Chicago, on Lake Michigan, in August, 1863. Many of us were without blankets, and all without overcoats. Although the nights were already cold, the authorities refused to furnish either blankets or overcoats. Those of us who had friends within the Federal lines were, however, permitted to write to them. In December we were stripped of the overcoats we had procured, the officers stating, as an excuse, that they might assist us in making our escape. Cotton jackets and condemned Federal coats of light material, with the skirts cut off, were issued in their stead. On New Year's eve the snow fell and the cold became intense. No words can describe the agony we endured while this pinching weather lasted. None more severe had been known for twenty years. The floors of our barracks had been torn up to prevent our digging tunnels to escape by, and the wind had full play about our feet. Most of the windows were more or less broken; some of them had no glass in them. There were large crevices on the sides of the barracks, through which the snow drifted in upon our bunks. Icicles hung from the roof within two inches of the stove-pipe, and the breath froze upon our beards as it left our mouths. Six or seven blankets were issued one day to a barrack containing 120 to 160 men, for which we drew lots. These were, as far as I knew, the only blankets issued during the winter. Although the guards were well clad in heavy overcoats and provided with furs and blankets, some of them were frostbitten. They were all ordered into our quarters at dusk, the cold being too severe for them to do duty outside. Our own sufferings can hardly be imagined. We were forced to be economical with fuel, as we did not know what we were to be allowed; and we were almost afraid to venture out into the air, even should we receive orders to go for wood. But it was plain we must go to the wood-yard or freeze. Few of those who were detailed to bring in fuel returned without being frostbitten or frozen. Many were brought back insensible or in a helpless condition. Four of my company started for our allowance. All suffered extremely. Two of them could not speak on their return; one of them had to be carried into an adjoining barrack, another had his arms frozen stiff around the wood and could not open them. Going after water was nearly as bad. Many died from exposure this winter. Pneumonias, colds, and rheumatism became very common. Our rations at first were ample, and aided us greatly in contending with the cold. Afterwards they were cut down fearfully, and living was reduced to a science. We had bread and water for breakfast, and a small piece of meat and bread for dinner, with a few beans and potatoes occasionally. We were allowed no supper. There are no words to describe our sufferings. I had known what it was to be on allowance for some time, and even to be without food for a day or two in the field, but I never knew till now the horrors of starvation. It was terrible to go to bed suffering from the gnawings of hunger, to pass a long and restless night, dreaming perhaps of feasting, and to awake feeling weaker than ever. Shut up thus and starved, it is no wonder that we cried bread! bread! when strangers visited the camp. For this we were severely punished, and in some barracks even the scanty rations of bread allowed were discontinued for a time. Rats and dogs were luxuries, and frequently eaten in prison. There was a very scanty supply of medicine for the hospital. I have heard surgeons tell men they had nothing to give them, and that they could do nothing for them. I have seen men left to die for want of a little physic or restorative. From the summer of 1864 to the spring of 1865, when I was exchanged, there was a great want of medicines of all kinds.

"Many modes of cruelty and punishment were inflicted upon us during the administration of Col. Charles V. de Land, and also during that of Col. B. J. Sweet. We were tied up by the thumbs for attempting to escape. We were beaten by the guards with heavy sticks for the slightest offence, and often for nothing at all. We were ridden upon 'Morgan's mule'; that is, we were forced to straddle a narrow scantling placed high above the ground, not being permitted to derive any support from our hands. We were placed in this position at the bidding of the guard, and kept there at his pleasure, from ten minutes to two hours. We were taken out into the cold and forced to mark time, for standing too long near the fire. The guards frequently became intoxicated, and while they were in this condition, were permitted to inflict punishments for imaginary offences. The prisoners in barrack No. 10 were ordered out and made to pull down their clothes and sit naked upon the ice. The crime committed was bespattering the spit-box too much. Sometimes men would be ordered out at night, and forced to lean over, without bending the knee, and touch the ground with the forefinger. This was termed 'pointing for grub.' Many frequently fell in this position from rush of blood to the head. Many prisoners were shot down by the guards without any provocation whatever. Boxes and barrels were often placed over the shoulders of prisoners, and kept there for several days, as punishment for breaking rules unknown to them. While Colonel Sweet was in command, and Lieutenant-colonel L. C. Skinner was commissary-general of prisoners, we were forced to go to bed at sun-down summer and winter, after which, if a word was spoken, the offender was ordered out and punished cruelly. Inspection took place once a week. The whole camp was ordered out at once, and not by barracks. We were forced to stand until inspection was through. Numbers used to drop, fainting from weakness. The number of prisoners was 12,000. As I write, many terrible scenes occur to me. In barrack No. 9 a prisoner was caught at night standing by the stove, a guard entered, and presenting a revolver at the poor fellow's head, beat him mercilessly with his waist-belt, telling him that he intended to brand the letters of the brass plate U. S. on his back. Men talk of the horrors of Andersonville. If those who now sleep on the shores of Lake Michigan could tell the story of their sufferings, Andersonville would appear as a paradise in comparison."

Point Lookout.

A prisoner, who was confined eight months at Point Lookout, in Maryland, writes:—"We reached here about the middle of June, 1864. At the provost-marshal's office we were partially stripped of our clothing, and our persons were strictly searched. Our money, watches, and little valuables were taken from us. We were then marched into the camp-enclosure and initiated in prison regulations. We were deprived of most of our baggage, a small supply of clothing only being allowed us. What was taken from us was appropriated and disposed of by the officers in charge. When we entered the prison we found that all the new prisoners—those captured during the spring of 1864—were placed in small tents, capable of holding five men, with great discomfort. When we lay down together, one of us was always pressed tightly against the canvas. In our tent we had three blankets, which we brought with us, but none were issued for some time after our arrival. During this period, most of the men who came in with us slept on the ground. When it rained, our situation was truly deplorable. The tents were not high enough for a man to stand erect, so we sat all day upon the damp ground floor. On the morning of our arrival they gave us each a small loaf of bread. This was our scant allowance for the day; the next day when we applied for more, they told us our supply for that day was drawn the day before, we therefore had no bread till late in the afternoon. This explanation was always given when rations were not issued. At dinner we had a small slice of fat salt meat and a cup of soup. The ingredients of this soup are known only to those who made it; it smelt like dish-water, and strongly resembled it in appearance and consistency. Our voracious appetites rendered the most repugnant food palatable, yet I have often seen this abominable compound left untouched by those who would eagerly have devoured whatever their morbid stomachs could retain. Many tried to eat the meat, but could not. Rats were eagerly eaten, and hard cabbagestalk, with raw potato-peelings, which had been thrown into the sewers, was used for food. The scurvy, brought on by this wretched diet, was prevalent in its most awful form. The greatest of our troubles arose from want of good water. The salt meat created intense thirst, which we had no means of slaking. There were about thirty wells within the encampment, but all the water was strongly impregnated with copper and other minerals, and the surgeons pronounced it poisonous. We were advised by them to drink as little of it as possible. It turned the teeth and tongue, in many instances, perfectly black. In some of these wells the water was much better than others. These were strictly guarded, and no one was allowed to use them without a written permit. The best well was used only by the hospital. The handle of this pump was taken off and kept in the wards, to prevent the use of the well; but there was a small hole in the platform around the pump, and I have seen crowds of men collect there, with small tin cans tied to a string, which they would let down through this hole, and so reach the water. It was perfectly clear and invitingly cool when first drawn; but after standing a short time, a greenish scum formed on it. I have seen tea made with it, and when boiled it became black as ink.

"The enclosure around the camp was, I suppose, about half a mile square. Belting it on the outside, about four feet from the top, was a platform on which the sentinels always walked. When we first arrived, the negroes came on post every third day; on the intermediate days we were guarded by white soldiers. Afterwards we had the negroes only for several consecutive weeks. Around the entire encampment was a ditch, about fifteen feet from the fence, called 'the dead line.' The sentry fired upon any one who crossed it. The cook houses were situated upon one side of the camp, and in front of them was another ditch, also guarded by sentinels, who walked between the buildings. Before each door fronting this ditch was a small bridge, which we crossed at meal-times. The cooks were all prisoners, but they had access to these houses at all times, and the sentry would frequently permit others to pass on any special business. One evening about dusk I was sitting in my tent with the door open, when I saw a flash and heard the report of a musket; immediately followed a groan. I was sick at the time and did not leave my tent, but one of my tent-mates ran immediately to the spot, where a crowd of men soon collected, and found an unfortunate prisoner mortally wounded. He was a sick man, who had taken a walk for exercise, when, finding himself exhausted, he sat down on one of the bridges to rest. The negro sentinel did not speak to him, but fired without warning. The surgeons, General Barnes (the commandant of the post), and other officers came in soon afterwards. The poor prisoner died about three hours later, and we heard no more of the affair. No one was surprised at this atrocious outrage, or at the indifference with which it was treated by the authorities. This instance took place before my eyes. Many others of the same nature were witnessed by hundreds. Groups of men were sometimes fired into, and persons killed and wounded who had committed no offence. The brutality of these negroes was in another way fearfully exercised. During the day we had access to the sinks, built on piles driven in the water, a short distance from the beach; but at night the gates were closed, and boxes were placed in the lower part of the camp, to which the men were allowed to go at all hours of the night. There were hundreds of sick who were never admitted into the hospital; cases of violent diarrhœa of long continuance, reducing the patient almost to a skeleton. These men would sometimes go out twenty times during the night, and not unfrequently were compelled by the negroes to run for long distances at the point of the bayonet, and often, in their enervated condition, forced to carry some negro soldier on their backs. They were sometimes ordered to kneel and 'pray for Abraham Lincoln and the success of the colored troops,' and then to dance, stand on their heads, or in any other way made to contribute to the amusement of these heartless brutes. During the coldest days of winter, sick men might be seen running along the bleak streets to keep up rapid circulation of the blood; without sufficient clothing to hide their nakedness, a tattered blanket scarcely covering their shoulders, and their attenuated limbs shivering with cold. Sometimes men would huddle together in their tents all day to prevent actual freezing. Their feet in many instances were dreadfully frost-bitten. The supply of wood at best was scarcely sufficient to prevent actual freezing. Three small sticks, about three feet in length, was the usual allowance for twenty-four hours. Sometimes none was issued. This was generally the case when a sudden severe spell set in, and no preparation had been made for it. Bronchitis, pneumonia and dysentery became fearfully prevalent as the winter set in. I have actually tracked men coming to the hospital, and along the streets of the camp, by the blood spit up during a hemorrhage.

"When an exchange took place, the surgeons would order all the sick who were strong enough to walk, to assemble on a long platform in front of the wards, extending nearly a quarter of a mile. They generally appeared in hospital clothing, consisting of a thin shirt and drawers, and a blanket around their shoulders. This sometimes occurred in very cold weather. After forming into a line, they were marched several times up and down the platform; and after they returned to their beds, selections were made of the fit subjects for exchange. On these occasions, bribes were offered, and accepted, by the United States contract physicians. Men in perfect health were sent off in every boat-load of sick, when sick only should have been selected. Comparatively few of the number whose strength had been tried by the march on the platform, were chosen. Many were moved to superhuman exertions by the hope of release, and when disappointed, sunk in despair. The mortality after one of these occasions was terrific. The supply of medicine was generally entirely insufficient and unsuitable. One of the best Confederate physicians told me one morning that he had written sixty prescriptions for a ward that day, and had only eight of them filled. From men who were employed in the dispensary, and from all the physicians and ward-masters, I heard the same assertions and complaints. The hospital accommodation was totally insufficient. I have seen men brought from camp on a litter, where they had been lying ill for days upon the floor of their tents, with only one thin blanket; and, after getting to the hospital, they were put on the floor of the ward, instead of in a bed. Frequently, while they were making room for a patient, the poor wretch would lie shivering from cold outside the tent; and once I saw the litter set down upon the snow, and remain there some minutes, with a very ill man upon it. The dead were placed in a large tent, and I have gone there and found the tent almost blown away, and the bodies half buried in snow. I was a prisoner for eight long months, and the suffering I witnessed during this time I never before had any conception of. I am told, by those who experienced the tortures of Fort Delaware, that they were still worse."

Another prisoner, who was also at Point Lookout, writes:—"Each sentinel on the fence had orders to shoot any person crossing the 'dead-line,' and the order was not only carried out to the letter, but in several instances was made an excuse by negroes to shoot their former masters, on account of some fancied grievances they had suffered years previous to the war. Negro soldiers were urged on by their officers to shoot 'the d—d rebels'; and in one instance, when a negro had shot into a crowd of over two hundred, without any provocation, killing and wounding five men, the officer of the day, in presence of the prisoners, told him when his ammunition gave out to let him know and he would furnish more. . . . Last winter men were frozen to death by being forced to sleep on the ground, with only one blanket and no fire. . . . The rations were just enough to keep soul and body together. During the spring tides, the camp in some places was from two to three feet under water, and yet men were not allowed to move their tents to a dry place. The fiendish brutality practised by the Fifth Massachusetts Cavalry on the defenceless unfortunates at this post can never be forgotten. Prisoners who were going to the sinks were made to double-quick back and forth for half an hour or more; sometimes, with a pistol placed at each ear, made to dance; or forced, under penalty of death, to carry the negro patrol for two hundred yards on their backs. The negroes coming in camp on patrol-duty were frequently drunk, and they roamed up and down the streets, shooting indiscriminately at every one they saw, and, in several instances, killing each other."

Fort Delaware.

J. S. G., who was a prisoner in Fort Delaware, in the State of Delaware, writes:—"When we arrived at the fort, every man was thoroughly searched, and his money, watch, and extra clothing were taken from him. This was the last we saw of these articles. We were then driven with curses and kicks into a miserable pen, which already contained 8000 Confederates, hundreds of whom were sick, and all of whom were suffering from hunger. The sick were examined every morning, and a few of those who were thought fit for the hospital were sent there. The hospital arrangements were wretched. Men died there rapidly from want of care, unwholesome food, and bad water. The accommodations were entirely insufficient, and I have known sick men to stand by the bedside of the dying, waiting to get possession of the cot. Many prisoners died in barracks during the winter. Many of them were frozen to death. The rations were very meagre. At eight o'clock every morning, one small piece of mixed corn and wheat bread, and about an ounce of salt meat, were issued to each man. The same quantity was issued at two o'clock, with the addition of a pint of filthy soup. This was all we had. The water was

11

from the Delaware Bay, and was very brackish and foul. The tide flowed into the moat around. Our supply of water was drawn from the moat, into which the wash and the filth of the whole fort emptied. Prisoners who were fortunate enough to have a little money — and they were few — would offer one dollar for a pint of pure water. The prison was very strictly guarded, and the sentinels did not hesitate to shoot down the prisoners on the most trifling occurrences. A poor boy from Charlottesville, Va., was shot dead for throwing some water from a cup out of a window of the barracks. It was not the fault of the guard that many more were not killed, for they fired upon us for the slightest infraction of prison rules, of which we were often ignorant. If a prisoner did not happen to hear the bugle sound 'taps' and his light was not immediately extinguished, the sentinels always shot through the barracks without any warning whatever. I recollect that, in one instance alone, two men lying peaceably in their blankets were killed in this way. Tying up by the thumbs was a punishment practised daily for a very slight infraction of rigid prison rules. I have seen men tied up for two or three hours at a time, on the coldest winter day, until their arms and hands were as black as an African's. The average number of deaths at Fort Delaware, at one time, was twenty *per diem*. Want of food, bad water, absence of clothing, and insufficient protection made fearful ravages among the men. The barracks were mere shelters. Each barrack contained five hundred men. One stove was all that was allowed in the coldest winter months. A portion of the prisoners only had blankets. Those who could get them were fortunate. They were the exception, and not the rule. There was a stone walk through the centre of the prison-yard, upon which sentries had their beats. I have known them in the severest winter nights make barefooted men double-quick up and down the walk for being out of place after 'lights out,' or for some such trifling offence.

R., who was also a prisoner at Fort Delaware, writes: "During my confinement, I gleaned from the unhappy sufferer an account of most atrocious torture practised upon him by General Schoepf, who was in command. Lieut. H., adjutant in one of the battalions of Breckenridge's division, had written two letters to friends in the South, and had given them to one of the guards, who promised to mail them. There was nothing either particular or important in the letters, although it was in violation of prison rules to attempt to get them off. Lieut. H. acknowledged that he had written the letters, but refused to betray the name of the guard who had received them. General Schoepf, after much abuse, declared that he would force the names from him, and handed him over to the provost-marshal for torture. His hands were manacled and pinioned behind his back. He was then suspended by the elbows, and kept hanging in the air until he fainted from excruciating agony. A surgeon was detailed to watch the operation, and to replace the shoulders of the unfortunate sufferer when they became dislocated. This was repeated several times, after which Lieut. H. was placed in solitary confinement for ten days.

The Rev. Dr. Handy, in his recent work entitled *U. S. Bonds; or, Duress by Federal Authority*, favors us with the following specimens of barbarity practised by the Federals at Fort Delaware on Confederate soldiers, as witnessed by him during his captivity at that place. This eminent divine, who suffered untold miseries in this modern Bastile, has furnished the world with a history of this particular prison. His pictures are certainly not overdrawn A genial, sociable gentleman, a pure Christian, and a man of just conception, his statements must be taken as embodying nothing but the truth. He says (p. 189) that, "We had another spectacle of torment, this forenoon, in the case of two poor Irishmen, members of Co. 'Q,' who were hung up by their thumbs and wrists, in front of their own quarters, and in presence of their comrades.

They were tied by a rope to a cross-beam, which was thrown over the parapet, and then drawn up until they could only just stand upon the ends of their toes. They appeared to suffer very much, and one of them looked every moment as though he would faint from pain and exhaustion. The hands of each were purple and distended with blood. The weaker of the two finding it impossible to retain his water, was agonised with this additional mortification. This scene of barbarism was under the immediate direction of Captain Ahl and provost-marshal Hawkins; the occasion of the present infliction was the independence of one of the Irishmen in returning a blow given by the provost-marshal, an act which was considered by the Irishman as unmilitary and unjust. The other man was punished for cursing one of the 'galvanised rebs.' They both, no doubt, deserved punishment; but this heathenish method can receive no reasonable justification from any penal statute among a civilized people. . . Alas! for the humanity of the Lincoln rule." Again (p. 473):—"A lamentable affair occurred at 'the rear' about dusk this evening. Many persons are now suffering with diarrhœa, and crowds are frequenting that neighborhood. The orders are to go by one path, and return by the other. Two lines of men, going and coming, are in continual movement. I was returning from the frequented spot, and in much weakness making my way back, when suddenly I heard the sentinel challenge from the top of the water-house. I had no idea he was speaking to me, until some friends called my attention to the order. I suppose my pace was too slow for him. I passed on; and as frequent inquiries were made in regard to my health, I was obliged to say to friends, 'We have no time to talk; the sentinel is evidently restless or alarmed, and we are in danger.' I had scarcely reached my quarters before a musket fired, and it was immediately reported that Col. E. P. Jones had been shot. The murder of Col. Jones is the meanest and most inexcusable affair that has occurred in the officers' quarters, or that has

MURDER OF COL. JONES.

come under my observation since my imprisonment at Fort Delaware. I did not see him fall, but have learned from Capt. J. B. Cole, who was an eye-witness to the whole scene, that although he was standing within ten steps of the man that killed him, he heard no challenge, nor any order to move on. The first intimation he had of the sentinel's displeasure was the discharge of the musket, and the simultaneous exclamation of the Colonel, 'Oh, God! oh, God! My God! what did you shoot me for? Why didn't you tell me to go on? I never heard you say anything to me.' And with a few such exclamations, he sank upon the ground, and then fell, or rather rolled down the embankment. Col. Jones had been in the barracks so short a time, that I have not had the pleasure of making his acquaintance. I have only learned that he is an intelligent physician of considerable property and influence, and that he is from Middlesex County, Va. Since he came to Fort Delaware he has been constantly suffering with some affection of the feet, causing lameness. At the time he was shot he was hobbling along with one shoe, and was carefully stepping down a rough place near the water-house, buttoning his pants. He could not have been more than twenty steps from the point of the musket. It is said that the murderer seemed all day to be seeking an opportunity to shoot some one. It is, also, reported that Capt. Ahl was seen on the top of the shanty, giving some orders, only a few moments before the catastrophe. These are all the facts that I can learn concerning this melancholy affair, except that Colonel Jones has been taken to the hospital. . . The boy who shot Col. Jones is again on guard this morning, and it is reported that he has been promoted to a corporalcy. He belongs, I think, to an Ohio regiment, is about eighteen years old, and is known as 'Bill Douglas.' . . Colonel Jones died last night at the hospital, but the Yankees are silent, and we hear very little about him."

ELMIRA.

W. S., who was a prisoner at Elmira, states:—"The mortality there was frightful. The number of men confined in this prison-pen ranged from seven to nine thousand. On one day in the autumn of 1864 there were thirty-three deaths; and during my imprisonment the deaths averaged about one to every five. The rations were miserably insufficient, and consisted of bread and a piece of meat, salt or fresh, for breakfast, and a slice of bread and a cup of soup for dinner. This was all. Upon one occasion, a prisoner who was detected searching in a sewer that led from the hospital cook-house, for food to appease the intense craving of hunger, was fired upon by a sentinel. The ball missed him, but entered the gangrene hospital and wounded one of the patients in the leg. One man in my ward was fortunate enough to get hold of a dog, which was soon devoured. He was severely punished for appeasing hunger in this way. He was tied up by the thumbs, his rations were cut down to bread alone; a pork-barrel, weighing fifty pounds, was placed over his head and shoulders, labelled 'Dog-eater,' and he was forced to march up and down for seven hours a day in front of the guard-house in this way for two weeks. The small-pox was very violent. On some days there were twenty fresh cases. The men were inoculated in a very rough manner. They were made to stand up with bared arms, the surgeon came along, took up a piece of skin between the forefinger and thumb, and jobbed his vaccine knife through it. The inoculating matter was impure. There was much inflammation after this operation. Gangrene frequently made its appearance, and in several instances arms had to be amputated. The small-pox hospital was within the camp. Those who died of this horrible disease were buried in the enclosure, within two hundred yards of our mess-hall. Those who died from other causes were buried outside. The authorities informed us that the citizens of Elmira objected to having the small-pox corpses brought outside of the prison lines. Upon several occasions, corpses were permitted to remain on the snow, for want of coffins. Many deaths occurred from the refusal to give hospital tickets to the sick, and from the bad treatment they received in the wards. The conduct of incompetent under-surgeons was shocking and barbarous. Men were often refused hospital passes when at death's door. There was a great deal of punishment for petty offences. There was a sweat-box, made like a coffin, in which men were shut up, and in which they could hardly breathe. There was much petty persecution. On one occasion, when the thermometer was ten degrees below zero, I procured some shavings, to put in my bed to keep me warm. They were ordered to be removed by the commandant of the post, who said they were too luxurious for a rebel."

Camp Chase.

A released prisoner, writing of the sufferings of Camp Chase, Ohio, says:—"There were barbarities committed here from which the mind shrinks with horror and disgust. One prisoner was shot crossing the dead-line. His body was left lying where it fell, until it was nearly devoured by vermin, and the stench became so offensive that its removal was ordered. At another time, prisoners who had attempted to escape were put on half rations, and the leaders placed in a dungeon. This dungeon was made of wood. It was perfectly dark and very close. It was raised from the ground and built over a mud-puddle. There were a few auger-holes in the centre of the floor, and others immediately above, to let the air escape. In hot weather, no constitution could stand this confinement. Men saved themselves from suffocation by lying with their noses over the auger-holes, inhaling the stench from the muddy water below. Men confined here fainted from suffocation, and loss of blood produced by bleeding of the lungs. At one time the rations were greatly reduced, and the prisoners were allowed just sufficient to keep them from absolute starvation. Half-famished men fought over their food like wolves over a carcass. Various other modes of torture were resorted to. Gagging and corporeal punishment were matters of every-day occurrence. At Todd Barracks, a neighboring prison, one man was hung up by the toes, too far from the ground to obtain any support from his hands. During the latter part of 1864, prisoners were marched over the frozen ground, in bare feet and without coats to their backs. A squad of half-naked prisoners was marched from Todd Barracks to Camp Chase, during the coldest nights of 1864, without the slightest necessity. All were frozen. Many of them were unable to draw their hands from their pockets. The corpses of prisoners were sold and bodies taken from the graves, for the use of the medical colleges and surgeons. This fact is notorious."

S. L. says:—"One method of persecution practised here was to refuse hospital tickets to prisoners who were seriously ill. These invalids were forced to remain in barracks, where there were no accommodations whatever. Men scarcely able to walk were forced to drag themselves out to the sinks in the severest weather, where they were repeatedly found in the morning stark and stiff."

Johnson's Island.

G. L. writes of this prison, situated on Lake Erie:—"Bread made of inferior flour, which was occasionally sour, was issued. The meat was rusty bacon or beef-neck. Twice in one year we had good cuts of beef, but it was so far decayed as to be offensive. Occasionally we had a few worm-eaten peas, and twice I saw some small potatoes. The hospital was poorly supplied with inferior medicines for about half the time. The quarterly supplies of laudanum, morphia, and a cheap substitute for quinine, which we were told was too dear to buy, generally gave out about the seventh week after their receipt. Money was tendered from friends in New York to supply the needed drugs, but the permission was refused. Many of the prisoners were wretchedly clad. Two boxes, for which General

Archer, himself a prisoner, had succeeded in obtaining a special permit, containing one hundred overcoats and one hundred and twenty pairs of trousers, reached Johnson's Island in December. The cold was intense. The thermometer stood at 20° below zero. Many of the prisoners had ragged trousers, and no coats at all. This clothing was kept in the yard for five weeks before it was delivered. The prisoners had one blanket apiece. They were not allowed wood enough to keep up fires in the scanty supply of stoves, more than twelve out of the twenty-four hours. After 'taps'—nine o'clock—prisoners were only allowed to leave their quarters to go to the sink. At one period, for about two months, four or five men were deliberately fired at nightly by the sentinels; one sentinel shot into the barracks and wounded two men, upon which the prisoners declared that they would rather die in attacking their assassins than be thus cruelly murdered. This put a check to the shooting. Rats were caught in and about the sinks, and sold freely. The slop-barrels were raked, and bread-crusts were fished out, to be dried in the sun and eaten."

J. H., speaking of his experiences in this prison, says:—"The discipline was very severe. Men suffered from want of clothing, and from want of food. It was a common thing to have the scanty rations stopped on men because they would not fall promptly into line at roll-call. Men died from want of common medicines. Every kind of cruelty was practised. Men were placed in close confinement; were tied up by the thumbs, and were made to stand on one foot, holding the other up with one of their hands, and pointing with a finger of the other to the ground. Men were wantonly killed on slight pretexts. On one occasion, a sentinel seeing a light from the hospital shining through one of the prison buildings after 'taps,' mistook it for a light in quarters. He fired through the windows and wounded one or two men."

MORRIS ISLAND AND FORT PULASKI.

G. H. says:—"Our men were assassinated by the negro troops who guarded us. Colonel Owings was deliberately murdered. He was lame, and could not walk as fast as he was ordered, on return to quarters. He was shot, and died soon after. Several others were shot."

B. S. D. writes:—"Our rations consisted of ten ounces of hard-tack, full of worms; two ounces of salt beef, half a pint of beef soup, and half a pint of boiled rice. At one time our bread ration was cut off, and half a pint of mush, made of spoiled corn-meal, substituted. One of the men on one occasion picked one hundred and fifty worms out of three rations of this meal. The rations were not sufficient to sustain life. Some of these prisoners were removed to Fort Pulaski, Ga., others were taken to Hilton Head."

G. H. writes from Fort Pulaski:—"I have never seen so much suffering. About one-half of the prisoners have the scurvy in its most violent form. We bury constantly one or two each day. The sour, wormy meal does the work bravely. Out of 282 men, 82 have died in 42 days."

B. S. D. writes of Hilton Head, S. C.:—"Our rations were ten ounces of spoiled corn-meal and a half a pint of pickles. We were restricted to this by order of General Foster, commanding the district. He refused to permit us to receive aid from our friends. We lived on these rations for forty-two days. The result of this treatment was that fifty of the six hundred died, and, when the rest of us were transferred to Fort Delaware, one hundred and fifty were sent to the hospital, most of them suffering from scurvy in its worst form."

Quoting from the same work, the writer says:—"The facts recorded above were collected without any particular care or effort, and were furnished from time to time by the parties, without any knowledge that they were to be made public. They give in reality but a faint idea of the individual sufferings endured by gallant gentlemen, or witnessed by them, of which no written statement has as yet been made. More detailed and accurate accounts of the cruelties practised in Northern forts and jails could readily be collected from hundreds of former captives, for the purpose of publication. Enough, however, has been told to show the extreme persecution to which Confederate prisoners of war were subjected. Many were killed outright. Thousands died, and many more took the oath of allegiance, to obtain relief from tortures they could not endure. One young man, who had been confined for a long period in one of these forts, was recaptured soon after his exchange. He took the oath of allegiance rather than return to prison. 'I know,' said he, 'I have disgraced myself, and that my family will refuse to receive me; but I feel that I have not the strength to bear up again under the ills of prison-life.'"

It must be borne in mind that there was no excuse whatever for the systematic ill-treatment which Southern prisoners received at the hands of the Federals. In the North, supplies were abundant, clothing was plenty, and both were freely and gratuitously offered by citizens of Maryland and Kentucky, and indeed of New York and other Northern States. Medicines could be readily obtained. Transportation was easy. There was no deficiency of men for police-duty, and no difficulty in guarding prisoners and preventing their escape, without resorting to torture and assassination for the purpose of intimidation. In the South, on the contrary, people were put to their greatest straits. Houses were bared of their carpets to supply coverings for the soldiers in the field; churches were stripped of their cushions to provide couches for the wounded in the hospitals. Medicines could be had only at exorbitant rates, and then in but small quantities; the Federal Government having inaugurated a most cruel precedent, in declaring them, together with surgical instruments, contraband of war. Transportation became difficult, as the railroads wore out, and during the latter part of the war many of the supplies for the Army of Virginia had to be wagoned three hundred miles over country roads. Men were spared from the field with the greatest difficulty, every soldier under arms being required, in fact, to do the duty of two or three men, and it was impossible to detail any large or even sufficient force to guard prisoners. Notwithstanding all these difficulties; notwithstanding the outrages committed by Northern troops, and the cruelties committed by Northern jailors, it is a fact well-known to the intimate friends of Mr. Davis, that he persistently turned a deaf ear to the entreaties of extreme men, and that he steadfastly refused to inaugurate in the Confederacy a system of persecution which was utterly repugnant to every sentiment of his nature, and to the feelings of every brave and high-toned leader in the South. The fact is, that it was the intention and desire of the Confederate Government to provide for its prisoners of war as it did for its own men. When, however, there was a scarcity of food, the preference was naturally given to Southern soldiers in the field. Speaking of the difficulty of providing even for these, Major-general Heth said:—"If the soldiers last winter under my command had been in prison, and had been restricted to the rations allowed them, they would have been found miserably insufficient. Some days they had no meat; at other times they had no meal. I, myself, have repeatedly gone to my horse's feed-trough, and robbed him of corn, which I parched to appease my hunger. Had my men been in confinement, their sufferings would have been intense. But they were in open air; they were free; they were active; they were constantly skirmishing; they had opportunities of amusing themselves, and they had other things to think about besides their own personal discomforts. Had it been otherwise, the troops of my division would have been decimated by disease."

I now insert the following, by Mr. Wade, of Ohio, as referred to in the beginning of this chapter; and if the Congress did not adopt it, from the evidence of Southern prisoners the keepers of Northern prisons certainly practised it. It reads as follows:

"Joint Resolution, advising retaliation for the cruel treatment of prisoners by the insurgents.

"WHEREAS, It has come to the knowledge of Congress that great numbers of our soldiers, who have fallen as prisoners of war into the hands of the insurgents, have been subjected to treatment unexampled for cruelty in the history of civilised war, and finding its parallels only in the conduct of savage tribes; a treatment resulting in the death of multitudes by the slow but designed process of starvation, and by mortal diseases occasioned by insufficient and unhealthy food, by wanton exposure of their persons to the inclemency of the weather, and by deliberate assassination of unoffending men, and the murder, in cold blood, of prisoners after surrender; and, whereas, a continuance of these barbarities, in contempt of the laws of war and in disregard of the remonstrances of the national authorities, has presented to us the alternative of suffering our brave soldiers thus to be destroyed, or to apply the principle of retaliation for their protection. Therefore,

"*Resolved*, By the Senate and House of Representatives of the United States of America, in Congress assembled, That, in the judgment of Congress, it has become justifiable and necessary that the President should, in order to prevent the continuance and recurrence of such barbarities, and to insure the observance, by the insurgents, of the laws of civilised war, resort at once to measures of retaliation. That, in our opinion, such retaliation ought to be inflicted upon the insurgent officers now in our hands, or hereafter to fall into our hands, as prisoners; that such officers ought to be subjected to like treatment, practised towards our officers or soldiers in the hands of the insurgents, in respect to quantity and quality of food, clothing, fuel, medicine, medical attendance, personal exposure, or other mode of dealing with them; that, with a view to the same ends, the insurgent prisoners in our hands ought to be placed under the control and in the keeping of officers and men who have themselves been prisoners in the hands of the insurgents, and have thus acquired a knowledge of their mode of treating Union prisoners; that explicit instructions ought to be given to the forces having the charge of such insurgent prisoners, requiring them to carry out strictly and promptly the principles of this resolution in every case, until the President, having received satisfactory information of the abandonment by the insurgents of such barbarous practices, shall revoke or modify said instructions. Congress do not, however, intend by this resolution to limit or restrict the power of the President to the modes or principles of retaliation herein mentioned, but only to advise a resort to them as demanded by the occasion."

This resolution was not adopted, because Mr. Sumner and Secretaries Seward and Stanton argued that it was useless to commit Congress to an odious act that lay in the power of the Government to enforce, and was already being enforced, without legislation. It was then agreed, for the double purpose of apparent magnanimity, and as a means to fill up the Federal ranks with recruits, that Mr. Sumner offer the following substitute for the resolution of the Committee:

"*Resolved,* That retaliation is harsh always, even in the simplest cases; and is permissible only where, in the first place, it may reasonably be expected to effect its object; and where, in the second place, it is consistent with the usages of civilised society; and that, in the absence of these essential conditions, it is a useless barbarism, having no other end than vengeance, which is forbidden, alike to nations and to men.

"*Resolved,* That the treatment of our officers and soldiers in rebel prisons is cruel, savage, and heartrending beyond all precedent; that it is shocking to morals, that it is an offence against human nature itself; that it adds new guilt to the great crime of the rebellion, and constitutes an example from which history will turn with sorrow and disgust.

"*Resolved,* That any attempted imitation of rebel barbarism in the treatment of prisoners would be plainly impracticable, on account of its inconsistency with the prevailing sentiments of humanity among us; that it would be injurious at home, for it would barbarise the whole community; that it would be utterly useless, for it could not affect the cruel authors of the revolting conduct which we seek to overcome; that it would be immoral, inasmuch as it proceeded from vengeance alone; that it could have no other result than to degrade the national character and the national name, and to bring down upon our country the reprobation of history; and that, being thus impracticable, useless, immoral, and degrading, it must be rejected as a measure of retaliation, precisely as the barbarism of roasting or eating prisoners is always rejected by civilised powers.

"*Resolved*, That th United States, filled with grief and sympathy for cherished citizens, who, as officers and soldiers, have become the victims of heaven-defying outrage, hereby declare their solemn determination to put an end to this great iniquity, by putting an end to the rebellion of which it is the natural fruit; that to secure this humane and righteous consummation, they pledge anew their best energies and all the resources of the whole people, and they call upon all to bear witness, that in this necessary warfare with barbarism, they renounce all vengeance, and every evil example, and plant themselves firmly on the sacred landmarks of Christian civilisation, under the protection of that God who is present with every prisoner, and enables heroic souls to suffer for their country."

I presume the trail of Sherman's raid through Georgia, Sheridan's grand march through the Valley of Virginia, and the charred remains of Columbia, S. C., are the "landmarks of Christian civilisation" to which Mr. Sumner so eloquently refers. This cant about the "national honor" is shown and well illustrated by the little regard which some of the Federal officers held for their own "private characters," much less for the character of the nation. It will be remembered that during the winter of 1864–5 a large number of Federal officers were confined in "Camp Asylum Prison" at Columbia, South Carolina. The base ingratitude of these men is shown in the following statement of J. C. Gibbs, who furnished them with means from his own private resources to procure (besides the usual Confederate ration) a better quality of food, and even, in some instances, luxuries that were to be occasionally found in this once wealthy city. The following is the statement of Mr. Gibbs:

"During 1864 a large number of Federal officers were held as prisoners at Columbia, S. C. At that time I was doing a very large mercantile business in Columbia, controlling, perhaps, as much means as any business house in the Confederate States. I was applied to by the Federal prisoners to advance them money, by cashing their drafts on their friends at home. I notified them that I could do nothing for them unless in accordance with the wishes of the Confederate authorities or the officers in charge. I was then applied to by General Winder, the commandant in charge of the prisoners, and Captain J. S. Richardson, quartermaster, who made very earnest appeals to me to do anything I could for the prisoners. There were about 1200, I think, then in Columbia. General Winder told me that he would be pleased for me to aid them; that it was very difficult indeed to provide properly for them, and that the same provisions that were provided for our Confederate soldiers were not considered by the prisoners as anything like what they wanted or expected. At that time, communication between the prisoners and their friends at the North was very uncertain and irregular. The prisoners had been getting assistance to a small extent from various parties, who advanced them Confederate money in return for their drafts, but 'shaving' them fearfully. It was this that induced them to apply to me. After the request of General Winder, I informed them that they could get anything they wished from me. My motive in this was purely a kind and benevolent one. I was a true, loyal Confederate, and would do nothing in opposition to the wishes of our authorities; at the same time I was glad to relieve those in distress. The idea of making money out of it never entered my mind. The prisoners, on hearing from me, passed resolutions thanking me, and pledging about thirty of them (the most important officers) in a written contract, that for my kindness they would send me no draft or orders except such as were perfectly good and certain to be paid. I then informed them that I would advance them double whatever they were in the habit of getting from other parties for their drafts. The rate that they had been getting was about ten dollars in Confederate money for one of their exchange. I therefore advanced them over one million dollars in Confederate currency. When the city of Columbia was destroyed by General Sherman on the 17th of February, 1865, everything I had was destroyed, most of my property being in cotton, 3500 bales of which were burned in one night. After the war, having lost everything, I made an effort to collect the drafts I had taken; and out of nearly 1000 drafts, not one single dollar have I ever been able to collect. The drafts were drawn as follows:

COLUMBIA, S. C., *November 25th*, 1864.

At sight pay to ——————, or order, one hundred dollars in gold, and charge to

Yours, &c.,

S. T. MUFFLY, *Adjt.* 184*th Pa. Regt.*

Major J. R. MUFFLY, *Harrisburg, Penn.*

Endorsed on the back thus:

This draft is given for the equivalent value in Confederate funds, kindly advanced me while a prisoner of war in Columbia, S. C., and I desire it promptly and honorably paid.

S. T. MUFFLY, *Adjt.* 184*th Pa. Regt.*

"On sending the drafts on for collection, I found that about one-half of them were drawn on fictitious parties, evidently done as a swindle from the beginning. Where this was not the case, the reply to my efforts to collect was, that I was a rebel, and that it was all right to get what they could out of me. Most of them refused to take any notice of my letters, and as I had only the address of the parties drawn on, I could not make them responsible, not knowing anything of the drawers. Where I did succeed in getting their address, their replies were generally as stated above; either that it was all right to cheat a rebel, or that they were forbidden to pay by order of a special circular of instructions issued by Stanton, Secretary of War. The only instance of which I had a polite or gentlemanly reply to my letters, was one from Lieutenant G. H. Rowley, 2d U. S. Infantry, who had given me a draft on J. W. Joyne, Patent Office, Washington. He declined to pay, on the grounds that the Secretary of War had forbidden it; still, he expressed his regret at it, and acknowledged the favor done him. I presented one draft for one hundred dollars, in person, to Hugh Nealy, of Washington, drawn by his son, O. H. Nealy, Lieutenant U. S. Infantry, and was received with curses and threats; was informed that I was a swindler, and that his son never intended at the time to pay it. It is very strange, indeed, that in such a number of drafts, over one thousand, and given, too, in return for kindness shown them, that not a *single instance* has occurred in which the obligations were acknowledged. Amongst the drafts were two for $400, drawn by Lieutenant G. E. Saber, 2d R. I. Cavalry, on Globe Bank, Providence, R. I. He denied the draft *in toto*, and claimed as proof that his real name was G. E. Sabre, and not *Saber*, as written.

"JAMES G. GIBBS.

"QUINCY, FLORIDA, *February* 15*th*, 1874."

When we take into consideration the impoverished condition of the Confederacy at this late date, in regard to food and clothing, and the kind and humane efforts of General Winder, through private sources, to ameliorate the sufferings of the Federal officers, we cannot but feel the force of the unprincipled acts of these men. Certainly, if it had not been that these means were resorted to, in order to procure healthy diet for the officers, their condition at Columbia would have been but little better than the poor privates of Andersonville. Their position, if nothing else, ought to have dictated more gratitude. Whilst the soldiers at Andersonville were starving, for want of proper diet, vegetables, and anti-scorbutics, the officers at Columbia were living on the best that the land could afford. Whilst the graveyard at Andersonville is without a parallel, the deaths amongst the Federal officers at Columbia did not exceed half-a-dozen. That there were amongst these Federal officers, gentlemen—men of honor—I do not deny; but it certainly does appear strange that no single instance is on record whereby any one of them has denied this act of kindness of Mr. Gibbs, or had the manliness to come forward and denounce the slanders that have, from time to time, been charged against those who had the care of Federal prisoners of war.

CHAPTER X.

In this chapter I shall again avail myself of some extracts from the *Southern Review*. The writer from whom I quote says:—

Some few accounts have, from time to time, been published of the treatment of Confederate soldiers in particular Northern forts and prisons; though no general comparison has ever been made of the condition of the captives in the respective prisons of the existing Government. Southern men have had little opportunity to defend themselves, and the Confederate Government has ceased to be. No occasion, however, has been neglected, and no means spared, on the part of the Northern press and the Federal administration, to vilify the South and to cast a stigma upon the name of its most irreproachable men. The incidents of the trial of Captain Wirz, for a long time in charge of the Andersonville prison in Georgia, by a military commission in Washington in the autumn of 1865, the record of which has been carefully preserved and widely disseminated, afford abundant evidence of this malignant spirit. In their eagerness, however, to condemn others, the principal actors in the "Star Chamber trial" have condemned themselves. Their wickedness has recoiled on their own heads. The execution was a disgrace to the administration at Washington. It must forever remain a stain upon the annals of the age. The men who sentenced him, Generals Lew. Wallace, Underwood, Geary, Gersham, Mott, Thomas, and others, have, together with Colonel Chipman, the Judge-advocate, rendered their names as odious as that of the infamous Jeffries. . . .

If Captain Wirz had committed one-half of the atrocities charged against him—if he had wantonly shot, mutilated, or starved helpless prisoners—there might have been some excuse for the lawless vengeance which was visited upon him, even had he been convicted by a hostile and prejudiced judicial tribunal. But there was no reason why the President and his Cabinet should yield to a clamorous cry from a bloodthirsty people, and no excuse for the delivery of a civil prisoner, in time of peace, to a military commission, of all tribunals the most irresponsible, and one which, in this instance, had no authority whatever to sit in judgment upon the prisoner who was arraigned before it. Captain Wirz was a military officer, and as such, amenable to his superiors. If there is any responsibility on the part of recognised belligerents to their antagonists, for the treatment of prisoners of war, it attaches to those who issue, and not to those who execute, orders. No one who has read the proceedings in this infamous trial, who has seen how one indictment was deliberately altered, after being systematically prepared and regularly made, without any notice at all being given to the counsel for the defence; who has noted how the proceedings were conducted in violation of all law and precedent, and how the counsel, Messrs. Hughes, Denver and Peck, who were first retained, withdrew from a court which proceeded in so extraordinary a manner, convinced that they could do justice neither to their client nor to themselves; no one who has noticed how, as the trial proceeded, nearly every objection on the part of the prisoner's counsel was overruled; how the witnesses on the one side were not only encouraged, but permitted to introduce hearsay evidence, and even to testify as to their impressions, while the timid witnesses for the prisoner were browbeaten and bullied, and the more fearless ones imprisoned and not allowed to testify at all; and how access to public documents was denied to the counsel for the defence, and accorded to the prosecution; no one who has noted these things can honestly doubt for one moment that this friendless man was condemned from the hour he was arraigned. The cry of a political mob was yielded to, and he was given up a victim to their violence and brutality. "His blood be upon their heads and upon their children."

But behind all this there was a hidden purpose on the part of the administration, which it failed to accomplish. The real object of the trial was, not so much the conviction of Wirz, as the implication of Mr. Davis and General Lee in an imaginary plot to torture Federal prisoners, to withhold from them clothing, to deprive them of food, to poison them with foul water, and, by deliberate and atrocious barbarity and cruelty, to murder them as rapidly as possible. The utter failure of this design can excite no surprise. Even the bitterest enemies of Mr. Davis cannot stain his name with such reproach as this; and those who know aught of General Lee, can but smile at such attempt to defame his high character. It is hard to conceive, in this enlightened age, that such charges could be made against any civilised human being. It is difficult to believe that any people, boasting high education and refinement, could imagine that Christian men could be guilty of such wanton barbarities. But the truth is, the idea was suggested by the people of the North. The system was inaugurated, practised, and, if one may use the term, perfected by them. They sought to subjugate the South, not by civilised warfare, but savage atrocity, by fire as well as sword, by ruthless cruelty and inhuman torture. They condemned thousands of captive men to months of dreary prison confinement, for the purpose of draining the life from the South, and of rendering it unable to do battle against the North. And they persisted in their refusal to exchange prisoners, with this intention and for this purpose. This fact has been fully confirmed by General Butler's statement of the instructions received by him from General Grant. General Grant wrote him that he was determined that the South should not have a man, and directed him to make any pretext he chose, *but on no account to grant an exchange of prisoners.* If any doubts exist on this subject in the minds of impartial men, they will be put at rest by the following testimony of the Confederate Agent of Exchange. . . . Judge Ould's reputation is in itself a sufficient guaranty of the truth of the statement. We give it in his own words. He says:

"In January, 1864, in consequence of the complication of the controversy in relation to the exchange of prisoners, it became very manifest that the large bulk of prisoners on both sides would remain in captivity for many long and weary months, if not for the duration of the war. Prompted by an earnest desire to alleviate the hardships and confinement on both sides, I addressed the following communication to General E. A. Hitchcock, Commissioner of Exchange, and on or about the day of its date, delivered the same to the Federal authorities:

CONFEDERATE STATES OF AMERICA, WAR DEPARTMENT,
RICHMOND, VA., *January 24th*, 1864.

Major-general E. A. HITCHCOCK, *Agent of Exchange:*

SIR:—In view of the present difficulties attending the exchange and release of prisoners, I propose that all such, on either side, shall be attended by a proper number of their own surgeons, who, under rules to be established, shall be permitted to take charge of their health and comfort. I also propose that these surgeons shall act as commissaries, with power to receive and distribute such contributions of money, food, clothing, and medicines, as may be forwarded for the relief of prisoners. I further propose that these surgeons be selected by their own Government, and that they shall have full liberty, at any and all times, through the agents of exchange, to make reports, not only of their own acts, but of any matters relating to the welfare of prisoners.

Respectfully your obedient servant,
Ro. Ould, *Agent of Exchange.*

"To this communication no reply was ever made. I need not state how much suffering or misrepresentation would have been prevented, if this offer had been met in the spirit in which it was dictated. Just one year afterwards, to wit, on the 24th of January, 1865, the proposition was renewed to General Grant, but no notice was taken of it by him. Before the battle of Gettysburg, the Confederates held a majority of prisoners, and continued to send them off as fast as the United States authorities furnished transportation. After that time the Federals had a majority, and they refused to deliver according to the requirements of the cartel, offering, however, to exchange officer and man for man, thus leaving the excess in confinement. This was resisted by the Confederate authorities, as being in open violation of the cartel, until about the summer of 1864, when the latter relinquished their rights under the cartel, and offered to accept the proposition of the exchange of officer and man for man. Thereupon the Federal authorities retreated from their offer, and declined even to exchange officer for officer and man for man. Under this latter proposal quite a large surplus would have remained in Northern prisons, owing to the excess held by the United States. In this state of affairs I was instructed by the Confederate authorities to offer to the United States Government their sick and wounded, without requiring any equivalents. Accordingly, in the summer of 1864, I did offer to deliver from ten to fifteen thousand sick and wounded at the mouth of the Savannah river, without requiring any equivalents;

promising the United States agent that if the number for which he might send transportation could not be made up from sick and wounded, I would supply the difference with well men. Although this offer was made in the summer of 1864, transportation was not sent to the Savannah river until December, and then I delivered as many prisoners as could be transported, amongst which were more than five thousand well men. More than once I urged the mortality of Andersonville as a reason for haste on the part of the United States. About the same time, that is, in the summer of 1864, the Surgeon-general of the Confederate States informed me that he was almost entirely destitute of medicines, requesting me to offer to make purchases of medicines from the United States authorities to be used exclusively for the relief of Federal prisoners. On the first opportunity I did make such proposal, offering to pay gold, cotton, or tobacco for them, and even two or three prices if required. At the same time I gave assurance that the medicines would be used exclusively in the treatment of Federal prisoners, and moreover agreed, if it was insisted on, thst such medicines might be brought into the Confederate lines by United States surgeons, and dispensed by them. To this offer, like the first, I never received any reply.

RO. OULD."

In every large prison in the North, cruelty was systematically practised for the purpose of forcing prisoners to take the oath of allegiance to the Federal Government, or, in case of their refusal, of enfeebling their health to such an extent as to render them unfit for military service on their return to the South. During the trial of Captain Wirz, the names of witnesses were handed to Mr. Baker, the assistant counsel to the Judge-advocate, to be summoned to testify in behalf of the prisoner. It was intended to prove by them what was the customary mode of treatment of prisoners in Northern forts. Not one witness, however, appeared. Since the close of the trial, it has been ascertained that the subpœnas for these witnesses were never issued. They were suppressed by the Judge-advocate; "it was not proper that such testimony should see the light." The Judge-advocate demanded of Judge Ould, who had been summoned for the defence, to surrender his subpœna. He refused to surrender it, as it was his only passport in Washington City. Without it he might have been incarcerated with other unfortunate Confederates in Old Capitol Prison; whereupon the Judge-advocate cancelled it, and he (Ould) was thereby not permitted to testify in behalf of the accused. Judge-advocate Chipman has since publicly admitted that he refused to have subpœnas issued for a few "rebel" functionaries whose testimony was considered important for the defence. How many the Judge-advocate considered "a few," it is hard to say. We know, however, that General Lee was among them. His name had been stricken from the list of those with whom Captain Wirz had originally been accused of conspiring. He must have been regarded as a perfectly competent witness by any court in the world, and his evidence was more material to the accused than that of all the other witnesses together. His word would have been believed in the North as well as the South. The Government refused to permit him to testify, and the public must draw its own conclusions as to the motives by which it was influenced. There were evidently considerations of importance which rendered it impolitic and inexpedient that the truth about Andersonville should be made known.

In addition to the appeal of Colonel Robert Ould to the Federal Government for food, medicines, clothing, &c., to be furnished by the United States Government for the Federal prisoners, and dispensed, if necessary, by Federal surgeons, I will insert a few "extracts" from a petition which was composed by the captors of Andersonville, in August, 1864, and addressed to President Lincoln. This memorial was suppressed by the Federal Secretary of War, Mr. Stanton, for the base purpose (as time and circumstances have proved) of trying to fasten the odium of cruelty to Federal prisoners on the leaders of the Confederate Government. It is as follows:

"The Memorial of the Union prisoners confined at Andersonville, Georgia, to the President of the United States:

"CONFEDERATE STATES PRISON,
CHARLESTON, S. C., *August*, 1864.

"*To the President of the United States:*

"The condition of the enlisted men belonging to the Union armies, now prisoners to the Confederate rebel forces, is such that it becomes our duty, and the duty of every commissioned officer, to make known the facts in the case to the Government of the United States, and to use every honorable effort to secure a general exchange of prisoners, thereby relieving thousands of our comrades from the horrors now surrounding them. For some time past there has been a concentration of prisoners from all parts of the rebel territory to the State of Georgia; the commissioned officers being confined at Macon, and the enlisted men at Andersonville. . . . Thirty-five thousand men are confined here in a field of some thirty or forty acres, enclosed and heavily guarded. . . . To these men, as indeed to all prisoners, there are issued three-quarters of a pound of bread or meal and one-eighth of a pound of meat per day. This is the entire ration, and upon it the prisoner must live or die. . . . Such are the rations upon which Union soldiers are fed by the rebel authorities, and by which they are barely holding on to life. But to starvation and exposure to sun and storm, add the sickness which prevails to a most alarming and terrible extent. On an average, one hundred die daily. . . . In behalf of these men, we most earnestly appeal to the President of the United States. Few of them have been captured, except in the front of battle, in the deadly encounter, and only when overpowered by numbers. They constitute as gallant a portion of our armies as carry our banners anywhere. If released, they would soon return to again do vigorous battle for our cause. We are told that the only obstacle in the way of exchange is the status of enlisted negroes, captured from our armies; the United States claiming that the cartel covers all who serve under its flag, and the Confederate States refusing to consider the colored soldiers, heretofore slaves, as prisoners of war. We beg leave to suggest some facts bearing upon the question of exchange, which we would urge upon this consideration. Is it not consistent with the national honor, without waiving the claim that the negro soldiers shall be treated as prisoners of war, to effect an exchange of the white soldiers? The two classes are treated differently by the enemy. The whites are confined in such prisons as Libby and Andersonville. . . The blacks, on the contrary, are seldom imprisoned. They are distributed among the citizens or employed on Government works. Under these circumstances they receive enough to eat, and are worked no harder than they have been accustomed to be. . . It is true, they are again made slaves; but their slavery is freedom and happiness compared with the cruel existence of our gallant men. They are not bereft of hope as are the white soldiers, dying by piecemeal. . . While, therefore, believing the claims of our Government, in matters of exchange, to be just, we are profoundly impressed with the conviction that the circumstances of the two classes of soldiers are so widely different that the Government can honorably consent to an exchange, waiving for a time the established principle justly claimed to be applicable in the case. Let thirty-five thousand suffering, starving, and enlisted men aid this appeal. By prompt and decided action in their behalf, thirty-five thousand heroes will be made happy. For the eighteen hundred commissioned officers, now prisoners, we urge nothing. Although desirous of returning to our duty, we can bear imprisonment with more fortitude, if the enlisted men, whose sufferings we know to be intolerable, were restored to liberty and life."

Here we have evidence of the strongest nature that the Confederate Government, as well as the prisoners, were appealing in language that cannot be mistaken, for a general exchange of prisoners. Nor do we wonder that General Grant and the Federal Secretary of War were anxious, at the close of the war, through their representative "Judge-advocate Chipman," to cover up their own guilt in the matter of exchange, and by the trial of Captain Wirz, endeavor to shift the responsibility of the sufferings endured by Northern captives, on to the shoulders of the Confederate Government. It was not reasonable to suppose that the Federal prisoners would charge their own Government with neglect and cruelty, when it ostentatiously claimed to be considered "the best Government the world ever saw." Sergeant Goss, in his "Soldier's Story," which will be taken as good authority by the North, says:—"Rumors and statements of an exchange were so frequently made, and backed by evidence which looked plausible, that the prisoners were expectant and despondent by turns, during July and August, 1864. These two months were the most terrible of any experienced by the prisoners. Nine thousand are said to have died during that space of time. . . Many of the deaths were hastened by despondency, after an unusual excitement about exchange — expecting to be called out to be released at any moment, followed by disappointment — deaths were most frequent."

Again, speaking on the same subject, he says:—"Rumors of exchange continued to pervade the prison; men were crazy with the idea of freedom and home, and wandered up and down the prison, clinging to every rumor, 'like drowning men to straws.'"

Abbott, in his "Prison Life in the South," speaking on the subject of exchange, says:—"We had many discussions over this subject *pro* and *con*. It was urged there was no principle involved. If there had been, how come so many 'special exchanges' to take place? More or less of them were constantly occurring; and if the Government could exchange forty or fifty, could it not all? Did the negro question stop it? Had not our Government a sufficient number of rebel prisoners, so that they could afford to exchange all our white soldiers, and then have a sufficient number of rebels left as hostages for the negro captives? Has the Government forgotten us? If not, why prevent our friends ministering to our necessities? Have our services ceased to be as valuable to our Government as before we were captured?"

These, and many other suggestions, presented themselves to this Federal officer, when in prison, in common with thousands of Federal captives. The real object of the Federal Government in stopping the exchange, was to keep the Confederate army from being recruited by Southern soldiers held in Northern forts; it being a well-known fact that the Southern prisoners, as soon as released, and sufficiently recruited in health, hastened to rejoin their comrades on the field of battle; whilst the number that rejoined the Northern ranks from Southern prisons were exceedingly few. It has been stated, in this work, that General Grant instructed General Butler to put the question of exchange to the Confederates in any shape he chose, but on no account to permit any more exchanges to be made. In order to corroborate the above, I will insert a letter from General Butler to Colonel Ould on the subject; and I must say, that the sagacity displayed in this letter is characteristic of the shrewdness of the Federal Commissioner of Exchange in carrying out General Grant's instructions. It reads as follows:

HEADQUARTERS OF VIRGINIA AND NORTH CAROLINA,
IN THE FIELD, *August*, 1864.

Hon. ROBERT OULD, *Commissioner of Exchange.*

SIR:—Your note to Major Mulford, assistant agent of exchange, under date of August 10th, 1864, has been referred to me. You therein state that Major Mulford has several times proposed "to exchange prisoners respectively held by the two belligerents — officer for officer, and man for man"; and that "the offer has also been made by other officials having charge of matters connected with the exchange of prisoners"; and that "this proposal has been heretofore declined by the Confederate authorities." That you now consent to the above proposition, and agree to deliver to you (Major Mulford) the prisoners held in captivity by the Confederate authorities, provided you agree to deliver an equal number of officers and men. As equal numbers are delivered from time to time, they will be declared exchanged. This proposal is made with the understanding that the officers and men on both sides, who have been longest in captivity, will be first delivered where it is practicable. From a slight ambiguity in your phraseology, but more, perhaps, from the antecedent action of your authorities, and because of your acceptance of it, I am in doubt whether you have stated the proposition with entire accuracy. It is true a proposition was made by Major Mulford, and myself, as agent of exchange, to exchange all prisoners of war taken by either belligerent party — man for man, and officer for officer — of equal rank or their equivalents. It was made by me as early as the first of the winter of 1863–4, and has not been accepted. In May last I forwarded to you a note, desiring to know *whether the Confederate authorities intended to treat colored soldiers of the United States army as prisoners of war.* To that inquiry no answer has yet been made. To avoid all possible misapprehension, or mistake hereafter, as to your offer now, will you now say whether you mean by "prisoners held in captivity," colored men duly enrolled and mustered into the service of the United States, who have been captured by the Confederate forces; and if your authorities are willing to exchange all soldiers so mustered into the United States army, whether colored or otherwise, and the officers commanding them — man for man, officer for officer? At the interview which was held between yourself and the agent of exchange, on the part of the United States, at Fortress Monroe, in March last, you will do me the favor to remember the principal discussion turned upon this very point; you, on behalf of the Confederate Government, claiming the right to hold all negroes who had heretofore been slaves, and not emancipated by their masters, enrolled and mustered into the service of the United States, when captured by your forces, not as prisoners of war, but, upon capture, to be turned over to their supposed masters or claimants, whoever they might be, to be held by them as slaves.

By the advertisements in your newspapers, calling upon masters to come forward and claim these men so captured, I suppose that your authorities still adhere to that claim; that is to say, that whenever a colored soldier of the United States is captured by you, upon whom any claim can be made by any person residing within the States now in insurrection, such soldier is not to be treated as a prisoner of war, but is to be turned over to his supposed owner or claimant, and put at such labor or service as that owner or claimant may choose; and the officers in command of such soldiers, in the language of a supposed act of the Confederate States, are to be turned over to the Governors of States, upon requisitions, for the purpose of being punished by the laws of such States for acts done in war in the armies of the United States.

You may be aware that there is still a proclamation by Jefferson Davis, claiming to be the chief executive of the Confederate States, declaring in substance that all officers of colored troops, mustered into the service of the United States, were not to be treated as prisoners of war, but were to be turned over for punishment to the Governors of States. I am reciting these public acts from memory, and will be pardoned for not giving the exact words, although I believe I do not vary the substance and effect. These declarations, on the part of those whom you represent, yet remain unrepealed, unannulled, unrevoked, and must therefore be still supposed to be authoritative. By your acceptance of our proposition, is the Government of the United States to understand that these several claims, enactments, and proclaimed declarations are to be given up, set aside, revoked, and held for naught by the Confederate authorities; and that you are ready and willing to exchange man for man those colored soldiers of the United States, duly mustered and enrolled as such, who have heretofore been claimed as slaves by the Confederate States, as well as white soldiers? If this be so, and you are so willing to exchange these colored men claimed as slaves, and you will so officially inform the Government of the United States, then, as I am instructed, a principal difficulty in effecting exchanges will be removed. As I informed you personally, in my judgment, it is neither consistent with the policy, dignity, nor honor of the United States, upon any consideration, to allow those who, by our laws solemnly enacted, are made soldiers of the Union, and who have been duly enlisted, enrolled, and mustered as such soldiers; who have borne arms in behalf of this country, and who have been captured while fighting in vindication of the rights of that country, not to be treated as prisoners of war, and remain unchanged, and in the service of those who claim them as masters; and I cannot believe that the Government of the United States will ever be found to consent to so gross a wrong. Pardon me if I misunderstand you in supposing that your acceptance of our proposition does not, in good faith, mean to include all the soldiers of the Union, and that you still intend, if your acceptance is agreed to, to hold the colored soldiers of the Union unexchanged, and at labor or service; because I am informed that very lately, and almost contemporaneously with this offer on your part to exchange prisoners, and which seems to include all prisoners of war, the Confederate authorities have made a declaration that the negroes heretofore held to service by owners in the States of Delaware, Maryland, and Missouri, are to be treated as prisoners of war, when captured in arms in the service of the United States. Such declaration that a part of the colored soldiers of the United States were to be treated as prisoners of war, would seem most strongly to imply that others were not to be so treated, or, in other words, that the colored men from the insurrectionary States are to be held to labor and returned to their masters if captured by the Confederate forces, while duly enrolled and mustered into and actually in the armies of the United States.

In the view which the Government of the United States takes of the claim made by you to the persons and services of these negroes, it is not to be supported upon any principle of national or municipal law. Looking upon these men only as property, upon your theory of property in them, we do not see how this claim can be made, certainly not how it can be yielded. It is believed to be a well-settled rule of public international law, and a custom and part of the laws of war, that the capture of movable property vests the title to that property in the captor; and therefore, where one belligerent gets into full possession of property belonging to the subjects or citizens of the other belligerent, the owner of that property is at once divested of his title, which rests in the belligerent government capturing and holding possession. Upon this rule of international law, all civilised nations have acted, and by it both belligerents have dealt with all property, save slaves, taken from each other during the present war. If the Confederate forces capture a number of horses from the United States, the animals are claimed to be, and, as we understand it, become the property of the Confederate authorities. If the United States capture any movable property in the rebellion, by our regulations and laws, in conformity with international law and the laws of war, such property is turned over to our government as its property. Therefore, if we obtain possession of that species of property known to the laws of the insurrectionary States as slaves, why should there be any doubt that that property, like any other, vests in the United States? If the property in the slave does so vest, then the *jus disponendi*, the right of disposing of that property, vests in the United States. Now, the United States have disposed of the property which they have acquired by capture in slaves taken by them, *i. e.*, by emancipating them, and declaring them free forever; so that, if we have not mistaken the principles of international law and the laws of war, we have no slaves in the armies of the United States. All are free men, being made so in such manner as we have chosen to dispose of our property in them which we acquired by capture. Slaves being captured by us, and the right of property in them thereby vested in us, that right of property has been disposed of by us by manumitting them, as has already been the acknowledged right of the owner to do to his slave.

The manner in which we dispose of our property while it is in our possession certainly cannot be questioned by you. Nor is the case altered if the property is not actually captured in battle, but comes either voluntarily or involuntarily from the belligerent owner into the possession of the other belligerent. I take it, no one would doubt the right of the United States to a drove of Confederate mules or a herd of Confederate cattle, which should wander or rush across the Confederate lines into the lines of the United States army. So, it seems to me, treating the negro as property merely, if that piece of property passes the Confederate lines and comes into the lines of the United States, that property is as much lost to its owner in the Confederate States as would be the mule or the ox, the property of the resident of the Confederate States which should fall into our hands. If, therefore, the principles of international law and the laws of war used in this discussion are correctly stated, then it would seem that the deduction logically flows therefrom, in natural sequence, that the Confederate States can have no claim upon the negro soldiers captured by them from the armies of the United States because of the former ownership of them by their citizens or subjects, and only claim such as result under the laws of war, from their captor merely.

Do the Confederate authorities claim the right to reduce to a state of slavery, free men, prisoners of war, captured by them? This claim our fathers fought against under Bainbridge and Decatur, when set up by the Barbary Powers on the northern shore of Africa about the year 1800, and in 1864 their children will hardly yield upon their own soil. This point I will not pursue further, because I understand you to repudiate the idea that you will reduce free men to slaves because of capture in war, and that you base the claim of the Confederate authorities to reënslave our negro soldiers, when captured by you, on the *jus postliminii*, or that principle of the law of nations which inhabilitates the former owner with the property taken by an enemy, when such property is recovered by the forces of his own country. Or, in other words, you claim that, by the laws of nations and of war, when property of the subjects of one belligerent power, captured by the forces of the other belligerent, is recaptured by the armies of the former owner, then such property is to be restored to its prior possessor, as if it had never been captured; and, therefore, under this principle your authorities propose to restore to their masters the slaves which heretofore belonged to them, which you may capture from us. But this postliminary right under which you claim to act, as understood and defined by all writers on national law, is applicable simply to immovable property, and, that too, only after complete subjugation of that portion of the country in which the property is situated, upon which this right fastens itself. By the laws and customs of war, this right has never been applied to movable property. True it is, I believe, that the Romans attempted to apply it to the case of slaves; but for two thousand years no other nation has attempted to set up this right as ground for treating slaves differently from other property. But the Romans even refused to reënslave men captured from opposing belligerents in a civil war, such as ours unhappily is. Consistently then with any principle of the law of nations, treating slaves as property merely, it would seem to be impossible for the Government of the United States to permit the negroes in their ranks to be reënslaved when captured, or treated otherwise than as prisoners of war.

I have forborne, sir, in this discussion, to argue the question upon any other or different ground of right than those adopted by your authorities in claiming the negro as property, because I understand that your fabric of opposition to the Government of the United States has the right of property in man as its corner-stone. Of course, it would not be profitable, in settling a question of exchange of prisoners of war, to attempt to argue the question of abandonment of the very corner-stone of their attempted political edifice. Therefore I have admitted all the considerations which should apply to the negro soldier as a man, and dealt with him upon the Confederate theory of property only.

I unite with you most cordially, sir, in desiring a speedy settlement of all these questions, in view of the great suffering endured by our prisoners in the hands of your authorities, of which you so feelingly speak. Let me ask, in view of that suffering, why you have delayed eight months to answer a proposition which, by now accepting, you admit to be right, just, and humane, allowing that suffering to continue so long? One cannot help thinking, even at the risk of being deemed uncharitable, that the benevolent sympathies of the Confederate authorities have been lately stirred by the depleted condition of their armies, and a desire to get into the field, to affect the present campaign, the hale, hearty, well-fed prisoners held by the United States, in exchange for the half-starved, sick, emaciated, and unserviceable soldiers of the United States, now languishing in your prisons. The events of this war, if we did not know it before, have taught us that it is not the Northern people alone who know how to drive sharp bargains. The wrongs, indignities, and privations suffered by our soldiers would move me to consent to anything to procure their exchange, except to barter away the honor and faith of the Government of the United States, which has been so solemnly pledged to the colored soldiers in its ranks. Consistently with national faith and justice, we cannot relinquish this position. With your authorities it is a question of property merely. It seems to address itself to you in this form: Will you suffer your soldier captured in fighting your battles, to be in confinement for months rather than release him by giving for him that which you call a piece of property, and which we are willing to accept as a man? You certainly appear to place less value upon your soldier than you do upon your negro. I assure you, much as we of the North are accused of loving property, our citizens would have no difficulty in yielding up any piece of property they have, in exchange for one of their brothers or sons languishing in your prisons; certainly there could be no doubt that they would do so were that piece of property less in value than five thousand dollars in Confederate money, which is believed to be the price of an able-bodied negro in the insurrectionary States.

Trusting that I may receive such a reply to the questions propounded in this note, as will tend to a speedy resumption of the negotiations, in a full exchange of all prisoners, and a delivery of them to their respective authorities, I have the honor to be,

Very respectfully your obedient servant,

BENJAMIN F. BUTLER,

Major-general and Commissioner of Exchange.

The following notes from Colonel Ould to Major Mulford and General Hitchcock, upon the subject, will be found of interest and significance. We are left to infer from General Butler's letter to Colonel Ould, that the whole matter of exchange was left to him, as the most suitable "tool" that the Federal Government could select to perform its perfidious acts. They read as follows:

RICHMOND, VA., *August 10th*, 1864.

Major JOHN E. MULFORD, *Assistant Agent of Exchange.*

SIR:—You have several times proposed to me to exchange the prisoners respectively held by the two belligerents, officer for officer and man for man. The same offer has also been made by other officials having charge of matters connected with the exchange of prisoners. This proposal has heretofore been declined by the Confederate authorities, they insisting upon the terms of the cartel, which required the delivery of the excess on either side upon parole. In view, however, of the very large number of prisoners now held by each party, and the suffering consequent upon their continued confinement, I now consent to the above proposal, and agree to deliver to you the prisoners held in captivity by the Confederate authorities, provided you agree to deliver an equal number of Confederate officers and men. As equal numbers are delivered, from time to time, they will be declared exchanged. This proposal is made with the understanding that the officers and men, on both sides, who have been longest in captivity, will be first delivered, where it is practicable. I shall be happy to hear from you, as speedily as possible, whether this arrangement can be carried out.

Respectfully your obedient servant,

RO. OULD, *Agent of Exchange.*

The delivery of this letter (says Colonel Ould) was accompanied with a statement of the mortality which was hurrying so many prisoners at Andersonville to the grave. Major Mulford returned with flag-of-truce steamer on the 20th of the same month, and, in a conversation with Colonel Ould, told him that he had no reply to make to his communication of the 10th, nor was he authorised by his Government to make any. Colonel Ould, fearing that some technicality might be urged against his note to Major Mulford, addressed the following letter to Major-general E. A. Hitchcock, one of the Federal Commissioners of Exchange, residing at Washington City, with an enclosure of his note to Major Mulford of the 10th of August:

RICHMOND, *August 22d*, 1864.

Major-general E. A. HITCHCOCK, *U. S. Com. of Exchange.*

SIR:—Enclosed is a copy of a communication which, on the 10th inst., I addressed and delivered to Major John E. Mulford, Assistant Agent of Exchange. Under the circumstances of the case, I deem it proper to forward this paper to you, in order that you may fully understand the position which is taken by the Confederate authorities. I shall be glad if the proposition therein made is accepted by your Government.

Respectfully your obedient servant,
RO. OULD, *Agent of Exchange.*

No answer being had from this communication, Colonel Ould again, on the 30th of August, when the flag-of-truce steamer made its appearance at Varina, addressed the following note to Major Mulford, as follows:

RICHMOND, *August 31st*, 1864.

Major JOHN E. MULFORD, *Assistant Agent of Exchange.*

SIR:—On the 10th of this month I addressed you a communication, to which I have received no answer. On the 22d inst. I also addressed a communication to Major-general E. A. Hitchcock, U. S. Commissioner of Exchange, enclosing a copy of my letter to you of the 10th inst. I now respectfully ask you to state, in writing, whether you have any reply to either of said communications; and if not, whether you have any reason to give why no reply has been made.

Respectfully your obedient servant,
RO. OULD, *Agent of Exchange.*

To this communication Colonel Ould received the following reply:

FLAG-OF-TRUCE STEAMER "NEW YORK,"
VARINA, VA., *August* 31*st*, 1864.

HON. ROBERT OULD, *Agent of Exchange:*

SIR:—I have the honor to acknowledge the receipt of your favor of to-day, requesting answer, &c., to your communication of the 10th inst. on the question of the exchange of prisoners. To which, in reply, I would say, I have no communication on the subject from our authorities. Nor am I authorised to make answer.

I am, Sir, very respectfully your obedient servant,

JNO. E. MULFORD, *Assistant Agent of Exchange.*

During the long suspense and agonising horrors of prison life endured by Northern and Southern captives, we find the Northern Government still inventing excuses for retarding a general exchange of prisoners. The negro question seems to have been the most prominent at this late period. Was it really for the honor of the Federal flag, and in the name of liberty, that General Butler openly violated the cartel and obstructed the exchange of prisoners? I can best answer this question by quoting from the narrative of A. M. Keely, Esq., of Petersburg, who was a prisoner at the North during the war, and is the author of that little work entitled *In Vinculis*. His testimony is trustworthy. He tells us that, "On approaching Butler's quarters, which were quite handsomely located, out of reach of all intrusion, the first thing that attracted attention was the presence and prominence of the negro. So far we had only seen one or two negro soldiers on duty at the pontoon bridge, and the night being as dark as themselves, we could with difficulty distinguish them; but there, Abyssinia ruled the roast. It was 'nigger' everywhere; and although the white soldiers were obviously annoyed at the companionship, the terrors of Butler's rule crushed all resistance even of opinion, and the colored brethren knew, and presumed on their secured position and importance. . . That he (Butler) established and maintained order in New Orleans and Norfolk in undeniable; but it was such order as reigned in Sicily in days of old, and in Warsaw in later times—the order of sullen, abject, physical fear—a political *coma*, which is itself death, yet in which there is one thing lively—stealing. The world will never know the truth of this creature's vileness and success, until it shall become safe for the hundreds he has robbed and outraged, to tell the story of their wrongs and his robberies. . . Quite a long conversation ensued between myself and Butler, which proceeded on this wise, the clerk busily recording it:

"'What is your name?'

"'Mr. ——— ———.'

"'Your profession or pursuit?'

"'I am a lawyer.'

"'You were captured yesterday near Petersburg?'

"'I was.'

"'How many men were in the trenches with you?'

"'About one hundred and twenty or thirty.'

"'All militia-men?'

"'All, with less than half a dozen exceptions.'

"'And you repulsed, I learn, for two hours, General Kautz's brigade of cavalry?'

"'You have been rightly informed.' . .

"'Will you tell me how many soldiers were in Petersburg at the time of General Kautz's first appearance?' . .

"'I decline answering.'

"'Oh, you need not decline; I know there was not a soldier there.'

"'Well, Sir, there is no need to ask if you know; but I am curious to know how you know that.'

"'By this infallible deduction: if there was a soldier in town, no lawyer would get into the trenches.'

"I joined in the smile that followed—and which Butler enjoyed hugely—more in compliment to the truth than the wit of his inference, and replied: 'You speak of Northern lawyers,

I presume. We have contributed our full share to this fight for freedom. If I may speak for myself, I entered the service on the 19th of April, 1861, and thousands of the profession volunteered as early.'

"'Yes, yes, I understand all that. I volunteered a couple of days before you, but I never got into the trenches, and by the help of heaven I never shall. That is quite another matter, you perceive.' Here he took up a note from his desk, held it within four inches of his left eye — what marvel that a man should have a *sinister* expression whose vision is left-handed? — and continued: 'I would like to know the position of your Government, and particularly of your people, on the subject of negro exchange. I have just received this note from Colonel Ould, in which the question is not met at all, and it is now a month since I applied for a categorical statement of the position of Mr. Davis's Government on this topic.'

"'As I have no official character, I am, of course, not entitled to speak by authority; and as to the President's individual views, I know nothing.'

"'Of course I know you are not a commissioner, but I would be glad to hear your views. I think a white man is as good as a negro, and would be willing to give one of your negroes, if a soldier, for one of my white soldiers. But your Government takes the position that the negro is better than a white man, and you will not give up one of my negroes to get back one of your best soldiers.'

"'My Government, I presume, takes no such absurd position. She merely contends that the right of property in a slave is no more affected by his running away to your army, than by his flying to your States — least of all by your kidnapping. You are entitled to demand the exchange of your negro soldiers not slaves, just as England would be entitled to claim her Sepoys, and France her Algerines, in the event of war between us and either of those powers. But both your Constitution and your positive statutory enactments, guard the title of the owner against disturbance from any quarter without the jurisdiction of the master's State.'

"'Ah, yes, but that is the law of peace; you claim the slave as a chattel. Now, if I capture land, and it is recaptured, it reverts to the original owner; but if I capture a chattel, a horse for example, on its recapture it becomes the property, not of the original owner, but of your Government, and is, doubtless, so treated. Thus the capture of realty divests the title only during occupancy; the capture of personalty divests it forever. How do you make the slave the exception?'

"'There is plainly no reason in the nature of things why one description of property should be less sacred than another, and the discrimination against personal property only arises, I presume, from the difficulty of identification — which does not exist in the case of the slave. Hence the Roman law, if I rightly remember, excepted slaves, and common sense excepts them from the general rule regarding personalty. For example, a Federal General goes to New Orleans or Norfolk, and steals my house and all that it contains — furniture, pictures, clothing, jewelry, everything; but before he has a chance to send them to his wife in Boston or New York, the city is recaptured. I presume my Government would restore me my house with all its contents, and the conquering General would hardly think of holding an auction on my premises.'

"'I am not certain that he would have the right. But how do you answer this? Public law authorises the United States to declare that a slave fleeing to her shall be free; she so does declare in the case of every slave that comes to her.'

"'I answer that, by denial first of the facts, and then of the right. And though both were true, I do not see how they could affect the power of our own Government and laws to reëstablish the original relation between master and slave, when all parties come again within the jurisdiction.'

"'Well, Sir, it is to be regretted that our Government cannot agree about this, *as there will be no more exchanges and no communication till this point is yielded.*'

"'How is it then, General, that while you made this demand on my Government a month ago, you continue to communicate, as I see from Colonel Ould's despatch?'

"'Oh, Mr. Davis moves very slowly, and I was giving him time to make up his mind. *He has now had abundant time, and I am going to stop all intercourse.*'"

Quoting from the same author, I will give some of his experience when an order came to Elmira for the surgeons to make out a list for exchange of all the sick and wounded who would be unfit for duty for the next sixty days. He says:—

"For several days past the rumor has been current in camp that an exchange of the sick and wounded on both sides is on the carpet. . . . What wonder that many a paling eye flashes up now with unusual fire, and many a poor feeble pulse, that for weeks past has been fighting an unequal battle with fever, starvation, memory, and despair, bounds now with a fresh impetus, as in the distance, not very remote, there looms up the enchanting vision of wife and child, mother, sister, HOME. Many, alas! who are indulging themselves with this fair prospect, will turn their trembling, tottering feet towards another home ere the light of the earthly one can answer their longings, *pulsat pede.*

"To-day (October 1st) the rumor takes definite shape as the surgeons make their rounds through the wards examining the sick, and excluding from the roll all but those whose convalescence is apparent, and those who will never get better here; and it leaks out that the order from Washington is, that a list must be made of those only who will be unfit for duty for sixty days. Having beat up England, Ireland, Scotland, France, Germany, Switzerland, Asia, and Africa, for recruits, these invincible twenty millions of Yanks admit that they are still not a match for five millions of Southerners, and they still cling with the tenacity of death to every able-bodied 'reb' they can clutch, lest he may again enter the Southern army. The negro question, which they plead as their excuse, is all bosh of the first water. The Northern people—and I speak from long acquaintance with them—care much less for negroes than we. . . . It is not, therefore, black love, but white fear, which is interposing difficulties in the way of a general exchange of prisoners; and so controlling is this latter motive, that the prisoners at Andersonville might forever have sung their sorrows to deaf ears, but for the advent of that crucible of parties and policies—election-day. The McClellan men have proclaimed a general exchange as a plank in their platform. . . . So the ingenious Yankees make a compromise between justice and expediency, by exchanging only those who will not be fit for fighting until the present campaign is over, and thus take the wind out of the democratic sails, without sending a man to that army which the veracious Grant affirms is deserting to him at the rate of a regiment a day. . . . At last, on the 8th, the lists were completed, some fifteen hundred were found 'unfit for duty for sixty days'—one-sixth of the whole—and, on the morning of the 9th, notice was given that the 'paroles' would be taken that day. . . . As soon as the announcement was made in the various hospitals, that the parole lists were ready, those who had been notified that they had been entered for exchange began to crawl from their cots, and turn their faces toward the door. On they came, a ghastly tide—with skeleton bodies and lustreless eyes, and brains bereft of but one thought, and hearts purged of all feelings but one—the thought of freedom, the love of home; and they came on their crutches, on their cots, borne in the arms of their friends; creeping, some of them, on hands and knees, pale, gaunt, emaciated; some with the seal of death stamped on their wasted cheeks and shrivelled limbs, yet fearing less death than the added agony of death in the hands of enemies, where no kindred hand should give them reassuring grasp as they tottered forth into the dark valley, and their bones should lie in unhonored graves, amid aliens and foemen. Such haggard, miserable, helpless, hopeless wretches I never saw; and I saw more than one consignment of Federal prisoners on their way home. Several died between the signing of the paroles and the day fixed for their departure—paroled by an authority that permits no official perfidy to go behind the record."

CHAPTER XI.

I shall now avail myself of an opportunity afforded me by quoting freely from that able work on the "Constitutional View of the War between the States," written by the Hon. Alexander H. Stephens, the statesman, patriot, and historian. I consider myself fortunate in my vindication to the claims of humanity, that his testimony has made its appearance in an official and tangible form. The work needs no eulogy from my feeble pen. I could not, if I were to make an attempt, add anything to its imperishable truths. I may, therefore, be pardoned for giving his statements as they appear in the body of his work in regard to prisoners of war, in full. Treating on the subject of the formation of the Confederate navy, he says:

Meantime the privateer *Savannah*, under command of T. Harrison Baker, with a crew of twenty men, had been captured on the 3d of June, 1861, off Charleston, by the U. S. Brig *Perry*. Her crew had been placed in irons and sent to New York, where they were to be tried for piracy under Mr. Lincoln's proclamation. It was now that the question about prisoners arose for the first time, between the parties belligerent, which, from the importance this question assumed in the subsequent conduct of the war, deserves special notice here. News of the treatment of these prisoners taken on the privateer

Savannah having reached Richmond through the public press, Mr. Davis immediately addressed a communication to Mr. Lincoln, and committed it to the hands of a special messenger, Col. Taylor, an officer of the Confederate army, with directions to obtain, if possible, a passage by flag-of-truce through the Federal lines, and to deliver it in person. In this communication, dated Richmond, July 16th, 1861, he said to Mr. Lincoln:

"Having learned that the schooner *Savannah*, a private armed vessel in the service, and sailing under a commission issued by authority of the Confederate States of America, had been captured by one of the vessels forming the blockading squadron off Charleston harbor, I directed a proposition to be made to the officer commanding that squadron for the exchange of the officers and crew of the *Savannah*, for prisoners of war held by this Government, 'according to number and rank.' To this proposition, made on the 19th ultimo, Captain Mercer, the officer in command of the blockading squadron, made answer on the same day that the 'prisoners (referred to) are not on board of any of the vessels under my command.'

"It now appears, by statements made without contradiction in newspapers published in New York, that the prisoners above mentioned were conveyed to that city, and have been treated, not as prisoners of war, but as criminals; that they have been put in irons, confined in jail, brought before the courts of justice on charges of piracy and treason, and it is even rumored that they have been actually convicted of the offences charged, for no other reason than that they bore arms in defence of the rights of this Government, and under the authority of its commission. I could not, without grave discourtesy, have made the newspaper statements above referred to the subject of this communication, if the threat of treating as pirates the citizens of this Confederacy, armed for its service on the high seas, had not been contained in your proclamation of the 19th of April last. That proclamation seems to afford a sufficient justification for considering these published statements as not devoid of probability.

"It is the desire of this Government so to conduct the war now existing as to mitigate its horrors as far as may be possible; and with this intent, its treatment of the prisoners captured by its forces has been marked by the greatest humanity and leniency consistent with public obligation. Some have been permitted to return home on parole, others to remain at large under similar conditions, within this Confederacy, and all have been furnished with rations for their subsistence, such as are allowed our own troops. It is only since the news has been received of the treatment of the prisoners taken on the *Savannah* that I have been compelled to withdraw these indulgences, and to hold the prisoners taken by us in strict confinement.

"A just regard to humanity and to the honor of this Government, now requires me to state explicitly that, painful as will be the necessity, this Government will deal out to the prisoners held by it, the same treatment and the same fate as shall be experienced by those captured on the *Savannah*; and if driven to the terrible necessity of retaliation by your execution of any of the officers or crew of the *Savannah*, that retaliation will be extended so far as shall be requisite to secure the abandonment of a practice unknown to the warfare of civilised man, and so barbarous as to disgrace the nation which shall be guilty of inaugurating it.

"With this view, and because it may not have reached you, I now renew the proposition made to the commander of the blockading squadron, to exchange for the prisoners taken on the *Savannah*, an equal number of those now held by us, according to rank."

Says Mr. Stevens:—This overture of Mr. Davis was so far respected as to let Colonel Taylor, the bearer of it, pass the enemy's lines and go to Washington; but a personal interview with Mr. Lincoln was denied. He was permitted to return the next day, with a verbal reply from General Scott, that the communication had been delivered to Mr. Lincoln, and that he would answer it in writing as soon as possible. No answer in writing, or in any other way, however, was made by Mr. Lincoln to the communication. The only resort left to Mr. Davis, therefore, was the extreme one of retaliation, recognised by the most civilised nations. A number of Northern prisoners were selected by lot, to meet whatever fate should be measured out to these and other privateers taken on the high seas. Amongst the Federal officers thus selected for retaliation were Colonels Corcoran, Lee, Cogswell, Wilcox, Woodruff and Wood, Majors Potter, Revere and Vogdes, Captains Rockwood, Bowman and Keffer. Bowman and Keffer were substituted in like manner by lot, in lieu of Captains Rickett and McQuade, who were wounded, and who, in consequence, were exempted from the lot, which fell on them in the first instance. The end of this whole matter, so revolting to the common sentiment of the age in all enlightened countries, was a desistance by Mr. Lincoln from the position and doctrines assumed in his proclamation. These prisoners, on both sides, were all subsequently duly exchanged. Whether the authorities at Washington were induced to change their policy and purpose, in this particular, by a recognition of the laws of war, or from a sense of humanity, or from fears excited in another quarter, will perhaps be left forever to conjecture; for no explanation of it has ever been given to the public, as far as I am aware.

No further reply was ever made to Mr. Davis's communication referred to. Judging, therefore, from the subsequent course of the Federal authorities upon the subject of prisoners, who were permitted by these authorities to suffer and die in Southern stockades, from wounds and diseases incident to a climate to which the men were not accustomed, rather than to agree upon just terms of exchange, as we shall see, it is not an illegitimate conclusion that the desistance in this case was induced from no considerations of the sufferings or impending fate of the gallant officers of their army thus held as hostages. The change of policy evidently came more from fear than from any sense of humanity, or the acknowledgment of the universally recognised principles of civilised warfare. That fear was excited by the position of England on the subject. This was made known by what occurred in the British House of Lords on the 16th of May, soon after Mr. Lincoln's most extraordinary proclamation of the 19th of April reached that country. On this day, in that body, the Earl of Derby said:

"He apprehended *that if one thing was clearer than another, it was that privateering was not piracy*, and that no law could make that piracy, as regarded the subjects of one nation, which was not piracy by the law of nations. Consequently, the United States *must not be allowed to entertain this doctrine,* and to call upon her Majesty's Government not to interfere. He knew it was said that the United States treated the Confederate States of the South as mere rebels, and that as rebels these expeditions were liable to all the penalties of high treason. That was not the doctrine of this country, because we have declared that they are entitled to all the rights of belligerents. *The Northern States could not claim the rights of belligerents for themselves, and, on the other hand, deal with other parties not as belligerents, but as rebels.*"

Lord Brougham said that "it was clear that privateering was not piracy by the law of nations." Lord Kingsdown took the same view. "What was to be the operation of the Presidential proclamation upon this subject was a matter for the consideration of the United States." But he expressed the opinion that the enforcement of the doctrine of that proclamation "would be an act of barbarity which would produce an outcry throughout the civilised world."

"It is no strain of presumption," says Mr. Stephens, "to assign this change of policy in reference to the privateersmen, on the part of the Federal authorities, to apprehensions and fears awakened by this voice from England, especially in view of their subsequent conduct in relation to the exchange of prisoners."

Speaking on the subject of the violation of the cartel of exchange by the Federal authorities, in another part of his work, he says:—"Another matter of this period (February 1862) to be specially noted is, that during this winter, while the Confederates had a very large excess of Federal prisoners, the authorities at Washington, under very great pressure of public sentiment in the Northern States, were induced to enter into a cartel for an exchange, upon the basis that the Confederates had offered at the beginning. This arrangement was entered into on the 14th day of February, 1862, by General Howell Cobb, on the part of the Confederate States, and General John E. Wool, on the part of the United States. According to the agreement then made, the privateersmen were put upon the footing of other prisoners of war. But no sooner had the Federals an excess of prisoners, by the capture of the garrison of about 10,000 officers and men at Fort Donelson, than the terms of this agreement were violated by their again refusing to send forward the privateersmen in exchange, as well as their failing to comply with the cartel in other respects."

This brings us to a point when the important subject of the exchange of prisoners of war began to take definite shape. A cartel of exchange was agreed upon by the two Governments, and a distinct and fair understanding was supposed to exist on this vexed ouestion. This important document reads as follows:

HAXALL'S LANDING, on James River, *July 22d*, 1862.

The undersigned having been commissioned by the authorities they respectively represent to make arrangements for a general exchange of prisoners of war, have agreed to the following articles:

ARTICLE I.—It is hereby agreed and stipulated, that all prisoners of war, held by either party, including those taken on private armed vessels, known as privateers, shall be exchanged upon the conditions and terms following:

Prisoners to be exchanged man for man and officer for officer. Privateers to be placed upon the footing of officers and men of the navy.

Men and officers of lower grades may be exchanged for officers of a higher grade, and men and officers of different services may be exchanged according to the following scale of equivalents:

A general-commanding-in-chief, or an admiral, shall be exchanged for officers of equal rank, or for sixty privates or common seamen.

A commodore, carrying a broad pennant, or a brigadier-general, shall be exchanged for officers of equal rank, or twenty privates or common seamen.

A captain in the navy, or a colonel, shall be exchanged for officers of equal rank, or for fifteen privates or common seamen.

A lieutenant-colonel, or commander in the navy, shall be exchanged for officers of equal rank, or for ten privates or common seamen.

A lieutenant-commander, or a major, shall be exchanged for officers of equal rank, or eight privates or common seamen.

A lieutenant, or a master in the navy, or a captain in the army or marines, shall be exchanged for officers of equal rank, or six privates or common seamen.

Master's-mates in the navy, or lieutenants or ensigns in the army, shall be exchanged for officers of equal rank, or four privates or common seamen. Midshipmen, warrant-officers in the navy, masters of merchant vessels and commanders of privateers, shall be exchanged for officers of equal rank, or three privates or common seamen; second captains, lieutenants or mates of merchant vessels or privateers, and all petty officers in the navy, and all non-commissioned officers in the army or marines, shall be severally exchanged for persons of equal rank, or for two privates or common seamen; and private soldiers or common seamen shall be exchanged for each other man for man.

Article II.—Local, state, civil and militia rank held by persons not in actual military service will not be recognised; the basis of exchange being the grade actually held in the naval and military service of the respective parties.

Article III.—If citizens held by either party on charges of disloyalty, or any alleged civil offence, are exchanged, it shall only be for citizens. Captured sutlers, teamsters, and all civilians in the actual service of either party, to be exchanged for persons in similar positions.

Article IV.—All prisoners of war to be discharged on parole in ten days after their capture; and the prisoners now held, and those hereafter taken, to be transported to the points mutually agreed upon, at the expense of the capturing party. The surplus prisoners not exchanged shall not be permitted to take up arms again, nor to serve as military police or constabulary force in any fort, garrison, or field-work, held by either of the respective parties, nor as guards of prisoners, deposit or stores, nor to discharge any duty usually performed by soldiers, until exchanged under the provisions of this cartel. The exchange is not to be considered complete until the officer or soldier exchanged for has been actually restored to the lines to which he belongs.

Article V.—Each party upon the discharge of prisoners of the other party is authorised to discharge an equal number of their own officers or men from parole, furnishing, at the same time, to the other party a list of their prisoners discharged, and of their own officers and men relieved from parole; thus enabling each party to relieve from parole such of their officers and men as the party may choose. The lists thus mutually furnished, will keep both parties advised of the true condition of the exchange of prisoners.

Article VI.—The stipulations and provisions above mentioned to be of binding obligation, during the continuance of the war, it matters not which party may have the surplus of prisoners; the great principles involved being, 1st. An equitable exchange of prisoners, man for man, or officer for officer, or officers of higher grade exchanged for officers of lower grade, or for privates, according to scale of equivalents. 2d. That privates and officers and men of different services may be exchanged according to same scale of equivalents. 3d. That all prisoners, of whatever arm of service, are to be exchanged or paroled in ten days from the time of their capture, if it be practicable to transfer them to their own lines in that time; if not, as soon thereafter as practicable. 4th. That no officer, or soldier, employed in service of either party, is to be considered as exchanged and absolved from his parole until his equivalent has actually reached the lines of his friends. 5th. That parole forbids the performance of field, garrison, police, or guard or constabulary duty.

JOHN A. DIX, *Major-general.*
D. H. HILL, *Major-general C. S. A.*

SUPPLEMENTARY ARTICLES.

ARTICLE VII.—All prisoners of war now held on either side, and all prisoners hereafter taken, shall be sent with all reasonable dispatch to A. M. Aiken's, below Dutch Gap, on the James River in Virginia, or to Vicksburg on the Mississippi river, in the State of Mississippi, and there exchanged or paroled until such exchange can be effected, notice being previously given by each party of the number of prisoners it will send, and the time when they will be delivered at those points respectively; and in case the vicissitudes of war shall change the military relations of the places designated in this article to the contending parties, so as to render the same inconvenient for the delivery and exchange of prisoners, other places bearing as nearly as may be the present local relations of said places to the lines of said parties, shall be, by mutual agreement, substituted. But nothing in this article contained shall prevent the commanders of two opposing armies from exchanging prisoners or releasing them on parole, at other points mutually agreed on by said commanders.

ARTICLE VIII.—For the purpose of carrying into effect the foregoing articles of agreement, each party will appoint two agents, to be called agents for the exchange of prisoners of war, whose duty it shall be to communicate with each other by correspondence and otherwise; to prepare the lists of prisoners; to attend to the delivery of the prisoners at the places agreed on, and to carry out promptly, effectually, and in good faith, all the details and provisions of the said articles of agreement.

ARTICLE IX.—And, in case any misunderstanding shall arise in regard to any clause or stipulation in the foregoing articles, it is mutually agreed that such misunderstanding shall not interrupt the release of prisoners on parole, as herein provided, but shall be made the subject of friendly explanation, in order that the object of this agreement may neither be defeated nor postponed.

JOHN A. DIX, *Major-general.*
D. H. HILL, *Major-general C. S. A.*

Colonel Robert Ould, a gentleman of high legal attainments, was appointed under this cartel as the agent of exchange on the part of the Confederate Government; and upon his statement it appears that the Confederates held an excess of prisoners up to July, 1863, and that the Federals neglected to send sufficient transportation, although repeatedly urged to do so by him. It was about this time that a misunderstanding also arose between the agents of exchange on the subject of the release of paroled prisoners after capture. This portion of the cartel was rendered null, it seems, by the authorities at Washington. It also appears that Lieutenant-colonel Ludlow, acting as agent on the part of the Federal Government, was dismissed on account of his integrity in endeavoring to carry out the provisions of the cartel of exchange. This is proven by a letter addressed to him on the 26th July, 1863, by Colonel Ould, in which he uses the following forcible and impressive language, in justification of his own course and in vindication of his Government:—"Now that our official connection is being terminated, I say to you, in the fear of God—and I appeal to Him for the truth of the declaration—that there has been no single moment from the time we were first brought together, in connection with the matter of exchange, to the present hour, during which there has not been an open and notorious violation of the cartel by your authorities. Officers and men numbering over hundreds have been, during your whole connection with the cartel, kept in cruel confinement, sometimes in irons, or doomed to cells, without charges or trial. They are in prison now, unless God, in His mercy, has released them. *In our parting moments, let me do you the justice to say, that I do not believe it is so much your fault as that of your authorities. Nay, more, I believe your removal from your position has been owing to the personal efforts you have made for a faithful observance, not only of the cartel, but of humanity in the conduct of the war.* Again and again have I importuned you to tell me of one officer or man, now held in confinement by us, who was declared exchanged. You have to those appeals furnished [the name of?] one, Spencer Kellogg. For him I have searched in vain. On the other hand, I appeal to your own records for the cases where your reports have shown that our officers and men have been held for long months, and even years, in violation of the cartel and our agreements. The last phase of the enormity, however, exceeds all others. Although you have many thousands of our soldiers now in confinement in your prisons, and especially in that horrible hold of death, Fort Delaware, you have not for several weeks sent us any prisoners. During those weeks you have despatched Captain Mulford with the steamer 'New York' to City Point three or four times without any prisoners. For the first two or three times, some sort of an excuse was attempted. None is given at this present arrival. I do not mean to be offensive when I say that effrontery could not give one. I ask you, with no purpose of disrespect, what can you think of this covert attempt to secure the delivery of all your prisoners in our hands without the release of those of ours who are languishing in hopeless misery in your prisons and dungeons?"

The facts in the case show that the Federals had no lists of paroled prisoners (released on capture) to be charged against the Confederates, Colonel Ould having paid off his debts from the large number of captives in the hands of the Confederates. The Federals, it seems, received their prisoners on parole without returning to Colonel Ould a like equivalent. Upon his remonstrating, the Federal Government informed him on the 8th of April, 1863, that exchanges, in the future, would be confined to "such equivalents as are held in confinement on either side." This Colonel Ould indignantly refused, as it was a direct and palpable violation of the cartel agreed upon. The effect of this would have been that the Confederates, after delivering their prisoners, would have had the paroles of ten times as many prisoners as the enemy held in captivity, leaving at the same time thousands of their men in Northern bastiles. The only resource left for Colonel Ould, was to declare all the officers and men captured at Vicksburg exchanged, to balance against those that had, in violation of their parole, entered the Federal ranks before they were duly exchanged. After this, the provision of the cartel, that "all prisoners of war were to be discharged on parole in ten days after their capture," &c., was practically nullified by the Federal Government. Almost all the exchanges that took place subsequently, were made by special orders or agreement.

In corroboration of the facts which I have presented, I cite the following letter, written by Colonel Ould after the close of the war, to the *National Intelligencer*, at Washington:

RICHMOND, VA., *August* 17, 1868.

To the Editors of the National Intelligencer:

GENTLEMEN:—I have recently seen so many misrepresentations of the action of the late Confederate authorities in relation to prisoners, that I feel it due to the truth of history, and peculiarly incumbent on me as their Agent of Exchange, to bring to the attention of the country the facts set forth in this paper:

I.

The cartel of exchange bears date July 22d, 1862. Its chief purpose was to secure the delivery of all prisoners of war.

To that end, the fourth article provided that all prisoners of war should be discharged on parole in ten days after their capture. From the date of the cartel until the summer of 1863, the Confederate authorities had the excess of prisoners. During the interval, deliveries were made as fast as the Federal Government furnished transportation. Indeed, upon more than one occasion, I urged the Federal authorities to send increased means of transportation. It has never been alleged that the Confederate authorities failed or neglected to make prompt deliveries of prisoners who were not held under charges, when they had the excess. On the other hand, during the same time, the cartel was openly and notoriously violated by the Federal authorities. Officers and men were kept in confinement, sometimes in irons, or doomed to cells, without charge or trial. Many officers were kept in confinement even after the notices published by the Federal authorities had declared them exchanged.

In the summer of 1863 the Federal authorities insisted upon limiting exchanges to such as were in confinement on either side. This I resisted, as being in violation of the cartel. Such a construction not only kept in confinement the excess on either side, but ignored all paroles which were held by the Confederate Government. These were very many, being the paroles of officers and men who had been released on capture. The Federal Government at that time held few or no paroles. They had all, or nearly all, been surrendered, the Confederate authorities giving prisoners as equivalent for them. Thus it will be seen, that as long as the Confederate Government had the excess of prisoners, matters went on smoothly enough; but as soon as the posture of affairs in that respect was changed, the cartel could no longer be observed. So, as long as the Federal Government held the paroles of Confederate officers and men, they were respected, and made the basis of an exchange; but when equivalents were obtained for them, and no more were in hand, the paroles which were held by the Confederate authorities could not be recognised. In consequence of the position thus assumed by the Federal Government, the requirement of the cartel, that all prisoners should be delivered within ten days, was practically nullified. The deliveries which were afterwards made were the results of special agreements.

The Confederate authorities adhered to their position until the 10th of August, 1864, when, moved by the sufferings of the men in the prisons of each belligerent, they determined to abate their just demand. Accordingly, on the last named day, I addressed the following communication to Brigadier-general John E. Mulford, (then Major,) Assistant Agent of Exchange:

RICHMOND, *August* 10, 1864.

Major JOHN E. MULFORD, *Assistant Agent of Exchange:*

SIR,—You have several times proposed to me to exchange the prisoners respectively held by the two belligerents—officer for officer and man for man. The same offer has also been made by other officials having charge of matters connected with the exchange of prisoners.

This proposal has heretofore been declined by the Confederate authorities; they insisted upon the terms of the cartel, which required the delivery of the excess on either side on parole. In view, however, of the very large number of prisoners now held by each party, and the suffering consequent upon their continued confinement, I now consent to the above proposal, and agree to deliver to you the prisoners held in captivity by the Confederate authorities, provided you agree to deliver an equal number of Confederate officers and men. As equal numbers are delivered from time to time, they will be declared exchanged. This proposal is made with the understanding that the officers and men on both sides who have been longest in captivity will be first delivered, where it is practicable.

I shall be happy to hear from you as speedily as possible, whether this arrangement can be carried out.

Respectfully, your obedient servant,

Ro. Ould, *Agent of Exchange.*

The delivery of this letter was accompanied with a statement of the mortality which was hurrying so many Federal prisoners at Andersonville to the grave.

On the 22d day of August, 1864, not having heard anything in response, I addressed a communication to Major-general E. A. Hitchcock, United States Commissioner of Exchange, covering a copy of the foregoing letter to General Mulford, and requesting an acceptance of my propositions.

No answer was received to either of these letters. General Mulford, on the 31st of August, 1864, informed me in writing that he had no communication on the subject from the United States authorities, and that he was not at that time authorised to make any answer.

This offer, which would have instantly restored to freedom thousands of suffering captives—which would have released every Federal soldier in confinement in Confederate prisons—was not even noticed. Was that because the Federal officials did not deem it worthy of a reply, or because they feared to make one? As the Federal authorities at that time had a large excess of prisoners, the effect of the proposal which I had made, if carried out, would have been to release all Union prisoners; while a large number of the Confederates would have remained in prison, awaiting the chances of the capture of their equivalents.

II.

In January, 1864, and, indeed, some time earlier, it became very manifest, that in consequence of the complication in relation to exchanges, the large bulk of prisoners on both sides would remain in captivity for many long and weary months, if not for the duration of the war. Prompted by an earnest desire to alleviate the hardships of confinement on both sides, I addressed the following communication to General E. A. Hitchcock, United States Commissioner of Exchange, and on or about the day of its date delivered the same to the Federal authority:

CONFEDERATE STATES OF AMERICA, WAR DEPARTMENT,
RICHMOND, VA., *January 24th*, 1868.

Major-general E. A. HITCHCOCK, *Agent of Exchange:*

SIR:—In view of the present difficulties attending the exchange and release of prisoners, I propose that all such on each side shall be attended by a proper number of their own surgeons, who, under rules to be established, shall be permitted to take charge of their health and comfort.

I also propose that these surgeons shall act as commissaries, with power to receive and distribute such contributions of money, food, clothing, and medicines as may be forwarded for the relief of prisoners. I further propose that these surgeons be selected by their own Governments, and that they shall have full liberty at any and all times, through the agents of exchange, to make reports, not only of their own acts, but of any matters relating to the welfare of prisoners.

Respectfully your obedient servant,

ROBERT OULD, *Agent of Exchange.*

To this communication no reply of any kind was ever made. I need not state how much suffering would have been prevented if this offer had been met in the spirit in which it was dictated. In addition, the world would have had truthful accounts of the treatment of prisoners on both sides, by officers of character, and thus much of that misrepresentation which has flooded the country would never have been poured forth. The jury-box in the case of Wirz would have had different witnesses, with a different story. It will be borne in mind that nearly all of the suffering endured by Federal prisoners happened after January, 1864. The acceptance of the proposition made by me, on behalf of the Confederate Government, would not only have furnished to the sick, medicines and physicians, but to the well an abundance of food and clothing from the ample stores of the United States.

The good faith of the Confederate Government in making this offer cannot be successfully questioned, for food and clothing (without the surgeons) were sent in 1865, and were allowed to be distributed by Federal officers to Federal prisoners.

Why could not the more humane proposal of January, 1864, have been accepted?

III.

When it was ascertained that exchanges could not be made, either on the basis of the cartel, or officer for officer and man for man, I was instructed by the Confederate authorities to offer to the United States Government their sick and wounded, *without requiring any equivalents.* Accordingly, in the summer of 1864, I did offer to deliver from ten to fifteen thousand of the sick and wounded at the mouth of the Savannah river, without requiring any equivalents, assuring, at the same time, the Agent of the United States, General Mulford, that if the number for which he might send transportation could not readily be made up from sick and wounded, I would supply the difference with well men. Although this offer was made in the summer of 1864, transportation was not sent to the Savannah river until about the middle or last of November, and then I delivered as many prisoners as could be transported—some thirteen thousand in number—amongst whom were more than five thousand well men.

More than once I urged the mortality at Andersonville as a reason of haste on the part of the United States authorities. I know, personally, that it was the purpose of the Confederate Government to send off from all its prisons all the sick and wounded, and to continue to do the same, from time to time, without requiring any equivalents for them. It was because the sick and wounded at points distant from Georgia could not be brought to Savannah within a reasonable time, that the five thousand well men were substituted.

Although the terms of my offer did not require the Federal authorities to deliver any for the ten or fifteen thousand which I promised, yet some three thousand sick and wounded were delivered by them at the mouth of the Savannah river. I call upon every Federal and Confederate officer and man, who saw the cargo of living death, and who is familiar with the character of the deliveries made by the Confederate authorities, to bear witness that none such was ever made by the latter, even when the very sick and desperately wounded alone were requested. For, on two occasions at least, such were specially asked for, and particular request was made for those who were so desperately sick that it would be doubtful whether they would survive a removal a few miles down James river. Accordingly, the hospitals were searched for the worst cases, and after they were delivered they were taken to Annapolis, and there photographed as specimen prisoners. The photographs at Annapolis were terrible indeed; but the misery they portrayed was surpassed at Savannah.

The original rolls showed that some thirty-five hundred had started from Northern prisons, and that death had reduced the number during the transit to about three thousand. The mortality, amongst those who were delivered alive, during the following three months, was equally frightful.

But why was there this delay between the summer and November in sending transportation for sick and wounded, for whom no equivalents were asked? Were Union prisoners made to suffer in order to aid the photographs "in firing the popular heart of the North"?

IV.

In the summer of 1864, in consequence of certain information communicated to me by the Surgeon-general of the Confederate States as to the deficiency of medicines, I offered to make purchases of medicines from the United States authorities, to be used exclusively for the relief of Federal prisoners. I offered to pay gold, cotton or tobacco for them, and even two or three prices, if required. At the same time I gave assurances that the medicines would be used exclusively in the treatment of Federal prisoners; and moreover agreed, on behalf of the Confederate States, if it was insisted on, that such medicines might be brought into the Confederate lines by the United States surgeons, and dispensed by them. To this offer I never received any reply. Incredible as this appears, it is strictly true.

V.

General John E. Mulford is personally cognisant of the truth of most, if not all, the facts which I have narrated. He was connected with the cartel from its date until the close of the war. During a portion of the time he was Assistant Agent of Exchange on the part of the United States. I always found him to be an honorable and truthful gentleman. While he discharged his duties with great fidelity to his own Government, he was kind, and, I might almost say, tender to Confederate prisoners. With that portion of the correspondence with which his name is connected he is, of course, familiar. He is equally so with the delivery made at Savannah, and its attending circumstances, and with the offer I made as to the purchase of medicines for the Federal sick and wounded. I appeal to him for the truth of what I have written. There are other Federal corroborations to portions of my statements.

They are found in the report of Major-general B. F. Butler to the "Committee on the Conduct of the War." About the last of March, 1864, I had several conferences with General Butler at Fortress Monroe in relation to the difficulties attending the exchange of prisoners, and we reached what we both thought a tolerably satisfactory basis.

The day that I left there, General Grant arrived. General Butler says he communicated to him the state of the negotiations, and "most emphatic verbal directions were received from the Lieutenant-general not to take any step by which another able-bodied man should be exchanged until further orders from him"; and that on April 30, 1864, he received a telegram from General Grant, "to receive all the sick and wounded the Confederate authorities may send you, but send no more in exchange." Unless my recollection fails me, General Butler also, in an address to his constituents, substantially declared that he was directed in his management of the question of exchange with the Confederate authorities, to put the matter offensively, *for the purpose of preventing an exchange.*

The facts which I have stated are also well known to the officers connected with the Confederate Bureau of Exchange.

At one time I thought an excellent opportunity was offered of bringing some of them to the attention of the country. I was named by poor Wirz as a witness in his behalf. The summons was issued by Chipman, the Judge-advocate of the military court. I obeyed the summons, and was in attendance upon the court for some ten days. The investigation had taken a wide range as to the conduct of the Confederate and Federal Governments in the matter of the treatment of prisoners, and I thought the time had come when I could put before the world these humane offers of the Confederate authorities, and the manner in which they had been treated. I so expressed myself more than once—perhaps too publicly. But it was a vain thought.

Early in the morning of the day on which I expected to give my testimony, I received a note from Chipman, the judge advocate, requiring me to surrender my subpœna. I refused, as it was my protection in Washington. Without it the doors of the Old Capitol might have been opened and closed upon me. I engaged, however, to appear before the court, and I did so the same morning. I still refused to surrender my subpœna, and thereupon the judge-advocate endorsed on it these words: "The within subpœna is hereby revoked; the person named is discharged from further attendance." I have got the curious document before me now, signed with the name of "N. P. Chipman, Colonel," &c. I intend to keep it, if I can, as the evidence of the first case *in any court of any sort*, where a witness who was summoned *for the defence* was dismissed *by the prosecution.* I hastened to depart, confident that Richmond was a safer place for me than the metropolis.

Some time ago a committee was appointed by the House of Representatives to investigate the treatment of Union prisoners in Southern prisons. After the appointment of the committee —the Hon. Mr. Shanks, of Indiana, being its chairman—I wrote to the Hon. Charles A. Eldridge and the Hon. Mr. Mungen (the latter a member of the committee) some of the facts herein detailed. Both of these gentlemen made an effort to extend the authority of the committee, so that it might inquire into the treatment of prisoners North as well as South, and especially that it might inquire into the truth of the matters which I had alleged. All these attempts were frustrated by the Radical majority, although several of the party voted to extend the inquiry. As several thousand dollars of the money of the people have been spent by this committee, will not they demand that the investigation shall be thorough and impartial? The House of Representatives have declined the inquiry; let the people take it up.

Respectfully, your obedient servant,

ROBERT OULD.

CHAPTER XII.

Mr. Stephens says further, in his testimony in regard to the alleged differences as to the "external" and "internal" policy of the Government of the Confederate States, between himself and Mr. Davis, that, "These differences, however wide and thorough they were, as we shall see, caused no personal breach between us. None of them, moreover, related to the general treatment of prisoners. *On that point there was no disagreement between us.*" Says he:—This whole subject of the treatment of prisoners, which has become so prominent a feature in considering the conduct of the war on both sides, from the turn which has been given to it, I may as well dispose of here, at once and finally. This I do, by stating broadly that the charge of cruelty and inhumanity towards prisoners, which has been so extensively made at the North against Mr. Davis and the Confederate authorities, is utterly without foundation in fact. From the commencement and throughout the war, the whole course of Mr. Davis toward prisoners shows conclusively the perfect recklessness of the charge. His position on this subject in the beginning clearly appears from what we have seen, and that fully sustains this statement. The efforts which have been so industriously made to fix the odium of cruelty and barbarity upon him and other high officials under the Confederate Government, in the matter of prisoners, in the face of all the facts, constitute one of the boldest and baldest attempted outrages upon the truth of history which has ever been essayed; not less so than the infamous attempt to fix upon him and other high officials on the Confederate side, the guilt of Mr. Lincoln's assassination! Whatever unnecessary privations and sufferings prisoners on both sides were subjected to, the responsibility of the whole rested not upon Mr. Davis or the Confederate authorities. It is (says he) not my purpose to go into a full history of the subject. This would take more time than is at all necessary. A few leading facts will settle the matter.

Let it be borne in mind then, that the Confederates were ever anxious for a speedy exchange, and that after the interruption of the exchange under the cartel first agreed upon. As before stated, another arrangement was entered into by the Federals, under pressure of public sentiment at the North, when the excess was against them. This was afterward likewise broken. It was broken, not by the Confederates, but by the Federals, upon some pretext or other. Throughout the struggle, Mr. Davis's conduct and bearing upon this point not only challenge the severest scrutiny of the fair-minded of this day, but will command the admiration of the just and generous for all time to come. In addition to what has been shown heretofore, what higher evidence on this point could be desired than that furnished by his congratulatory address to the army of Gen. Lee, for the successes achieved in the battles around Richmond, when McClellan, with his newly organised host of at least one hundred and twenty thousand men, made the second unsuccessful attempt to take the Confederate capital in 1862, and when over *ten thousand Federal prisoners* had fallen into our hands? In this hour of triumph, mark the significant, as well as magnanimous, and even chivalrous language, which came spontaneously from his heart on that occasion:—*You are fighting for all that is dearest to men; and though opposed to a foe who disregards many of the usages of civilised war, your humanity to the wounded and to the prisoners was the fit and crowning glory to your valor.*"

Prof. Norton.—Yes, but how did he act toward these same prisoners afterward? What did he do to relieve the horrors they suffered in Libby and on Belle Island, almost in the range of his sight, to say nothing of the sufferings of those at Salisbury and Andersonville, of which he must have been apprised? Why was his humanity and magnanimity so deaf to the appeals and dying wails of these men, which went up from those places so near his own doors, and almost within his hearing?

Mr. Stephens.—The horrors of Libby and Belle Island, as well as of Salisbury and Andersonville, so pathetically set forth by many, and great as they really were, were not his fault, or in any way justly chargeable upon him.

Prof. Norton.—Whose fault was it? Was he not at the head of the Government? Did he not know of these sufferings, and who but himself could be justly responsible for them?

Mr. Stephens.—It was the fault of the Federal authorities, in not agreeing to and carrying out an immediate exchange, which Mr. Davis was at all times anxious to do. The men at the head of affairs at Washington were solely responsible for all these sufferings. Upon these officials, and upon them only, can these sufferings be justly charged. Neither Libby, nor Belle Island, nor Salisbury, nor Andersonville would have had a groaning prisoner of war, but for the refusal of the Federal authorities to comply with the earnest desire of the Richmond Government for an immediate exchange upon the most liberal and humane principles. Had Mr. Davis's repeated offers been accepted, no prisoner on either side would have been retained in confinement a day. All the sufferings and loss of life, therefore, during the entire war, growing out of these imprisonments on both sides (it is not my wish to understate or underrate them on either) are justly chargeable to but one side, and that is the Federal side.

Prof. Norton.—But if the Federal authorities did refuse to carry out an exchange of prisoners for any cause whatever, this certainly did not justify the Confederates in adopting a regular systematic policy of starving the unfortunate men taken by them in arms, and of withholding proper medical remedies and attention from the wounded and sick, nor mitigate, in the least, the savage cruelties which were perpetrated upon them by such men as Wirz?

Mr. Stephens.—It certainly did not, or would not have justified such policy or acts. But it is not true that there was any such thing as the systematic policy you speak of, either in starving the well, or withholding medical remedies and attention from the sick and wounded. The policy of the Confederates in these particulars was established by law. By an Act of Congress, passed soon after the war was inaugurated, as I have shown, it was provided that prisoners of war should have the same rations in quantity and quality as the Confederate soldiers in the field. By an act afterwards passed, all hospitals for sick and wounded prisoners were put upon the same footing with hospitals for sick and wounded Confederates. This policy was never changed. Whatever food or fare the Confederate soldiers had, whether good or bad, full or short, the Federal prisoners shared *equally* with them. Whatever medical attention the sick and wounded Confederate soldiers had, the Federal prisoners in like condition also received. When the supply of the usual standard medicines was exhausted, and could not be replenished, in consequence of the action of the Federal Government in holding them to be contraband of war, and in preventing their introduction, by blockade and severe penalties—when resort was had to the virtue of the healing herbs of the country as substitutes for more efficient remedial agents, the suffering Federal shared these equally with like suffering Confederates. Did the requirements of perfect justice and right go beyond this? Could humanity ask more? As for particular instances of cruelty on the part of subordinates who may have been untrue to their trusts, that is a very different matter. There were unquestionably very great wrongs of this sort on both sides. Wirz, to whom you have alluded, may have committed some of these. How this was I really don't know.* He, by-the-by, was not one of our people. He was a European by birth,

* No full and authentic account of "Captain Wirz and Andersonville" had yet been published by any Southern author. Hence Mr. Stephens could give no positive opinions or data upon the subject.

who obtained position in our service through letters of recommendation which warranted confidence in his intelligence and good character. I know nothing to his discredit in either of these respects, except the allegations you refer to. Whether they were true or false, as I have said, I do not know. It is due to his memory, however, to recollect, that his own dying declarations were against the truth of these accusations. This, moreover, I can, and do venture to say, that acts of much greater cruelty and barbarity than any which were proven against him could have been easily established, and would have been established on his trial, against numerous subordinates on the Federal side, if the tendered proof had not been rejected. I have been informed by returned Confederate prisoners, of unquestionable truth and veracity, from Camp Douglas, Rock Island, Elmira, and Point Lookout, of numerous instances which came under their immediate observation, of much greater atrocity than anything alleged against Wirz. These acts, many of which were of the most inhuman and barbarous character, were perpetrated by Federal subordinates having control of Confederate prisoners at these points. There may have been, therefore, and I do not question but that there were, great wrongs of this sort on the part of Confederate subordinates, as there certainly were on the part of the Federals. But what I maintain is, that such conduct never met the approval of the Confederate authorities. They never, in a single instance, *sanctioned*, much less ordered, well demeaning and unoffending prisoners of war to be confined in unwholesome dungeons, and to be manacled with cuffs and irons, as was repeatedly done, by orders from the authorities at Washington, in utter violation of the well-established usages of modern civilised warfare. But apart from this marked difference between the two Governments in their highest official character, in sanctioning and ordering acts of wanton cruelty, I insist upon the irrefutable fact, that but for the refusal of the Federals to carry out an exchange, none of the wrongs or outrages you speak of, none of the sufferings incident to prison-life on either side, could have occurred.

Prof. Norton.—If there was no such systematic purpose to torture and literally to kill Federal prisoners, why were thirty thousand of them huddled together at Andersonville, in the sickly region of southwestern Georgia, where, from the malarious influences prevailing under a burning sun, so many of them died, as must have been necessarily expected?

Mr. Stephens.—Large numbers of them were taken to southwestern Georgia in 1864, because it was a section most remote and secure from the invading Federals, and because, too, it was a country of all others then within the Confederate limits, not thus threatened with an invasion, most abundant with food, and all resources at command for health and comfort of prisoners. *They were put in one stockade for the want of men to guard more than one.* The section of country, moreover, was not regarded as more unhealthy or more subject to malarious influences than any in the central part of the State. The official order for the erection of the stockade enjoined that it should be in a healthy locality, plenty of pure water, a running stream, and, if possible, shade trees, and in the immediate neighborhood of grist and saw-mills. The very selection of the locality, so far from being, as you suppose, made with cruel designs against the prisoners, was governed by the most humane considerations. Your question might, with much more point, be retorted by asking, Why were Southern prisoners taken in the dead of winter, with their thin clothing, to Camp Douglas, Rock Island and Johnson's Island—icy regions of the North—where it is a notorious fact that many of them actually froze to death? As far as mortuary returns afford evidence of the general treatment of prisoners on both sides, the figures show nothing to the disadvantage of the Confederates, notwithstanding all that has been said of the horrible sacrifice of life at Andersonville. It now appears that a larger number of Confederates died in Northern, than Federals in Southern prisons or stockades. The report of Mr. Stanton, as Secretary of War, on the 19th of July, 1866, exhibits the fact that of the Federal prisoners in Confederate hands during the war, only 22,576 died; while of the Confederate prisoners in Federal hands, 26,436 died. This report does not set forth the exact number of prisoners held by each side respectively. These facts were given more in detail in a subsequent report by Surgeon-general Barnes, of the United States Army. His report I have not seen, but according to a statement, editorially, in the *National Intelligencer*—very high authority—it appears, from the Surgeon-general's report, that the whole number of Federal prisoners captured by the Confederates, and held in Southern prisons, from first to last during the war, was in round numbers 270,000; while the whole number of Confederates captured and held in prisons by the Federals was, in like round numbers, only 220,000. From these two reports, it appears that, with 50,000 more prisoners in Southern stockades or other modes of confinement, the deaths were nearly 4000 less! According to these figures, the *percentum* of Federal deaths in Southern prisons was *under nine;* while the percentum of Confederate deaths in Northern prisons was *over twelve.* These mortality statistics are of no small weight in determining on which side there was the most neglect, cruelty, and inhumanity. But the great question in this matter is, *upon whom rests the tremendous responsibility of all this sacrifice of human life, with all its indescribable miseries and sufferings?* The facts, beyond question or doubt, show that it rests *entirely* upon the authorities at Washington. It is now well understood to have been a part of *their settled policy,* in conducting the war, not to exchange prisoners. The grounds upon which this extraordinary course was adopted were: That it was humanity to the men in the field, on their side, to let their captured comrades perish in prison, rather than to let an equal number of Confederate soldiers be released on exchange to meet them in battle. *Upon the Federal authorities, and upon them only, with this policy as their excuse, rests the whole of this responsibility. To avert the indignation which the open avowal of this policy by them at the time would have excited throughout the North, and throughout the civilised world, the false cry of cruelty towards prisoners was raised against the Confederates. This was but a pretext to cover up their own violation of the usages of war in this respect among civilised nations.*

Mr. Stephens still further pursuing his vindication of the Confederate authorities on the subject of humanity to prisoners of war, says:—There was also a difference between myself and some of the Confederate authorities, as to the best course to be pursued toward the Andersonville prisoners, to whom you (Prof. Norton) have especially referred, in the year 1864, as well as prisoners of war generally, then held by the Confederates after the Federals had refused all proffered terms for their relief by exchange. This difference, however, did not relate to their *treatment*, but to the most *politic* manner of disposing of them. On this point I thought policy and humanity were united. I did not confer directly with Mr. Davis upon it, but I did with several officers high in authority. To General Howell Cobb, who, then, as Major-general of the reserves in the military district of Georgia, had the general control of the custody and safe-keeping of the prisoners at Andersonville, I specially presented my views on the whole subject.

The condition of those at Andersonville at the time was indeed most pitiable and deplorable. . . Now, to General Cobb I suggested the propriety and expediency in a political point of view, as well as from the promptings of humanity, of sending these prisoners, as well as those confined at other points, home without any equivalent in return. My views presented to him, and to be presented by him, if he concurred, to Mr. Davis, were that Mr. Davis himself should visit and address the prisoners in person, in a way and manner in which I knew he was well fitted to do, if he approved the object; and after recapitulating all the facts in relation to exchange — after setting forth the nature of the war, and the objects for which we were struggling — after stating distinctly we were not fighting against the Union, but for the principles upon which the Union was based—for the rights of our common ancestors, which were as dear to them as to us — in short, after a full review of all the questions in issue by him thus to be presented, for him to extend to the prisoners an unconditional discharge. Such an unexampled act of generosity on his part, with copies of his address given to them by thousands, not only to be read and pondered by them, but to be distributed through the Northern States in the Presidential election pending that fall, I thought would effect a vast deal in determining the doubtful issue between the then opposing parties there, and upon which the most momentous results in my judgment depended; results of no less importance to us than to the friends of constitutional liberty there. My sympathies throughout the contest were, of course, thoroughly with those who were attempting at the ballot-box to put out of power the centralists, whose executive and congressional usurpations had already awakened an extensive alarm in most, if not all, the Northern States. The object of the centralists throughout the war had been, as the object of most of the writers since has been, to impress upon the minds of the people in the Northern States, that the Confederates were but a set of conspirators, whose chief design was to subvert the Constitution and overthrow the Government. It was my object, in this way, and in quarters which could not so well otherwise be reached, to disabuse the public mind there of this very erroneous sentiment; and that too by evidences almost as strong as those which the doubting Thomas required. These very unfortunate suffering prisoners—suffering from the inhumanity of their own high officials, who had beguiled them by false pretexts into this crusade against unoffending neighbors—so relieved and sent home to the bosom of their families and friends by such an act of mercy on our part, I thought would be the most effective instruments at our command for accomplishing this great end. The humblest one of them might, in my view, be a diplomat, with more power for good in the cause for which we were contending, than either of our able and accomplished commissioners abroad, seeking sympathy or favor at foreign courts.

The reply of General Cobb, as well as that of others to whom I presented these views, for the purpose of bringing them to the consideration of the administration at Richmond, was in substance, that if the Federal prisoners should be thus discharged, there would be no security for the safety of the gallant and equally suffering Confederates in Northern prisons. They might, he said, be tried and executed for treason, as the privateers-men had been tried and condemned to death for piracy. These had been saved only by the retaliatory course to which the Confederates had been compelled to resort; and that the only security the Confederates had against so monstrous an outrage upon their soldiers, was the Federal prisoners of war in hand, to be kept until regularly exchanged, as hostages against such threatened barbarity. General Cobb, as well as all others with whom I conferred on the subject, fully concurred with me in general sympathy for the condition of prisoners on both sides, and expressed an earnest desire to do all in their power for their relief consistent with public security, and with what was considered by them to be due to Confederates then in the hands and power of the Federals, who openly proclaimed their purpose to treat them and deal with them as traitors. . . .

It is proper also to state, that I did not concur to the full extent in the apprehensions entertained by General Cobb and others, as to the fate of Confederate prisoners, which might result from the course advised. The retention of a few thousand of the officers of the highest grade among the Federal prisoners in Confederate hands, would be ample security, I thought, against the judicial execution of any Confederate prisoner under the charge of piracy or treason; while the unconditional release of so many prisoners of war on our part, under all the circumstances of the case, would, in my judgment then and now, have produced a profound sensation with the masses of the people throughout the entire North, overwhelming in its effects upon the men in authority at Washington. It might have produced a general release of prisoners, as well as the removal of these officials from place and power.

Under a Cabinet consultation, Mr. Davis accepted the generous offer of Mr. Stephens, who wished to proceed to Washington for the purpose of treating with the Federal Government on the subject of the release of the prisoners, by seeking to reëstablish the cartel of exchange on a fair basis, as well as endeavoring to stay the barbarous and cruel acts of such Federal officers as Major-general D. Hunter, and others, in their useless and uncalled-for treatment of women, children and non-combatants. Mr. Davis's commission to Mr. Stephens reads as follows:

RICHMOND, *July 2d*, 1863

Hon. ALEXANDER H. STEPHENS, *Richmond, Va.*

SIR:—Having accepted your patriotic offer to proceed, as a military commissioner, under flag-of-truce, to Washington, you will herewith receive your letter of authority to the Commander-in-Chief of the Army and Navy of the United States.

This letter is signed by me as Commander-in-Chief of the Confederate land and naval forces.

You will perceive, from the terms of the letter, that it is so worded as to avoid any political difficulties in its reception. Intended exclusively as one of those communications between belligerents which public law recognises as necessary and proper between hostile forces, care has been taken to give no pretext for refusing to receive it on the ground that it would involve a tacit recognition of the independence of the Confederacy.

Your mission is simply one of humanity, and has no political aspect.

If objection is made to receive your letter on the ground that it is not addressed to Abraham Lincoln as President, instead of Commander-in-Chief, &c., then you will present the duplicate letter, which is addressed to him as President, and signed by me as President. To this letter, objection may be made on the ground that I am not recognised to be President of the Confederacy. In this event, you will decline any further attempt to confer on the subject of your mission, as such conference is admissible only on a footing of perfect equality.

My recent interviews with you have put you so fully in possession of my views, that it is scarcely necessary to give you any detailed instructions, even were I at this moment well enough to attempt it.

My whole purpose is, in one word, to place this war on the footing of such as are waged by civilised people in modern times, and to divest it of the savage character which has been impressed on it by our enemies, in spite of all our efforts and protests. War is full enough of unavoidable horrors, under all its aspects, to justify, and even to demand of any Christian ruler, who may be unhappily engaged in carrying it on, to seek to restrict its calamities, and to divest it of all unnecessary severities.

You will endeavor to establish the cartel for the exchange of prisoners on such a basis as to avoid the constant difficulties and complaints which arise, and to prevent for the future what we deem the unfair conduct of our enemies, in evading the delivery of prisoners who fall into their hands, in retarding it by sending them on circuitous routes, and by detaining them sometimes for months in camps and prisons, and in persisting in taking captive non-combatants.

Your attention is also called to the unheard-of conduct of Federal officers in driving from their homes entire communities of women and children, as well as of men, whom they find in districts occupied by their troops, for no other reason than because these unfortunates are faithful to the allegiance due to their States, and refuse to take an oath of fidelity to their enemies.

The putting to death of unarmed prisoners has been a ground of just complaint in more than one instance; and the recent execution of officers of our army in Kentucky, for the sole cause that they were engaged in recruiting service in a State which is claimed as still one of the United States, but is also claimed by us as one of the Confederate States, must be repressed by retaliation, if not unconditionally abandoned, because it would justify the like execution in every other State of the Confederacy; and the practice is barbarous, uselessly cruel, and can only lead to the slaughter of prisoners on both sides, a result too horrible to contemplate without making every effort to avoid it.

On this and all kindred subjects you will consider your authority full and ample, to make such arrangements as will temper the present cruel character of the contest; and full confidence is placed in your judgment, patriotism, and discretion, that, while carrying out the objects of your mission, you will take care that the equal rights of the Confederacy be always preserved.

Very respectfully,

JEFFERSON DAVIS.

The results of this mission are given by Mr. Stephens in his work on the "Constitutional View of the War," in which he says:—"At first, the arrangement was for me to proceed by land in the route taken by General Lee's army, and communicate with the Washington authorities from his headquarters. Excessive rains, badness of roads, and tardiness of travelling in consequence, caused a change in this arrangement. A small steamer was put in readiness by orders of Mr. Mallory, of the Navy Department, and I, with Mr. Robert Ould, the distinguished agent for the exchange of prisoners on our side, a gentleman of high accomplishments and attainments, who had been appointed secretary of the commission, set out in this way directly for Washington City, if we should be permitted to pass the Federal lines at Fortress Monroe. The sequel is known; the great battles of Gettysburg were fought before we reached Newport News. There our arrival and proposal were telegraphed to Washington by Acting Rear Admiral S. P. Lee, of the U. S. Navy, commanding the blockade squadron at that point. We were detained two days, while the proposition for the conference was held under consideration at Washington. In the meantime, Vicksburg was surrendered by General Pemberton on the 4th day of July — earlier than was expected. The reply from Washington then came, that '*no special commissioner on the subjects embraced in the proposed conference would be received.*' "

CHAPTER XIII.

We now approach the last official acts of the Confederate Government on the subject of the treatment of prisoners of war. With the sagacity and foresight for which he was characterised, Colonel Robert Ould, true to the cause he had espoused, and in the interest of the reputation of the Southern people, succeeded in getting a joint congressional committee at Richmond, whose duty it was to investigate the condition of the prisoners of both sides. A large amount of testimony was taken before it; but unfortunately the papers were destroyed by fire. This committee made a report, however, based on the testimony taken before it, some time in February, 1865, which has been preserved. It is an important document, and fully sustains the points given throughout this work. It reads as follows

Report of the Joint Select Committee of the Confederate Congress, appointed to investigate the condition and treatment of prisoners of war.

The duties assigned to the committee, under the several resolutions of Congress designating them, are, "to investigate and report upon the condition and treatment of the prisoners of war respectively held by the Confederate and United States Governments, upon the causes of their detention and the refusal to exchange; and also upon the violations by the enemy of the rules of civilised warfare in the conduct of the war." These subjects are broad in extent and importance; and in order fully to investigate and present them, the committee propose to continue their labors in obtaining evidence, and deducing from it a truthful report of facts illustrative of the spirit in which the war has been conducted.

But we deem it proper, at this time, to make a preliminary report, founded upon evidence recently taken, relating to the treatment of prisoners of war by both belligerents. This report is rendered especially important, by reason of persistent efforts lately made by the Government of the United States, and by associations and individuals connected or coöperating with it, to asperse the honor of the Confederate authorities, and to charge them with deliberate and wilful cruelty to prisoners of war. Two publications have been issued at the North within the past year, and have been circulated not only in the United States, but in some parts of the South and in Europe. One of these is the report of the joint select committee of the Northern Congress on the conduct of the war, known as "Report No. 67"; the other purports to be a "Narrative of the privations and sufferings of United States officers and soldiers while prisoners of war," and is issued as a report of a commission of inquiry, appointed by "the United States Sanitary Commission." This body is alleged to consist of Valentine Mott, M. D., Edward Delafield, M. D., Gouverneur Morris Wilkins, Esq., Ellerslie Wallace, M. D., Hon. J.

J. Clark Hare, and Rev. Treadwell Walden. Although these persons are not of sufficient public importance and weight to give authority to their publication, yet your committee have deemed it proper to notice it in connection with the "Report No. 67," before mentioned, because the Sanitary Commission has been understood to have acted to a greater extent under the control and by authority of the United States Government, and because their report claims to be founded on evidence taken in solemn form.

A candid reader of these publications will not fail to discover that, whether the statements they make be true or not, their spirit is not adapted to promote a better feeling between the hostile powers. They are not intended for the humane purpose of ameliorating the condition of the unhappy prisoners held in captivity. They are designed to inflame the evil passions of the North, to keep up the war-spirit among their own people; to represent the South as acting under a spirit of cruelty, inhumanity and interested malice, and thus to vilify her people in the eyes of all on whom these publications can work. They are justly characterised by the Hon. James M. Mason, as belonging to that class of literature called the "sensational," a style of writing which has been prevalent for many years at the North, and which, beginning with the writers of newspaper narratives and cheap fiction, has gradually extended itself, until it is now the favorite mode adopted by medical professors, judges of courts, and reverend clergymen, and is even chosen as the proper style for a report by a committee of their Congress.

Nothing can better illustrate the truth of this view than the "Report No. 67," and its appendages. It is accompanied by eight pictures or photographs, alleged to represent United States prisoners of war returned from Richmond in a sad state of emaciation and suffering. Concerning these cases your committee will have other remarks, to be presently submitted. They are only alluded to now, to show that this report does really belong to the "sensational" class of literature, and that *prima facie* it is open to the same criticism to which the yellow-covered novels, the "narratives of noted highwaymen," and the "awful beacons" of the Northern bookstalls, should be subjected.

The intent and spirit of this report may be gathered from the following extract:—"The evidence proves, beyond all manner of doubt, a determination on the part of rebel authorities, deliberately and persistently practised for a long time past, to subject those of our soldiers who have been so unfortunate as to fall into their hands, to a system of treatment which has resulted in reducing many of those who have survived and been permitted to return to us, to a condition, both physically and mentally, which no language can adequately describe." (Report, p. 1.)

And they give also a letter from Edwin M. Stanton, the Northern Secretary of War, from which the following is an extract:—"The enormity of the crime committed by the rebels toward our prisoners for the last several months, is not known or realised by our people, and cannot but fill with horror the civilised world, when the facts are fully revealed. There appears to have been a deliberate system of savage and barbarous treatment and starvation, the result of which will be that few, if any, of the prisoners that have been in their hands during the past winter, will ever again be in a condition to render any service, or even to enjoy life." (Report, p. 4.)

The Sanitary Commission, in their pamphlet, after picturing many scenes of privations and sufferings, and bringing many charges of cruelty against the Confederate authorities, declare as follows:—"The conclusion is unavoidable therefore, that these privations and sufferings have been designedly inflicted by the military and other authorities of the rebel government, and could not have been due to causes which such authorities could not control." (p. 95.)

After examining these publications, your committee approached the subject with an earnest desire to ascertain the truth. If their investigation should result in ascertaining that these charges, or any of them, were true, the committee desired, as far as might be in their power, and as far as they could influence the Congress, to remove the evils complained of, and to conform to the most humane spirit of civilisation; and if these charges were unfounded and false, they deemed it a sacred duty, without delay, to present to the Confederate Congress and people, and to the public eye of the enlightened world, a vindication of their country, and to relieve her authorities from the injurious slanders brought against her by her enemies. With these views, we have taken a considerable amount of testimony bearing on the subject. We have sought to obtain witnesses whose position or duties made them familiar with the facts testified to, and whose characters entitled them to full credit. We have not hesitated to examine Northern prisoners of war upon points and experience specially within their knowledge. We now present the testimony taken by us, and submit a report of facts and inferences fairly deducible from the evidence, from the admission of our enemies, and from public records of undoubted authority.

First in order, your committee will notice the charge contained both in "Report No. 67" and in the "Sanitary" publication, founded on the appearance and condition of the sick prisoners sent from Richmond to Annapolis and Baltimore, about the last of April, 1864. These are the men, some of whom form the subjects of the photographs with which the United States Congressional Committee have adorned their report. The disingenuous attempt is made in both these publications, to produce the impression that these sick and emaciated men were fair representatives of the general state of the prisoners held by the South, and that all their prisoners were being rapidly reduced to the same state by starvation and cruelty, and by neglect, ill-treatment, and denial of proper food, stimulants, and medicines in the Confederate hospitals. Your committee

INSPECTION OF SICK FOR EXCHANGE.

take pleasure in saying that, not only is this charge proved to be wholly false, but the evidence ascertains facts as to the Confederate hospitals, in which Northern prisoners of war are treated, highly creditable to the authorities who established them, and to the surgeons and their aids who have so humanely conducted them. The facts are simply these:

The Federal authorities, in violation of the cartel, having for a long time refused exchange of prisoners, finally consented to partial exchange of the sick and wounded on both sides. Accordingly, a number of such prisoners were sent from the hospitals in Richmond. General directions had been given that none should be sent except those who might be expected to endure the removal and passage with safety to their lives; but in some cases the surgeons were induced to depart from this rule, by the entreaties of some officers and men in the last stages of emaciation, suffering not only with excessive debility, but with "nostalgia," or home-sickness, whose cases were regarded as desperate, and who could not live if they remained, and might possibly improve if carried home. Thus it happened that some very sick and emaciated men were carried to Annapolis, but their illness was not the result of ill-treatment or neglect. Such cases might be found in any large hospital, North or South. They might even be found in private families, where the sufferer would be surrounded by every comfort that love could bestow. Yet these are the cases which, with hideous violation of decency, the Northern Committee have paraded in pictures and photographs. They have taken their own sick and enfeebled soldiers, have stripped them naked, have exposed them before a daguerrean apparatus, have pictured every shrunken limb and muscle, and all for the purpose, not of relieving their sufferings, but of bringing a false and slanderous charge against the South.

The evidence is overwhelming that the illness of these (Federal) prisoners was not the result of ill-treatment and neglect. The testimony of surgeons Semple and Spence, of assistant-surgeons Tinsley, Marriott and Miller, and of the Federal prisoners, E. P. Dalrymble, George Henry Brown, and Freeman B. Teague, ascertains this to the satisfaction of every candid mind. But in refuting this charge your committee are compelled, by the evidence, to bring a counter-charge against the Northern authorities, which they fear will not be so easily refuted. In exchange, a number of Confederate sick and wounded prisoners have been, at various times, delivered at Richmond and at Savannah. The mortality among these on their passage, and their condition when delivered, were so deplorable as to justify the charge that they had been treated with inhuman neglect by the Northern authorities. Assistant-surgeon Tinsley testifies:—"I have seen many of our prisoners, returned from the North, who were nothing but skin and bones. They were as emaciated as a man could be to retain life, and the photographs (appended to Report No. 67) would not be exaggerated representations of our returned prisoners to whom I thus allude. I saw two hundred and fifty of our sick brought in on litters from the steamer at Rockett's; thirteen dead bodies were brought off the steamer the same night. At least thirty died in one night after they were received." Surgeon Spence testifies:—"I was at Savannah, and saw rather over three thousand prisoners received. The list showed that a large number had died on the passage from Baltimore to Savannah. The number sent from the Federal prisons was three thousand and twenty-eight, to the best of my recollection. Captain Hatch can give you the exact number. I was told that sixty-seven dead bodies had been taken from one train of cars between Elmira and Baltimore. After being received at Savannah, they had the best attention possible, yet many died in a few days." In carrying out the exchange of disabled, sick, and wounded men, we delivered at Savannah and Charleston about eleven thousand Federal prisoners, and their physical condition compared most favorably with those we received in exchange, although of course the worst cases among the Confederates had been removed by death during the passage.

Richard H. Dibrell, a merchant of Richmond, and a member of the "ambulance committee," whose labors in mitigating the sufferings of the wounded have been acknowledged both by Confederate and Northern men, thus testifies concerning our sick and wounded soldiers at Savannah, returned from Northern prisons and hospitals:—"I have never seen a set of men in worse condition. They were so enfeebled and emaciated that we lifted them like little children. Many of them were like living skeletons. Indeed, there was one poor boy, about seventeen years old, who presented the most distressing and deplorable appearance I ever saw. He was nothing but skin and bone, and besides this, he was literally eaten up with vermin. He died in the hospital a few days after being removed thither, notwithstanding the kindest treatment and the use of the most judicious nourishment. Our men were in so reduced a condition, that on more than one trip upon the short passage of ten miles from the transports to the city, as many as five died. The clothing of the privates was in a wretched state of tatters and filth. The mortality on the passage from Maryland was very great, as well as that on the passage from the prisons to the port from which they started. I cannot state the exact number, but I think I heard that three thousand five hundred were started, and we only received about three thousand and twenty-seven. Thus about 473 died on the passage. I have looked at the photographs appended to 'Report No. 67' of the committee of the Federal Congress, and do not hesitate to declare that several of our men were worse cases of emaciation and sickness than any represented in these photographs." The testimony of Mr. Dibrell is confirmed by that of Andrew Johnston, also a merchant of Richmond, and a member of the "ambulance committee."

Thus it appears that the sick and wounded Federal prisoners at Annapolis, whose condition has been made a subject of outcry and of widespread complaint by the Northern Congress, were not in a worse state than were the Confederate prisoners returned from Northern hospitals and prisons, of which the humanity and superior management are made subjects of special boasting by the United States Sanitary Commission.

In connection with this subject, your committee take pleasure in reporting the facts ascertained by their investigations concerning the Confederate hospitals for sick and wounded Federal prisoners. They have made personal examination, and have taken evidence, especially in relation to "Hospital No. 21," in Richmond, because this has been made subject of distinct charge in the publication last mentioned. It has been shown, not only by the evidence of the surgeons and their assistants, but by that of Federal prisoners, that the treatment of the Northern prisoners in these hospitals has been everything that humanity could dictate; that their wards have been well ventilated and clean, their food the best that could be procured for them; and, in fact, that no distinction had been made between their treatment and that of our own sick and wounded men. Moreover, it is proved that it has been the constant practice to supply to the patients, out of the hospital funds, such articles as milk, butter, eggs, tea and other delicacies, when they were required by the condition of the patients. This is proved by the testimony of E. P. Dalrymble, of New York; George Henry Brown, of Pennsylvania; and Freeman B. Teague, of New Hampshire, whose depositions accompany this report.

This humane and considerate usage was not adopted in the United States hospital on Johnson's Island, where Confederate sick and wounded officers were treated. Col. J. H. Hilman thus testifies:—"The Federal authorities did not furnish to the sick prisoners the nutriment and other articles which were prescribed by their own surgeons. All they would do was to permit the prisoners to buy the nutriment or stimulants needed; and if they had no money, they could not get them. I know this, for I was in the hospital sick myself, and I had to buy myself such articles as eggs, milk, flour, chickens and butter, after their doctors had prescribed them. And I know this was generally the case, for we had to get up a fund among ourselves for this purpose, to aid those who were not well supplied with money." This statement is confirmed by the testimony of Acting-assistant John J. Miller, who was at Johnson's Island for more than eight months. When it is remembered that such articles as eggs, milk and butter were very scarce and high-priced in Richmond, and plentiful and cheap at the North, the contrast thus presented may well put to shame the "Sanitary Commission," and dissipate the self-complacency with which they have boasted of the superior humanity in the Northern prisons and hospitals.

Your committee now proceed to notice other charges in these publications. It is said that their prisoners were habitually stripped of their blankets and other property, on being captured. What pillage may have been committed on the battle-field, after the excitement of combat, your committee cannot know. But they feel well assured that such pillage was never encouraged by the Confederate generals, and bore no comparison to the wholesale robbery and destruction to which the Federal armies have abandoned themselves, in possessing parts of our territory. It is certain that after the prisoners were brought to the Libby and other prisons in Richmond, no such pillage was permitted. Only articles which came properly under the head of munitions of war, were taken from them.

The next charge noticed is, that the guards around the Libby prison were in the habit of recklessly and inhumanly shooting at the prisoners, upon the most frivolous pretexts; and that the Confederate officers, so far from forbidding this, rather encouraged it, and made it a subject of sportive remark. This charge is wholly false and baseless. The "Rules and Regulations," appended tc the deposition of Major Thomas P. Turner, expressly provide, "Nor shall any prisoner be fired upon by a sentinel or other person, except in case of revolt or attempted escape." Five or six cases have occurred in which prisoners have been fired on and killed or hurt; but every case has been made the subject of careful investigation and report, as will appear by the evidence. As a proper comment on this charge, your committee report that the practice of firing on our prisoners by the guards in the Northern prisons appears to have been indulged in to a most brutal and atrocious extent. See the depositions of C. C. Herrington, Wm. F. Gordon, Jr., J. B. McCreary, Dr. Thomas P. Holloway, and John P. Fennell. At Fort Delaware, a cruel regulation, as to the use of the sinks, was made the pretext for firing on and murdering several of our men and. officers, among them Lieut. Col. Jones, who was lame, and who was shot down by the sentinel while helpless and feeble, and while seeking to explain his condition. Yet this sentinel was not only not punished, but was promoted for his act. At Camp Douglas, as many as eighteen of our men are reported to have been shot in a single month. These facts may well produce a conviction in the candid observer, that it is the North, and not the South, that is open to the charge of deliberately and wilfully destroying the lives of the prisoners held by her.

The next charge is, that the Libby and Belle Isle prisoners were habitually kept in a filthy condition, and that the officers and men confined there were prevented from keeping themselves sufficiently clean to avoid vermin and similar discomforts. The evidence clearly contradicts this charge. It is proved by the depositions of Major Turner, Lieut. Bossieux, Rev. Dr. McCabe, and others, that the prisoners were kept constantly and systematically policed and cleansed; that in the Libby there was an ample supply of water conducted to each floor by the city pipes, and that the prisoners were not only not restricted in its use, but urged to keep themselves clean. At Belle Isle, for a brief season, (about three weeks) in consequence of a sudden increase in the number of prisoners, the police was interrupted; but it was soon restored, and ample means for washing, both themselves and their clothes, were at all times furnished to the prisoners. It is doubtless true, that notwithstanding these facilities, many of the prisoners were lousy and filthy; but it was the result of their own habits, and not of neglect in the discipline or arrangements of the prison. Many of the prisoners were captured and brought in while in this condition. The Federal general, Neal Dow, well expressed their character and habits. When he came to distribute clothing among them, he was met by profane abuse, and he said to the Confederate officer in charge, "You have here the scrapings and rakings of Europe." That such men should be filthy in their habits might be expected.

We next notice the charge that the boxes of provisions and clothing sent to the prisoners from the North, were not delivered to them, and were habitually robbed and plundered, by the permission of the Confederate authorities. The evidence satisfies your committee that this charge is, in all substantial points, untrue. For a period of about a month there was a stoppage in the delivery of boxes, caused by a report that the Federal authorities were forbidding the delivery of similar supplies to our prisoners. But the boxes were put in a warehouse, and afterward delivered. For some time no search was made of boxes from the "Sanitary Committee," intended for the prisoners' hospital. But a letter was intercepted, advising that money should be sent in these boxes, as they were never searched; which money was to be used in bribing the guard, and thus releasing the prisoners. After this, it was deemed necessary to search every box, which necessarily produced some delay. Your committee are satisfied that if these boxes, or their contents, were robbed, the prison officials are not responsible therefor. Beyond doubt, robberies were often committed by prisoners themselves, to whom the contents were delivered for distribution to their owners. Notwithstanding all this alleged pillage, the supplies seem to have been sufficient to keep the quarters of the prisons so well furnished that they frequently presented, in the language of a witness, "the appearance of a large grocery store." In connection with this point, your committee refer to the testimony of a Federal officer, Col. James M. Sanderson, whose letter is annexed to the deposition of Major Turner. He testifies to the full delivery of the clothing and supplies from the North, and to the humanity and kindness of the Confederate officers, specially mentioning Lieut. Bossieux, commanding on Belle Isle. His letter was addressed to the President of the United States Sanitary Commission, and was, beyond doubt, received by them, having been forwarded by the regular flag-of-truce. Yet the scrupulous and honest gentlemen composing that commission, have not found it convenient for their purposes to insert this letter in their publication. Had they been really searching for the truth, this letter would have aided them in finding it.

Your committee proceed next to notice the allegation that the Confederate authorities had prepared a mine under the Libby prison, and placed in it a quantity of gunpowder for the purpose of blowing up the buildings with their inmates, in case of an attempt to rescue them. After ascertaining all the facts bearing on this subject, your committee believe that what was done under the circumstances, will meet a verdict of approval from all whose prejudices do not blind them to the truth. The state of things was unprecedented in history, and must be judged of according to the motives at work, and the result accomplished. A large number of Northern raiders, under one Col. Dahlgren, was approaching Richmond. It was ascertained, by the reports of the prisoners captured from them, and other evidence, that their design was to enter the city to set fire to the buildings, public and private, for which purpose turpentine balls in great number had been prepared; to murder the President of the Confederate States, and other prominent men; to release the prisoners of war, then numbering five or six thousand; to put arms into their hands, and to turn over the city to indiscriminte pillage, rape, and slaughter. At the same time a plot was discovered among the prisoners to coöperate in this scheme, and a large number of knives and slung-shot (made by putting stones into woollen stockings) were detected in places of concealment about their quarters. To defeat a plan so diabolical, assuredly the sternest means were justified. If it would have been right to put to death any one prisoner attempting to escape under such circumstances, it seems logically certain that it would have been equally right to put to death any number making such attempt. But in truth, the means adopted were those of humanity and prevention, rather than of execution. The Confederate authorities felt able to meet and repulse Dahlgren and his raiders, if they could prevent the escape of the prisoners. The real object was to save their lives, as well as those of our citizens. The guard force at the prison was small, and all the local troops in and around Richmond were needed to meet the threatened attack. Had the prisoners escaped, the women and children of the city, as well as their homes, would have been at the mercy of five thousand outlaws. Humanity required that the most summary measures should be used to deter them from any attempt at escape. A mine was prepared under the Libby prison; a sufficient quantity of gunpowder was put into it, and pains were taken to inform the prisoners that any attempt at escape made by them would be effectually defeated. The plan succeeded perfectly. The prisoners were awed and kept quiet. Dahlgren and his party were defeated and scattered. The danger passed away, and in a few weeks the gunpowder was removed. Such are the facts. Your committee do not hesitate to make them known, feeling assured that the conscience of the enlightened world and the great law of self-preservation will justify all that was done by our country and her officers.

We now proceed to notice, under one head, the last and gravest charge made in these publications. They assert that the Northern prisoners in the hands of the Confederate authorities have been starved, frozen, inhumanly punished, often confined in foul and loathsome quarters, deprived of fresh air and exercise, and neglected and maltreated in sickness; and that all this was done upon a deliberate, wilful, and long-conceived plan of the Confederate Government and officers, for the purpose of destroying the lives of these prisoners, or of rendering them forever incapable of military service. This charge accuses the Southern Government of a crime so horrible and unnatural, that it could never have been made except by those ready to blacken with slander men whom they have long injured and hated. Your committee feel bound to reply to it calmly, but emphatically. They pronounce it false in fact and in design; false in the basis on which it assumes to rest, and false in its estimate of the motives which have controlled the Southern authorities.

At an early period in the present contest, the Confederate Government recognised their obligation to treat prisoners of war with humanity and consideration. Before any laws were passed on the subject, the Executive Department provided such prisoners as fell into their hands, with proper quarters and barracks to shelter them, and with rations the same in quantity and quality as those furnished to the Confederate soldiers who guarded these prisoners. They also showed an earnest wish to mitigate the sad condition of prisoners of war, by a system of fair and prompt exchange; and the Confederate Congress coöperated in these humane views. By their act, approved on the 21st day of May, 1861, they provided that "all prisoners of war taken, whether on land or on sea, during the pending hostilities with the United States, shall be transferred by the captors, from time to time, and as often as convenient, to the Department of War; and it shall be the duty of the Secretary of War, with the approval of the President, to issue such instructions to the Quartermaster-general and his subordinates, as shall provide for the safe custody and sustenance of prisoners of war; and the rations furnished prisoners of war shall be the same in quantity and quality as those furnished to enlisted men in the army of the Confederacy." Such were the declared purpose and policy of the Confederate Government toward prisoners of war: amid all the privations and losses to which enemies have subjected them, they have sought to carry them into effect. Our investigations for this preliminary report have been confined chiefly to the rations and treatment of prisoners of war at the Libby and other prisons in Richmond and Belle Isle. This we have done, because the publications to which we have alluded chiefly refer to them, and because the "Report No. 67" of the Northern Congress plainly intimates the belief that the treatment in and around Richmond was worse than it was farther South. That report says:—"It will be observed from the testimony, that all the witnesses who testify upon that point, state that the treatment they received while confined at Columbia, South Carolina, Dalton, Georgia, and other places, was far more humane than that they received at Richmond, where the authorities of the so-called Confederacy were congregated." (Report, p. 3.)

The evidence proves that the rations furnished to prisoners of war, in Richmond and Belle Isle, have been never less than those furnished to the Confederate soldiers who guarded them, and have at some seasons been larger in quantity and better in quality than those furnished to Confederate troops in the field. This has been because, until February, 1864, the Quartermaster's department furnished the prisoners, and often had provisions or funds, when the Commissary department was not so well provided. Once, and only once, for a few weeks, the prisoners were without meat; but a larger quantity of bread and vegetable food was in consequence supplied to them. How often the gallant men composing the Confederate army have been without meat for even longer intervals, your committee do not deem it necessary to say. Not less than sixteen ounces of bread and four ounces of bacon, or six ounces of beef, together with beans and soup, have been furnished per day to the prisoners. During most of the time the quantity of meat furnished to them has been greater than these amounts; and even in times of the greatest scarcity, they have received as much as the Southern soldiers who guarded them. The scarcity of meat and of breadstuffs in the South, in certain places, has been the result of the savage policy of our enemies, in burning barns filled with wheat or corn, destroying agricultural implements, and driving off or wantonly butchering hogs and cattle. Yet, amid all these privations, we have given to their prisoners the rations above mentioned. It is well known that this quantity of food is sufficient to keep in health a man who does not labor hard. All the learned disquisitions of Dr. Ellerslie Wallace on the subject of starvation, might have been spared, for they are all founded on a false basis. It will be observed that few (if any) of the witnesses examined by the "Sanitary Commission," speak with any accuracy of the quantity (in weight) of the food actually furnished them. Their statements are merely conjectural and comparative, and cannot weigh against the positive testimony of those who superintended the delivery of large quantities of food, cooked and distributed according to fixed ratio for the number of men to be fed.

The statements of the "Sanitary Commission" as to prisoners freezing to death on Belle Isle, are absurdly false. According to that statement, it was common, during a cold spell in winter, to see several prisoners frozen to death every morning in the places in which they had slept. This picture, if correct, might well excite our horror; but, unhappily for its sensational power, it is but a clumsy daub, founded on the fancy of the painter. The facts are, that tents were furnished sufficient to shelter all the prisoners; that the Confederate commandant and soldiers on the island were lodged in similar tents; that a fire was furnished in each of them; that the prisoners fared as well as their guards; and that only one of them was ever frozen to death, and he was frozen by the cruelty of his own fellow-prisoners, who thrust him out of the tent in a freezing night, because he was infested with vermin. The proof as to the healthiness of the prisoners on Belle Isle, and the small amount of mortality, is remarkable, and presents a fit comment on the lugubrious pictures drawn by the "Sanitary Commission," either from their own fancies, or from the fictions put forth by their false witnesses. Lieut. Bossieux proves that from the establishment of the prison-camp on Belle Isle in June, 1862, to the 10th of February, 1865, more than twenty thousand prisoners had been, at various times, there received, and yet, that the whole number of deaths during this time was only one hundred and sixty-four. And this is confirmed by the Federal Colonel Sanderson, who states that the average number of deaths per month on Belle Isle was "from two to five, more frequently the lesser number." The sick were promptly removed from the island to the city. Doubtless, the "Sanitary Commission" have been, to some extent, led astray by their own witnesses, whose character has been portrayed by Gen. Neal Dow, and also by the editor of the *New York Times*, who, in his issue of January 6th, 1865, describes the material for recruiting the Federal army as "wretched vagabonds, of depraved morals, decrepit in body, without courage, self-respect, or conscience. They are dirty, disorderly, thievish, and incapable."

In reviewing the charges of cruelty, harshness, and starvation to prisoners, made by the North, your committee have taken testimony as to the treatment of our own officers and soldiers in the hands of the enemy. It gives us no pleasure to be compelled to speak of the suffering inflicted upon our gallant men; but the self-laudatory style in which the "Sanitary Commission" have spoken of their prisons, makes it proper that the truth should be presented. Your committee gladly acknowledge that in many cases our prisoners received kind and considerate treatment; but we are equally assured, that in nearly all the prison stations of the North—at Point Lookout, Fort

McHenry, Fort Delaware, Johnson's Island, Elmira, Camp Chase, Camp Douglas, Alton, Camp Morton, the Ohio Penitentiary, and the prisons of St. Louis, Missouri, our men have suffered from insufficient food, and have been subjected to ignominious, cruel, and barbarous practices, of which there is no parallel in anything that has occurred in the South. The witnesses who were at Point Lookout, Fort Delaware, Camp Morton, and Camp Douglas, testify that they have often seen our men picking up the scraps and refuse thrown out from the kitchens, with which to appease their hunger. Dr. Herrington proves that at Fort Delaware, unwholesome bread and water produced diarrhœa in numberless cases among our prisoners, and that "their sufferings were greatly aggravated by the regulations of the camp, which forbade more than twenty men at a time at night to go to the sinks. I have seen as many as five hundred men in a row waiting their time. The consequence was, that they were obliged to use the places where they were. This produced great want of cleanliness, and aggravated the disease." Our men were compelled to labor in unloading Federal vessels and in putting up buildings for Federal officers, and if they refused, were driven to work with clubs.

The treatment of Brigadier-general J. H. Morgan and his officers was brutal and ignominious in the extreme. It will be found stated in the depositions of Captain M. D. Logan, Lieutenant W. P. Crow, Lieutenant-colonel James B. McCreary, and Captain B. A. Tracy, that they were put in the Ohio Penitentiary, and compelled to submit to the treatment of felons. Their beards were shaved, and their hair was cut close to the head. They were confined in convict's cells, and forbidden to speak to each other. For attempts to escape, and for other offences of a very light character, they were subjected to the horrible punishment of the dungeon. In mid-winter, with the atmosphere many degrees below zero, without blanket or overcoat, they were confined in a cell, without fire or light, with a fetid and poisonous air to breathe; and here they were kept until life was nearly extinct. Their condition, on coming out, was so deplorable as to draw tears from their comrades. The blood was oozing from their hands and faces. The treatment in the St. Louis prison was equally barbarous. Captain William H. Sebring testifies:—"Two of us, A. C. Grimes and myself, were carried out into the open air, in the prison-yard, on the 25th of December, 1863, and handcuffed to a post. Here we were kept all night in sleet, snow, and cold. We were relieved in the daytime, but again brought to the post and handcuffed to it in the evening; and thus we were kept all night until the 2d of January, 1864. I was badly frost-bitten, and my health much impaired. This cruel infliction was done by order of Captain Byrnes, commandant of prisons in St. Louis. He was barbarous and insulting to the last degree."

But even a greater inhumanity than any we have mentioned was perpetrated upon our prisoners at Camp Douglas and Camp Chase. It is proved by the testimony of Thomas P. Holloway, John P. Fennel, H. H. Barlow, H. C. Barton, C. D. Bracken, and J. S. Barlow, that our prisoners in large numbers were put into "condemned camps," where small-pox was prevailing, and speedily contracted this loathsome disease, and that as many as forty new cases often appeared daily among them. Even the Federal officers who guarded them to the camp protested against this unnatural atrocity; yet it was done. The men who contracted the disease were removed to a hospital about a mile off, but the plague was already introduced, and continued to prevail. For a period of more than twelve months the disease was constantly in the camp, yet our prisoners during all this time were continually brought to it, and subjected to certain infection. Neither do we find evidences of amendment on the part of our enemies, notwithstanding the boasts of the "Sanitary Commission." At Nashville, prisoners recently captured from General Hood's army, even when sick and wounded, have been cruelly deprived of all nourishment suited to their condition; and other prisoners from the same army have been carried into the infected camps Douglas and Chase. Many of the soldiers of General Hood's army were frost-bitten by being kept day and night in an exposed condition before they were put into Camp Douglas. Their sufferings are truthfully depicted in the evidence. At Alton and Camp Morton the same inhuman practice of putting our prisoners into camps infected by small-pox, prevailed. It was equivalent to murdering many of them by the torture of a contagious disease. The insufficient rations at Camp Morton forced our men to appease their hunger by pounding up and boiling bones, picking up scraps of meat and cabbage from the hospital slop-tubs, and even eating rats and dogs. The depositions of Wm. Ayres and J. Chambers Brent prove these privations.

The punishments often inflicted on our men for slight offences, have been shameful and barbarous. They have been compelled to ride a plank only four inches wide, called "Morgan's horse," to sit down with their naked bodies in the snow for ten or fifteen minutes, and have been subjected to the ignominy of stripes from the belts of their guards. The pretext has been used, that many of their acts of cruelty have been by way of retaliation; but no evidence has been found to prove such acts on the part of the Confederate authorities.

We do not deem it necessary to dwell further on these subjects. Enough has been proved to show that great privations and sufferings have been borne by the prisoners on both sides.

Why have not Prisoners of War been Exchanged?

But the question forces itself upon us, Why have these sufferings been so long continued? why have not the prisoners of war been exchanged, and thus some of the darkest pages of history spared the world? In the answer to this question must be found the test of responsibility for all the sufferings, sickness, and heart-broken sorrow, that have visited more than eighty thousand prisoners within the past two years. On this question your committee can only say, that the Confederate authorities have always desired a prompt and fair exchange of prisoners. Even before the establishment of a cartel they urged such exchange; but could never effect it by agreement, until the large preponderance of prisoners in our hands made it the interest of the Federal authorities to consent to the cartel of July 22d, 1862. The ninth article of that agreement expressly provided, that in case any misunderstanding should arise, it should not interrupt the release of prisoners on parole, but should be made the subject of friendly explanation. Soon after this cartel was established, the policy of the enemy in seducing negro slaves from their masters, arming them and putting white officers over them to lead them against us, gave rise to a few cases in which questions of crime under the internal laws of the Southern States appeared. Whether men who encouraged insurrection and murder could be held entitled to the privileges of prisoners of war under the cartel, was a grave question. But these cases were few in number, and ought never to have interrupted the general exchange. We were always ready and anxious to carry out the cartel in its true meaning; and it is certain that the ninth article required that the prisoners on both sides should be released, and that the few cases as to which misunderstanding occurred should be left for final decision. Doubtless, if the preponderance of prisoners had continued with us, exchanges would have continued; but the fortunes of war threw the larger number into the hands of our enemies. Then they refused further exchanges, and for twenty-two months this policy has continued. Our Commissioner of Exchange has made constant efforts to renew them. In August 1864 he consented to a proposition which had been repeatedly made, to exchange officer for officer and man for man, leaving the surplus in captivity. Though this was a departure from the cartel, our anxiety for the exchange induced us to consent; yet the Federal authorities repudiated their previous offer, and refused even this partial compliance with the cartel. Secretary Stanton, who has unjustly charged the Confederate authorities with inhumanity, is open to the charge of having done all in his power to prevent a fair exchange, and thus to prolong the sufferings of which he speaks; and very recently, in a letter over his signature, Benjamin F. Butler has declared that in April 1864 the Federal Lieutenant-general Grant forbade him "to deliver to the rebels a single able-bodied man"; and, moreover, General Butler acknowledges that, in answer to Col. Ould's letter consenting to the exchange of officer for officer and man and man, he wrote a reply, "*not diplomatically, but obtrusively and demonstratively; not for the purpose of furthering exchange of prisoners, but for the purpose of preventing and stopping the exchange, and furnishing a ground on which we could fairly stand.*" These facts abundantly show that the responsibility of refusing to exchange prisoners of war rests with the Government of the United States, and the people who have sustained that Government; and every sigh of captivity, every groan of suffering, every heart broken by hope deferred among these eighty thousand prisoners, will accuse them in the judgment of the just.

With regard to the prison-stations at Andersonville, Salisbury, and other places south of Richmond, your committee have not made extended examination, for reasons which have already been stated. We are satisfied that privation, suffering and mortality, to an extent much to be regretted, did prevail among the prisoners there; but they were not the result of neglect, still less of design, on the part of the Confederate Government. Haste in preparation, crowded quarters prepared only for a small number, frequent removals to prevent recapture, want of transportation and scarcity of food, have all resulted from the pressure of the war, and the barbarous manner in which it has been conducted by our enemies. Upon these subjects your committee propose to take further evidence, and to report more fully hereafter.

But even now, enough is known to vindicate the South, and to furnish an overwhelming answer to all complaints on the part of the United States Government or people, that their prisoners were stinted in food or supplies. Their own savage warfare has wrought all the evil. They have blockaded our ports; have excluded from us food, clothing and medicines; have even declared medicines and surgical instruments contraband of war, and have repeatedly destroyed the contents of drug-stores, and the supplies of private physicians in the country: have ravaged our country, burned our houses, and destroyed growing crops and farming implements. One of their officers (General Sheridan) has boasted, in his official report, that in the Shenandoah Valley alone he burned two thousand barns filled with wheat and corn; that he burned all the mills in the whole tract of country, destroyed all the factories of cloth, and killed or drove off every animal, even to the poultry, that could contribute to human sustenance. These desolations have been repeated again and again in different parts of the South. Thousands of our families have been driven from their homes as helpless and destitute refugees. Our enemies have destroyed the railroads and other means of transportation, by which food could be supplied from abundant districts to those without it. While thus desolating our country, in violation of the usages of civilised warfare, they have refused to exchange prisoners, have forced us to keep fifty thousand of their men in captivity; and yet have attempted to attribute to us sufferings and privations caused by their own acts. We cannot doubt that in the view of civilisation we shall stand acquitted, while they must be condemned.

In concluding this preliminary report, we will notice the strange perversity of "interpretation" which has induced the "Sanitary Commission" to affix, as a motto to their pamphlet, the words of the compassionate Redeemer of mankind, "For

I was an hungered, and ye gave me *no* meat; I was thirsty and ye gave me *no* drink; I was a stranger, and ye took me *not* in; naked, and ye clothed me *not;* sick and in prison, and ye visited me *not.*" We have yet to learn on what principle the Federal soldiers, sent with arms in their hands to destroy the lives of our people, to waste our land, burn our houses and barns and drive us from our homes, can be regarded by us as the meek and lowly Redeemer, so as to claim the benefit of his words. Yet even these soldiers, when taken captive by us, have been treated with proper humanity. The cruelties inflicted on our prisoners at the North may well justify us in applying to the "Sanitary Commission" the stern words of the Divine Teacher: "Thou hypocrite, first cast out the beam out of thine own eye, and then shalt thou see clearly to cast out the mote out of thy brother's eye."

We believe that there are many thousands of just, honorable, and humane people in the United States, upon whom this subject, thus presented, will not be lost; that they will do all they can to mitigate the horrors of war; to complete the exchange of prisoners now happily in progress, and to prevent the recurrence of such sufferings as have been narrated. And we repeat the words of the Confederate Congress in their manifesto of the 14th of June, 1864:—"We commit our cause to the enlightened judgment of the world, to the sober reflections of our adversaries themselves, and to the solemn and righteous arbitrament of heaven."

The humane proposition of General Lee to General Grant, to exchange prisoners man for man, is a matter of history. That General Grant and the Federal authorities refused to accede to this generous proposal is also a fact. As corroborative of this statement, I am permitted to insert the following extract from a letter, written since the war, from General R. E. Lee to a gentleman in Philadelphia, kindly furnished the author by his son, Colonel G. W. C. Lee:

"LEXINGTON VA., 17*th April*, 1867.

". . . I have a great repugnance to be brought before the public in any manner. Sufficient information has been officially published, I think, to show, that whatever sufferings the Federal prisoners at the South underwent, were incident to their position as prisoners, and produced by the destitute condition of the country arising from the operations of war. The laws of the Confederate Congress, and the orders of the War Department, directed that the rations furnished prisoners of war should be the same in quantity and quality as those furnished enlisted men in the army of the Confederacy; and that the hospitals for prisoners should be placed on the same footing as other Confederate States hospitals, in all respects. It was the desire of the Confederate authorities to effect a continuous and speedy exchange of prisoners of war; for it was their true policy to do so, as their retention was not only a calamity to them, but a heavy expenditure of their scanty means of subsistence, and a privation of the services of a veteran army. Mr. ——, or Bishop ——, has confounded my offers for the exchange of prisoners with those made by Mr. Ould, the commissioner on the part of the Confederate States. It was he that offered, when all hopes of effecting the exchange had ceased, to deliver all the Federal sick and wounded, to the amount of fifteen thousand, without an equivalent, provided transportation was furnished. Previously to this, I think, I offered to General Grant to send into his lines all the prisoners within my department, which then embraced Virginia and North Carolina, provided he would return me man for man; and when I informed the Confederate authorities of my proposition, I was told that if it was accepted they would place all the prisoners at the South at my disposal. I offered subsequently, I think, to the Committee of the U. S. Sanitary Commission, who visited Petersburg for the purpose of ameliorating the condition of their prisoners, to do the same. *But my propositions were not accepted.*

"R. E. LEE."

Still pursuing my chain of evidence in vindication of truth and justice, I cannot do better than to close this chapter with the following letter from Mr. Davis, written to me after his release from Fortress Monroe. It bears on its face the impress of truth and integrity of purpose, that has marked his life and character in either victory or defeat—whether as the leader of a host of warriors, or in exile. It reads as follows:—

MONTREAL, 20*th June*, 1867.

R. R. STEVENSON, M. D.

My Dear Sir:—I have just received your very kind letter of the 7th inst., and have read with much gratification your remarks in regard to the care and treatment of the prisoners at Andersonville. Without personal observation on which to base an opinion, I have never doubted that all had been done for the comfort and preservation of the prisoners at that place which the circumstances rendered possible. General Winder I had known, from my first entrance into the United States army, as a gallant soldier and an honorable gentleman. Cruelty to those in his power, defenceless and sick men, was inconsistent with the character of either a soldier or a gentleman. I was always, therefore, confident that the charge was unjustly imputed. But to those who have been deceived by false statements, the proofs in your hands will be useful; and to me it is most desirable that no stain should be left upon the conduct of those who unsuccessfully struggled to maintain their inheritance to State sovereignty and self-government. The efforts made to exchange the prisoners will be found in the published reports of our Commissioner of Exchange, and they were referred to in several of my messages to the Confederate Congress. They show the anxiety felt on our part to relieve the captives, on both sides, of the sufferings incident to imprisonment, and how that humane purpose was obstructed by the enemy, in disregard of the cartel which had been agreed upon.

It is probably unnecessary to say to you that I have no

records, and can therefore give you no aid by extracts from "Official Documents." The work you suggest would, I think, meet a want of the public mind; and not only the generous, but the just, of every land must hail with satisfaction an authentic vindication of the victim Wirz, and all others, the dead or living, who have suffered in body or in repute.

Sincerely thanking you for your kind expressions towards myself, and with the best wishes for your professional success and individual happiness,

I am very respectfully and truly yours,

JEFFERSON DAVIS.

CHAPTER XIV

The vandalism of General Sherman, in Georgia and South Carolina, furnishes us with some of the most striking illustrations of the mode of warfare adopted by many of the Northern Generals during the conflict. He commenced his last track of desolation and ruin from Atlanta, on the night of the 14th of November, 1864. He first applied the torch to every portion of the city, and soon it was enveloped in one broad expanse of fire; the troops marching out with the bands playing "John Brown's soul goes marching on." After leaving Atlanta, this immense horde moved off in two columns, in the direction of Savannah, the right wing under General Howard and the left under General Slocum. They met with but little resistance; in fact, the small amount of Confederate cavalry that could be brought against them only served to keep the straggling Federals more closely in ranks.

The conduct of the Federal officers and soldiers in this "great march to the sea," which has been compared by Northern historians to "Napoleon's march to Moscow," is best illustrated by one of General Sherman's war-correspondents to the Northern press, who writes as follows:—"Such little freaks as taking the last chicken, the last pound of meal, the last bit of bacon, and the only remaining scraggy cow, from a poor woman and her flock of children, black or white not considered, came under the order of legitimate business. Even crockery, bed-covering, or clothes, were fair spoils. As for plate, or jewelry, or watches, these were things rebels had no use for. Men with pockets plethoric with silver and gold coin; soldiers sinking under the weight of plate and fine bedding materials; lean mules and horses, with the richest trappings of Brussels carpets and hangings of fine chenille; negro wenches, particularly good-looking ones, decked in satin and silks and sporting diamond ornaments; officers with sparkling rings that would set Tiffany in raptures;—gave color to the stories of hanging up or fleshing an 'old cuss' to make him shell out. A planter's house was overrun in a jiffy; boxes, drawers and escritoires were ransacked with a laudable zeal, and emptied of their contents. If the spoils were ample, the depredators were satisfied and went off in peace; if not, everything was torn and destroyed, and most likely the owner was tickled with sharp bayonets into a confession where he had his treasures hid. If he escaped and was hiding in a thicket, this was *prima facie* evidence that he was a skulking rebel; and most likely some ruffian, in his zeal to get rid of such vipers, gave him a dose of lead, which cured him of his secesh tendencies. Sorghum barrels were knocked open, bee-hives rifled while their angry swarms rushed frantically about; indeed, I have seen a soldier knock a planter down because a bee stung him. Should the house be deserted, the furniture is smashed in pieces; music was pounded out of four hundred dollar pianos with the ends of muskets; mirrors were wonderfully multiplied; and rich cushions and carpets carried off to adorn teams and war-steeds. After all was cleared out, most likely some set of stragglers wanted to enjoy a good fire, and set the house, debris of furniture and all the surroundings, in a blaze. This is the way Sherman's army lived on the country."

After General Sherman reached Savannah, he announced in his dispatch to Mr. Lincoln, that "he has wasted and destroyed in subsistence to the enemy, eighty millions of dollars' worth"; that "his march was most agreeable," and might be compared to a "pleasure trip."

The author of this book was on duty in the prison department at Columbia, S. C., when that ill-fated city was ravaged and pillaged by General Sherman's hosts. His track through Georgia, from Atlanta to Savannah, was sorely marked by desolation and ruin. The sword was sheathed for a time, and the "torch" was brandished instead. All modes of civilised warfare were laid aside. It is no part of my plan or purpose to discuss points and questions of statesmanship or strategy in this work. Whether the act of Mr. Davis, in substituting, at a most critical moment, for the tried and skilful strategist Johnston, the magnanimous but unfortunate Hood, was a wise one, or the reverse; whether the former general, if left in command of the Confederate forces, would have saved the country and the world from that disgraceful blot upon the pages of military history—Sherman's "March to the Sea"—I must leave to others to discuss—that is, if the discussion should seem to them to promise aught of profit. My province is to call attention to some of the countless iniquities of that celebrated "march," and to describe a few of its characteristic scenes. Scarcely had General Sherman's forces crossed the Savannah river into South Carolina, when a free license was given to the soldiers, to plunder and pillage to their utmost desire. Each day the news came to Columbia of the atrocities of the enemy in the outlying country districts. The roads were lined with fugitives. Long trains of wagons with women and children, together with what little stock they could gather up, were flying by thousands before the destroying hosts. Thinly-clad women and children, in the dead of winter, might be seen in the thickets, under bush tents, in railroad sheds, in old barns, out-houses and old cars. The sad scenes presented by these poor, suffering, poverty-stricken beings, "exiles in their own domains," can never be erased from my memory. They knew not whither they were going; they moved on with their flocks and herds, leaving their homesteads to be destroyed by the pursuing foe. Friends and neighbors that had started together, in the rush and confusion had become separated; children were lost from their mothers. Squads of these poor wanderers, when nightfall came on, might be seen encamped by the side of some brook or friendly spring. The piteous lowing of hungry herds, the moans and cries of weary children, and the sobs of exhausted mothers, lent a gloom to the scene that neither pen nor pencil can ever portray.

Going through the country, some distance from Columbia, a few days previous to its destruction, (on business connected with my department), I had occasion to pass by one of these camps. I noticed sitting at the foot of an old pine-tree a woman, with the corpse of an infant on her lap. Upon addressing her, she told me that her husband was in the army, and that her child, eighteen months old, had fallen sick on the road and had died a few hours since. On further inquiry, I learned that her old patriarchal father was then engaged in digging a grave in the sand a few yards from the road, in which to deposit the remains of her little cherub. And thus, by the pale, flickering light of the camp-fire, the little one was deposited in its last resting-place, and its desolate mother was left to mingle her moanings over her lost babe with the mournful dirge of the pines of the forest. This was but a fairly illustrative instance. Scenes of a similar nature could be given, which were enacted under "Butler's rule" and in Sherman's raids, sufficient to fill a volume; but my pen naturally shrinks from recording these horrors of a war, inflicted upon defenceless women and children, under the guise of perpetuating the Union! Homestead after homestead, village after village, all gave way to the

BURIAL OF AN INFANT IN SOUTH CAROLINA.

torch of the invader. Horses, mules, cattle, hogs, and everything that contributed to the sustenance of the people, were either driven off or shot. Eyery implement of the mechanic or farmer was destroyed. Tools, plows, hoes, gins, looms, wagons, mills, factories—all were burned.

On the approach of the Federals to Columbia, the Confederate authorities removed whatever stores they could to Charlotte and Salisbury, N. C. The necessity of removing the Federal officers, who were confined here in "Asylum Prison," together with the limited amount of transportation at our command, made it impossible to remove any considerable number of the inhabitants of the "doomed city"; hence the suffering and misery attending its destruction were appalling. Visiting the place shortly after its evacuation by the Federal troops, I found nothing but blackened and charred ruins. The torch of the foe had well performed its work. The State House at Columbia, a building that promised to be one of the finest in the South, or in the United States, was in course of construction when the war broke out. This was injured and defaced, as well as the "Palmetto Monument," erected in the State House yard, in memory of the gallant South Carolinians who fell in the Mexican War. For a full description of the burning and sacking of Columbia, I am indebted to the gifted pen of Dr. William Gilmore Simms, and I can cheerfully vouch for the veracity of his statements. This gentleman, in a pamphlet published shortly after the war, says:—

"Hardly had the troops reached the head of Main street, when the work of pillage was begun. Stores were broken open within the first hour after their arrival, and gold, silver, jewels, and liquors eagerly sought. The authorities, officers, soldiers, all seemed to consider it a matter of course. And woe to him who carried a watch with gold chain pendant; or who wore a choice hat, or overcoat, or boots or shoes. He was stripped in the twinkling of an eye. It is computed that, from first to last, twelve hundred watches were transferred from the pockets of their owners to those of the soldiers. Purses shared the same fate, nor was the Confederate money repudiated. But of all these things hereafter in more detail.

At about 12 o'clock the jail was discovered to be on fire from within. This building was immediately in rear of the market or City Hall, and in a densely built portion of the city. The supposition is that it was fired by some of the prisoners—all of whom were released, and subsequently followed the army. The fire of the jail had been preceded by that of some cotton piled in the streets. Both fires were soon subdued by the firemen. At about half-past one P. M. that of the jail was rekindled, and was again extinguished. Some of the prisoners who had been confined at the Asylum, had made their escape, in some instances, a few days before, and were secreted and protected by citizens. No one felt safe in his own dwelling; and in the faith that General Sherman would respect the Convent, and have it properly guarded, numbers of young ladies were confided to the care of the Mother Superior, and even trunks of clothes and treasure were sent thither, in full confidence that they would find safety. Vain delusions! The Irish Catholic troops, it appears, were not brought into the city at all; were kept on the other side of the river. But a few Catholics were collected among the corps which occupied the city, and of the conduct of these a favorable account is given. One of them rescued a silver goblet of the church, used as a drinking-cup by a soldier, and restored it to the Rev. Dr. O'Connell. This priest, by the way, was severely handled by the soldiers. Such also was the fortune of the Rev. Mr. Shand, of Trinity (the Episcopal) Church, who sought in vain to save a trunk containing the sacred vessels of his church. It was violently wrested from his keeping, and his struggle to save it provoked the rougher usage. We are since told, that on reaching Camden, General Sherman restored what he believed were these vessels to Bishop Davis. It has since been discovered that the plate belonged to St. Peter's

Church in Charleston. And here, it may be well to mention, as suggestive of many clues, an incident which presented a sad commentary on that confidence in the security of the Convent which was entertained by the great portion of the people. This establishment, under the charge of the sister of the Right Rev. Bishop Lynch, was at once a convent and an academy of the highest class. Hither were sent for education the daughters of Protestants of the most wealthy classes throughout the State; and these, with the nuns and those young ladies sent thither on the emergency, probably exceeded one hundred. The Lady Superior herself entertained the fullest confidence in the immunities of the establishment. But her confidence was clouded after she had enjoyed a conference with a certain Major of the Yankee army, who described himself as an editor from Detroit. He visited her at an early hour of the day, and announced his friendly sympathies with the Lady Superior and the sisterhood; professed his anxiety for their safety; his purpose to do all that he could to insure it; declared that he would instantly go to Sherman and secure a chosen guard; and altogether made such professions of love and service, as to disarm those suspicions, which his bad looks and bad manners, inflated speech and pompous carriage, might have otherwise provoked. The Lady Superior, with such a charge in her hands, was naturally glad to welcome all shows and prospects of support, and expressed her gratitude. He disappeared, and soon after reappeared, bringing with him no less than eight or ten men; none of them were Catholics, as he admitted. He had some specious argument to show that, perhaps, her guard had better be one of Protestants. This suggestion staggered the lady a little, but he seemed to convey a more potent reason, when he added in a whisper, "For I must tell you, sister, that *Columbia is a doomed city.*" Terrible doom! This officer, leaving his men behind him, disappeared, to show himself no more. The guards so left behind were finally among the most busy as plunderers. The moment that the inmates, driven out by the fire, were forced to abandon their house, they began to revel in its contents. *Quis custodiet ipsos custodes?*—who shall guard the guards? asks the proverb. In a number of instances, the guards provided for the citizens were among the most active plunderers; were quick to betray their trusts, abandon their posts, and bring their comrades in to join in the general pillage. The most dexterous and adroit of these, it is the opinion of most persons, were chiefly Eastern men, or men of immediate Eastern origin. The Western men, including Indiana and a portion of Illinois and Iowa troops, were neither so dexterous nor unscrupulous; were frequently faithful and respectful; and, perhaps, it would be safe to assert, that many of the houses which escaped the sack and fire owed their safety to the presence or the contiguity of some of these men. But we must retrace our steps; the reign of terror did not fairly begin till night. In some instances, where parties complained of the misrule and robbery, their guards said to them, with a chuckle, "This is nothing; *wait till to-night*, and you will see hell."

Among the first fires at evening was one about dark, which broke out in a filthy purlieu of low houses of wood, on Gervais street, occupied mostly as brothels. Almost at the same time, a body of the soldiers scattered over the eastern outskirts of the city fired severally the dwellings of Secretary Trenholm, General Wade Hampton, Dr. John Wallace, J. U. Adams, Mrs. Starke, Mrs. Latta, Mrs. English, and many others. There were then some twenty fires in full blast, in as many different quarters; and while the alarm sounded from these quarters, a similar alarm was sent up almost simultaneously from Cotton Town, the northernmost limit of the city, and from Main street in its very centre, at the several stores or houses of O. Z. Bates, C. D. Eberhardt, and some others in the heart of the most densely settled portion of the town; thus enveloping in flames almost every section of the devoted city. At this period, thus early in the evening, there were few shows of that drunkenness which prevailed at a late hour in the night, and only after all the grocery shops on Main street had been rifled. The men engaged in this were well prepared with all the appliances essential to their work. They did not need the torch. They carried with them, from house to house, pots and vessels containing liquids, composed probably of phosphorus and other similar agents, turpentine, &c., and with balls of cotton saturated in this liquid, with which they also overspread floors and walls, they conveyed the flames with wonderful rapidity from dwelling to dwelling. Each had his ready box of lucifer-matches, and with a scrape upon the walls the flames began to rage. Where houses were closely contiguous, a brand from one was the means of conveying destruction to the other. The winds favored. They had been high throughout the day, and steadily prevailed from southwest by west and bore the flames eastward. To this fact we owe the preservation of the portions of the city west of Assembly street. The work, begun thus vigorously, went on without impediment and with hourly increase throughout the night. Engines and hose were brought out by the firemen, but these were soon driven from their labors — which were, indeed, idle against such a storm of fire — by the pertinacious hostility of the soldiers; the hose was hewn to pieces, and the firemen, dreading worse usage to themselves, left the field in despair. Meanwhile the flames spread from side to side, from front to rear, from street to street; and where their natural and inevitable progress was too slow for those who had kindled them, they helped them on by the application of fresh combustibles and more rapid agencies of conflagration. By midnight, Main street, from its northern to its southern extremity, was a solid wall of fire. By 12 o'clock, the great blocks, which included the banking-houses and the Treasury buildings, were consumed. Janney's (Congaree) and Nickerson's hotels, the magnificent manufactories of Evans and Cogswell — indeed, every large block in the business portion of the city, the Old Capitol and all the adjacent buildings — were in ruins. The range called the "Granite" was beginning to flame at 12, and might have been saved by ten vigorous men resolutely working. At one o'clock the hour was struck by the clock of the Market hall, which was even then illuminated from within. It was its own last hour which it sounded, and its tongue was silenced forevermore. In less than five minutes after, its spire went down with a crash; and by this time almost all the buildings within the precinct were a mass of ruins.

Very grand, and terrible beyond description, was the awful spectacle. It was a scene for the painter of the terrible. It was the blending of a range of burning mountains, stretched in a continuous series for more than a mile. Here was Ætna, sending up its spouts of lava; Vesuvius, emulous of like display, shooting up with loftier torrents; and Stromboli struggling, with awful throes, to shame both, by its superior volumes of fluid flame. The winds were tributary to these convulsive efforts, and tossed the volcanic torrents hundreds of feet in the air. Great spouts of flame spread aloft in canopies of sulphur-cloud. Wreaths of sable, edged with sheeted lightnings, wrapped the skies; and, at short intervals, the falling tower and the tottering wall, avalanche-like, went down with thunderous sound, sending up at every crash great billowing showers of glowing, fiery embers.

Throughout the whole of this terrible scene, the soldiers continued their search after spoil. The houses were severally and soon gutted of their contents. Hundreds of iron safes, warranted "impenetrable to fire and the burglar," it was soon satisfactorily demonstrated were not "Yankee proof." They were split open and robbed, yielding in some cases very largely of Confederate bonds and money, if not of gold and silver. Jewelry and plate in abundance were found. Men could be seen staggering off with huge waiters, vases, candelabra, to say nothing of cups, goblets, and smaller vessels, all of solid silver. Clothes and shoes, when new, were appropriated, the rest left to burn. . . . In one vault on Main street, seventeen casks of wine were stored away, which, an eyewitness tells us, barely sufficed, once broken into, for the draughts of a single hour—such were the appetites at work and the numbers in possession of them. Rye, corn, claret, and Madeira, all found their way into the same channels; and we are not to wonder when told that no less than one hundred and fifty of the drunken creatures perished miserably among the flames, kindled by their own comrades, and from which they were unable to escape. The estimate will not be thought extravagant by those who saw the condition of hundreds after one o'clock A. M. By others, however, the estimate is reduced to thirty; but the number will never be known. Sherman's officers themselves are reported to have said that they lost more men in the sack and burning of the city (including certain explosions) than in all their fights while approaching it. It is also suggested that the orders which Sherman issued at daylight on Saturday morning for the arrest of the fire, were issued in consequence of the loss of men which he had thus sustained.

One or more of his men were shot, by parties unknown, in some dark passages or alleys—it is supposed in consequence of some attempted outrages which humanity could not endure; the assassin taking advantage of the obscurity of the situation and adroitly mingling with the crowd without. And while these scenes were at their worst, while the flames were at their highest and most extensively raging, groups might be seen at the several corners of the streets, drinking, roaring, revelling, while the fiddle and accordeon were playing their popular airs among them. There was no cessation of the work till 5 A. M. on Saturday. . . . Ladies were hustled from their chambers, their ornaments plucked from their persons and their bundles from their hands. It was in vain that the mother appealed for the garments of her children; they were torn from her grasp and hurled into the flames. The young girl, striving to save a single frock, had it rent to fibres in her grasp. Men and women, bearing off their trunks, were seized, despoiled in a moment, the trunk burst asunder with the stroke of an axe or gun-butt, the contents laid bare, rifled of all the objects of desire, and the residue sacrificed to the fire. You might see the ruined owner, standing woe-begone, aghast, gazing at his tumbling dwelling, his scattered property, with a dumb agony in his face that was inexpressibly touching. . . . Your watch, your money, was the demand. Frequently no demand was made. Rarely, indeed, was a word spoken, where the watch or chain, or ring or bracelet, presented itself conspicuously to the eye. It was incontinently plucked away from the neck, breast, or bosom. Hundreds of women, still greater numbers of old men, were thus despoiled. The slightest show of resistance provoked violence to the person. The venerable Mr. Alfred Huger was thus robbed in the chamber and presence of his family, and in the eye of an almost dying wife. He offered resistance, and was collared and dispossessed by violence. We are told that the venerable ex-Senator, Colonel Arthur P. Hayne, was treated even more roughly. . . .

Within the dwellings, the scenes were of more harsh and tragical character, rarely softened by any ludicrous aspects, as they were screened by the privacy of the apartment, with but few eyes to witness. The pistol to the bosom or head of woman, the patient mother, the trembling daughter, was the ordinary introduction to the demand, your gold, silver, watch jewels. They gave no time, allowed no pause or hesitation. It was in vain that the woman offered her keys, or proceeded to open drawer or wardrobe, or cabinet or trunk. It was dashed to pieces by axe or gun-butt, with the cry, "We have a shorter way than that!" It was in vain that she pleaded to spare her furniture, and she would give up all its contents. All the precious things of a family, such as the heart loves to pore on in quiet hours when alone with memory —the dear miniature, the photograph, the portrait—these were dashed to pieces, crushed under foot, and the more the trembler pleaded for the object so precious, the more violent the rage which destroyed it. Nothing was sacred in their eyes, save the gold and silver which they bore away. Nor were these acts those of common soldiers. Commissioned officers of rank, so high as that of Colonel, were frequently among the most active in spoliation, and not always the most tender or considerate in the manner and acting of their crimes; and after glutting themselves with spoil, would often utter the foulest speeches, coupled with oaths as condiment, dealing in what they assumed besides to be bitter sarcasms upon the cause and country. And what do you think of the Yankees now? was a frequent question. Do you not fear us now? What do you think of secession? &c., &c. "We mean to wipe you out." "Will burn the very stones of South Carolina." Even General Howard, who is said to have been once a *pious* parson, is reported to have made this reply to a citizen who had expostulated with him on the monstrous crime of which his army had been guilty, "It is only what the country deserves. It is her fit punishment; and if this does not quiet rebellion, and we have to return, we will do this work thoroughly. We will not leave woman or child." . . .

There are some horrors which the historian dare not pursue, which the painter dare not delineate. They both drop the curtain over crimes which humanity bleeds to contemplate. A lady, undergoing the pains of labor, had to be borne out on a mattress in the open air to escape the fire. It was in vain that her situation was described as the soldiers applied the torch within and without the house, after they had penetrated every chamber, and robbed them of all that was either valuable or portable. They beheld the situation of the sufferer, and laughed to scorn the prayer for her safety. Another lady, Mrs. J——, was but recently confined; her condition was very helpless, her life hung upon a hair. The men were apprised of all the facts in the case. They burst into the chamber, took the rings from the lady's fingers, plucked the watch from beneath her pillow, and so overwhelmed her with terror, that she sank under the treatment, surviving their departure but a day or two. . . . In several cases newly-made graves were opened, the coffins taken out, broken open in search of buried treasure, and the corpses left exposed. Every spot in graveyard or garden which seemed to have been recently disturbed, was sounded with sword or bayonet or ramrod, in their desperate search after spoil.

These villainies summed up, find no equal amongst civilised nations. Cowardly mobs may dwell on the martial glory of Northern generals, but the execrations of an enlightened people will forever rest on their cruel acts. Fourth of July oratory and Centennial celebrations may vainly attempt to renew the old bond of union. Southern women may be permitted to decorate the graves of the Confederate dead, social reunions may be held by the veteran soldiers of both sides; but the names of Butler, Hunter, Turchin, Howard, Milroy, Sheridan, and Sherman, must forever be remembered by all true Southern people with feelings of contempt horror and disgust.

Vice-President Stephens* on this subject says:—"A comparison between the acts of the two Governments in these particulars, during the whole conduct of the war, will forever clearly exhibit on which side in the contest was the higher standard of 'moral ideas,' and with it the higher type of civilisation."

The character of the two Governments is so fully and forcibly expressed in the sentiments laid down by the historian of the "Chatham Artillery," (Confederate) that I cannot refrain from quoting them in this connection. They read as follows:

"Although the rich goal of national independence was not attained, the happy consciousness remains of self-respect preserved, of honor vindicated, of manhood declared, and of every honest effort expended in the brave defence of principle and

* *Constitutional View of the War.* Vol. II., p. 514.

property. Overcome, but not conquered; defeated, but not humiliated; impoverished, but not degraded; oppressed, and yet proud in spirit — snch to-day is the condition of the South. Federal armies, attracting to themselves, under the stimulus of extraordinary exertions, and by virtue of most prodigal bounties, multitudes of recruits from the New, and mercenaries from the Old, World, obedience to the commands of a military dictator, and at the expense of blood and treasure and right, compassed a physical solution of the question of comparative strength in favor of superior numbers and greater resources. They did not determine the validity or impropriety of the moral propositions involved in this gigantic struggle. The sword never does, it never has, and it never can submit any other than a physical arbitrament in matters of conscience, of abstract principle, and of inalienable right. The dismemberment of Poland was accomplished by warlike measures which commended themselves to the entire approbation of the arbitrary, grasping monarchs by whom they were inaugurated and sustained; and yet the life-blood of that nation has ever been held sacred, and its death-agonies perpetuated in honor, in story, and in song; and the action of the invading armies, which blotted out from the sisterhood of nations a brave people struggling for liberty and national existence, condemned by every lover of freedom, by the voice of civilisation, and the verdict of impartial history. To-day, the causes which brought about the Confederate revolution are morally as unaffected by the issues of the contest as they were at the moment of its inception. The Roman motto, *exitus acta probat,* is as fallacious as it is antiquated. The subsequent acts of Radical rule justify each day, more and more emphatically, the necessity which was laid upon the South to maintain her honor and manhood and self-respect, even at the expense of wounds and desolations and death. Clouds of fanaticism cannot forever darken the sunlight of truth and justice. The error of the present will be corrected by the calm verdict of the future; and the day will come when the moral record of the struggle of the Confederate States, for life and right and liberty and property, shall stand forth, justified and honored and admired in the hearts of all men who possess the knowledge to discern, the honesty to appreciate, and the candor to confess."

CHAPTER XV.

Up to this point, I have occupied the position of a witness simply, in the cause under consideration; and I trust that I may, without presumption, lay claim to some measure of success in my efforts to restrain within the bounds of modesty, a natural inclination toward the expression of my own sentiments and opinions concerning the facts and testimony herein submitted to the consideration and judgment of the reader. Indeed, so studiously and consistently have I refrained from breaking or interfering with the chain of documentary evidence, by obtruding my own opinions or the rhetoric of others, as to afford, if not a ground for fear that enough has not been said, at least a hope that a few words further will not be deemed too much. It should be remembered that I have a personal interest in the decision of this question, aside from the love that I feel for my country. If the world should return an unfavorable verdict—of which I have no fear; if the South should be declared guilty of the heinous "Crime of Andersonville"; then am I also, and my devoted comrades and co-laborers in the midst of plague, pestilence and famine, deep-dyed in guilt. Yet, as my conscience holds me guiltless here, so will the voice of Christendom declare my beloved country and her chosen Government void of offence in the matter charged against her.

And now, what do the facts, as fairly exhibited in the

foregoing pages, warrant the compiler in saying, by way of conclusion? Are the people and officials of the South longer to bear the odium of "the Crime of Andersonville"; or has the tremendous burden of that guilt been fairly shifted to other shoulders?

It will be remembered that the aim of this work has been to show:

First, That the sufferings at Andersonville were the results of a malignant pestilence, coupled with the uncontrollable events of a fierce and bitter war.

Second, That Captain Wirz expiated his alleged crimes under the form of a trial that can reflect no credit on the Government that tried him; and that his life was taken away by suborned testimony and perjury.

Third, That his alleged co-conspirators were as innocent of the crimes charged as himself.

Fourth, The Federal authorities at Washington prevented the exchange of prisoners of war; and,

Fifth, That by their consenting to an exchange, as urged by the Confederate authorities, three-fourths of all the lives lost in prisons, North and South, could have been saved.

I think I can safely assert, that I have conclusively and satisfactorily proved all these points; and I now call on an impartial public opinion, to reverse the unjust verdict against the South, of intentional cruelty to Federal prisoners of war.

For ten years the South has borne in silence, and with unshaken fortitude, the taunts and insults of her conquerors. To the writer it has appeared, that the time had at length come, when it behooved some one among her sons to raise a voice in her defence; and in so far as the charge of systematic cruelty to the prisoners at Andersonville was concerned, circumstances seemed to indicate him (the writer) as the proper person to undertake the duty of its refutation.

The defence of the conquered has ever been regarded as a difficult task, and in most cases one promising poor requital.

Especially may this be considered true when, as in the present case, the line of defence necessitates the proving of a negative. Perhaps the greatest difficulty arises from the world's indisposition and reluctance to grant a hearing to an unsuccessful party—the representatives, in fine, of *failure*, than which the world knows no graver nor more unpardonable crime. How often has the writer been advised, by well-meaning friends, to desist from the prosecution of what, he was told, was a most hopeless and unprofitable undertaking. The verdict has been found, said they, and no appeal will be permitted. "Besides," said many, "why stir up these old matters? Let them be; they will be forgotten within a generation." But there are some yet living, in both the South and the North, who prefer truth to falsehood, even though the attainment of the former costs some trouble. This policy of forgetfulness—a convenient repudiation of ugly recollections—would be, doubtless, a pleasant thing for those who hurried to death the poor and defenceless soldier, Henry Wirz, and the gray-haired matron, Mrs. Surratt, whose only crime was that she loved her children and did not close her doors against them. It is not to be wondered at if these are earnest advocates of forgetfulness and forgiveness. But first let it be known what we have to forget, and what to forgive.

Meanwhile, how stands the case? Arraigned before the bar of enlightened public sentiment, under charges of stupendous iniquity—crimes whose enormity is limited only by the powers of imagination of her accusers and their estimate of popular credulity—the South continues to bear the brunt of these charges, as they ring unchallenged throughout the world, until, by sheer force of persistent repetition, they have extorted credence from even her own slandered people. It is with these charges, and collateral subjects, that I have undertaken to deal. The causes of the war, and the fortunes of battle that placed in prisons a half-million of Federal and Confederate soldiers, I have not discussed. But this reticence is not due to any want of firm convictions on these points. On the contrary, my opinions on the matters mentioned are of a character very positive indeed. One of them, which I may perhaps express here without apology, is this, that one great fact stands out preëminent over all the vexed questions relating to the late war between the States, either as cause or consequence, and that is, that the real seceders from the principles of the American Republic were the people of the North, misguided by a destructive political faction, known successively as the "Abolitionist," "Free-Soil," and "Republican" party—a faction who first arrayed section against section, refused to be bound by solemn and deliberate compacts, first disregarded and then openly violated the Constitution, and gave general approval and sympathy to acts of brigandage committed during peace in the South.

Leaving the discussion of such questions, however, let us get back to our proper subject. An interesting inquiry is — What was the real meaning of the Wirz trial? As Mr. Davis, though sick and enfeebled, was manacled in order that "the iron might enter into the soul of his people," so was the entire South put on trial in the person of this unhappy officer, Henry Wirz. And, having noted the brutality and malignity by which those memorable transactions were so peculiarly marked, we are not to wonder if the motives which impelled to such enormities should still continue to bring forth bitter fruit in the shape of calumny and detraction. And are there no indications by which we may be guided to a correct estimate or conjecture as to the real character of those motives? Let us see. The South — like her chosen leader, who was vicariously suffering indignities for her sake — was already conquered, disarmed, prostrate, and utterly impotent for further harm to her victorious antagonist. Captain Wirz had been paroled, like any other officer of the defeated armies of the South, and, conscious of no crime, was resting quietly at Andersonville, never dreaming of molestation. What was the necessity, real or imagined, of the ostentatious and expensive arraignment of this man and his "co-conspirators," and especially the indecent haste and malignant energy which characterised the prosecution? If, to quote the rhetorical flourish of the prosecution, it was because "the blood of those who died at Andersonville cried aloud for vengeance," is it not most probable that it was for vengeance on the real, not the pretended, authors of their woes? And why were not those alleged "co-conspirators,"—those "more guilty" men, whose humble instrument poor Wirz was declared to have been,—why were not they, also, tried, condemned and hung? In his argument against the prisoner, Judge Advocate-general Chipman used the following language:—

"If Mr. Davis be ever brought to trial for his many crimes—and may heaven spare the temple of justice if he is not—it will not do for him to upbraid and accuse his willing tools, Winder and Wirz, as King John did Hubert for the death of Prince Arthur; they will turn upon him and say:

> 'Here is your hand and seal for all I did,
> And in the winking of authority
> Did we understand a law.'"

This neat specimen of forensic eloquence receives a brilliant illustration from poor Wirz's dying declaration of Mr. Davis's innocence; but we cannot stop to admire it. The question again recurs: *Why* was not Mr. Davis, with the rest of "the more guilty men," brought to trial? If guilty, they were not hard to find. Mr. Davis lay ironed in Fortress Monroe, and asked nothing more than a fair trial, which was persistently refused him. Mr. Stephens, our honored Vice-President, a man exceptionally inoffensive, and moderate in all his actions, was in Fort Warren. Mr. Seddon, our Secretary of War, was also a prisoner. So were all, except two—Captain W. S. Winder and the author of this work—who were self-exiled in self-defence. Was it magnanimity—an indisposition to further humiliate these incarcerated "conspirators"—that dictated forbearance after hanging the humblest, and, according to Judge-advocate Chipman, the *least guilty* one of the number?

It is impossible for a candid mind, in view of all the facts as presented in this work, to avoid the inference that some sinister motive, even more unworthy than the desire of revenge, underlay the cloud of turgid rhetoric and denunciation, sham indignation, and abuse, in which this notable state trial was enveloped. As the flying thief, when hard pressed by his pursuers, adroitly joins the hue and cry, and saves himself as much by strength of lungs as fleetness of foot, so did the Stantonian clique at Washington endeavor (and with ill-merited success) to avert from their guilty heads the impending storm of indignation, justly aroused by their inhuman "policy of exhaustion" by refusing exchange. The war was ended: the Andersonville prisoners were pouring homeward by thousands, with the cry of angry inquiry on every tongue: "*Why were we not exchanged? Who and where are the men that are responsible for our long martyrdom?*" The Wirz trial was the parry to this attack.

CHAPTER XVI.

A great deal of foolish clamor has been raised about the use of hounds at Andersonville to track escaped prisoners, and so aid in their recapture. But, divested of sensational flourishes, the questions pertinent to this subject are two:—First, was the practice of pursuing and recapturing escaping prisoners of war by means of hounds cruel and inhuman in itself, contrary to civilised precedent and the usages of honorable warfare? and, second, was the method as adopted at Andersonville, under direction of Captain Wirz, distinguished by any peculiar features of cruelty? A negative reply to the first of these questions will be promptly returned, I believe, by any one who has taken the trouble to inform himself on the following points, which, for the sake of brevity and because they are true, I put in the form of assertions:

1st, The part and province of a soldier is to obey orders and to perform faithfully the duties assigned him. If those orders and those duties are to prevent the escape of prisoners, he must prevent it. If, despite his vigilance, they escape, he must recapture them; and to this end he must use the most effective means within his reach.

2d, A fugitive pursued in a forest country has extraordinary opportunities of escape, and special means must be used for his capture, not necessary in regions thickly settled.

3d, On the score of humanity, the method was far preferable to the bullets with which the Federal prison authorities were accustomed to overtake the hapless Confederate who attempted an escape.

4th, (as regards precedent) The mode of pursuit and capture that was deemed by the beneficent United States Government proper for a Seminole chief, his wife and little children, guiltless of offence save the crime of owning land which his pursuers coveted, was good enough for a paroled prisoner, who had taken an oath not to attempt to escape, but to look after the wants of his sick and dying comrades.

As regards the second proposition, that is sufficiently negatived by the statements of the prisoners themselves—excepting, of course, the few who were selected as being favorable subjects for Chipman's manipulations, and pliant enough for the purposes of the "Commission." Statements, sworn or otherwise, are hardly necessary to prove that when the fleeing men found that the dogs were nearing them and escape was hopeless, they "took to a tree," until the huntsman rode up and called off the hounds—a proceeding obviously dictated by the commonest instinct of self-protection. In point of fact, the animals referred to under the terrific name of "bloodhounds," were neither intended for, nor qualified for, any furious assault or laceration; but were ordinary, inoffensive hounds, whose power of scent enabled them to render the one service they were needed for, that of following the trail of the fugitive. This fact and the nature of these dogs were shown in the statements of several of the witnesses. Corbitt, on the "Wirz trial," testified that he had escaped, "and on being hard pressed by the hounds, I took refuge in a thicket of underbrush, and lay down, when one of these ferocious dogs came up to me and rubbed his nose against my own." When asked by the Judge-advocate why the animal did not tear him to pieces, he replied, "the same Power which protected Daniel in the lions' den protected me"!

The ingenious Mr. Goss unintentionally testifies to the natural timidity and comparative harmlessness of "the hounds," by relating his exploit of prowess in intimidating and keeping off the entire pack by wielding a piece of rotton fence-rail. Hamlin also tells, in *Martyria*, (p. 65,) that "the ordinary bloodhound of these regions (the South) is cowardly from degeneration, and dare not face the look nor disregard the voice of man." From all the evidence that I could collect on the subject, during my official duties at Andersonville, I know of but two instances of the dogs even attempting to take hold of an escaping fugitive. One of these was a paroled prisoner, the other a detailed negro teamster. Both had their clothes slightly torn; otherwise they were not injured.

Next to this "bloodhound horror," we are treated with whole chapters on the "negro question," in some of their slanderous productions on the Andersonville prison. This subject is so old, hackneyed, and worn-out, that I would not even condescend to give it a passing notice; but as Butler and the Federal Government made the "negro question" a *sine qua non* in the exchange of prisoners, and most of the authors referred to seem to have been incapable of writing on any other theme, I shall be compelled to notice one or two paragraphs, and then dismiss the subject.

The candid reader of their works does not fail to detect the fact that these men are about as competent to write histories of "Southern Prisons" as the authors of the "Impending Crisis" and "Uncle Tom's Cabin" were to discuss the "negro question" during the existence of slavery. Says one of this sect*:—"After their long existence and progress, what have the slave faction left for the historian to contemplate with satisfaction?" It is true, it may not be a "satisfaction" for us to "contemplate" that we have been overcome in war; but even in this we have left us a rich legacy—the memory of our dead. The principles for which they fell will never die with us. Their acts of courage and devotion to our cause will ever be the admiration of the brave and generous of every civilised nation on the globe; and the fair hands of the daughters of the South, with each returning spring, will strew fresh flowers over the hallowed mounds beneath which their dead defenders sleep. Their heroic deeds will be the theme of "song and story" long after these Northern versions of Southern prisons have been buried in dust or consumed by moth. Perhaps it would be as well for some of the defamers of the South to "contemplate" (that is, if the period has arrived for them to be in a contemplative mood) some of the truths that are couched in the words which Lord Macaulay, the great English historian, puts in the mouth of Milton. "When will rulers learn," says he, "that where liberty is not, security and order can never be? We talk of absolute power; but all power hath limits, which, if not fixed by the moderation of the governors, will be fixed by the force of the governed. Sovereigns may send their opposers to dungeons; they may clear out a senate-house with soldiers; they may enlist armies of spies; they may hang scores of the disaffected in chains at every cross-road; but what power shall stand in that frightful time when rebellion hath become a less evil than endurance? Who shall dissolve that terrible tribunal which, in the hearts of the oppressed, denounces against the

*Augustus C. Hamlin, author of "Martyria: or Andersonville Prison."

oppressor the doom of its wild justice? Who shall repeal the law of self-defence? What arms or discipline shall resist the strength of famine or despair?" Methinks it would be far wiser for Northern historians, as well as some of the present legislators and rulers of the country, to "contemplate" on the dark abyss to which the maelstrom of centralised power is gradually drifting them since the war, than to be writing philippics against an overpowered foe, whose only crime was to stand by the old landmarks of Republicanism as laid down by our forefathers.

We fully recognise and admit the fact that slavery on this continent is dead, that we would not resuscitate it if we could; but we also recognise another significant fact,—that the index of futurity points to a much greater trouble than ever existed in the "slave faction," as they are wont to term the Southern people, viz. the sacrificing of the true principles of Republicanism for a centralised power. These are some of the living issues of the day that should engage the pens of their historians, the thoughts of their statesmen, and the judgment of their rulers. Again says this enthusiastic defender of the "dead issues of the past":—"What besides misery, violence and crime have they (the Southern people) bequeathed to the black man?" This, like the foregoing, is but a divergence in order to strike a cowardly blow at the South. I would just here ask our defamers and the Negrophilists of the North, who was it that took a race of people that in their native jungles of Africa are but little removed from the gorilla, and in the short space of two centuries accomplished for them that which forty centuries had failed to do? The wisdom and learning of the ancient Egyptians kindled no light for them. The seeds of Christianity perished in the soil of Africa; and not until the nineteenth century, on American soil, has the negro been admitted to equal privileges and equal rights with the white man. If it is true that he is in all respects equal to the white race, who was it that prepared him for his sudden change and escape from bondage to freedom? Was it the people of the North? No! It was the Southern people who raised him from his savage condition, taught him as much of the great principles of virtue and morality as he was capablo of acquiring, and transformed him into a being who, according to Mr. Hamlin's theory, is the peer of the Anglo-Saxon. Has the South anything to blush for in this?

The dilemma is palpable. If the Negro is capable of spontaneous development and progress, why, in his native land, has he never risen out of his savage state? If slavery was the brutalising and degrading system that its enemies asserted, how is it that its product, the Southern blacks, are so fit to discharge the duties of citizens? All the difference, be it more or less, between them and their savage ancestors, has been the fruit of a few generations of slavery.

It is to be hoped that these troubles cannot be of long duration. While the thirty-seven millions of whites are augmenting in a constantly increasing ratio, their natural increase being aided by immigration, the three and a half millions of negroes, not recruited from without, show a steadily diminishing rate of reproduction. The solution of the great problem is now growing plain. The longevity of the negro in slavery was above the average; in freedom it steadily declines. In slavery, his food, his lodging, his health and vigor were cared for; care was taken of, and medical attendance provided for, women during pregnancy and in confinement, and young children: these now must take whatever chance poverty, ignorance, indifference or brutality will leave them. The unnatural mixture of the white and black races produces a hybrid type that is physically weaker, more liable to disease, and shorter lived than either of its progenitors. All indications point to the fact that the extinction of the negro race on this continent is merely a question of time.

The control of the once free and sovereign States of the South by this race, that ages of slavery have made ignorant of just laws or good government, cannot be of long duration, or else I am mistaken in the judgment and common sense of a large majority of the American people. Either the utter annihilation of the pernicious and ruinous system of legislation of the past twelve or fifteen years must take place, or else, judging the future by the past, a central despotism must be the inevitable consequence. We have the form of a republican government, but have lost the substance; our rights and liberties have silently and secretly disappeared through the fascinating charms of hero-worship. Without a speedy change in the affairs of the nation, the fate of republican institutions in all ages will inevitably overtake this much-boasted "land of the free and home of the brave."

Our would-be historians have vainly attempted to shift all the horrors of the war and its sequences to the shoulders of the South; happily, up to the present, they have failed to prove a single point in their tremendous indictments. Volumes have been written, and language has been tortured, to find invectives of sufficient force and bitterness in which to vent their spleen. The pencil and brush have endeavored to portray what the pen failed to supply; but the "Banner of the South" to-day is as stainless as it was when folded at Appomattox Court-house by the hand that drew the sword in defence of the rights and liberties of the people of the South. No foul blot marked their fair escutcheon during the mighty contest; and they now have the proud satisfaction to know that their flag was borne by men like Lee and Jackson and Johnston, and not by such as Hunter, Milroy, Butler, and Turchin. That virtue and patriotism were the beacon-stars that guided the former in their efforts for freedom and independence, and not empire, plunder, and the spoils of war, under the guise of devotion to the Union and the Constitution.

I would say, in conclusion, that for the victim Wirz or the slandered Winder I have no defence to make; as the impartial historian must always place a just estimate on their efforts in behalf of humanity towards defenceless prisoners of war. The unbiassed reader of these pages will justly appreciate the difficulties under which they labored amid the terrible trials of unequal warfare. That they may have erred in some instances, in their attempts to ameliorate the condition of the suffering captives, may be true; but their desire and intention to mitigate the severities of imprisonment, as far as their means and their duty permitted, are evident from the record. For myself and alleged co-conspirators, justice demanded that the world should know how unfairly our antagonists have dealt with us, in seeking through false statements to pervert the truth in the matter of Federal prisoners of war. I am fully conscious that in discharging the duty of vindicating myself and countrymen, I have said nothing in a spirit of malice. The impartial tribunal of the civilised world must judge our acts and motives by the facts as recorded in these pages. Another Tribunal will fix the penalty upon those who were responsible for the violation of the "Cartel of Exchange," and the consequent sufferings and mortality at *Andersonville Prison.*

APPENDIX.

A

List of Federal soldiers that died and were buried at Andersonville, Ga., registered by Surgeon J. H. White, Surgeon R. R. Stevenson, and Surgeon H. H. Clayton, on the C. S. M. Prison Hospital Register, from the organisation of the prison in February 1864 to the surrender of the Confederate armies in May 1865; alphabetically arranged by States and names, showing the regiments and companies to which they belonged, and date of death. The numbers refer to the graves, as previously described in the body of the work.

It is proper to state, that up to the present date I have been debarred from my Hospital Register, now in possession of the authorities at Washington City, and have had to depend mainly for the preparation, arrangement and correctness of this record on the published statements of Northern writers on the same subject.

ALABAMA.

7524	Barton Wm	1 Cav Co	L	Sept 1 64
2111	Berry J M, Sgt	"	A	May 17 64
4623	Belle Robert	"	A	Aug 3 64
5505	Boobar Wm	"	E	Aug 13 64
8425	Brice J C	"	L	Sept 11 64
8147	Guthrie J	"	I	Sept 8 64
2514	Henry P	"	F	June 26 64
996	Jones Jno F	"	K	Mar 15 64
4735	Mitchell Jno D	1 Co	A	Aug 4 64
5077	Ponders J	1 Cav Co	H	Aug 8 64
5763	Panter R	1 "	L	Aug 15 64
6886	Patterson W D	1 "	K	Aug 25 64
2504	Prett J R	1 "	F	June 3 64
10903	Redman W R	1 Cav "	G	Oct 14 64
4731	Stubbs W	1 "	I	Aug 4 64

TOTAL 15

CONNECTICUT.

2380	Anderson A	14	Co K	June 23 64
3461	Batchelder Benj	16	" C	July 17 64
3664	Baty John	16	" C	July 19 64
7306	Brunkissell H	14	" D	Aug 30 64
2833	Brennon M	14	" B	July 3 64
3224	Burns Jno	7	" I	July 12 64
10414	Blumly E	8	" D	Oct 6 64
545	Bigelow Wm	7	" B	Apr 14 64
11965	Ball H A	3	" B	Nov 11 64
12089	Brookmeyer T W	8	" H	Nov 18 64
12152	Burke H	16	" D	Nov 24 64
12209	Bone A	1	" E	Dec 1 64
10682	Burnham F, Corpl	14	" I	Oct 11 64
10690	Barlow O L	16	" E	Oct 11 64
10876	Bennett N	18	" H	Oct 13 64
5806	Brown C H	1	" H	Aug 15 64
5919	Boyce Wm	7	" B	Aug 17 64
6083	Bishop B H	1 Cav	" I	Aug 18 64
6184	Bushnell Wm	14	" D	Aug 19 64
1763	Bailey F	16	" E	Sept 4 64
2054	Brewer G E	21	" A	June 16 64
5596	Burns B	6	" G	Aug 14 64
5632	Balcomb	11	" B	Aug 14 64
5754	Beers James C	16	" A	Aug 15 64
11636	Birdsell D	16	" D	Oct 28 64
4296	Blakeslee H	1 Cav	" L	July 30 64
3900	Bishop A	18	" A	July 24 64
1493	Besannon Peter	14	" B	June 2 64
2720	Babcock R	30	" A	July 1 64
2818	Baldwin Thomas	1 Cav	" L	July 3 64
2256	Bosworth A M	16	" D	June 21 64
5132	Bougin John	11	" C	Aug 8 64
5152	Brooks Wm D, Corpl	16	" F	Aug 9 64
5308	Bower John	16	" E	Aug 11 64
5452	Bently F	6	" H	Aug 12 64
5464	Bently James	1 Cav	" I	Aug 12 64
4830	Blackman A, Corpl	2 Art	" C	Aug 6 64
7742	Banning J F	16	" E	Sept 3 64
8018	Ballentine Robert	16	" A	Sept 6 64
12408	Bassett J B	11	" B	Jany 6 65
12540	Bohine C	2	" E	Jany 27 65
12620	Bennis Charles	7	" K	Feby 8 65
3707	Chapin J L	16	" A	July 21 64
3949	Cottrell P	7	" C	July 25 64
3941	Clarkson	11	" H	July 25 64
4367	Culler M	7	" E	July 31 64
4449	Connor D	18	" F	Aug 1 64
4818	Carrier D B	16	" D	Aug 6 64
6060	Cook W H	1 Cav	" G	Aug 18 64
6153	Clark H H	13	" F	Aug 15 64
6846	Clark W	6	" A	Aug 25 64
5799	Champlain H	10	" F	Aug 15 64
836	Cane John	9	" H	Apl 2 64
620	Christian A M	1	" A	Apl 19 64
775	Crawford James	14	" A	Apl 28 64
7316	Chapman M	16	" E	Aug 30 64
7348	Cleary P	1 Cav	" B	Aug 31 64
7395	Campbell Robert	7	" E	Aug 31 64
7418	Culler M	16	" K	Aug 31 64
7685	Carver John G	16	Co B	Sept 3 64
7780	Cain Thomas	14	" G	Sept 4 64
9984	Crossley B	8	" G	Sept 29 64
10272	Coltier W	16	" B	Oct 3 64
11175	Callahan J	11	" I	Oct 19 64
11361	Candee D M	2 Art	" A	Oct 23 64
25	Dowd F	7	" I	Mch 8 64
7325	Davis W	1 Cav	" L	Aug 30 64
2813	Davis W	10	" E	July 3 64
3614	Damery John	6	" A	July 20 64
7597	Diebenthal H	11	" C	Sept 2 64
8568	Donoway J	1 Cav	" A	Sept 12 64
8769	Dutton W H	16	" K	Sept 14 64
5446	Dugan Charles	16	" K	Aug 12 64
11339	Dean R	16	" H	Oct 23 64
11481	Demmings G A	16	" I	Oct 24 64
11889	Downer S	18	" C	Nov 7 64
11991	Demming B J	16	" G	Nov 13 64
3482	Emmonds A	16	" K	July 17 64
4437	Easterly Thomas	14	" G	July 31 64
4558	Earnest H C	6	" I	Aug 2 64
7346	Ensworth John	16	" C	Aug 31 64
7603	Edwards O J, Corpl	8	" G	Sept 2 64
8368	Evans N L	16	" I	Sept 10 64
11608	Emmett W	16	" K	Oct 28 64
12442	Eaton W	6	" F	Jany 12 65
186	Fluit C W	14	" G	Mch 27 64
1277	Francell Otto	6	" C	May 22 64
2612	Fry S	7	" D	June 28 64
4144	Fibbles H	16	" G	Aug 1 64
4465	Fisher H	1	" E	Aug 1 64
5123	Florence J J, Corpl	16	" C	Aug 8 64
5382	Fuller H S	24	" H	Aug 11 64
5913	Frisbie Levi	1 Cav	" G	Aug 17 64
5556	Fogg C, Sgt	7	" K	Aug 13 64
8028	Feely M	7	" I	Sept 6 64
9089	Filby A	14	" C	Sept 18 64
10255	Frederick John	7	" A	Oct 3 64
12188	Fagan P D	11	" A	Nov 28 64
3028	Gordon John	14	" G	July 7 64
4096	Gray Pat	9	" H	July 27 64
4974	Grammon Jas	1 Cav	" K	July 7 64
4005	Gulterman J	Mus 1	" E	July 26 64
5173	Gilmore J	16	" C	Aug 9 64
7057	Gallagher P	16	" D	Aug 28 64
7337	Gott G	Mus 18		Aug 30 64
7592	Goodrich J W	16	" C	Sept 2 64
7646	Graigg W	16	" B	Sept 3 64
9423	Guina H M	11	" G	Sept 21 64
10300	Grady M	11	" B	Oct 4 64
10397	Gladstone Wm	6	" K	Oct 6 64
49	Holt Thomas	1 Cav	" A	Mar 15 64
2336	Hughes Ed	14	" D	June 22 64
3195	Hitchcock Wm A	16	" C	July 12 64
3148	Hall Wm G	1	" K	July 17 64
3559	Holcomb D	14	" D	July 18 64
1350	Hilenthal Jas	14	" C	May 25 64
3033	Haskins Jas	16	" D	July 8 64
5029	Hollister A	1 Cav	" L	Aug 8 64

Connecticut— (*Continued.*)

5162	Hally Thomas	16 Co	F	Aug 9 64
5353	Hanson F A	15 "	I	Aug 11 64
6695	Hodges Geo	1 Cav "	H	Aug 24 64
4937	Harwood G	15 "	A	Aug 7 64
6964	Hoyt E S	17 "	B	Aug 27 64
7012	Hull M	16 "	E	Aug 27 64
7380	Holcomb A A	16 "	E	Aug 31 64
7642	Haley W	16 "	D	Sept 3 64
7757	Hubbard H D	16 "	D	Sept 4 64
8043	Haywood	18 "	E	Sept 11 64
8613	Heath I, Sgt	16 "	K	Sept 13 64
9129	Hall B	16 "	G	Sept 18 64
9369	Heart W	11 "	F	Sept 20 64
9981	Hurley R A	16 "	I	Sept 29 64
12086	Hibbard A	18 "	D	Nov 18 64
12117	Hancock W	14 "	G	Nov 22 64
12163	Hudson Chas	11 "	C	Nov 26 64
8148	Hubbard B	16 "	A	Nov 8 64
9340	Islay H	11		Sept 4 64
737	Jamieson Charles	7 "	D	Apl 26 64
5221	Johnson John	16 "	E	Aug 10 64
7083	Johnson G W	11 "	G	Aug 28 64
7365	Jamison J S, Q M S	1 Cav		Aug 31 64
7570	Jones Jno J	16 "	B	Sept 2 64
7961	Jones James R	6 "	G	Sept 6 64
8502	Johnson F	1 "	D	Sept 12 64
11970	Johnson C S	16 "	E	Nov 12 64
12340	Johnson W	16 "	E	Dec 26 64
1590	Kingsbury C	14 "	K	June 3 64
5186	Klineland L	11 "	C	Aug 9 64
6374	Kempton B F	8 "	G	Aug 21 64
6705	Kershoff B	6 "	H	Aug 25 64
6748	Kelley F	14 "	I	Aug 25 64
7749	Kalty J	1 Cav "	L	Sept 3 64
8065	Kimball H H	7 "	H	Sept 7 64
8866	Kohlenburg C	7 "	D	Sept 15 64
10233	Kearn T	16 "	A	Oct 2 64
3401	Lendon H	16 "	D	July 16 64
5893	Lastry J	10 "	I	Aug 16 64
5499	Lewis J	8 "	E	Aug 12 64
6124	Leonard W	14 "	H	Aug 19 64
7912	Lavanaugh W O, Sgt	16 "	C	Sept 5 64
7956	Linker C	8 "	G	Sept 6 64
9219	Lewis G H	7 "	G	Sept 19 64
10228	Lee, farrier	1 Cav "	F	Oct 2 64
74	Mills W J	6 "	D	Mar 20 64
119	McCaulley Jas	14 "	D	Mar 20 64
2295	Miller Charles	14 "	I	June 21 64
3516	McCord P	16 "	G	July 18 64
3644	Miller A	14 "	D	July 19 64
3410	Mould James	11 "	E	July 16 64
3932	McGinnis J W	15 "	E	Aug 17 64
4079	Miller D	1 Cav "	E	July 27 64
4417	Messenger A	16 "	G	July 31 64
4492	McLean Wm	11 "	F	Aug 1 64
4595	Marshalls B	8 "	H	Aug 3 64
5238	Mickallis F	16 "	F	Aug 10 64
7852	Miller F D	16 "	B	Sept 64
8150	Modger A	10 "	I	Sept 8 64
6902	Mape George	11 Co	B	Aug 25 64
6240	Marshall L	8 "	H	July 20 64
7547	Moore A P, Sgt	1 Cav "	H	Sept 2 64
8446	Mathews S J	16 "	K	Sept 11 64
8501	Myers L	1 Cav		Sept 12 64
9170	Merts C	11 Co	C	Sept 18 64
9321	Milor W, Sgt	14 "	F	Sept 20 64
5328	Miller H	16 "	A	Aug 11 64
6342	Malone John	16 "	B	Aug 22 64
6426	Messey M	7 "	E	Aug 22 64
6451	McGee Thomas	11 "	D	Aug 22 64
6570	McDavid James	1 "	K	Aug 23 64
6800	Meal John	11 "	D	Aug 25 64
10595	McCreieth A	14 "	H	Oct 10 64
10914	McKeon J	7 "	H	Oct 14 64
11487	Murphy W	16 "	C	Oct 26 64
11538	McDowell J	11 "	D	Oct 27 64
12134	Montjoy T	5 "	C	Nov 23 64
5044	Nichols C	16 "	G	Aug 8 64
6222	Northrop John	7 "	D	Aug 20 64
7331	North S S, Sgt	1 Cav "	D	Aug 30 64
10895	Nichols M	7 "	I	Oct 14 64
4565	Orton H C	6 "	I	Aug 9 64
7511	Olena R	1 Cav "	E	Sept 1 64
8276	Orr A	14 "	H	Sept 14 64
2960	Pendalton W	14 "	C	July 6 64
3868	Pompey C	14 "	B	July 24 64
4356	Parker S B	10 "	B	July 31 64
3803	Phelps S G	1 "	H	July 22 64
4934	Pimble A	16 "	I	Aug 7 64
5002	Plum James	11 "	G	Aug 8 64
5386	Patchey J	1 Cav "	I	Aug 12 64
7487	Post C, Sgt	16 "	K	Sept 1 64
7688	Potache A	7 "	G	Sept 3 64
9248	Phillips J I	8 "	B	Sept 19 64
9444	Padfrey Sylvanus	8 "	H	Sept 21 64
9533	Painter N P	7 "	C	Sept 22 64
10676	Puritan O	1 Cav "	L	Oct 11 64
11616	Peir A	7 "	D	Oct 28 64
2804	Ruther J, Sgt	1 Cav "	E	July 3 64
2871	Reed H H	2 Art "	H	July 4 64
3674	Risley E, Sgt	10 "	B	July 20 64
4636	Reins Wm	11 "	I	Aug 3 64
5902	Ross D	10 "	K	Aug 16 64
6400	Robinson H	21 "	K	Aug 21 64
6796	Ringwood R	14 "	I	Aug 25 64
8078	Reed John	7 "	B	Sept 7 64
8170	Richardson C S	16 "	E	Sept 9 64
8345	Ray A	11 "	G	Sept 10 64
7310	Reed Robt K	7 "	A	Aug 30 64
8662	Roper H	16 "	G	Sept 13 64
10029	Robinson J W	18 "	D	Sept 29 64
10196	Richardson D T	16 "	G	Oct 2 64
10416	Reynolds E	1 "	E	Oct 6 64
12031	Rathbone B	2 "	A	Nov 15 64
4	Stone H I	1 Cav "	A	Mar 3 64
234	Smith Horace	7 "	D	Mar 29 64
2405	Seward G H	14 "	A	June 24 64
2474	Stephens E W	1 Cav "	L	June 25 64

Connecticut — (*Continued.*)

3010	Scott W	14	Co D	July 7 64
3026	Sutcliff B	21	" G	Jul. 7 64
3041	Stuart J	7		July 8 64
3522	Smith J	14	" I	July 18 64
3598	Sherwood D	1	" D	July 18 64
4212	Smith C E, Sergt	1 Cav	" L	July 27 64
4316	Stranbell L	11	" C	July 30 64
4555	Straum James	2 Art	" L	Aug 2 64
4722	Sullivan M	16	" D	Aug 4 64
4892	Steel Sam	14	" C	Aug 6 64
5385	Shults C T	14	" I	Aug 12 64
5563	Stino P	16	" K	Aug 13 64
5712	Steele Sam	16	" C	Aug 15 64
5725	Smith S	7	" B	Aug 15 64
6734	Steele James M	16	" F	Aug 18 64
7070	Stephens B H	14		Aug 28 64
7975	Smith Henry	5	Co H	Sept 6 64
8088	Short L C	18	" K	Sept 7 64
8235	Smally L	16	" E	Sept 9 64
9304	Starkweather E M	1 Cav	" L	Sept 20 64
9435	Sutliff J	16	" C	Sept 21 64
9648	See L	1	" G	Sept 24 64
9987	Sling D	7	" F	Sept 29 64
10138	Schubert K	16	" K	Oct 1 64
10247	Sparring T	7	" K	Oct 3 64
10476	Steele H	16	" F	Oct 7 64
10787	Stauff J	1 Cav	" L	Oct 12 64
12005	Swift J	1	Co K	Nov 14 64
12288	Smith J T	7	" D	Dec 13 64
541	Taylor Moses	14	" E	Apl 14 64
4443	Thompson Wm T	14	" I	Aug 1 64
5427	Thompson F	14	" A	Aug 12 64
5479	Tibbels Wm	16	" G	Aug 12 64
7723	Tredway J H, Sgt	15	" E	Aug 3 64
10035	Tisdale Ed F	1 Cav	" B	Sept 29 64
10142	Taylor J	14	" I	Oct 1 64
11089	Turner H	11	" A	Oct 18 64
8107	Valter H	14	" A	July 10 64
401	Winship J H	18	" C	Apl 6 64
2158	Weldon Henry	7	" E	June 19 64
2601	Warner E	1 Cav	" E	June 28 64
5543	Wickert Henry	14	" C	Aug 13 64
5222	Wright C	16	" B	Aug 10 64
4649	Wheely James	10	" G	Aug 3 64
5675	Wenchell John L	16	" E	Aug 14 64
6138	Way H C	16	" K	Aug 19 64
6918	Wiggleworth M L	2 Art	" H	Aug 26 64
8024	West Chas H	16	" I	Sept 6 64
9028	Williams H D, Sgt	16	" F	Sept 17 64
9165	Wheeler J	1 Cav	" M	Sept 19 64
9512	Ward Gilbert, Sgt	11	"	Sept 22 64
10033	Weins John	6	" K	Sept 29 64
12600	Ward G W	18	" C	Feb 6 65
6394	Young C S, Sgt	16	" C	Aug 21 64

TOTAL 290.

DELAWARE.

8812	Aiken Wm	7	Co G	Sept 15 64
5529	Boice J	4		Aug 13 64
7016	Brown J H	2	Co I	Aug 27 64
1709	Callihan Jno	1	" B	June 7 64
2698	Conoway F	1	" K	June 30 64
4394	Conley J H	2	" F	July 31 64
12253	Connor G	1 Cav	" D	Dec 9 64
10868	Conner C	2	" F	Oct 13 64
11245	Cunningham K	1	" F	Oct 13 64
6217	Donohue H	2	" D	Aug 20 64
6677	Emmett W	1	" K	Aug 24 64
2091	Field S	2	" D	June 17 64
9004	Hanning H, Drum	2	" F	Sept 17 64
8346	Hills W	2	" K	Sept 10 64
5504	Hobson W	1 Cav	" E	Aug 13 64
9839	Hudson G W, Sgt	2		Sept 27 64
11634	Hussey J R	1 Cav	Co D	Oct 28 64
790	Joseph W C	1	" E	Apl 28 64
5340	Jones H	2	" B	Aug 11 64
11410	Kinney M	1	" D	Oct 24 64
8292	Laughlin R M	1	" C	Sept 9 64
483	Limpkins J H	2	" D	Apl 9 64
5956	Maham Jas	2	" C	Aug 17 64
8972	Moxworthy Geo	2	Co D	Sept 16 64
9580	Martin J	1	" G	Sept 23 64
9043	Manner C	2	" K	Sept 28 64
1671	McCracklin H	1	" B	June 6 64
11570	McKinney J	1	" F	Oct 27 64
12407	McBride	2	" F	Jan 6 65
9450	Norris Clarence	1 Cav	" L	Sept 21 64
6307	Peterson P	4	" F	Aug 20 64
8743	Piffer W	2	" F	Aug 14 64
7551	Reitter G	2	" F	Sept 2 64
11534	Riddler H A	1	" H	Oct 27 64
6618	Saurot John	2	" E	Aug 23 64
6479	Sholder Ed	2	" H	Aug 22 64
6593	Simble Wm	1 Cav	" C	Aug 23 64
12707	Sill James	2	" K	Feby 28 65
5764	Smith E E	2	" E	Aug 15 64
276	Taylor Robert	1	" G	Mch 31 64
8082	Thorn H I	2	" D	Sept 8 64
9324	Tilbrick E L	1 Cav	" L	Sept 20 64
11921	Warner G	2	" K	Nov 13 64
10302	Wilds J	2	" K	Oct 4 64
198	Wilburn Geo	2	" G	Mch 27 64

TOTAL 55.

DISTRICT OF COLUMBIA.

8449	Boissonnault F M	1 Cav	Co H	Sept 11 64
11700	Clark Theodore	1 "	" I	Oct 31 64
11180	Farrell C	1 "	" E	Oct 19 64
5736	Gray G S	1 "	" K	Aug 15 64
9463	Pillman John	1 Cav	Co D	Sept 21 64
6873	Ridley A C	1 "	" M	Aug 26 64
11716	Russell T	1 "	" D	Nov 1 64
6847	Stretch J	1 "	" G	Aug 25 64

District of Columbia—(*Continued.*)

8189	Sergeant L, Sgt	1 Cav	Co G	Sept 8 64
11742	Stanhope W H	1 "	" I	Nov 2 64
12457	Veasie F	1 "	" K	Jan 15 65
8172	Winworth G	1 Cav	Co G	Sept 8 64
8307	Wiggins Nat	1 "	" M	Sept 15 64
10301	Wilson W	1 "	" E	Oct 3 64

TOTAL 14.

ILLINOIS.

8402	Adams H F, Sgt	17	Co E	Sept 11 64
12430	Adder W	80	" C	Jan 4 65
3840	Adlet John	119	" K	July 23 64
8249	Adrian F	Cav 9	" E	Sept 9 64
5876	Akens C, Sgt	78	" F	Aug 16 64
8331	Albany D	22	" D	Sept 10 64
1264	Aldridge A	Cav 16	" L	May 20 64
8127	Alexander B	123	" B	Sept 8 64
1423	Allen R C	17	" I	May 28 64
10762	Alf H	89	" A	Oct 12 64
2400	Allison L J	21	" B	June 24 64
6710	Anderson A	19	" K	Aug 24 64
10242	Anderson A	98	" E	Oct 3 64
9946	Anderson W	89	" C	Sept 28 64
10271	Anthony E	3	" E	Oct 3 64
7339	Armstrong R	89	" A	Aug 30 64
12792	Arnold L	137	" I	Mch 18 65
10979	Atkins E	6	" C	Oct 15 64
9783	Atkinson James	Cav 14	" D	Sept 25 64
11777	Atwood A	23	" G	Nov 3 64
8046	Augustine J	100	" I	Sept 6 64
3709	Babbitt John	7	" K	July 21 64
2593	Babcock F	44	" G	June 28 64
3783	Bailey P, Sgt	38	" B	July 22 64
12530	Baker James	25	" H	Jan 26 65
2892	Baker John	89	" B	July 4 64
3308	Baker Thomas	Cav 16	" M	July 14 64
1034	Bales Thomas	Art 2	" M	May 11 64
5848	Barber C F	112	" I	Aug 16 64
3829	Barclay P	42	" I	July 23 64
12758	Barnard W	14	" F	Mch 12 65
10480	Barnes Thomas	135	" F	Oct 7 64
8458	Barnett J	120	" I	Sept 11 64
8762	Barrett A, Sgt	25	" A	Sept 14 64
12687	Bass J	Cav 2	" C	Feb 22 65
977	Basting C	47	" B	May 9 64
3275	Bathrick J	Cav 1	" A	July 14 64
4618	Batsdorf M	93	" F	Aug 3 64
3603	Bayley Frank	Cav 16	" E	July 19 64
11917	Beaver M	29	" B	Nov 8 64
11652	Beard J	14	" K	Oct 30 64
1870	Beal John	78		June 12 64
6644	Bear D	93	Co B	Aug 28 64
4573	Beck J	21	" G	Aug 2 64
411	Beliskey J	Cav 16	" D	Apl 18 64
1230	Bender George	12	" C	May 20 64
5242	Bennet A	16	" B	Aug 10 64
6412	Benning John	Cav 6	" G	Aug 22 64
3315	Benstill John	27	" H	July 15 64
10653	Benton C W	29	" B	Oct 11 64
8188	Berlizer B	Cav 16	" F	Sept 8 64
10681	Best William	88	" E	Oct 11 64

4215	Black John, Sgt	31	Co A	July 30 64
2904	Black J H	21	" E	July 5 64
1665	Blanchard L, Sgt	16 Cav	" D	June 6 64
1983	Bloss P	21	" A	June 15 64
11085	Bodkins E L	103	" D	Oct 18 64
2890	Bogley J E	21	" D	July 4 64
12456	Bohem J	Cav 14	" B	Jan 14 65
9899	Boles William	89	" C	Sept 27 64
10795	Bolton N P	100	" B	Nov 4 64
10791	Bowman J	108	" D	Oct 12 64
3008	Boorem O	64	" B	July 7 64
12621	Borem M	35	" G	Feby 9 65
11921	Bonser G	89	" F	Nov 8 64
5475	Bowden W		" F	Aug 13 64
5046	Bowen A O	113	" C	Aug 8 64
5943	Bowman E	123	" F	Aug 17 64
9328	Boyd B F	Cav 6	" D	Sept 25 64
11678	Boyd H P	14	" I	Oct 31 64
1971	Boyd J E	84	" B	June 15 64
10984	Boyer J, Sgt	14	" H	Oct 16 64
11729	Boyle F	4	" B	Nov 1 64
12840	Bradford D	85	" C	Apl 25 65
4259	Branch J	38	" C	July 29 64
1815	Brandiger F	24	" K	June 10 64
1619	Brannock C, Sgt	79	" K	June 4 64
1578	Brayheyer H	Cav 7	" M	June 3 64
3940	Brett James	88	" K	July 24 64
1669	Brewer Henry, Sgt	24	" C	June 6 64
6421	Brewer H	78	" F	Aug 22 64
3264	Bridges W H	30	" K	July 13 64
9570	Bridges W J	122	" F	Sept 23 64
1613	Bridewell H C	38	" D	June 4 64
2367	Brinkey M, Sgt	16 Cav	" L	June 25 64
3056	Britsnyder J	65	" G	July 9 64
2927	Brockhill J	Cav 4	" M	July 5 64
3717	Brookman J E, Corpl	44	" I	July 21 64
8911	Brothers D	48	" H	Sept 16 64
9350	Brown A F, Sgt	73	" C	Sept 20 64
12450	Brown H	15	" F	Jany 14 65
5978	Brown J	73	" B	Aug 17 64
9011	Brown J H	12	" F	Sept 17 64
5924	Brown J M	29	" B	Aug 17 64
6826	Brown William	Cav 1	" G	Aug 26 64
8962	Brown William	16	" C	Sept 16 64
6256	Bryant William C	107	" A	Aug 20 64
10763	Briden E	35	" E	Oct 12 64
5785	Buck B F	30	" I	Aug 15 64
4963	Buchman	Cav 16	" H	Aug 7 64
10888	Buckmaster J	79	" C	Oct 13 64
12362	Buffington B	74	" F	Dec 30 64
5457	Burdes G	89	" A	Aug 12 64
4299	Burrows J	90	" L	July 30 64

Illinois — (*Continued.*)

7055	Burns John	100	Co K	Aug 23 64
6936	Burns H, Sgt	Cav 16	" D	Aug 17 64
526	Burr W B	112	" E	Apl 13 64
1858	Burton O L	35	" I	Nov 6 64
11858	Butler H J	89	" D	Oct 10 64
10362	Butler N, Sgt	89	" D	Oct 5 64
8776	Butler J	89	" A	Sept 14 64
11668	utton A R	79	" E	Oct 30 64
9824	Butts John	22	" F	Sept 27 64
626	Byres George	65	" B	Apl 19 64
12348	Cadding J C	89	" B	Dec 27 64
6356	Callahan C	39	" F	Aug 21 64
6505	Campbell J M	120	" G	Aug 22 64
10026	Capell C	87	" D	Sept 29 64
10257	Capsey J, Sgt	90	" D	Oct 3 64
3556	Carl C C	38	" H	July 18 64
666	Carroll J	3	" H	Apl 22 64
7037	Carroll J Q, Sgt	78	" I	Aug 27 64
3393	Carren O	38	" H	July 16 64
6693	Carirt Robert	113	" D	Aug 24 64
446	Cault Albert	116	" A	Apl 9 64
1844	Castle F	103	" E	June 10 64
7502	Center E R	115	" H	Sept 1 64
3907	Charles R J	5 Cav	" M	July 24 64
6109	Chase E S	23	" C	Aug 18 64
9095	Chattenay S	82	" H	Sept 18 64
10459	Chenly S	79	" A	Oct 7 64
4319	Chitwood T C	16 Cav	" H	July 30 64
3205	Chlunworth Wm	9	" G	July 12 64
10551	Choate Wm	Cav 6	" D	Oct 10 64
9935	Chunberg A	89	" G	Sept 28 64
6935	Christiansen J	82	" F	Aug 26 64
7863	Clancey J W	38	" E	Sept 5 64
504	Clark A E	Cav 16	" M	Apl 12 64
7760	Clark C	51	" K	Sept 4 64
9560	Clark C	29	" B	Sept 23 64
8834	Clark F J	Cav 6	" B	Sept 15 64
12672	Clark R	114	" F	Feb 18 65
5143	Clark Wm	Cav 14	" K	Aug 9 64
9925	Cleaver M	Cav 3	" H	Sept 28 64
8750	Cleggett M, Sgt	36	" I	Sept 14 64
5787	Cline John	Cav 12	" I	Aug 15 64
12726	Cline M	14	" B	Mar 4 65
12051	Cline T	15	" E	Nov 16 64
2237	Clusterman	16 Cav	" D	June 21 64
2048	Coalman H	16 Cav		June 15 64
2753	Colbern M	73	Co I	July 1 64
2244	Colburn Thomas	16 Cav	" G	June 20 64
5597	Colburn Wm	16 "	" G	Aug 14 64
300	Cole John	112	" E	Apl 1 64
7211	Cole W H	112	" A	Aug 29 64
6971	Coller John	6	" B	Aug 27 64
256	Collins Wm	93	" G	Mch 30 64
1198	Coddington M J	93	" G	May 18 64
11719	Compton H H	21	" K	Nov 1 64
2933	Cooret D	78	" F	July 5 64
46[illegible]3	Carey J	38	" I	Aug 4 64
2758	Corey O C	106	" D	July 1 64
6738	Cornelius Jas	Cav 9	" H	Aug 24 64

3856	Corwin J	Cav 7	Co K	July 24 64
2677	Corwin J V	Cav 6	" L	July 20 64
6091	Cotton J, Sergt	100	" H	Aug 18 64
9704	Craig G	23	" B	Sept 25 64
9307	Craig J	38	" I	Sept 20 64
12506	Craig J	Art 3	" B	Jan 22 63
9704	Craig S	23	" B	Sept 25 64
10087	Craig F	9	" K	Sept 30 64
1[illegible]74	Crandall W M	93	" A	June 15 64
2329	Crane M	23	" E	June 23 64
2253	Crawford Wm	Cav 16	" K	June 21 64
10912	Crelley C W	29	" B	Oct 14 64
4879	Cook G P	Cav 16	" L	Aug 6 64
12433	Crosbey J	90	" C	Jan 11 65
1417	Cross E	111	" C	May 27 64
8859	Cross J D	Cav 14	" I	Sept 15 64
7982	Cross J T	21	" D	Sept 6 64
6744	Crouse J, Sergt	16	" I	Aug 24 64
2032	Cruse J	79	" D	June 15 64
2179	Creman George	24	" C	June 19 64
10026	Cupell C	82	" D	Sept 29 64
10257	Cupsay J, Corpl	90	" D	Oct 3 64
3887	Curtis A	16	" D	July 24 64
8626	Dake G, Corpl	100	" D	Sept 13 64
4063	Dalby James	73	" H	Aug 3 64
1826	Darling D W	93	" B	June 10 64
10961	Darum J J	112	" I	Oct 15 64
356	Davis And	112	" A	Apl 2 64
8553	Davis C	112	" E	Sept 12 64
10603	Davis J	113	" D	Oct 10 64
4150	Davis W	Cav 16	" M	July 28 64
4048	Davis H, Sergt	38	" A	July 27 64
12311	Delancey L D	Art 2	" F	Dec 9 64
7013	Day W H	111	" H	Aug 27 64
9073	Decker C	Cav 7	" M	Sept 17 64
4608	Decker J P	119	" C	Aug 3 64
7150	Demos B F	78	" F	Aug 29 64
2497	Denhart W	Cav 16	" K	June 26 64
4423	Denior E, Sergt	79	" B	July 31 64
7514	Deming Joseph	31	" D	Sept 1 64
12060	Denton E, Corpl	15	" B	Feby 16 65
2231	Detreeman D, Sgt	44	" E	June 20 64
5165	DePue J W	16	" C	Aug 9 64
352	Deraus G W	21	" B	Apl 2 64
2365	Dricks Henry	89	" C	June 23 64
12547	Dilley A	15	" E	Jany 28 65
1314	Dodson M, Sgt	Cav 3	" H	May 23 64
8187	Dock C	Cav 9	" H	Sept 8 64
3834	Dodd G W	21	" F	July 23 64
4207	Dodson R B	Cav 6	" B	July 29 64
2867	Dooley James	Cav 16	" L	July 4 64
1441	Doran W H	78	" I	May 28 64
1103	Donen C	6	" I	May 15 64
1727	Dowd J W	38	" G	June 8 64
1342	Dowdy John	16	" K	May 24 64
10143	Dowell J W	112	" K	Oct 1 64
10496	Downer A	24	" H	Oct 8 64
12436	Doyle P	65	" H	Jany 11 65
12476	Doyle J	112	" I	Jany 17 65

Illinois—(*Continued.*)

5053	Drake R R	34 Co H	Aug 8 65
10302	Dresser C	24 " G	Oct 4 65
9378	Drum G	89	Sept 24 65
8123	Dudley J W	89 Co F	July 10 65
2666	Dumond P	35 " E	June 29 65
9947	Dunn Alexander	75 " A	Sept 28 65
12496	Dunsing A	30 " C	Jany 21 65
9037	Dyer J C	30 " D	Sept 17 64
12686	Drew E	53 " D	Feby 20 65
209	Eadley Levi	26 " H	Mch 28 64
8045	Easinbeck M	100 " D	Sept 6 64
10909	Easley W A, Sgt	21 " G	Oct 14 64
5992	Eastman Wm	36 " F	Aug 17 64
4962	Edwards C D	51 " K	Aug 7 64
8084	Elliott Ed	92 " B	Sept 7 64
9703	Ellis William	26 " G	Sept 25 64
9734	Ellison W	Cav 14 " F	Sept 25 64
2249	Elslin James	112 " E	July 24 64
4502	Emery J	22 " K	Aug 1 64
4979	Emmerson J	Cav 16 " L	Aug 7 64
9717	Erb J	9 " C	Sept 25 64
12628	Ermains F	Cav 14 " M	Feb 14 65
214	Errickson	Cav 16 " M	Mch 28 64
2211	Ench W	29 " H	June 20 64
11727	Enrow W	Cav 7 " M	Nov 1 64
2936	Evans J	9 " C	Sept 25 64
3373	Eydroner R	74 " F	July 15 64
6268	Fagan O	23 " G	Aug 20 64
2436	Fandish S	Art 1 " A	June 25 64
2230	Farmer F	21 " A	June 20 64
4991	Farnham C A	51 " D	Aug 7 64
10740	Ferguson L, Corpl	115 " K	Oct 14 64
2512	File R	11 " K	June 26 64
12628	Fermer J	14 " M	Feb 20 65
3854	Finch F M	21 " G	July 24 64
10097	Fink J P	53 " F	Sept 30 64
11541	Fish J	65 " G	Oct 27 64
9845	Fisher S F	123 " F	Sep 27 64
2129	Fitzgerald H	Cav 16 " I	June 18 64
9992	Flanagan J	42 " H	Sept 29 64
6972	Floyd A	7 " A	Aug 27 64
10881	Ford W J, Sergt	17 " I	Oct 13 64
161	Folk A P	112 " G	Mch 26 64
2564	Forney D	93 " G	June 27 64
8230	Foster A J	Cav 16 " M	Sept 8 64
7720	Foster B B	112 " G	Sept 12 64
12473	Foster E S, Corpl	9 " A	Jan 17 65
531	Fowler John	14 " D	Apr 13 64
12275	Frame W	120 " E	Dec 17 64
12837	Francis J F	12 " I	Apr 19 65
5933	Franklin H	81 " F	Aug 17 64
432	Frass Louis	16 " E	Apr 8 64
4031	Freeman D	Cav 11 " L	July 26 64
2080	French J	129 " B	June 17 63
2210	Fritz P, Sergt	38 " C	June 20 64
1055	Fremont James	Cav 7 " B	May 13 64
497	Fuller Ira B	112 " D	Apr 11 64
8114	Funk Wm	26 " F	Sept 8 64
2021	Furlough H	23 " B	June 15 64
9926	Gaines C	20 Co B	Sept 28 64
1347	Gallagher P	21 " C	May 24 64
579	Garvin John, Sergt	59	Apr 16 64
12801	Gerlock D	30 Co C	Mch 30 65
1340	German P	24 " G	May 24 64
1416	Gibson H D	93 " K	May 27 64
4201	Gibson L F	78 " I	July 29 64
4485	Gichma J, Sergt	Cav 16 " G	Aug 1 64
1652	Giles J V	89 " H	June 5 64
7988	Giles S P	112 " A	Sept 6 64
5144	Gillespie J W	84 " H	Aug 9 64
1499	Gillgrease J	Cav 16 " I	May 30 64
1868	Gilmore J	Cav 16 " E	June 12 64
12731	Gleason G M	Cav 14 " A	Mch 4 65
1850	Glidwell F, Corpl	73 " K	June 11 64
2001	Goffinet P	51 " D	June 15 64
10307	Goddard H	89 " G	Oct 4 64
4203	Gooles H F, Sergt	47 " B	July 29 64
12847	Gordon I	114 " B	Apr 25 65
7953	Gore F	36 " I	Sept 5 64
7761	Gore N	15 " C	Sept 4 64
6111	Garrig J	78 " F	Aug 18 64
12161	Gott H	39 " C	Jany 15 65
9403	Graber J	24 " H	Sept 21 64
9312	Graber J F	81 " D	Sept 20 64
2164	Grace W	21 " D	June 19 64
6617	Graham M J	41 " E	Aug 23 64
10998	Gravel J	51 " C	Oct 16 64
2942	Greadley H	20 " A	July 6 64
4560	Greathouse J	6 " I	Aug 2 64
783	Greaves George	16 " K	Apl 28 64
12116	Green C	79 " A	Nov 22 64
11155	Green John	23 " H	Oct 19 64
7836	Green M	9 " C	Sept 4 64
3111	Greenwall B	Cav 16 " L	July 11 64
11778	Greer George, Corpl	120 " D	Nov 3 64
10594	Gress J	29 " B	Oct 10 64
12834	Grimmins M A	42 " H	Apl 17 65
4083	Griswold J P	79 " E	July 27 64
2501	Grogan H	66 " B	June 26 64
10466	Grower H	42 " K	Oct 7 64
3730	Gulk P	79 " B	July 21 64
5025	Guyen William	72 " E	Aug 8 64
5961	Gonder H	Cav 16 " B	Aug 17 64
5074	Hageman James	Cav 16 " E	Aug 8 64
4094	Haggard E	Cav 16 " K	July 27 64
11959	Haginis W	89 " B	Nov 11 64
2825	Haines Theodore	Cav 14 " M	July 3 64
63	Haks William	16 " E	Mch 19 64
11572	Hall G H	Cav 7 " B	Oct 27 64
12314	Hall H C, Corpl	41 " D	Dec 20 64
7194	Hall J L	9 " C	Aug 29 64
12223	Hall J L	89 " G	Dec 4 64
11[illegible]33	Hall Peter, Corpl	103 " D	Nov 5 64
10061	Haley C H	22 " H	Sept 30 64
1241	Hallam Wm	82 " H	May 20 64
2605	Hanna P	21 " G	June 28 64
187	Hanna H, Corpl	107 " C	Mch 24 64
11188	Hansom D	39 " E	Oct 19 64

Illinois—(*Continued.*)

318	Harken John	65	Co E	Apl 2 64
6634	Harlan J C	7	" L	Aug 24 64
6113	Harrell G	120	" K	Aug 19 64
2633	Harrington S M	112	" A	June 29 64
11725	Harris E K	79	" C	Nov 1 64
10447	Harris G W	9	" G	Oct 7 64
8715	Harshman Peter	84	" H	Sept 14 64
2677	Hart George	Cav 16	" K	June 30 64
2202	Hart W	Cav 16	" K	June 19 64
1980	Harney E	39	" B	June 15 64
10606	Hathaway S	Cav 15	" B	Oct 10 64
12791	Hanch L	15	" D	Mch 18 65
8608	Hawkins J W	79	" I	Sept 12 64
2326	Hayward W G, Corpl	16	" I	June 22 64
5192	Hayworth F	Cav 7	" I	Aug 10 64
1852	Hegenberg W	24	" F	June 11 64
8798	Helch S	77	" K	Sept 15 64
6489	Hendson Geo B	31	" C	Aug 22 64
1162	Henry Wm P	23	" A	July 17 64
6035	Herdson Wm H	107	" C	Aug 18 64
8428	Herrell Wm	Cav 14	" K	Sept 11 64
2365	Hess H	84	" G	June 27 64
1906	Hester John	38	" G	June 13 64
7863	Hicks Geo W	65	" F	Sept 5 64
8303	Hicks H	11	" G	Sept 10 64
1102	Hicks W	85	" D	May 15 64
12070	Highland C	Cav 14	" C	Nov 17 64
725	Hilderbrand N	24	" G	Apr 25 64
8830	Hill Aaron	115	" C	Sept 15 64
67	Hill David, Corpl	36	" A	Mch 19 64
8721	Hill Henry	11		Sept 14 64
4489	Hill J	Cav 9	Co F	Aug 1 64
12683	Hinchcliff J	8	" B	Feb 20 65
6117	Hoen Peter	112	" H	Aug 19 64
3835	Hoffman J	Cav 7	" I	July 23 64
11847	Hofman R	35	" C	Nov 5 64
2098	Hook Jas J, Sergt	93	" E	June 17 64
8255	Hoppock I	112	" F	July 13 64
9880	Honeson A F	88	" F	Sept 27 64
9214	Hormer J	38	" F	Sept 19 64
12090	Horn T	86	" A	Nov 18 64
89	Horseman W	Cav 16	" I	Mch 21 64
5812	Howard D N, Sergt	79	" E	Aug 16 64
10782	Howard G S, Corpl	127	" K	Nov 3 64
3211	Howell J W	78	" F	July 12 64
11506	Hoye J	100	" A	Oct 26 64
5741	Hude C	24	" F	Aug 15 64
6035	Hudson W H	107	" C	Aug 13 64
9962	Hughes D L	125	" H	Sept 28 64
12755	Huise A B	14	" D	Mch 12 65
11140	Hungerford N	108	" I	Oct 19 64
6085	Huntley R	89	" F	Aug 18 64
1136	Hurlburt D	84	" C	May 16 64
1162	Hurry W B	23	" A	May 16 64
5019	Hutchins S	104	" A	Aug 8 64
4583	Hustand B F, Sgt	92	" D	Aug 2 64
4091	Hyber John	Cav 6	" A	July 27 64
3312	Iverson J S	Cav 16	" I	July 14 64
4132	Jaccards S A, Sgt	29	" E	July 28 64
2658	Jackson H	51	Co C	June 29 64
10287	Jackson M	123	" F	Oct 4 64
12797	Janks J P	Cav 3	" A	Mch 18 65
3686	Jarvis J	73	" K	July 20 64
6733	Jenningsen G B	30	" E	Aug 24 64
1845	Jenny E H, Corpl	79	" F	June 11 64
2135	Jewett F	14	" A	June 18 64
1996	Johnson C W	Cav 7	" F	June 15 64
9458	Johnson Joseph	125	" K	Sept 21 64
1412	Johnson J S	7	" C	May 27 64
5395	Johnson Samuel	100	" B	Aug 12 64
9827	Jones G W	27	" E	Sept 27 64
8971	Jones J	117	" E	Sept 16 64
4889	Jones P	41	" G	Aug 6 64
644	Jones Thomas	112	" E	Apl 12 64
2567	Jones Thomas	Cav 16	" F	June 27 64
2990	Jones Wm	27	" D	July 7 64
1764	Jordan B W	84	" D	June 9 64
9153	Jordan M	38	" C	Sept 18 64
2961	Joy B	16	" I	July 6 64
2241	Joyce A	90	" D	June 20 64
10513	Justice H	Cav 7	" H	Oct 8 64
12052	Kane H	95	" A	Nov 16 64
4308	Kappel H	29	" H	July 30 64
4743	Keefe James P	Art 2	" M	Aug 5 64
8348	Kelaze E	29	" G	Sept 10 64
18	Kell M R, Corpl	49	" D	Mch 7 64
7183	Kelly John	75	" F	Aug 29 64
6795	Kelley William	94	" I	Aug 25 64
5518	Kennedy M	38	" C	Aug 13 64
12488	Kent J	14	" F	Jany 19 65
5707	Kerbey John	96	" H	Aug 15 64
396	Kiger John	22	" E	Apl 6 64
10520	Kilkreath J	42	" A	Oct 8 64
82	Kimball James	Art 25	" L	Mch 20 64
158	Kinkle John	16	" G	Mch 25 64
696	Kinderman G	82	" D	Apl 26 64
7807	Kingham J	38	" G	Sept 4 64
685	Klinehaus D	65	" G	Apl 23 64
4766	Kenigge A	113	" C	Aug 5 64
4908	Knight J	9	" H	Aug 6 64
11891	Knoble P	108	" E	Nov 7 64
4700	Koahl J	Cav 16	" H	Aug 4 64
2754	Krail J	Cav 16	" I	July 1 64
12685	Kreiger J	14	" E	Feby 20 65
652	Kalber John	16	" D	Apl 20 64
1809	Keyser John	82	" I	June 10 64
7927	Lacost J M	89	" E	Sept 5 64
7299	Ladien J	100	" H	Aug 23 64
7175	Lambert C	38	" D	Aug 29 64
10419	Lamsden W H	78	" A	Oct 6 64
12044	Lance V	59	" D	Nov 16 64
12270	Langley G	14	" K	Dec 12 64
5906	Lanner W A	Cav 9	" E	Aug 16 64
1233	Law Henry	93	" G	May 20 64
9635	Lawrene L G	89	" G	Sept 21 64
10179	Lape J	125	" A	Oct 1 64
10896	Leatherman M	98	" E	Oct 14 64
8464	Leach W	115	" B	Sept 11 64

Illinois—(*Continued.*)

4172	Lee A	112	Co B	July 28 64
8524	Lee P, Corpl	16	" A	Sept 12 64
963	Lee Thomas	8	" E	May 9 64
1297	Lee W E	Cav 16	" I	May 23 64
11258	Lewis Charles	79	" A	Oct 21 64
6238	Lewis Thomas	2	" L	Aug 20 64
10148	Lickey J B, Sgt	96	" F	Oct 1 64
8295	Liday J	113	" I	Sept 9 64
6295	Liken John, Sgt	112	" I	Aug 20 64
1685	Linday B	57	" H	June 6 64
7768	Linderman H A	99	" B	Sept 4 64
6414	Lindsay A	113	" D	Aug 22 64
1818	Linebergh I, Corpl	16	" F	June 10 64
11449	Linwood J	79	" F	Oct 25 64
12358	Lipsey D, Corpl	Cav 2	" C	Dec 30 64
10405	Lord L B, Corpl	112	" B	Oct 6 64
11222	Lorsam C	89	" C	Oct 20 64
2268	London L	Cav 16	" D	June 21 64
1017	Lowry Frank	35	" E	May 11 64
2342	Lusk John	29	" B	June 23 64
1456	Lutz John	23	" H	May 29 64
8196	Lyman J	100	" D	Sept 8 64
11467	Lynch V, Corpl	38	" C	Oct 26 64
10849	Mack J	Cav 14	" G	Oct 13 64
5390	Madden L	96	" D	Aug 12 64
11358	Maddock J W, Sergt	79	" A	Oct 23 64
10982	Madrill A	12	" A	Aug 12 64
3935	Malcolm J R	38	" K	July 25 64
2838	Manning A	215	" A	July 4 64
953	Manty P, Sergt	Cav 16	" E	May 8 64
2050	Markman Wm	Cav 16	" K	June 16 64
6333	Marritt H	Cav 16	" L	Aug 21 64
2762	Marshall A, Corpl	96	" C	July 2 64
8444	Martin A	Cav 16	" L	May 28 64
4071	Martin I	9	" K	July 27 64
12757	Masman S	42	" G	Mch 12 65
863	Mason Thos B	93	" B	May 3 64
1428	Massey W H	111	" D	May 28 64
746	Master Wm	12	" A	Apl 26 64
429	Mathening A D, Sergt	79	" I	Apl 8 64
12744	Matthews F M	32	" G	Mch 7 65
1061	Maxem H C	19	" H	May 13 64
3280	Maxwell S	Cav 8	" C	July 13 64
10019	May M H	89	" I	Sept 29 64
3100	McCampbell D	104	" B	July 10 64
56	McCleary Thos	Cav 16	" L	Mch 17 64
1315	McClusky James	Cav 16	" K	May 27 64
4850	McCray A	103	" A	Aug 6 64
1617	McCready Wm	96	" C	June 4 64
6513	McCreary J	119	" C	Aug 22 64
5724	McCone R	Cav 16	" K	Aug 15 64
3050	McCunne H	13	" C	July 8 64
3470	McEntire L	Cav 16	" K	July 17 64
5283	McGee Wm	30	" D	Aug 11 64
11623	McGivens J	119	" A	Oct 28 64
11952	McLarens B	89	" A	Nov 10 64
1634	McLaughlin B	90	" I	June 5 64
3169	McLing Benj, Corpl	23	" E	July 11 64
4725	McMahon M	93	" E	Aug 4 64
1337	McMillan W B, Corpl	112	Co E	May 24 64
9763	McMiller W B	78	" D	Sept 25 64
692	McShaw B	80	" B	Apl 23 64
9710	McWorthy W M	92	" G	Sept 25 64
3279	Mead G	19	" H	July 14 64
4648	Medler H	38	" I	Aug 3 64
6266	Mee William	51	" C	Aug 20 64
2177	Meher Charles	Cav 16	" F	June 19 64
2049	Mercenner Charles	90	" A	June 16 64
2637	Merritt F, Sgt	89	" F	June 29 64
7464	Merg F	44	" K	Sept 1 64
9145	Meyers A, Corpl	24	" H	Sept 18 64
5608	Meyers J	24	" K	Aug 14 64
2097	Meyers J K	116	" C	June 17 64
5432	Myers Samuel	25	" A	Aug 12 64
9188	Miller F, Corpl	16	" B	Sept 18 64
3139	Miller H	92	" F	July 10 64
11721	Miller J	21	" C	Nov 1 64
2257	Miller J M, Sgt	31	" I	June 21 64
9795	Miller M	92	" A	Sept 27 64
4515	Miller Mac	Cav 16	" C	Aug 18 64
3955	Mills N	11	" K	July 25 64
10721	Mills S	Cav 14	" F	Oct 14 64
7989	Mind D	8	" D	Sept 6 64
381	Mitchan A	92	" E	Apl 5 64
11617	Mitchell J R	89	" G	Oct 27 64
9753	Mix C	22	" C	Sept 25 64
4680	Mixwell L B	38	" F	Aug 4 64
4526	Monecal J	21	" G	Aug 2 64
2646	Morehead J	9	" E	June 29 64
2539	Morley H	Cav 16	" M	June 26 64
9187	Moran F	89	" C	Sept 18 64
7428	Moran W	11	" C	Aug 31 64
10645	Morbley B	48	" H	Oct 11 64
6402	Mounty R	6	" B	Aug 21 64
3263	Morris B	Cav 8	" F	July 13 64
816	Morris J	15	" H	Apl 30 64
1320	Morris James	66	" K	May 23 64
12757	Mossman S	42	" G	Mch 12 65
2993	Mulford W R, Sergt	23	"	July 7 64
2334	Mulkey D	89	" D	July 3 64
11900	Munz P	14	" I	Nov 7 64
50	Myers Charles	Cav 16	" B	Mch 16 64
3080	Myers C H, Corpl	24	" F	July 9 64
5038	Myers F	Cav 16	" L	Aug 8 64
1407	Myers P	24	" F	May 27 64
438	Nashen Ed	65	" A	Apl 8 64
283	Neal Joseph	16	" K	Apl 1 64
7439	Needham L H, Sergt	42	" K	Sept 1 64
9331	Nelson J, Corpl	3	" K	Sept 22 64
8166	Newberg H	22	" F	Sept 8 64
299	Newberg Wm	Art 2	" M	Apl 1 64
5778	Newby E	123	" A	Aug 15 64
8129	Newlan H	25	" B	Sept 8 64
4896	Nicely F	82	" A	Aug 6 64
6945	Nicholas L C	14	" F	Aug 26 64
7847	Nicholson R H	123	" B	Sept 4 64
7086	Nugent T	103	" E	Aug 23 64
12460	Nully C	120	" A	Jan 15 65

Illinois—(*Continued.*)

6519	Obevre O B, Corpl	112	Co C	Aug 22 64
10851	O'Brian D	89	" C	Oct 13 64
11274	Ochley Wm	24	" K	Oct 20 64
3817	O'Connor M	2	" F	July 24 64
1921	O'Dean Thomas	78	" F	June 14 64
1533	O'David J H	9	" A	June 1 64
7151	O'Donnell	34	" I	Sept 3 64
3609	Odom W	7	" G	July 19 64
1502	Oglesby D	Cav 16	" M	May 31 64
1214	O'Keefe M	Art 2	" G	May 19 64
7856	Olderfield J R	Cav 6	" B	Sept 5 64
9196	Oley O S, Corpl	21	" I	Sept 18 64
10042	Oleny A	108	" K	Sept 29 64
9885	Olson J	112	" K	Sept 27 64
6098	Olson J	89	" D	Aug 18 64
30	O'Neil D	Cav 16	" K	Apl 19 64
10469	Osborn J W	9	" H	Oct 7 64
6774	Oss	89	" D	Aug 25 64
4123	Ottway D	Cav 8	" A	July 28 64
8414	Owens C	120		Sept 11 64
10279	O'Mine D J, Corpl	Cav 9	Co E	Oct 3 64
5511	Padon C	12	" F	Aug 13 64
6095	Paine S	88	" B	Aug 18 64
3408	Paisley F F	120	" E	July 16 64
6301	Parshall J M	114	" A	Aug 20 64
12357	Parkhurst B	14	" H	Dec 30 64
6303	Partridge W J, Sergt	30	" F	Aug 20 64
12677	Patterson F J	14	" F	Feby 19 65
393	Penny James	Cav 14	" D	Apl 6 64
12707	Penny W	114	" F	Feby 26 65
7700	Peeter H M	107	" C	Sept 3 64
2621	Perkins A E	89	" A	June 28 64
4853	Perry George	89	" G	Aug 6 64
9313	Perry J	Cav 9	" G	Sept 20 64
3953	Perry N	Cav 1	" B	July 18 64
12179	Peterson J B	112	" I	Nov 27 64
1686	Pettas Wm	65	" I	June 6 64
5889	Pettijohn J	21	" F	Aug 16 64
12594	Philbrook A, Sgt	Cav 17	" F	Feby 5 65
410	Phillips W, Corpl	Cav 16	" L	Apl 6 64
4887	Pierce C, Corpl	Cav 6	" H	Aug 6 64
1506	Pierce W B	Cav 8	" H	May 31 64
3764	Place S	44	" F	July 22 64
10059	Plamerly H	14	" D	Sept 30 64
3679	Porterlange Wm	24	" K	July 24 64
1862	Pollard F	127	" A	June 12 64
9602	Post George	Cav 7	" L	Sept 23 64
5783	Powell A	122	" C	Aug 15 64
3058	Powell D	Cav 16	" K	July 9 64
3422	Powers James	44	" C	July 16 64
23	Preston C W	Cav 8	" M	Mch 8 64
6007	Price J M	79	" D	Aug 17 64
9059	Prickett F	30	" E	Sept 17 64
12597	Pratt W	16	" F	Feby 6 65
10893	Prime D	103	" K	Oct 14 64
7972	Puck John	122	" D	Sept 5 64
1143	Puhrer Fred	27	" A	May 16 64
10412	Pyner T	89	" D	Oct 6 64
10531	Quinn P	52	" A	Oct 8 64

3039	Ralston John	79	Co I	July 8 64
1011	Ramsay J C	21	" B	May 10 64
1765	Ramsay A B	45	" K	June 9 64
12763	Ramsey T	79	" A	Mch 12 65
10772	Randall C F	124	" I	Oct 12 64
8578	Rankin W A, Crpl	Cav 1	" I	Sept 12 64
12780	Ransom J	Cav 4	" B	Feb 19 65
7604	Reany J H, Sgt	Cav 6	" B	Sept 2 64
5908	Redmont John	112	" H	Aug 17 64
8571	Reed A	98	" I	Sept 12 64
3496	Reed D	26	" H	July 18 64
12024	Richardson T	34	" E	Dec 23 64
1616	Richards H	79	" I	June 4 64
3809	Rickold W	16	" G	July 23 64
2836	Rictor Charles, Corpl	82	" H	July 3 64
8632	Ripley J	9	" B	Sept 13 64
7748	Riller D	Art 14	" D	Sept 3 64
2074	Roberts W W	Cav 16	" I	June 17 64
8410	Robinson E H	36	" A	Sept 11 64
4460	Robinson H B, Sgt	Cav 6	" B	Aug 1 64
6080	Robinson J B	79	" A	Aug 18 64
10751	Roder F	Cav 16	" G	Oct 12 64
2596	Rodenberger N	96	" E	June 29 64
10184	Roferty J O	Cav 6	" H	Oct 1 64
747	Rodgers O	12	" A	Apl 26 64
1807	Rogers Silas	65	" D	June 10 64
7228	Rogers George	Cav 16	" G	June 29 64
528	Rolla E J	103	" G	Apl 13 64
4389	Rosecrans H	113	" A	July 31 64
11473	Ross J W	45	" F	Oct 26 64
8465	Ross Thomas	113	" K	Sept 11 64
306	Rudd Eras, Sergt	100	" K	Apl 2 64
1294	Rudd F	Cav 16	" L	May 23 64
2557	Ryan M	89	" A	June 27 64
2000	Saddle M	27	" G	June 15 [illegible]
9345	Saler J B, Sergt	14	" F	Sept 20
10512	Sandler L, Corpl	19	" D	Oct 8 [illegible]
11289	Sargeant M, Sergt	14	" K	Oct 22 64
1902	Savage P P	13		June 13 64
9915	Sanin B	36	Co C	Sept 28 64
7558	Schrider D	23	" A	Sept 2 64
7163	Schrider John	44	" K	Aug 29 64
3493	Schaunoller C	24	" H	July 17 64
10559	Schurtz W	44	" F	Oct 5 64
1573	Scitaz Victor	Cav 16	" L	June 3 64
11077	Scott H	28	" G	Oct 17 64
4524	Scuyner N, Corpl	64	" G	Aug 2 64
12034	See S	11	" G	Oct 15 64
1787	Seeley Charles	41	" G	June 10 64
9325	Sern C	Cav 8	" D	Sept 20 64
4872	Serens R B	112	" I	Aug 6 64
1333	Setters Geo H	38	" G	May 24 64
12827	Seward R	61	" E	Apl 8 65
5350	Seybert A J	39	" E	Aug 11 64
9322	Shadrach G H	Cav 7	" C	Sept 20 64
1661	Shauback Ed	44	" E	June 6 64
8831	Shark L F	113	" D	Sept 15 64
12149	Sharp A	Cav 7	" B	Nov 21 64
2579	Sharp A H	22	" A	June 27 64

Illinois — (*Continued.*)

1899	Sharp E D T	89		June 13 64
2317	Shaw J	89	Co E	June 29 64
7315	Shaw Joseph	98	" D	Aug 30 64
4135	Sheeby John, Sgt	42	" G	July 23 64
8336	Sherwood J F	Cav 16	" I	Sept 10 64
7270	Shields J A	Cav 6	" E	Aug 30 64
12016	Siebert H C	Cav 7	" M	Nov 16 64
10441	Sifle H	Cav 7	" M	Oct 7 64
2130	Silkwood H M	89	" D	June 21 64
1717	Silter John	Cav 16	" I	June 9 64
12713	Simmons W D	42	" H	Mch 1 65
7630	Simpson C	14	" D	Sept 2 64
12334	Simmons M A	42	" H	Apl 17 65
309	Sipple A	107	" E	Apl 2 64
12390	Skinner H	11	" C	Jan 4 65
10382	Skinner Wm	16	" G	Sept 30 64
2585	Slasher H, Corpl	93	" E	June 23 64
10663	Slick P	9	" E	Oct 11 64
9492	Smith C W	16	" K	Sept 21 64
5960	Smith George	53	" E	Aug 17 64
362	Smith Jno B	Cav 7	" L	Apl 2 64
12566	Smith J S	115	" D	Feb 1 65
10866	Smith N P	23	" G	Oct 13 64
10975	Smith O	114	" H	Oct 15 64
4659	Smith William	Cav 16	" M	Aug 3 64
8223	Snyder B	Cav 6	" B	Sept 8 64
8079	Sommers W	40	" F	Sept 7 64
2165	Soms	82	" A	June 19 64
4283	Spangler H J	Cav 16	" L	July 30 64
9022	Spindler W	113	" F	Sept 18 64
11359	Spurlock A	79	" E	Oct 23 64
4598	Sprague W	Cav 8	" K	Aug 3 64
1067	Springer M	112	" E	Jan 6 64
12132	Steilhoult A	92	" H	Nov 23 64
2532	Standsfield H	96	" H	June 26 64
1718	Stark F	78	" H	June 8 64
1018	Stegall J	Cav 16	" L	May 11 64
10737	Stevens S	44	" D	Oct 11 64
6292	Stewart F	78	" I	Aug 20 64
4878	Stillwell F H	79	" L	Aug 6 64
1340	Stillwell James	38	" I	June 5 64
10828	Stine A	14	" H	Oct 13 64
4724	Stopes S W	89	" E	Aug 4 64
8451	Storem A	89	" D	Sept 11 64
12190	Storem C	98	" C	Nov 23 64
10440	Strand John	9	" H	Oct 6 64
8549	Striker J	11	" K	Sept 12 64
12522	Stringer P	15	" B	Apl 5 65
9013	Strong S M	95	" B	Sept 17 64
855	Stune S L	40	" G	May 3 64
8615	Sullivan J	Cav 16	" I	Sept 13 64
12482	Sullivan M	15	" E	Jany 17 65
9325	Sunn C	Cav 8	" D	Sept 20 64
11808	Suter B F	Cav 4	" L	Nov 4 64
5515	Sutton M	Cav 9	" M	Aug 13 64
4442	Swanson P	9	" K	July 31 64
12725	Steinhaus J	15	" B	Mch 3 65
6292	Stewart F	73	" I	Aug 20 64
12557	Swarts E, Corpl	24	" G	Jany 30 65
6105	Swartz A	Cav 7	Co M	Aug 18 64
505	Sweet Wm	89	" E	Apl 12 64
10515	Tanner J		" A	Oct 8 64
592	Taylor George	Cav 16	" M	Apl 12 64
10036	Taylor H, Corpl	Cav 7	" I	Sept 29 64
809	Taylor James	Cav 4	" F	Apl 30 64
12526	Taylor M P	14	" I	Jany 26 65
1925	Temple I	100	" H	June 10 64
4466	Terry John	Cav 16	" M	Aug 1 64
12437	Thayer D	64	" E	Jany 12 65
2415	Thomas A	16	" A	June 24 64
10411	Thompson D	24	" K	Oct 6 64
6491	Thompson F	10	" B	Aug 22 64
7128	Thompson G G	Cav 1	" M	Aug 28 63
2453	Thompson John	Cav 16	" I	June 25 64
6331	Thompson T	2	" M	Aug 25 64
10347	Thornsburg N C	70	" A	Oct 5 64
8863	Thorn J	Cav 16	" K	Sept 15 64
9833	Thurmain J	84	" E	Sept 27 64
46	Tuiler W	Cav 16	" D	Mch 15 64
3074	Topp A	19	" C	July 9 64
547	Trailer Van Buren	Cav 16	" I	Apl 14 64
11550	Trask J J	Cav 7	" B	Oct 27 64
751	Trowbridge L	Cav 16	" M	Apl 26 64
1915	Trout E	21	" F	June 14 64
2502	Turnerholm S H	19	" K	June 26 64
3032	Tucker E	38	" B	July 8 64
12736	Tucker J	7	" F	Mch 6 65
10832	Tucker J P	Cav 8	" G	Oct 13 64
10988	Turner S	120	" A	Oct 16 64
11091	Underwood D	11	" E	Oct 18 64
5183	Vase	Cav 15	" H	Aug 9 64
1078	Vaugh James	Cav 16	" L	May 14 64
7765	Vincent L D	Cav 7	" G	Sept 4 64
1026	Voris Ross	Cav 16	" I	May 11 64
8271	Volter George	9	" C	July 13 64
2015	Vought Wm	24	" H	July 15 64
5028	Vox Wm	24	" E	Aug 14 64
6767	Waddle J, Sergt	112	" C	Aug 24 64
2364	Wahl M	Cav 16	" I	July 6 64
9218	Walker George	81	" K	Sept 19 64
12072	Ward R S	15	" C	Nov 13 64
11345	Ward G B	Cav 7	" E	Nov 23 64
2488	Ward W J	Cav 16	" M	June 26 64
12392	Wareck N	120	" D	Jany 4 65
7895	Warkwich J	93	" C	Sept 5 64
5398	Watts Wm	Cav 16	" L	Aug 16 64
11619	Waterman L	95	" D	Nov 23 64
6173	Weaver G	Cav 16	" L	Aug 19 64
9317	Weaver Alex	93	" A	Sept 20 64
722	Weeks Benj	Cav 16	" L	Apl 25 64
10785	Weedman J W, Corpl	38	" I	Oct 12 64
4941	Weinmiller J, Sergt	56	" G	Aug 7 64
10091	Welch John	7	" E	Sept 20 64
11751	Welch L	24	" F	Nov 2 64
10385	Welch G, Sergt	95	" A	Sept 30 64
4358	Wentworth Charles	27	" D	July 31 64
7423	Westbrook B D	Cav 6	" B	Aug 31 64
8867	Whalin M	23	" B	July 9 64

Illinois — (*Continued.*)

3910	Wham T	21	Co G	July 24 64
9184	Wheeler J	61	" F	Sept 18 64
92	Wheelock A	96	" H	May 10 64
1496	Whitmore B	Cav 16	" D	May 31 64
1699	Whitmore L	104	" I	June 7 64
5998	Whitney J F	89	" G	Aug 17 64
8718	Whipp Charles	Cav 9	" E	Sept 14 64
5613	Wildberger P	Cav 6	" B	Aug 14 64
5158	Wiley T	7	" M	May 15 64
12732	Wiley W P	32	" C	Mch 5 65
12671	Wilkes R	81	" A	Feb 18 65
7840	Wilhelm G A	9	" C	Sept 4 64
90	Will Gustavus	Cav 16	" E	Mch 21 64
9785	Will J	36	" B	Sept 23 64
8310	Williams A	22	" H	Sept 10 64
3254	Williams E	49	" D	July 13 64
10899	Williams G W	Bat 15		Oct 14 64
11497	Williams G B	15	Co B	Oct 26 64
12780	Willis A P	84	" A	Mch 15 65
4737	Wilson D	Cav 16	Co M	Aug 4 64
9531	Wilson J, Corpl		" K	Sept 22 64
11712	Wilson W, Sgt	89	" F	Nov 15 64
1120	Wimmer G	Cav 16	" I	May 15 64
989	Wink Lewis	Cav 16	" C	May 10 64
8755	Winning D	125	" C	Sept 14 64
6079	Winters Wm	24	" H	Aug 18 64
8743	Wismer J, Corpl	74	" G	July 21 64
2301	Wing John	Cav 7	" H	June 22 64
8815	Wood	21	" G	Sept 15 64
1042	Woodcock R	Cav 16	" L	May 12 64
3695	Workman James	7	" G	July 21 64
10582	Worthy A A	21	" K	Oct 10 64
2624	Wright J W	35	" C	June 23 64
5265	Wright M	59	" E	Aug 10 64
12309	Yates J	120	" E	Dec 19 64
10766	Yagle C	24	" B	Oct 12 64
2391	Zimmerman Philip	Art 1		June 24 64
72	Zoran Philip	44	Co I	Mch 20 64

TOTAL 850.

INDIANA.

571	Allen Jesse, Corpl	116	Co K	Apl 15 64
1917	Adkins George	Cav 6	" D	June 14 64
3991	Andrews E L	Cav 6	" K	July 26 64
4270	Anderson D	76	" E	July 29 64
5630	Ault J W	40	" D	Aug 14 64
6921	Alexander S	93	" D	Aug 26 64
7124	Alexander J D	Cav 5	" K	Aug 28 64
9292	Auburn C	65	" H	Sept 19 64
9445	Atkins J F	Cav 2	" H	Sept 21 64
9584	Adams H	35	" A	Sept 23 64
9613	Allen D B, Sgt	29		Sept 24 64
9759	Alfred W J	117	Co K	Sept 25 64
10473	Allyn D	88	" K	Oct 7 64
10793	Atland C	32	" C	Oct 12 64
11186	Albin I	89	" D	Oct 19 64
12183	Austin Alfred	5	" K	Nov 27 64
12513	Amick W	93	" B	Jan 23 65
313	Bash David	117	" C	Apl 2 64
576	Bee Thomas	Cav		Apl 16 64
596	Bock Samuel	75	Co I	Apl 17 64
838	Brown T	63	" D	May 1 64
1514	Barry Henry	84	" D	May 31 64
1603	Boley A J	66	" C	June 4 64
1759	Barra John	65	" H	June 9 64
2016	Burnett Wm	Cav 6	" G	June 15 64
2191	Buckhart E	27	" F	June 19 64
2222	Brasier S, Mus	19	" I	June 20 64
2299	Bumgardner	44	" D	June 22 64
2458	Barrett E	42	" I	June 25 64
2874	Bowman John	42	" C	July 4 64
3041	Bruce J W	Cav 5	" M	July 8 64
3359	Broughton D	7	" K	July 15 64
3366	Bricker J	68	" C	July 15 64
4027	Barton J F	52	" G	July 26 64
4035	Ballinger Robert	39	" I	July 26 64
4251	Bonly James	81	" C	July 29 64
4479	Baker J	9	Co G	Aug 1 64
4563	Baker D W	13	" B	Aug 2 64
4948	Bayer F	129	" H	Aug 7 64
5039	Brenton J W	29	" I	Aug 8 64
5093	Bowlin Wm	53	" G	Aug 8 64
5220	Barton E	Cav 2	" G	Aug 10 64
2275	Busick W A, Corp'l	101	" F	Aug 10 64
5442	Bryer P	81	" K	Aug 12 64
5590	Bohems Philip	79	" A	Aug 14 64
5690	Baker J P	Cav 7	" H	Aug 15 64
5794	Boom W P	31	" F	Aug 15 64
5981	Barton George	130	" F	Aug 17 64
6163	Brookers J M	112	" E	Aug 19 64
6410	Brown J M	66	" F	Aug 22 64
6518	Bartholomew I	99	" A	Aug 22 64
7370	Bamgroover J A	101	" H	Aug 31 64
7794	Barnes Thomas M	Cav 5	" C	Sept 4 64
8314	Babbitt W H	29	" I	Sept 10 64
8397	Bassinger H	14	" C	Sept 10 64
8519	Boyd W F	125	" F	Sept 12 64
9098	Bortley S	88	" I	Sept 18 64
9548	Bray T E	79	" K	Sept 23 64
9708	Brown J, Sergt	Cav 1	" A	Sept 24 64
9777	Birch T A	58	" L	Sept 26 64
9793	Bozell J F	40	" B	Sept 26 64
9346	Bixter D	5	" B	Sept 27 64
10350	Blackaber Wm H	42	" I	Oct 5 64
10939	Benton L	30	" H	Oct 14 64
11559	Bennett R N	72	" D	Oct 27 64
11604	Bemis J M, Sergt	87	" F	Oct 28 64
11919	Brown D	128	" B	Nov 8 64
11930	Bailey George	72	" A	Nov 8 64
12019	Bennet A	29	" G	Nov 15 64
12128	Booth J	32	" E	Nov 22 64
12294	Bennett C	6	" H	Dec 15 64
12486	Barrey H	66	" I	Jan 19 65

Indiana—(*Continued.*)

12504	Balstrum J	93	Co F	Jan 22 65
12596	Branson E	57	" A	Feb 6 65
301	Charles James	6	" G	April 1 64
625	Connell P	Cav 6	" M	April 19 64
634	Claycome S A, Sgt	66	" G	April 20 64
1117	Cox Joseph, Sgt	42	" B	May 15 64
1146	Carter Henry	2	" C	May 16 64
1172	Curry J W	30	" F	May 17 64
1433	Currier Wm	87	" K	May 30 64
1523	Crest J D	31	" F	May 31 64
2234	Carpenter O C, Corp'l	29	" D	June 21 64
2307	Cottrell M, Sgt	Cav 6	" G	June 22 64
2776	Cooley A	38	" C	July 2 64
3043	Clark W	82	" C	July 8 64
3922	Connolley D	9	" I	July 25 64
4192	Cox S	66	" E	July 28 64
4917	Clifford H C	Cav 7	" I	Aug 6 64
5262	Courtney J F	Cav 2	" L	Aug 10 64
5654	Collar E	120	" G	Aug 14 64
5660	Crews E M	Cav 5	" A	Aug 14 64
5901	Clark A	54	" A	Aug 16 64
6203	Chrichfula S	93	" A	Aug 19 64
6477	Croane J J	22	" C	Aug 22 64
6646	Cornelius E	58	" B	Aug 23 64
6926	Carnahan A W, Sgt	6	" E	Aug 26 64
7383	Carpenter S	66	" I	Aug 31 64
7726	Callings W	120	" F	Sept 3 64
7737	Cramer A	30	" H	Sept 3 64
7899	Cheny James	Cav 7	" I	Sept 5 64
8051	Cramton R	101	" I	Sept 6 64
8108	Crazen J	53	" G	Sept 7 64
8133	Crager J	13	" C	Sept 8 64
8144	Cooper J	80	" E	Sept 8 64
9294	Christman J E	Cav 6	" G	Sept 19 64
9535	Collins G	56	" F	Sept 22 64
9980	Connett Daniel	130	" F	Sept 28 64
10084	Conel J	13	" D	Sept 30 64
10305	Callan M	85	" B	Oct 13 64
11423	Cafer J H	87	" K	Oct 24 64
11631	Cummings J W	93	" F	Oct 28 64
12062	Clark M	101	" B	Nov 17 64
12173	Cannon A	42	" F	Nov 26 64
12213	Cregs Wm	Cav 5	" E	Dec 3 64
12415	Collins W A, Sgt	5	" G	Jan 8 65
12559	Calvert G F	Cav 8	" I	Jan 30 65
4234	Curry W F	Cav 4	" I	July 29 64
426	Dummond J H	65	" F	Apl 7 64
508	Davis J M	66	" I	Apl 12 64
964	Darker Wm	12	" C	May 8 64
2205	Denny John	44	" E	June 19 64
3157	Detrich C	29	" K	July 11 64
3419	Dusan J	6	" D	July 16 64
4021	Develin E	35	" B	July 26 64
4029	Decer P	32	" K	July 26 64
4124	Dill C P	42	" F	July 27 64
5255	Davis K	13	" D	Aug 10 64
5367	Dunben M	36	" E	Aug 11 64
5420	Delup Z S	13	" D	Aug 12 64
5681	Dallinger W C	38	" E	Aug 14 64
6147	Denton Philip	81	Co D	Aug 19 64
6 34	Downey S M	116	" I	Aug 25 64
6944	Dowell W L	6	" C	Aug 23 64
9638	Dunlap W	30	" A	Sept 24 64
10010	Downs J R	Cav 5	" I	Sept 29 64
10435	Dane Andrew	36	" I	Oct 6 64
10446	Dignon L	35	" B	Oct 7 64
10916	Dawson L F	29	" I	Oct 14 64
10954	Dial R	1	" B	Oct 14 64
12037	Daffendall P H	58	" D	Nov 18 64
12172	Davenport J	Cav 6	" I	Nov 24 64
12236	Delashment F, Sgt	14	" B	Dec 6 64
12533	Duckworth J	85	" F	Jan 27 65
12545	Dawley J	73	" I	Jan 27 65
12580	Dawson J	124	" D	Feb 3 65
9236	Diver O	19	" F	Sept 19 64
916	Evans G H	Cav 1	" A	May 6 64
917	Edwards G H, Mus	6	" G	May 7 64
1083	Ellis H C	Cav 6	" D	May 14 64
1279	Evans W	75	" I	May 22 64
1346	Eskridge Oakley	29	" D	May 24 64
1994	Edwards J W	38	" G	June 15 64
2481	Esenthal F	Cav 5	" D	June 25 64
4075	Eaton W H	58	" B	July 27 64
4913	Ecker J	39	" I	Aug 17 64
5076	Evans J	Cav 6	" I	Aug 8 64
7917	Ells D	20	" I	Sept 5 64
11320	Elston F	9	" B	Oct 22 64
11429	Estelle E W, Sgt	Cav 2	" L	Oct 24 64
11712	Eldridge E	38		Nov 1 64
11774	Earl D, Corpl	Cav 2	Co B	Nov 3 64
12285	Emmons W	5	" D	Dec 14 64
1482	Frecks F	35	" D	May 30 64
1803	Fitter B	66	" I	June 10 64
2143	Fike Tobias	30	" D	June 18 64
3014	Fitzgerald I	30	" D	July 7 64
3453	Fescher D	32	" E	July 17 64
3637	Fuget W	Cav 3	" C	July 20 64
8379	Fields N	Cav 6	" F	Sept 10 64
8547	Fenton I	72	" D	Sept 12 64
8766	Forward S	Cav 8	" I	Sept 14 64
9847	Forshua W	25	" H	Sept 27 64
10509	Farmingham W C	Cav 14	" K	Oct 8 64
11311	Fanier F	Cav 6	" I	Oct 22 64
11526	Fish C	Cav 2	" H	Oct 26 64
12012	Falkerson J, Sgt	93	" B	Nov 14 64
12144	Francis F, Mus	93		Nov 21 65
12320	Fross John, Sgt	Cav 5	Co D	Dec 24 64
12723	Felnick H	10	" F	Mch 4 65
93	Graham Wm	6	" G	Mch 22 64
322	Gladman H	110	" B	Apl 2 64
1048	Goodwin Wm	Cav 2	" M	May 12 64
1165	Grimes F O	66	" I	May 17 64
1215	Garver John	29	" F	May 19 64
1312	Gullsen William	Cav 7	" L	May 23 64
1594	Griffin William	Cav 6	" I	June 3 64
2337	Gray D L	22	" I	June 22 64
2386	Guthrie W B	80	" C	June 24 64
2418	Gillard Wm	120	" C	June 24 64

Indiana—(*Continued.*)

No.	Name	Regt.	Co.	Date
8573	Gibbons W T	128	Co I	July 19 64
4[illegible]9	Gould Wm	66	" E	July 28 64
4273	Gilbert H A, Sgt	Cav 2	" K	July 29 64
4[illegible]47	Galliger Wm	7	" B	July 31 64
4901	Gerard H	35	" G	Aug 6 64
6189	Goodwin I	20	" F	Aug 19 64
6398	Gordon W M	74	" G	Aug 21 64
6493	Goodridge E, Corpl	91	" H	Aug 23 64
7293	Grass C	32	" H	Aug 30 64
7321	Gray H F	Cav 2	" H	Aug 30 64
7698	Gerber I	30	" C	Sept 3 64
8746	Galliger P	58	" C	Sept 12 64
8791	Gagham Wm	25	" K	Sept 14 64
9112	Green S	73	" E	Sept 18 64
9114	Gillan J	29	" F	Sep 18 64
10782	Griswold Thomas	2	" F	Oct 12 64
11409	Gordon J W	13	" D	Oct 24 64
11581	Greenwood W	8	" C	Oct 28 64
12216	Grant H G	5	" G	Dec 3 64
12398	Garnet T	6	" E	Jan 5 65
12483	Green Wm	89	" E	Jan 19 65
630	Hollar John	Cav 5	" I	April 19 64
879	Henick Wm	30	" F	May 4 64
1933	Hall L S	117	" C	June 14 64
2118	Hilliard J	116	" D	June 17 64
2130	Hodges J	7	" C	June 18 64
2379	Hustin James	74	" B	June 23 64
2392	Hodges S	9	" F	June 24 64
2629	Humphrey I	3	" C	June 28 64
2768	Hendricks J	Cav 2	" C	July 2 64
2768	Higgins M P	Cav 3	" C	July 2 64
2793	Hodges W J	5	" F	July 2 64
2812	Hillman H	65	" G	July 3 64
2974	Hamilton James	7	" K	July 7 64
3289	Hine S	63	" A	July 14 64
3507	Hodgen J W	80	" G	July 18 64
4487	Hanger L S	65	" A	July 1 64
5362	Hart J R	88	" H	Aug 11 64
5678	Hittle B	Cav 6	" L	Aug 14 64
5695	Helville N C	20	" F	Aug 15 64
5872	Heah Jacob	20	" G	Aug 16 64
6016	Hearne John	Cav 5	" F	Aug 18 64
6198	Hershton A	4	" M	Aug 19 64
6491	Hendricks I	129	" H	Aug 23 64
7031	Hartsock I	80	" A	Aug 27 64
7790	Hunter J M	42	" F	Sept 4 64
7837	Hammond G W, Sgt	65	" D	Sept 4 64
7903	Halfree J A	82	" A	Sept 5 64
7971	Hamilton P S	7	" E	Sept 6 64
8091	Hughes W H, Corp'l	81	" D	Sept 7 64
8347	Hart A	7	" A	Sept 10 64
8541	Haff M	Bat 4		Sept 12 64
8681	Hunter H	42	Co F	Sept 13 64
8778	Haynes W	30	" G	Sept 14 64
8836	Higgins John W	Cav 3	" C	Sept 15 64
8967	Holloway J	Cav 5	" M	Sept 16 64
9073	Hubbner F	Cav 4	" E	Sept 18 64
9329	Hurst R V, Corp'l	86	" B	Sept 20 64
9429	Higgins W E	53	" H	Sept 21 64
9911	Haghton J	2	Co D	Sept 28 64
9933	Harrington O	30	" I	Sept 28 64
10123	Hoffman J	80	" C	Oct 1 64
10193	Hunstler W H, Sgt	38	" E	Oct 4 64
10322	Hoagler N C	39	" E	Oct 8 64
10613	Harris W C	13	" D	Oct 10 64
10820	Hector E	13	" D	Oct 12 64
11231	Haskins H	99	" A	Oct 20 64
11243	Hasfle J, Mus	1	" F	Oct 21 64
11790	Hill R	14	" D	Nov 4 64
12249	Hamilton D	13	" B	Dec 9 64
12536	Hall H H	2	" E	Jan 27 65
6414	Ihn C	129	" B	Aug 22 64
8963	Igo T, Corp'l	4	" E	Sept 16 64
670	Johnson Isaac	5	" C	Apl 22 64
1931	Jennings C, Corpl	Cav 6	" I	June 14 64
2212	Jackson John	23	" C	June 20 64
2353	Jones Wm M	63	" D	June 23 64
3311	Jasper Wm	38	" I	July 10 64
5245	Judd Henry, Sgt	2	" D	Aug 10 64
6172	Julerso H	Cav 2	" D	Aug 19 64
6311	Jones H C	5	" C	Aug 20 64
7100	Jones A	88	" I	Aug 28 64
9948	Johnson J	Cav 7	" A	Sept 28 64
12517	Jones J	120	" C	Jan 24 65
12709	Johnson H	40	" C	Mch 19 65
417	Kistner George	42	" B	Apl 7 64
618	Kinnan A	56	" G	Apl 18 64
858	Ketchum G W, Sgt	Cav 5	" I	May 3 64
2036	Kelly John, Sgt	Cav 5		June 1 64
2407	Kennedy Amos	2	Co H	June 24 64
1908	Kelso E O	Cav 3	" C	June 13 64
2527	Kanga J	74	" E	June 26 64
3347	Kennedy J W, Corpl	3	" I	July 8 64
4024	Keys Wm	72	" E	July 26 64
5149	Keiler W J, Sgt	Cav 4	" H	Aug 9 64
5253	K[illegible]cher T	29	" I	Aug 10 64
5722	Kern W	25	" H	Aug 15 64
6796	Kelly John	32	" C	Aug 23 64
7085	Kames J	128	" F	Aug 28 64
8621	King D	81	" A	Sept 13 64
10689	Kell[illegible]r I	49	" B	Oct 11 64
12278	Kuling I	79	" A	Dec 12 64
12587	Keef P, Corpl	Cav 10	" C	Feb 4 65
1041	Lewis J	6	" H	May 12 64
1239	Lawrence R J	30	" G	May 20 64
1261	Lower N G	116	" I	May 21 64
2615	Lewis James	65	" F	June 28 64
2745	Luff C	58	" I	July 1 64
3029	Lewis J	Cav 3	" C	July 7 64
3767	Lannon J S	128	" F	July 22 64
3890	Lawrence D	80	" A	July 24 64
4548	Lyons Wm	35	" A	Aug 2 64
5014	Lee John	Cav 3	" C	Aug 8 64
5585	Lawson William	75	" A	Aug 14 64
5616	Lawyer James	80	" B	Aug 14 64
6775	Lyons Wm	1	" E	Aug 25 64
7[illegible]63	Lowery D	Cav 2	" G	Aug 29 64
8697	Lunger A	Cav 7	" M	Sept 12 64

Indiana—(*Continued.*)

9256	Liggett	52	Co G	Sept 10 64
10508	Lewis R	Cav 7	" C	Oct 8 64
11152	Lash J	101	" B	Oct 18 64
11715	Lakin A	Cav 7		Nov 1 64
12250	Lawrence B T	42	Co D	Dec 9 64
130	McCarty John	66	" D	Mch 23 64
6[illegible]1	Mullen James	Cav 6	" G	Apl 19 64
746	Masters Wm	65	" G	Apl 26 64
841	Milton John	18	" C	May 1 64
903	Mytinger Wm	117	" F	May 5 64
954	Milburn J	6	" K	May 8 64
1090	Moore Peter	6	" I	May 14 64
1405	Miller Jacob	74	" E	May 27 64
1516	Martin Geo, Sgt	Cav 3	" C	May 31 64
1860	Merritt H	30	" G	June 12 64
2240	Mitchell J J	30	" D	June 20 64
2397	Milliken S L	Cav 1	" G	June 24 64
2511	Moneyhon B	38	" D	June 26 64
2[illegible]08	Marsh J	88	" D	June 28 64
5	Moodie Z	119	" K	Mch 31 64
3387	Mank E	80	" E	July 16 64
3633	Marlit J	80	" H	July 20 64
3884	Mulchy J	35	" A	July 24 64
4010	Mercer John	12	" F	July 26 64
4388	Malsby F	Cav 14	" A	July 31 64
4959	McDall R	19	" A	Aug 7 64
5562	Manihan J	38	" D	Aug 13 64
5618	Mageson J	Cav 7	" A	Aug 14 64
5703	Mensome S, Sergt	42	" E	Aug 15 64
5713	Monroe S	33	" F	Aug 15 64
5767	Montgomery R	80	" F	Aug 15 64
5863	Michael S	7	" I	Aug 16 64
6461	Mitchell J H	30	" I	Aug 22 64
6521	Monroe H J, Sgt	44	" G	Aug 22 64
6566	Mathews M	42	" K	Aug 23 64
7043	Milsker J	5	" D	Aug 27 64
72[illegible]3	Matheny N, Sgt	42	" A	Aug 29 64
7272	McQueston J O	13	" B	Aug 30 64
7510	Myers A	29	" E	Sept 1 64
7820	Moore G, Corp'l	101	" F	Sept 4 64
7973	Mine John N	2	" H	Sept 6 64
8007	Miller W W	101	" B	Sept 6 64
8176	McCoy W, Segt	66	" B	Sept 8 64
8389	Murphy J	9	" E	Sept 10 64
8[illegible]51	McElvain J	93	" E	Sept 15 64
8925	Myers J	143	" D	Sept 16 64
9575	Morrison J	4	" B	Sept 23 64
9600	Miller J	Cav 7	" G	Sept 23 64
9856	Murgu A	35	" D	Sept 27 64
10231	Monay G W	7	" E	Oct 2 64
10245	McFarney J	93	" B	Oct 3 64
10391	Maples H	29	" H	Oct 6 64
10891	Murphy F	35	" B	Oct 13 64
10995	McDonald I	74	" B	Oct 16 64
11166	Mills Milton	26	" D	Oct 18 64
11271	Mitchell I	7	" K	Oct 21 64
11585	McCarty A	7	" A	Oct 23 64
11665	McBeth I C	28	" K	Oct 30 64
11680	Murphy F	35	" C	Oct 31 64
11746	McCarty A	7	Co A	Nov 2 64
11857	McCarty I	6	" A	Nov 6 64
11946	Miller F B	30	" C	Nov 10 64
12548	Madlener L	12	" K	Jan 27 65
12563	McFall I	30	" A	Jan 31 65
12624	Manifold W	Cav 6	" I	Feb 9 65
12639	Montgomery W	Cav 5	" G	Feb 17 65
12709	Maloy I	Cav 11	" G	Feb 28 65
2007	Nossman G	117	" G	June 15 64
3205	Newcomb George	22	" A	July 12 64
3519	Nucha S	Cav 3	" I	July 18 64
4627	Napper W H, Sgt	6	" I	Aug 3 64
6528	Norton N A	38	" B	Aug 23 64
10187	Note John H	39	" F	Oct 1 64
12226	Nichols J	38	" G	Dec 5 64
9494	Newberry M	Cav 7	" L	Sept 21 64
342	O'Niel Thomas	6	" G	Apl 2 64
1874	Oliver John, Corpl	42		June 12 64
2778	Oliver H H	Cav 5	Co M	July 2 64
5226	Oliver J	120	" K	Aug 10 64
5361	Osborn J	73	" E	Aug 11 64
7863	Oliver J	19	" D	Sept 5 64
7911	O'Conner Thomas	Cav 5	" B	Sept 5 64
10940	Olinger E	65	" A	Oct 14 64
12514	Ortell M	35	" G	Jan 27 64
12590	Ousley W J	7	" A	Feb 5 65
287	Peache Cyrus	66	" D	Apl 1 64
559	Pashby John	Cav 6	" C	Apl 15 64
3434	Pavy W	123	" A	July 17 64
3738	Palmer A	42	" F	July 21 64
4068	Parker E, Sgt	29	" A	July 27 64
4171	Park John	129	" B	July 28 64
4551	Pettis H	53	" C	Aug 2 64
4553	Pruitt H C	Cav 7	" K	Aug 2 64
5627	Prentice J M	22	" K	Aug 14 64
6159	Penat Alexander	38	" B	Aug 19 64
6278	Patterson E	Cav 4	" G	Aug 20 64
6374	Parten D R	65	" F	Aug 26 64
7710	Plough J W, Sgt	89	" D	Sept 3 64
8661	Pratt William	29	" F	Sept 13 64
9196	Plumer A	2	" D	Sept 18 64
9705	Pope I T, Sgt	Cav 5	" G	Sept 24 64
9709	Patterson N S	93	" G	Sept 24 64
10128	Packett T C, Sgt	39	" F	Oct 1 64
11880	Pangburn, Sgt	20	" B	Nov 6 64
12572	Potts I	99	" H	Feb 2 65
12588	Phepps A	30	" D	Feb 4 65
1249	Packer Samuel B	Cav 6	" G	May 20 64
872	Remy John	66	" B	May 4 64
914	Reed R	57	" F	May 7 64
1065	Remcett L	65	" H	May 13 64
1558	Roll N C	117	" F	June 2 64
1696	Reese L	116	" I	June 7 64
2140	Robinson L	7	" I	June 18 64
4039	Rogman	38	" I	July 26 64
4165	Reiggs K N	39	" K	July 28 64
4406	Richardson I	35	" I	July 31 64
5180	Rawlings J W	117	" F	Aug 9 64
5259	Rains G D	4	" G	Aug 10 64

Indiana—(*Continued.*)

5454	Ritter Benjamin	29 Co	K	Aug 12 64
5542	Ralph G	68 "	F	Aug 13 64
6247	Roundbush Daniel	6 "	B	Aug 20 64
6383	Redyard A	65 "	F	Aug 21 64
6754	Russell J	7 "	K	Aug 24 64
7677	Ringold I	Cav 7 "	I	Sept 3 64
8488	Russmore E	Cav 2 "	C	Sept 11 64
8577	Redman N E	80 "	F	Sept 12 64
9521	Richardson John	86 "	D	Sept 21 64
9547	Riggs L	19 "	E	Aug 23 64
10829	Reeves Wm	42 "	F	Oct 13 64
11416	Rierdon M D	Bat 5		Oct 24 64
11451	Rutger W, Corpl	44 Co	D	Oct 25 64
11935	Russell W H	13 "	C	Nov 9 64
12454	Robinson R	8 "	G	Jan 14 65
12523	Richardson E	127 "	E	Jan 26 65
1440	Ryan Mart'n	35 "	B	May 28 64
6707	Rawlings E, Sgt	66 "	C	Aug 24 64
86	Smiley ——	65 "	I	Mch 21 64
129	Stein Thomas	66 "	D	Mch 23 64
205	Stouts ——	65 "	I	Mch 28 64
768	Sanderson H	Cav 6 "	G	Apl 27 64
817	Sears I	65 "	I	Apl 30 64
901	Shick Eli	20 "	C	May 5 64
1039	Smith M C, Corp	Bat 24		May 12 64
1331	Smith H	86 Co	A	May 24 64
1400	Sapp A J	44 "	H	May 26 64
1430	Swindle T O, Sgt	82 "	A	May 28 64
1501	Smith L	116 "	A	May 31 64
1611	Schroder W	42 "	A	June 4 64
1690	Sparks L D	66 "	D	June 7 64
1732	Search C	Cav 5 "	D	June 8 64
2079	Shigley T W	10 "	H	June 17 64
2083	Stinit D	Cav 6 "	L	June 17 64
2218	Smudley W	5 "	E	June 20 64
2318	Swain J W	20 "	A	June 22 64
2420	Snow J	Cav 5 "	G	June 24 64
2447	Stafford J W	68 "	I	May 25 64
2740	Smith J	65 "	H	July 1 64
2799	Stanchley Wm	5 "	K	July 2 64
2923	Stofer L, Sgt	29 "	B	July 5 64
3416	Spencer M	80 "	K	July 16 64
4014	Shields J	128 "	F	July 26 64
4054	Smith J W	38 "	G	July 27 64
4062	Smith H	79 "	H	July 27 64
4088	Schneider S A	Cav 3		July 27 64
4229	Sollman C, Sgt	35 Co	D	July 29 64
4418	Stevens M	Cav 6 "	M	July 31 64
4630	Snider D	117 "	K	Aug 3 64
4799	Summersvolt V	29 "	A	Aug 5 64
5254	Scott B	9 "	D	Aug 10 64
5418	Smith Samuel E	9 "	C	Aug 12 64
5513	Shoemaker E W	Cav 5 "	I	Aug 13 64
5514	Sims S	101 "	B	Aug 13 64
5571	Sackett I	Cav 6 "	G	Aug 14 64
5611	Stockman L M	68 "	E	Aug 14 64
5884	Standish M	66 "	B	Aug 16 64
5977	St[illegible]ckh ff G	19 "	I	Aug 17 64
6041	Stout H	7 "	G	Aug 18 64
6736	Sipe J	82 Co	A	Aug 24 64
6330	Strong L	9 "	F	Aug 25 64
7120	Spellman J	80 "	F	Aug 28 64
7264	Shaver F	129 "	I	Aug 30 64
7633	Snyder L	Cav 6 "	A	Sept 3 64
7822	Sanders D	7 "	I	Sept 4 64
8058	Suthien J H	66 "	E	Sept 7 64
8107	Starkey I	Cav 6 "	I	Sept 7 64
8262	Sizeman I	123 "	B	Sept 9 64
8313	Stagewald J M, Sgt	22 "	K	Sept 10 64
8 23	Swillenbarger F	21 "	I	Sept 13 64
8606	Sylvanus J J	35 "	G	Sept 13 64
8727	Shoel J P	30 "	B	Sept 14 64
8910	Storm L M, Sgt	6 "	A	Sept 16 64
9093	Simmons J	84 "	I	Sept 18 64
9232	Sharp D M	13 "	E	Sept 19 64
9546	Sharpless W	43 "	G	Sept 23 64
9623	Smith S B	17 "	F	Sept 24 64
9707	Skeels W	65 "	A	Sept 26 64
10790	Smith George	131 "	D	Oct 12 64
10949	Smith I	39 "	I	Oct 14 64
11036	Sloat G W, Sgt	44 "	B	Oct 16 64
111 7	Seigferd G H	Cav 4 "	I	Oct 19 64
11427	Sweitzer J	2 "	G	Oct 24 64
11842	Shaw W R	99 "	B	Nov 5 64
11969	Shoe G W	74 "	E	Nov 12 64
11984	Steamer F	29 "	F	Nov 13 64
12113	Scarff F	Cav 6 "	D	Nov 21 64
12381	Starke M S	93 "	D	Jan 2 65
12492	Salts H C	Cav 4 "	F	Jan 20 65
12582	Smith D H	Cav 12 "	H	Feb 3 65
12615	Sides G	66 "	A	Feb 8 65
12666	Smare C	Cav 2 "	G	Feb 17 65
12724	Stewart E B	38 "	E	Mar 3 65
12809	Staley G W	72 "	A	Mar 24 65
2625	Sattershwait A	82 "	I	June 28 64
518	Tenher James	117 "	I	Apl 18 64
3778	Tunblora B	65 "	B	July 22 64
3791	Thompson T	Cav 6 "	C	July 22 64
4733	Tooley G W	42 "	H	Aug 4 64
5065	Truman L H, Sgt	Cav 6 "	G	Aug 8 64
5403	Taylor N	63 "	I	Aug 12 64
6509	Tooley W R, Corpl	42 "	H	Aug 22 64
6719	Todd T	6 "	B	Aug 24 64
7096	Thomas H D	42 "	I	Aug 28 64
7442	Taylor George H	Cav 4 "	M	Sept 1 64
8405	Trumble D A	30 "	A	Sept 11 64
8525	Taylor E	25 "	I	Sept 12 64
10438	Thomas M	Cav 2		Oct 6 64
12337	Tucer B, Cit			Nov 26 64
12609	Terhune C	Cav 9 Co	A	Feb 7 65
10219	Tasnahet Charles, Sgt	33 "	E	Oct 2 64
10356	Underwood P	Cav 7 "	C	Sept 5 64
10760	Upton F M	52 "	A	Oct 12 64
1717	Voit T	Cav 6 "	K	June 8 64
5363	Venome James	39 "	K	Aug 11 64
6250	Vanose J	93 "	B	Aug 20 64
7691	Verhouse D	42 "	A	Sept 3 64
135	Windinger J	117 "	G	Mch 24 64

Indiana— (*Continued.*)

886	Walters J H, Corpl	Cav 6	Co G	May 5 64
934	Williams A	6	" G	May 7 64
1194	Wright Samuel	Cav 6	" I	May 18 64
1776	White P	Cav 6	" C	June 9 64
1812	Wise Eli	88	" D	June 10 64
1918	Warren E	65	" H	June 14 64
2107	Williams F	38	" F	June 17 64
2242	West E	Cav 7	" H	June 20 64
2363	Woodward W W	29	" A	June 23 64
2417	Wilson J N	75	" G	June 24 64
2467	Warden I	44	" B	June 25 64
2554	Warren E	37	" I	June 27 64
2670	Ward J	79	" F	June 29 64
2900	Wyn W E	13	" D	July 5 64
2929	Wislake I	116	" I	July 5 64
2934	Wicks L	Cav 6	" H	July 6 64
4528	Whitehead J	29	" I	Aug 2 64
4639	Winship James	36	" K	Aug 4 64
4826	Witt T	125	" D	Aug 5 64
5399	Wade C	81	" K	Aug 12 64
5547	Waynin J H	Cav 4	" I	Aug 13 64
6132	Washburn R H	Cav 6	" A	Aug 19 64
6405	Winders A	120	" I	Aug 21 64
6524	Wagner M	Cav 5	" I	Aug 25 64
7184	Winters F W	84	" C	Aug 29 64
7191	Wagoner E	42	Co A	Aug 29 64
7349	Witzgall John	2	" D	Aug 31 64
8943	Weiber Charles	13	" F	Sept 16 64
9228	White W	7	" E	Sept 19 64
9316	Watkins J	81	" A	Sept 20 64
6418	Wellington H	129	" I	Sept 21 64
9501	Wilson J B	6	" E	Sept 21 64
9998	Wagner F	7	" D	Sept 29 64
10643	Ward J	29	" G	Oct 11 64
11141	Whitehead N B	Cav 5	" L	Oct 18 64
11424	White R B	6	" D	Oct 24 64
11602	Walters J	5	" I	Oct 28 64
12708	Winebrook P	35	" B	Nov 18 64
12316	Werper J	32	" E	Dec 20 64
12341	White J	7	" A	Dec 26 64
12412	Welis J M	13	" D	Jan 16 65
12497	What J	93	" B	Jany 21 65
12737	Wade W	Cav 10	" M	Mch 6 65
3837	Weltz Ira, Sergt	4	" B	July 23 64
6060	West S N, Corpl	7	" B	Aug 17 64
9920	Williams J A, Sergt	38	" C	Sept 28 64
5055	Younce Chas. A	Cav 7	" I	Aug 8 64
5858	Yorker Daniel	28	" B	Aug 16 64
1540	Zuet J	65	" H	June 1 64

TOTAL 593.

IOWA.

5560	Allen N	3	Co K	Aug 13 64
8974	Ankebus L, Corpl	6	" I	Sept 17 64
9472	Ashford A W	11	" C	Sept 21 64
11784	Alderman W W	31	" F	Nov 4 64
11896	Austin Wm	Cav 3	" A	Nov 7 64
1293	Bartche C P	5	" K	May 23 64
1570	Bingman W H	39	" H	June 3 64
5276	Blanchard A	7	" A	Aug 10 64
6164	Bursford M	7	" F	Aug 19 64
7779	Baird J J	26	" H	Sept 4 64
8265	Buckmaster F	15	" K	Sept 9 64
9301	Buell J	4	" D	Sept 20 64
9456	Boylan C	14	" G	Sept 21 64
9691	Boles M B		" I	Sept 24 64
10749	Bellings J	5	" B	Oct 12 64
11334	Blakeley Geo	3	" G	Oct 23 64
167	Collins Henry, Sergt	4	" G	Mch 26 64
328	Chenworth Wm	1	" K	April 2 64
4582	Cromwell G W	27	" F	Aug 2 64
5101	Cooper S	5	" B	Aug 9 64
5244	Cox E E, Corp'l	5	" G	Aug 9 64
5620	Cox W A	5	" G	Aug 14 64
5999	Coder E	31	" E	Aug 17 64
6378	Cox H	5	" I	Aug 21 64
6604	Clamson Henry	26	" I	Aug 23 64
6848	Collins M	3	" L	Aug 25 64
8062	Culbertson S, Corp'l	5	" H	Sept 7 64
8352	Crow B	4	" E	Sept 10 64
9784	Coles J W, Sergt	8	" K	Sept 26 64
9820	Cobb E	Cav 3	" C	Sept 26 64
10037	Cramer J M	Cav 5	" B	Sept 29 64
10901	Chapman J	3	Co G	Oct 14 64
12230	Chamberlain J B	Cav 8	" A	Dec 6 64
2903	Davis S	3	" E	June 30 64
4206	Davis J	15	" D	July 29 64
9229	Davis H	17	" A	Sept 19 64
4675	Dermott L	5	" G	Aug 4 64
6349	Discol S	26	" I	Aug 25 64
9852	Dingman W	31	" D	Sept 27 64
11098	Denoya W H	5	" M	Oct 18 64
11753	Dutlin S	Cav 6	" C	Nov 2 64
12245	Durochis Wm	12	" H	Dec 8 64
12657	Derickson W W, Cor.	Cav 8	" M	Feby 15 65
262	Ennis Wm	4	" B	Mch 31 64
11414	England G	9	" F	Oct 24 64
3705	Field Jacob	5	" K	July 21 64
4503	Farnsworth S	2	" H	Aug 1 64
1316	Forney James M	10	" K	May 23 64
7715	Frue J	10		Sept 3 64
7878	Frederick J A	16	Co C	Sept 5 64
8380	Frussell G W	6	" D	Sept 10 64
10048	Fordson Michael	16	" H	Sept 29 64
11078	Fener J W	Cav 3	" B	Oct 17 64
12701	Ferguson A W	15	" A	Feby 28 65
750	Gain L	6	" C	April 26 64
1474	Gender Jacob	5	" I	May 30 64
5004	Gentle G	4	" G	Aug 8 64
5836	Gunshaw C	26		Aug 16 64
10511	Gray J	11	Co C	Oct 7 64
10306	Gothard J	8	" G	Oct 11 64
5461	Harris J	Cav 8	" H	Aug 13 64
8106	Hastings J, Sergt	11	" B	Sept 7 64

Iowa—(*Continued.*)

9379	Hird D, Corp'l	3	Co G	Sept 20 64
9417	Hudson M	16	" B	Sept 21 64
2168	Huffman R J	5	" H	June 19 64
862	Heeler A	5	" D	May 3 64
1633	Harper D	7	" K	June 5 64
1816	Hurlay J	8	" H	June 11 64
12749	Hubanks C, Sergt	17	" H	Mch 8 65
10360	Ireland J S	Cav 5	" H	Oct 5 64
4461	Jones C	4	" B	Aug 1 64
8656	Jenks G A, Sergt	8	" C	Sept 13 64
9401	Jones J	5	" C	Sept 21 64
3[illegible]04	Kolenbrander H	17	" K	July 12 64
7	King Alexander	17	" H	April 5 64
6464	King E	Cav 2	" C	Aug 22 64
3560	Kesler F	4	" B	July 18 64
11281	Knight J H, Sergt	9	" I	Oct 22 64
892	Lambert Chas. Corp'l	39	" K	May 5 64
2045	Littleton J	5		May 15 64
7959	Lord L	13	Co G	Sept 6 64
8263	Lanning A	13	" I	Sept 9 64
9438	Lowdenbeck N	5	" B	Sept 21 64
10224	Lowelenbuck D R	5	" B	Oct 2 64
10881	Layers W	5	" E	Oct 14 64
11752	Luther J, Corp'l	9	" B	Nov 2 64
1[illegible]629	Littlejohn L D	Cav 4	" B	Feby 10 65
257	Moore John	39	" H	Mch 31 64
307	Myers M	4	" K	April 2 64
450	Moon James	39	" H	April 9 64
1192	McMullen James	4	" C	May 18 64
1317	Miller F	5	" H	May 23 64
1472	McCameron W	4	" A	May 30 64
2027	McAllister A P	14	" E	June 15 64
3423	McNeil J W	11	" I	July 16 64
4804	Moore Wm	13	" A	Aug 5 64
5445	Murray J J	17	" I	Aug 12 64
6167	McCall Thomas	Cav 8	" M	Aug 19 64
6315	Merchant Wm	13	" G	Aug 25 64
6878	Maynard J D	4	" B	Aug 26 64
7143	McDonald D B, Sgt	Cav 5	" M	Aug 29 64
8120	McClure Z, Sergt	16	" C	Sept 8 64
9274	Martin S S	11	" G	Sept 19 64
9585	Mann J	16		Sept 23 64
10110	Miller J	5	Co D	Oct 1 64
10827	McCoy G B, Corp'l	5	" G	Oct 13 64
10950	Mercer John	4	" C	Oct 14 64
11745	Miller E, Corp'l	31	" D	Nov 2 64
12484	Martin J B	5	" B	Jany 19 65
12561	Macy C S	Cav 8	" C	Jany 31 65
6959	O'Connor P	26	" D	Aug 27 64
9509	O'Verturf P W	5	" H	Sept 22 64
12160	Osborn F L	16	" A	Nov 26 64
1972	Peterson J	76	" E	June 15 64
2869	Palmer L H	9	" D	July 4 64
6209	Phillpot C P	31	" B	Aug 19 64
9370	Putnam O	27	" F	Aug 20 64
10270	Pitts J	16	" I	Oct 3 64
10297	Pugh A, Corp'l	8	Co M	Oct 3 64
10413	Parker D	4	" I	Oct 6 64
18	Rule Y A	10	" A	April 12 64
1796	Ryan Charles	5	Co G	June 10 64
1820	Richardson John	Cav 5	" I	June 11 64
1951	Ratcliff J	4	" I	June 14 64
5878	Reed R	16	" I	Aug 16 64
6572	Robinson D	13	" G	Aug 23 64
7100	Rice H M, Sut's Clerk	9		Aug 31 64
9413	Riley M	5	Co A	Sept 21 64
9483	Reeves S J	9	" D	Sept 21 64
10015	Reed C	2	" C	Sept 29 64
10017	Rogers L	4	" F	Sept 29 64
12264	Russel E	4	" G	Dec 12 64
12287	Raiser A	8	" C	Dec 14 64
451	Stout John	5	" A	April 9 64
599	Shuffleton J	5	" H	April 17 64
641	Seeley Norman	9	" B	April 20 64
2712	Smith R F, Corp'l	10	" H	July 1 64
2845	Shutter J	30	" K	July 3 64
3060	Sparks M J	5	" K	July 9 64
4178	Sutton S	5	" H	July 28 64
4773	Smith Charles, Corp'l	20	" F	Aug 4 64
5410	Starr C F	30	" H	Aug 12 64
5892	Sheddle G	16	" C	Aug 16 64
7954	Seims Wm	3	" D	Sept 6 64
8200	Smith J	13	" A	Sept 8 64
9209	Smith O	5	" D	Sept 19 64
9125	Sherman J W	3	" I	Sept 17 64
9234	Spears J	Cav 5	" H	Sept 19 64
9367	Smith D	Cav 3	" B	Sept 20 64
11789	Shaw W W	5	" H	Nov 4 64
12729	Smice W	16	" E	Mch 4 65
10884	Sayres W	5	" E	Oct 14 64
1981	Taiping Wm	5	" K	June 15 64
8936	Thopson M	5	" G	July 25 64
6687	Tivis C	5	" A	Aug 24 64
9720	Tomme B	Cav 4	" M	Sept 25 64
11708	Thier A F	3		Nov 1 64
10351	Voke John C, Corp'l	5	Co E	Oct 5 64
1674	Whitman O R, Corp'l	5	" E	June 6 64
2161	Wells F, Sergt	5	" I	June 19 64
2213	Wittesrick A K	9	" K	June 20 64
2855	Wolf B F	8	" E	July 4 64
4916	Wolfe J H	2	" C	Aug 6 64
6934	Wheelan J, Sergt	26	" D	Aug 26 64
8101	Walworth C, Sergt	5	" K	Sept 17 64
8131	Woolston S P, Sergt	13	" H	Sept 8 64
9221	Ward O R	3	" E	Sept 19 64
9186	Wagner Joseph	13	" E	Sept 21 64
9727	Wersbrod Y	31	" A	Sept 25 64
10843	Wilson P D	10	" G	Oct 13 64
10942	Woodward J, Sut	9		Oct 14 64
11114	Whiting J	5	Co H	Oct 18 64
11141	Whitehead N B	Cav 5	" L	Oct 19 64
12741	Wen C	57	" C	Mch 6 65

TOTAL 174.

KANSAS.

1614	Freeman F J, Sergt	8 Co	F	June 4 64
1935	Gensarde Thos	8 "	A	June 14 64
12127	Sweeney M	1 "	H	Nov 22 64
11189	Weidman W	8 Co	B	Oct 19 64
1663	Williams C A	8 "	A	June 6 64

TOTAL 5.

KENTUCKY.

329	Allen Sam'l S, Corp'l	13 Co	F	April 2 64
674	Alford George	Cav 11 "	B	April 22 64
1575	Anderson S	Cav 11 "	D	May 3 64
3385	Adams J D	Cav 1 "	I	July 16 64
3759	Ashley J M	Cav 1 "	L	July 22 64
4723	Allen Wm, Corp'l	Cav 11 "	C	Aug 4 64
4894	Atkins A	Cav 39 "	H	Aug 6 64
6093	Anghlin J A, Cor'l	Cav 18 "	B	Aug 18 64
6720	Arnett H S	Cav 13 "	A	Aug 24 64
10514	Adamson Wm	Cav 15 "	K	Oct 8 64
11759	Adams J L	27 "	G	Nov 3 64
12426	Arthur D	4 "	G	Jany 9 65
12528	Ayers E	52 "	A	Jany 26 65
12703	Ayers S	52 "	A	Jany 26 65
12593	Arnett T	Cav 4 "	F	Jany 5 65
193	Bow James	Cav 1		Mch 27 64
261	Burrows Wm	Cav 1 Co	K	Mch 31 64
366	Byesly Wm	Cav 11 "	E	April 2 64
379	Baker Isaac	Cav 1 "	H	April 5 64
413	Basham S	Cav 12 "	E	April 7 64
419	Button Ed	Cav 11 "	D	April 18 64
608	Burrett B	Cav 6 "	D	April 18 64
609	Bloomer H	Cav 4 "	G	April 18 64
803	Baker A W	Cav 3 "	C	April 29 64
832	Boley Peter	12 "	L	May 1 64
891	Bird W T	Cav 11 "	H	May 5 64
857	Bailey A W	14 "	G	May 2 64
1167	Burton Tillman	Cav 1 "	F	May 17 64
1200	Butner L B, Sergt	Cav 6 "	I	May 18 64
1263	Bell P B	Cav 11 "	I	May 21 64
1362	Barnett James	Cav 8 "	H	May 25 64
1566	Baird Sam'l J	Cav 12 "	D	June 2 64
1789	Bishop D L	Cav 11 "	A	June 10 64
2022	Bowman G	Cav 11 "	D	June 15 64
2423	Bray H N, Corp'l	Cav 9 "	H	June 24 64
2529	Buchanan S	Cav 12 "	F	June 26 64
2760	Ball David	Cav 11 "	B	July 2 64
3087	Beard J C, Sergt	Cav 1 "	C	July 9 64
3228	Brophy M	Cav 5 "	I	July 12 64
3433	Bailey F M	Cav 4 "	G	July 17 64
3909	Banner J	Cav 11 "	C	July 24 64
3998	Bridell S, Corp'l	Cav 3 "	F	July 26 64
4562	Booth Z, Sergt	Cav 16 "	E	Aug 2 64
4653	Barger George	Cav 5 "	I	Aug 3 64
4835	Baker Wm	Cav 3 "	I	Aug 6 64
4971	Bigler A	Cav 6 "	B	Aug 7 64
5471	Bailey J H	Cav 11 "	A	Aug 12 64
5644	Branan H	Cav 1 "	G	Aug 14 64
6576	Boston J	Cav 27 "	E	Aug 23 64
6727	Bottoms J M	Cav 1 "	H	Aug 24 64
9551	Brinton W J, Sgt	Cav 11 "	C	Aug 23 64
9568	Barnett A	Cav 12 "	K	Sept 23 64
9628	Brown J	Cav 10 "	I	Sept 24 64
9740	Boyd M	Cav 13 "	A	Sept 25 64
10147	Batt W	5 Co	G	Oct 1 64
10202	Byron H M, Sgt	Cav 1 "	I	Oct 2 64
10451	Bill B S	Cav 1 "	K	Oct 7 64
10816	Bodkins P, Corp'l	Cav 1 "	K	Oct 12 64
10859	Bagley T	Cav 11		Oct 13 64
11052	Brickey W L	4 Co	F	Oct 17 64
11256	Baldwin J W	11 "	H	Oct 21 64
11303	Brown E W	4 "	F	Oct 22 64
11491	Barber T	Cav 4 "	H	Oct 26 64
12006	Brannon J	3 "	B	Nov 13 64
12104	Beatty R	5 "	B	Dec 18 64
12333	Barnes J	11 "	D	Dec 25 64
12360	Brodus O	Cav 11 "	A	Dec 30 64
12421	Britton J	45 "	F	Jany 9 65
5098	Bowman Henry	Cav 11 "	F	Aug 9 64
12777	Balson L	12 "	B	Mch 15 64
11483	Cranch J P	10 "	D	Oct 26 64
240	Conler Wm	14 "	I	Mch 30 64
484	Caldwell Wm	Cav 12 "	I	April 9 64
509	Cook Theo	Cav 12 "	D	April 12 64
672	Colvin George	Cav 11 "	D	April 22 64
877	Christmas J	Cav 11 "	F	May 4 64
966	Collague M	Cav 12 "	E	May 8 64
1268	Cash Philip	Cav 1 "	I	May 21 64
1600	Cole W C	Cav 1 "	C	June 4 64
1676	Christenburg R I,	Cav 12 "	G	June 6 64
1687	Callihan Pat	Cav 11 "	A	June 6 64
1856	Clane H	Cav 11 "	E	June 12 64
2152	Clinge W H	40 "	A	June 18 64
2293	Cox A B	Cav 6 "	I	June 21 64
2339	Chippendale C	Cav 1 "	B	June 22 64
2446	Carlisle J	Cav 6 "	I	June 25 64
2823	Cummings J	11 "	F	July 3 64
2912	Cleming Thos	18 "	I	July 5 64
3184	Carter W	Cav 11 "	H	July 11 64
60	Cristian John	Cav 4 "	C	July 4 64
4044	Clark A H	11 "	I	July 27 64
4809	Chapman	11 "	H	Aug 5 64
6387	Coulter M	23 "	B	Aug 21 64
9835	Conrad R P	4 "	B	Sept 27 64
11179	Clun W H	Cav 11 "	L	Oct 19 64
11486	Chatsin W M	Cav 6 "	H	Oct 26 64
12447	Carcanright	4 "	C	Jany 13 65
12700	Cook J P	4 "	G	Jany 26 65
2223	Corbitt Thos	5 "	A	June 20 64
8113	Coyle C	Cav 11 "	I	Sept 7 64
4740	Chance A J	Cav 1 "	C	Aug 5 64
421	Dupon F	12 "	G	Apl 7 64
1388	Delaney M	Cav 11 "	I	May 26 64
1414	Dugean J R, Sgt	" 12 "	K	May 27 64
1568	DeBarnes P M	" 11 "	C	June 2 64
1627	Demody Thos	" 1 "	H	June 4 64
1867	Drake J H	" 12 "	G	June 12 64
2736	Davis B	5 "	C	July 1 64

Kentucky—(*Continued.*)

23	Duncan E	Cav 12	Co G	Apl 15 64
3623	Dodson E	39	" H	July 20 64
27	Derine George	Cav 1	" I	Apl 17 64
3924	Davis G C	" 12	" F	July 25 64
3966	Derringer H	" 11	" I	July 25 64
4510	Dulrebeck H	11	" E	Aug 1 64
4556	Delaney H	Cav 4	" H	Aug 2 64
5088	Dounty P	5	" F	Aug 8 64
5899	Daniel R	9	" F	Aug 16 64
11405	Disque F, Sgt	Cav 6	" G	Oct 21 64
12250	Duland D W	3	" K	Dec 13 64
12523	Dannard W	4	" D	Feb 9 65
12684	Dipple S	4	" E	Feb 21 65
1109	Dinsman H	Cav 4	" E	May 15 64
2805	Davis J P	13	" A	July 3 64
2117	Davis C	Cav 6	" D	June 30 64
639	Eodus James	" 1	" F	Apl 20 64
1174	Edmiston J W	" 11	" A	May 17 64
1439	Edwards H S, Corpl	" 8	" K	May 27 64
2544	Emery J	10	" G	June 27 64
2341	Errbanks J	Cav 1	" A	Aug 11 64
12277	Esteff J	" 1	" L	Oct 22 64
1447	Fast R	" 1	" G	May 29 64
384	Falconburg I K	" 1	" A	Apl 5 64
2540	Fleming R	" 4	" D	June 27 64
3640	Forteen John	8	" A	July 20 64
4344	Fenkstine M	1	" D	July 30 64
6763	Featherstone J	6	" C	Aug 25 64
7068	Fritz J	Cav 4	" G	Aug 28 64
10280	Funk L	" 1	" I	Oct 4 64
11549	Frazier C R	23	" H	Oct 27 64
11720	Fletcher T	17	" E	Nov 1 64
1612	Gritton G	Cav 11	" D	June 4 64
1618	Graves G	18	" C	June 4 64
1841	Gritton M	Cav 11	" B	June 11 64
2583	Gibson John	" 6	" L	June 27 64
3670	Griffin B	11	" E	July 20 64
3663	Glessman P	Cav 4	" B	July 20 64
3888	Gonns J M	4	" H	July 24 64
4438	Gather M	Cav 4	" F	July 31 64
5779	Gullett A	45	" K	Aug 15 64
7197	Green J B, Sgt	11	" I	Aug 29 64
7817	Grabul B	1	" F	Sept 4 64
8049	Gury J	4	" H	Sept 6 64
8903	Gray C D	20	" G	Sept 18 64
9318	Gett John, Sgt	40	" G	Sept 20 64
9950	Gill W J	Cav 11	" H	Sept 28 64
10053	Gower J C	13	" A	Sept 30 64
10650	Gibson A	Cav 8	" K	Oct 10 64
10831	Grulach J, Sgt	4	" K	Oct 13 64
11910	Grimstead J R	1	" E	Nov 8 64
12022	Griffin R	11	" E	Nov 15 64
1235	Gregory H	Cav 12	" D	May 20 64
81	Hauns J B	12	" K	Mch 20 64
237	Holloway Richard	4	" I	Mch 29 64
289	Harley Alfred	40	" K	Apl 1 64
292	Hood G	Cav 5	" F	Apl 1 64
348	Hammond J W	" 1	" G	Apl 2 64
376	Harper J	1	" C	Apl 5 64
402	Harlow Harvey	13	Co I	Apl 6 64
614	Hess Wm F	Cav 12	" M	Apl 18 64
613	Hendree A, Sgt	11	" F	Apl 20 64
1023	Hillard Geo	11	" D	May 11 64
1127	Hoffman C	Cav 11	" E	May 15 64
1584	Hughes Thos, Sgt	9	" G	June 3 64
1760	Hennessey J	28	" D	June 9 64
1378	Hundley Geo W	Cav 4		June 12 64
1956	Hazlewood J H	18	Co G	June 14 64
1999	Hamner A	9	" B	June 15 64
2490	Huison J W, Sgt	9	" B	June 26 64
2705	Hillard S	Cav 1	" I	June 30 64
3239	Henderson J	18	" B	July 12 64
26	Hooper Saml	Cav 11	" D	Apl 16 64
3944	Hooper J	" 1	" D	July 25 64
3994	Hickworth J	45	" D	July 26 64
4313	Hall J H	Cav 1	" C	July 30 64
4420	Hammontius P	" 6	" L	June 30 64
4970	Hayner E	" 1	" D	Aug 7 64
5059	Haines J	" 12	" D	Aug 8 64
5091	Harrington C	15	" K	Aug 8 64
5793	Hatfield L	1	" F	Aug 15 64
6193	Hendrie Wm	Cav 11	" F	Aug 19 64
6801	Hardison G	23	" I	Aug 25 64
8032	Hise P	4	" I	Sept 6 64
8111	Hicks P	Cav 11	" F	Sept 7 64
8181	Heglen C	Cav 4	" I	Sept 8 64
9376	Hanker R	Cav 18	" F	Sept 20 64
9599	Hyrommus Jas	Cav 11	" D	Sept 23 64
10683	Halton S M	2	" K	Oct 11 64
11054	Halligan J	4	" A	Oct 17 64
11095	Hall F	Cav 1	" F	Oct 18 64
11182	Hazer John	11	" I	Oct 18 64
11251	Harter F	Cav 12	" M	Oct 21 64
12253	Hays J F	5	" A	Dec 15 64
12518	Hasting J	4	" H	Jany 24 65
12638	Hudson B F	4	" A	Feby 11 65
5734	Inman John	24	" A	Aug 15 64
9757	Isabell J M	3	" H	Sept 25 64
11392	Inman W	Cav 11	" D	Oct 24 64
12203	Isabel A	1	" K	Dec 1 64
649	Jackson John	45	" D	April 20 64
2679	Jeffries Wm	Cav 1	" A	June 30 64
5229	Jacobs John W	Cav 4	" I	Aug 10 64
7294	Johnson A	10	" H	Aug 31 64
7371	Jenkins S	Cav 6	" A	Aug 31 64
7594	Justin J	39	" F	Sept 2 64
7754	James W	5	" K	Sept 4 64
9654	Jarvis W D	12	" D	Sept 24 64
11000	Jordan J	Cav 5	" B	Oct 16 64
11143	Jones D	Cav 1	" L	Oct 18 64
12541	Jones J	16	" E	Jany 27 65
87	Kennedy James	Cav 11	" E	Mch 21 64
191	Knotts Fred	Cav 11	" E	Mch 27 64
926	Kessmer John	Cav 12	" I	May 7 64
1045	Kennedy S B	39	" B	May 12 64
1173	Keilling M	Cav 11	" D	May 17 64
3928	Keystone C	6	" E	July 25 64
4321	Kennedy A, Corpl	Cav 1	" A	July 6 64

Kentucky — (*Continued.*)

5553	Knapp Thomas	Cav 6	Co M	July 13 64
5925	Kressler P	Cav 4	" K	July 17 64
12265	Knapp J	Cav 5	" B	Dec 12 64
48	Lenniert L	1	" K	Mch 15 64
310	Lambert R	Cav 11	" F	April 2 64
1135	Lay Wm	Cav 11	" D	May 16 64
1726	Lossman A	Cav 4	" E	June 8 64
1802	Larger W	Cav 1	" L	June 10 64
1912	Ledford J A	16	" B	June 13 64
2109	Little J	1	" D	June 17 64
2352	Lononey B	Cav 1	" K	June 23 64
2668	Lasper Otto	15	" H	June 29 64
837	Lublett M L	13	" E	June 3 64
3310	Leville Thomas	4	" D	July 15 64
3398	Lee S	Cav 1	" A	July 16 64
3658	Loy W B	Cav 8	" L	July 20 64
3776	Lanhart J	Cav 6	" G	July 22 64
3839	Lowry Jas W	Cav 12	" G	July 23 64
6024	Lewis T	Cav 2	" C	Aug 18 64
7132	Landers, Corp'l	36	" I	Aug 28 64
7934	Luster W	Cav 1	" B	Sept 5 64
8634	Little J F	Cav 12	" D	Sept 13 64
11870	Lindusky G	11	" G	Nov 6 64
12175	Ledwick A	7	" C	Nov 27 64
9175	Lord Wm	20	" G	Sept 18 64
271	McMannus Sam'l	11	" D	Mch 31 64
369	Miller John	3	" A	April 5 64
525	McDougal W C	14	" K	April 13 64
795	Mills John	1	" H	April 29 64
991	McClure P	Cav 11	" C	May 10 64
1232	Marshall Wm	Cav 5	" I	May 19 64
1380	Montgomery W A	Cav 5	" H	May 26 64
1391	Moreland H	Cav 1	" F	May 26 64
1969	Merix J	Cav 45	" D	June 14 64
2024	Morton W	Cav 7	" I	June 15 64
2137	Meldown D	Cav 11	" E	June 18 64
2669	Miller W C	Cav 27	" A	June 29 64
3152	Mitchell James	Cav 12	" C	July 11 64
64	Mullins W W	Cav 1	" H	Aug 8 64
3418	Morgan J	Cav 4	" D	July 17 64
4513	Masters J	Cav 11	" A	Aug 1 64
4550	McDonald J	Cav 4	" I	Aug 2 64
4646	Mitchell R M	Cav 17	" E	Aug 3 64
5601	Mooney Pat	Cav 11	" G	Aug 15 64
7951	McCarty E	Cav 5	" K	Sept 6 64
8455	McCarty John	Cav 6	" K	Sept 9 64
8635	McCarter W	Cav 9	" B	Sept 13 64
9239	Munch J	Cav 28	" F	Sept 19 64
9498	Macary C	Cav 11	" M	Sept 21 64
9711	Moore Wm	Cav 12	" D	Sept 24 64
7336	Martin F P	Cav 12	" D	Aug 30 64
10170	Marshall L	Cav 1	" F	Oct 1 64
10460	Mills George	Cav 4	" H	Oct 7 64
11455	Murphy W M	Cav 2	" H	Oct 25 64
11478	Miller E	Cav 4	" I	Oct 26 64
12[illegible]6	Miller J	Cav 4	" K	Jany 16 65
12491	Myers J	Cav 4	" C	Jany 20 65
12720	Meach A J	Cav 1	" A	Mch 3 65
12764	Morgan F, Corp'l	3	" I	Mch 12 65
212	New Geo W	Cav 1	Co F	Mch 28 64
447	Neely B W	Cav 1	" G	April 9 64
63	Nelson John	Cav 1	" D	July 19 64
7693	Northcraft J	Cav 6	" H	Sept 3 64
9230	Newton A, Corp'l	Cav 4	" H	Sept 19 64
2499	O'Bannon Wm	Cav 11	" B	June 20 64
2513	Oper L	Cav 4	" B	June 20 64
11943	Owen W, Corp'l	Cav 1	" L	Nov 9 64
1178	Pott J	Cav 7	" C	May 17 64
1925	Porter J F	Cav 18		June 13 64
3654	Pulliam J	2		July 20 64
4220	Plyman Wm	39		July 27 64
5761	Pally S C, Sergt	Cav 12	" B	Aug 15 64
6616	Phelps Wm E	Cav 6	" F	Aug 23 64
6632	Pruils W H	Cav 1	" F	Aug 23 64
7222	Pope Frank, Corpl	Cav 5	" B	Aug 29 64
8070	Pott Samuel	Cav 4	" G	Sept 17 64
8207	Patterson J	Cav 2	" B	Sept 8 64
9359	Phelps F M, Sergt	Cav 11	" I	Sept 20 64
10249	Partis J R	Cav 1	" F	Oct 3 64
12220	Pace John	" 3	" G	Dec 4 64
12327	Purcell J	" 1	" G	Dec 23 64
2144	Qucata J	" 11	" E	June 18 64
452	Rurves E, Sgt	" 4	" F	Apl 9 64
577	Roberts R	" 12	" H	Apl 16 64
590	Ramy Lester	" 39	" H	Apl 17 64
637	Raberie Geo	" 1	" A	Apl 20 64
825	Richardson M, Corpl	3	" H	May 1 64
1097	Runs T	Cav 11	" H	May 14 64
1193	Russell Jacob	" 12	" B	May 18 64
1355	Ritter B B	" 6	" L	May 25 64
1555	Rose R C, Corpl	" 6	" B	June 2 64
1571	Rogers W	1	" F	June 3 64
2163	Reve F N	11	" F	June 25 64
2731	Reilly Thos	1	" D	July 1 64
4018	Ramsay Robert	45	" A	July 26 64
4482	Robertson H	Cav 11	" D	Aug 1 64
4549	Rodes James	" 1	" F	Aug 2 64
4919	Rockwell W W, Cl	" 1	" C	Aug 6 64
5775	Roberts L	" 1	" K	Aug 15 64
5967	Rieff R	Art 1		Aug 17 64
5976	Roberts Andrew	Cav 1	Co K	Aug 17 64
6274	Readman W	" 11	" I	Aug 20 64
7215	Rogers Henry	" 12	" A	Aug 29 64
10124	Robny F	" 15	" E	Oct 1 64
11369	Racine P	" 12	" I	Oct 27 64
11583	Ryan W	" 1	" I	Oct 28 64
11642	Riddle J H	" 1	" I	Oct 30 64
11644	Rogers Wm	" 2	" I	Oct 30 64
11873	Rusby J	" 2	" F	Nov 6 64
12828	Rice P D, Sgt	3	" I	April 9 65
1202	Ruble L, Corpl	Cav 11	" D	May 19 64
4206	Rankin J H, Sgt	Cav 18	" G	July 27 64
213	Simpson W	" 1	" C	Mch 23 64
277	Sims Geo, Sgt	40	" I	Mch 31 64
567	Summers W H	Cav 11	" D	April 15 64
797	Smith Geo	" 13	" G	April 29 64
925	Sallac Geo, Corp'l	" 11	" C	May 7 64
995	Smith Wm A	" 4	" K	May 10 64

Kentucky — (*Continued.*)

1003	Smith H	Cav 16	Co B	May 10 64	6257	Tapp George	Cav 13	Co I	Aug 20 64
1101	Smith R C	" 1	" I	May 14 64	6508	Tracy James	Cav 11	" L	Aug 22 64
1180	Schafer J E	" 4	" A	May 18 64	6956	Thorp J	Cav 4	" K	Aug 26 64
1500	Stempf Lewis	" 12	" G	May 31 64	7205	Tucker Robert	Cav 17	" G	Aug 29 64
1659	Sutherland J E, Sgt,	" 1	" C	June 6 64	10028	Tucker J A	Cav 15	" A	Sept 29 64
1681	Sebastian J W	45	" C	June 6 64	10[illegible]08	Thornburg B	Cav 2	" G	Oct 6 64
1691	Sanders J S	Cav 12	" E	June 7 64	10[illegible]88	Tussey E D	Cav 24	" A	Oct 10 64
1708	Stine C	" 4	" K	June 7 64	10809	Terry Wm	Cav 1	" A	Oct 12 64
1716	Sandfer Jno	" 11	" B	June 8 64	108[illegible]2	Thomas W E, Sgt	Cav 11	" G	Oct 14 64
1811	Summers Wm	" 11	" D	June 10 64	10657	Vandevier J	Cav 11	" C	Oct 11 64
1827	Sweeney M	" 5	" I	June 11 64	278	West John C	Cav 11	" E	Mch 31 64
1952	Shirley John	" 28	" E	June 14 64	494	White A	Cav 6	" K	April 12 64
1964	Stanley C O	" 17	" E	June 14 64	735	Wailar M R	Cav 16	" C	April 24 64
2063	Salmond P	" 18	" H	June 16 64	1125	White John	Cav 11	" D	May 15 64
2094	Shanks W L	" 6	" B	June 17 64	1706	Westfall J	Cav 4	" D	June 7 64
2766	Show J	" 11	" I	July 6 64	1734	Wickles John	40	" K	June 8 64
44	Smith John	" 2	" I	May 13 64	1745	Walsh J E	Cav 6	" L	June 8 64
51	Shaggs I P	" 11	" G	June 2 64	1894	Wright John E	Cav 1		June 13 64
3402	Shuman J	" 4	" A	July 16 64	2199	Wheelan James	Cav 18	Co C	June 19 64
4258	Smith B, Corp'l	" 5	" A	July 29 64	2584	White C	Cav 1	" H	June 27 64
4829	Schmal Andrew	Cav 4	" B	Aug 6 64	2901	Wiser R M	Cav 1	" B	July 5 64
4831	Schottsman F, Cor	Cav 1	" D	Aug 6 64	40	Ward F W	Cav 1	" A	May 3 64
4976	Snyder H M	Cav 10	" B	Aug 7 64	4374	Warren W P	Cav 34	" K	July 30 64
5297	Smith W H, Corp'l	27	" E	Aug 11 64	4624	Wallace H	Cav 14	" E	Aug 3 64
62[illegible]0	Stevens P L, Sgt	Cav 12	" G	Aug 20 64	4697	West P H	Cav 6	" K	Aug 3 64
6280	Schransburg R	Cav 1	" K	Aug 20 64	1[illegible]057	Webb J	Cav 6	" F	Aug 8 64
8226	Stimett J	Cav 6	" K	Sept 9 64	5762	Welch T C	Cav 5	" G	Aug 15 64
8487	Sutton Thomas	Cav 6	" A	Sept 11 64	5790	Walsh John	Cav 6	" H	Aug 15 64
88[illegible]7	Shulds J	Cav 2	" K	Sept 15 64	6101	Winter H	Cav 11	" E	Aug 18 64
10154	Sanders B	Cav 4	" F	Oct 1 64	6121	Winfries W S	Cav 3	" A	Aug 19 64
10673	Sheppard T L	Cav 5	" H	Oct 11 64	6893	White S A	Cav 17	" G	Aug 26 64
11456	Sapp B	Cav 1	" B	Oct 25 64	7038	Willser J	Cav 11	" I	Aug 27 64
11898	Selors W H	Cav 1	" C	Nov 7 64	7694	Wells J W	Cav 12	" C	Aug 3 64
12556	Stewart E	Cav 4	" A	Jany 30 65	8533	Wallace J, Sergt	Cav 11	" K	Sept 12 64
10197	Sawney Wm	Cav 5	" H	Oct 2 64	9258	Warner D	Cav 12	" A	Sept 19 64
2654	Sutherland H	32	" G	June 29 64	9541	Wicog S	Cav 4	" I	Sept 23 64
253	Taylor Thos, Corp	Cav 11	" H	Mch 30 64	9636	Wagoner H, Corp'l	Cav 4	" I	Sept 24 64
391	Thrope H	Cav 1	" B	April 6 64	10770	Warner Thos	Cav 15	" F	Oct 12 64
781	Tucker Wm	Cav 12	" I	April 28 64	10898	Walton J J	Cav 8	" A	Oct 14 64
1009	Travis Geo	Cav 16	" E	May 10 64	11749	Willit M	Cav 4	" I	Nov 2 64
1628	Truney J	Cav 11	" C	June 4 64	12279	Weasett A	Cav 1	" D	Nov 13 64
2116	Tutune J, Sergt	Cav 11	" A	June 17 64	904	Yocombs H	Cav 11	" D	May 5 64
2371	Tudor Ab'm, Corp	Cav 11	" A	June 23 64	1166	Yoam J	Cav 10	" D	May 17 64
3701	Tullor G W	28	" A	July 21 64	2689	Yeager L, Sgt	Cav 11	" C	June 30 64
5424	Tabu Silas	27	" D	Aug 12 64	3757	Yeast R	Cav 1	" I	July 22 64
6234	Templeton W H	Cav 11	" B	Aug 20 64	5257	Zertes G	Cav 4	" G	Aug 10 64

TOTAL 436.

LOUISIANA.

6778 Kimball Jas Cav 2 Co A Aug 25 64

MAINE.

2604	Anderson John	19	Co I	June 28 64	6211	Bachelor P, Sergt	3	Co K	Aug 19 64
3093	Allen A	32	" K	July 10 64	9162	Baker James	17	" H	Sept 18 64
7024	Arnold E W	17	" G	Aug 27 64	10669	Ballast J	19	" G	Oct 11 64
22	Butler C A	3	" K	Mch 7 64	7663	Bartlett H	17	" C	Sept 3 64
269	Brown E M	5	" G	Mch 31 64	7255	Barney G S	32	" I	Aug 30 64
3953	Buner A E	31	" E	July 25 64	6683	Bean G W	8	" C	Aug 24 64

Maine—(*Continued.*)

6603	Bennett L	Art 1	Aug 23 64
9097	Berry C H	6 Co H	Sept 18 64
7645	Bigelow C	19 " H	Sept 3 64
5290	Blaizdell H	8 " F	Aug 11 64
12055	Boren W	16 " I	Nov 16 64
9408	Bowden ——	7 " A	Sept 21 64
4776	Braley J	3 " E	Aug 4 64
5015	Briggs J C	19 " F	Aug 8 64
8542	Brinkerman L	9 " D	Sept 11 64
8247	Broadstreet C B	Cav 1 " B	Sept 9 64
6811	Brown J	8 " G	Aug 25 64
11980	Bryant C D	16 " E	Nov 13 64
5719	Bullsen E T, Sgt	Cav 5 " B	Aug 15 64
5757	Bunker S A	Art 1 " A	Aug 15 64
8174	Burgen A	4 " I	Sept 11 64
7017	Cardoney C	17 " G	Aug 27 64
7746	Carlen M	Cav 1 " F	Sept 3 64
8374	Carr J	19 " E	Sept 10 64
6246	Carlton J S	31 " D	Aug 19 64
5989	Chase F W	Art 1 " D	Aug 17 64
2316	Clark James	Cav 1 " C	June 26 64
8143	Clark P M, Sergt	Cav 1 " C	Sept 8 64
10376	Clark L	19 " D	Oct 5 64
10421	Clayton E B	1 " F	Oct 6 64
28	Cohan D	3 " K	Mch 7 64
6950	Conder W H	16 " G	Aug 26 64
8037	Conley W	5 " F	Sept 6 64
8943	Cook James	4 " D	July 25 64
8433	Condon D H	20 " K	Sept 11 64
425	Craw H	3 " B	April 7 64
12061	Cressy N F	11 " G	Nov 17 64
10936	Cromwell S R, Corp	Art 1 " M	Sept 14 64
11211	Cromwell W H	19 " D	Oct 20 64
8625	Curtiss John	16 " I	Sept 13 64
12367	Cutts O M	16 " D	Jany 1 65
80	Cutler A	20 " E	Mch 20 64
5171	Cross Noah	Art 1 " A	Aug 9 64
8581	Crosby W	4 " A	Sept 12 64
8445	Davis D	3 " C	Sept 11 64
227	Davis Wm L	20 " E	Mch 20 64
5615	Dougherty Thomas	8 " G	Aug 14 64
6612	Donnell F	8 " E	Aug 23 64
9624	Downes J	8 " G	Sept 23 64
1359	Doyle Wm	6 " D	May 25 64
5181	Drisdale F	1 " H	Aug 13 64
4435	Duffy A	3 " G	July 31 64
6115	Dugan D	32 " A	Aug 21 64
6128	Dunning S P	29 " G	Aug 21 64
7240	Dunnie G	5 " G	Aug 29 64
6357	Dye John	Cav 1 " E	Aug 21 64
8035	Dittener H	20 " A	Aug 8 64
10608	Eckhard H	7 " C	Sept 10 64
7212	Edwards N S	Cav 1 " F	Aug 29 64
8588	Ellis A	Art 2 " H	Sept 11 64
1877	Emmerson H H	3	June 12 46
2628	Farewell E	31 " E	June 28 64
8401	Ferrell P	6 " H	Sept 10 64
4765	Fish Wm	7 " A	Aug 5 64
5243	Flagg J B	5 " K	Aug 10 64
69	Flanders L G	20 Co E	Mch 19 64
1989	Foley John	19 " E	June 15 64
2362	Forrest Thomas	Cav 1 " E	June 23 64
2482	Foster A, Corp'l	6 " K	June 25 64
8145	Foster E R	16 " C	Sept 8 64
7073	Foster Samuel C	16 " K	Aug 23 64
6191	Frisble L	7 " C	Aug 19 64
10957	Fitzgerald Joseph	8 " E	Oct 14 64
5907	Gardner W H, Sergt	4	Aug 16 64
12515	Gibbs R	19 Co K	Jany 23 65
2906	Gilgan W	7 " C	July 5 64
6107	Goodward A	Art 1 " I	Aug 18 64
5580	Goodwin M T	8 " F	Aug 14 64
4141	Grant G	Art 1 " F	July 23 64
7391	Grant Frank	16 " F	Aug 30 64
8392	Griffith S	8 " G	Sept 10 64
9190	Gunney C	31 " A	Sept 18 64
10031	Gunney J F, Sergt	1 " I	Sept 29 64
11823	Gilgrist ——	31 " E	Nov 5 64
8306	Hammond J	19 " G	Sept 10 64
12343	Harris J S	1 " F	Dec 26 64
3506	Hassen H	7 " G	July 18 64
3274	Hatch J S	3 " G	July 13 64
6112	Hatch S, Sergt	8 " F	Aug 19 64
9311	Heath B	3 " F	Sept 20 64
4174	Heninger ——	19	July 28 64
12349	Hopes H	19 Co D	Dec 27 64
7474	Howard D H	17 " D	Sept 1 64
3844	Howe Samuel W	1 " K	July 23 64
7186	Hoyt A D	3 " K	Aug 29 64
3237	Hudson W	17 " E	July 12 64
8797	Hughes Wm	31 " K	Sept 15 64
9652	Humphrey ——	Cav 3 " L	Sept 24 64
3484	Hunkey E B	1 " L	July 17 64
4703	Henly D	8 " G	Aug 4 64
5355	Ingols L	16 " H	Aug 11 64
9379	Ingerson P	7 " I	Sept 29 64
11189	Jackson A J	17 " I	Oct 26 64
10619	Jackson R	7 " B	Oct 10 64
10710	Jackson R W	7 " D	Oct 11 64
12602	Jerdan J	19 " F	Feby 6 65
7385	Johnson B	7 " K	Aug 30 64
5845	Jones Wm	19 " E	Aug 16 64
10243	Jory G F	8 " F	Oct 3 64
11586	Kellar J	19 " J	Oct 28 64
8237	Kelley L	11 " D	Sept 9 64
3313	Kennedy W	17 " G	July 14 64
6169	Kilpatrick C	3 " C	Aug 19 64
5376	Ladd C	6 " I	Aug 11 64
8350	Lamber W	17 " K	Sept 10 64
11707	Levitt H	19 " A	Nov 1 64
7967	Lincoln A	16 " I	Sept 6 64
10981	Littlefield C	Cav 1 " F	Oct 14 64
6340	Lord Geo H	3 " B	Aug 21 64
5549	Ludovice F	13 " F	Aug 13 64
490	Lowell B	4 " G	April 12 64
9126	Macon L	8 " A	Sept 21 64
709	Malcolm H M	16 " A	April 21 64
6606	Marshall B F	1 " H	Aug 23 64

Maine—(*Continued.*)

12122	Maston A	19	Co D	Nov 22 64
10392	Mathews James	32	" F	Oct 14 64
12011	Maxwell J	8	" E	Nov 14 64
3679	McFarland G	3	" G	July 21 64
9538	McGinley J	7	" A	Sept 22 64
2200	McKinney G	3	" I	June 19 64
12084	McFarland E S	8	" I	Nov 18 64
4391	Metcalf Oliver	8	" H	July 31 64
12768	McFarland W, Corp'l	19	" K	Mch 13 64
5200	Melgar J	7		Aug 10 64
5614	Messer C R	7	Co F	Aug 14 64
9399	Miller C J	Cav 1	" B	Sept 21 64
2002	Miller J O	2	" D	June 15 64
7573	Mills M	1		Sept 2 64
2808	Moore Charles W	8	Co B	July [illegible] 64
11042	Moore G	18	" D	Oct 17 64
7273	Moore J D	Cav 1	" B	Aug 30 64
6940	Moore W C	7	" A	Aug 26 64
8118	Moyes F	32	" F	Sept 8 64
7046	Newton C	9	" K	Aug 27 64
1507	Nickerson D	4	" F	May 31 64
8020	Nolton H	7	" B	Sept 6 64
2131	O'Brien W	16	" A	June 18 64
6325	Opease S	19		Aug 21 64
143	Osborn A J	8		Mch 24 64
10866	Owens O H	10		Nov 6 64
3710	Parker A	Cav 1	Co E	July 21 64
7979	Parsons James W	16	" D	Sept 6 64
9362	Patrick F	14	" F	Sept 20 64
2272	Peabody F S, Sergt	5	" I	June 20 64
12543	Pequette P	4	" G	Jany 28 65
1486	Perkins D	Cav 1	" I	May 31 64
5197	Perkins T	1	" H	Aug 10 64
6911	Peters H	4	" E	Aug 23 64
12056	Phillbrook F	Art 1	" A	Nov 17 64
2064	Phelps W H	Cav 1	" H	June 16 64
3436	Pinkham U W	Art 1	" A	July 17 64
1361	Pottle A E	Cav 1		May 25 64
5398	Pratt A M	Cav 1	Co L	Aug 15 64
8441	Pulerman G	16	" D	Sept 11 64
12410	Prescott C	19	" H	Jany 7 65
7785	Richardson C	31	" L	Sept 4 64
6762	Richardson J K	8	" G	Aug 24 64
10465	Richardson W, Cor	Cav 1	" B	Oct 7 64
5532	Ricker Wm, Corpl	Cav 1	" D	Aug 13 64
8480	Ridlon N	7	" D	Sept 11 64
900	Riseck R	3	" I	May 5 64
3921	Roberts H	19	" K	July 25 64
5236	Rowe L	1	" A	Aug 10 64
166	Rosmer Frank	4	" C	Mch 26 64
5796	Ruet H	2	" H	Aug 15 64
8557	Russell G A	Cav 1	Co E	Sept 12 64
5150	Sampson E	1	" F	Aug 12 64
4532	Sawyer Enos	Art 1	" H	Aug 2 64
3132	Sawyer John	31	" K	July 11 64
11462	Shorey S	Cav 1	" K	Oct 20 64
2143	Simmons G F	6	" K	June 20 64
3159	Smith W	9	" K	July 11 64
3331	Smith W A	6	" F	July 14 64
1782	Snowdale F	4	" C	June 10 64
9974	Snower S C	19	" A	Sept 28 64
1978	Springer H W	36	" A	June 15 64
4596	Steward G	20	" H	Aug 3 64
11562	St Peter F	19	" F	Oct 27 64
7001	Swaney P	19	" F	Aug 27 64
199	Swan H B, Corp'l	3	" F	Mch 28 64
1936	Swan F	3	" F	June 14 64
8632	Thompson F	9	" E	Sept 13 64
10455	Thompson John	3	" E	Oct 7 64
621	Thorn E	9	" I	April 19 64
10928	Toothache J	7	" G	Oct 14 64
1106	Turner C C	4	" E	May 15 64
5090	Tufts J	32	" C	Aug 8 64
11875	Taylor G	9	" C	Nov 16 64
12322	Tattle D L	32	" F	Dec 20 64
12196	Tuttle L S, Corp'l	32	" F	Nov 30 64
12706	Thorndie W B, Corp'l	19	" I	Mch 2 65
6245	Valley F	32	" K	Aug 19 64
3335	Venill C	32	" G	July 15 64
7226	Walker A B, Corpl	1	" K	Aug 29 64
3894	Walker M C	5	" I	July 24 64
7722	Wall A	Cav 1	" K	Sept 4 64
5042	Walsh Thomas	20	" H	Aug 17 64
6750	Watson B	7	" K	Aug 24 64
10558	Webber Oliver	3	" A	Oct 9 64
4559	Whiteman A M, Corp'l	5	" I	Aug 2 64
1648	Whitcomb T O	4	" F	June 5 64
6251	Whittier J K P	32	" C	Aug 19 64
10415	Willard W	20	" B	Oct 7 64
7711	Williams C	6	" G	Sept 3 64
6900	Wilson George	32	" C	Aug 26 64
3639	Wilson G W	16	" H	July 20 64
3132	Willey D H	19	" E	July 10 64
3860	Winslow E I	4	" B	July 24 64
5512	Winslow N L	4	" K	Aug 13 64
6372	Wyman A	32	" C	Aug 21 64
2095	Wyman J	16	" A	June 17 64
12470	Wyer R	3	" K	Jany 16 65
12043	Wright C	1	" G	Nov 16 64
178	Young E W, Sergt	3	" H	Mch 26 64
6369	Young J	3	" H	Aug 21 64
8140	Young J, Corpl	8	" I	Sept 8 64

TOTAL 233.

MARYLAND.

850	Allen W H	1	Co H	May 3 64
1023	Anderson Wm	2	" C	May 11 64
1379	Aikens A	Cav 1	" I	May 26 64
1928	Adams Jas T	6	" H	May 14 64
10288	Abbott D E	2	Co D	Oct 4 64
2325	Archer H	1	" I	Dec 24 64
112	Babb Samuel	8	" I	Mch 23 64
238	Berlin Jas	Cav 2	" F	April 1 64

Maryland—(*Continued.*)

472	Beltz W W	2 Co	H	April 9 64
1036	Bowers A	1 "	I	May 14 64
1155	Brown Augustus	2 "	G	May 29 64
1437	Braddock Wm	2 "	D	May 30 64
1549	Buck H	Cav 1 "	B	June 2 64
1641	Buckley Geo	9 "	B	June 5 64
2404	Bennett C B	1 "	D	June 21 64
3263	Brant D B	2 "	H	July 13 64
4602	Betson James	Bat 1 "	A	Aug 3 64
5261	Ball J A	2 "	B	Aug 10 64
8525	Brown J C	Art 1 "	B	Aug 23 64
6540	Brown E R	2 "	C	Aug 13 64
7727	Brown E	2 "	D	Sept 3 64
8975	Buckley A M	1 "	B	Sept 17 64
1184	Beale R	Cav 1 "	D	Sept 19 64
11761	Buckner George	2 "	K	Nov 3 64
11620	Bell J R	8 "	D	Oct 28 64
12373	Bloom J, Corp'l	7 "	F	Jany 1 65
12679	Book C	8 "	G	Feby 19 65
54	Carpenter Wm	Cav 2 "	I	Mch 17 64
394	Cook Lewis	9 "	E	April 1 64
469	Coombs E A	9 "	I	April 9 64
524	Carter Wm	2 "	C	April 13 64
728	Cary W H	9 "	F	April 25 64
1357	Carl J M	6 "	E	May 25 64
1371	Cabbage C H	2 "	H	May 25 64
2012	Cullin John	2 "	D	June 15 64
4182	Crasby M	1 "	G	July 23 64
4610	Carter John	2 "	C	Aug 3 64
5036	Carr Wm	Cav 1 "	D	Aug 8 64
5063	Childs G A	9 "	I	Aug 8 64
5826	Crisle J	6 "	G	Aug 16 64
8008	Crouse W A, Cole's Cav	"	E	Sept 9 64
8035	Conway Wm E	4 "	E	Sept 6 64
8266	Crabb H	4 "	E	Sept 9 64
8357	Coon H S	1 "	E	Sept 10 64
8618	Crouse J A	Cav 1 "	A	Sept 13 64
10600	Collins D	1 "	C	Sept 10 64
12395	Callahan P	1 "	F	Jany 4 65
181	Duff Chas, Corpl	8 "	A	Mch 27 64
1410	Dunn John, Corpl	9 "	H	May 27 64
2296	Davis Thomas	9		June 24 64
3912	Drew C	35 Co	B	July 24 64
4138	Dennis Benj	2 "	A	July 28 64
4211	Davis G	Cav 1 "	F	July 29 64
6510	Dickwall Wm	2 "	F	Aug 22 64
8199	Deller F	1 "	E	Sept 8 64
6788	Dennissen T	42 "	I	Aug 25 64
8428	Ellis C	4 "	D	Sept 12 64
10410	Eli W	7 "	C	Oct 6 64
3849	Fecker L	2 "	I	July 24 64
1321	Fairbanks J E	9 "	C	May 23 64
2539	Francis J, Corpl	2 "	K	June 27 64
2600	Flage F J	2 "	H	June 23 64
2824	Farrass Jas	7 "	G	July 2 64
6016	Frantz F	2 "	H	Aug 17 64
7104	Fink L	2 "	H	Aug 31 64
9220	Frederick J E	9 "	I	Sept 19 64
12752	Freare W	8 "	A	Mch 10 65
1271	Gordon A B	9 Co	E	May 22 64
2138	Gerard Fred	Cav 1 "	B	June 18 64
3013	Green Thomas	2 "	D	July 7 64
3739	Gregg F	2 "	I	July 22 64
6072	Gilson J E, Sgt	Cav 1 "	C	Aug 18 64
6731	Ganon J W	2 "	K	Aug 24 64
12735	Goff John	1 "	I	Mch 6 65
1767	Houck J, Corpl	2 "	H	April 27 64
826	Hickley John	9 "	G	May 1 64
1625	Howell L H	Cav 1 "	M	June 4 64
1720	Hoop H	2 "	I	June 8 64
2357	Hickley J S	2 "	H	June 23 64
2404	Hidderick H	1 "	I	June 26 64
2078	Hite J E	2 "	I	July 7 64
3364	Hering P, Sergt	2 "	C	July 24 64
4767	Hank Thomas	Bat 1 "	D	Aug 5 64
5202	Hilligar ——	1 "	E	Aug 11 64
5108	Hood John	8 "	C	Aug 12 64
5917	Holmes L	2 "	H	Aug 17 64
6184	Hour S	8 "	E	Aug 22 64
6504	Harris J E	1 "	A	Aug 22 64
7434	Hazel J	9 "	C	Sept 1 64
8165	Himick F	Cav 1 "	E	Sept 8 64
8393	Hall J	7 "	D	Sept 10 64
9932	Holden J R	9 "	C	Sept 23 64
11109	Hakalon F	2 "	K	Oct 18 64
12422	Hoover J	Cav 2 "	C	Jany 9 65
2895	Isaac Henry	2 "	H	July 4 64
93	Jones David	Bat 1 "	A	Mch 22 64
669	Jenkins M	2 "	A	April 23 64
460	Keplinger J	2 "	H	April 9 64
544	Keefe Lewis	7 "	F	April 14 64
7243	Kirby J	9 "	F	Aug 29 64
1019	Laird Corbin	Cav 1 "	F	May 11 64
1036	Lees W H	2 "	C	May 13 64
3913	Louis J, Sergt	2 "	B	July 24 64
11385	Little D	Cav 2 "	K	Oct 24 64
12361	Lebud J	Cav 1 "	D	Dec 30 64
12367	Lambert W	1 "	I	Feby 17 65
206	McCarle James	Cav 1 "	B	Mch 28 64
471	Moland B	2 "	F	April 9 64
896	Myers Noah	9 "	G	May 5 64
1190	McGuigen S K	Bat 1 "	D	May 18 64
1307	Myers L S	1 "	B	May 23 64
1797	Moore Frank	9 "	A	June 10 64
1898	Moffitt Thomas	6		June 13 64
2079	Martz G H	2 Co	H	June 16 64
3429	Machler C S	Bat 1 "	A	July 17 64
3797	McKinsay Jno	2 "	I	July 22 64
4051	Miller F	6 "	C	July 27 64
4146	Mathews F	8 "	G	July 28 64
4831	Macomber John	Cav 1 "	B	Aug 6 64
5170	Marvin J	2 "	H	Aug 9 64
6757	Moon J J	1 "	D	Aug 25 64
7281	McCullough J	1 "	I	Aug 30 64
7327	McLamas J	7 "	C	Aug 30 64
8043	Markell S	2 "	H	Sept 6 64
10150	Munroe J, Corpl	4 "	H	Oct 1 64
10861	Markin W	1 "	F	Oct 13 64

Maryland—(*Continued.*)

11547	Mathews J	8			Oct 27 64
12608	McMiller J A	1	Co	E	Feby 7 65
91	Nice Jacob	Cav 5	"	M	Mch 21 64
371	Nace Harrison	9	"	H	April 5 64
9752	Norris N	1			Sept 25 64
153	Pool Hanson	2	Co	H	Mch 25 64
7590	Porter G	1	"	I	Sept 2 64
7981	Pindiville M	7	"	H	Sept 6 64
5069	Papple D, Corpl	2	"	H	Aug 8 64
252	Rusk John	9	"	E	Mch 30 64
918	Russell A P	2	"	C	May 6 64
1606	Rodk Simon	9	"	E	June 4 64
1901	Robinson J	9			June 13 64
2050	Rynedollar Wm	Cav 1	Co	D	June 23 64
6599	Reed Thos P	Art 1	"	B	Aug 23 64
155	Seberger F	9	"	F	Mch 25 64
817	Scarboro Rob't	9	"	I	April 2 64
478	Suffecol S	1	"	I	April 9 64
718	Sinder John	2	"	H	April 24 64
899	Snooks W	9	"	E	May 5 64
1205	Spence Levi	9	"	D	May 19 64
1272	Scarlett Jas	1	"	D	May 22 64
1926	Smith Ed, Sgt	9	"	I	June 14 64
2004	Stafford John	9	"	G	June 15 64
2361	Shipley W	9	"	G	June 23 64
2489	Schineder J	Bat 1	"	B	June 26 64
5797	Smith John	Cav 1	"	B	Aug 15 64
6751	Shelley B	2	"	F	Aug 24 64
6816	Shiver G H, Corpl	1	"	C	Aug 25 64
6919	Stull G E	Cav 1	"	D	Aug 26 64
7580	Shilling Wm	2	"	K	Sept 2 64
7833	Stolz ——	7	"	K	Sept 4 64
8296	Smitzer J	1	"	D	Sept 9 64
8716	Segar Chas	6	"	F	Sept 14 64
9309	Snyder F	2	Co	K	Sept 20 64
9451	Stratten J A	Art 1	"	C	Sept 21 64
10215	Shafer J N	Cav 1	"	A	Oct 22 64
11159	Samon L W	1	"	I	Oct 19 64
11160	Speaker H	1	"	F	Oct 19 64
12195	Spaulding J	4	"	C	Nov 29 64
12704	Smith G C	1	"	I	Feby 26 65
149	Tyson J T	9	"	D	Mch 25 64
1022	Tysen J T	9	"	I	May 11 64
677	Turner Wm F	Cav 1	"	D	April 22 64
1029	Turner A	Cav 1	"	B	May 11 64
1356	Tindle E, Corpl	9	"	G	May 25 64
1377	Turner C	9	"	E	May 26 64
7872	Thompson J	13	"	I	Sept 5 64
8689	Thompson John	2	"	S	Sept 14 64
9246	Tucker ——	2	"	D	Sept 19 64
9335	Tindell Wm	11	"	B	Sept 20 64
11450	Tilton J	Cav 1	"	F	Oct 25 64
1583	Ulrich Daniel	9	"	I	June 3 64
1305	Veach Jesse	2	"	H	May 25 64
8209	Viscounts A J	Art 1	"	E	Sept 9 64
78	Wise John	9	"	D	Mch 20 64
21	White Wm	9	"	C	Mch 7 64
553	Widdons D	1	"	E	April 14 64
537	Webster Samuel, Corp	9	"	G	April 17 64
1171	Wharton Samuel	2	"	F	May 17 64
2275	Worthen Wm	9	"	C	June 20 64
4748	West M	4	"	D	Aug 5 64
9409	Weaver George	1	"	B	Sept 2 64
11578	Witman D	13	"	D	Sept 23 64
12147	Wolfe H	1	"	B	Nov 24 64
455	Yieldhan R	9	"	C	April 9 64
1030	Zeck Wm J, Corpl	7	"	E	May 13 64
3223	Zimmerman C	9	"	E	July 12 64

TOTAL 194.

MASSACHUSETTS.

12286	Adams I B	16	Co	G	Oct 22 64
9561	Adams S B	18	"	G	Sept 23 64
6360	Akers H H	2	"	I	Aug 21 64
4290	Aldrich H	36	"	G	July 30 64
10973	Aldrich H W	27	"	I	Oct 15 64
5650	Alger W A, Corpl	15	"	D	Aug 14 64
8730	Allen Francis	Art 1	"	M	Sept 14 64
5334	Allen G H	2	"	E	Aug 11 64
9748	Allen John	19	"	B	Sept 25 64
2236	Ames H	35	"	A	June 25 64
8349	Ames M L	32	"	G	Sept 10 64
8373	Analstine ——	54			Sept 10 64
1084	Anchey J	61	Co	F	May 4 64
8583	Armington H	13	"	C	Sept 12 64
10693	Armstrong G	28	"	A	Oct 11 64
9781	Atmore C	Cav 2	"	A	Sept 25 64
4065	Avery John W	Art 1	"	G	July 27 64
5372	Avigron F	53	"	I	Aug 11 64
10767	Bacey Wm	27	"	H	Oct 12 64
7116	Baggard F	Art 1	"	B	Aug 28 64
8338	Baice G A	27	"	G	Sept 10 64
6324	Barley R	20	Co	A	Aug 23 64
6735	Baker E E	34	"	C	Aug 25 64
11475	Baldwin W	35	"	A	Oct 24 64
9078	Banner M	20	"	B	Sept 17 64
642	Barge Henry	20	"	E	April 20 64
6274	Barnes L A	19	"	F	Aug 27 64
1607	Barnes W L	Cav 2	"	M	June 7 64
7358	Barlen E F	18	"	E	Sept 5 64
3341	Barnsh John	17	"	H	July 23 64
6952	Barnett G H	25	"	G	Aug 26 64
8348	Bassett B C	Art 1	"	I	Sept 15 64
4055	Batten Geo C, Sgt	Art 2	"	G	July 31 64
8303	Baxten H	Art 2	"	G	Sept 12 64
2525	Bear G W	56	"	I	June 26 64
6386	Beannian Wm	Art 2	"	G	Aug 21 64
6499	Beary Henry	59	"	B	Aug 22 64
3801	Beels H	59	"	C	July 22 64
8110	Bell Wm	Cav 2	"	M	Sept [illegible] 64
8442	Bemis Albert	57	"	B	Sept 11 64
11955	Berry George	18	"	K	Nov 10 64
6403	Besson Wm	Cav 2	"	H	Aug 21 64

Massachusetts — (*Continued.*)

8657	Biglow G	34	Co E	Sept 13 64
5321	Biglow John	22	" F	Aug 11 64
2908	Black James	9	" E	July 5 64
109	Blanchard Oscar	Cav 2	" E	Mch 23 64
4067	Blanchard O S	52	" G	July 27 64
3337	Blair J W	27	" C	July 15 64
3973	Blair D	27	" B	July 25 64
10753	Blake Wm	19	" K	Oct 12 64
7166	Blodgett A Z	34	" A	Aug 29 64
137	Blood T B	18	" F	Mch 24 64
470	Bodge S D	18	" D	Aug 1 64
3030	Bosworth H	25	" B	July 8 64
7466	Bowler H A	Art 1	" C	Sept 10 64
12013	Boyd F	18	" A	Nov 10 64
1796	Boynton Henry	32	" A	June 10 64
1857	Bracketts L	23	" C	June 12 64
4059	Brackin Dennis	46		July 27 64
6512	Bradford J	Cav 2	Co F	Aug 22 64
3178	Brady F	27	" G	July 11 64
11903	Bradish F	19	" B	Nov 11 64
12030	Branagan C	Art 2	" H	Nov 15 64
4070	Brand S C	57	" K	Oct 12 64
2565	Briggs W	Art 2	" G	July 2 64
993	Briggs W W	36	" H	May 10 64
8799	Bromley A	1	" K	Sept 15 64
465	Broadley James	17	" A	April 9 64
3587	Bronagan M	17	" E	July 19 64
11932	Brotherton W H, Cor	29	" G	Aug 26 64
2341	Brown A	56	" D	June 29 64
6057	Brown D	13	" K	Aug 18 64
6177	Brown J	25	" A	Aug 19 64
9660	Brown J	11	" E	Sept 24 64
10819	Brown John, Corpl	57	" E	Oct 12 64
7440	Brown L	27	" I	Sept 1 64
8780	Brown Samuel	56	" E	Sept 14 64
5339	Brown Wm	Art 2	" H	Aug 11 64
6342	Brownell A G	58	" B	Aug 25 64
6903	Bryant W A	Art 2	" H	Aug 26 64
7738	Buchanan J	27	" A	Sept 4 64
5775	Buldas L	56	" I	Aug 9 64
10746	Bullen J W	60	" C	Oct 11 64
11517	Bubler J W	40	" C	Oct 26 64
1734	Bullock W D	24	" K	July 22 64
11154	Burns W H, Corpl	Art 2	" H	Oct 19 64
2307	Burt C E	Art 2	" K	July 5 64
7134	Burgan L	25	" G	Aug 28 64
3699	Burgess W F	16	" H	July 21 64
5540	Burnham J	12	" I	Aug 13 64
7777	Burton John	19	" E	Sept 4 64
2429	Butler A	72	" H	June 24 64
4956	Buxton Thomas	Art 1	" G	Aug 7 64
9868	Byerns I	Art 1	" I	Sept 27 64
7230	Callihan J	57	" B	Aug 29 64
8158	Callihan P	57	" A	July 11 64
12663	Campbell D A	15	" G	Feb 16 65
4031	Carr Wm, Corpl	Art 1	" H	July 27 64
456	Carroll J	Art 2	" D	Aug 1 64
4363	Carroll O J	Art 2	" G	July 31 64
4168	Casey M	23	" C	July 28 64

4569	Casey M	17	Co H	Aug 2 64
4226	Castle M	22	" H	July 29 64
6724	Caughlin B	56	" E	Aug 24 64
7070	Caswell James	18	" F	Aug 18 64
7313	Chase John	25	" F	Aug 30 64
8686	Chase M M	Art 2	" G	Sept 13 64
6230	Child A F	Cav 1	" E	Aug 20 64
3344	Chiselson P	Cav 1	" B	July 15 64
1684	Church W H	Cav 1	" E	June 6 64
2416	Churchill F J	39	" G	June 24 64
7674	Chute A M	23	" B	June 11 64
4516	Claflin F G	Art 1	" F	Aug 1 64
11178	Claug J H	Art 1	" E	Oct 19 64
3016	Clausky J, Corpl	17	" E	July 7 64
10099	Clark ——, Corpl	27	" A	Sept 30 64
3648	Clark E	27	" H	July 20 64
4295	Clark George	16	" I	July 30 64
6492	Clark S	27	" I	Aug 27 64
7928	Clemens J	19	" B	Sept 5 64
12825	Cloonan P	Art 1	" E	April 7 65
5315	Coffin A R	Cav 2	" M	Aug 11 64
11590	Cohash John	23	" I	Oct 28 64
8099	Cole W H	16	" K	Sept 7 64
8	Coleman Leonard	Cav 1	" A	Mch 5 64
10773	Coalman C S	37	" I	Oct 12 64
11853	Collins A J	Art 2	" D	Nov 6 64
6714	Collins C R	27	" D	Aug 21 64
5409	Colt J	20	" K	Aug 12 64
9081	Colyer B	Art 1	" G	Sept 18 64
6362	Coney C W	Art 1	" L	Aug 18 64
6591	Congden E	Cav 2	" G	Aug 23 64
9332	Connell J D	24	" E	Sept 19 64
1848	Conner D	17	" H	June 11 64
6673	Conner John	11	" F	Aug 24 64
11892	Conner P	Cav 2	" H	Nov 7 64
11575	Conner F	9	" C	Oct 28 64
4547	Conlin Tim	Art 1	" L	Aug 2 64
7593	Cook W H	37	" H	Sept 2 64
8841	Coombs George	Art 2		Sept 15 64
1088	Coones J M	Cav 1	Co E	May 14 64
11171	Copeland J	15	" D	Oct 19 64
7802	Corbet W M	Art 1	" M	Sept 4 64
4210	Cox D O	59	" F	July 29 64
687	Cox Joseph	7	" G	May 23 64
11030	Cox P, Sergt	Art 1	" G	Oct 16 64
4483	Crockett A W	17	" K	Aug 1 64
174	Crofts E P	17	" E	Mch 26 64
7619	Cromian John	Art 1	" E	Sept 2 64
9026	Crowninshield T	37	" I	Sept 17 64
6812	Crosby E	40	" A	Aug 25 64
15	Cross Ira M	16	" G	Mch 6 64
3592	Cross Geo W	Art 1	" L	July 19 64
5243	Crosser E P	9	" C	Aug 10 64
5150	Crossman E J	20	" L	Aug 9 64
1290	Cummings A B, Sgt	29	" C	May 22 64
3746	Culligan Joseph	Cav 2	" A	July 22 64
574	Cunell H G	39	" C	April 16 64
7873	Curren F	58	" I	Sept 5 64
1309	Cushing C E	12		June 13 64

Massachusetts — (*Continued.*)

10172	Cutler C F	Art 2	Co G	Oct 1 64
8579	Dalber S A	17	" B	July 19 64
787	Daly John	28	" F	April 28 64
9421	Davis C	27	" B	Sept 21 64
7180	Davis C A	58	" I	Aug 29 64
1518	Davis Thomas	Cav 1	" H	May 31 64
12037	Davidson W	27	" H	Nov 16 64
7239	Day D B	25		Aug 29 64
2390	Decker C	Art 1	Co E	June 24 64
11763	Delano E	19	" E	Nov 3 64
7848	Densmore Wm	9	" F	Sept 4 64
6883	Dewry L A	27	" C	Aug 26 64
4042	Dexter G	Cav 2	" M	July 27 64
7069	Dill Z	58	" A	Aug 28 64
10964	Dimmick George H	27	" I	Oct 15 64
8430	Dodge Thomas A	Cav 1	" A	Sept 11 64
3059	Downing G	Bat 14		July 9 64
5501	Dcggett L	22	Co L	Aug 13 64
9577	Dolan J	Cav 1	" D	Sept 23 64
8732	Dole Charles H,	10	" H	Sept 4 64
6676	Dones S M	58	" A	Aug 24 64
12004	Douglass B	10	" H	Sept 14 64
12829	Dow H A, Corpl	Art 1	" E	April 10 65
3 78	Dowlin J	27	" H	July 20 64
1677	Downey Joel	Art 2	" M	June 6 64
2676	Drake E C	57	" E	June 30 64
12773	Drake T	4	" D	Mch 14 65
7115	Dansfield John	19	" E	Aug 28 64
5856	Drawn George	32	" C	Aug 16 64
2717	Drickarm L	Cav 1	" K	July 1 64
8294	Dromantle W	25	" G	Sept 9 64
3570	Drum R	19	" G	July 19 64
9251	Duffey J	Art 2	" H	Sept 19 64
15 2	Duffey James	18	" A	May 31 64
4613	Dull W	Art 2	" H	Aug 31 64
11666	Dunmett S	4	" D	Oct 30 64
10660	Dunn J	Art 2	" G	Oct 11 64
11319	Dunn I	20	" H	Oct 22 64
4471	Dunn P	Art 2	" H	Aug 1 64
4964	Dyer G W	Art 2	" H	Aug 7 64
8212	Eaff N	56	" H	Sept 8 64
8616	Earl G W, Sergt	Art 1	" I	Sept 13 64
8157	Eastman D	35	" I	Sept 8 64
10000	Eaton F W	5	" D	Sept 29 64
7281	Edes W, Corpl	11	" F	Aug 20 64
11809	Edwards C	19	" A	Nov 4 64
63[illegible]4	Edwards C F	Art 2	" H	Aug 21 64
171	Eagan Charles	17	" K	Mch 26 64
10822	Eibers Henry	19		Oct 12 64
6994	Emerson G W	57	Co A	Aug 27 64
418	Emerson Wm	12	" D	April 7 64
5619	Emery J	Art 1	" F	Aug 14 64
5539	Emmerson F F	Art 1	" B	Aug 13 64
8300	Empay Robert	25	" E	July 14 64
10542	Emusin D G	21	" B	Oct 8 64
5236	Evans H	Cav 1	" K	Aug 10 64
2785	Evans J	17	" H	July 2 64
7889	Ester W A	Art 1	" A	Sept 5 64
4399	Evarts T P	Art 2	" G	July 31 64
8556	Farmer G S, Sgt	Art 1	Co H	Sept 12 64
11908	Farralle G	19	" K	Nov 7 64
9443	Farisdale H	Art 1	" G	Sept 21 64
8926	Fearing J I	Art 1	" F	July 25 64
4987	Feamley Wm	25	" E	Aug 7 64
6450	Fegan John	Art 2	" H	Aug 21 64
12812	Fellows H	15	" E	Mch 19 64
7803	Felyer Wm	20	" E	Sept 4 64
7611	Fenis J	Cav 1	" C	Sept 2 64
5795	Fields E	37	" F	Aug 15 64
11401	Finjay W	Cav 1	" K	Oct 24 64
6723	Finigan B	19		Aug 24 64
8974	Fisher C B	Art 2	Co G	July 25 64
441	Fisher John	Cav 2	" E	April 9 64
3451	Flanders Charles	Art 1	" E	July 17 64
286	Fleming M	17	" E	April 1 64
2476	Floyd George E	Art 2	" H	June 25 64
4187	Forbs H	Art 1	" B	July 28 64
70	Fosgate Henry S	17	" K	Mch 19 64
5649	Fowler Samuel	Art 1	" M	Aug 14 64
10601	Frahar P	Art 2	" D	Oct 10 64
11135	Fraser L	20	" C	Oct 18 64
3848	Fray Patrick	17	" C	July 24 64
4267	Frederick C	20	" A	July 29 64
8186	Frisby A	12	" G	Sept 8 64
9502	Frost B	16	" H	Sept 21 64
10205	Frost B	16	" H	Oct 2 64
7170	Fuller A	Cav 2	" G	Aug 29 64
12681	Fuller H	15	" E	Feby 20 65
5467	Fuller S	27	" D	Aug 13 64
7392	Fuller George A	Art 2	" G	Aug 31 64
7154	Funold C G	23	" G	Aug 29 64
9304	Gadkin G H	21	" H	Sept 22 64
4333	Gaffering John	11	" F	July 30 64
8927	Galligher F	18	" B	Sept 19 64
2787	Galse I E, Corpl	27	" B	July 2 64
7569	Gardner D	25	" E	Sept 2 64
126[illegible]0	Garland W	Art 1	" M	Feby 10 65
8882	Gannan E	Art 2		Sept 16 64
11470	Gay C	Cav 1	Co K	Oct 6 64
7910	Gay George C	Art 2	" G	Sept 5 64
8312	Gibson D E	33	" F	Sept 10 64
8364	Gibson H H	25	" B	Sept 10 64
4464	Gifford J	40	" A	Aug 1 64
4250	Gilbert S	Art 2	" H	July 29 64
159	Gilchrist J R, Corpl	17	" A	Mch 25 64
11157	Gilliland J	17	" H	Oct 19 64
7110	Gilsby P	36	" G	Aug 28 64
10918	Glancey P	59	" A	Oct 18 64
9471	Goanney G	Art 2	" G	Sept 21 64
2114	Godbold F A	29	" K	June 24 64
3585	Gooding N	54	" C	July 19 64
9202	Goodman J	25		Sept 18 64
5983	Goodman S	Art 2	Co B	Aug 17 64
9817	Goodridge G J	Art 1	" F	Sept 25 64
12844	Gonier D	4	" D	April 23 65
179	Gordon Charles	17	" C	Mch 26 64
3436	Gordon W L	Art 2	" H	July 17 64
10501	Goriche H	Art 2	" G	Oct 8 64

Massachusetts—(*Continued.*)

893	Gould Wm	17	Co G	May 5 64
8092	Gore J	Art 2	" G	Sept 7 64
8339	Gowen J	11	" C	Sept 10 64
7885	Grant Geo W	Art 1	" E	Sept 5 64
8277	Grant J	15	" E	Sept 9 64
10491	Grant Wm	15	" E	Oct 7 64
8898	Gray C	28	" D	Sept 16 64
2018	Green John	18	" A	June 15 64
9417	Gayson C W	25	" I	Sept 21 64
3166	Guild C	Art 2	" C	Aug 9 64
12568	Guilford J	Art 1	" I	Feb 1 65
10108	Gutherson G	Art 1	" B	Sept 30 64
3056	Haggert P, Corpl	Cav 2	" M	Sept 7 64
7408	Haley Wm	16	" F	Aug 31 64
151	Halstead J W, Cor	Cav 2	" M	Mch 25 64
11086	Hall G H	Art 1	" E	Oct 18 64
1742	Hamlin H P	Cav 2	" M	June 8 64
9342	Hammond Geo, Corpl	77	" G	Sept 19 64
7374	Handy George	Art 1	" K	Aug 31 64
10126	Handy Moses	59	" A	Oct 1 64
8273	Hane J H	Art 1	" I	Sept 9 64
8804	Hanks Nelson	98	" D	Sept 15 64
6582	Hanley M	Cav 1	" L	Aug 23 64
12276	Hare F	27	" H	Dec 13 64
8697	Harding C	58	" G	Sept 14 64
556	Harrison Henry	12	" I	April 14 64
7626	Hamesworth F	27	" A	Sept 2 64
3901	Harrington F	12	" H	July 24 64
7957	Hart W	15	" G	Sept 6 64
6923	Hartret M	34	" I	Aug 26 64
766	Harty John, Cop'l	Cav 2	" M	April 27 64
3505	Harvey S J	Art 2	" G	July 7 64
10024	Hash Wm	Art 1	" H	Sept 29 64
3242	Hav Wm	Art 2	" H	July 13 64
5789	Havmouth N	Cav 2	" M	Aug 15 64
4209	Haynes Charles E	Art 2	" H	July 29 64
9604	Hayes P	37	" A	Sept 23 64
3508	Heart John	28	" G	July 18 64
7416	Hebban Thomas	28	" B	Aug 31 64
3168	Henrie E W	17	" H	July 14 64
5606	Henry D	16	" H	Aug 14 64
4604	Henry J	Art 2	" K	Aug 3 64
1093	Hermans John	11	" G	May 24 64
7297	Hervey George W, Cpl	33	" I	Aug 30 64
6242	Higgin A	23	" B	Aug 20 64
4906	Hill F	9	" I	Aug 6 64
1740	Hills J B	Cav 2	" G	June 8 64
11762	Hillman G	16	" H	Nov 3 64
6056	Hines S	59	" C	Aug 10 64
9223	Hitchcock J C	27	" C	Sept 19 64
6907	Hogan Pat	Art 2	" G	Aug 26 64
6067	Hogan S	19	" E	Aug 18 64
9260	Hoit D	19	" B	Sept 19 64
4811	Hoitt J F	Art 2	" D	Aug 5 64
6228	Holbrook Charles	Art 2	" H	Aug 20 64
6826	Holden Pat	Art 2	" G	Aug 25 64
1986	Holland P	17	" I	June 15 64
905	Holland Pat	11	" C	May 5 64
4816	Holmes S	12	" I	Aug 5 64
8712	Holt E K	Art 1		Sept 14 64
6716	Holt T E	22	Co H	Aug 24 64
8575	Howard C	24	" C	Sept 12 64
10864	Howard James	59	" D	Oct 13 64
7025	Howe C H	36	" G	Aug 27 64
222	Howe E H	36	" H	May 29 64
3871	Howe John W	24	" B	July 24 64
5973	Hubbard E	34	" B	Aug 17 64
11045	Hubert G W	27	" I	Oct 17 64
11960	Hunt J	84	" D	Nov 11 64
4323	Hunting John W	25	" I	July 30 64
12299	Hartshaw L E	56	" A	Dec 16 64
6161	Hyde N L	Cav 2	" B	Aug 19 64
5470	Hyde Richard	39	" E	Aug 13 64
3487	Jackson N S	Art 1	" K	July 17 64
3501	Jackson N S	17	" K	July 17 64
8129	Jackson Wm R	Cav 2	" B	Sept 11 64
5733	Jaquirions C	57	" D	Aug 15 64
2308	Jaynes H	59	" G	June 22 64
10561	Jeff M	16	" I	Oct 9 64
5915	Jeffrey A	58	" B	Aug 17 64
9951	Jewett E	27	" I	Sept 28 64
12820	Jewett G	4	" A	April 11 65
5473	Johnson M	34	" G	Aug 13 64
5850	Johnson R A	19	" G	Aug 16 64
3684	Johnson Wm	Art 2	" H	July 21 64
10702	Jones J	59	" E	Oct 11 64
603	Jones John	Cav 2	" M	April 18 64
8875	Jones N P	32	" F	Sept 16 64
6054	Jones Thomas	11	" A	Aug 18 64
6183	Kavanaugh Jas	32	" K	Aug 19 64
8658	Kelly Charles	Art 3	" C	Sept 13 64
6579	Kelley Henry	20	" E	Aug 23 64
9983	Kelley M	Art 2	" H	Sept 17 64
6275	Kelsey E	27	" D	Aug 20 64
6712	Kempton E	Art 2	" G	Aug 24 64
5708	Kennedy Wm	59	" F	Aug 15 64
6529	Kenney J	Cav 3	" G	Aug 23 64
8252	Kent S	27	" H	Sept 9 64
12490	Kerr William, Sgt	56	" D	Jan 20 65
6036	Keyes J C	Art 2	" G	Aug 18 64
868	Kice Thomas	Cav 2	" B	May 3 64
296	Kilan M, Sgt	17	" I	April 1 64
4544	Kimball A	Art 1	" B	Aug 2 64
1754	Kinnely F, Sgt	17	" E	June 9 64
12813	Kluener F	27	" A	Mch 25 65
554	Knapp David	Cav 2	" M	April 14 64
3842	Knight——	25	" A	July 23 64
11119	Keephart M	Art 2	" E	Oct 18 64
5037	Kuppy H	Art 1	" K	Aug 8 64
8648	Krote Huer	20	" G	Sept 13 64
12549	Langley L F, Sgt	28	" B	Jan 23 65
6735	Lain S	12	" I	Aug 24 64
10885	Lane J H, Sgt	23		Oct 13 64
9738	Latham W	25	Co K	Sept 25 64
8835	Lathrop W O	58	" C	Sept 15 64
2175	Laurens John	23	" E	June 15 64
9621	Leach C W	20	" I	Sept 23 64
2781	Leary D	Cav 2	" A	July 2 64

Massachusetts — (*Continued.*)

7707	Leavey W H	12	Co A	Sept 3 64
7210	Lecraw W P	Art 1	" G	Aug 29 64
7548	Leonard W E	59	" H	Sept 2 64
7725	Leonard I G	Art 1	" K	Sept 3 64
7598	Lewin Charles	19	" I	Sept 3 64
2448	Lewis F	Art 2	" G	June 25 64
10068	Lewis G C	Art 2	" G	Sept 30 64
4082	Lewis L	Cav 5	" L	July 27 64
10750	Lewis L	Art 1	" A	Oct 12 64
5401	Lindsay J	18	" A	Aug 12 64
12413	Liswell L	27	" F	Jan 8 65
8748	Livingston R	39	" C	Sept 14 64
1156	Lochlen Joel	Cav 1	" E	May 16 64
480	Lohem E D	18	" H	April 9 64
3163	Lombard B K	58	" A	July 11 64
12256	Loring G	20	" A	Dec 10 64
10744	London Ed	22	" G	Oct 11 64
8437	Lovely Francis	25	" I	Sept 11 64
3217	Lovett A W	39	" E	July 12 64
3175	Lowell George	22	" E	July 11 64
9957	Lucier J	2	" G	Sept 28 64
4090	Lugby Z	Art 2	" G	July 27 64
8593	Lyons E	27	" I	Sept 12 64
3633	Lynch John	56	" K	July 21 64
7521	Macey Charles	18	" I	Sept 1 64
4264	Macomber J	20	" H	July 29 64
4034	Mahan E	56	" I	July 26 64
3383	Marintine G H	18	" I	July 16 64
9940	Mann N C, Saddler	16	" F	Sept 28 64
6220	Mansfield D R	58	" G	Aug 20 64
503	Marden G O	17	" I	April 12 64
1350	Mariland W H	17	" D	May 25 64
7147	Marchet C	28	" F	Aug 29 64
8450	Martin C M	Art 2	" H	Sept 11 64
6272	Maxwell M	Art 1	" I	Aug 20 64
5060	McAllister J, Corpl	17		Aug 8 64
7823	McCaffrey J	27	Co E	Sept 4 64
3835	McCloud J	56	" K	July 23 64
9342	McCord J G	32	" H	Sept 28 64
12176	McCorner J	19	" F	Nov 27 64
8905	McDarle J	Art 8	" M	Sept 15 64
6162	McDermott J	Art 2	" B	Aug 19 64
4409	McDevitt Wm	25	" E	July 31 64
9439	McDonald R	18	" D	Sept 21 64
430	McDonnell P	2	" B	April 8 64
7459	McDonough P, Corpl	25	" E	Sept 1 64
1984	McGiven J	22	" K	June 15 64
6375	McGovern B	34	" D	Aug 21 64
2632	McGowen John	Art 2	" H	June 29 64
5280	McGowen Wm	12	" A	Aug 11 64
4260	McGonegal R	16	" K	July 29 64
5124	McGuire A	58	" D	Aug 9 64
6460	McHenry James	Art 2	" G	Aug 21 64
6544	McIntire H	Art 1	" K	Aug 23 64
11531	McKarren E	Art 1	" I	Oct 26 64
11849	McKenny B	34	" A	Nov 5 64
6358	McKinzie George	27	" I	Aug 5 64
5223	McKnight B	Cav 3	" G	Aug 10 64
3174	McLaughlin E, Sergt	9	" C	July 11 64
10030	McMasters ——	57	Co A	Sept 29 64
2675	McMillan Jos	24	" B	July 20 64
522	McNamara	17	" I	April 13 64
5185	McNaury R	27	" I	Aug 9 64
11381	McNulty P	Art 2	" G	Oct 24 64
5194	McWilliams W	77	" D	Aug 10 64
7586	Medren W	20	" G	Sept 2 64
5808	Mehan B	Art 2	" H	Aug 16 64
1424	Milan A	18	" F	May 28 64
9735	Melvin S	Art 1	" K	Sept 25 64
2269	Merritt M	27	" C	June 20 64
1258	Merriman W H	17	" D	May 25 64
9117	Messers W	Art 1	" B	Sept 18 64
9597	Mesters E	34	" H	Sept 23 64
6286	Meyer ——	Cav 1	" K	Aug 20 64
8631	Miland John	Art 2	" H	Sept 13 64
11514	Millard P S	19	" G	Oct 26 64
1219	Miller A	23	" F	May 19 64
4329	Miller J M	11	" A	July 30 64
10169	Miller L	20		Oct 1 64
4050	Miller Joseph, Sergt	57	Co C	July 27 64
7178	Millrean M W, Cor	Cav 2	" E	Aug 29 64
9539	Milton C	21	" A	Sept 22 64
8506	Mitchell W C	23	" A	Sept 11 64
11867	Mitchell F	14	" A	Nov 6 64
11771	Mitchell John	19	" C	Nov 3 64
8243	Mittance L	20	" G	Sept 10 64
4053	Mixter G L	Cav 1	" E	July 27 64
6235	Monroe J	Art 2	" M	Aug 20 64
2455	Morgan C H	27	" H	June 25 64
8077	Morgan Pat	23	" B	Sept 7 64
3160	Moore A	56	" C	July 11 64
5490	Moore C A, Mus	Art 2	" N	Aug 13 64
10593	Moore M	57	" A	Oct 10 64
3411	Moore P	18	" F	July 16 64
3990	Morris N G	Art 1		July 26 64
1004	Morris R, Sergt	23	Co F	May 10 64
9627	Mortimer L	19	" E	Sept 24 64
8272	Morton G H	42	" C	Sept 9 64
5360	Morton J	34	" A	Aug 11 64
6982	Moss Charles	Art 2	" H	Aug 27 64
12516	Moulton H	15	" F	Jan 23 65
12619	Murdock A B, Corpl	27	" D	Feb 8 65
321	Murley D	9	" D	April 2 64
7862	Murphy C	17	" D	Sept 5 64
5488	Murphy F	17	" D	Aug 13 64
1630	Murphy Michael	12	" K	June 6 64
12783	Murphy P	27	" H	Mch 15 65
5041	Murray Thomas	19	" A	Aug 8 64
9241	Needham J A	Art 1	" B	Sept 19 64
9278	Nelson J	Art 2		Sept 19 64
7006	Newcomb John E	Art 2	Co G	Aug 27 64
9694	Nitchman A	19	" B	Sept 24 64
1282	Noble David	17	" D	May 22 64
12439	Norman E	Art 1	" E	Jan 12 65
350	Norton F F	39	" H	April 14 64
10058	Nottage I L	2	" F	Sept 30 64
7193	O'Brien James	Art 2	" G	Aug 29 64
2509	O'Brien John	36	" K	June 26 64

Massachusetts—(*Continued.*)

5117	O'Connell J	9 Co	C	Aug 9 64
12189	O'Connell J	15 "	H	Nov 28 64
9789	O'Connell M	2 "	H	Sept 26 64
11080	O'Conner Wm	29 "	K	Oct 17 64
11493	O'Donnell W	11 "	G	Oct 26 64
10592	Oliver J	39 "	E	Oct 10 64
4649	Oliver S E	27 "	B	Aug 3 64
7161	O'Neil Charles	25 "	B	Aug 29 64
4884	O'Neil D	25 "	E	Aug 6 64
4975	Osborn W	19 "	K	Aug 7 64
5340	Packard N M	27 "	C	Aug 11 64
6629	Page Wm	16 "	D	Aug 23 64
598	Paisley Wm	17 "	D	April 17 64
10695	Palmer T	59 "	E	Oct 11 64
4714	Panier J M	17 "	K	Aug 4 64
11059	Pantins A J	15 "	H	Oct 17 64
6899	Pandes L	Art 3 "	G	Aug 26 64
7811	Parrish Charles	Cav 1 "	C	Sept 4 64
5380	Pains F	Art 2 "	E	Aug 12 64
1074	Parker D H	36 "	C	May 13 64
2327	Parsons W D	23 "	E	June 22 64
6860	Pasco J M	58 "	D	Aug 26 64
1231	Patterson H W	33 "	G	May 20 64
8888	Payne G A	57 "	H	Sept 16 64
4[illegible]67	Payne Wm A	Art 1 "	M	Aug 7 64
7556	Peabody W F	37		Sept 2 64
6471	Peckham A P	15 Co	B	Aug 21 64
5441	Peeto A	36 "	A	Aug 12 64
4003	Pennington R A	Art 1		July 26 64
9603	Perry N	Art 1 Co	F	Sept 23 64
274	Perry Samuel K	39 "	D	Mch 31 64
4986	Pettie C	Art 2 "	H	Aug 7 64
7671	Phillbrook J E	56 "	F	Sept 3 64
7708	Phillips A	50 "	B	Sept 3 64
10383	Phillips L M, Sgt	17 "	D	Oct 5 64
69[illegible]6	Phipps H B, Corpl	Art 1 "	B	Aug 20 64
4763	Phipps M M	27 "	C	Aug 4 64
11079	Pierson R, Sergt	Art 2 "	H	Oct 17 64
20	Pilhuton John	11 "	E	April 14 64
5128	Piper Charles	28 "	G	Aug 9 64
6740	Piper F	25 "	E	Aug 24 64
7080	Polshon F B	17 "	D	Aug 28 64
703	Poole Charles, Corpl	"	G	April 23 64
6583	Pratt Daniel	27 "	I	Aug 27 64
12135	Pratt D W	Art 2 "	G	Nov 23 64
5742	Pratt Henry	23 "	C	Aug 15 64
2008	Price Edward	Art 2 "	M	June 15 64
12475	Prichard J, Corpl	2 "	G	Jany 18 65
5404	Prior Michael	56 "	I	Aug 12 64
11975	Puffer E D	34 "	A	Nov 1[illegible] 64
4218	Quinn James	15 "	M	July 29 64
12804	Quirk M J	1 "	D	Mch 20 65
12094	Ragan C, Corpl	27 "	H	Nov 19 64
10156	Ramstell H	37 "	H	Oct 1 64
5500	Rand M	Art 2 "	G	Aug 13 64
3358	Randall J	2 "	F	July 15 64
54	Raymond C	20 "	I	June 12 64
8072	Reed Charles	Art 2 "	H	Sept 7 64
1725	Rensseller C N	54 "	C	June 8 64
6122	Rapp James	28 Co	A	Aug 19 64
2970	Reynolds N A	26 "	C	July 7 64
3272	Rice C A J	Art 2 "	G	July 13 64
1235	Rich C	2 "	D	May 22 64
42[illegible]3	Rich Samuel	27 "	B	July 29 64
4918	Richards G	16 "	I	Aug 6 64
3156	Richards James	27 "	C	July 11 64
11553	Richardson L	Art 1 "	G	Oct 27 64
4167	Richardson S R	Art 1 "	M	July 28 64
7546	Richards Thomas	20 "	B	Sept 2 64
7199	Ridlaw James	19 "	C	Aug 29 64
10638	Riley H J	Art 2 "	G	Oct 10 64
8642	Riley M	56 "	K	Sept 13 64
7200	Ripley M A	32 "	F	Aug 29 64
6650	Rippon Wm	58 "	G	Aug 23 64
6166	Roach J	35 "	F	Aug 19 64
11552	Roberts J H	18 "	I	Oct 27 64
9448	Roberts Joseph	Cav 1 "	K	Sept 21 64
12505	Roberts L	13 "	F	Jan 22 65
11699	Robinson J	19 "	H	Oct 31 64
3833	Robinson R	27 "	F	July 23 64
5659	Roe Wm	Art 2 "	H	Aug 14 64
4875	Roferty John	2 "	K	Aug 6 64
12[illegible]93	Rome R	1 "	I	Jan 4 65
4219	Rover F	4 "	E	July 29 64
6654	Rope A R	11 "	I	Aug 23 64
5336	Rowe Asa	Art 1 "	K	Aug 11 64
11521	Rowley Charles	19 "	K	Oct 26 64
8455	Russell	27 "	C	July 17 64
9349	Rustar R	27 "	A	Sept 19 64
5987	Ruth F	36 "	C	Aug 17 64
6086	Ryes J C	Art 2 "	G	Aug 18 64
5276	Sabines Edward	19 "	K	Aug 11 64
9465	Samlett P V	1 "	A	Sept 21 64
8074	Sanborn G B	Cav 2 "	B	Sept 7 64
10256	Smith C	27 "	D	Oct 3 64
8002	Smith C A	Art 1 "	C	Sept 6 64
4[illegible]52	Smith D H	1 "	I	Aug 7 64
12499	Smith E	27 "	G	Jan 21 65
11804	Smith E M	1 "	D	Nov 4 64
7158	Smith H	57 "	D	Aug 29 64
7443	Smith J, Corp'l	20 "	E	Sept 1 64
967	Smith John	17 "	K	May 8 64
7538	Smith J P	Art 1 "	A	Sept 2 64
5780	Smith J H	19 "	G	Aug 15 64
8184	Smith W	23 "	B	Sept 8 64
154	Smith W H	12 "	I	Mch 25 64
2304	Smith Wm	54		June 22 64
12748	Smith V	57 Co	K	Mch 6 65
3745	Snow W	16 "	E	July 21 64
12063	Somers F	19 "	G	Nov 17 64
5316	Switzer L	16 "	E	Aug 11 64
8280	Southworth J	18 "	G	Sept 9 64
2469	Southworth John	18 "	E	June 25 64
2188	Spalding J	2 "	E	June 19 64
12160	Spar H	19 "	H	Nov 25 64
10342	Spellman B F	Art 2		Oct 4 64
6179	Spence David	19 Co	D	Aug 19 64
4153	Spooner C L	27 "	H	July 28 64

Massachusetts — (*Continued.*)

5600	Spooner E O	27 Co A	Aug 14 64
4632	Spooner F	18 " A	Aug 3 64
8397	Stalder E P	17 " H	July 16 64
9873	Stauf J	20 " D	Sept 27 64
6501	Steadson W	16 " G	Aug 22 64
5028	Stelle F	Art 1 " J	Aug 8 64
7991	Stevens H	28 " F	Sept 6 64
9183	Stevens N	1 " E	Sept 18 64
392	Sanborn T	17 " D	April 6 64
8281	Sanders F	Art 2 " G	Sept 9 64
10637	Sandwich J	1 " G	Oct 10 64
3405	Sanford J D	40 " A	July 16 64
10406	Savin J H	34 " C	Oct 6 64
11888	Sawer John	33 " F	Nov 7 64
4180	Sawyer S F	Art 1 " B	July 28 64
11203	Sayer G D	11 " I	Oct 20 64
5834	Schalster S	25 " G	Aug 16 64
5623	Seeley Charles H	Art 2 " G	Aug 14 64
11731	Sergeant J C	19 " E	Nov 2 64
11338	Shamrock I	19 " H	Oct 23 64
6782	Shaw Andrew	25 " K	Aug 25 64
12303	Shaw C L, Corp'l	15 " E	Dec 18 64
7827	Shea J	Art 2 " H	Sept 4 64
7481	Shehan James	Art 2 " G	Sept 1 64
2324	Sherman P H	37 " E	June 23 64
8822	Sherwood F	76 " B	Sept 15 64
4950	Shindler John	Art 1 " I	Aug 7 64
6602	Shore J J	1 " F	Aug 23 64
10946	Short J	2 " B	Oct 14 64
7735	Shultes A M	23 " B	Sept 3 64
10415	Shults George	28 " H	Oct 6 64
1458	Simmonds E	17 " D	May 29 64
6957	Simons A	Art 2 " M	Aug 26 64
4186	Simpson D O	34 " D	July 28 64
9842	Simpson W	Art 2 " H	Sept 27 64
6141	Sinclair A	1 " G	Aug 19 64
11189	Sloan S	20 " K	Oct 19 64
8375	Small Z	Art 1 " G	Sept 11 64
10404	Smalley J H	2 " G	Oct 6 64
9	Smith Warren	12 " F	Mch 5 64
2881	Stevens Thomas	2 " H	July 4 64
1758	Stewart J	11 " H	June 9 64
11291	Stewart E	52 " D	Oct 22 64
12420	Stone F P	27 " A	Jany 9 65
10181	Stone A	Art 2 " H	Oct 1 64
5957	Sullivan Jno	16 " A	Aug 17 64
7401	Sullivan Jno	2 " K	Aug 31 64
10890	Sullivan M	2 " D	Oct 4 64
8203	Sullivan P	9	Sept 8 64
10792	Sullivan P	15 Co I	Oct 12 64
11671	Sullivan F	59 " B	Oct 30 64
12788	Sylvester D	1 " B	Mch 17 65
8325	Sylvester E	Art 2 " H	Sept 10 64
12053	Sylvester J	4 " A	Nov 16 64
11957	Tabor B	35 " C	Nov 11 64
10697	Tabor F	16 " E	Oct 11 64
2067	Taggerd John	17 " E	June 19 64
8368	Taylor N	37 " D	July 15 64
2515	Taylor Thos	Cav 2 " G	June 26 64
8805	Temerts T J	110 Co D	Sept 15 64
4386	Tenney Wm	3 " G	July 31 64
3812	Thayer J	27 " A	July 23 64
8312	Thomas J	Art 2 " H	Sept 13 64
11123	Thomas J A	32 " G	Oct 18 64
2421	Thomas J W	56 " I	June 24 64
12527	Thompson C	Art 1 " B	Jany 26 65
1890	Thompson Geo	16	June 13 64
4536	Thompson Geo	58 Co F	Aug 2 64
3908	Thompson J M	27 " H	July 24 64
3596	Thompson W W	58 " G	July 19 64
4634	Tibbett A	23 " F	Aug 3 64
7468	Tiffany J	4 " F	Sept 1 64
6549	Tilden A	27 " B	Aug 23 64
3898	Tillson C E	29 " E	July 24 64
3549	Tooma Jno	28 " E	July 18 64
407	Torey L	12 " H	April 7 64
6019	Torrey C L	7 " G	Aug 17 64
10131	Townley J J	1 " F	Oct 1 64
9108	Travern W	Art 2 " G	Sept 18 64
7860	Travis H C	59 " C	Sept 5 64
7993	Trescutt W M	15 " I	Sept 6 64
8132	Turner H	34 " F	Sept 8 64
12161	Tuith F	20 " F	Nov 25 64
5428	Twichell J	17 " K	Aug 12 64
6332	Twichell ——	36 " C	Aug 21 64
9517	Usher Samuel	17 " I	Sept 22 64
8466	Wade A D L	Art 2 " G	Sept 11 64
5959	Waldon Wm	36 " B	Aug 17 64
12444	Walker A	19 " F	Jan 12 65
8377	Wallace P	57 " B	July 16 64
11494	Walsh M	4 " C	Oct 26 64
5191	Walton E A	57 " H	Aug 19 64
8724	Walton Nat	59 " E	Sept 14 64
8304	Wanderfelt ——	6 " C	Sept 10 64
1733	Wardin H	17 " I	June 8 64
5217	Ware Sam	1 " H	Aug 10 64
8864	Warffender J W	27 " C	Sept 15 64
12131	Warner A F	19 " D	Nov 22 64
6454	Washburne W E	27 " I	Aug 21 64
4721	Weiden H	17 " H	Aug 4 64
1066	Welsh Frank	17 " B	May 13 64
6224	Weldon Charles	Art 1 " D	Aug 20 64
11796	Wells S	1 " A	Nov 14 64
5214	Wellington G W	2 " G	Aug 10 64
3547	Welworth C W	18 " D	July 18 64
3247	Werdler W	58 " G	July 13 64
1334	West E	24 " A	May 24 64
7002	West J G	Art 1 " E	Aug 27 64
4577	White F	15 " K	Aug 2 64
6307	White Joseph	Art 2 " G	Aug 25 64
7138	White Joseph	2 " G	Aug 29 64
7902	Whiting A	27 " H	Sept 5 64
6867	Whitney F P	1 " G	Aug 26 64
635	Whittaker S	17 " D	April 20 64
1115	Wiggard Geo	22 " A	May 15 64
6715	Wilber E	27 " G	Aug 24 64
4339	Wilcox A	Art 14 " C	Aug 2 64
5519	Wilder L E	2 " G	Aug 15 64

Massachusetts—(*Continued.*,

7318	Wilkins S O	1	Co G	Aug 30 64
661	Williams Chas	27	" G	Aug 21 64
668	Williams J	58	" G	Sept 13 64
469	Willis C	17	" K	July 17 64
7549	Wilson J	Art 2	" H	Sept 2 64
769	Wilson Robert	34	" A	Aug 25 64
6742	Wilson S	Art 2	" G	Aug 24 64
10545	Wilson W	18	" B	Oct 9 64
13	Witherill O	47	" C	Aug 20 64
6483	Woodbury B	17	Co A	Aug 21 64
6561	Woodward W A	27	" B	Aug 23 64
6368	Wright C E	27	" B	Aug 21 64
6288	Wright M E .	27	" C	Aug 20 64
4923	Wyman H C	Art 2	" H	Aug 6 64
3562	Wright W M	Art 3	" G	July 18 64
7152	Young N C	1	" I	Aug 29 64
8882	Young E	2		Sept 16 64
6922	Young G W	Art 2	Co H	Aug 26 64

TOTAL 768.

MICHIGAN.

2198	Ayres J B	22	Co C	June 17 64
2247	Acker J	22	" K	June 20 64
2161	Atkinson P	22	" C	June 22 64
2516	Anderson George	23	" E	June 27 64
3257	Abbott C M	5	" E	July 13 64
4947	Ammerman H H	23	" A	Aug 7 64
5472	Aulger George	10	" F	Aug 13 64
5601	Ackler W	Cav 3	" C	Aug 14 64
6119	Austin D	8	" C	Aug 19 64
6713	Allen A A	14	" I	Aug 24 64
9156	Anderson F	Cav 1	" G	Sept 18 64
12250	Arsnoe W	7	" E	Dec 27 64
12571	Allen J	9	" H	Feby 2 65
12606	Adams A	4	" B	Feby 7 65
121	Brockway O	11	" K	Mch 23 64
1154	Banghart J	Cav 9	" G	May 16 64
1288	Broman C	4	" H	May 22 64
1511	Beckwith E	Cav 6	" I	May 31 64
1513	Bishop C	27	" F	May 31 64
1664	Beard J	6	" E	June 6 64
2004	Bostwick R S	2	" F	June 15 64
2025	Bowerman R	22	" H	June 17 64
2201	Bryant George	Cav 6	" H	June 17 64
2271	Bush Thomas	8	" A	June 20 64
2303	Brigham David	22	" D	June 22 64
2381	Bowlin J	27	" E	June 23 64
2478	Briggs I	6	" E	June 25 64
2595	Berry Henry	15	" E	June 28 64
2700	Broo F	A	" I	June 30 64
2946	Bailey John	Cav 4	" M	July 6 64
3149	Briggs W H	20	" G	July 11 64
3215	Bibl y J	3	" C	July 12 64
3479	Brannock F	3	" C	July 17 64
3517	Brush J	16	" K	July 18 64
3531	Bradley Geo	17	" B	July 18 64
3591	Bulit F	Art 3	" A	July 19 64
3777	Bohnmiller J	Cav 10	" H	July 22 64
3798	Beardslee M A	22	" D	July 22 64
4109	Billiams Jno	2	" K	July 27 64
4339	Binder Jno	2	" A	Aug 30 64
4395	Brown G	Cav 4	" E	July 31 64
4810	Baker A	Cav 5	" F	Aug 5 64
5573	Betts P	1	" C	Aug 14 64
8333	Brookiniger F	7	" D	Sept 10 64
5950	Bertan I	Cav 8	" B	Aug 16 64
5970	Burnett J	7	" G	Aug 17 64
6013	Burkhart C	22	Co G	Aug 17 64
6065	Brower L F	17	" H	Aug 18 64
6290	Bilby Geo	9	" E	Aug 20 64
6388	Burcham J	5	" B	Aug 21 64
6990	Burdick Theo	Cav 6	" I	Aug 27 64
7148	Beirs S	18	" B	Aug 29 64
7227	Billingsby J	Bat 1		Aug 29 64
7536	Bradley B	Cav 9	Co E	Sept 1 64
7796	Blair Jno	7	" E	Sept 4 64
7932	Barr W	Cav 8	" L	Sept 5 64
8391	Brown H S	Cav 8	" F	Sept 10 64
8505	Bradley E	11	" K	Sept 12 64
8814	Blanchard Jas	7	" G	Sept 15 64
8869	Brown A	3	" G	Sept 15 64
9226	Beckley W	Cav 1	" E	Sept 19 64
9240	Brown H	13	" A	Sept 19 64
9305	Beebe Jno	1	" A	Sept 20 64
9430	Baker Jno	Cav 1	" H	Sept 21 64
9545	Birdsey J	7	" D	Sept 23 64
9553	Barber J M	26	" C	Sept 23 64
9637	Baxter S	Cav 6	" L	Sept 24 64
9330	Batt W H	Cav 6	" L	Sept 27 64
9834	Bunker R B	1	" D	Sept 27 64
9853	Barnard G	Cav 7	" M	Sept 27 64
9856	Beekley L	10	" F	Sept 27 64
10044	Barney H	17	" D	Sept 29 64
10240	Blackburn Jas	5	" G	Oct 4 64
10490	Bentley H	24	" I	Oct 7 64
10835	Bittman J	Cav 1	" C	Oct 13 64
11275	Baldwin L A	24	" B	Oct 22 64
12130	Beck G	Cav 1	" H	Nov 23 64
12162	Bennett W L	26	" G	Nov 26 64
12187	Barnett I	2	" E	Nov 28 64
12745	Bearves M	15	" G	Mch 7 65
34	Colan Fred	17	" F	Feby 9 64
210	Chilcote Jas C	20	" G	Feby 28 64
398	Chambers J R	Cav 5	" K	April 5 64
439	Cowill Ed	Cav 8	" G	April 8 64
593	Cowell John	Cav 10	" H	April 15 64
1037	Conrad Edson	Cav 8	" G	May 12 64
1077	Cripper G F	Cav 5	" C	May 14 64
1164	Coastner J D	Cav 5	" L	May 16 64
1330	Chapman H	Cav 5	" E	May 24 64
1371	Cameron Jas	27	" H	May 25 64
1305	Constank John	9	" B	May 31 64
1392	Cronkwhite John	22	" K	June 7 64

Michigan—(*Continued.*)

1711	Cook J	Cav 4	Co D	June 7 64
1811	Churchward A R	9	" C	June 10 64
1943	Clear James	22	" F	June 14 64
2317	Cussick B	7	" C	June 28 64
3071	Collins James	5	" I	July 9 64
3462	Cartney A	Cav 2	" E	July 17 64
3595	Cameron D	Cav 1	" L	July 19 64
3800	Cummings W	2	" F	July 22 64
3989	Clements Wm	S S 1	" C	July 26 64
4002	Cook J	10	" F	July 23 64
4620	Cronk Jas	Cav 5	" G	Aug 3 64
4920	Cooper J	7	" K	Aug 6 64
4956	Curtis M D	8	" C	Aug 7 64
5201	Crunch J	Cav 1		Aug 10 64
5685	Cummings D	Cav 5	Co I	Aug 15 64
5686	Churchill G W	3	" A	Aug 15 64
5905	Carr C B	25	" K	Aug 16 64
6263	Coft Jas	20	" F	Aug 20 64
6285	Cobb G	4	" D	Aug 20 64
6446	Cook Geo	Cav 10	" H	Aug 22 64
6904	Cahon W J	1	" H	Aug 26 64
7004	Carp J S	1	" K	Aug 23 64
7164	Caten M	Cav 7	" E	Aug 29 64
7496	Cling Jacob	2	" K	Sept 1 64
7534	Campbell S B	2	" H	Sept 1 64
7383	Coldwell W	124	" H	Sept 5 64
8406	Cope J B	17	" A	Sept 11 64
8993	Cornice J D	7	" F	Sept 17 64
9341	Carver J H	Cav 4		Sept 20 64
10644	Cooley G	3	Co A	Oct 9 64
10759	Clago S	7	" C	Oct 12 64
10788	Crain R O	17	" A	Oct 12 64
10871	Cooley Henry	34	" G	Oct 13 64
11743	Collins C	2	" K	Nov 2 64
11903	Clark G W	Art 1	" C	Nov 7 64
12143	Cameron F	17	" E	Nov 24 64
12258	Cook N	1	" K	Dec 10 64
12391	Case S	Cav 5	" L	Jan 4 65
12474	Coras E	Cav 6	" C	Jan 17 65
12634	Chambers W	Cav 8	" G	Feb 10 65
1345	Davis Wilson	8	" A	May 21 64
43	Diets Jno	Cav 6	" I	Feb 14 64
195	Dunay Jno	6	" C	Feb 27 64
315	Deas Abe	Cav 7	" L	April 2 64
716	Decker L	10	" H	April 24 64
1270	Drummond Jno	27	" E	May 21 64
1292	Dolf Sylvanus	27	" G	May 23 64
1296	Denter W A	5	" E	May 23 64
1683	Dougherty D	8	" C	June 6 64
2090	Demerie D	Bat 1		June 17 64
2218	Dillingham W O	20	Co I	June 20 64
2683	Dennison H	Cav 5	" G	June 30 64
2882	Dreal D	Cav 2	" B	July 4 64
3237	Dusalt A	17	" H	July 12 64
3314	Dyre Wm	17	" B	July 14 64
3610	Davy R	22	" C	July 19 64
3619	De Realt F	5	" C	July 20 64
4660	Decker G S	Cav 5	" K	Aug 3 64
4669	Darct S	5	" I	Aug 4 64
4670	Dugan D	21	Co I	Aug 4 64
5070	Dawson D	17	" H	Aug 8 64
5351	Dalzell Wm	6	" A	Aug 10 64
5666	Dolph S	8	" B	Aug 14 64
6235	Duinz G W	Cav 5	" I	Aug 20 64
6401	Denton G	5	" E	Aug 21 64
7654	Derffy Wm	1	" H	Sept 3 64
7709	Dumont W	83	" H	Sept 4 64
8351	Daly A	Cav 7	" E	Sept 13 64
9995	Dyer J	5	" I	Sept 29 64
10161	Doass M	Cav 1	" L	Oct 1 64
10922	Dixon Jno	Cav 5	" L	Oct 14 64
11125	Dennis C	1	" H	Oct 18 64
12224	Dunroe P	24	" H	Oct 22 64
12574	Drake O	22	" D	Feby 2 65
2350	Egsillim P H	22	" K	July 4 64
5318	Eggleston Wm	Cav 7	" E	Aug 10 64
3981	Elliot J	24	" G	July 26 64
1210	Eaton R	22	" H	May 19 64
1240	Ellis E	Cav 2	" B	May 20 64
2788	Ensign J	11	" A	July 2 64
7901	Edwards S	6	" E	Sept 5 64
8255	Edmonds B	1	" H	Sept 9 64
11065	English James	17	" B	Oct 17 64
5817	Everett J	77	" K	Aug 13 64
890	Force F	27	" D	May 3 64
1064	Fitzpatrick M	Cav 1	" B	May 13 64
1337	Folk C	14	" E	May 25 64
2197	Fitse T	Cav 1	" C	June 19 64
2272	Fairbanks J	Cav 15	" G	June 20 64
2343	Face W H	6		June 23 64
4194	Fisher F	22	Co G	June 29 64
5081	Farmer M	22	" D	Aug 8 64
5831	Flanigan John	5	" D	Aug 16 64
6135	Farnham A	5	" A	Aug 19 64
6353	Fox James	3	" H	Aug 21 64
6680	Fritchie M	22	" G	Aug 24 64
6983	Fitzpatrick M	8	" E	Aug 27 64
7027	Fox Charles	1	" B	Aug 27 64
7060	Forsythe H	5	" F	Aug 28 64
7171	Forbs C	Cav 1	" B	Aug 27 64
8785	Fethton F	Cav 1	" G	Sept 12 64
10275	Fliflin H	27	" F	Oct 3 64
11500	Freeman B	S S 1		Oct 26 64
11709	Fredenburg F	7		Nov 1 64
12638	Findlater H	Cav 7	Co C	Feb 22 65
12845	Frederick G	9	" G	April 23 65
8270	Face C	S S 1	" B	Sept 9 64
11509	Fox W	22	" E	Oct 26 64
145	Goodenough G M	23	" K	Mar 25 64
566	Grover Jas	20	" H	April 15 64
784	Grippman J	Cav 5	" M	April 28 64
956	Graham Geo W	5	" C	May 8, 64
1049	Goodbold Wm	Cav 2	" L	May 12 64
1131	German E	13	" H	May 16 64
1234	Garrett S H	Cav 2	" G	May 20 64
1927	Grimley Jas	22	" D	June 14 64
2192	Ganigan J	Cav 9	" L	June 19 64
2614	Gorden Jas	1	" D	June 28 64

Michigan—(*Continued.*)

2862	Gilbert F	3	Co K	July 3 64
2923	Gibbons M	6	" C	July 5 64
3863	Goodman W	5	" I	July 24 64
4092	Griffin G	11	" H	July 27 64
4225	Green E	11	" H	July 29 64
5716	Galvin M	23	" I	Aug 15 64
6482	Greek C H	Cav 1	" K	Aug 22 64
6866	Gillis Jno	Cav 4	" F	Aug 26 64
7476	Gaines A	22	" F	Sept 1 64
7518	Guilz H	1	" A	Sept 1 64
7624	Griens G D	8	" I	Sept 2 64
7659	Graff Jacob	17	" H	Sept 3 64
7741	Gibson J	1	" K	Sept 3 64
7968	Grant A H	7	" D	Sept 6 64
8623	Gray Geo	Cav 1	" E	Sept 13 64
10671	Gallitt L	22	" F	Oct 9 64
10726	Gibbs J	7	" B	Oct 11 64
11207	Gask I	Cav 8	" C	Oct 20 64
11302	Gray James	Cav 6	" A	Oct 22 64
11352	Groucher J	Cav 6	" B	Oct 23 64
11647	Grabaugh J	5	" G	Oct 30 64
12164	Gifford L	61		Nov 26 64
12443	Gowell N	19	Co F	Jan 12 65
12573	Goodel M	5	" C	Feb 2 65
5818	Gurmane B S	77	" K	Aug 16 67
4511	Grasman E	23	" I	Aug 1 64
12207	Gabulison J	Cav 5	" F	Dec 1 64
6	Hall William	Cav 2	" M	Feb 5 64
339	Holton S M	1	" B	April 20 64
367	Henry Jas	8	" A	April 5 64
409	Hartsell Geo	Cav 7	" B	April 6 64
818	Hutton S	Cav 9	" G	April 30 64
860	Hood Jas D	22	" H	May 3 64
917	Hart J R	6	" E	May 7 64
1452	Hannah Jno	22	" C	May 29 64
1519	Hunter F A	22	" F	May 31 64
1656	Herriman D	22	" D	June 6 64
1788	Huntley W	Cav 5	" E	June 8 64
1813	Haines R	Cav 9	" G	June 10 64
1904	Hough M	22		June 13 64
1910	Harty J S	16	Co F	June 13 64
2660	Hayes C	6	" H	June 29 64
3015	Hardy Jno	4	" H	July 7 64
3040	Hughey Jas	17	" B	July 8 64
3206	Hopkins N	Cav 6	" E	July 12 64
4	Halson David	Cav 8	" A	Mch 27 64
3343	Heil H	9	" G	July 15 64
3483	Honsigner W L	7	" C	July 17 64
3889	Hance C, Bugler	7	" D	July 24 64
3927	Hawkins George	12	" H	July 25 64
4166	Hunter M W	22	" D	July 28 64
4286	Heron Jno	5	" F	July 30 64
4426	Heath M	21	" C	July 31 64
4674	Hale S B	Cav 7	" D	Aug 4 64
5332	Hollen Geo	Cav 1	" L	Aug 11 64
5370	Haynes P	Cav 1	" H	Aug 11 64
5376	Husted J	10	" C	Aug 10 64
5556	Henrich J	3	" C	Aug 13 64
5931	Hall W	26	" I	Aug 17 64
6110	Holmes J F	42	Co H	Aug 18 64
6276	Hibler A	Cav 9	" D	Aug 20 64
6992	Henny A	27	" B	Aug 27 64
6998	Hungerford C	20	" E	Aug 27 64
6999	Hunt L	2	" C	Aug 27 64
8100	Holcomb J	Cav 6	" K	Sept 7 64
8624	Harrington G	Cav 6	" D	Sept 13 64
9233	Hawley C	4	" F	Sept 19 64
9386	Hartman H	29	" A	Sept 24 64
9968	Hinkley G C	20	" F	Sept 28 64
10348	Hoag J M	20	" H	Oct 5 64
11027	Hankins E	5	" E	Oct 16 64
11057	Hayes Jas I		" E	Oct 17 64
11070	Haywood J B	Cav 1	" H	Oct 17 64
11260	Hamlin J H	S S 1	" K	Oct 20 64
11336	Hoag J M	20	" H	Oct 23 64
11412	Hill W	S S 1		Oct 24 64
11480	Howard F S	8	Co E	Oct 26 64
11593	Hawk H L	24	" I	Oct 28 64
11757	Hodges M	22	" I	Nov 3 64
11835	Hilmer C	Cav 6	" M	Nov 5 64
12067	Howe J	Cav 7	" F	Nov 17 64
12612	Hicks C	8	" B	Feby 8 65
9718	Harper D	3	" E	Sept 25 64
5141	Ingraham W L	Cav 5	" B	Aug 9 64
1317	Jackson James	7	" I	June 7 64
2776	Jones A	6	" E	June 27 64
3564	Jagnet E B	Cav 7	" C	July 19 64
3621	Jackson Geo G	22	" F	July 20 64
4736	Johnson J H	7	" G	Aug 4 64
6578	Johnson J	24	" I	Aug 23 64
7520	Jump D O	1	" A	Sept 1 64
7753	Johnson H	Cav 9	" L	Sept 2 64
9746	Jackland C	Cav 8	" E	Sept 25 64
12010	Jamieson H	Cav 5	" H	Nov 14 64
12396	Jondro M	1	" K	Jany 5 65
12463	Johnson A	5	" C	Jany 16 65
368	King Leander	8	" G	April 5 64
488	Keintzler R	Cav 5	" F	April 12 64
706	Karl Wm	2	" A	April 21 64
4140	Klunder Charles	Cav 5	" F	July 28 64
4397	Kennedy H	27	" H	July 31 64
4424	Kinney John	17	" H	July 31 64
4728	Kendall W	6	" D	Aug 4 64
8389	Kessler J	11	" G	Sept 9 64
10789	Kinsell George	Cav 5	" B	Oct 12 64
10903	Kenkham H C	Cav 5	" E	Oct 14 64
12431	Kenney C	Cav 5	" H	Jany 11 65
1882	Lewis F L	Cav 9		June 12 64
223	Lossing John	Cav 8	Co B	Mch 29 64
960	Loring Jno	27	" E	May 8 64
1187	Lewis P	5	" D	May 18 64
1331	Lancreed M	14	" B	May 23 64
37	Lumer Jno	17	" F	Mch 28 64
3303	Lanning H B	22	" H	July 14 64
3700	Lyon A D	Cav 5	" G	July 21 64
4243	Lonsey L	Cav 1	" L	July 29 64
4913	Luce F	Art 1	" A	Aug 6 64
4992	Lu Duc Jas	17	" G	Aug 7 64

Michigan—(*Continued.*)

5142	Larke J A	23	Co F	Aug 9 64
5216	Lowell Jas	Cav 7	" E	Aug 10 64
5776	Laribee L	8	" H	Aug 15 64
5923	Lofler E E	17	" H	Aug 17 64
6667	Lord M	8	" M	Aug 24 64
8085	Leamon G	Cav 8	" H	Sept 7 64
9685	Lard H O	22	" D	Sept 24 64
9760	Lund Jas	Cav 6	" H	Sept 25 64
10877	Laidham G	1	" D	Oct 13 64
11969	Lutz Wm	Cav 6	" F	Nov 11 64
218	McCartney H	Cav 6	" K	Mch 29 64
268	McGuire Jno	20	" A	Mch 31 64
542	Markham D	Cav 5	" B	April 14 64
612	McCarter Jas	22	" H	April 18 64
1059	Mum A F	27	" F	May 13 64
1062	Miller Chas	Cav 5	" D	May 13 64
1710	Miller J	3	" C	June 7 64
2255	Maby Ed	Cav 8	" K	June 20 74
2586	McDowell J	Cav 8	" F	June 28 64
2739	McSpoulding W	22	" E	July 2 64
2828	Manwaring Wm	22	" D	July 3 64
2976	Man Thos G	5	" A	July 7 64
3090	Marshall H E	27	" B	July 9 64
3150	Morris A T	14	" K	July 9 64
3537	Marvey Andrew	17	" G	July 18 64
3697	Miller W E	2	" K	July 21 64
3936	McCabe F	22	" H	July 25 64
3954	Morgan M	2	" E	July 26 64
4078	McFall H	17	" E	July 27 64
4144	Miller G	5	" I	July 28 64
4304	Monny Jno	Cav 5	" L	July 30 64
4783	Monroe D	Cav 6	" A	Aug 4 64
4942	Morgan E C	23	" G	Aug 7 64
5153	Miller L	7	" F	Aug 9 64
5630	Monch C	20	" I	Aug 14 64
6249	McCarty Chas	26	" I	Aug 20 64
6229	Meyers J	6	" H	Aug 21 64
6830	Myer J	4	" I	Aug 25 64
7114	Moore J	27	" B	Aug 28 64
7269	Merrill S B	5	" G	Aug 30 64
7279	McLaine Thos	1	" I	Aug 30 64
7473	McCloud A	21	" I	Sept 1 64
7513	Mason F	Cav 7	" L	Sept 1 64
7918	Martin Peter	17	" H	Sept 5 64
7936	Musket J	Cav 4	" K	Sept 5 64
7962	Miller F	22	" G	Sept 6 64
8025	Munday E	17	" G	Sept 6 64
8387	McClure R	7	" D	Sept 9 64
8518	Miles C S	Cav 1	" F	Sept 12 64
8590	McGinis P	16		Sept 12 64
8050	McKay K	10		Sept 6 64
8876	Munson H C	30	Co E	Sept 16 64
8307	Morrison J	21	" F	Sept 16 64
8994	Maher S L	Cav 7	" I	Sept 17 64
9185	Marine Wm	22	" E	Sept 18 64
9750	McArthur W	Cav 7	" D	Sept 25 64
9791	Moore John	Cav 6	" G	Sept 26 64
10011	Moses C	Cav 5	" I	Sept 29 64
10134	Moses A	Cav 6	" M	Oct 1 64
10423	Migelo J	9	Co A	Oct 6 64
10575	May Thomas	Cav 6	" H	Oct 9 64
10958	McMillen Alex	Cav 5	" M	Sept 14 64
11126	Miller John A	10	" F	Oct 18 64
11536	Molash F	3	" D	Oct 27 64
11548	McMann W	17	" A	Oct 27 64
11582	Mongby D	22	" C	Oct 28 64
11798	Merrill C	4	" K	Nov 4 64
12085	Miller H	9	" A	Nov 18 64
12093	Magram J	S S 1		Nov 19 64
12252	McCame W	7	Co B	Dec 9 64
12458	Morton J	1	" I	Jany 15 65
11511	Mackswarer W	S S 1	" K	Oct 26 64
12674	Marshall G	4	" M	Feby 19 65
12733	McNeill C	Cav 8	" M	Mch 5 65
3799	Major Wm	22	" D	July 22 64
7916	Monroe John	7	" I	Sept 5 64
9791	Moore John	Cav 6	" G	Sept 26 64
9965	McClary W	Cav 7	" H	Sept 28 64
513	Nicholson E	Cav 6	" G	April 12 64
1209	Newbury James	Cav	" A	May 19 64
2077	Nash Charles	22	" H	June 17 64
3343	Nail	9	" F	June 15 64
4102	Neck H	4	" K	July 27 64
5092	Nirthhammer J	20	" D	Aug 8 64
5400	Nagle C	11	" G	Aug 11 64
5493	Narrane A	17	" E	Aug 13 64
11021	Noyes James E	1		Oct 16 64
11911	Niland H	8	Co D	Nov 9 64
1005	Nurse H W	Cav 5	" L	May 10 64
9812	Northam O H	6	" M	Sept 26 64
285	O'Brien Austin	Cav 9	" H	April 1 64
499	Oliver Alex	Cav 8	" G	April 12 64
1189	Orrison Geo	Cav 9	" M	May 18 64
2267	O'ney G W	4	" A	June 20 64
4384	Osborn S	27	" B	July 31 64
4374	Overmeyer J F	Cav 6	" E	Aug 6 64
5574	O'Neil J	22	" K	Aug 14 64
5846	Orcutt C	3	" F	Aug 16 64
8141	Ornig S W	20	" C	Sept 8 64
8511	O'Brian W H	Cav 7	" A	Sept 13 64
9011	Ogden E S	Cav 5	" M	Sept 17 64
11940	O'Leary J	S S 1	" H	Nov 9 64
11999	Osborn J L	6	" E	Nov 13 64
12500	Oathart D	18	" C	Jan 17 65
443	Parsons G	7	" I	April 9 64
515	Pullman Geo	5	" I	April 12 64
1038	Parker B C	Cav 8	" C	May 12 64
1276	Perigo Jno	Cav 2	" D	May 22 64
1374	Parish Thos	6	" I	May 26 64
1892	Paisley A G	22		June 13 64
1937	Payne R H	6	Co I	June 15 64
2533	Piffer J	Cav 6	" I	June 26 64
3546	Pierson Daniel	Cav 3	" C	July 18 64
3591	Palmerly J	Cav 7	" C	July 19 64
4100	Post R L	10	" H	July 27 64
4253	Pratt M	22	" E	July 29 64
4436	Pelton A	21	" A	Aug 1 64
4662	Philbrook F	Art 1		Aug 3 64

Michigan — (*Continued.*)

5056	Podroff D	13 Co	D	Aug 8 64
5546	Peck J H	Cav 1 "	D	Aug 13 64
5612	Pond C	1 "	I	Aug 14 64
5745	Pettibone E E	7 "	D	Aug 15 64
4564	Porter L	S S 1 "	C	Aug 2 64
5760	Pentecost W G	18		Aug 15 64
5852	Palmer D	5 Co	D	Aug 16 64
7389	Parks	7 "	C	Aug 31 64
7354	Perrin N	Cav 8 "	B	Aug 31 64
7960	Parks F	Cav 5 "	E	Sept 6 64
8195	Pearmell J	23 "	B	Sept 8 64
8636	Pike B H	Cav 2 "	C	Sept 13 64
8986	Plant Wm	16 "	G	Sept 16 64
9331	Pharrett Wm	22 "	D	Sept 20 64
11046	Platt R	22 "	A	Oct 17 64
11177	Palmer P	5 "	H	Oct 19 64
11986	Preston B	7 "	K	Nov 13 64
12273	Plins Wm	Cav 5 "	C	Dec 12 64
12409	Preston J	6 "	C	Jan 7 65
12578	Pratt L	Cav 8 "	C	Feb 3 65
12762	Parmalee C	Cav 8 "	M	Feb 12 65
77	Roloff Jno	Cav 5 "	E	Mch 20 64
324	Russell Peter	23 "	G	April 2 64
623	Rowland B	6 "	M	April 19 64
922	Robinson Wm	2 "	H	May 6 64
1804	Rhinehart D	Cav 5 "	C	June 10 64
2291	Rolland J	6 "	G	June 21 64
2402	Ruggles O	32 "	H	June 24 64
3296	Rassan A	28 "	I	July 14 64
3732	Riley Charles	6 "	I	July 21 64
3710	Riggs J	22 "	I	July 21 64
3876	Russ W J	22 "	C	July 24 64
5176	Rood C	22 "	C	Aug 9 64
5885	Roman John	5 "	C	Aug 16 64
6154	Relu A	17 "	G	Aug 19 64
5707	Ryan W	1 "	E	Sept 1 64
7750	Robinson H	Cav 5 "	L	Sept 2 64
7955	Rich A	11 "	B	Sept 6 64
8617	Riley Miles	Cav 7 "	F	Sept 13 64
9254	Rimer J C	Cav 1 "	C	Sept 19 64
9914	Ryan T	22 "	I	Sept 28 64
10156	Robinson T	27 "	F	Oct 1 64
10380	Randall H D	6 "	D	Oct 5 64
11151	Riley R	24 "	H	Oct 19 64
11457	Ramsay J	5 "	H	Oct 25 64
11675	Raley H	Cav 21 "	L	Oct 30 64
11705	Ricott S	S S 1 "	K	Nov 1 64
12573	Richardson M B	1 "	L	Jany 29 65
12589	Rodgers W	26 "	G	Feby 5 65
12740	Robbins A	Cav 4 "	H	Mch 6 65
12745	Reaves M	15 "	G	Mch 8 65
134	Snyder E	17 "	F	Mch 24 64
172	Smith Wm	Cav 7 "	L	Mch 26 64
236	Soper Calvin	27 "	H	Mch 29 64
330	Sheldon H S	1 "	A	April 2 64
520	Shannon John	20 "	H	April 13 64
842	Smith W W	Cav 5 "	D	May 2 64
854	Stillman L D	6 "	M	May 3 64
1082	Stuck L H	Cav 2 "	B	May 14 64
1328	Schemerhorn J	Cav 7 Co	C	May 24 64
1406	Samborn H	22 "	K	May 27 64
1446	Snow Levi	20 "	H	May 28 64
1626	Smith A	Cav 1 "	L	June 4 64
1801	Smith S	17 "	C	June 10 64
1741	Stevens S	22 "	K	June 8 64
1948	Shafer W	22 "	G	June 11 64
1966	Strickland Thos	10 "	E	June 14 64
2209	Sanburn H	22 "	K	June 20 64
2507	Smith C	Art 1 "	E	June 26 64
2651	Sarmyes C	24 "	C	June 29 64
2664	Stevens L	Cav 6 "	M	June 29 64
2685	Stewart C A	7 "	F	June 30 64
2807	Sprague W B	11 "	I	July 3 64
2936	Shaw F N	2 "	K	July 7 64
3001	Steele E	Cav 2 "	C	July 7 64
3035	Sibley J E	1 "	G	July 9 64
3373	Stubbs J	Cav 9 "	L	July 15 64
3518	Simpson E T	Art 6 "	G	July 18 64
3234	Shultz C	5 "	B	July 18 64
3544	Shummay Wm	Cav 8 "	L	July 18 64
3942	Shaw F F	7 "	D	July 25 64
3951	Sharp Jas	6		July 25 64
4103	Stines H	4 Co	K	July 27 64
4311	Sprague B	Cav 7 "	E	July 30 64
4433	Sale Thos	17 "	G	July 31 64
4859	Smith Wm	17 "	H	Aug 6 64
5193	Swain D	Cav 6 "	H	Aug 10 64
5972	Stow Geo	10 "	C	Aug 17 64
6323	Simpson T	8 "	I	Aug 21 64
6306	Simons A	17 "	B	Aug 22 64
6686	Smoke H B	6 "	H	Aug 24 64
7014	Sullivan Jno	27 "	E	Aug 27 64
7303	Sherman Fred	22 "	G	Aug 30 64
7330	Sayrrer J M	1 "	G	Aug 31 64
7328	Schofield C	27 "	G	Sept 1 64
7376	Satterly H J	Cav 6 "	E	Sept 2 64
8300	Sutherland J	1 "	I	Sept 6 64
8380	Stanning G W	Art 5 "	G	Sept 12 64
9100	Suthphar H W	15 "	F	Sept 18 64
9469	Stewart F	Cav 6 "	E	Sept 21 64
9431	Stewart W V	5 "	E	Sept 21 64
9629	Snyder J	Cav 5 "	M	Sept 24 64
10080	Straut C A	Cav 5 "	F	Sept 30 64
10117	Spencer Geo	21 "	H	Oct 1 64
10254	Sammonds A	7 "	E	Oct 3 64
10285	Spencer John	2 "	I	Oct 3 64
10417	Skull Wm	7 "	B	Oct 6 64
10444	Simpson J P	22 "	A	Oct 7 64
11128	Swart M M	3 "	F	Oct 19 64
11148	Swester C	5 "	K	Oct 19 64
11234	Sutton H	22 "	I	Oct 21 64
11265	Strander A	6 "	G	Oct 21 64
11354	Stoddard S	Cav 5 "	F	Oct 23 64
11701	Steadman S	10 "	H	Oct 30 64
11717	Smith S	7 "	H	Nov 1 64
11773	Sickles M	14 "	I	Nov 3 64
12020	Seeley H	Cav 6 "	B	Nov 15 64
12225	Spondle C	Cav 1 "	C	Dec 5 64

Michigan—(*Continued.*)

12229	Sumner H	27	Co B	Dec 6 64
12261	Stedman S D	10	" H	Dec 11 64
12300	South Peter	S S 1	" K	Dec 19 64
12678	Smith C B	Cav 8	" L	Feby 19 65
12803	Smith Geo	8	" B	Mch 20 65
12254	Stickner J	16	" D	Dec 10 64
11508	Sockem A	S S 1	" K	Oct 26 64
11510	Springer J	Cav 7	" K	Oct 26 64
1304	Turrell Henry	22	" H	May 23 64
2945	Tubbs P	7	" K	July 6 64
48	Tilt George	Cav 2	" D	May 24 64
3498	Thatcher E H	Cav 6	" F	July 18 64
6603	Tompkins N R	1	" B	Aug 24 64
7009	Tift H	Cav 5	" M	Aug 27 64
7544	Thompson W	8	" F	Sept 2 64
7599	Tracy D	Cav 7	" K	Sept 2 64
7797	Thompson M C	Cav 5	" I	Sept 4 64
9103	Taylor H	32	" F	Sept 18 64
11113	Taylor J M	11	" A	Oct 18 64
11148	Twesler C	5	" K	Oct 19 64
3945	Udell W O	2	" D	July 25 64
731	Vanderhoof Jas	Cav 6	" G	April 25 64
1126	Vangieson L	Cav 5	" D	May 15 64
1467	Vogle Jacob	27	" D	May 29 64
2270	Van Dyke Jno	Cav 6	" D	June 20 64
2994	Van Brant W H	Cav 9	" E	July 7 64
3278	Vanlin C	6	" F	July 14 64
6864	Vanshoten W H	Cav 6	" K	Aug 26 64
7595	Vansickle L	Cav 5	" G	Sept 2 64
8958	Vanmke F	16	" G	Sept 15 64
9536	York C	5	" K	Sept 22 64
9936	Vleight A	22	" D	Sept 28 64
12166	Vanallen C	27	" K	Nov 26 64
12690	Vincient J	8	" K	Feb 22 65
840	Whittaker J	7	" B	April 2 64
733	Whipper G	4	" A	April 25 64
741	Wilson Byron	Cav 5	" D	April 26 64
749	Wright Wm A	7	Co K	April 26 64
957	Wilson J	22	" K	May 8 64
2102	Wilson W	11	" I	June 17 64
4961	Winegardner A S	Cav 1	" K	Aug 7 64
12723	White C	5	" F	Mch 3 65
12796	Whitmore C	Cav 8	" M	Mch 18 65
6781	Wiley E T	1	" E	Aug 25 64
749	Wright Wm A	7	" K	April 6 64
1089	Woolsey R	22	" E	May 14 64
1701	Walker J	22	" C	June 7 64
1920	Wolf F	13	" E	June 14 64
3301	Wentdarbly ——	5	" G	July 14 64
2899	Whitlock M	2	" B	July 5 64
3380	Wilet S	22	" K	July 11 64
3269	Wright W	Cav 5	" K	July 13 64
3437	Wolverton C	6	" B	July 17 64
3992	Woodruff H	Cav 1	" E	July 26 64
4119	Warren H	4	" B	July 31 64
4860	Walker Geo	22	" G	Aug 6 64
5051	Williams M	1	" A	Aug 8 64
5786	Williams T	Cav 2	" L	Aug 15 64
11323	Wolfinger J M	20	H	Oct 23 64
12307	Windless S	Cav 8	K	Dec 18 64
5559	Warner C		F	Aug 13 64
11096	Warner J	Cav 5	" K	Oct 18 64
9844	Wheeler E	24	" A	Sept 27 64
5930	Wisner Jno	Cav 6	" I	Aug 17 64
8331	Wood A O	Cav 8	" M	Sept 10 64
8076	Wilder H S	23	" K	Sept 7 64
6996	Wolverton J S	Cav 5	" A	Aug 26 64
7362	Way F	7	" C	Aug 31 64
7812	Whalen H	6	" I	Sept 4 64
7882	Wells F	7	" F	Sept 5 64
9022	Wing A	17	" G	Sept 17 64
9525	Whitworth W G	Cav 6	" A	Sept 2 64
2910	Yacht E	22	" E	July 5 64
2626	Zett J	22	" D	June 28 64

TOTAL 638.

MINNESOTA.

5964	Atkinson Geo	9	Co F	Mch 17 64
6567	Adcock Jas	9	" B	Mch 23 64
11977	Abrian G	1	" B	Nov 12 64
4224	Becker G	9	" E	July 29 64
5715	Barnard H A	9	" A	Aug 15 64
6630	Buyton M	9	" H	Aug 23 64
7841	Brese D	9	" E	Sept 4 64
7892	Brayton J M	9	" B	Sept 5 64
8053	Buckley J F	9	" G	Sept 7 64
8253	Burrows H	9	" K	Sept 9 64
9474	Babcock L A	9	" D	Sept 21 64
9800	Besgrove Isaac	9	" E	Sept 26 64
12778	Baker J G	1	" A	Mch 15 65
2747	Conner P	11	" A	July 1 64
3575	Clabaugh J	9	" D	July 19 64
4111	Conklin S	9	" I	July 27 64
6970	Conklin E	9	" C	July 27 64
10724	Cassady J	9	" F	Oct 6 64
7692	Dunham R H		Co K	Sept 3 64
10971	Davis E J	9	" E	Oct 15 64
8517	Fitch W F	9	" F	Sept 12 64
12656	Fuchs H	9	" D	Feby 14 65
9905	Freeschelz F	9	" F	Sept 27 64
3237	Geer O	9	" F	July 14 64
10401	Goodfellow E C	9	" D	Oct 6 64
10579	Goodwin G	9	" A	Oct 9 64
4130	Gordon W C	17	" I	July 28 64
6033	Higly M F	9	" G	Aug 18 64
6064	Hill C J	9	" K	Aug 18 64
6605	Handy J	9	" I	Aug 23 64
9144	Heaway J E	9	" K	Sept 18 64
4176	Holts A	9	" F	July 28 64
7809	Johnson N	9	" H	July 4 64
1211	Kerrick Sam	4	" K	May 19 64
9127	Kloss L	9	" H	Sept 18 64
5079	Lindley C	9	" B	Aug 8 64

Minnesota — (*Continued.*)

7795	Large M	9 Co	G	Sept 4 64
12165	Lewis L	9 "	E	Nov 26 64
12510	Latimore W H	9 "	D	Jany 22 65
9312	Lenyer M	9 "	G	Aug 30 64
5460	Myers J	3 "	I	Aug 13 64
7288	Mander J W	9 "	A	Aug 30 64
8130	McDougal J	9 "	A	Sept 8 64
9195	Montenary J	9 "	G	Sept 18 64
2829	Nichols John	15 "	A	July 3 64
7789	Ollman Wm	9 "	B	Sept 4 64
8384	Orcutt J	2 "	C	Sept 10 64
2341	Pitcher E	5 "	B	July 3 64
4813	Packett C	9 "	K	" Aug 5 64
5506	Pericle J	9 "	H	Aug 13 64
5909	Pence Geo	9 "	H	Aug 16 64
8353	Poinder T	9 "	B	Sept 10 64
8823	Pettijohn S W	9 "	H	Sept 11 64
4277	Roberts J G	9 "	E	July 29 64
5588	Roovin J	1 "	H	Aug 14 64
10327	Robertson Jno	9 "	B	Oct 4 64
10715	Reese Wm	9 "	E	Oct 11 64
5941	Short M	9 "	K	Aug 17 64
6216	Spence C	9 Co	G	Aug 20 64
6276	Sontor C	9 "	H	Aug 20 64
7185	Scheffer H	9 "	G	Aug 20 64
12038	Shiver F	9 "	E	Nov 17 64
12803	Sarf H	5 "	E	Mar 22 65
8478	Thompson W	9 "	A	Sept 11 64
10196	Tiltan N M	9 "	B	Oct 1 64
11603	Thomas W R	9 "	E	Oct 23 64
12106	Ulrici A	9 "	E	Nov 20 64
11505	Vanhouse B A	9 "	C	Oct 26 64
11568	Vittam E W	9 "	B	Oct 27 64
986	Wood A	2 "	B	May 9 64
3867	Walrich P	1 "	C	July 24 64
4498	Wheeler A	9 "	C	Aug 1 64
4588	Woodbury J	9 "	C	Aug 2 64
5637	Wilson F C	9 "	E	Aug 11 64
8228	Waiter G	9 "	H	Sept 9 64
8416	Whipple O C	9 "	F	Sept 11 64
8459	Westover J	9 "	E	Sept 9 64
8777	Warren E F (mus)	9 "	A	Sept 14 64
5006	Young D S	9 "	I	Aug 8 64

TOTAL 79.

MISSOURI.

281	Burns Jno	17 Co	I	April 1 64
1251	Burk J H	2 "	H	May 2 64
1464	Buel J	4 "	C	May 29 64
2217	Bishop P	15 "	I	June 20 64
2306	Bloomker Wm	2 "	F	June 22 64
4269	Broyer J	2 "	E	July 29 64
5355	Birley Peter	29 "	I	Aug 16 64
8664	Berger J	2 "	I	Sept 13 64
8772	Bitter H	29 "	F	Sept 14 64
11223	Bullard Jas	19 "	D	Oct 20 64
12795	Bates B	44 "	F	Mch 18 65
2351	Clarg C	2 "	I	July 4 64
4328	Clements Jas	Cav 2 "	A	July 30 64
6533	Cornell Jas	Cav 9 "	H	Aug 23 64
12351	Coon F	15 "	K	Dec 28 64
12776	Chapman R	24 "	B	Mch 14 65
5260	Dicksen D	18		Aug 10 64
1641	Daley M	Cav 10 Co	H	June 5 64
343	Eddington G W	29 "	A	April 2 64
3963	Engler Jno	15 "	B	July 25 64
6937	Fogg B F	Cav 1 "	H	Aug 27 64
8633	Folk L	18 "	C	Sept 13 64
11266	Fay J W	2 "	K	Sept 21 64
12305	Fry M	Cav 12 "	L	Mch 21 65
6914	Frick S	2 "	E	Aug 26 64
2770	Guffy R	18 "	E	July 2 64
3725	Gallegher F	2 "	G	July 21 64
223	Houston W E	18 "	E	Mch 29 64
4505	Hunter W	Cav 1 "	H	Aug 1 64
4563	Hartman V	29 "	G	Aug 2 64
4727	Huntsley A	22 "	H	Aug 4 64
7064	Haginey F	2 "	K	Aug 28 64
226	Houston W E	18 "	E	Mch 29 64
1552	Head B J	23 "	B	June 2 64
2655	Heltgen G	12 "	E	June 29 64
8026	Hasse Jno	Cav 14 Co	L	Sept 6 64
9042	Hamilton W	31 "	A	Sept 17 64
11941	Hanahan A	29 "	D	Nov 9 64
4410	Isenhour J	9 "	I	July 31 64
5709	Keyan M	2 "	D	Aug 15 64
7414	Keiler A	29 "	H	Aug 31 64
8178	Kline C S	2 "	F	Sept 8 64
10546	Kaunst H	18 "	G	Oct 9 64
12821	Keller I	40 "	H	April 65
7713	Kuhn Jacob	15 "	E	Sept 3 64
3249	Lowe Jno	18 "	E	July 13 64
4803	Lavilley Wm	29 "	K	Aug 5 64
7035	Lang C	Cav 10 "	B	Aug 27 64
12232	Litch J	4 "	A	Dec 6 64
5401	Lindsay J	18 "	A	Aug 12 64
7438	Miller W	Cav 4 "	E	Sept 1 64
8913	Morgan E	Cav 12 "	F	Sept 16 64
11035	Manning S H	30 "	A	Oct 16 64
11459	Menzt W	15 "	G	Jany 15 65
12706	Martin J	44 "	H	Feby 27 65
12754	McGuire O	Cav 2 "	I	Mch 12 65
12760	McDowell J	2 "	F	Mch 12 65
8456	Newkirk Chas	15 "	F	July 17 64
3539	Neclout W	2 "	E	July 18 64
4109	Nelson Jno	29 "	A	July 28 64
12774	O'Dell E	44 "	B	Mch 14 65
12823	Purcell J R	44 "	G	April 5 65
735	Phillips Pat	11 "	E	April 27 64
25	Payne Jos	29 "	A	April 16 64
4978	Perkins A H	29 "	L	Aug 7 64
6732	Plasmine A	26 "	D	Aug 24 64
10539	Plumer E D	24 "	B	Oct 8 64
1348	Reilly P	29 "	B	May 25 64
3540	Riddle F	8 "	D	July 13 64
5110	Ritteman John	15 "	F	Aug 9 64

Missouri—(*Continued.*)

6915	Remers J	4 Co G	Aug 26 64
2422	Robertson J C	Cav 10 " F	June 25 64
1424	Schenck Philip	15 " B	May 26 64
1478	Scebel A	12 " G	May 30 64
1023	Search Henry	15 " D	June 4 64
2464	Stickle D	4 " D	June 24 64
2480	Stofacke F	15 " D	June 25 64
28	Stiner Gottlieb	29 " A	April 17 64
5239	Stormn F	58 " E	Aug 9 64
5667	Schmas G	15 " G	Aug 14 64
63 6	Segin C	2 " H	Aug 26 64
6930	Shuman Jos	1 " B	Aug 26 64
7535	Sherman H	15 " G	Sept 1 64
9821	Schaat D B	18 " E	Sept 26 64
536	Trask Geo K	29 Co A	April 14 64
770	Terrill Christian	27 " E	April 27 64
1509	Terrell J	12 " A	May 31 64
5672	Tresler H W	4 " I	Aug 14 64
12730	Turman D	44 " B	Mch 4 65
2803	Vance H J	26 " B	July 3 64
373	Walham H	4 " C	April 5 64
678	Watson J J	18 " A	April 22 64
3106	Wigan M	2 " F	July 10 64
7494	Williams J M	31 " H	Sept 1 64
10889	Weidam J	2 " B	Oct 14 64
12550	Ware J B	40 " K	Jan 29 65
12739	West J	40 " K	Mch 6 65

TOTAL 97.

NEW HAMPSHIRE.

26	Ames John C	2 Co F	Mch 18 64
29	Allen E S	2 " H	Mch 9 64
4656	Allen S	9 " C	Aug 3 64
4746	Abbott C	7 " K	Aug 5 64
7130	Arches J L	9 " A	Aug 28 64
9518	Atmore G W	3 " C	Sept 22 64
9832	Anderson J N	7 " E	Sept 24 64
11765	Avery J	Cav 1 " H	Nov 3 64
5721	Austendalph J	3 " D	Aug 15 64
833	Bushbey N	7 " C	May 1 64
3346	Bailey A D	7 " C	July 15 64
3380	Bush A	4 " H	July 16 64
4447	Bachelor J R	1	Aug 1 64
4965	Baker Wm	4 Co H	Aug 7 64
4938	Babb Jas	7 " D	Aug 7 64
6871	Brown W F	2 " B	Aug 26 64
6765	Breakman A	12 " I	Aug 25 64
7857	Baker D W	3 " G	Sept 5 64
8463	Bell Geo	5 " C	Sept 11 64
10294	Bond J	12 " F	Oct 4 64
2228	Clark G M	7 " C	May 20 64
8326	Combs John	7 " B	July 14 64
4230	Coon Charles	7 " G	July 29 64
5137	Colbry John N	13 " D	Aug 9 64
7072	Cooney Thomas	9 " C	Aug 28 64
8551	Connelly M	4 " C	Sept 12 64
2796	Chadwick C E	7 " H	July 2 64
11192	Carr P	1 " H	Oct 20 64
1370	Downs E	7 " I	May 25 64
2986	Doer S	7 " D	June 17 64
3668	Dodge C F	7 " K	July 20 64
5577	Drake Chas C	Cav 1 " B	Aug 14 64
3566	Eschoymer H	Cav 1 " B	July 19 64
5337	Estey E E	4 " C	Aug 10 64
8126	Edwards John	9 " H	Sept 11 64
12841	Elliott A	7 " I	April 21 65
1596	Fuller George	7 " B	May 26 64
5240	Faucett J	7 " C	Aug 10 64
6678	Flanders O	9 " F	Aug 24 64
6894	Ford W	7 " K	Aug 26 64
9460	Faggerty Jackson	Cav 1 " A	Sept 21 64
12440	Felch G P	7 " H	Jany 12 65
2838	Guingoelett H	3 " E	July 3 64
4413	Gill N	7 Co A	July 31 64
4687	Gooley J	7 " G	Aug 4 64
11905	Goodwin A	1 " I	Nov 7 64
9671	Gardiner A	4 " C	Sept 24 64
6516	Gray G H	4 " E	Aug 22 64
6143	Hunter C	4 " K	Aug 19 64
6875	Hurd Wm	6 " I	Aug 26 64
7869	Hartford H	4 " A	Sept 5 64
8537	Hally H	7 " C	Sept 12 64
10269	Huse W	11 " H	Oct 3 64
11156	Hamlin G W	Cav 1 " I	Oct 19 64
11439	Holmes J	7	Oct 24 64
11463	Holmes J	7	Oct 26 64
7733	Janes J B	9 Co K	Sept 3 64
9198	Johnson O O	5 " F	Sept 18 64
11216	Juntplute F	12 " E	Oct 20 64
11758	Johnson P	9 " E	Nov 3 64
4314	Keyes C	Cav 1 " K	July 30 64
5114	Kemp C H	7 " A	Aug 9 64
5151	Kingsbury H R	9 " R	Aug 9 64
5444	Karson H B	2 " C	Aug 12 64
7394	Kreaser M	4 " I	Aug 31 64
11877	Klinsmith J	10 " I	Nov 6 64
11994	Kingsbury J H	Cav 1 " A	Nov 13 64
6144	Lawrence A	Cav 1 " C	Aug 19 64
6787	Lenert D	9 " K	Aug 25 64
8048	Libby A G	4 " H	Sept 6 64
11415	Leport J	Cav 3 " I	Oct 24 64
11484	Lucht P	5 " C	Oct 26 64
2687	Mumford A	12 " A	June 30 64
3652	Mantove J	4 " H	June 20 64
4284	Miller F	11 " G	July 30 64
4629	Miller R	11 " H	Aug 3 64
7203	Milliot P	5 " I	Aug 29 64
7423	Morrison O P	9 " C	Aug 31 64
79 8	Morten J	4 " C	Sept 6 64
8573	McCann M	9 " G	Sept 12 64
9921	Matheson F	7 " B	Sept 28 64
11207	McCann O	13 " E	Oct 20 64
12234	Montyan P	35 " F	Dec 6 64
1658	O'Brien Chas	7 " I	June 6 64
11698	Osmore J	Cav 1 " C	Oct 31 64
6185	Patch John	3 " T	Aug 19 64

New Hampshire — (*Continued.*)

819	Poore Samuel	2	Co H	April 30 64
8260	Puny J	3	" G	July 13 64
4764	Place I K	7	" F	Aug 5 64
7011	Patterson N	9	" I	Aug 27 64
11121	Parsons Samuel	5	" H	Oct 18 64
11828	Perven H A	7	" A	Nov 5 64
11837	Phelps M F	9	" D	Nov 5 64
5383	Paschal E	7	" E	Aug 12 64
1572	Reed F K	2	" H	June 3 64
2771	Ramsay Wm	7	" G	July 2 64
3406	Richards W R	7	" C	July 16 64
11 00	Ringer I K, Sgt Maj	11		Oct 22 64
1336	Smith John	7	Co K	May 24 64
2330	Sanburn W	7	" H	June 22 64
2505	Sanlay E	9	" E	June 26 64
2708	Simms S	9	" C	June 30 64
2925	Searle I R	7	" E	July 5 64
3472	Smith L F	13	" C	July 17 64
4779	Steward George	10	" A	Aug 5 64
5140	Smith J	7	" B	Aug 9 64
5198	Schean W	7	" A	Aug 9 64
5405	Shorey Ed	1	" C	Aug 12 64
5438	Salsbur I	4	" K	Aug 12 64
5621	Stanley John	9	" A	Aug 14 64
6547	Smith I	11	" E	Aug 23 64
7040	Swain C	7	" D	Aug 27 64
8629	Smith C	3	" F	Sept 13 64
8652	Stark S	15	" A	Sept 13 64
8980	Smith John	3	" T	Sept 17 64
9412	Smith L	12	Co B	Sept 21 64
10503	Shantz I	11	" G	Oct 8 64
11887	Spaulding T C	4	" K	Nov 7 64
8396	Taylor A B	5	" H	July 16 64
3131	Tobine T	6	" A	July 17 64
4072	Tilton D B	7	" G	July 26 64
8098	Thompson A	9	" K	Sept 8 64
10734	Tilton L G	11	" B	Oct 11 64
10493	Upkins A	Cav 1	" B	Oct 7 64
5191	Valley John	10	" K	Aug 12 64
794	Woodward L A	7	" K	April 29 64
1991	Williams I	7	" I	June 15 64
2345	Woodbury A	7	" H	June 23 64
2545	Whipple A	7	" H	June 23 64
4156	Webster I	6	" I	July 28 64
2710	Welson W	4	" F	July 1 64
4104	Whalen M	9	" H	July 27 64
4750	Weston W W	8	" A	Aug 5 64
4749	Welch Jas	7	" I	Aug 5 64
5702	Wagner John	7	" H	Aug 15 64
7559	Welsh I	7	" C	Sept 2 64
7834	Wolf John D	3	" F	Sept 4 64
8083	Wultramsen F	9	" I	Sept 7 64
11278	Williams P	3	" H	Oct 22 64
11472	Wingerd D	3	" G	Oct 26 64
11768	Wilson I	11	" I	Nov 3 64
11878	Warren E	Cav 1	" H	Nov 6 64
12734	Whitman G E	Cav 1	" B	Mch 6 65
8736	York Charles	Cav 1	" B	Sept 14 64

TOTAL 144.

NEW JERSEY.

3347	Aaron Thos	2	Co B	July 15 64
3354	Aney G	1	" K	July 15 64
4098	Austin D B	2	" I	July 27 64
7138	Anderson T	2	" E	Aug 28 64
8513	Albright ——	Cav 3	" I	Sept 12 64
11389	Alexander W L	Cav 3	" C	Oct 24 64
12646	Amps C	33	" I	Feb 13 65
909	Broderick I S	2	" A	May 5 64
1548	Beach I H	11	" E	June 1 64
2181	Brannin Pat	11	" B	June 19 64
2260	Bells I H	2	" H	June 21 64
2577	Buckley John	1	" G	June 27 64
2980	Bloon Adam	2	" I	July 4 84
3099	Buffman A C	Art 1	" B	July 10 64
5761	Baily L	7	" A	Aug 9 94
5272	Brann Geo	Cav 1	" B	Aug 10 64
5357	Burns P	Cav 3	" C	Aug 11 64
5379	Baker Wm	Cav 1	" K	Aug 12 64
5483	Blanchard G	7	" K	Aug 13 64
5934	Bennet C	14	" B	Aug 17 64
11682	Brant Chas	1	" E	Oct 31 64
12283	Buver A	6	" I	Dec 7 64
12640	Brewer W H	10	" D	Feb 12 65
715	Corley Daniel	11	" A	April 24 64
1437	Creamer E	35	" A	May 28 64
6929	Creamer E	10	" B	Aug 26 64
3209	Chamberlain R	Cav 1	" D	July 12 64
5730	Clark C H	2	Co C	Aug 15 64
8249	Coonan J	2	" C	Sept 9 64
10552	Collar H	2	" D	Sept 9 64
11990	Clayton L	10	" B	Nov 13 64
3176	Curtis W O	Cav 1	" L	July 17 64
8041	Coykendall D	15	" K	Sept 6 64
335	Disbrow J P	14	" K	April 2 64
2473	Davenport J	7	" I	June 25 64
3441	Davis H	12	" F	July 17 64
4926	Dayton C	2	" C	Aug 6 64
5138	Dorland A H	10	" I	Aug 9 64
6306	Dewinger J	2	" G	Aug 20 64
7076	Dunham L	35	" H	Aug 28 64
7304	Dilan Edward	9	" G	Aug 30 64
7409	Dermer J L	9	" G	Sept 1 64
7734	Doremus C	Cav 2	" A	Sept 3 64
7804	Duncan H P	2	" G	Sept 4 64
8440	Doyle H	16	" C	Sept 11 64
10533	Dunn G	1	" F	Sept 18 64
1426	Ebner Chas	Cav 1	" K	May 23 64
1715	Egbert Jas	15	" B	June 8 64
4303	Esligh Jacob	10	" D	July 13 64
1522	Farrell J H	5	" G	May 31 64
3938	Foliand M	Cav 1	" K	July 25 64
4393	Fitch F	35	" F	Aug 4 64
5327	Fry Jno	9	" G	Aug 4 64
6737	Fisher Wm	9	" C	Aug 24 64

New Jersey — (*Continued.*)

7285	Farran J	3		Aug 30 64
9972	Fairbrother H	35	Co D	Sept 28 64
11584	Ford A	7	" K	Oct 28 64
7338	Fisher N O	9	" I	Aug 30 64
5900	Gade B	9	" D	Aug 16 64
7039	Galloway F C	12	" K	Aug 27 64
11165	Glenn C H	4	" I	Oct 19 64
11120	Guier G	7	" D	Oct 20 64
1508	Hallman H	6	" C	May 31 64
3072	Hemis Daniel	Cav 1	" D	July 9 64
3819	Hick James	9	" G	July 23 64
4151	Hegamann J	14	" K	July 28 64
4189	Hammle A	Cav 1		July 28 64
4744	Huber C	9	Co G	Aug 5 64
4862	Herbert J S	Cav 2	" I	Aug 6 64
4911	Halman M	Cav 1	" A	Aug 6 64
821	Hull Alex	7	" C	Sept 4 64
7870	Howell J	1	" K	Sept 5 64
7900	Hilgard P F	10	" A	Sept 5 64
10761	Hatter W	3	" I	Oct 12 64
12302	Humes E M	2	" M	Dec 17 64
12416	Hook J M	Cav 2	" D	Jany 8 65
5252	Jennings G H	Cav 2	" A	Aug 10 64
9519	Jone A	Cav 1	" A	Sept 22 64
11117	Jay H	5	" K	Oct 18 64
11399	Jomson G W	6	" G	Oct 24 64
12344	Johnson A F	9	" D	Dec 26 64
3762	Kronk Peter	Cav 2	" H	July 22 64
5085	Kuhn R	9	" A	Aug 8 64
8649	Kitchell S	7	" K	Sept 13 64
12023	King C	15	" G	Nov 15 64
1935	Lyons D	Cav 1	" K	June 15 64
795	Layton Stephen	11	" A	April 29 64
1769	Lindsley Samuel	10	" H	June 9 64
3622	Lewis S	Cav 3		July 20 64
4095	Leadbeater J H	6	" B	July 27 64
5944	Leighton Wm	5	" H	Aug 17 64
6157	Luney Ed	8	" G	Aug 19 64
12102	Larime C	15	" C	Nov 20 64
2019	Menner Jacob	11	" H	June 15 64
2852	Miller J	Cav 1	" K	July 4 64
3323	McIntire R	8	" I	July 14 64
3548	Marks Chas	Cav 2	" G	July 18 64
4594	Mulrainy I	4	" B	Aug 3 64
4645	Miller S S	Cav 2	" G	Aug 3 64
5250	Morell A	5	" K	Aug 10 64
5832	Mahler Jno	35	" I	Aug 16 64
6986	Munn Chas	4	" K	Aug 27 64
8019	McElroy E	10	" I	Sept 6 64
8332	Mount C H	9	" D	Sept 10 64
8592	Miller J	7	" K	Sept 13 64
10959	Mullan A	39	" B	Oct 14 64
12232	Mills F	2	" I	Oct 21 64
11564	Millington J	Cav 1	" H	Oct 27 64
6780	Noll M	9	" A	Aug 25 64
4983	Nichols J	S S 1	" C	Aug 7 64
7131	Osborne E	14	" E	Aug 23 64
10463	Osborn J M	9	" H	Oct 7 64
1071	Pratt J F	1	Co M	May 13 64
1072	Purdee Chas	11	" C	May 13 64
5206	Peterson Henry	Cav 3	" H	Aug 10 64
6298	Peer T	9	" K	Aug 20 64
6963	Pelger M	10	" G	Aug 27 64
7451	Peterson G	12	" I	Sept 1 64
8017	Post G J	4	" I	Sept 6 64
9990	Parker W	2	" I	Sept 29 64
12221	Prink J	2		Dec 4 64
2145	Rooks H	5	Co H	June 18 64
2321	Riley M	Cav 1	" L	July 3 64
4066	Robinson Jacob	Cav 1	" B	July 27 64
4858	Radford Wm	13	" B	Aug 6 64
8232	Reed A	9	" D	Sept 9 64
10461	Ray J	10	" A	Oct 7 64
10708	Regan D O	8	" C	Oct 11 64
11292	Reevis F	2	" I	Oct 21 64
2548	Starr N	5	" H	June 27 64
5067	Simonds J	9	" K	Aug 8 64
5807	Shanahan W	9	" C	Aug 16 64
7364	Stout L	2	" C	Aug 21 64
7565	Street John J	9	" D	Sept 2 64
7577	Stiflin H	3	" M	Sept 2 64
7729	Skell C W	Cav 3	" M	Sept 3 64
8637	Swetser P	9	" G	Sept 13 64
8751	Stevenson W	Cav 2	" M	Sept 14 64
9328	Shay H H	7	" I	Sept 19 64
10346	Smith A	5	" G	Oct 13 64
10615	Sutton T	12	" K	Oct 28 64
11653	Stimmell I	5	" A	Oct 30 64
11793	Sullivan I	8	" C	Nov 8 64
11882	Steele George	2	" B	Nov 6 64
10882	Sweet B F	10	" K	Oct 13 64
1853	Tindel E	1	" B	June 11 64
5112	Taylor Peter	9		Aug 9 64
6131	Towsend J	35	Co I	Aug 19 64
7937	Turner B	4	" G	Sept 5 64
9398	Townsend F	10	" C	Sept 21 64
11304	Thompson S	4	" I	Oct 21 64
12451	Thatcher J	8	" H	Jan 14 65
12705	Toy J	7	" G	Feb 27 65
10212	Thomas Henry	10	" B	Oct 2 64
6148	Traittman Jas	9	" D	Aug 22 64
2634	Utter Stephen	Art 1	" B	June 29 64
12100	Vallett W	Art 5	" A	Nov 19 64
1955	Weed Wm	15	" I	June 14 64
2246	Wood W J	12	" E	June 20 64
4643	Widder W	5	" G	Aug 3 64
4998	Wainwright	9	" C	Aug 7 64
5031	Wolverton	1	" I	Aug 8 64
5099	Warner A	4	" A	Aug 9 64
5333	Willey J	Cav 2	" M	Aug 10 64
6168	Winard Wm	2	" I	Aug 19 64
7560	Willis A	35	" I	Sept 2 64
8142	Wright S M	7	" K	Sept 8 64
8307	Ward J	Cav 1	" H	Sept 10 64
12157	Williams W	1	" D	Nov 20 64
12658	Wells G	10	" C	Feb 15 65

TOTAL 170.

NEW YORK.

2038	Abbey O	174	June 15 64
2141	Abbey W H	85 Co E	June 18 64
4719	Abel C	Art 15 " C	Aug 4 64
4612	Aber J	104 " I	Aug 3 64
5626	Ackerman Sam'l	97 " K	Aug 14 64
64	Ackheart David	20 " A	Mch 19 64
8497	Adams H	98 " G	Sept 11 64
4581	Adams J A	10 " F	Aug 2 64
6467	Adams O	61 " C	Aug 22 64
8559	Adams S	100	Sept 12 64
8226	Adams T R	85 Co H	July 12 64
1700	Ades Ed	Cav 8 " C	June 7 64
5047	Adeler A	8 " D	Aug 8 64
6575	Adney F	85 " K	Aug 23 64
4382	Ahearn Daniel	170	July 31 64
8349	Aiken J W	85 " H	July 15 64
8001	Akerman M	Art 7 " L	Sept 6 64
7062	Albarson J	42 " C	Aug 28 64
6698	Albert Wm	Bat 24	Aug 24 64
7007	Alderman F	Cav 15 Co F	Aug 27 64
1755	Alexander J	125 " C	June 9 64
11212	Alford B C	152 " F	Oct 20 64
8293	Allen A W	Art 14	July 14 64
12453	Allen J I	82 Co A	Jan 14 65
5768	Allen W	Cav 1 " H	Aug 13 64
5844	Allenburger J	39 " B	Aug 16 64
7478	Allenberens E	39 " D	Sept 1 64
11479	Allinger L	48 " I	Oct 26 64
7587	Allman Chas	Art 7 " C	Sept 2 64
6941	Almy F	111 " K	Aug 26 64
5938	Alphord J	75 " G	Aug 17 64
7739	Alsaver S	47 " H	Sept 3 64
806	Ambler Fred	47 " H	April 29 64
2344	Ambrose Jacob	Cav 2 " C	June 23 64
10642	Ames Henry	Art 2	Oct 10 64
4654	Ames J R	Art 14 Co I	Aug 3 64
7743	Amgere G	47 " E	Sept 3 64
1954	Amigh A	162 " K	June 14 64
8739	Anderson A	100 " I	July 21 64
4890	Anderson A	99 " F	Aug 6 64
537	Anderson H	Cav 20 " M	April 14 64
8819	Anderson J	39 " E	Sept 15 64
4110	Anderson L	14 " D	July 27 64
1389	Andrews G	111 " I	May 26 64
7533	Andrews W	85 " K	Sept 1 64
8717	Ansom Robert	Cav 1 " K	Sept 14 64
6548	Answell J	Cav 15 " A	Aug 23 64
8220	Antisdale Geo	Cav 5	Sept 4 64
6976	Appleby S W	85 Co K	Aug 27 64
9741	Argt C	6	Sept 25 64
11172	Armond W	7 Co F	Oct 19 64
9475	Armstrong H	140 " G	Sept 21 64
10818	Armstrong J	164 " C	Oct 12 64
11571	Armstrong W	Bat 24	Oct 27 64
7470	Arnold R B	Art 7 Co L	Sept 1 64
6551	Arnott C	47 " C	Aug 26 64
1580	Asley C G	146 " G	June 3 64
12202	Auster F	39 " B	Dec 1 64
12622	Ashley S, Citizen		Feb 9 65
5541	Ashton ——	10 Co I	Aug 13 64
7207	Atwood G S	Bat 24	Aug 29 64
930	Aubray K	14 Co A	May 8 64
11748	Augh J	66 " D	Nov 2 64
5027	Augustine F	52 " A	Aug 8 64
1736	Austin A	147 " H	June 8 64
3094	Austin J	Art 7 " M	July 10 64
8218	Austin G	147 " H	Sept 3 64
12810	Ayers G S	147 " G	Mch 29 65
12347	Babcock J M	140 " I	Dec 27 64
1712	Babcock H	111 " G	May 7 64
3066	Babcock J	72 " E	July 9 64
5335	Babcock J	55 " E	Aug 11 64
4338	Babcock J S	140 " D	Aug 3 64
4893	Babcock R	9 " L	Aug 9 64
11831	Babcock W H	Cav 13 " L	Nov 5 64
5692	Babst M	9 " D	Aug 15 64
754	Bacon E P	154 " B	April 27 64
9101	Bacon J	154 " E	Sept 13 64
2870	Bacchus A	169 " A	July 4 64
11272	Bacchus E R	Art 15 " F	Oct 22 64
3147	Bachelder B F	Bat 24	July 17 64
3115	Backley C	Bat 24	July 10 64
3771	Badger P	47 Co E	July 22 64
7890	Bailey A	5 " K	Sept 5 64
10163	Bailey C	76 " K	Oct 1 64
5697	Bailey G W	154 " G	Aug 15 64
7493	Bailey Jno	Cav 12 " A	Sept 1 64
8215	Baker J	Bat 24	Sept 8 64
10636	Baker A	9 Co B	Oct 10 64
4463	Baker Chas	52 " G	Aug 1 64
3550	Baker E	85 " E	July 18 64
12376	Baker Geo	40 " H	Jan 1 65
8759	Baker H	146 " F	Sept 14 64
8052	Baker Ira	85 " H	Sept 7 64
11848	Baker J	24 " F	Nov 5 64
11660	Baker J	Cav 16 " K	Oct 31 64
61	Baker Wm	7 " D	Mch 18 64
7591	Baldwin C	Cav 24 " M	Sept 2 64
6853	Baldwin G	154 " C	Aug 25 64
4457	Ballard Robt B	85 " C	Aug 1 64
4364	Barnard Wm	85 " K	July 31 64
5347	Bancroff A H	85	Aug 11 64
8592	Barrett G M	184 Co E	Sept 8 64
11605	Banigan A	82 " A	Oct 28 64
5536	Banker J M	118 " K	Aug 13 64
9319	Banker J T	152 " G	Sept 26 64
8443	Bannan H	39 " H	Sept 11 64
11056	Bannyer F	126 " K	Oct 17 64
12315	Barber H	96 " D	Dec 20 64
1680	Barge H	120 " A	June 6 64
3748	Barnes J	Cav 12 " F	July 22 64
6771	Barnes J S	Cav 10 " K	Aug 25 64
11243	Barnes M	115 " F	Oct 23 64
6933	Barnes A C	85 " D	Aug 27 64
8321	Barnes R W	Bat 24	Sept 15 64
12418	Barnes Thos	76 Co B	Oct 6 64
1835	Barrett J	132 " C	June 11 64
8361	Barnum H	39 " H	Sept 10 64

New York—(*Continued.*)

7877	Barklatt H	Bat 24		Sept 5 64
8192	Barrett G M	184	Co A	Sept 8 64
10153	Barratt G	22	" A	Oct 1 64
588	Barrett D	13	" H	April 16 64
9979	Barron C L	Bat 12		Sept 28 64
3580	Barrows M	14	Co G	July 19 64
11612	Bartill R	164	" F	Oct 28 64
4769	Bartlett L	118	" I	Aug 5 64
8409	Barton D	85	" I	Sept 11 64
6552	Bass Chas	Art 7	" B	Aug 23 64
8217	Bass Geo, Teamster	63		Sept 8 64
8097	Bassford J	Cav 12	Co G	Sept 7 64
5555	Bates G	5	" A	Aug 13 64
530	Bates J	97	" A	April 13 64
3845	Bates Jno	14	" I	July 24 64
1069	Bates Lester	97	" A	May 13 64
10556	Baters W	139	" G	Oct 9 64
10999	Baty A	132	" K	Oct 16 64
61	Bayne Daniel	57	" D	July 4 64
9380	Baywood J	Cav 1	" I	Sept 20 64
6021	Beam B	Cav 2	" M	Aug 17 64
4302	Beck John	97	" H	July 30 64
6034	Beckham F B	Cav 10	" A	Aug 18 64
9216	Beckshire J	Cav 12	" F	Sept 19 64
8472	Beckwith C	Art 14	" D	Sept 11 64
5012	Bce George	119	" F	Aug 8 64
8992	Beebe J E	11		Sept 17 64
3843	Beekman J	43	Co A	July 23 64
11933	Beers W	82	" B	Nov 8 64
8010	Belden Wm	82	" E	Sept 6 64
3267	Bell D S, State Mil	20	" D	July 13 64
9136	Bell J	6	" B	Sept 18 64
11124	Bell J C	120	" D	Oct 18 64
8942	Bell Wm	39	" K	Sept 16 64
11694	Bellvea O	179	" F	Oct 31 64
3089	Bennett J H	85	" E	July 9 64
3138	Bennett ——	146	" B	July 10 64
5945	Bentley C	Cav 22	" L	Aug 17 64
6670	Bentner Josh	100	" I	Aug 24 64
6979	Benway C	Art 6	" K	Aug 27 64
10955	Berges E	146	" B	Oct 14 64
6598	Benall M L	125	" A	Aug 23 64
5749	Beat Isaac	42	" G	Aug 15 64
6039	Bertin F	69	" G	Aug 18 64
6137	Besrha John	Art 15	" B	Aug 19 64
8234	Buell J	85	" B	Sept 9 64
5230	Beyers H	24	" K	Aug 10 64
351	Bidon S	52	" A	April 2 64
10635	Bidwell J	Cav 5	" G	Oct 10 64
3232	Bigelow L	85	" D	July 12 64
10555	Billings J	Cav 2	" M	Oct 8 64
601	Billings W W	52	" G	April 17 64
10945	Bings G	Art 5	" B	Oct 14 64
10005	Bingham C E	Cav 5	" D	Sept 29 64
12831	Bird M	Art 7	" K	April 14 65
4780	Bird P	Art 7	" K	Aug 5 64
6590	Bishop C	Art 7	" M	Aug 23 64
5786	Bissell J S	85	" D	Aug 15 64
11018	Black J	42	" G	Oct 16 64
2574	Black L	9	Co A	June 27 64
11971	Black H C	42	" F	Nov 12 64
1885	Blackman J	85		June 13 64
4076	Blackwood W	115	Co G	July 27 64
7989	Blair D	15	" C	Sept 5 64
12469	Blair Jas	Cav 8	" K	Jan 16 65
498	Blaize H	Art 3	" H	April 12 64
3236	Blake W D	Bat 24		July 22 64
2439	Blake Geo	100	Co I	June 25 64
6129	Blanchard E	Cav 12	" F	Aug 19 64
8340	Blanchard L	100	" K	Sept 10 64
10083	Blancolt Wm	95	" B	Sept 30 64
1861	Blank J M	95	" A	June 12 64
4933	Bliss Jas H	Cav 22	" I	Aug 7 64
8959	Block J P	100	" F	Sept 16 64
7206	Blood L	7	" C	Aug 29 64
2777	Blyme S	85	" G	July 2 64
12521	Boaman J	Cav 1	" D	Jan 25 65
6371	Boares A	178	" D	Aug 21 64
5285	Bode A	85	" B	Aug 11 64
2989	Bodishay J	7	" F	July 7 64
474	Boermaster J	14	" A	April 9 64
3073	Bohl H	Cav 10	" E	July 9 64
6918	Bolan E	35	" F	Aug 17 64
11718	Bolby O	Art 14	" D	Nov 1 64
8267	Boles J	Cav 22	" D	Sept 9 64
3606	Bomsteel S A	20	" G	July 19 64
5269	Borst J	Cav 5	" B	Aug 10 64
4401	Bodler D	7	" D	July 31 64
51	Boughton H	77	" A	Mch 16 64
7627	Boulton T	43	" G	Sept 2 64
10066	Bowden P	Cav 16	" M	Oct 17 64
6744	Bowen J H	65	" D	Aug 24 64
4601	Bowin J	Cav 7	" K	Aug 3 64
11944	Bowman H	84	" K	Nov 10 64
12521	Bowman I	Cav 1	" D	Jan 25 65
3635	Bowman S	147	" H	July 20 64
1275	Box G	111	" D	May 22 64
9728	Boyce A	Cav 3	" I	Sept 25 64
2673	Boyce R	Cav 6	" M	June 30 64
10	Boyle Pat	63	" A	Mch 5 64
8912	Boyle Pat	48	" F	Sept 16 64
11974	Boyle I	16	" D	Nov 12 64
4365	Bradford D B	Art 7	" B	July 31 64
5232	Bradley Jno	69	" K	Aug 10 64
6685	Bradshaw R	120	" E	Aug 24 64
12219	Brady J	140	" E	Dec 4 64
3979	Bragg J C	Cav 2	" E	July 26 64
12263	Brain Wm	Art 5	" B	Dec 12 64
7704	Brandon O	Art 15	" A	Sept 3 64
1800	Breny Jas	178	" K	June 10 64
5134	Brewer Fred	39	" C	Aug 9 64
11685	Brewer Henry	Cav 2	" G	Oct 31 64
10221	Brewer J S	6	" B	Oct 2 64
1365	Brewer S	15	" K	May 25 64
519	Brewer Thos	111	" F	April 13 64
9690	Bryant L A	146	" B	Sept 24 64
8116	Bright ——	104	" C	Sept 8 64
11627	Brightman E	7	" D	Oct 28 64

New York—(*Continued.*)

8415	Brill C	140	Co F	Sept 11 64
6953	Brink C	109	" K	Aug 26 64
9787	Britansky J	52	" E	Sept 26 64
2997	Brobst J	52	" B	July 7 64
9148	Brock W	76	" F	Sept 18 64
6882	Broder H	76	" F	Aug 26 64
12002	Brogan J M	85	" B	Nov 14 64
1324	Brooks W	Cav 10	" E	May 24 64
1221	Brott A	Cav 1	" K	May 19 64
9838	Broscang C	150	" C	Sept 27 64
7517	Brought Chas	Art 14	" I	Sept 1 64
51	Broughten H	77	" H	Mch 16 64
10668	Brown A	140	" K	Oct 11 64
5538	Brown B M	85	" I	Aug 13 64
4112	Brown C	103	" C	July 27 64
9556	Brown C	66	" K	Sept 23 64
11953	Brown C	39	" H	Nov 10 64
11928	Brown C	Cav 1	" M	Nov 8 64
6623	Brown Chas	97	" F	Aug 23 64
7501	Brown D	118	" B	Sept 1 64
3659	Brown E G	Art 7	" L	July 20 64
9674	Brown G H	85	" H	Sept 24 64
7985	Brown G H	63	" C	Sept 6 64
2465	Brown H	72	" C	June 25 64
1879	Brown H	Cav 12		June 12 64
7266	Brown H	39	Co F	Aug 30 64
1887	Brown J	125		June 13 64
7658	Brown J	16		Sept 3 64
6655	Brown James	Cav 4	Co E	Aug 24 64
6691	Brown James	170	" K	Aug 24 64
7526	Brown John	66		Sept 1 64
7615	Brown Wm	5	Co D	Sept 2 64
552	Brown Warren	120	" K	April 14 64
428	Brown Wm	42	" A	April 8 64
7390	Broxmire Thos	15	" E	Aug 31 64
1559	Brumaghin T	125	" E	June 2 64
4475	Bryant D	179	" B	Aug 1 64
7248	Bryant H	82	" F	Aug 30 64
7668	Bryan Wm	Cav 1	" I	Sept 3 64
3814	Buck	24	" H	July 23 64
9975	Buckbier J	Art 7	" F	Sept 28 64
10585	Buckley Wm	122	" D	Oct 10 64
5714	Buel G W	115	" E	Aug 15 64
331	Buel S	42	" B	April 2 64
12417	Buffman L	100	" K	Jan 8 65
7567	Buckley E A	97	" E	Sept 2 64
12509	Burfield C	Citizen		Jan 22 65
5953	Bullier Wm	Cav 23	Co B	Aug 17 64
9642	Bullock E	85	" E	Sept 24 64
4137	Bundy Josh	Art 7	" B	July 28 64
540	Bunn W H	132	" F	April 14 64
9870	Bunnell W	59	" C	Sept 27 64
6452	Burbanks J	85	" D	Aug 22 64
10924	Burdick A	85	" C	Oct 14 64
978	Burdick C	47	" F	May 9 64
2134	Burdick Sam'l	125	" A	June 18 64
7838	Burdock L	Cav 22	" L	Sept 4 61
10016	Burleigh L	Art 6	" F	Sept 29 64
12389	Burley C	3	" B	Jan 4 65
619	Burns E J	Cav 13	Co D	April 19 64
477	Burns Jno	40	" I	April 9 64
924	Burns Jno	99	" H	May 6 64
11881	Burns J	118	" F	Nov 6 64
8745	Burns W	Cav 3	" C	Sept 14 64
5991	Burns Daniel	Art 5	" D	Aug 17 64
7247	Burr H	59	" C	Aug 30 64
6171	Bursha Thos	Art 2	" M	Aug 19 64
3165	Burshen F	54	" C	July 11 64
2875	Burt J	Cav 2	" A	July 4 64
7214	Burton G E	85	" K	Aug 29 64
217	Burton Henry	140		March 29 64
5847	Buserman E	97	Co E	Aug 16 64
6457	Bush E	20	" D	Aug 22 64
1415	Bushnell A	65	" D	May 27 64
487	Bushan J R	132	" G	April 11 64
11366	Bushley Wm	Art 5	" A	Oct 23 64
1360	Buskirk A	47	" A	May 25 64
2047	Buskirt O	13		June 15 64
721	Butler Thos	132	Co G	April 25 64
4189	Butler W	43	" D	July 28 64
12651	Butoff R	124	" C	Feb 13 65
10848	Butler Jas	Cav 2	" D	Oct 13 64
9235	Butter P	126	" D	Sept 19 64
5805	Button Jas	Art 24	" B	Aug 16 64
3446	Butts A	111	" C	July 17 64
9790	Byron J	69	" A	Sept 26 64
1224	Burke W H	120	" I	May 19 64
5196	Burk Jno	69	" K	Aug 10 64
1073	Brower Jno A	Art 5	" D	Oct 17 64
12190	Cademus C	48	" A	June 19 64
10765	Cady Geo	66	" G	Oct 12 64
2377	Cady J	77	" E	June 23 64
10721	Cady J J	14	" H	Oct 11 64
3062	Cane M	132	" E	July 9 64
2136	Cale J	85	" G	June 18 64
9040	Caldham L C	Cav 8	" L	Sept 17 64
11807	Caldwell A	42	" A	Nov 4 64
1530	Caling Ed	7	" H	Oct 26 64
9706	Calkins S V	120	" D	Sept 25 64
8411	Callbrook J	147	" B	Sept 11 64
2348	Cameron John	Cav 1	" H	July 4 64
1770	Camp H	Cav 2	" F	June 9 64
1238	Campbell D	Cav 8	" H	May 20 64
7236	Campbell J	99	" I	Aug 29 64
946	Campbell L R	104	" B	May 7 64
8793	Campbell M	169	" K	Sept 15 64
11294	Campbell W	2	" C	Oct 22 64
7378	Campbell Wm	76	" B	Aug 31 64
12178	Card A	152	" C	Nov 27 64
5034	Card G	109	" F	Aug 8 64
8136	Carbolnes W	39	" C	Sept 8 64
6433	Cardon E	115	" A	Aug 22 64
7555	Carey D	57	" A	Sept 2 64
11512	Carey F	65	" E	Oct 26 64
372	Carl Josh	14	" A	April 5 64
5545	Carl L	120	" G	Aug 13 64
12339	Carle ——→	Cav 1	" D	Dec 26 64
12268	Carmac F	2	" D	Dec 12 64

New York—(*Continued.*)

7655	Carmer A	85	Co B	Sept 3 64
11640	Carney M	Cav 9	" L	Oct 30 64
8470	Carnehan Chas	Bat 24		Sept 11 64
5258	Carney D J	132	Co G	Aug 10 64
9379	Carney Francis	Art 2	" C	Sept 27 64
3102	Carnes P	Cav 13	" B	July 10 64
10806	Carpenter Frank	Art 7	" C	Oct 12 64
8854	Carpenter G	7	" D	Sept 15 64
4632	Carpenter H A	Art 2	" A	Aug 3 64
3916	Carpenter L	Art 2	" B	July 25 64
3977	Carpenter M B	85	" B	July 26 64
6743	Carr Andrew	22		Aug 24 64
3859	Carr D	25	Co B	July 24 64
531	Carr F	Art 3	" K	April 16 64
6470	Carr Geo A	Art 3	" K	Aug 22 64
5673	Carr Wm	125	" K	Aug 14 64
6304	Carr Wm	97	" E	Aug 20 64
4139	Carroll James	69	" A	July 28 64
10293	Carroll P	95	" E	Oct 4 64
2061	Carroll F	132	" F	June 15 64
12015	Carroll W	42	" D	Nov 15 64
8563	Carson J G	100	" B	Sept 12 64
8023	Cart M A	118	" F	Sept 6 64
1937	Carter A	146	" E	June 15 64
5212	Carter Ed	Art 7	" A	Aug 10 64
6433	Carson E	115	" A	Aug 22 64
11640	Carney M	Cav 9	" L	Oct 30 64
8479	Case A F	Cav 8	" A	Sept 11 64
8377	Case E	Cav 8	" M	Sept 10 64
6296	Case H J	Cav 12	" A	Aug 20 64
3832	Casey J	100	" G	July 23 64
5271	Casey P	174	" A	Aug 10 64
8241	Cassells Saml	52	" D	Sept 11 64
2643	Cassine John S	Bat 24		June 29 64
1177	Castano J	104	Co H	May 16 64
10482	Cashel C	Art 7	" I	Oct 7 64
1785	Castle J W	147	" H	June 10 64
6128	Castle Wm	Art 1	" E	Aug 19 64
1534	Cavenaugh John	146	" H	June 1 64
5971	Cæsar D	Art 7	" B	July 7 64
1456	Centre A	16	" A	May 29 64
9632	Chaffe R A	Cav 5	" H	Sept 24 64
11101	Chambers J	140	" F	Oct 18 64
6557	Chambers J	147	" E	Aug 23 64
5360	Chamberlain C	154	" D	Aug 16 64
4768	Champlin W	85	" E	Aug 5 64
4726	Chapel A	85	" D	Aug 4 64
5478	Chapel R	Cav 6	" A	Aug 13 64
5831	Chappell A	39	" E	Aug 16 64
10748	Chappell E	76	" K	Oct 12 64
3222	Chapin F	Cav 24	" A	July 12 64
3236	Chapman J	85	" K	July 14 64
1393	Chase A	111	" H	June 3 64
4356	Chase D	98	" I	Aug 6 74
5439	Chase N F	85	" K	Aug 13 64
7450	Chase S M	Art 4	" D	Sept 1 64
2157	Chatbrim H	Bat 23		June 18 64
8033	Chatman C	Art 6	" I	Sept 6 64
6658	Chatman S M	2	" F	Aug 23 64

9919	Chatterton J	95	Co B	Sept 28 64
7865	Chagnon E	Cav 12	" F	Sept 25 64
7189	Chesley P S	Cav 10	" G	Aug 29 64
7539	Chestey Jno	174	" G	Sept 2 64
10680	Chickchester C H	57	" I	Oct 11 64
6317	Childs A	85	" I	Aug 20 64
4141	Childs Wm	73	" A	July 28 64
11555	Chile H	47	" E	Oct 27 64
10612	Christey J	Drag 1	" I	Oct 10 64
5824	Church C L	Cav 5	" C	Aug 16 64
5413	Church F M	Cav 2	" D	Aug 12 64
4257	Churchill C	99	" I	July 29 64
3449	Clancey Robb	164	" E	July 17 64
2114	Clark A	85	" E	June 17 64
5167	Clark Chas	Cav 12	" F	Aug 19 64
2947	Clark F	Cav 8	" B	July 6 64
12114	Clark J	Cav 8	" K	Nov 21 64
12403	Clark J B	Art 7	" L	Jan 6 65
2154	Clark Jno	48	" D	June 18 64
11304	Clark L	100	" G	Oct 22 64
10611	Clark P	42	" B	Oct 10 64
5802	Clemens A	Cav 15	" F	Aug 15 64
6909	Clements H	65	" F	Aug 26 64
11028	Cleaver W	43	" F	Oct 16 64
813	Clifford Chas	16	" B	April 30 64
740	Clifford Geo	132	" K	April 26 64
6494	Cline B	85	" K	Aug 22 64
11437	Cline J W	85	" K	Oct 24 64
12021	Cline S M	Drag 1	" H	Nov 15 64
9721	Cline W	76	" F	Sept 25 64
6243	Clingman J	150	" L	Aug 20 64
12471	Clinton R	102	" D	Jan 17 65
1497	Clute H V	Bat 24		May 31 64
5955	Clyen J P	147	Co B	Aug 17 64
7343	Coanas W	73	" D	Aug 31 64
5365	Coburn C	122	" E	Aug 11 64
10129	Coburn A	116	" H	Oct 1 64
933	Coddington W	99	" H	May 7 64
7992	Cochran Jno	126	" K	Sept 6 64
11775	Cochran M	42	" A	Nov 3 64
9237	Cochson J	140	" C	Sept 19 64
10651	Cogger M	125	" B	Oct 11 64
3715	Cogswell L	Art 6	" M	July 21 64
10362	Cole E B	Art 14	" B	Sept 30 64
8456	Cole Geo	Cav 12	" A	Sept 11 64
6241	Cole Jno J	Cav 5	" M	Aug 20 64
5890	Cole M	Art 15	" M	Aug 16 64
4142	Cole R S	152	" H	July 28 64
11589	Cole F	109	" K	Oct 28 64
4519	Cole Wm	61	" H	Aug 2 64
7855	Coleby A	Cav 1	" M	Sept 5 64
10553	Coleman I	Art 2	" I	Oct 9 64
3070	Collins A	98	" B	July 9 64
7557	Colwell D C	Art 2	" E	Sept 2 64
5743	Colwell J	120	" A	Aug 15 64
6969	Comstock G E	Art 2	" A	Aug 27 64
3539	Condon Thos	Cav 22	" F	July 18 64
4320	Cone R	8	" A	July 30 64
9619	Conely John	125	" K	Sept 23 64

New York—(*Continued.*)

5528	Conely Pat	164	Co G	Aug 13 64
8919	Conger James	49	" A	Sept 13 64
11347	Corvier Chas	Cav 1	" C	Oct 25 64
2160	Conkin A	69	" A	June 19 64
10699	Conlin Daniel	5	" A	Oct 11 64
11513	Concll T	139	" C	Oct 23 64
2033	Connelly F	52		June 15 64
10006	Conners E	43	Co D	Sept 20 64
4025	Connor Henry	52	" D	July 23 64
936	Conners John	99	" D	May 7 64
7842	Cosgrove F	76	" H	Sept 4 64
11093	Cook C H	Cav 6	" E	Oct 13 64
11240	Cook Geo	65	" E	Oct 21 64
7485	Cook G W	146	" E	Sept 1 64
5228	Coombs B	69	" A	Aug 10 64
10626	Coombs J	96	" I	Oct 10 64
2195	Coons F	52	" B	June 10 64
11418	Coom Geo F	65	" K	Oct 24 64
3692	Cooney F	14	" G	July 21 64
10723	Cooney T	82	" E	Oct 11 64
5816	Cooper James	Cav 22	" G	Aug 16 64
12274	Cooper N	Cav 22	" F	Dec 13 64
1150	Copeland J	106	" I	May 16 64
1778	Corbit B F	Bat 24		June 9 64
10529	Corbit John	24	Co C	Oct 8 64
6662	Corless R	Art 7	" E	Aug 24 64
7182	Cornelius J	Cav 12	" F	Aug 20 64
1995	Corry P	99	" A	June 15 64
6729	Correll O B	Cav 1	" D	Aug 24 64
11331	Cornell P	100	" C	Oct 23 64
11347	Corrier Chas	Cav 1	" C	Oct 23 64
7471	Castin J	Cav 22	" C	Sept 1 64
12767	Corselman G	152	" K	Mch 13 65
7786	Cottin Z T	85	" E	Sept 4 64
5329	Countryman ——	120	" A	Aug 11 64
3899	Courtney W	Cav 12	" A	July 24 64
8976	Cowen J	4	" I	Sept 7 64
7058	Cox D	Cav 1	" H	Aug 23 64
7675	Coy Jno H	Cav 1	" L	Sept 3 64
11158	Coyne M	98	" H	Oct 19 64
7274	Cozin J	82	" E	Aug 30 64
3601	Craft B	48	" D	July 21 64
8221	Craig J	139	" H	Sept 8 64
8328	Crandall D	85	" E	Sept 10 64
8329	Crandall J	85	" C	Sept 10 64
2950	Crandall R	115	" I	July 6 64
3061	Crandle J F	120	" K	July 9 64
334	Craven J	134	" E	April 2 64
3432	Crawford Jno	61	" B	July 17 64
12649	Cripman S	2	" K	Feb 13 65
8733	Crissman Josh	140	" F	Sept 14 64
11471	Crine C	Cav 6	" C	Oct 26 64
2311	Criswell J	Cav 12	" F	June 22 64
2882	Crocker J	93	" E	July 3 64
5836	Cromark J	77	" B	Aug 16 64
2644	Crompter Jas	14	" F	June 20 64
8695	Cromwell T	Art 6		Sept 14 64
8324	Crosby M	Bat 24		July 14 64
2273	Crouse Geo	Bat 24		June 21 64
11297	Crowley S	2	Co B	Oct 22 64
5003	Cuff S	14	" E	Aug 17 64
7159	Culbert Wm	89	" D	Aug 29 64
4119	Culver N L	Bat 24		July 23 64
8003	Cunnings ——	22	Co D	Sept 16 64
11279	Cron F	115	" D	Oct 21 64
5473	Cunningham J	170	" E	Aug 13 64
6721	Cunningham J	41	" I	Aug 24 64
1447	Cunningham Wm	45	" B	May 29 64
1224	Curley P	125	" E	May 19 64
3327	Currey John	146	" B	July 20 64
4453	Custerman F	47	" G	Aug 1 64
9540	Cute A	Cav 8	" A	Sept 22 64
9311	Cuter C F	2	" G	Sept 23 64
12431	Cutler J P	99	" B	Jany 11 65
4346	Cutler Wm	59	" B	Aug 6 64
8193	Daher G	66	" D	Sept 8 64
8350	Daley T	42	" I	Sept 13 64
10711	Damon J D	Art 7	" K	Oct 11 64
8577	Dailey Wm	Cav 5	" I	July 19 64
11122	Daniels W O	76	" K	Oct 13 64
5509	Daratt Louis	111	" G	Aug 14 64
1480	Daly Jno	99		May 30 64
6341	Dawson J	47	Co K	Aug 23 64
8095	Darley J	Art 14	" D	Sept 7 64
6723	Darling G H	Cav 18	" F	Aug 24 64
5083	Darling J	Cav 4	" C	Aug 8 64
7362	Dart Chas W	85	" C	Sept 2 64
6404	Davidson M	Cav 15	" M	Aug 21 64
6301	Davis D	164	" G	Aug 21 64
6037	Davis G	1	" H	Aug 13 64
1383	Davis H	85	" I	May 23 64
7370	Davis H	Art 1	" D	Sept 3 64
8039	Davis H J	85	" C	Sept 7 64
931	Davis H R	99	" I	May 8 64
12052	Davis H T	Cav 5	" G	Feb 14 65
5120	Davis J	85	" H	Aug 9 64
7304	Davis J J	43	" B	Sept 5 64
11117	Davis Jno	47	" E	Nov 5 64
10241	Davis P	94	" I	Oct 3 64
10018	Davy J J	Cav 2	" A	Sept 20 64
5328	Day J W	32	" D	Aug 11 64
8866	Dean	13	" E	July 21 64
9400	Dean J	Cav 8	" G	Sept 21 64
2305	Dean Jno	Art 6	" K	June 22 64
10523	Debrass J	9	" A	Oct 8 64
9958	Decker A	82	" I	Sept 28 64
3300	Deckman J G	134	" B	July 20 64
7305	Declercy W E	Cav 22	" E	Sept 1 64
10355	Dedrich P	9	" K	Oct 9 64
12020	Deman W	26	" E	Dec 23 64
7059	Dessotell J	98	" D	Aug 23 64
7935	Deet F	90	" D	Sept 5 64
4400	Deiffer Louis	40	" H	July 31 64
4014	Degammo J	43	" E	Aug 6 64
6233	Degroff C	115	" H	Aug 20 64
12074	Degroot W	Art 7	" I	Nov 13 64
12228	Devit Chas	Art 7	" G	Dec 5 64
7261	Delane M	111	" C	Aug 30 64

New York—(*Continued.*)

11206	Delany C	52	Co H	Oct 20 64
12271	Demara Jno	108	" M	Dec 12 64
5709	Demeres D	5	" A	Aug 15 64
10123	Demerest H H	Cav 2	" M	Sept 30 64
8761	Demhart W	111	" F	Sept 14 64
9592	Demming F M	83	" H	Sept 23 64
7278	Dempsey Jno	85	" B	Aug 30 64
7623	Demming L	85	" D	Sept 2 64
9930	Dennis A A	106	" H	Sept 28 64
1439	Dennis Thos	132	" G	May 31 64
4090	Dennison J	Cav 12	" A	July 27 64
12257	Dennison J	155	" I	Dec 10 64
7471	Dennison W	Art 14	" M	Sept 1 64
3259	Denorf F	147	" B	July 13 64
2320	Densamore S F	115	" G	June 22 64
6324	Densmore E	85	" K	Aug 21 64
12603	Desmond D	82	" C	Feby 6 65
1799	Deveny H	99	" I	June 10 64
7593	Devlin A	Art 1	" M	Sept 2 64
5502	Devlin J	Cav 12	" F	Aug 13 64
10077	Dewise Dennis	7	" E	Sept 30 64
2839	De Witt S C	120	" E	July 3 64
9334	Dewitt J S	48	" H	Sept 20 64
9855	Dickinson N	152	" K	Sept 27 64
10597	Dickerman W B	Art 6	" A	Oct 10 64
11854	Difendorf R	Art 2	" L	Nov 6 64
2234	Dykeman F	47	" C	June 20 64
10089	Dingle J	122	" G	Sept 30 64
1821	Dingley C	Cav 4	" A	June 10 64
8588	Dighard F	Cav 15	" A	Sept 12 64
8245	Doan A	85	" C	Sept 9 64
3773	Dodson E	85	" C	July 22 64
1959	Dolan J	48	" E	June 14 64
11805	Dolan M	Cav 6	" F	Nov 4 64
5638	Dolan P	30	" I	Aug 14 64
11884	Domick E	Art 4	" E	Nov 6 64
4886	Donaghen J	16	" A	Aug 6 64
2809	Doud Daniel	155	" I	July 3 64
6149	Dondall B	111	" G	Aug 19 64
11357	Donely M	10	" F	Oct 23 64
3031	Donovan J	Art 14		July 9 64
229	Donley E J	M Rifles 2	Co K	Mch 29 64
12718	Donnell W	Art 4	" A	Mch 2 65
655	Donnelly Jas C	Cav 2	" D	April 21 64
10102	Doolittle W	76	" D	Sept 30 64
3533	Dorchester H S, V S	Cav 12		July 13 64
12715	Dormity M	Citizen		Mch 1 65
10320	Dotsey J	139	Co E	Oct 4 64
9416	Dougherty E S	85	" I	Sept 21 64
4630	Dougherty J	9	" C	Aug 3 64
2052	Dougherty O	99	" I	June 16 64
10992	Doughty E S	48	" A	Oct 16 64
9208	Downey H	11	" I	Sept 19 64
5735	Downey J A	85	" H	Aug 15 64
7275	Douglas M	48	" D	Aug 30 64
10353	Douglas P	147	" C	Oct 5 64
6149	Dondall B	111	" G	Aug 19 64
2361	Doyle Jno	Cav 5	" G	June 27 64
4827	Doyle Jas	130	" H	Aug 5 64
9112	Doyle W	Art 7	Co I	Sept 18 64
9378	Dow M	125	" H	Sept 20 64
3929	Drake D W	Art 2	" H	July 25 64
2317	Drake D B	158	" F	June 23 64
699	Driscoll ——	52	" B	April 23 64
2826	Drum A	155	" A	July 3 64
9857	Druse I	Art 15	" D	Sept 20 64
394	Derfee Jas	99	" H	April 6 64
3063	Dumfray Dennis	100	" I	July 9 64
3490	Dudley J C	Cav 10	" H	July 17 64
3957	Ducll R	Art 6	" F	July 25 64
5264	Dumond A	85	" E	Aug 10 64
5810	Dumond C	120	" A	Aug 16 64
6773	Dumond S	5	" B	Aug 25 64
10144	Dumond F	146	" A	Oct 1 64
9116	Dunlap C	85	" B	Sept 18 64
8639	Duane T	95	" E	Sept 13 64
8158	Dritman Wm	42	" C	Sept 11 64
6905	Duble Henry	61	" F	Aug 26 64
6087	Dule Levi	5	" B	Aug 18 64
10948	Duger P	67	" A	Oct 14 64
11104	Dunham R	Art 14	" G	Oct 18 64
7621	Dunn J	40	" G	Sept 2 64
8244	Dunn L H	Eng 50	" E	Sept 9 64
5732	Dunn Jas	88	" D	Aug 15 64
1695	Dunn J H	99	" I	June 7 64
10948	Devine P	67	" A	Oct 14 64
123	Dunbar Thos	2	" F	Mch 23 64
3234	Dunn M	99	" I	July 12 64
919	Dunn Owen	126	" H	May 6 64
1033	Dunn Pat	149	" A	May 11 64
3584	Dunning Wm	132	" G	July 19 64
2972	Dunsham Abr	120	" C	July 7 64
7554	Durand H	82	" K	Sept 2 64
4833	Durand Jas E	Cav 10	" E	Aug 6 64
9316	Dyer S	Art 7	" D	July 24 64
4086	Dyer Jno S	Cav 10	" M	Sept 25 64
3574	Dykeman D	Cav 22	" F	July 9 64
12271	Dunaram Jno	108	" F	Dec 12 64
9033	Earl C	85	" D	Sept 17 64
2443	Earl H	174	" H	June 25 64
3203	Eastern Thos	Cav 5	" L	July 12 64
3919	Eastman Wm	10	" C	July 25 64
4239	Easton E E	52	" F	July 29 64
4410	Eastwood E	Bat 24		July 31 64
7149	Eber Jas	76	Co B	Sept 1 64
3552	Edmonds L	Cav 5	" M	July 18 64
4283	Edwards S	52	" F	July 30 64
7309	Edson John	64	" D	Aug 30 64
7850	Edsen W	105	" E	Sept 5 64
2728	Egan John	125	" D	July 1 64
9454	Egerton H	Art 14	" L	Sept 20 64
2319	Elberson J	Cav 10	" E	June 21 64
7420	Eldeny B	146	" E	Aug 31 64
6407	Eldred H	125	" K	Aug 22 64
8597	Eldred I	76	" F	July 19 64
10309	Ellis J	2	" H	Oct 4 64
12071	Ellis P M	2	" E	Nov 17 64
9736	Ellis C	85	" G	Sept 25 64

New York—(*Continued.*)

7204	Ellis R H	76	Co F	Aug 29 64
8960	Elliott F F	76	" B	Sept 16 64
8163	Elliott L	Cav 3	" I	Sept 8 64
1107	Ellis Wm	119	" F	May 15 64
3526	Ells Perry	106	" I	Nov 18 64
8274	Ellison W	95	" F	Sept 9 64
6343	Elster James	Art 7	" E	Aug 21 64
9564	Elwell W	47	" B	Sept 23 64
8152	Emery C Z	48	" G	Sept 8 64
6096	Engal W	39	" B	Aug 18 64
9086	English G	Cav 7	" I	Sept 13 64
9961	Eagh John	Art 7	" E	Sept 28 64
2454	Easley W H	Cav 2	" H	June 25 64
10375	Erst J	51	" H	Oct 4 64
2731	Ethear J	Cav 13	" E	July 1 64
9459	Evans Franklin	140	" D	Sept 21 64
12365	Evans L	Art 7	" I	Dec 31 64
6786	Evens B	66	" B	Aug 25 64
6429	Everett J	58	" K	Aug 22 64
11263	Everly G	108	" I	Oct 21 64
11362	Faggerty C	Cav 2	" C	Oct 23 64
1321	Fallam Pat	Art 3	" K	June 3 64
11576	Famcle E	43	" D	Oct 28 64
7666	Fairfax Chas	111	" A	Sept 3 64
12091	Farland T	6	" I	Nov 19 64
11247	Farley W	Art 14	" F	Oct 21 64
10259	Farrell Jas	100	" C	Oct 3 64
5840	Farn C	169	" G	Aug 16 64
5946	Fairman H B	Art 6	" M	Aug 17 64
6995	Fawry Jno	Art 2	" C	Aug 27 64
7415	Face J	115	" E	Aug 31 64
10057	Fareclough R	2	" F	Sept 30 64
9609	Ferris C	100	" E	Sept 23 64
8439	Ferris Robt	Art 14	" I	Sept 3 64
3452	Ferris Jno	5	" E	July 17 64
4760	Felter F	69	" C	Aug 5 64
7260	Ferguson H C	14	" C	Aug 30 64
7498	Ferguson M	39	" G	Sept 1 64
7412	Felton Geo	164	" C	Aug 31 64
8407	Feasel H	Art 7	" F	Sept 3 64
9779	Ferguson J M	Cav 15	" G	Sept 26 64
12507	Finnerty P	155	" G	Jan 22 65
247	Fich Jno	8	" M	Mch 30 64
3869	Fincucum Jno	96	" E	July 24 64
6192	Fields F	Art 2	" L	Aug 19 64
6656	Finch Henry	Cav 22	" L	Aug 24 64
8699	Finch Jas	Cav 22	" L	Sept 14 64
10072	Findley Andrew	70	" D	Sept 20 64
11482	Finlay A	Art 7	" D	Oct 26 64
6215	Fish L V	Art 7	" B	Aug 20 64
4412	Fish H	179	" A	July 31 64
5752	Fish F	52	" K	Aug 15 64
9723	Fish J W	Cav 12	" C	Sept 25 64
279	Fish Wm	17	" H	April 1 64
11651	Fisher C P	124	" C	Oct 30 64
10049	Fisher Conrad	Cav 1	" E	Sept 29 64
5104	Fisher Daniel	45	" F	Aug 9 64
2389	Fisher D	125	" K	June 24 64
12542	Fisher H	59	" K	Jan 27 65
10966	Fisher L	39	Co D	Oct 15 64
10171	Fitch A	3	" F	Oct 1 64
4819	Fitch C	Bat 24		Aug 5 64
3569	Fitzgerald N	111	Co C	July 19 64
6453	Fitzgerald Thos	Bat 24		Aug 22 64
12400	Fitzpatrick	Cav 10	Co G	Jan 5 65
6961	Fitzpatrick O	100	" E	Aug 27 64
6500	Flagler Wm	Art 7	" M	Aug 22 64
7452	Flanigan Ed	Art 7	" C	Sept 1 64
5558	Flanigan P	40	" D	Aug 13 64
8583	Fleming P	Cav 22	" E	Sept 12 64
190	Fletcher Wm	Cav 13	" G	Mch 27 64
12537	Flintkoff F	102	" E	Jan 27 65
774	Florence B	99	" H	April 28 64
7690	Fluke J	76	" K	Sept 3 64
8379	Flynn J	Bat 24		Sept 10 64
11958	Flynn J	13	Co K	Nov 11 64
9212	Flynn Wm	71	" E	Sept 19 64
9283	Fohnsbelly C	169	" A	Sept 19 64
8042	Folden H	Art 7	" B	Sept 6 64
3987	Folet D	Cav 1	" A	July 26 64
10841	Follard Jas	Cav 1	" I	Oct 13 64
4807	Foulke Peter	100	" F	Aug 5 64
175	Ford E B	132	" K	Mch 26 64
7344	Foreber A	Cav 13	" F	Aug 31 64
11736	Foley F	77	" B	Nov 2 64
1589	Forget G H	85	" K	June 3 64
2470	Foster H	Cav 1	" B	June 25 64
759	Foster J	Cav 5	" G	April 27 64
408	Foster James	Cav 2	" D	April 6 64
6115	Fox A	49	" K	Aug 19 64
11173	Fox D	152	" A	Oct 19 64
2830	Fox M	Art 15	" K	July 3 64
9432	Frahworth F	57	" I	Sept 21 64
8393	Frake S	11	" G	Sept 10 64
2863	Francis P L	Cav 2	" H	July 4 64
9917	Franklin J	39	" I	Sept 28 64
4227	Franklin J C	Cav 22	" L	July 29 64
10484	Fraser J H	73	" C	Oct 7 64
11353	Freilander C	Cav 2	" B	Oct 23 64
4820	Freburg E	52	" F	Aug 5 64
6619	Fredinburg Jas	85	" H	Aug 23 64
6668	Free C	30	" B	Aug 24 64
11368	French J	Cav 2	" H	Oct 23 64
10963	French James	Cav 22	" G	Oct 15 64
6998	French John C	Cav 5	" H	Aug 27 64
1395	Freiser John	111	" K	May 26 64
5125	Frisby W L	111	" B	Aug 9 64
11421	Frositer F	Cav 16	" L	Oct 24 64
3806	Fuller A	49	" K	July 22 64
11638	Fuller C	52	" H	Oct 30 64
3713	Fuller J B	85	" F	July 21 64
11050	Fuller N	18	" C	Oct 17 64
10295	Fuller W	122	" A	Oct 4 64
10323	Funday F	39	" B	Oct 4 64
10140	Fricks A	62	" L	Oct 1 64
2472	Gagan Thos	85	" C	June 25 64
5773	Gale George	2	" A	Aug 15 64
1148	Gallagher G	Cav 5	" D	May 16 64

New York — (*Continued:*)

6106	Gallagher P	47	Co D	Aug 18 64
4699	Gallewin Thos	Art 20	" F	Aug 4 64
10489	Galush W	Cav 5	" F	Oct 7 64
7673	Gandley J	Cav 8	" F	Sept 3 64
6993	Gannon S	Art 7	" E	Aug 27 64
385	Gansey ——	94	" B	April 5 64
1133	Gardner H	52	" A	Oct 19 64
5251	Gardner R	155	" K	Aug 19 64
982	Gardner H	132	" E	May 9 64
13 3	Gardner O	149	" C	May 24 64
9206	Gardner Wm	Cav 7	" I	Sept 13 64
7926	Garlock Jno	46	" B	Sept 5 64
8982	Gaman J	126	" H	Sept 17 64
8333	Garney C	40	" A	Sept 10 64
7033	Garry Jas	95	" C	Aug 27 64
2688	Garrison J	65	" H	June 30 64
7216	Gartill H	Cav 22	" L	Aug 29 64
7044	Gartland ——	109		Aug 27 64
94	Garbey Jno	32	Co K	Mch 22 64
10339	Gatiff H	82	" D	Oct 8 64
5270	Garette C	134	" G	Aug 10 64
6808	Gear Jas	142	" A	Aug 23 64
7120	Gees A	95	" I	Aug 23 64
7930	Geiser Chas	39	" D	Sept 5 64
8878	Gemminge J	Art 6		Sept 16 64
7650	Ge ler Jas	65	Co E	Sept 8 64
6728	Glan Benj	11		Aug 24 64
10967	Gibbs Chas	Art 4	Co B	Oct 15 64
6259	Gibbs M H	Cav 22	" E	Aug 20 64
3218	Gibson J	170	" A	July 12 64
12017	Gibson J	82	" I	Nov 15 64
6912	Giddings J	115	" H	Aug 26 64
2042	Gifford H N	111		June 17 64
4185	Gilbert E	48	Co D	July 23 64
10925	Gilbert E	Cav 22	" B	Oct 14 64
1834	Gilbert J	111	" K	June 11 64
11270	Gillis G	85	" G	Oct 21 64
10160	Gill Jno F	Cav 1	" B	Oct 1 64
2413	Gill Jas	111	" K	June 24 64
3339	Gillen M	107	" E	July 15 64
7898	Gillett Wm	85	" F	Sept 5 64
12345	Gilmore M	17	" B	Dec 27 64
3106	Gimrich P, Bugl'r	Cav 2	" K	July 10 64
1678	Gleick Wm	Cav 1	" A	June 6 64
3946	Gleason Thos	97	" D	July 25 64
10336	Goaner F	16	" K	Oct 4 64
2553	Goffney J	104	" D	June 27 64
8639	Goldsmith Wm	2	" F	Sept 13 64
2962	Gond E	104	" C	July 6 64
7088	Goodbread J F	147	" B	Aug 28 64
12529	Goodell F	122	" K	Jan 26 65
4145	Goodenough Jas	140	" D	July 23 64
7342	Goodman J A	154	" A	Aug 31 64
3042	Goodrich F	154	" B	July 8 64
4561	Goodrich Geo	Cav 2	" D	Aug 2 64
1415	Gorman G	Art 3	" K	June 17 64
8223	Goodnow J	64	" I	Sept 9 64
12304	Golt C	49	" D	Feb 7 65
2203	Goss Jas	132	" G	June 19 64
8822	Gould Richard	61	Co D	July 14 64
11985	Gough H	146	" B	Nov 13 64
8703	Gower J	147	" B	July 22 64
10439	Graff F	Cav 14	" M	Oct 8 64
9347	Graham J	Cav 15	" L	Sept 20 64
7089	Graham Wm	Cav 12	" F	Aug 28 64
10093	Grampy M J	52	" D	Sept 30 64
2640	Grandine D S	111	" E	June 29 64
3333	Granger A	93	" I	July 20 64
5798	Granger John	107	" H	Aug 15 64
4131	Granner H	62	" I	July 28 64
3212	Grant C	96	" B	July 12 64
3875	Grant James	125	" K	July 24 64
6449	Grant J K	9	" D	Aug 22 64
9511	Grass H	42	" G	Sept 22 64
12200	Graves E	Cav 2	" I	Dec 1 64
4787	Graves W F	2	" H	Aug 5 64
5354	Gray John	Art 6	" H	Aug 11 64
1342	Green E	85	" C	May 24 64
12522	Green H W	146	" E	Jany 26 65
10277	Green J H	109	" K	Oct 3 64
6863	Greer John	76	" B	Aug 26 64
5202	Green O	154	" G	Aug 10 64
2184	Greenman J S	Cav 2	" D	June 19 64
7634	Gregory A D L	120	" E	Sept 2 64
4322	Gregory John	61	" E	July 30 64
7492	Gregory L	Art 7	" M	Sept 1 64
7201	Grenals H	70	" F	Aug 29 64
11502	Griffin J B	Cav 7	" D	Oct 26 64
8316	Griffin John	40	" H	July 23 64
5763	Griffin N	52	" F	Aug 15 64
3101	Griffith A	Bat 24		July 10 64
11185	Griffith E P	85	Co D	Oct 19 64
8351	Gilmartin A	69		Sept 10 64
8315	Griswold B F	109	Co F	July 23 64
1220	Groncly M	47	" E	May 19 64
10914	Gross C	63	" E	Oct 14 64
9553	Gross J	140	" I	Sept 24 64
9931	Gross J	151	" B	Sept 29 64
3092	Groven Josh	49	" F	July 10 64
10997	Grundy R J	73	" G	Oct 16 64
10813	Gunan Wm	Cav 8	" D	Oct 12 64
5867	Gundaloch F	95	" A	Aug 16 64
1459	Gunn Calvin	Cav 12	" G	May 29 64
6651	Gunnahan J	85	" G	Aug 23 64
9372	Gunnell Jno	Cav 2	" B	Sept 20 64
8317	Guile A L	154	" C	Sept 10 64
12145	Guyer F	Art 15	" A	Nov 24 64
12328	Gwin Chas	69	" H	Dec 24 64
6495	Hack J	12	" K	Aug 22 64
10194	Hackett C	43	" C	Oct 2 64
2323	Hackett ——	Cav 12	" F	June 28 64
7113	Hackett J	Art 7	" D	Aug 28 64
6376	Hagate Jacob	Cav 10	" F	Aug 26 64
4677	Hager ——	52	" H	Aug 4 64
3646	Hager J	59	" B	July 20 64
6369	Hagerty Wm	147	" E	Aug 26 64
8275	Hadden C	20		Sept 9 64
473	Haddish T	14	Co A	April 9 64

New York — (*Continued.*)

7721	Hadsell F	Art 2	Co L	Sept 3 64
8024	Haight J E	Art 8	" H	Sept 16 64
2887	Hair G	89	" A	July 4 64
11036	Halbert A H	85	" D	Oct 16 64
3342	Halbert L	1	" D	July 15 64
170	Haline Gotfried	Cav 12	" K	Mch 26 64
11310	Hall C	Drag 1	" H	Oct 28 64
2214	Hall Chas	Cav 12	" K	June 20 64
5003	Hall Chas	109	" G	Aug 8 64
12370	Hall C W	40	" I	Jan 1 65
870	Hall Ed	111	" C	May 3 64
2846	Hall Jas	Cav 9	" E	July 3 64
4459	Hall Jno	109	" E	Aug 1 64
9661	Hall S	Cav 14	" L	Sept 21 64
7731	Hall W C	Cav 8	" K	Sept 3 64
7819	Hall Wm	2	" K	Sept 4 64
10865	Hallembeck S	145	" B	Oct 13 64
4175	Halloway J	146	" D	July 28 64
9253	Halpin P	68		Sept 19 64
11049	Halper Jno	134	Co F	Oct 17 64
8213	Hamilton H	132	" D	Sept 8 64
12405	Hamilton J	111	" G	Jan 6 65
10032	Hamilton Jno	Art 6	" L	Sept 29 64
6601	Hamilton Thos	Art 6	" L	Aug 23 64
5634	Hammond M	66	" G	Aug 14 64
1104	Hand L	Cav 5	" C	May 15 64
9862	Hanlon Thos	180	" F	Sept 27 64
11076	Hand H S	169	" A	Oct 17 64
3589	Hanks J	Cav 1	" L	July 19 64
3857	Hanley D	22	" B	July 24 64
12448	Hanley Wm	29	" D	Jan 13 65
6009	Hancock R	Cav 2	" D	Aug 17 64
1207	Hanor Frank	12	" G	May 19 64
6432	Hansom C	67	" F	Aug 22 64
11149	Hardy J	96	" C	Oct 19 64
9363	Hardy J	Cav 5	" I	Sept 20 64
10101	Hardy W	95	" E	Sept 30 64
7929	Hannom Jno	164	" I	Sept 5 64
1411	Haines Philip	85	" I	May 27 64
2383	Harp M	95	" I	June 23 64
8323	Harper J	126	" G	Sept 10 64
10115	Hanen F J	52	" C	Oct 1 64
5550	Harris C	63	" E	Aug 13 64
5482	Haynes H	Cav 5	" I	Aug 13 64
6784	Harris Thos	85	" C	Aug 25 64
4056	Harris V S	Cav 8	" M	July 27 64
1378	Harrington Pat	71	" D	May 26 64
10384	Harrison Henry	76	" K	Oct 5 64
8362	Harrison O	14	" K	Sept 10 64
2326	Harry A	143	" K	June 26 64
4705	Hart D R	109	" D	Aug 4 64
5748	Hart J	Cav 12	" F	Aug 15 64
11524	Hart J	Art 7	" K	Oct 21 64
8287	Hart S	146	" B	Sept 9 64
8337	Hart S	Cav 22	" M	Sept 10 64
7432	Hartman J N	40	" H	Aug 31 64
766	Harty John	Cav 2	" M	April 27 64
10312	Hasket A	39	" I	Oct 12 64
8758	Hasler M	110	" C	Sept 14 64
11947	Hass J F	49	Co F	Nov 10 64
1891	Hathaway Chas	Bat 24		June 13 64
10878	Hause John	Cav 1	Co L	Oct 13 64
2262	Haveland H	Art 6		June 21 64
11461	Havens Geo	22	Co G	Oct 25 64
3826	Havens H	141	" A	July 23 64
4814	Havens S	104	" A	Aug 5 64
8523	Haverslight H	66	" E	July 13 64
11629	Hawley W L	Cav 2	" D	Oct 23 64
10646	Hawley F	76	" E	Oct 11 64
5355	Hayatt L P	Cav 1	" A	Aug 11 64
11786	Hayes C	2	" F	Nov 4 64
8022	Hayes Edward	69	" G	Sept 6 64
9080	Hayes J	6	" A	Sept 18 64
10904	Hayes James	39	" E	Oct 14 64
1264	Hayes P	85	" H	Oct 21 64
9134	Head Thos	Art 6	" A	Sept 18 64
3594	Haynes W C	Art 6	" G	July 16 64
10220	Hayner L	125	" H	Oct 2 64
10632	Heacock R	66	" H	Oct 11 64
3581	Hecker C	47	" C	July 19 64
6181	Heddle Wm	Cav 5	" M	Aug 19 64
3155	Hefferman D	132	" C	July 11 64
8135	Helafsattan J	63	" K	Sept 8 64
11382	Helf J C	Cav 1	" G	Oct 24 64
6828	Heller D	Art 14		Aug 25 64
7330	Henderson N J	85	Co K	Aug 30 64
10206	Hendfest J B	100	" K	Oct 2 64
11380	Henertes B	15	" I	Oct 24 64
11733	Hilbert G	5	" E	Nov 2 64
8336	Hennesy M	Art 3	" K	Sept 10 64
7196	Henyon W	85	" H	Aug 29 64
10870	Heratage Thos	8	" C	Oct 13 64
196	Herget Jno	111	" A	Mch 27 64
3119	Hermance F C	Stm 20	" A	July 10 64
11996	Hermance J	100	" C	Nov 13 64
4495	Herrick Chas	39	" M	Aug 1 64
6627	Henning C	140	" I	Aug 23 64
10566	Hestolate Jno	69		Oct 9 64
12104	Hewes J	Cav 1	Co A	Nov 20 64
11193	Hewes R	100	" C	Oct 20 64
7605	Hicks W H	99	" I	Sept 2 64
99	Hietzel C	52	" B	Mch 22 64
9937	Higgins J	43	" G	Sept 28 64
883	Higgins Wm	99	" B	May 4 64
4058	Higley Geo	85	" F	July 27 64
7632	Hildreth H	85	" K	Sept 3 64
3698	Hildreth L C	88	" D	July 21 64
777	Hill A A	44	" G	April 23 64
8643	Hill A J	2	" F	Sept 13 64
8970	Hill Frank	Cav 2	" K	July 25 64
11998	Hill L	22	" B	Nov 13 64
11912	Hill Wm	Cav 24	" E	Nov 8 64
3316	Hillman Geo	85	" B	July 14 64
4434	Hines J	126	" G	Aug 1 64
9060	Hingman A	140	" G	Sept 17 64
31	Hinkley B	Cav 9	" B	Mch 9 64
6255	Hinkley D	Cav 1	" E	Aug 20 64
5331	Hinton J	Art 14	" B	Aug 11 64

New York—(*Continued.*)

2967	Hinton Thos	Cav 12	Co E	July 6 64
7192	Hoag I	169	" A	Aug 29 64
395	Hoag Jno A	Cav 21	" L	April 6 64
11670	Hoar H J	120	" I	Oct 30 64
2083	Hobbs J	8	" H	June 17 64
2984	Hobson Wm	Cav 14	" F	July 7 64
6556	Hodge Jno	Cav 22	" A	Aug 23 64
6977	Hodgekiss A	Cav 8	" M	Aug 27 64
1027	Hofland Jno	132	" E	May 11 64
5010	Hoffman Fred	48	" B	Aug 8 64
3811	Hoffman H	47	" E	July 23 64
4932	Hoffman H	Art 7	" L	Aug 7 64
6248	Hoffman N	Cav 5	" F	Aug 20 64
7718	Hofyenneck T	Cav 21	" I	Sept 3 64
11317	Hogan J	63	" F	Oct 22 64
5449	Hogan Jno J	Art 6	" M	Aug 13 64
162	Horsenton E L	94	" B	Mch 26 64
6465	Holbrook G	76	" K	Aug 22 64
6327	Holbrook J E	85	" E	Aug 21 64
5013	Holcomb M D	95	" F	Aug 8 64
2204	Holcomb Theo	40	" K	June 19 64
11662	Holfe J	48	" E	Oct 30 64
6475	Holiday S	85	" E	Aug 23 64
2510	Hollands H	115	" E	June 26 64
7218	Hollen M	152	" A	Aug 29 64
2573	Hollendeck H J	120	" G	June 27 64
7051	Holliday S	85	" K	Aug 28 64
10624	Holmen J	50	" C	Oct 10 64
7952	Holmes C	85	" A	Sept 6 64
7104	Holmes E	Art 7	" K	Aug 28 64
5531	Holmes Henry	99	" H	Aug 13 64
12467	Holmes J	Art 4	" K	Jan 16 65
1504	Holstenstein H	48	" E	May 31 64
12298	Holtcaup B	96	" F	Dec 16 64
7826	Homvighausen F	140	" B	Sept 4 64
7117	Hooker T	111	" D	Aug 28 64
5369	Hoover A	Art 15	" H	Aug 11 64
514	Hoppock A	Art 15	" H	April 12 64
8040	Homstead H	22	" A	Sept 6 64
6114	Hose R	Cav 15	" L	Aug 19 64
2445	Hosford W F	Bat 24		June 25 64
6094	Houghdalinger M	120	Co D	Aug 18 64
10817	Houghteling C	Art 5	" A	Oct 12 64
5652	Hour Jas	119	" E	Aug 14 64
7457	Hous A R	96	" C	Sept 1 64
11099	Houslin E	95	" G	Oct 13 64
11693	Howard A	Art 2	" M	Oct 31 64
8477	Howard J	Cav 12	" F	Sept 11 64
4387	Howard Wm	39	" A	July 31 64
10114	Howe Geo	Cav 16	" M	Oct 1 64
12292	Howe S	59	" C	Dec 15 64
11064	Howell C R	Cav 2	" C	Oct 17 64
6622	Hoye J	Art 9	" I	Aug 23 64
7301	Hubbard A	76	" B	Aug 30 64
10666	Hudson J A	148	" A	Oct 11 64
9562	Hudson S R	Cav 13	" L	Sept 23 64
9387	Hull J E	Cav 24	" E	Sept 20 64
1462	Huff W S	140	" C	May 29 64
7931	Huganer A	85	" K	Sept 5 64
16	Huganer D M	64	Co I	Mch 6 64
7805	Hughes Jno	93	" K	Sept 4 64
11191	Hughes M	82	" K	Oct 20 64
7287	Hughes Thos	61	" G	Aug 30 64
2362	Hulet W	Cav 22	" L	June 27 64
7384	Hulse G	99	" I	Sept 2 64
1474	Hulse W S	47	" G	May 30 64
71[illegible]3	Humphrey H	85	" F	Aug 29 64
2618	Humphrey Jas	155	" I	June 23 64
2898	Hunnell J	100	" A	July 5 64
476	Hunt F J	46	" D	April 9 64
3365	Hunter E	Bat 24		July 15 64
10978	Hunter J	115		Oct 15 64
9802	Hanlon Thos	180	Co F	Sept 27 64
5841	Huntsmore G	66	" E	Aug 16 64
5497	Hurlburt S B	100	" F	Aug 13 64
4430	Hurley Jno	52	" A	July 31 64
12514	Hurrell J	Cav 10	" E	Feb 8 65
11851	Hutchings H W	Cav 1	" D	Nov 1 64
3112	Hutchings S A	Cav 5	" B	July 10 64
5024	Hutchings Wm	Art 6	" G	Aug 8 64
898	Hutchinson T	Cav 13	" D	May 4 64
8585	Hutchinson J	82	" A	Sept 12 64
10019	Hutchinson M	52	" G	Oct 16 64
9173	Huleson Wm E	Art 2	" B	Sept 18 64
8355	Hyde C	14	" F	Sept 16 64
11083	Hyde G	42	" C	Oct 18 64
8770	Hyde J F	76	" B	Sept 14 64
7625	Hyland O	5	" D	Sept 2 64
2103	Hyman J	45	" E	June 17 64
2187	Imhoff R	Cav 2	" G	June 19 64
4019	Imlay E	95	" A	July 26 64
4339	Imman J P	Cav 1	" A	July 31 64
10549	Ingerson S	Art 14	" G	Oct 9 64
4685	Ingraham C B	85	" B	Aug 4 64
3428	Inler I	Cav 1	" H	July 16 64
4587	Irish G	85	" C	Aug 2 64
11781	Ivespack W	Cav 15	" E	Nov 3 64
8159	Jaquays R	9	" L	Sept 8 64
7596	Jack J W	95	" H	Sept 2 64
6558	Jackson A	Cav 5	" E	Aug 23 64
9048	Jackson J	43	" K	Sept 17 64
11391	Jackson T A	122	" E	Oct 24 64
5402	Jackson John S	109	" F	Aug 12 64
7253	Jackson Wm	85	" F	Aug 30 64
6966	Jarmine Jas	115	" I	Aug 27 64
4795	Jamison A	51	" A	Aug 5 64
3645	Jarvis E	106	" H	July 20 64
11704	Jasper C	Art 7	" D	Oct 31 64
6671	Jay John	Art 8		Aug 24 64
9389	Jay John	Art 2	Co G	Sept 20 64
3384	Jeffrey B	Art 9	" D	July 26 64
1120	Jelley John	99	" K	May 15 64
29	Jenner Henry	Art 3	" K	April 19 64
10757	Jennings C	149	" K	Oct 12 64
744	Jewell J R	Art 3	" K	April 26 64
9934	Johnson A	74	" C	Sept 28 64
11182	Johnson A	Art 7	" A	Oct 19 64
12121	Johnson B	63	" D	Nov 22 64

New York—(*Continued.*)

12477	Johnson B F	82 Co H	Jany 17 65
10118	Johnson H S	85 " B	Oct 1 64
5916	Johnson H	115 " I	Aug 17 64
6232	Johnson H	Cav 10 " C	Aug 20 64
7712	Johnson J	89 " I	Sept 3 64
12546	Johnson J	146 " A	Jany 27 65
10043	Johnson L W	Art 14 " C	Sept 29 64
5935	Johnson M	96 " H	Aug 17 64
9495	Johnson P B	Bat 24	Sept 21 64
8054	Johnson R	111 Co A	Sept 7 64
3427	Johnson R	120 " I	July 16 64
4017	Joice Thos	22 " C	July 27 64
7113	Jolley F	93 " E	Aug 31 64
5980	Jones C N	Cav 10 " C	Aug 17 64
6803	Jones David	85 " H	Aug 26 64
10769	Jones E C	147 " E	Oct 13 64
3650	Jones E	134 " F	July 20 64
4373	Jones G C	20	July 31 64
3282	Jones G W	47 Co F	July 14 64
5753	Jones H	Cav 10 " I	Aug 15 64
5582	Jones Jno	76 " K	Aug 14 64
11855	Jones Jno	Cav 6 " A	Nov 6 64
2487	Jones R	99 " B	June 26 64
4403	Jones Thos	116 " B	July 31 64
5042	Jones Wm	52 " B	Aug 8 64
8867	Jones Wm, Farrier	Cav 5 " C	Sept 15 64
8771	Jones J B	22 " F	Sept 14 64
9523	Jourdan Barney	Art 7 " E	Sept 22 64
4188	Jule H	51 " E	July 23 64
9107	Jump O	Cav 8	Sept 18 64
5198	Kahbaum E	Cav 12 " F	Aug 10 64
12170	Kane F	82 " A	Nov 26 64
792	Kane Peter	Cav 20	April 23 64
8863	Kanope C	49	Sept 15 64
9194	Kapp D	100 Co F	Sept 18 64
10222	Kearney W	Cav 16 " A	Oct 2 64
8452	Keating M	146 " A	Sept 11 64
4434	Keating Thos	83 " L	Aug 1 64
11075	Kean W	47 " I	Oct 17 64
7337	Keers M	49 " A	Aug 31 64
11736	Kehoe T	155 " A	Nov 3 64
10341	Kelley M	Art 2 " L	Oct 4 64
10349	Kellar Jno	139 " E	Oct 4 64
6759	Kelley D	45 " C	Aug 21 64
11100	Kelley J	Art 4 " K	Oct 18 64
10675	Kelley Jas	146 " K	Oct 11 64
6997	Kelley Jas	40 " F	Aug 27 64
10333	Kelley M	63	Oct 5 64
9676	Kelley P	106 Co D	Sept 24 64
12209	Kelley T	82 " F	Dec 2 64
10960	Kenarm Alfred	70 " K	Oct 14 64
11425	Kennedy M E	82 " K	Oct 24 64
9365	Kennedy W	132 " D	Sept 27 64
11244	Kennion F	8 " H	Oct 21 64
8572	Kenney A W	85 " D	July 19 64
1250	Kenney G W	Bat 24	May 21 64
3671	Kenney M	2 Co F	July 20 64
4393	Kent E L	85 " I	July 21 64
7403	Kenwell R	Cav 5 " D	Aug 31 64
1079	Keogh Peter	132 Co C	May 14 64
5922	Kerritt Jacob	132 " D	Aug 17 64
5310	Kerr C L	85 " B	Aug 11 64
2434	Kerr H	Cav 2 " L	June 25 64
3915	Kertser T	173 " K	July 25 64
2707	Kester Chas	141 " F	July 2 64
1632	Kettle Sol	Art 2 " K	Oct 23 64
9015	Keys R	95 " C	Sept 17 64
630	Keyes O S	Cav 5 " E	April 20 64
1932	Kidd Owen	126 " K	June 14 64
4303	Killner Sanford	125 " F	Aug 3 64
1861	Kilmer J	5 " I	June 12 64
10614	Kilson J	115 " E	Oct 10 64
12026	Kimball S	Art 7 " F	Nov 15 64
3232	Kimberly C	76 " B	July 13 64
7999	King ——	99 " I	Sept 6 64
9316	King N	Cav 21 " G	Sept 26 64
8738	King Sylvanus	Bat 24	Sept 14 64
3737	King Richard	99 Co H	July 22 64
3095	Kinsley D	Cav 12 " H	July 10 64
9639	Kinsley Jas	Cav 5	Sept 24 64
239	Kinney Lucas	99 Co H	Mch 30 64
11553	Kinney M	42 " C	Oct 27 64
8409	Kinnie J	76 " F	Sept 10 64
564	Kinsey B B	132 " K	April 15 64
7977	Kinsman John E	Art 14 " I	Sept 6 64
12359	Kinsman W S	83 " I	April 20 65
4237	Kirby Chas	Cav 12 " F	July 30 64
7037	Kirkland I	Art 2 " D	Aug 28 64
12742	Kirkpatrick ——	Cav 12 " D	Mch 6 65
5339	Kittle E N	125 " E	Aug 14 64
8373	Kizer G W	73 " B	Sept 15 64
4525	Knapp Henry	Cav 24 " A	Aug 2 64
5233	Knapp Philip	Cav 10 " C	Aug 10 64
2504	Knabe [illegible]	48 " C	June 28 64
7949	Knight Wm	142 " C	Sept 6 64
12318	Knowl H	63 " C	Dec 21 64
11976	Kossuth W	54 " F	Nov 12 64
8360	Krasipars K	65 " L	Sept 15 64
9211	Krantz H	54 " E	Sept 19 64
12115	Kreit J K	Cav 1 " L	Nov 21 64
11043	Krelar A	Bat 13	Nov 10 64
3302	Kroom C E	64 Co G	July 24 64
1238	Krouger G R	173 " K	May 19 64
8956	Lahey P	1 " D	Sept 16 64
8447	Lacey P	Cav 12 " F	Sept 11 64
3301	Lacey Wm	85 " K	July 19 64
10736	Lackley P I	Cav 1	Oct 11 64
10379	Lacks Lee	22 Co G	Oct 13 64
8372	Lacoster H	85	Sept 10 64
10827	Lader A	9 " E	Oct 26 64
7156	Lagay Frank	118 " B	Aug 29 64
41	Lahey Daniel	82 " I	Mch 13 64
12775	Lahiff D	42 " K	Mch 14 65
12100	Lake Wm	146 " K	Nov 21 64
6437	Laman C	39 " H	Aug 22 64
6331	Lamareux J	76 " K	Aug 21 64
11593	Lambright A	Art 7 " K	Nov 7 64
11590	Lambly J	1 " I	Oct 28 64

New York—(*Continued.*)

No.	Name	Regiment	Co.	Date
11318	Lampman W S	Art 6	Co M	Oct 22 64
11213	Lampert R	98	" D	Oct 20 64
9336	Larrabee E	15	" D	Sept 27 64
8283	Landers C	Art 7		July 14 64
12214	Lane C	146	Co E	Dec 3 64
7462	Lane Chas	Cav 3	" E	Sept 1 64
2678	Lane G W	85	" C	June 30 64
11409	Lane J W	Cav 15	" M	Oct 23 64
2288	Lang A	85	" F	June 21 64
13	Lang Wm W	Drag 1		Mch 6 64
8238	Langdon A M	85	Co B	Sept 9 64
4375	Lansing Wm	Cav 12	" B	July 31 64
3788	Lansop J	85	" D	July 23 64
10036	Langen A	39	" I	Sept 20 64
4871	Lampan L H	Bat 24		Aug 6 64
8087	Larcks G	85	Co F	Sept 7 64
6631	Larkins M C	100	" A	Aug 23 64
14	Lasar Benj	Cav 6	" F	Mch 6 64
8956	Latey P	1	" D	Sept 19 64
851	Lattaratta J	Cav 1	" A	May 3 64
4107	Laugha W	Art 1	" M	July 27 64
8102	Lawton J	69	" E	Sept 8 64
10095	Lawrence J	Art 7	" G	Sept 30 64
4101	Lawson John	Cav 2	" D	July 27 64
6434	Layman C	120	" K	Aug 22 64
2374	Leabrook John	157	" B	June 23 64
2119	Leach S	Cav 10	" E	June 17 64
1737	Lean W H	Cav 21	" C	June 8 64
7142	Ledderer Wm	132	" G	Aug 29 64
1944	Lee A	Bat 24		June 14 64
2169	Lee F	15	Co F	June 19 64
2572	Lee P	Art 2	" A	June 27 64
9696	Lee Wm	Cav 6	" L	Sept 24 64
8514	Legrist W	11	" E	Sept 10 64
6399	Leichinger J	Cav 3	" D	Aug 21 64
3565	Leiner A	39	" B	July 19 64
11697	Lenot V	47	" I	Oct 31 64
2686	Lent A	Bat 24		June 30 64
7499	Leonard A	52	Co B	Sept 1 64
12076	Leonard C H	Art 7	" A	Nov 13 64
8937	Leonard J W	85	" K	Sept 17 64
10065	Lestraff C	Art 7	" A	Sept 30 64
6150	Letch John	Cav 5	" C	Aug 19 64
8774	Levalley C	140	" A	Sept 14 64
9045	Lewis C	85	" F	Sept 17 64
3727	Lewis C F	52	" E	July 21 64
1329	Lewis F A	9	" G	May 24 64
11515	Lewis G W	146	" G	Nov 8 64
8297	Lewis J	Art 1	" E	Sept 9 64
5115	Lewis P W	85	" B	Aug 9 64
10365	Lickley P	Cav 1	" E	Oct 5 64
11531	Limbach S	7	" D	Oct 27 64
8419	Linch J H	76	" I	Sept 11 64
5845	Linchler F	Cav 1	" E	Aug 15 64
10559	Lindlay D	127	" E	Oct 9 64
7815	Lineham Thos	125	" C	Sept 4 64
6759	Ling Jno	Art 4	" F	Aug 25 64
38	Link Gotlib	54	" K	Mch 12 64
10073	Little C	76	" F	Sept 30 64
10933	Livingstone A	Cav 1	Co C	Oct 14 64
4543	Locher Conrad	Art 15		Aug 2 64
5535	Lock A	98	Co B	Aug 13 64
2142	Lodge T	12	" A	June 18 64
8346	Loftern H	Cav 12	" F	Sept 9 64
9722	Loftus M	Cav 11	" E	Sept 24 64
7010	Longs R	Art 2	" A	Aug 27 64
11531	Long J	75	" A	Oct 28 64
7324	Long L	40	" I	Sept 5 64
4514	Longle Wm	Art 4	" B	Aug 1 64
5424	Loomis Jno	Art 14	" M	Aug 12 64
9712	Loony C	48	" A	Sept 25 64
9383	Lorzbran J	64	" E	Sept 29 64
11906	Louis C	Cav 16	" C	Nov 7 64
12339	Love J	125	" A	Dec 24 64
7146	Lovejoy F	Cav 1	" I	Aug 29 64
10248	Lovering F	Art 14	" I	Oct 3 64
12313	Lowery G	7	" A	Dec 20 64
2563	Lowery Jas F	140	" A	June 27 64
9663	Laws H	Cav 22	" E	Sept 24 64
8395	Lloyd S	47	" D	Sept 10 64
9354	Luce V	140	" D	Sept 20 64
10311	Lucia A	95	" H	Oct 4 64
7308	Lurcock E	Art 14	" M	Aug 30 64
9002	Lutton O	Art 14	" H	Sept 17 64
5772	Lynch D	164	" A	Aug 15 64
6395	Lynch F	43	" K	Aug 26 64
931	Lynch Pat	99	" H	May 7 64
12633	Lyons Chas	Cav 2	" M	Feb 10 65
1427	Lyons Michael	99	" E	May 28 64
8419	Luch J H	76	" I	Sept 11 64
6151	Lucha Jno	Cav 5	" C	Sept 19 64
8342	Lyons J H	Art 5		Sept 10 64
6156	Lyons Thos	Art 6	Co G	Aug 19 64
7913	Lyons W	47	" A	Sept 5 64
87	Mace Jeff	134	" I	Mch 12 64
6675	Mace L	48	" H	Aug 24 64
10830	Mack J	39	" D	Oct 13 64
5016	Mackin Wm	85	" F	Aug 8 64
3983	Madder P	155	" E	July 25 64
10306	Madden F	152	" E	Oct 8 64
4822	Madden ——	Cav 1	" D	Aug 5 64
11257	Madczan Jno	125	" B	Oct 21 64
9798	Madison D	75	" D	Sept 26 64
11714	Magrath G H	61	" D	Nov 1 64
4028	Mahon E	170	" G	July 26 64
122	Mahon Jas	132	" K	Mch 23 64
1423	Mahon Thos	120	" C	May 28 64
5842	Mailer J R	134	" B	Aug 16 64
11679	Maine F O	85	" A	Oct 31 64
11380	Mainhart F	39	" B	Oct 28 64
12369	Makay J	5	" E	Nov 17 64
7943	Malleck M	Cav 6	" D	Sept 5 64
9427	Malley S S	16	" K	Sept 21 64
9457	Malone Pat	133	" F	Sept 21 64
8234	Maloney C	6	" C	July 14 64
11417	Maloney J	73	" G	Oct 25 64
7690	Mandeville Wm	85	" F	Sept 2 64
2802	Mangin F	Art 7	" F	July 3 64

New York —(*Continued.*)

10623	Manning ——	83		Oct 9 64
7139	Manning M	Art 6	Co D	Aug 23 64
10540	Manning Thos	125	" B	Oct 8 64
2952	Mannilly J	74	" C	July 6 64
2356	March J	Cav 22	" C	July 4 64
4000	Marley John, Mus	53	" E	July 23 64
1123	Maron J	99	" I	May 15 64
11764	Martaugh J	Cav 6	" A	Sept 3 64
3824	Marsh Ira	Art 6	" M	July 23 64
5407	Marsh J	104	" D	Aug 12 64
11097	Marston A	65	" G	Nov 13 64
3441	Martin A	Cav 12	" F	July 17 64
435	Martin C	Cav 10	" A	April 8 64
6543	Martin Chas	42	" G	Aug 23 64
11600	Martin E A	Cav 5	" C	Oct 23 64
12208	Martin J	39	" G	Dec 2 64
4321	Martin H	76	" H	July 30 64
5086	Martin J C	Bat 24		Aug 8 64
9164	Martin P	99	Co H	Sept 18 64
6293	Martin John	Cav 16	" L	Aug 20 64
1256	Martin Peter	40	" I	May 21 64
8003	Martin W	142	" F	Sept 6 64
3039	Martin W B	12	" I	July 25 64
8746	Martin W H	Art 24	" M	Sept 14 64
1073	Martin Wm	Cav 13	" D	May 13 64
676	Marvoney James	132	" G	April 22 64
10483	Mason F	Art 14	" I	Oct 7 64
2315	Martin Samuel	85	" I	June 22 64
11290	Masterson E	2	" D	Oct 22 64
11296	Massen H L	86	" C	Oct 22 64
10498	Maxwell J	85	" D	Oct 8 64
1477	Maxwell Robt	48	" D	May 30 64
11788	Matthews W	155	" I	Nov 4 64
4472	Matthews H	Cav 12	" M	Aug 1 64
2100	Mattice H C	134	" E	June 17 64
5651	Mattison R	85	" D	Aug 14 64
4946	Maxum S G	Cav 12	" A	Aug 7 64
10519	McAllister J	125	" I	Oct 8 64
7995	McBride ——	52	" K	Sept 6 64
4508	McCabe Jas	88	" D	Aug 1 64
2517	McCabe P	Cav 12	" F	June 26 64
732	McCabe Peter	Cav 2	" E	April 25 64
2196	McCabe J	41	" C	June 19 64
8324	McCafferty W	100	" D	Sept 10 64
11716	McCain L	18	" C	Oct 11 64
9864	McCardell W	Cav 15	" H	Sept 27 64
7620	McCarten L	Art 9	" B	Sept 2 64
3413	McCarty D	155	" G	July 16 64
4480	McCarty Deni	Art 2	" D	Aug 1 64
5132	McCarty I	99	" H	Aug 9 64
9633	McCarty I	M R 2	" K	Sept 24 64
4759	McCarty Jno	69	" K	Aug 5 64
6136	McCarty Jno	104	" E	Aug 19 64
1035	McCarty P	132	" K	May 11 64
2965	McCarty S	99	" C	July 6 64
6227	McCarty W	Cav 9	" L	Aug 20 64
8242	McClusky F	173	" E	Sept 9 64
1544	McColligan Pat	99	" F	May 24 64
9266	McCauly J H	47	" G	Sept 19 64
6440	McCloud Jno	97	Co A	Aug 22 64
4416	McConnell E	Art 9		July 31 64
6012	McCord H	Art 7	Co G	Aug 17 64
11110	McCormic M	93	" K	Oct 18 64
6597	McCormick H	69	" K	Aug 29 64
9018	McCormick H	178	" F	Sept 17 64
3629	McCormick J	155	" H	July 20 64
6203	McCormick J	Bat 24		Aug 19 64
7441	McCormick J	43	Co F	Sept 1 64
10258	McCormick P	43	" D	Oct 3 64
1433	McCormick Peter	39	" I	May 28 64
5203	McCormick W	2	" I	Aug 10 64
7730	McCraker B	Art 7	" B	Sept 3 64
8644	McCrass J	148		Sept 13 64
2279	McCrember M	85	Co I	June 21 64
8507	McCullen D	57	" F	Sept 12 64
10778	McDavid J	5	" D	Oct 12 64
6012	McDermott P	164	" H	Aug 26 64
8969	McDonald A	Bat 24		Sept 16 64
7745	McDonald A H	85	Co E	Sept 8 64
7110	McDonald B	52	" D	Aug 29 64
4013	McDonald Jno	104	" E	July 26 64
12138	McDonald F	Cav 16	" L	Nov 23 64
10002	McDonald F	95	" A	Sept 29 64
7259	McDonnell Wm	Art 14	" D	Aug 30 64
8126	McDurie C	71		Sept 8 64
4089	McElray Jno	43	Co I	July 27 64
9581	McErmany P	Art 7	" G	Sept 23 64
338	McFarland A	72	" I	April 2 64
12478	McGiben I	170	" B	Jan 17 65
11116	McGowan Wm	Art 6	" L	Oct 18 64
4001	McFadden Jas	39	" F	July 26 64
2665	McGain I	99	" H	June 29 64
354	McGeatte	52	" D	April 2 64
3551	McGibney H	85	" E	July 18 64
2756	McGiven Wm	158	" B	July 1 64
8225	McGowan F	170	" H	Sept 9 64
248	McGowan Jno	132	" K	Mch 30 64
1112	McGrath M	Cav 12	" E	May 15 64
4709	McGucker A	Cav 1	" C	Aug 4 64
4935	McGuire P	140	" C	Aug 7 64
6827	McGuire P	10	" C	Aug 25 64
3220	McGuire Pat	101	" F	July 12 64
8354	McIlarty M	69	" A	Sept 10 64
3233	McKabe J	Cav 12	" F	July 12 64
1163	McKenley J	99	" I	May 16 64
12664	McKenna H	12	" F	Feby 16 65
5350	McKerchay J H	85	" F	Aug 11 64
9390	McKinney John	82	" D	Sept 20 64
10302	McLain R	42	" F	Oct 6 64
10055	McLaughlin O	9	" F	Sept 30 64
4263	McLorens R	Cav 20	" M	July 29 64
6350	McLaughlin J	63	" D	Aug 25 64
3311	McMahon C L	Cav 3	" E	July 19 64
6314	McMurrier Wm	Cav 2	" L	Aug 25 64
9030	McNamara Wm	Art 2	" L	Sept 28 64
10723	McNamirin B F	14	" A	Oct 11 64
5403	McNulty ——	85	" E	Aug 12 64
3724	McPeak W	Cav 2	" B	July 21 64

New York — (*Continued.*)

7271	McPherson Wm	Art 14	Co M	Aug 30 64
5868	McQuillen A	Art 6	" L	Aug 16 64
8889	McSorley G W	20	" M	Sept 16 64
3127	Mead P	Art 1	" C	July 10 64
150	Megrame W H	99	" E	Mch 25 64
10599	Melin A	Art 14	" L	Oct 10 64
11167	Melins W	82	" B	Oct 10 64
2068	Menzie A	Art 3	" K	June 16 64
6042	Meritt H D	76	" F	Aug 18 64
9353	Merkle J	15	" A	Sept 20 64
11204	Merwin A	Cav 2	" A	Oct 20 64
11214	Merz F A	5	" I	Oct 20 64
8906	Messing I	39	" A	Sept 16 64
10116	Messinger C	Cav 1	" L	Oct 1 64
6462	Messiric J M	Cav 1	" A	Aug 22 64
2523	Metcalf A	85	" G	June 26 64
3134	Meyers F	45	" G	July 10 64
8852	Meyer H	66	" F	Sept 10 64
11723	Meyers I	57	" F	Nov 1 64
2896	Meyers W	54	" C	July 5 64
4520	Michael ——	66	" A	Aug 2 64
11780	Michells W	Cav 2	" B	Nov 3 64
3750	Midlaw F	Cav 12	" A	July 22 64
2709	Migner H	54	" D	June 30 64
6202	Milard F J	Cav 12	" A	Aug 19 64
168	Millens Adam	125	" E	Mch 26 64
5520	Mille A W	52	" D	Aug 13 64
4647	Miller C	111	" I	Aug 3 64
6469	Miller Chas B	Cav 24	" E	Aug 22 64
3221	Miller F	182	" D	July 18 64
5155	Miller F	99		Aug 9 64
6865	Miller F	Art 15	Co D	Aug 26 64
11516	Miller G A	152	" C	Oct 26 64
6585	Milen Geo	61	" F	Aug 23 64
11522	Miller Geo	1	" G	Oct 26 64
3131	Miller H	Cav 1	" L	July 10 64
10627	Miller H W	96	" E	Oct 10 64
8278	Miller J	95	" E	Sept 9 64
5521	Miller Jacob	39	Co I	Aug 13 64
628	Miller J E, Bugler	Cav 2	" M	April 19 64
9505	Miller Jno	12	" A	Sept 22 64
708	Miller O	126	" G	April 24 64
9986	Miller Wm	Art 2	" C	Sept 29 64
8063	Millerman G	Cav 22	" B	Sept 7 64
8862	Mills J J	85		Sept 15 64
2844	Mills S	Cav 12	Co A	July 3 64
4854	Millspaugh Fred	Art 6	" A	Aug 6 64
79	Milline Jno	95	" G	Mch 20 64
1889	Mindler Peter	Cav 1		June 13 64
4771	Miner J G	Bat 24		Aug 5 64
3618	Minie F	99	Co F	July 20 64
8080	Mitchell J	125	" E	Sept 7 64
9939	Mitchell Jno	120	" I	Sept 28 64
7396	Milty Sam'l	Cav 12	" L	Aug 30 64
2486	Moe Jno	120	" I	June 25 64
4121	Moffat J	Art 7	" C	July 23 64
5720	Monaghan	66	" D	Aug 15 64
4441	Monihan J	85	" C	July 31 64
4392	Monohan J	73	" D	July 31 64
11537	Monahan P	88	Co D	Oct 27 64
4353	Monroe J R	111	" G	Aug 3 64
11961	Monroe A J	22	" G	Nov 11 64
7433	Morgan M	76	" B	Sept 1 64
8341	Monschitz J	65	" D	Sept 9 64
1933	Monson Wm	11	" G	June 14 64
7830	Monson Geo	6		Sept 4 64
5635	Monta Henry	52	Co B	Aug 14 64
3512	Montag Geo	39	" B	July 18 64
11050	Moran D G	40	" G	Oct 30 64
6565	Moran Thos	85	" A	Aug 23 64
7782	Moram M J	Cav 8		Sept 3 64
11621	Morearty I	1	Co M	Oct 28 64
10308	Morgraff Wm	64	" H	Oct 4 64
8461	Moody C R	100	" B	Sept 11 64
6423	Moody Thos	147	" B	Aug 22 64
3108	Moony P	Art 3	" K	July 10 64
3631	Moony I	188	" D	July 20 64
8117	Mooney J	52	" D	Sept 11 64
10386	Mooney Thos	139	" F	Oct 14 64
2766	Moore A, Bugler	Cav 22	" E	July 12 64
7636	Moore C C	Cav 1	" B	Sept 3 64
11829	Moore C	Art 2	" B	Nov 5 64
638	Moore Martin	74	" C	April 21 64
1694	Moore S	46	" H	June 7 64
442	Moore T H	Cav 5	" M	April 9 64
457	Moore W H	125	" F	April 9 64
7767	Moore Jno	39	" H	Sept 4 64
9778	Moore W S	85	" D	Sept 26 64
10781	Morgan E	Art 14		Oct 12 64
7563	Morgan E J	179	Co C	Sept 2 64
10631	Mortross D H	Art 7	" L	Oct 10 64
624	Morland H	Cav 21	" H	April 19 64
4636	Morris E	Art 7	" K	Aug 4 64
9314	Morris T	65	" C	Sept 28 64
3780	Morris H	71	" F	July 22 64
8331	Morris J	Cav 5	" D	Sept 6 64
11226	Morris J	99	" A	Oct 20 64
5835	Morris J A	Art 7	" G	Aug 16 64
6009	Morris Jno	70	" B	Aug 18 64
12317	Morris R	66	" G	Jan 3 65
9378	Morris L R	85	" B	Sept 20 64
7703	Morris T A	111	" E	Sept 3 64
4830	Morris Wm	102	" G	Aug 6 64
8633	Morrison W	5	" I	Sept 13 64
9371	Morrison W	Cav 5	" I	Sept 20 64
7958	Morse E	Cav 5	" L	Sept 6 64
12311	Morse I	1	" L	Jan 23 65
617	Martin Chas	47	" A	April 18 64
10325	Martin G H	Art 7	" L	Oct 10 64
3181	Martin Henry	61	" C	July 11 64
7672	Mortimer Wm	Art 5	" A	Sept 3 64
7079	Mosher E	Art 9	" D	Aug 28 64
10152	Mosier E	Art 9	" E	Oct 1 64
11016	Mosier M W	4	" G	Oct 16 64
2372	Moses L	85	" E	July 4 64
12003	Motts C	Bat 24		Nov 14 64
8711	Moss W S	Art 7		Sept 14 64
11466	Mulcady W	42	Co E	Oct 26 64

New York—(*Continued.*)

7997	Molcohy D D	76	Co F	Sept 6 64
11368	Mulgrave Jas	2	" C	Oct 23 64
12240	Mullen Chas	Art 7	" I	Dec 7 64
11224	Muller P	7	" H	Oct 23 61
6985	Mulligan J	34	" H	Aug 27 64
11485	Mulish R	48	" A	Oct 26 64
12155	Mullin J	82	" G	Nov 25 64
4720	Mullington C	Art 6	" H	Aug 4 64
8370	Munger D	Art 2	" C	Sept 10 64
8404	Murchison D	Cav 4	" D	Sept 11 64
145	Murphy Jno	99	" H	Mch 21 64
5804	Murphy F	61	" B	Aug 16 64
5918	Murphy L	170	" E	Aug 17 64
6550	Murphy W S	40	" K	Aug 23 64
11803	Murphy R	85	" E	Nov 4 64
10200	Murphy Martin	Cav 2	" D	Oct 2 64
12118	Murray J	Cav 23	" F	Nov 20 64
11273	Murray J	47	" I	Oct 23 64
3389	Murry A	118	" C	July 16 64
8947	Murry J	39	" C	Sept 15 64
11519	Murry M John	63	" F	Oct 25 64
6218	Murny ——	Bat 11		Aug 20 64
11954	Murrey M	98	Co D	Nov 10 64
1560	Murvillc S	1	" C	June 2 64
12494	Muselman J	2	" K	Jan 20 65
1384	Myers E	154	" D	May 25 64
4958	Myers H	47	" A	Aug 7 64
9913	Myers H	Cav 2	" G	Sept 23 64
5000	Myers H L	147	" H	Aug 7 64
8970	Myers J	Cav 20	" M	Sept 16 64
6221	Myers James	65	" K	Aug 20 64
8973	Neal J	22	" E	Sept 15 64
10587	Nedden J	82	" A	Oct 10 64
7922	Nellman A	66	" I	Sept 4 64
2541	Nelson B	39	" A	June 27 64
6551	Nelson John	82	" D	Aug 13 64
11062	Nelson John	Art 2	" D	Oct 17 64
3022	Nevens C	100	" F	July 7 64
2985	Newton L C	Art 14	" I	July 7 64
4469	Newton R J	Bat 24		Aug 1 64
4943	Newton Samuel D	85	Co G	Aug 7 64
5227	Newton C W	85	" K	Aug 10 64
2258	Nichols A S	2	" C	June 20 64
5109	Nichols D A	125	" D	Aug 9 64
7050	Nichols F E	Art 7	" F	Aug 27 64
9017	Nobles E	14	" A	Sept 17 64
11533	Nolan M	5	" I	Oct 25 64
11356	Nolan Pat	83	" D	Oct 23 64
5050	Noonan E	Cav 16	" L	Aug 8 64
4633	Norman J	Art 15	" H	Aug 3 64
633	Northrop D	125	" H	April 10 64
5228	Northrop V	10	" G	Aug 17 64
17	Norton Alonzo	154	" A	Mch 7 64
4451	Norwood D F	85	" E	Aug 1 64
4735	Nostrand C	Art 2	" I	Aug 4 64
12241	Nott S A	Cav 15	" E	Dec 7 64
2549	Nutt M	123	" D	June 27 64
11681	Nutterville W	8	" G	Oct 21 64
5439	O'Brien D	63	" F	Aug 12 64
9765	O'Brien M	Cav 1	Co A	Sept 25 64
8035	O'Brien S	Cav 5	" L	Sept 6 64
1533	O'Brien W	Cav 8	" A	June 2 64
6270	O'Carrell F	69	" A	Aug 20 64
7356	Och S	46	" D	Aug 31 64
8520	O'Connell Thos	72	" B	July 18 64
2755	O'Dougherty J	51		July 1 64
12007	O'Kay Peter	140	Co E	Jan 5 65
9727	O'Keif C	146	" C	Sept 25 64
9316	Olahan A	65	" F	Sept 23 64
10009	Olmstead F H	Art 2	" I	Sept 20 64
6435	Older W M	Cav 16	" L	Aug 23 64
1448	Omat M	178	" B	May 28 64
12110	Omma Jas	Art 7	" B	Nov 24 64
11404	O'Neil J	39	" H	Oct 24 64
1988	Ostenhal L	73	" C	June 15 64
12	Osterstuck W	154	" I	Mch 5 64
6456	Osborne R H	22	" E	Aug 22 64
2714	Osterhardt B S	120	" C	July 1 64
12239	Ostrander J	86	" A	Dec 12 64
103	Ostrander J H	120	" F	Mch 23 64
6326	Otis Jno	94	" A	Aug 21 64
8763	Otto Chas	100	" F	Sept 14 64
656	Otto Jas L	Cav 12	" E	April 21 64
5447	Owens Ed	47	" G	Aug 12 64
12227	Owens Wm	49	" I	Dec 5 64
7534	O'Reilly Philip	Art 2	" I	Sept 1 64
9519	Page O D	146	" F	Sept 20 64
2225	Palmer P H	85	" D	June 22 64
2533	Palmer F	17	" F	June 27 64
6753	Pallette D	Cav 15	" K	Aug 24 64
20	Palmiter R	86	" D	Mch 7 64
5958	Pamperin Wm	71	" H	Aug 17 64
8850	Pardy E	85	" K	July 15 64
5710	Parish D	146	" E	Aug 15 64
12150	Parker F	128	" C	Nov 27 64
2002	Parker I	85	" I	June 17 64
2319	Parker Isaac	124	" G	July 3 64
1302	Parker J	80	" I	May 26 64
2953	Parker J	154	" G	July 6 64
8883	Parker J	Cav 15	" F	July 16 64
4732	Parkinson A	Art 4	" C	Aug 4 64
11956	Parks Wm	109	" K	Nov 11 64
11218	Parsons W	64	" E	Oct 20 64
9187	Patterson D	76	" D	Sept 21 64
5330	Patterson E	Art 6	" M	Aug 16 64
8440	Patterson Geo W	Art 15	" M	July 17 64
6135	Patterson H	Cav 1		Aug 19 64
5279	Patterson I H	85	Co F	Aug 11 64
4738	Patterson J H	85	" G	Aug 4 64
10333	Paul P	39	" L	Oct 8 64
6393	Pease Martin	Cav 2	" C	Aug 24 64
2166	Peck J G	Cav 22	" F	June 19 64
11030	Peckins L	Cav 2	" A	Oct 28 64
11373	Pedro Francis	Cav 12	" E	Oct 30 64
1342	Pellet Ed	Cav 15	" I	June 1 64
8751	Pen R	Cav 2	" F	July 22 64
2773	Penablin Jno	69	" F	July 12 64
11343	Pen Chas	Art 6	" D	Oct 23 64

New York—(*Continued.*)

7898	Perkey D	85	Co B	Aug 31 64
7172	Perkins J P	Bat 24		Aug 29 64
10562	Perry A	89	Co G	Oct 9 64
4527	Perry Jno	84	" D	Aug 2 64
7866	Perry W	Cav 2	" B	Sept 5 64
3721	Perry Wm	99	" E	July 21 64
12183	Perry Wm	79	" A	Nov 27 64
4517	Person A	61	" H	Aug 2 64
8082	Persons W B	64	" B	July 9 64
5224	Peters Fritz	52	" C	Aug 10 64
3914	Peters J	114	" F	July 25 64
5684	Peterson C	178	" I	Aug 15 64
9120	Peterson H	48	" B	Sept 13 64
3202	Pettis L P	100	" F	July 14 64
5727	Petrie Josh	81	" I	Aug 13 64
486	Phelps Martin	132	" G	April 9 64
4235	Phillips Geo A	85	" B	July 29 64
12431	Phillips I	Cav 6	" E	Jany 17 65
7637	Phillips H	100	" H	Sept 2 64
3318	Phillips R	85	" B	July 14 64
4152	Pierce Albert	Art 2	" M	July 28 64
2459	Pierce Chas	73	" F	June 25 64
5371	Pierce H	85	" B	Aug 11 64
6027	Pierce J	85	" D	Aug 18 64
11663	Pierce J H	Cav 8		Oct 30 64
6005	Pierson J	76	Co B	Aug 17 64
9423	Pilseck E	61	" I	Sept 21 64
1532	Pinmon John	99	" I	May 31 64
9994	Pitts G	97	" K	Sept 29 64
11441	Pivant M	61	" D	Oct 25 64
6086	Place E	47	" F	Aug 13 64
815	Plass H	120	" G	April 30 64
11379	Plunkett J	146	" A	Oct 24 64
9549	Polack J	85	" C	Sept 23 64
4432	Poliock R	Cav 16	" L	July 21 64
1843	Pomroy C	Cav 21	" G	June 11 64
4531	Ponteis G	Cav 16	" K	Aug 2 64
1830	Popple W G	85	" B	June 11 64
11120	Pope Jas E	Art 15	" A	Oct 13 64
12291	Post H E	125	" G	Oct 15 64
12425	Post J A	94	" E	Jan 10 65
6385	Potter H	48	" E	Aug 21 64
1582	Potter W H	85	" F	June 8 64
5116	Powell Geo	Art 7	" H	Aug 9 64
2948	Powers J	Cav 24	" H	July 6 64
3367	Powers J	10	" K	July 15 64
6990	Powers O	Art 6	" I	Aug 21 64
5435	Pratt B F	146	" G	Aug 12 64
1294	Presselman C	Cav 4	" M	May 23 64
5523	Preston H G	9	" G	Aug 13 64
1096	Price David	134	" A	May 11 64
12346	Price J, Citizen			Dec 27 64
6455	Pratt P	Bat 24		Aug 23 64
1051	Priest W	132	Co E	June 5 64
1479	Pratt G B	Cav 10	" D	May 30 64
7964	Pringler Thos W	133	" A	Sept 6 64
6914	Prow Jno	Art 14	" L	Aug 23 64
9638	Prowman S H	149	" H	Sept 21 64
2937	Puff I	Art 15	"	Sept 23 64
2221	Puley Daniel	115	Co I	June 22 64
729	Pullers U H	132	" E	April 25 64
2395	Putnam L	Art 14	" L	June 24 64
1515	Purkey Jacob	84	" B	May 31 64
4063	Purstle S	40	" A	July 27 64
11432	Prunan L	147	" H	Oct 24 64
9046	Quackenbuss P	11	" K	Sept 17 64
8227	Quigley J	99	" I	Sept 9 64
8074	Quinn Edser	Cav 10	" B	Sept 27 64
4325	Randolph ——	9	" E	July 30 64
11643	Rafbrun W	59	" C	Oct 30 64
512	Rafferty M	132	" G	April 12 64
2534	Rafferty P	Cav 5	" M	June 26 64
11330	Rafferty T	Art 5	" B	Oct 23 64
4593	Raker L	Cav 1	" E	Aug 3 64
8751	Ranch J	100	" D	July 22 64
10875	Randall Jno	99	" A	Oct 13 64
6503	Ralinger J	47	" B	Aug 22 64
6794	Rangheart Jno	100	" A	Aug 25 64
7778	Rasterfer Jno	100	" A	Sept 4 64
4216	Rattery Jno	104	" I	July 26 64
10037	Ray C	Cav 3	" B	Oct 14 64
11246	Ray R S	154	" A	Oct 3 64
4336	Raynard F	175		July 30 64
3435	Rattersboon J	Art 3	Co K	July 17 64
2830	Ramsay Isaac	86	" I	July 4 64
1265	Ramsay Hiram	31	" K	May 21 64
2186	Reamer W C	111	" B	June 19 64
2820	Redman J	Art 3	" K	July 3 64
11093	Reddo D V	Cav 8	" M	Oct 31 64
7233	Reed F A	64	" E	Aug 30 64
8574	Reed J	140	" H	Sept 12 64
406	Reed S G	13	" B	April 6 64
6041	Reed W D	146	" H	Aug 18 64
10232	Reed W J	41	" I	Oct 2 64
8492	Reed Wm	Art 14	" I	Sept 11 64
7369	Reetz Jno	52	" A	Aug 31 64
5694	Reeve G	152	" C	Aug 5 64
1630	Reeves Jno	57	" H	June 6 64
10467	Redmond J	43	" C	Oct 7 64
10911	Regler W H	Cav 22	" M	Oct 14 64
9122	Reiley P O	164	" B	Sept 13 64
7195	Reuback C	29		Aug 29 64
12455	Rebman J	59	" C	Jany 15 65
8431	Rencermane J R	Cav 5	" B	Sept 11 64
9320	Randall A B	76	" F	Sept 20 64
8352	Remson C	Cav 2	" M	July 15 64
8269	Reynolds O	155	" E	Sept 8 64
6799	Reynolds O S	85	" E	Aug 25 64
10265	Reynolds Samuel	92	" H	Oct 3 64
6830	Reynolds Wm	140	" I	Aug 21 64
6546	Reidy J D	65	" I	Aug 23 64
4313	Rice F	39	" I	July 20 64
8077	Rich T D	Bat 24		July 9 64
12280	Rich J	82	Co C	Dec 15 64
8531	Richey R	66	" C	July 18 64
2127	Rider E	173	" E	June 24 64
8305	Rhenebault R H	21	" B	Sept 6 64
11904	Rehn W	Art 7	" C	Nov 7 64

New York — (*Continued.*)

3891	Richistine C	132 Co D		July 24 64
5317	Richards A	52 "	D	Aug 11 64
5674	Richards A	41 "	E	Aug 14 64
12243	Richards A	9 "	C	Dec 7 64
3692	Richards H	47 "	E	July 21 64
7578	Richards N J	146 "	C	Sept 2 64
4210	Richardson H M	Cav 20 "	M	July 29 64
12193	Ricker M	Art 2 "	M	Nov 29 64
8155	Rickhor J	85 "	E	Sept 8 64
415	Rikel Robert	125 "	G	April 7 64
12382	Riley I	73 "	E	Jany 2 65
2885	Riley J	99 "	C	July 4 64
5021	Riley John	176 "	C	Aug 8 64
6347	Riley John	39 "	D	Aug 21 64
11163	Ripley F A	152 "	C	Oct 19 64
11760	Ripp W	42 "	B	Nov 3 64
3514	Rising C	75 "	B	July 18 64
10310	Risley Geo W	46 "	G	Oct 4 64
2558	Ritcher F	132 "	D	June 27 64
7243	Ritson S	Cav 18 "	E	Aug 29 64
9224	Ritzmiller Jno	115		Sept 19 64
1775	Roach F	99 Co	F	June 9 64
1842	Roach Chas	85 "	E	June 11 64
2354	Robberger P H	46 "	B	June 23 64
11195	Roberson C A	122 "	B	Oct 20 64
2346	Robertson W H	131 "	B	June 23 64
8554	Robertson W M	96 "	B	Sept 12 64
9070	Robinson H	39 "	K	Sept 28 64
7607	Robinson A	111 "	I	Sept 2 64
3380	Robinson H C	95 "	I	July 21 64
6419	Robinson Jno	115 "	A	Aug 22 64
27	Robins L	154 "	K	Mch 8 64
7663	Roberts A	173 "	C	Sept 3 64
7535	Rockwell N C	Art 14 "	D	Sept 2 64
8318	Rockfeller R E	85 "	D	July 23 64
11342	Rockfeller H	Art 15 "	M	Oct 23 64
3959	Rock F	Art 6 "	F	July 25 64
4330	Rogers A	Art 7 "	I	July 31 64
6059	Rogers A	125 "	H	Aug 18 64
5791	Rogers G	Mus 85 "	F	Aug 15 64
3011	Rogers Jas	132 "	H	July 7 64
4287	Rogers H C	85 "	C	July 30 64
8369	Rogers H J	Art 2 "	E	Sept 10 64
4912	Rogers M	43 "	D	Aug 6 64
7208	Rogers O S	85 "	C	Aug 29 64
6824	Rogers Thos	12 "	F	Aug 25 64
11772	Romer F	9 "	A	Nov 3 64
8468	Rook G	Art 6 "	M	Sept 11 64
9663	Rooney Jno	152 "	G	Sept 28 64
9102	Rooney M	132 "	F	Sept 18 64
8922	Rooney P	Art 2 "	C	Sept 16 64
5669	Root A N	85 "	C	Aug 14 64
2998	Roots W T	120 "	H	July 7 64
1725	Root Legrand	Bat 24		June 8 64
10278	Rose A	16 Co	L	Oct 2 64
9550	Rosecrans J E	125 "	H	Sept 23 64
8171	Ross C	av 23 "	A	Sept 8 64
3874	Ross E F	111 "	I	July 24 64
5591	Ross David	27 "	D	Aug 14 64
6741	Ross G	76 Co	K	Aug 24 64
9751	Ross A	Cav 1 "	M	Sept 25 64
11963	Ross J H	121 "	G	Nov 11 64
5939	Rosenbarger Jno	4 "	D	Aug 17 64
3616	Rosser Lewis	84 "	A	July 20 64
2924	Rosenburg J	80 "	A	July 5 64
8737	Rosson Chas	Cav 24 "	E	Sept 14 64
12239	Roswell J	93 "	K	Dec 10 64
727	Ross Jacob	151 "	A	April 25 64
1940	Row W J	120 "	B	June 14 64
5097	Roth Louis	39 "	D	Aug 9 64
8304	Rothwell M	Cav 20 "	M	Sept 12 64
3720	Rouge Wm, Bug'l	Cav 12 "	F	July 21 64
7709	Rowbotham R	Cav 11 "	L	Sept 3 64
5857	Rowell J E	70 "	G	Aug 16 64
3492	Rowell L N	99 "	H	July 17 64
59	Roberts A B	Cav 8 "	B	Mch 18 64
2609	Ruddin C	120 "	H	June 28 64
837	Rudler Wm	120 "	M	May 3 64
40	Rue Newton	Cav 5 "	A	Mch 13 64
8667	Runey F	69 "	H	Sept 13 64
12635	Russ Jno	2 "	K	Feb 10 65
8856	Russell J	Art 7 "	A	Sept 15 64
5094	Ryan D	106 "	D	Aug 8 64
8599	Ryan J	95 "	E	Sept 12 64
8741	Ryan J	Cav 22 "	E	Sept 14 64
7258	Ryan Owen	12 "	A	Aug 30 64
4762	Ryonch Jno	66 "	I	Aug 5 64
6413	Ryson Jno	Art 7 "	L	Aug 22 64
6206	Ryne J M	69 "	E	Aug 9 64
684	Rush Jno	111 "	E	April 23 64
7234	Sackett R S	85 "	G	Aug 29 64
1920	Sadley M	77 "	H	June 14 64
1880	Safford B J	Bat 24		June 12 64
11870	Salsbury H	Art 1 Co	M	Nov 6 64
10652	Salisbury E	16 "	D	Oct 11 64
10928	Samlett ——	Cav 13 "	I	Oct 14 64
10880	Samet W	15 "	H	Oct 13 64
3769	Sampson J	106 "	K	July 22 64
346	Sanders Chas	Mil 9 "	A	April 2 64
3618	Sanders J	99 "	C	July 23 64
9857	Sanders J	Cav 12 "	A	Sept 27 64
4423	Sandford P O	Art 7 "	L	July 31 64
2341	Saughin J	Cav 12 "	F	June 23 64
7740	Sawyer J	Cav 2 "	L	Sept 3 64
11232	Sayles A	Cav 22 "	E	Oct 21 64
3612	Seaman A	85 "	H	July 19 64
10356	Seaman A	Art 2		Oct 13 64
1372	Sears F	Cav 2 Co	H	May 25 64
6120	Seagher J	8 "	M	Aug 19 64
4325	See Henry	11 "	K	July 30 64
8824	Seeley A J	140 "	A	Sept 15 64
11374	Seeley C B	15 "	H	Oct 24 64
4256	Seeley Thos	100 "	F	July 29 64
10027	Segam Ed	Cav 5 "	K	Sept 29 64
4204	Seigler Geo	10		July 29 64
7458	Seigle John R	120 "	K	Sept 1 64
11886	Selson H	59 "	C	Nov 6 64
3457	Serrier R	40 "	C	July 17 64

New York — (*Continued.*)

1746	Serine C	Cav 4	Co M	June 8 64
629	Settle Henry	99	" H	April 19 64
9828	Seyman F	Cav 1	" A	Sept 27 64
5951	Seard Louis	77	" E	Aug 17 64
6388	Schayler J W	Cav 21	" M	Aug 26 64
10794	Schadt Theo	100	" A	Oct 12 64
3557	Scheck B	Cav 2	" G	July 18 64
3190	Schemerhorn H	1[illegible]0	" G	July 12 64
11965	Schempp M	Art 7	" F	Nov 11 64
2795	Schermashie B	170	" A	July 2 64
1325	Schlotesser J	91	" H	May 24 64
11515	Schlotesser J	1	" L	Oct 26 64
9578	Schmaker Jno	8[illegible]	" B	Sept 23 64
10291	Schmaley J	1	" G	Oct 16 64
10550	Schmeager A	39	" A	Oct 9 64
5311	Schneider Chas	39	" A	Aug 11 64
8593	Shockney T T	Bat 24		Sept 12 64
8796	Schofield J	7	Co H	Sept 15 64
2441	Scholl Jno	54	" D	June 25 64
11422	Schriber H	59	" I	Oct 24 64
7814	Schroeder G	Art 7	" E	Sept 4 64
8550	Schrum J	Art 14	" K	Sept 12 64
1070	Schrimer Wm	20	" B	May 13 64
4280	Schware F	Cav 12	" K	July 20 64
6613	Schwick A	66	" G	Aug 23 64
4849	Scott J C	85	" K	Aug 6 64
6857	Scott P C	Cav 14	" G	Aug 26 64
8622	Scott W W	Cav 2	" F	Sept 13 64
8290	Sibble W	148	" G	Sept 9 64
4362	S[illegible]k R E			July 31 64
4557	Sickler E	Art 7	Co E	Aug 2 64
3210	Sickles A	120	" D	July 12 64
11950	Siddell G	40		Nov 10 64
12284	Simmons A	Art 8	Co H	Dec 13 64
6364	Simmons C G	85	" B	Aug 21 64
8316	Simon H	1[illegible]6	" B	Sept 10 64
6284	Simons H L	85	" E	Aug 20 64
142	Simondinger B	155	" I	Mch 24 64
242	Simpson D	99	" H	Mch 30 64
6345	Sisson P V	Art 22	" M	Aug 21 64
10067	Shaab J	50	" A	Sept 30 64
201	Shea Pat, drummer	61	" M	Mch 28 64
4801	Shaffer M	Art 7		Aug 5 64
4534	Shaffer J	66	Co E	Aug 2 64
782	Shafer H	103	" F	April 28 64
6747	Shaughnessey J	Cav 6	" A	Aug 24 64
4446	Shannan E	Art 6	" H	Aug 1 64
5645	Shenk S W	Bat 24		Aug 14 64
290	Shaw Alex	Art 3	Co K	April 1 64
9667	Shaw T I	Cav 15	" M	Sept 24 64
12814	Shaw W	Art 7	" F	Mch 25 65
7660	Shay John	69	" B	Sept 3 64
3360	Sheldon M	Art 7	" B	July 15 64
4[illegible]47	Shepardson L	Cav 22	" E	July 29 64
5474	Shaw J	Cav 2	" E	Aug 13 64
7798	Shuler Chas	52	" G	Sept 4 64
8335	Shaw M	76	" D	Sept 10 64
9924	Sheppard W H	9	" F	Sept 28 64
8205	Sherer H	Cav 5		Sept 8 64
10930	Sherridan J	Cav 2		Oct 14 64
4676	Sherwood J E	76	Co G	Aug 4 64
720	Shickls Richard	132	" F	April 25 64
701	Shilts E	52	" K	April 23 64
10495	Shidler Geo	97	" F	Oct 8 64
8206	Shindler J	Art 15	" E	Sept 8 64
7437	Shirlock R	85	" K	Sept 1 64
5337	Shippey F	85	" D	Aug 16 64
2430	Shirley P	Bat 24		June 23 64
2151	Shats C	1[illegible]1	Co F	June 18 64
5755	Shortey Robert	164	" B	Aug 15 64
5343	Shotliff J	Art 7	" L	Aug 11 64
2975	Shults Jno	118	" F	July 7 64
6633	Shultz F	76	" F	Aug 23 64
12194	Shultz Wm	Art 7	" C	Nov 29 64
11822	Shultz C	66	" F	Nov 5 64
11813	Shumaker P	100	" K	Nov 4 64
11280	Shuhps P D	1[illegible]5	" K	Oct 22 64
2462	Shuster ——	54	" C	June 25 64
2922	Slater F	48	" F	July 5 64
700	Slater Jno	1[illegible]0	" H	April 23 64
12534	Slater Jas	7	" K	Jan 27 65
11162	Slater Richard	2	" E	Oct 19 64
12811	Sleight C	32	" I	Mch 24 65
10377	Sloat Wm	140	" E	Oct 5 64
6819	Sloates F	76	" F	Aug 25 64
10125	Slimp W	146	" A	Oct 11 64
7628	Smades W	9	" D	Sept 2 64
12083	Small S	53	" F	Nov 18 64
7783	Smarty Jno	Cav 22	" G	Sept 4 64
7406	Smead L	Art 18	" D	Aug 31 64
762	Smalley Geo	140	" H	April 27 64
12503	Smith A	Art 7	" F	Jan 21 65
11371	Smith A	9	" A	Oct 23 64
7326	Smith A J	85	" D	Aug 30 64
802	Smith Bernard	132	" B	April 29 64
1310	Smith Benjamin	Cav 2	" H	May 23 64
2659	Smith Chas	61	" A	June 29 64
3735	Smith Chas	52	" E	July 21 64
4534	Smith Chas	100	" B	Aug 2 64
7612	Smith Chas	Art 15	" K	Sept 2 64
10052	Smith Chas	9	" G	Sept 30 64
11233	Smith E	61	" D	Oct 22 64
1819	Smith F	48	" F	June 10 64
1246	Smith Frank	99	" I	May 30 64
11839	Smith G R	Cav 2	" H	Nov 5 64
3372	Smith N	Cav 9	" C	July 15 64
1247	Smith Henry	132	" C	May 20 64
3238	Smith J	Cav 5		July 12 64
3504	Smith J	Cav 4	Co B	July 18 64
4834	Smith J	115	" G	Aug 6 64
9300	Smith J	52	" A	Sept 20 64
10456	Smith J	Cav 13	" D	Oct 7 64
12627	Smith J	46	" E	Feb 10 65
1215	Smith Jas	Cav 20	" M	May 20 64
7004	Smith Jas	6	" A	Aug 27 64
11787	Smith Jas	57	" B	Nov 4 64
7610	Smith Jackson	85	" I	Sept 2 64
11210	Smith J	52	" A	Oct 20 64

New York—(*Continued.*)

305	Smith Jno	71	Co C	April 1 64
534	Smith Jno	Cav 3	" E	April 14 64
5496	Smith Jno	41	" E	Aug 13 64
5602	Smith Jno	66	" F	Aug 14 64
6428	Smith Jno	95	" D	Aug 22 64
10547	Smith Jno	69	" G	Oct 9 64
5882	Smith Jno J	109	" C	Aug 16 64
11454	Smith J M	59	" A	Oct 25 64
10079	Smith K	Cav 22	" K	Sept 30 64
5009	Smith L A	115	" F	Aug 8 64
9973	Smith Levi	125	" B	Sept 28 64
7706	Smith John C	48	" E	Sept 3 64
2780	Smith S	11	" I	July 2 64
5854	Smith S A	132	" F	Aug 16 64
6709	Smith T	147	" E	Aug 24 64
6361	Smith Thos	47	" C	Aug 21 64
9199	Smith T R	2	" E	Sept 21 64
139	Smith Wm	99	" H	Mch 24 64
325	Smith Wm	Art 3	" K	April 2 64
532	Smith Wm	104	" A	April 14 64
812	Smith Wm	106	" B	April 30 64
7550	Smith Wm	2	" L	Sept 2 64
10164	Smith Wm	76	" K	Oct 1 64
12394	Smith H	7	" C	Jany 5 65
3708	Snedegar A J	111	" D	July 21 64
7173	Snyder A	25	" E	Aug 29 64
4448	Snyder B	2	" B	Aug 1 64
10076	Snyder Wm	Drag 1	" E	Sept 30 64
1319	Sombeck Geo	52	" I	May 23 64
5169	Somers John	2	" E	Aug 9 64
2773	Sopher James	132	" F	July 2 64
2403	Sopher S	102	" K	June 24 64
4352	Sotter J M	47	" C	July 31 64
3534	Southard H	Cav 5	" C	July 18 64
10526	Southard N	2	" H	Oct 8 64
11346	Southard W A	18	" I	Oct 23 64
2877	Souther Henry	69	" K	July 4 64
8124	Southworth R	Cav 22	" E	Sept 8 64
10488	Skall S	Art 7	" L	Oct 7 64
12029	Skeeley T	66	" H	Nov 15 64
9954	Spark G	Art 16	" C	Sept 28 64
6975	Sparks E	10	" B	Aug 27 64
5421	Spaulding H	Cav 1	" F	Aug 12 64
5567	Spellman John	66	" B	Aug 13 64
12712	Spencer A	93	" D	Feb 28 65
10989	Sperry A	51	" F	Oct 16 64
3532	Span Jas	147	" H	July 18 64
5982	Spanbury S	Art 14	" C	Aug 17 64
5821	Sprague E H	Bat 10		Aug 16 64
3593	Sprague J	85	Co I	July 19 64
10730	Sprig Jas A	Cav 24	" E	Oct 11 64
4877	Sprink A	146	" F	Aug 6 64
9035	Strats Jno	15	" A	Sept 17 64
889	Stacey Jno	99	" I	May 4 64
4574	Stadler J	39	" A	Aug 2 64
10078	Stancliff A B	106	" H	Sept 30 64
2570	Stanton H H	22	" E	June 27 64
5187	Stark J D	100	" A	Aug 9 64
11740	Starkweather L	146	" E	Nov 2 64

12650	Star C	15	Co D	Feb 13 65
7331	Stanton L H	Art 7	" K	Aug 31 64
2520	Stark J H	121	" A	June 26 64
1698	Stanley J C	85	" C	June 7 64
10290	St Dennis L	16	" F	Oc 4 64
9903	Stewart Peter	5	" B	Sept 27 64
7636	Stevens E	120	" C	Sept 2 64
95	Stevenson Wm	132	" G	Mch 22 64
3782	Sternhoff A	Art 15	" C	July 22 64
4678	Stevens Jno S	100	" F	Aug 4 64
5530	Steiner C	Art 7	" M	Aug 13 64
7028	Stevens Wm	99	" I	Aug 27 64
2346	Stead J	115	" F	June 27 64
6531	Stebins C	85	" C	Aug 23 64
3872	Sevenson W	10	" F	July 24 64
6443	Stead J	15	" D	Aug 22 64
2031	Stewart Jno	89		June 15 64
1863	Stebbins H	85	Co B	June 12 64
6049	Stelrocht D	Cav 22	" C	Aug 18 64
10149	Stickler E	169	" A	Oct 1 64
11755	Stivers R	111	" F	Nov 2 64
7075	Still D	132	" D	Aug 28 64
6102	Stump W	6	" K	Aug 18 64
4193	Still Jas	164	" E	July 29 64
4385	Stillwell S	Art 2	" E	July 31 64
915	Stone Jno, Mus	Cav 5	" C	May 16 64
11043	Stoddard J	111	" F	Oct 17 64
6722	Stone L	24	" E	Aug 24 64
2053	Stoup J	15	" A	June 16 64
3415	Strue G A	Art 1	" B	July 16 64
3997	Storing A	54	" B	July 26 64
8520	Strain A W	Cav 2	" I	Sept 12 64
3905	Streeter F	76	" F	July 24 64
4665	Storms A N	Art 7	" I	Aug 4 64
4798	Strale J	178	" B	Aug 5 64
5342	Strater Geo	85	" K	Aug 11 64
6988	Stratton J H	140	" H	Aug 27 64
11967	Strip W	42	" E	Nov 11 64
116	Streight Lewis	127	" A	Mch 23 64
2401	Stratten Chas	125	" K	June 24 64
7845	Sturdevant G	Cav 5	" I	Sept 4 64
5994	Stutzman P	39	" D	Aug 17 64
6102	Stump W	60	" K	Aug 18 64
11832	Styler G W	Art 7	" I	Nov 5 64
9953	Sughem I	H A	" B	Sept 28 64
640	Sullivan Ed	69	" A	April 20 64
6048	Sullivan M	69	" K	Aug 18 64
1492	Sullivan Pat	99	" H	May 31 64
7728	Sullivan P C	155	" E	Sept 3 64
5440	Susear Fred	39	" I	Aug 12 64
10661	Sutliff E	Cav 15	" M	Oct 11 64
1	Swarner J H	Cav 2	" H	Feby 27 64
4005	Swarner J, bugler	Cav 2	" H	July 26 64
6466	Swartz M	Cav 2	" M	Aug 22 64
12267	Swager G	103	" F	Dec 12 64
2322	Sweeney Jas	155	" I	June 22 64
5835	Sweeney M	122	" C	Aug 16 64
3527	Sweet E	93	" F	July 18 64
2921	Sweet L	Art 4	" M	July 5 64

New York—(*Continued.*)

4960 Sylurs S	140 Co E	Aug 7 64
12765 Swancent J	2 " A	Mch 13 65
10539 Stratton E	76 " E	Oct 10 64
1934 Taylor A	Cav 2 " F	June 14 64
4867 Taylor C	115 " F	Aug 6 64
551 Taylor Chas B	154	April 14 64
11321 Taylor D	149 Co D	Oct 22 64
2742 Taylor R H	125 " F	July 1 64
493 Taylor Thos B	Cav 10 " E	April 11 64
9993 Taylor L B	147 " K	Sept 29 64
12290 Taylor W	Cav 12 " A	Dec 15 64
124 0 Taylor W	42 " B	Jany 17 65
10370 Taylor W H	Art 7 " C	Oct 5 64
10738 Taylor W H	Cav 7 " C	Oct 11 64
10157 Taylor Wm	Cav 22 " C	Oct 1 64
8961 Taylor W W	2 " I	Sept 16 64
8988 Tarvis G W	Drag 1 " K	Sept 17 64
9480 Tare W	115 " D	Sept 21 64
3681 Tambrick A	Cav 16 " A	July 21 64
3976 Tanner M	1 " E	July 25 64
4326 Tanschivit Ed	Art 15 " E	July 30 64
7019 Tell Wm	59 " C	Aug 27 64
9143 Thompson A	9 " D	Sept 18 64
133 Terry Aaron	12 " K	Mch 24 64
9064 Teneyck M	Art 14 " E	Sept 17 64
4909 Tewey J	99 " H	Aug 6 64
6445 Terwilliger D R	85 " D	Aug 22 64
10352 Thomas J	Cav 2 " D	Oct 5 64
3598 Thomas H	88 " D	July 19 64
3711 Thomas W	3 " H	July 21 64
4619 Thomas J	85 " G	Aug 3 64
10361 Thearer J	Bat 1	Oct 5 64
8161 Thompson C W	85 Co K	Sept 8 64
4781 Thompson J	39 " H	Aug 5 64
5510 Thompkins Ira	Art 6	Aug 13 64
5524 Thompson P	10 Co E	Aug 13 64
6730 Thompson N B	146 " A	Aug 24 64
5784 Thompson J	104 " G	Aug 15 64
2613 Thompson T	Cav 12 " F	June 28 64
320 Thompson Daniel	142 " E	April 2 64
3538 Thresh G	Cav 5 " K	July 18 64
5147 Thruston N E	85 " C	Aug 9 64
11235 Thornton J	Art 14 " L	Oct 21 64
6309 Thorpe W C	82 " I	Aug 20 64
4393 Thurston G W	85 " E	July 31 64
12843 Thayer G	70 " E	April 22 65
679 Thierbach P M	39 " D	April 22 64
11230 Tilton H	Art 24	Oct 20 64
8283 Tillitson N P	51 Co A	Sept 9 64
8849 Timerson Wm	Art 2 " I	Sept 15 64
2680 Timmish ——	85 " C	June 30 64
659 Tiner David	79 " E	April 21 64
10422 Townsend W	111 " B	Oct 6 64
8068 Townsend L	Cav 22 " G	Sept 7 64
3883 Townsend Jno	52 " A	July 24 64
535 Townsend Geo M	111 " F	April 14 64
9050 Thornson E	22	Sept 17 64
4774 Toney L	100 Co D	Aug 5 64
10727 Tolal Pat	164 " K	Oct 11 64
5833 Towner L	Cav 5 Co G	Aug 16 64
6047 Tobias A	120 " G	Aug 18 64
2112 Toomey J F	85 " I	June 17 64
12465 Tourney P	99 " B	Jan 16 65
12636 Tocdt H	1 " K	Feb 10 65
12708 Tomlinson W F	22 " G	Feb 28 65
3193 Tripp Ira	77 " B	July 12 64
10442 Tripp O S	Art 3 " K	Oct 7 64
9507 Truman A M	Art 2 " D	Sept 22 64
7629 Trueman R	Art 7 " G	Sept 2 64
8544 Tremor M	76 " F	Sept 12 64
7317 Trumpp E	Cav 22 " F	Aug 30 64
3882 Trumbull H	115 " I	July 24 64
7187 Travis T	Cav 8 " G	Aug 29 64
4052 Truesdale W J	85 " H	July 27 64
3425 Trompter F	140 " B	July 16 64
100 Tracey Pat	99 " I	Mch 22 64
707 Turner Wm	Cav 5 " G	April 24 64
7970 Turner Jno	49 " A	Sept 5 64
11376 Turner J	Cav 22 " M	Oct 24 64
1688 Turner Thos	Cav 16 " B	June 6 64
2120 Turner J B	85 " C	June 17 64
10535 Tuthill C	Cav 22 " G	Oct 8 64
9687 Tuthill S D	Art 2 " M	Sept 24 64
10604 Tuft E	29 " C	Oct 10 64
7915 Turden E S	Cav 15 " D	Sept 5 64
7421 Turton W F	Art 2 " I	Aug 31 64
3796 Tubbs W H	85 " D	July 22 64
3084 Tupple H	154 " H	July 9 64
3129 Tucker L	120 " D	July 10 64
2893 Tuttle W	48 " K	July 4 64
10494 Tyrrell J	Cav 22 " A	Oct 8 64
4217 Uncer Jas	15 " H	July 29 64
416 Uber Chas	14 " A	April 7 64
12401 Udell J	Art 7 " H	Jany 5 65
10887 Ulmer H	Art 15 " K	Oct 14 64
2317 Underburg L W	77 " G	June 22 64
254 Underhill H	47 " E	Mch 30 64
1495 Underwriter A	62 " F	May 21 64
1091 Van Clarke Wm	106 " D	May 14 64
9087 Van Allen C	7 " E	Sept 18 64
1025 Van Buren J W	Art 3 " K	May 11 64
664 Van Buren Henry	Art 3 " K	April 21 64
10071 Van Bethysen H	Art 7 " I	Sept 30 64
12539 Van Bramin T	71 " K	Jany 27 65
1511 Van Derbreck A	132 " B	June 3 64
3163 Van Dugen ——	Cav 24 " M	July 17 64
6560 Van Hosen C	95 " A	Aug 23 64
10656 Van Housen B	Bat 12	Oct 11 64
3371 Van Haughton J	124 Co C	July 15 64
1418 Vanderbrogart W	104 " F	May 27 64
8957 Vanarsdale P	1 " G	Sept 16 64
8782 Vanalstine H	152 " A	Sept 14 64
8806 Vanclack F	5 " D	Sept 15 64
7564 Vanvelzer J M	85 " I	Sept 2 64
7635 Vanburen J	Cav 15 " B	Sept 2 64
11446 Vanscott L	59 " C	Oct 25 64
11596 Vanarnum J	Cav 8 " E	Oct 28 64
7054 Vanwagner C	Art 2 " F	Aug 28 64

New York—(*Continued.*)

7244	Vanesse M	Cav 2	Co K	Aug 29 64
7252	Vanzart Wm	Art 7	" E	Aug 30 64
6472	Varney C	169	" E	Aug 22 64
6634	Vanalstine C	Art 7	" C	Aug 23 64
3333	Vanest J H	Art 14	" B	July 15 64
83	Vanvelsen J	120	" A	Mch 21 64
2089	Vaughan W H	Cav 8	" K	June 17 64
973	Vespers Jas W	85	" D	May 9 64
7506	Van Osten C	52	" H	Sept 1 64
5661	Vencot L	Cav 2	H	Aug 14 64
4196	Veil Wm	Art 6	" F	July 29 64
1539	Vernon S	Cav 2	" M	June 1 64
7846	Vincent R	178	" I	Sept 4 64
2782	Vincent Richard	1	" K	July 2 64
2879	Vinsant G M	Art 14	" I	July 4 64
2715	Vish O	178	" E	July 1 64
6525	Vibbard Geo	Cav 22	" E	Aug 22 64
10023	Voerling H	Art 15	" C	Sept 29 64
4623	Vogle Anton	10	" C	Aug 3 64
5503	Voorhies A H	Cav 1	" H	Aug 13 64
11507	Voorhies E R	85	" C	Oct 26 64
6682	Voorhies Geo	85	" C	Aug 23 64
1184	Walls Peter	Cav 4	" D	May 18 64
5001	Wall Jas	15	" G	Aug 7 64
1398	Wallace Jno	Cav 11	" B	May 26 64
10211	Watt H	Cav 12	" A	Oct 2 64
9977	Watts C	6	" C	Sept 28 64
10313	Waters A L	Cav 8	" F	Oct 4 64
10477	Warner Chas L	Cav 2	" D	Oct 7 64
4026	Warren L	95	" I	July 26 64
7351	Warner P P	Art 14	" M	Aug 31 64
7444	Warner A J	76	" F	Sept 1 64
12449	Warner Luther	Cav 12	" A	Jan 9 65
10543	Ward Patrick	88	" C	Oct 8 64
5127	Ward J	99	" G	Aug 9 64
10920	Ward J	40	" H	Oct 14 64
2238	Ward H	95	" I	June 20 64
400	Ward W A	99	" B	April 6 64
12816	Warden H B	5	" B	Mch 25 65
9858	Walters D	125	" E	Sept 27 64
1557	Walters Nelson	120	" K	June 2 64
3381	Walterhouse Ed	9	" I	July 16 64
2827	Wallace J	Cav 2	" M	July 3 64
8939	Watson G	Art 6	" C	Sept 16 64
10965	Watson Jas	Art 15	" M	Oct 15 64
6947	Watson T	99	" I	Aug 26 64
9356	Wade M	Art 14	" D	Sept 20 64
8146	Walker J	Art 2	" D	Sept 8 64
8198	Wall J	64	" I	Sept 8 64
7276	Warhurst Sam'l	Art 7	" I	Aug 30 64
3731	Washington I	76	" G	July 21 64
5679	Washburn H	Cav 5	" D	Aug 14 64
2023	Wagner C	39	" E	June 15 64
10686	Wagner C	93	" K	Oct 11 64
11001	Warren P	Art 7	" G	Oct 16 64
16537	Warren E	Cav 22	" L	Aug 23 64
4120	Warren Geo R	2	" F	July 28 64
11082	Warrell E C	57	" I	Oct 17 64
11945	Waterman S	169	" K	Nov 10 64
6978	Waldron N	146	Co A	Aug 27 64
7249	Walz M	Art 14	" I	Aug 30 64
6425	Walling Geo	76	" B	Aug 22 64
6046	Watchler J	119	" G	Aug 18 64
4060	Walls C H	109	" K	July 27 64
3336	Walser Jno	Art 15	" D	July 15 64
1564	Walcott G P	67	" D	June 2 64
2294	Wales J	85	" D	June 22 64
1537	West Jas	Art 3	" H	June 1 64
9572	West T	Cav 13	" F	Sept 23 64
3964	West Wm	152	" E	July 25 64
739	West Jas	Cav 2	" E	April 25 64
10303	Weston L	115	" F	Oct 4 64
9731	Webster G	29	C	Sept 25 64
5593	Webster E	76	" E	Aug 14 64
1598	Webster James	137	" C	June 4 64
9889	Wendle John	Art 7	" E	Sept 27 64
9941	Wellstraff C	100	" D	Sept 28 64
10013	Welch W	76	" G	Sept 29 64
5030	Welch C	Cav 3	" B	Aug 8 64
8555	Welber E G	120	" K	Sept 15 64
8208	Weil E C	164	" B	Sept 8 64
7561	Welson Jas H	74	" K	Sept 2 64
8177	Welch C	39	" H	Sept 8 64
5181	Welch E	Bat 24		Aug 9 64
6692	Welch J	Cav 5	Co K	Aug 24 64
2310	Welsh L	146	" B	June 22 64
8855	Welber E G	120	" K	Sept 15 64
9428	Weaver J	Cav 1	" E	Sept 21 64
7078	Weaver B S	96	" I	Aug 28 64
9148	Webber C H	85	" C	Sept 21 64
9506	Westerfield P S	Art 7	" B	Sept 22 64
8731	Werting John	52	" D	Sept 14 64
7987	Wellington G R	Cav 12	" A	Sept 6 64
8204	Weeks J	7	" G	Sept 8 64
7472	Wells Jeff	1	" H	Sept 1 64
12036	Wells E	69	" K	Nov 16 64
7667	Weismere H	32	" I	Sept 3 64
4915	Wedder N C	184	" E	Aug 6 64
11061	Wellder C M	Cav 22	" G	Oct 17 64
11397	Westbrook D	155	" H	Oct 24 64
6927	Weafer Chas	115	" A	Aug 26 64
7256	Wertz Jas	Cav 12	" I	Aug 30 64
6370	Webb M E	Art 14	" F	Aug 21 64
11127	Welch J	Cav 5	" D	Oct 18 64
6002	Weiber J	Art 6	" E	Aug 17 64
4272	Weller W H	85	" E	July 29 64
3285	Westfall Jno	151	" H	July 12 64
265	Weldon Edson	Cav 20	" M	Mch 31 64
507	Westhrop H	125	" B	April 12 64
6755	Webster H	Cav 22	" A	Aug 24 64
10303	Weston L	115	" F	Oct 4 64
7543	Whitmore D	140	" I	Sept 2 64
10423	Wharton J R	Cav 5	" L	Oct 6 64
9743	Whittle J C	85	" E	Sept 25 64
9878	Whertmore M	Art 15	" M	Sept 13 64
8611	Whipple M	Cav 22	" D	Sept 13 64
8680	White Jas	Drag 1	" D	Sept 13 64
11879	White L	Art 8	" G	Nov 6 64

New York —(*Continued.*)

3034	White E	Cav 10 Co D	July 8 64
8792	Whiting M	85 " D	Sept 15 64
7417	Whitney John	39 " K	Aug 31 64
5207	Whitney J	104 " E	Aug 10 64
10972	Whitman I	16 " H	Oct 15 64
12049	Whitmans P	66 " E	Nov 16 64
11724	Whifbeck J	20 " D	Nov 1 64
6611	Wheeler D	147 " H	Aug 23 64
5770	Whitmore O B	40 " A	Aug 15 64
4155	Whitlock Wm	Art 14 " I	July 28 64
1133	Wilson James	132 " K	May 16 64
3757	Wilson John	95 " A	July 22 64
6832	Wilson M	Art 2 " H	Aug 25 64
11983	Wilson W	155 " H	Nov 13 64
5870	Wilson A	57 " A	Aug 16 64
1645	Wilson D	48 " H	June 5 64
6233	Windness A	Art 15 " C	Aug 20 64
4080	Williams F	125 " A	July 27 64
4522	Williams Ed	42 " A	Aug 2 64
11130	Williams H	Cav 2 " M	Oct 18 64
12697	Williams S	94 " I	Feb 23 65
9516	Williams L D	85 " G	Sept 22 64
8478	Wilcox T E	85 " B	Sept 11 64
7945	Williams Jas	63 " G	Sept 5 64
4603	Williams Geo	Cav 1 " K	Aug 3 64
4701	Williams John	52 " K	Aug 4 64
3947	Williams O	Bat 24	July 25 64
1567	Williams H	9 Co A	June 2 64
6861	Williams L	16 " A	Aug 26 64
7112	Williams I B	Cav 24 " C	Aug 28 64
6219	Williams C R	85 " E	Aug 20 64
3069	Wiron P	Cav 20 " M	July 9 64
3273	Wicks D	63 " D	July 13 64
1938	Wilcox Geo	Cav 12 " F	June 14 64
2044	Wilcox R	14	June 15 64
9496	Wilcox W	43 Co G	Sept 21 64
3576	Wilcox J	85 " D	July 19 64
11111	Wilcox H R	55 " C	Oct 18 64
11428	Wilcox C	Cav 5 " G	Oct 24 64
12607	Wiley I	59 " B	Feb 7 65
10122	Willis I	121 " G	Oct 1 64
9057	Willsey D	7	Sept 17 64
8729	Wiggins James	52 Co D	Sept 14 64
7980	Winn James	Art 7 " I	Sept 6 64
8208	Will E C	164 " B	Sept 8 64
7622	Wiley W	115 " G	Sept 2 64
3728	Wilkey S	8 " B	July 21 64
10977	Wilkinson I N	42 Co A	Oct 15 64
5663	Wicks Frank	Art 1 " K	Aug 14 64
11474	Winney G A	100 " D	Oct 25 64
11520	Winter G	Cav 10 " L	Oct 26 64
11689	Wilds I	154 " B	Oct 31 64
7122	Winser I	117 " I	Aug 28 64
7581	Wood E G	Bat 24	Sept 2 64
3607	Wood F	Cav 5 Co I	July 19 64
9874	Wood H	115 " G	Sept 27 64
10063	Wood H	15 " B	Sept 30 64
9715	Wood J	Cav 10 " H	Sept 25 64
7686	Wood John	97 " D	Sept 3 64
3881	Wood M	111 " H	July 24 64
5039	Wood J S	Art 6 " A	Aug 8 64
9132	Woodmancy D M	Cav 3 " H	Sept 18 64
10141	Wood W J	95 " H	Oct 1 64
8382	Woodworth B	56 " D	Sept 10 64
7884	Woodland H	1 " I	Sept 5 64
5696	Woodhull D T	8 " E	Aug 15 64
12356	Wooley G C	Art 7 " K	Dec 30 64
11821	Wolf T	88 " D	Nov 5 64
11031	Wolf W	Art 2 " H	Oct 16 64
6130	Wood Fred	Cav 24 " E	Aug 19 64
591	Wolpan A	52 " C	April 16 64
4847	Wright Chas S	118 " E	Aug 6 64
10941	Wright D	43 " G	Oct 14 64
5126	Wright I I	148 " I	Aug 9 64
4281	Wang C	39 " E	July 30 64
7784	Wulslager John	85 " G	Sept 4 64
4589	Wyatt James	147 " G	Aug 2 64
7334	Wyncoop G	Cav 12 " H	Aug 30 64
2104	Winegardener L	18 " G	June 17 64
7433	Yales W G	71 " H	Sept 1 64
4984	Yencer I D	Bat 24	Aug 7 64
12501	Yeomand G	7 Co A	Jany 21 65
6539	Young C	41 " D	Aug 23 64
5598	Young Chas	15 " C	Aug 14 64
8224	Young E	Art 2 " I	Sept 8 64
1306	Young Eugene	111 " G	May 23 64
8733	Young George	22 " H	Sept 14 64
6946	Young J	Cav 1 " B	Aug 26 64
7411	Young T B	148 " A	Aug 31 64
10481	Yonker W	Art 10 " B	Oct 7 64
7480	Zaphan H P	Art 7 " E	Sept 1 64
12204	Zolber F W	40 " D	Dec 1 64
12617	Zegler S	145 " G	Feby 9 65

TOTAL 2571.

NORTH CAROLINA.

1596	Barker J	2 Co F	June 3 64
849	Briggs Wilson	1 " A	May 3 64
275	Callowhill B	2 " F	Mch 31 64
475	Cox William C	2 " F	April 9 64
864	Check W F	2 " F	May 8 64
144	Dunbar Alex	2 " F	Mch 25 64
1057	Miller J, Drummer	2 " D	May 13 64
10705	Macey Henry	7	Oct 11 64
11844	Moss Wm	1 Co F	Nov 5 64
8690	Norfleld Warren	1 Co G	Sept 14 64
370	Stone Jno A	2 " F	April 5 64
2636	Smith Jas	2 " F	June 29 64
4899	Smith George	2 " E	Aug 5 64
333	Turner F	2 " I	April 2 64
798	Turner H, Colored	2 " I	April 29 64
204	Weeks Nathan	2 " F	Mch 28 64
712	Williams Thos	2 " D	April 24 64

TOTAL 17.

OHIO.

12846 Akers J W	4	Co B	April 24 65
251 Arthur George	7	" B	Mch 30 64
789 Arrowsmith W R	45	" K	April 28 64
1118 Ames George	100	" K	May 15 64
1550 Allen W	45	" B	June 1 64
1569 Alinger D	51	" C	June 2 64
1724 Anderson D	111	" B	June 8 64
1779 Augustus T	89	" K	June 9 64
1805 Akers A A	94	" F	June 10 64
2040 Aldridge C W	33		June 15 64
2935 Adam Miller	103	Co I	July 5 64
3046 Anderson R	93	" C	July 8 64
3197 Aldbrook C W	60		July 12 64
3485 Arthur I C	89	Co A	July 17 64
3852 Armebrish A	21	" A	July 24 64
3932 Almond A	72	" A	July 25 64
4529 Arnold Chas	Cav 9	" G	Aug 2 64
4990 Ailes T G	20	" I	Aug 7 64
5048 Andrews Sam'l G			Aug 8 64
6422 Adams E	Cav 2	Co C	Aug 22 64
7429 Allen A B	121	" C	Aug 31 64
7482 Alward A	135	" B	Sept 1 64
7436 Arthur J	69	" I	Sept 3 64
7843 Arne I	64	" D	Sept 4 64
9818 Alown A	34	" D	Sept 26 64
10393 Andrews I R	63	" K	Oct 6 64
10425 Adams I	122	" I	Oct 6 64
10874 Allen James C	91	" F	Oct 13 64
11198 Andermill John	24	" K	Oct 20 64
12495 Allen J W	1	" G	Jan 20 65
188 Baiel W T	45	" F	Mch 27 64
207 Bodin Thomas S	44		Mch 28 64
691 Beaver George E	111	Co B	April 23 64
829 Beeman Richard	125	" E	May 1 64
861 Biddinger M, Mus	94	" K	May 3 64
952 Branigan James	82	" F	May 8 64
1094 Blangy S	70	" B	May 14 64
1212 Botkins A S	45	" G	May 19 64
1236 Black G W	99	" F	May 20 64
1366 Bates L B	Cav 1	" A	May 25 64
1368 Bodkin W	45	" K	May 25 64
1376 Baldwin N	Cav 9	" T	May 26 64
1385 Bowers James	89	" A	May 26 64
1468 Boyd H I	7	" H	May 30 64
1602 Boman John	2	" C	June 4 64
1609 Bryan R	16	" C	June 4 64
1781 Balcomb D	19	" F	June 9 64
1919 Brownles John	7	" I	June 14 64
1937 Brooks J	135	" I	June 14 64
1970 Bothin W J	45	" F	June 15 64
1993 Bartholomew E W	205	" C	June 15 64
2065 Belding F	105	" D	June 16 64
2067 Brookheart W	45	" I	June 16 64
2087 Benor H	100	" E	June 17 64
2110 Bishop S	49	" K	June 17 64
2170 Berry J C	90	" E	June 19 64
2264 Beers A	45	" A	June 20 64
2292 Burnham W	Art 1	" K	June 21 64
2415 Bird I	43	" A	June 24 64
2492 Bratt G	21	Co G	June 26 64
2599 Broughfman I	39	" C	June 28 64
2696 Brandon John	15	" F	June 30 64
3053 Barnes V H	92	" H	July 9 64
3245 Brown Charles	23	" D	July 13 64
3299 Burns M G	111	" B	July 13 64
3608 Brackneck H	Cav 7	" A	July 19 64
3656 Bogart John	9	" G	July 20 64
3706 Bontrell C	6	" G	July 21 64
3756 Butch O	45	" I	July 22 64
3831 Bowman S	51	" K	July 23 64
4073 Brockway M	Art 2	" D	July 27 64
4279 Boyle W H	11	" H	July 30 64
4684 Britton B H	125	" H	Aug 4 64
4968 Berdy M J	45	" D	Aug 7 64
5138 Buckle J J	126	" E	Aug 9 64
5219 Brabham George	Cav 9	" B	Aug 10 64
5493 Baldwin George	Cav 9	" G	Aug 13 64
5653 Bonestine W H	107	" I	Aug 14 64
5656 Burna J M	121	" K	Aug 14 64
5758 Balmet J	19	" I	Aug 15 64
5771 Brutch E	Cav 10	" I	Aug 15 64
5819 Bond S T	123	" B	Aug 16 64
5825 Boyle H	130	" B	Aug 16 64
5937 Bower F	61	" I	Aug 17 64
5985 Birch L T	31	" H	Aug 17 64
6008 Bowman A	104	" E	Aug 17 64
6020 Bright N	6	" E	July 17 64
6152 Brown G S	111	" F	Aug 18 64
6 39 Buren T J	89	" A	Aug 25 64
7280 Barrett S C	26	" F	Aug 30 64
7283 Bell A	70	" B	Aug 30 64
7484 Baxter P D	121	" D	Sept 1 64
7490 Brenning C	14	" G	Sept 1 64
7529 Brown W	26	" G	Sept 1 64
7806 Bear E	33	" A	Sept 4 64
7983 Bender C	54	" G	Sept 6 64
7998 Brown M	110	" F	Sept 6 64
7994 Barnes T S	31	" B	Sept 6 64
8365 Benear W A	135	" F	Sept 10 64
8376 Barston G H	135	" F	Sept 10 64
8476 Brenner N	60	" F	Sept 11 64
8496 Barnes A	36	" G	Sept 11 64
8508 Blythe C	1	" I	Sept 12 64
8509 Brinhomer J	65	" C	Sept 12 64
8676 Brown H H	41	" A	Sept 13 64
8693 Bell James	135	" B	Sept 14 64
8872 Buckley J G	126	" A	Sept 15 64
8939 Blessing C	9	" F	Sept 16 64
9287 Baker W C	94		Sept 19 64
9446 Brookover Geo	135	Co B	Sept 21 64
9473 Briace J R	122	" C	Sept 21 64
9625 Bradley A	101	" A	Sept 24 64
9679 Blackman S	72	" G	Sept 24 64
9897 Birchfield Eli	14		Sept 27 64
9949 Beant H T	34	Co D	Sept 28 64
10120 Brewer D C	43	" K	Oct 1 64
10199 Brown E N	21	" E	Oct 2 64
10281 Brum W H	20	" B	Oct 4 64

Ohio—(*Continued.*)

10591	Briggs F	17	Co G	Oct 10 64
11072	Baymher L G	153	" A	Oct 17 64
11307	Boles G	112	" H	Oct 22 64
11308	Bunker J	11	" K	Oct 22 64
11313	Burns M	12	" K	Oct 22 64
11626	Bricker J J	126	" H	Oct 28 64
11920	Bumgardner Joel	3	" C	Nov 8 64
11939	Barber B	Cav 10	" D	Nov 9 64
12296	Bissel J	2	" E	Dec 16 64
12383	Beckley G	102	" F	Jan 3 65
12524	Barnes E H	2	" D	Jan 26 65
12641	Bower A	37	" F	Feb 12 65
517	Blackwood I H	92	" I	April 12 64
12772	Bowens W	100	" A	Mch 13 65
5	Carpenter W	92	" D	Mch 4 64
458	Copeland C	1	" A	April 9 64
561	Coates Geo	Cav 7	" I	April 15 64
563	Campbell Jas	Cav 7	" H	April 15 64
723	Callaway Wm	Cav 7	" F	April 25 64
763	Coleman G	101	" A	April 27 64
911	Chapman G	75	" A	May 1 64
928	Crosser M	111	" B	May 7 64
965	Corby W C	111	" B	May 8 64
1269	Cruat Wm	89	" C	May 21 64
1291	Collins Thos	21	" G	May 22 64
1521	Capeheart H	70	" I	May 31 64
1537	Clark H S	62	" E	June 3 64
1631	Conklin W	121	" B	June 5 64
1679	Clark D V	111	" B	June 6 64
1900	Childers Wm	89	" B	June 13 64
1945	Crocker Geo	Art 1	" A	June 14 64
1992	Christy W	89	" K	June 15 64
2017	Curtis N	45	" D	June 15 64
2025	Careahan G M	65	" F	June 15 64
2101	Caldwell J	15	" D	June 17 64
2162	Cornelius L C	89	" C	June 19 64
2207	Cochrane James	22	" G	June 20 64
2468	Church E	2	" G	June 25 64
2578	Combston J	Cav 7	" I	June 27 64
2953	Cameron H	69	" B	July 6 64
3002	Callahan H	34	" C	July 7 64
3241	Caynee Geo M	89	" D	July 13 64
3307	Canard J Q A	14	" G	July 13 64
3356	Cruer J W	60	" B	July 15 64
3541	Cole B	82	" A	July 18 64
3578	Collins T	15	" I	July 19 64
3604	Cook L B	Cav 2	" C	July 19 64
3617	Clark J C	31	" H	July 20 64
3774	Clayton D J	Cav 9	" D	July 22 64
3937	Cover L	49	" B	July 25 64
4128	Clayton J	89	" G	July 28 64
4342	Conway J	103	" A	July 30 64
4493	Cordray J J	89	" G	Aug 1 64
4865	Cahill J N	90	" C	Aug 6 64
5105	Charles F	10	" A	Aug 9 64
5451	Collyer J	11	" G	Aug 12 64
5548	Chandler M	124	" E	Aug 13 64
5922	Clark James	89	" I	Aug 17 64
6022	Cline K	111	" B	Aug 17 64
6108	Church Geo E	14	Co C	Aug 18 64
6188	Chambers R S	89	" A	Aug 19 64
6258	Copir S A	33	" C	Aug 20 64
6281	Conklin J R	45	" I	Aug 20 64
6562	Craig D	2	" D	Aug 23 64
7483	Caswell G	21	" C	Sept 1 64
7486	Coons David	57	" C	Sept 1 64
7495	Crooks J M	92	" K	Sept 1 64
7695	Chard C W	2	" H	Sept 3 64
7800	Cregg I	49	" K	Sept 4 64
7896	Cline M	2	" E	Sept 4 64
7919	Clark George	60	" D	Sept 5 64
7998	Clokir J W, S Major	49		Sept 6 64
8130	Cummings W S	35	Co I	Sept 8 64
8454	Cattlehock T	35	" A	Sept 14 64
8457	Campbell W C	5	" I	Sept 11 64
8694	Chapin Jas	135	" F	Sept 14 64
8701	Crooke W B	135	" B	Sept 14 64
8810	Clarke J R	135	" F	Sept 15 64
9243	Constein W	98	" C	Sept 19 64
9288	Cramblet A J	123	" H	Sept 19 64
9452	Campbell Sam'l	74	" G	Sept 21 64
9476	Cadwell A T	3	" E	Sept 21 64
9491	Clay O	122	" D	Sept 21 64
9662	Cort W	11	" D	Sept 24 64
9770	Cummings A	Cav 6	" E	Sept 25 64
9772	Clark S	24	" H	Sept 26 64
9895	Conner J B	Cav 9	" G	Sept 27 64
9971	Castable I	51	" A	Sept 28 64
10381	Cotes Rufus	Cav 2		Oct 5 64
10796	Colts R E	2	Co C	Oct 12 64
10834	Cepp J	14	" I	Oct 13 64
10968	Cary A	21	" E	Oct 16 64
11103	Carter J B	89	" I	Oct 18 64
11224	Craven A J	15	" C	Oct 20 64
11262	Cromwell W H	59	" H	Oct 21 64
11409	Cutsdaghner W J	95	" D	Oct 24 64
11540	Crominberger J C	23	" I	Oct 27 64
11567	Cantwright L	51	" F	Oct 27 64
11587	Chapin J A	135	" F	Oct 28 64
11618	Clark H M	21	" A	Oct 28 64
11641	Clingan A P	26	" K	Oct 30 64
11766	Cohyen J H	6	" K	Nov 3 64
12082	Cahill Wm	51	" A	Nov 18 64
12385	Calvington R	72	" C	Jan 3 65
12435	Chambers J C	15	" C	Jan 11 65
12691	Crampton A	79	" C	Feb 22 65
12798	Conover S	175	" B	Mch 19 65
690	Davis Wm E	7	" H	April 23 64
930	Downing George	45	" C	May 7 64
981	Dumar R	45	" D	May 9 64
1267	Dugan Thos	Cav 1	" B	May 21 64
1748	Davis I	7	" T	June 9 64
2251	Decker B F	111	" B	June 21 64
2296	Dumas J P	2	" H	June 21 64
2351	Douglass W	24	" F	June 23 64
2674	Davis B	22	" B	June 30 64
2909	Davis G H	45	" E	July 5 64
2973	Dandelion T	Ind Cav 3		July 7 64

Ohio—(*Continued.*)

3703	Dodson L	Cav 7 Co H	July 21 64
3802	Dille Chas	23 " I	July 22 64
4455	Dodge ——	2 " I	Aug 1 64
4501	Diecy C	26 " C	Aug 1 64
4772	Denton John	Cav 7 " E	Aug 5 64
5020	Desselbem M	1 " I	Aug 8 64
5268	Dorson L	12 " I	Aug 10 64
5299	Doty E E	41 " H	Aug 11 64
5368	Dyke F	Cav 5 " K	Aug 11 64
5465	Donley James	Cav 1 " F	Aug 13 64
5620	Davis W H	33 " D	Aug 14 64
6043	Decker J	111 " B	Aug 18 64
6223	Durant B	95 " D	Aug 20 64
6312	Downer A P	52 " B	Aug 20 64
6708	Dougherty W H	15 " H	Aug 24 64
7229	Dildine J	33 " K	Aug 29 64
7376	Deming W	111 " B	Aug 31 64
7419	Daley S	33 " D	Aug 31 64
7427	Dick Chas	53 " G	Aug 31 64
7479	Drake M	59 " D	Sept 1 64
7500	Doran James	60 " A	Sept 1 64
7609	Ditto John	51 " A	Sept 2 64
7631	De Mastoris J	54 " B	Sept 2 64
8034	Davison P S	21 " K	Sept 6 64
8483	Donley M	59 " G	Sept 11 64
8498	Drake J F	135 " C	Sept 11 64
8779	Diver J	4	Sept 14 64
8820	Davere J	49 Co D	Sept 15 64
9293	Diver J	123 " H	Sept 19 64
9605	Decker S	12 " C	Sept 23 64
9702	Dobson J R	99 " H	Sept 25 64
9849	Duffy G	45 " C	Sept 27 64
10112	Dunbar J	122 " F	Oct 1 64
10113	Diven J	135 " F	Oct 1 64
10130	Duncan A	49 " K	Oct 1 64
10190	Dunhand Jas	Cav 8 " H	Oct 1 64
10424	Dewit Joseph	65 " G	Oct 6 64
10596	Dibble F	101 " H	Oct 10 64
11017	Diper O	128 " I	Oct 16 64
11102	Danton W H	105 " E	Oct 18 64
12159	Donahue P	72 " K	Oct 25 64
12224	Drith C	33 " K	Dec 4 64
12675	Dunken T	20 " K	Feb 19 64
12738	Deputy W	21 " H	Feb 6 65
7431	Davis G W	21 " G	Aug 31 65
1629	DeRush Sam'l	94 " F	June 5 64
327	Elijah Baker	45 " B	April 2 64
341	Evalt E J	10 " M	April 12 64
1047	Eppart Sam'l	9 " B	May 12 64
2221	Earles William	Cav 4 " G	June 20 64
3376	Ellis Charles	29 " B	July 16 64
4504	Elliott W	20 " F	Aug 1 64
5304	Evans Sam'l	33 " C	Aug 11 64
5349	Eastman J	18 " C	Aug 11 64
5717	Evans Chas	Art 1 " D	Aug 15 64
5887	Ensly William	135 " T	Aug 16 64
6015	Eckhart J	2 " B	Aug 17 64
7448	Elmann A	28 " F	Sept 1 64
8981	Entulin B C	104 " K	Sept 17 64
11051	Evans W	51 Co I	Oct 17 64
11169	Evans E M	20 " I	Oct 19 64
11542	Elha D	8 " A	Oct 25 64
11654	Ewing D	135 " D	Oct 30 64
12321	Ellerman N	59 " K	Dec 22 64
75	Falman A	82 " H	Mch 20 64
176	Fairbanks Alph	45 " A	Mch 26 64
246	Ferris Joseph	Cav 2 " H	Mch 30 64
311	Foster A M	100 " A	April 2 64
572	Frayer Daniel	99 " I	April 5 64
636	Facer Wm	111 " K	April 20 64
830	Fisher Chas	Cav 3 " C	May 1 64
1054	Free M	Bat 22	May 13 64
1381	Freenough Geo	Cav 3	May 26 64
1786	Fraiser James	2 Co E	June 10 64
2457	Fry W L	123 " H	June 25 64
2479	Fenton J M	35 " I	June 25 64
2761	Finlan Jas	18 " K	July 2 64
4231	Fry Jacob	99 " I	July 29 64
4317	Fitch E P	40 " G	July 30 64
4337	Fulkinson H	2 " I	July 30 64
4651	Fife J	33 " E	Aug 3 64
4868	Fling T I	27 " A	Aug 6 64
5249	Ferce R S	2 " C	Aug 10 64
5626	Falk W	82 " D	Aug 14 64
5864	Fullerston W	18 " K	Aug 16 64
6212	Foreman A	64 " E	Aug 19 64
6308	Fisher D	89 " I	Aug 20 64
6891	Futers John H	82 " F	Aug 26 64
7873	Franks R L	122 " E	Sept 5 64
7976	Forney W O	123 " D	Sept 6 64
9158	Firman V	Cav	Sept 18 64
9225	Ferguson H	Cav 3 Co D	Sept 19 64
9530	Fowler C	100 " A	Sept 22 64
9557	Finch C	" B	Sept 23 64
9976	Franklinburg C	72 " G	Sept 28 64
10045	Farshay A	116 " F	Sept 29 64
10915	Freely P	10 " G	Sept 14 64
11819	Flowers W T	116 " D	Nov 5 64
11914	Forest Wm	21 " K	Nov 8 64
12108	Fargrove M B	135 " F	Nov 21 64
12637	Fusselman J	20 " H	Feb 11 65
12781	Foults M	183 " D	Mch 15 65
12427	Fike W P	95 " H	Jan 9 65
197	Griling Daniel	13 " A	Mch 27 64
245	Gardner A	100 " H	Mch 30 64
386	Grescanst S	Cav 6 " G	April 2 64
611	Gillinghar B	Cav 7 " I	April 18 64
681	Godfrey Amos	45 " C	April 23 64
693	Greek Samuel	100 " C	April 23 64
906	Gibson Collins	40 " H	May 5 64
1465	Greer R J	Cav 6 " C	May 29 64
2152	Gillanni J	35 " K	June 27 64
2926	Garner C	Cav 1 " K	July 5 64
3130	Goff P E	19 " K	July 10 64
3251	Gaunt Wm	14 " I	July 13 64
3327	Gibson R	40 " B	July 15 64
3962	Ginging P S	21 " E	July 25 64
4037	Gillett G W	6 " G	July 26 64

Ohio — (*Continued.*)

4242	Gilbert J	19 Co	B	July 29 64
4301	Grafton D	118 "	D	July 30 64
4383	Graham J W	31 "	C	July 31 64
4445	Goffy P	113 "	G	Aug 1 64
4655	Gragrer H	125 "	H	Aug 3 64
4802	Greer G G	49 "	D	Aug 5 64
4902	Granbaugh	85 "	E	Aug 6 64
6023	Gordon Wm	45 "	B	Aug 17 64
6075	Gallagher James	38 "	F	Aug 18 64
6207	Green E	Cav 4 "	D	Aug 19 64
6346	Gordon W	10 "	G	Aug 21 64
6408	Greff A J	13 "	E	Aug 22 64
6486	Gates H	13 "	G	Aug 22 64
6821	Grooves L	12 "	C	Aug 25 64
7111	Gilland A	27 "	F	Aug 28 64
8330	Goodrich J S	9 "	A	Sept 10 64
8367	Ganold L	60 "	A	Sept 10 64
9566	Gould J M	124 "	A	Sept 23 64
9813	Graft P	Bat 20		Sept 26 64
9927	Galbraith J S	Cav 6 Co	H	Sept 28 64
1121	Gaither J	60 "	B	Oct 20 64
11850	Gardner G	1 "	K	Nov 5 64
1203	Glissin A	Cav 2 "	M	Nov 15 64
1206	Gillinbuck I	77 "	E	Nov 17 64
1210	Goodbrath C	28 "	G	Nov 21 64
12560	Griffith J H	58 "	C	Jan 31 65
12842	Gassler P	64 "	A	April 22 65
85	Hall J W	4 "	A	Mch 9 64
295	Hochenburg N	45 "	C	April 1 64
420	Hanney W T	45 "	A	April 7 64
424	Hill J	Cav 7 "	I	April 7 64
437	Henry Jas	Cav 7 "	I	April 8 64
464	Haner Jacob	45 "	B	April 9 64
527	Hickcox M R	Cav 2 "	B	April 13 64
580	Holdman F	Bat 1 "	D	April 16 64
748	Hanning Mark	Cav 7 "	I	April 26 64
758	Harvey Chas	76 "	E	April 26 64
875	Henry G W	95 "	E	May 4 64
949	Hawkins W W	103 "	G	May 3 64
112	Hudsonpilfer R L	Cav 7 "	I	May 15 64
1354	Hind George	103 "	H	May 25 64
1390	Holloway G W	1 "	C	May 28 64
1524	Harrison J	21 "	I	May 31 64
1666	Hazlett Wm	2 "	K	June 6 64
182	Hull S	21 "	E	June 10 64
1979	Harris E D	99 "	I	June 15 64
2029	Hengle John	Cav 1 "	C	June 15 64
2185	Humphreys W	45 "	C	June 19 64
2263	Hanley C	15 "	F	June 20 64
2300	Henderson S W	40 "	H	June 22 64
2369	Howard J, Mus	70 "	D	June 23 64
2424	Hayford A E	125 "	C	June 24 64
2997	Harrington S J	103 "	I	June 28 64
2671	Hurles I	126 "	C	June 30 64
2775	Hurlburt O	14 "	H	July 2 64
2842	Hadison J	111 "	B	July 3 64
3185	Hall T	2 "	H	July 11 64
31	Heaton Amos	45 "	T	April 20 64
3388	Hudsen Wm	74 "	G	July 16 64
3420	Hunt W H	113 "	G	July 16 64
3736	Harman L	9 "	F	July 21 64
4030	Hansbury E A	6 "	G	July 26 64
4408	Hindershot John	45 "	D	July 31 64
4411	Harris J	1 "	E	July 31 64
4506	Hartman H	73 "	K	Aug 1 64
4599	Harrison J M	105 "	H	Aug 3 64
4993	Hendrickson O	19 "	F	Aug 7 64
5293	Hollbaugh J A	23 "	E	Aug 11 64
5296	Hatfield G W	126 "	K	Aug 11 64
5396	Holman A	68 "	K	Aug 12 64
5554	Honnihill T R	9 "	G	Aug 13 64
5636	Hany B T	89 "	C	Aug 14 64
5813	Hicks F	40 "	H	Aug 16 64
5853	Hibbett Wm	21 "	D	Aug 19 64
5858	Holt P	116 "	B	Aug 16 64
6058	Hamm E J	"	K	Aug 18 64
6123	Higgins I W	14 "	C	Aug 18 64
6774	Houser W R	89 "	K	Aug 18 64
6522	Hicks I	11 "	D	Aug 23 64
6625	Hughes Henry	33 "	A	Aug 23 64
6639	Henricks E	34 "	H	Aug 23 64
6647	Hartman I	2 "	K	Aug 23 64
6793	Herrig N	Cav 7 "	D	Aug 25 64
6802	Hine T E	Cav 2 "	D	Aug 25 64
7022	Hull O	89 "	B	Aug 27 64
7388	Hubbell W A	23 "	A	Aug 31 64
7446	Hurdnell O	72 "	C	Sept 1 64
7825	Holley V H	100 "	B	Sept 4 64
7946	Hughes I	12 "	E	Sept 5 64
8060	Herbolt Dan'l	115 "	T	Sept 7 64
8067	Harper I H	60 "	I	Sept 7 64
8284	Halshult A	12 "	C	Sept 9 64
8481	Hechler John	86 "	G	Sept 11 64
8696	Hitchcock G	34 "	G	Sept 14 64
8725	Hifner G	86 "	C	Sept 14 64
9189	Hoyt R	7 "	K	Sept 18 64
9210	Hart E	10 "	H	Sept 19 64
9538	Hall S	126 "	F	Sept 20 64
9415	Hood F	13 "	F	Sept 21 64
9510	Hamilton J	13 "	A	Sept 22 64
9582	Hoover J	18 "	K	Sept 23 64
9622	Hurley J C	124 "	C	Sept 23 64
10094	Holmes Wesley	135 "	F	Sept 30 64
10207	Harrison J	Cav 2 "	A	Oct 2 64
10208	Holcomb L	7 "	I	Oct 2 64
10225	Harkins M	60 "	D	Oct 2 64
10390	Hinton Wm	72 "	A	Oct 5 64
10492	Hererlin B	32		Oct 7 64
10518	Herbert Wm	4 Co	I	Oct 8 64
10524	Homich C	110 "	D	Oct 8 64
10647	Herman R	135 "	F	Oct 11 64
11029	Hilyard J	98 "	F	Oct 16 64
11032	Hubber D	5 "	A	Oct 16 64
11053	Heymers B	2 "	G	Oct 17 64
11209	Hanard J B	123 "	C	Oct 20 64
11228	Hoyt W B	29 "	A	Oct 20 64
11335	Henderson D F	122 "	H	Oct 23 64
11588	Hintz D	1 "	B	Oct 28 64

Ohio—(*Continued.*)

11592	Hutchins G W	135	Co A	Oct 28 64
11696	Hutchins I W	133	" A	Oct 31 64
11856	Hayner B	135	" A	Nov 6 64
11938	Hatfield A G	114	" E	Nov 9 64
12353	Hume J A	32	" F	Dec 29 64
12371	Haines N S	72	" E	Jan 1 65
12404	Hill W L	54	" A	Jan 6 65
12416	Hill E P	89	" G	Jan 13 65
12512	Hagerman R	33	" B	Jan 23 65
12569	Hart H C	2	" C	Feb 1 65
12611	Hagerly D G	72	" E	Feb 7 65
12743	Holtz W	101	" I	Mch 7 65
1129	Hudson R L	Cav 7	" I	May 15 64
1132	Hank George B	7	" I	May 16 64
2607	Hander L C	92	" E	June 28 64
1280	Irving Ester	114	" H	May 23 64
1967	Ingler Wm	31	" C	June 14 64
7489	Imboden J	44	" E	Sept 1 64
8744	Irwin A	1	" I	Sept 14 64
10700	Idold A	Cav 7	" C	Oct 11 64
12579	Isham D	89	" G	Feb 3 65
354	Justice G W	45	" B	April 2 64
1637	Johnson J H	98	" D	June 5 64
3590	Jacobs P O	45	" E	July 19 64
3754	Jones R	45	" C	July 23 64
3903	Jones S	111	" B	July 24 64
4381	Jewell I	99	" F	July 31 64
5120	Johnston J W	89	" H	Aug 9 64
5508	Johnson M	126	" C	Aug 13 64
5583	Jones H	40	" G	Aug 14 64
5624	Jewell W A	126	" G	Aug 14 64
5839	Jolly G	21	" K	Aug 15 64
6265	Jeffries H	86	" I	Aug 20 64
6810	Jones John	40	" G	Aug 25 64
7308	Johnson E	124	" I	Aug 30 64
7861	Jones R W	118	" F	Sept 5 64
8647	Jenkins Wm	Bat 3		Sept 13 64
8757	Johnson D	43	Co B	Sept 14 64
8760	Johnson I	51	" A	Sept 14 64
9306	Jordan A	103	" G	Sept 20 64
9700	Jones I B	3	" M	Sept 25 64
9744	Johnson I B	2	" C	Sept 25 64
9850	Jones Wm	84	" B	Sept 27 64
11014	Jones S D	135	" F	Oct 16 64
11203	Jennings Jno	24	" K	Oct 29 64
11942	Jones G L	135	" G	Nov 9 64
12126	Jarvitt W	15	" A	Nov 22 64
12231	Johnson A S	45	" I	Dec 6 64
12335	Jones W H	2	" C	Dec 23 64
12428	Jackson S	72	" E	Jan 10 65
7947	Jacobs H	26	" F	Sept 6 64
836	Kelly Josiah	45	" C	May 1 64
4615	Kimble S	98	" A	Aug 1 64
4715	Knight J	21	" E	Aug 4 64
5331	Kelly E	21	" D	Aug 12 64
5448	Knidler J W	33	" H	Aug 12 64
5576	Kelly H	1	" I	Aug 14 64
6195	Kelsey Jno	3	" I	Aug 19 64
7177	Kennedy S J B	45	" E	Aug 29 64
7424	Kelly G	15	Co E	Oct 31 64
9377	Kelly Wm	46	" C	Sept 20 64
9436	Kerr J H	122	" C	Sept 21 64
9630	Knapp J	54	" E	Sept 24 64
10139	Killar J	15	" D	Oct 1 64
10607	Kirby A	Cav 4	" A	Oct 10 64
10853	Keanshoff L	28	" I	Oct 13 64
11055	Kerr A	13	" I	Oct 17 64
11732	Kingkade S	18	" C	Nov 2 64
12061	Kennedy J	70	" K	Jan 16 65
12746	Kaler J	72	" B	Mch 8 65
12802	Karch J	183	" B	Mch 20 65
765	Kinney Jno	67	" E	April 27 64
2406	Knowlton E	Cav 6	" B	June 24 64
13	Kiger J H	45	" E	April 9 64
834	Lowry Jas	49	" I	May 1 64
935	Lewis Frank	103	" D	May 7 64
1236	Larme Chas	45	" K	May 22 64
1354	Larkin Joseph	Art 1		May 25 64
1470	Logan Frank	89	Co F	May 30 64
1615	Logan H	Cav 6	" E	June 4 64
1838	Leonard Jno	21	" A	June 11 64
2173	Lever H B	2	" C	June 19 64
2372	Lisure Samuel	7	" A	June 23 64
2426	Lemons M	89	" E	June 24 64
3495	Lutz M	14	" C	July 18 64
3497	Love John	96	" E	July 18 64
3649	Linsay J	21	" D	July 20 64
4097	Lyon L L	Art 1	" E	July 27 64
4354	Law S S	124	" I	July 31 64
4262	Lawson J	2	" E	July 29 64
4641	Lucas J	89	" H	Aug 3 64
4628	Legrand D	111	" B	Aug 3 64
4692	Long John	45	" H	Aug 4 64
5195	Lightfoot Wm	Cav 9	" G	Aug 10 64
5246	Latta W H	89	" H	Aug 10 64
5449	Lehigh W	22	" B	Aug 12 64
5635	Lamphare G W	125	" K	Aug 14 64
5676	Larison A	63	" D	Aug 14 64
6066	Lowe G H	72	" C	Aug 18 64
6314	Leasure Isaac	122	" K	Aug 21 64
7123	Leasure F	45	" K	Aug 28 64
7744	Linway J	2	" H	Sept 3 64
8016	Lambert Jas	89	" A	Sept 6 64
8739	Lickliter Henry	135	" B	Sept 14 54
8874	Lindsley A K	99	" K	Sept 16 64
9036	Leonard T M	12	" H	Sept 20 64
9318	Lovely John	100	" K	Sept 20 64
9351	Lawyer J B	89	" L	Sept 20 64
7419	Lefarer W E, Citizen Gardener, Athens Co			
10039	Laley ——	28		Sept 29 64
11161	Lepe A	7	Co K	Oct 19 64
11193	Lantz A W	45	" A	Oct 20 64
11344	Lochner M	72	" E	Oct 23 64
11440	Laughlin M W	1	" I	Oct 24 64
11490	Lips F	2	" H	Oct 26 64
11316	Lane D	91	" D	Nov 4 64
12007	Lay John	123	" K	Nov 19 64
12201	Lohmeyer H	35	" K	Nov 30 64

Ohio — (*Continued.*)

12297	Livingood C B	35	Co G	Dec 16 64
12525	Longstreet W F	81	" A	Jan 26 65
12698	Lewis D	7	" A	Jan 23 65
12826	Little Wm	175	" D	April 7 65
66	Metcalf Milo R	100	" E	Mch 19 64
96	Malsbray Asa	Cav 40	" A	Mch 22 64
113	Moore T J	2	" D	Mch 23 64
141	McKeever Jas	8	" G	Mch 24 64
165	Mickey Samuel	45	" E	Mch 26 64
215	Murphy Jno	Cav 7	" B	Mch 28 64
412	Mitchell J	120	" F	April 7 64
444	McKindry M	7	" I	April 9 64
573	Malone R J	40	" H	April 16 64
880	McCormick J W E	33	" B	May 4 64
984	Musser D	45	" B	May 9 64
998	Meek David	111	" K	May 10 64
1262	McKnight H	11	" G	May 21 64
1283	McMunny Geo	21	" G	May 22 64
1630	Moore Chas	19	" H	June 5 64
1849	Masters Samuel	17	" I	June 11 64
1930	Martin G	105	" F	June 14 64
2075	McCling B	Cav 7	" I	June 17 64
2139	Maloney A	4	" H	June 18 64
2150	Mitchell W H	31	" D	June 18 64
2290	Massey J C	33	" A	June 21 64
2471	Mullin J	65	" K	June 25 64
2667	McCloud A	35	" G	June 29 64
2682	Miller T	Cav 4	" A	June 30 64
2743	McFarland L	2	" I	July 1 64
2806	McInnes A	45	" B	July 3 64
2873	Moriatt Joseph	5	" K	July 4 64
2991	Mitchell Jas	17	" D	July 7 64
3104	Malone L B	Cav 7	" L	July 10 64
3122	Mitchell C	1	" K	July 10 64
3137	Minchell R	45	" C	July 10 64
3290	Mahin B	51	" I	July 13 64
3491	Master J	13	" A	July 17 64
3718	Miller E	4	" E	July 21 64
4040	Marshall T	21	" G	July 23 64
4199	Myer C	21	" I	July 29 64
4252	Meek J	19	" E	July 29 64
4298	McKell M J	89	" D	July 30 64
4331	Mooney Jas	50	" D	July 31 64
4421	Morris C E	11	" H	July 31 64
4501	McCann A	33	" C	Aug 3 64
4657	Maher P	7	" E	Aug 3 64
4789	Martin D	Cav 3	" L	Aug 5 64
5738	McCabe H	12	" C	Aug 15 64
5777	Manson W	9	" G	Aug 15 64
5883	McIntosh D	50	" D	Aug 16 64
6026	Manahan Thos	21	" D	Aug 18 64
6040	McKee Jas	51	" A	Aug 18 64
6055	McHugh W S	2	" D	Aug 18 64
6063	McClair P M	27	" A	Aug 18 64
6478	McCabe J	63	" C	Aug 22 64
6841	McCormick W P	2	" G	Aug 25 64
6855	McSorley D	49	" F	Aug 25 64
6862	McCoy J B	93	" A	Aug 26 64
6920	McDell Wm	89	" K	Aug 26 64
7108	McDonald J	99	Co H	Aug 28 64
7133	Mason J	45	" D	Aug 28 64
7136	More Jno H	60	" D	Aug 28 64
7515	Myers L H	135	" B	Sept 1 64
7896	Morris J	105	" A	Sept 5 64
8021	Meek Robert	111	" K	Sept 6 64
8044	Myers A	51	" I	Sept 6 64
8385	Maymer R	68	" D	Sept 10 64
8408	McCabe J	70	" C	Sept 11 64
8482	Morens H	51	" A	Sept 11 64
8688	Moore T H	59	" C	Sept 13 64
8726	Miller Samuel	135	" F	Sept 14 64
8838	Mackrill R	50	" I	Sept 15 64
8885	Manlig S	60	" A	Sept 16 64
9039	Miller C	28	" I	Sept 17 64
9096	McMillan J F	123	" A	Sept 18 64
9241	McComb J S	14	" K	Sept 19 94
9348	Maxwell P	12	" A	Sept 20 64
8236	Moor D D	2	" A	Sept 9 64
9359	Manly J	7	" M	Sept 24 64
9867	Mitchell R C	Cav 10		Sept 27 64
10064	Morgan R O	Cav 12	Co H	Sept 30 64
10081	McIntosh Wm	23	" I	Sept 30 64
10106	Morals Wm	135	" F	Sept 30 64
10517	Montgomery J	2	" G	Oct 8 64
10563	Myer L, Blacksmith	1	" A	Oct 9 64
10936	Martin F	Cav 10	" A	Oct 14 64
11156	McElroy Jno	92	" B	Oct 18 64
11200	Martin W	15	" A	Oct 20 64
11341	McQuilken F	1	" I	Oct 23 64
11400	Mark J	135	" B	Oct 24 64
11811	Miller J	135	" I	Nov 4 64
12050	Moore R F	101	" C	Nov 16 64
12054	Mills G W	60	" F	Nov 16 64
12184	Morrison J H	21	" B	Nov 28 64
12535	McDonald H H, Citizen			Jan 27 65
12717	Milholland R	183	Co B	Mch 1 65
12872	McGrath D	115	" G	Mch 15 65
12875	Martin M	135	" B	Mch 16 65
983	Neal Jno	45	" C	May 9 64
2328	Nash C D	45	" B	May 22 64
4994	Nelson J	Cav 1	" K	Aug 7 64
5897	Neff B	95	" H	Aug 16 64
7103	Nelson Thos	Cav 1		Aug 28 64
10584	Nelder S	89	Co G	Oct 10 64
11012	Nott J	153	" H	Oct 16 64
11448	Norman G L	135	" B	Oct 25 64
12815	Norris E J	102	" K	Mch 25 65
2183	Niver Edward	Cav 3	" I	June 19 64
2245	Ostrander E W	100	" A	June 20 64
2412	Ott C	51	" C	June 25 64
4552	O'Neil Jas	126	" F	Aug 2 64
12024	O'Connor F	103	" F	Nov 15 64
12247	Oliver J	122	" C	Dec 8 64
12429	Olinger J	63	" F	Dec 10 64
12835	Ornig J B	101	" I	April 17 65
11349	O'Brien Jno	2	" D	Oct 23 64
65	Pusey Jas	45	" H	Mch 19 64
724	Parker Wm E	45	" H	April 25 64

Ohio — (*Continued.*)

913	Penny A	59	Co C	May 6 64
1326	Prouty Wm	Cav 9	" L	May 24 64
2692	Phenix A H	21	" H	June 20 64
9	Price Barney	45	" I	April 5 64
3391	Pile Wilson	33	" F	July 16 64
3555	Pierce H	100	" A	July 18 64
4020	Perkins W B	89	" G	July 26 64
5190	Piffer G	123	" A	Aug 9 64
5377	Parker W	124	" H	Aug 11 64
5426	Perrin N	72	" A	Aug 12 64
6463	Parlice Geo W	94		Aug 22 64
6589	Potter H	72	Co E	Aug 23 64
6590	Pullen Sam'l	33	" B	Aug 24 64
6717	Post J	Art 1	" D	Aug 24 64
6984	Palmer Sam'l	135	" I	Aug 27 64
7021	Pease G E	Cav 10	" I	Aug 27 64
7157	Plunket M	124	" E	Aug 29 64
7329	Pelterson F	113	" G	Aug 30 64
7368	Purcell Jno	72	" D	Aug 31 64
7384	Pierson J	125	" B	Aug 31 64
7399	Palmer F G	Cav 2	" D	Aug 31 64
7519	Patten W	21	" D	Sept 1 64
7644	Pierce Wm	75	" H	Sept 3 64
7701	Pruser H	1	" B	Sept 3 64
7724	Payne J	89	" E	Sept 3 64
8109	Potts Jas	122	" E	Sept 7 64
8238	Phillips H	33	" I	Sept 9 64
8534	Powell F	9	" G	Sept 12 64
8597	Pror A M	Cav 135	" B	Sept 12 64
8620	Pinert F	21	" C	Sept 13 64
8733	Parker Z	124	" E	Sept 14 64
9111	Parks J W	Cav 6	" G	Sept 18 64
9327	Parker J	40	" H	Sept 20 64
9470	Perrin G	6	" B	Sept 21 64
9768	Pipenbring Geo	13	" K	Sept 25 64
9822	Preston Wm	M I 24	" B	Sept 27 64
10056	Parks E F	86	" D	Sept 30 64
11321	Piper E A	23	" B	Oct 20 64
11453	Patterson F	Cav 28	" F	Oct 25 64
11676	Prouse P I	1	" I	Oct 30 64
11779	Preshall J A	116	" C	Nov 3 64
12038	Peasly J	65	" H	Nov 16 64
12040	Porter W C	40	" H	Nov 16 64
12322	Powers J	21	" K	Dec 28 64
12551	Poistan J	133	" F	Jan 29 65
12645	Piper I	64	" F	Feb 13 65
344	Ricker Henry	Cav 2	" E	April 2 64
908	Rush D	107	" H	May 5 64
1642	Radabaugh W H	63	" A	June 5 64
2030	Ralston W J	89	" C	June 15 64
2124	Rawlings S	45	" E	June 17 64
2156	Rancey A K	111	" B	June 18 64
2281	Rickards W V	33	" B	June 20 64
2410	Rowe A	124	" F	June 24 64
2378	Rees Thos	98	" C	July 4 64
3074	Rix Wm	2	" K	July 9 64
49	Reed Harmon	103	" E	May 25 64
3400	Rogers T	51	" C	July 16 64
3426	Ralston J M	89	" C	July 16 64
3613	Russell L F	111	Co B	July 20 64
3832	Regman O	2	" D	July 24 64
3961	Robinson H H	110	" H	July 25 64
4061	Reiggs H	21	" F	July 27 64
4335	Rex J W	Cav 3	" K	July 30 64
4777	Robbins A	Cav 6	" D	Aug 5 64
5570	Reichardson G	82	" G	Aug 14 64
5631	Russell J G	115	" G	Aug 14 64
5639	Read Geo H	21	" H	Aug 14 64
5641	Redder G	45	" G	Aug 14 64
6488	Robbins D B	89	" I	Aug 22 64
6511	Ross J	59	" A	Aug 22 64
6835	Ridgeway Jno	23	" D	Aug 25 64
6948	Redd C	122	" H	Aug 26 64
7174	Ross A	45	" H	Aug 29 64
7353	Roberts Ed	75	" K	Aug 31 64
7639	Rutain E B	41	" E	Sept 2 64
7844	Russell Jas	9	" E	Sept 4 64
8521	Rhotin W	2	" C	Sept 12 64
8747	Riley W M	89	" B	Sept 14 64
8818	Robertson R	120	" D	Sept 15 64
9614	Robinson J	65	" D	Sept 23 64
9617	Rose Jno	72	" H	Sept 23 64
10165	Riper O H	110	" G	Oct 1 64
10354	Rogers C	13	" H	Oct 5 64
10538	Rochelle Jno	135	" F	Oct 11 64
11279	Romain J	59	" H	Oct 21 64
11360	Reese A	80	" C	Oct 23 64
11413	Reese R	59	" D	Oct 24 64
11646	Rapp N	19	" A	Oct 30 64
11657	Robbins P	122	" H	Oct 30 64
11672	Robinson C	Cav 2	" E	Oct 30 64
11859	Rourk J	6	" G	Nov 6 64
12366	Repan A	47	" A	Dec 31 64
12647	Rapp D C	2	" C	Feb 13 65
12692	Ramsbottom A F	99	" D	Feb 22 65
1763	Rei J	124	" K	June 6 64
33	Smith J E	Cav 7	" C	Mch 9 64
44	Smith H B	82	" B	Mch 14 64
58	Strill Michael	100	" K	Mch 18 64
231	Sears Samuel	Cav 2	" F	Mch 29 64
260	Stephen H	100	" B	Mch 31 64
263	Shields Geo	Cav 7	" L	Mch 31 64
284	Saughessy Jno	45	" B	April 1 64
481	Steele Abraham	80	" H	April 9 64
594	Swench W	45	" A	April 16 64
653	Snyder Lewis	80	" C	April 20 64
726	Sweeny Samuel	Cav 7	" G	April 25 64
771	Shannon Chas	45	" I	April 23 64
804	Starbuck F	62	" E	April 29 64
937	Storer Jno	17	" A	May 7 64
962	Smith Jno	Cav 7	" F	May 8 64
994	Smith Wm	103	" E	May 10 64
1160	Samse Wm	14	" H	May 17 64
1179	Smith Conrad	100	" A	May 18 64
1183	Smith Wm	2	" G	May 18 64
1229	Spangler A	45	" E	May 20 64
1231	Swineheart J W	111	" B	May 22 64
1404	Seyman Aaron	89	" D	May 27 64

Ohio—(*Continued.*)

1672	Sprague W L	Cav 6	Co K	June 6 64
1773	Simmons Jno	Bat 22		June 9 64
2220	Shannon E	85	Co A	June 20 64
2230	Stanett J	45	" C	June 20 64
2376	Stiver J	93	" C	June 23 64
2524	Smith G W	11	" K	June 26 64
2575	Sampson C	89	" D	June 27 64
2638	Stults P	45	" F	June 29 64
2783	Shiver L	31	" B	July 2 64
2792	Smith N H	1	" H	July 2 64
3116	Smith G	21	" I	July 10 64
42	Sabine Alonzo	100	" A	May 11 64
3252	Short Jas	Cav 4	" A	July 13 64
3288	Smith D	7	" H	July 13 64
3361	Safle J	2	" E	July 15 64
3536	Steward C S	33	" K	July 18 64
3602	Stevenson D	111	" B	July 19 64
3698	Squires Thos	49	" C	July 20 64
3744	Snyder Thos	9	" G	July 21 64
3770	Smith D	2	" I	July 22 64
3794	Sever H H	2	" C	July 22 64
4249	Shephard J H	2	" E	July 29 64
4275	Smith J B	1	" B	July 29 64
4294	Steward J	2	" K	July 30 64
4745	Steiner M J	72	" F	Aug 5 64
5018	Smock A	93	" D	Aug 8 64
5054	Smarz A	93	" E	Aug 8 64
5066	Shipple John	Cav 6	" G	Aug 8 64
5133	Scott S E	4	" I	Aug 9 64
5287	Stevenson John	111	" B	Aug 11 64
5330	Spegle F	14	" D	Aug 11 64
5373	Schem J	101	" K	Aug 11 64
5435	Stevens G W	101	" K	Aug 12 64
5896	Sullivan W	78	" D	Aug 16 64
6010	Staley G	89	" A	Aug 17 64
6032	Smith Wm	Cav 9	" G	Aug 18 64
6178	Simpson W J	82	" F	Aug 19 64
6199	Sheddy G	2	" K	Aug 19 64
6214	Shaw Geo W	105	" A	Aug 20 64
6253	Shoulder E	24	" F	Aug 20 64
6779	Soper P	72	" G	Aug 25 64
6870	Scarberry O	89	" D	Aug 26 64
7034	Sutton J	4	" A	Aug 27 64
7065	Shoemaker J	47	" E	Aug 28 64
7436	Stinchear F E	101	" A	Sept 1 64
7475	Shafer J	9	" G	Sept 1 64
7540	Sell Adam	125	" E	Sept 2 64
7788	Stewart John S	19	" B	Sept 4 64
7897	Smith H H	Cav 2	" A	Sept 5 64
7986	Selb Jacob	23		Sept 6 64
8014	Shriver Geo	45	Co K	Sept 6 64
8015	Snider Jas	4	" C	Sept 6 64
8156	Sturtevant W	72	" A	Sept 8 64
8197	Shrouds J	Bat 6		Sept 8 64
8200	Stroufe A	7	Co E	Sept 8 64
8229	Shaw W	15	" I	Sept 9 64
8300	Smith N	121	" H	Sept 9 64
8319	Sheldon W	49	" E	Sept 10 64
8422	Sullivan Jno	135	" F	Sept 11 64
8728	Sisson P B	18	Co H	Sept 14 64
8752	Sickles J	51	" I	Sept 14 64
8914	Simmonds S P	1	" A	Sept 16 64
8931	Stull G	15	" G	Sept 16 64
9009	Sharp F S	63	" K	Sept 17 64
9244	Schmall J D	12	" E	Sept 19 64
9336	Smith L	153	" H	Sept 20 64
9345	Scott J H	33	" H	Sept 24 64
9649	Skiver J	114	" H	Sept 24 64
10250	Sheets W	81	" A	Oct 3 64
10312	Spencer S M	89	" E	Oct 4 64
10434	Shingle D	Cav 2	" L	Oct 6 64
10437	Stanford P W	Cav 2	" A	Oct 6 64
10576	Stonchecks J D	51	" F	Oct 9 64
10618	Schafer P	101	" I	Oct 10 64
10703	Stout Samson	2	" F	Oct 11 64
10833	Sheppard Jno	84	" D	Oct 13 64
11139	Shark H	72	" F	Oct 17 64
11146	Smith G A	45	" F	Oct 19 64
11249	Sullivan F	76	" C	Oct 21 64
11433	Swaney E	124	" A	Oct 24 64
11579	Smith P	69	" I	Oct 28 64
11595	Sapp W N	20	" E	Oct 28 64
11711	Spiker J	122		Nov 1 64
11797	Shaler F	72	Co E	Nov 4 64
12105	Sly F	89	" G	Nov 20 64
12231	Singer J	6	" G	Dec 13 64
12305	Sweet M	49	" F	Dec 18 64
12441	Shoemaker C	8	" F	Jan 12 65
12538	Stewart A F	2	" D	Jan 27 65
12562	Sponcerlar Geo	71	" B	Jan 31 65
12668	Shorter W	89	" K	Feb 17 65
12769	Sloan L	123	" D	Mch 13 65
12789	Stroup S	50	" B	Mch 17 65
12793	Seeley N	132	" D	Mch 18 65
12810	Scott R	75	" G	Mch 24 65
730	Tweedy R	Cav 1	" A	April 25 64
743	Trescott Samuel	2	" C	April 26 64
909	Trimmer Wm	40	" H	May 10 64
1196	Turney U S	Cav 2	" G	May 18 64
1496	Thomas Wm	Cav 10	" M	May 30 64
4784	Thompson J	2	" E	Aug 5 64
4951	Toroman W R	13	" E	Aug 7 64
5356	Tierney W	Art 1	" L	Aug 11 64
5532	Tinsley M	90	" B	Aug 13 64
5668	Terilliger N	12	" C	Aug 14 64
6830	Tanner A	82	" G	Aug 21 64
7224	Thompson V B	26	" C	Aug 29 64
7246	Turner S B	45	" B	Aug 30 64
7340	Thomas Jas	44	" C	Sept 2 64
8850	Talbert R	135	" F	Sept 15 64
9774	Thomas N	103	" B	Sept 26 64
9945	Townsend J	26	" C	Sept 28 64
10471	Tattman B	153	" C	Oct 7 64
10800	Tinway P	93		Oct 12 64
11820	Townsley E M	89	Co B	Nov 5 64
12377	Tensdale T H	Cav 2	" E	Feb 3 65
12271	Uchre S	12	" E	Dec 9 64
2194	Vining W H H	45	" G	June 19 64

Ohio—(*Continued.*)

3902	Valentine C	123 Co H	July 24 64
4450	Vaugh B	125 " F	Aug 1 64
4497	Vangrider H	103 " H	Aug 1 64
5263	Vatier J F	Cav 6	Aug 10 64
6170	Vail Jno L	17 Co C	Aug 19 64
6859	Vanaman M	21 " E	Aug 26 64
6985	Vanderveer A	6 " H	Aug 27 64
7756	Victor H	Art 1 " D	Sept 4 64
9576	Volis J	34 " H	Sept 23 64
10252	Vail N	12 " K	Oct 3 64
10389	Vail G M	7 " D	Oct 5 64
10472	Van Fleet H	14 " I	Oct 7 64
11095	Van Kirk G	135 " B	Oct 18 64
11097	Van Malley J M	89 " G	Oct 18 64
12554	Vanhorn S	Cav 9 " C	Jan 30 65
7	Wiley Samuel	82 " A	Mch 5 64
185	Wickman Wm	111 " B	Mch 27 64
779	Wooley Jno	45 " B	April 28 64
807	Werts Louis	45 " D	April 30 64
1085	Wood Wm	89 " A	May 14 64
1449	Wentling Joseph	100 " K	May 29 64
1604	Wood Joseph	15 " B	June 4 64
1836	Wilkinson W	89 " D	June 11 64
1913	Wilson Jas	93 " I	June 13 64
2020	Way Jno	44 " I	June 15 64
2041	Windgrove S R	15	June 15 64
2172	Webb E	45 Co A	June 19 64
2358	Walters F	9 " E	June 23 64
2536	Wing	Cav 2 " M	June 26 64
2815	Willis A	89 " A	July 3 64
2840	Wroten L	89 " H	July 3 64
3188	Williams D	90 " A	July 12 64
34	Wright Wm	7 " H	April 24 64
3310	White H	15 " A	July 15 64
3325	Whitten G	75 " K	July 14 64
4214	West J B	89 " B	July 29 64
4631	Witt Jno T	93 " G	Aug 4 64
4688	Won J	111 " B	Aug 4 64
4695	Wile A	33 " D	Aug 4 64
5121	Winder I	70 " D	Aug 9 64
5211	Wood N L	Cav 4 " L	Aug 10 64
5726	Winters Geo	145 " K	Aug 15 64
6314	Wainwright S G	89 " G	Aug 20 64
6318	Wisser F J	35 " A	Aug 20 64
6362	Wistman N	Cav 9 Co G	Aug 21 64
6397	Wilson E	4 " A	Aug 21 64
6700	Watson G	21 " A	Aug 24 64
6761	Wood S	123 " A	Aug 25 64
7036	Wood W H	59 " E	Aug 28 64
7373	Wyatt J	90 " B	Aug 31 64
7382	Wentworth L	73 " A	Sept 1 64
8298	Wright J S	89 " E	Sept 9 64
8396	Warner T	14 " C	Sept 10 64
8907	Wyckman D	73 " G	Sept 16 64
9334	Worte J	116	Sept 20 64
9527	Woodruff J M	135 Co F	Sept 22 64
9691	Wagner J	93 " F	Sept 24 64
10007	Whitney E	21 " K	Sept 29 64
10230	Williams Orland	Cav 7 " K	Oct 2 64
10309	Weaver M	72 " H	Oct 4 64
10402	Ward Francis	21 " H	Oct 6 64
10464	Whitehead A B	33 " E	Oct 7 64
10528	Wiley A	26 " I	Oct 8 64
10733	White I	73 " E	Oct 11 64
10844	Westbrook R L	135 " F	Oct 13 64
11013	Walker C	63 " I	Oct 16 64
11031	Waldron H	14 " A	Oct 16 64
11418	Williams S M	60 " F	Oct 24 64
11770	Worthen D	122 " B	Nov 3 64
11874	Weason J	36 " F	Nov 6 64
12042	Wickham J	14 " H	Nov 16 64
12073	White R M	15 " D	Nov 18 64
12158	Warner B F	35 " E	Nov 25 64
12584	Whitaker E	72 " A	Feb 4 65
12722	Wella E	57 " A	Mch 3 65
12759	Winklet T, McL's Sqn		Mch 12 65
12786	Warner M	122 Co G	Mch 16 65
4333	Webricks Josh H	9 " G	Aug 6 64
638	Yuterler W A	45 " E	April 20 64
5477	Younker S	80 " F	Aug 13 64
6068	Young Jno	7 " E	Aug 18 64
7816	Yeager Jno	Cav 7 " B	Sept 4 64
7876	Young J	9 " F	Sept 5 64
10583	Young W	6 " G	Oct 10 64
12659	Young W	15 " A	Feb 16 65
3225	Zubers J M	100 " B	July 12 64
11253	Zink A J	72 " E	Oct 21 64

TOTAL 1031.

PENNSYLVANIA.

224	Attwood Abr'm	Cav 18 Co I	Mch 29 64
250	Armidster M	Cav 4 " A	Mch 30 64
468	Ackerman C	8 " B	April 9 64
758	Arb Simon	Cav 4 " C	April 27 64
846	Allbeck G B	52 " F	May 3 64
975	Algert H K	54 " F	May 9 64
1382	Arble Thos	Cav 13 " A	May 26 64
1837	Alt M	21 " K	June 11 64
2348	Akers Geo	90 " H	June 23 64
2398	Allison E	55 " K	June 24 64
2547	Anderson D	103 " K	June 27 64
2648	Able J	54 " F	June 29 64
2956	Amagart Eli	103 " F	July 6 64
3018	Ackley G B	Art 3 Co B	July 7 64
3317	Alexander M	Cav 1 " F	July 14 64
3937	Ardray J F	13 " F	July 25 64
4035	Anderson J	79 " I	July 27 64
4143	Aches T J	7 " H	July 28 64
4149	Alcorn Geo W	145 " F	July 28 64
4195	Archart H	51 " C	July 29 64
4673	Allen C	Cav 8 " K	Aug 4 64
4973	Andertin J	Cav 4 " L	Aug 7 64
5236	Aler B	103 " D	Aug 11 64
5311	Ault J L	101 " C	Aug 13 64
5332	Armstrong Chas	Cav 4 " C	Aug 16 64
6029	Anersen Jno	91 " C	Aug 18 64

Pennsylvania—(*Continued.*)

7163	Arnold Daniel	134 Co	C	Aug 29 64
7887	Angstedt Geo W	1 "	F	Sept 5 64
8185	Allen J L	101 "	I	Sept 8 64
8232	Ambler C	Cav 13 "	D	Sept 9 64
8388	Alexander W	Reserve 2 "	I	Sept 10 64
8653	Armstrong A	7 "	K	Sept 13 64
8655	Arnold L	73 "	A	Sept 13 64
8765	Altimus Wm	7 "	E	Sept 14 64
1743	Ainley Wm	Cav 3 "	E	June 8 61
9150	Alcorn J W	Cav 18 "	D	Sept 18 64
9896	Allison D B	55 "	K	Sept 27 64
10487	Anderson A	135 "	F	Oct 7 61
10570	Allen D	125 "	A	Oct 9 64
10823	Allin S	Cav 7 "	H	Oct 13 61
11419	Applebay T M	149 "	K	Oct 24 64
11607	Antill J	61 "	I	Oct 28 64
11710	Auger W	118		Nov 1 64
11852	Affleck T	2 Co	F	Nov 6 64
11860	Amandt J	131 "	D	Nov 6 64
12520	Atchinson W P	142 "	F	Jan 25 65
228	Bull Frank	Cav 4 "	H	Mch 29 64
249	Burton Lafayette	Cav 18 "	D	Mch 30 64
332	Briggs Andrew	Cav 13 "	H	April 2 64
427	Begler A	27 "	C	April 8 64
543	Breel Jacob	27 "	H	April 14 64
569	Black Jas A	Cav 14 "	D	April 15 64
661	Bradley Alex	Cav 3 "	F	April 21 64
671	Burns Sam'l	73 "	K	April 22 64
673	Barra J	54 "	F	April 22 64
822	Bayne Wm	145 "	I	May 1 64
874	Bradley M	Art 3 "	A	May 4 64
897	Brown Henry	90 "	H	May 5 64
938	Brown D	4 "	C	May 7 64
974	Batting Isaac	Cav 8 "	H	May 9 64
1046	Baker J D	57 "	F	May 12 64
1183	Butler Wm	90 "	B	May 18 61
1300	Boyd Thomas	9 "	D	May 23 61
1309	Bryson J	Cav 2 "	D	May 23 64
1327	Brining J	Cav 13 "	B	May 24 64
1375	Burney J	Cav 13 "	G	May 26 64
1393	Brown J B	Cav 4 "	K	May 26 64
1576	Boman Saml	Art 3 "	B	June 3 64
1601	Berfert R	103 "	B	June 4 64
1654	Brumley Geo	Cav 4 "	I	June 5 64
1790	Butler J D	76 "	B	June 10 64
1859	Berkhawn H	73 "	G	June 12 64
1872	Brooks D S	79		June 12 64
1923	Brian Chas	183 Co	F	June 14 64
1909	Bixter R	73 "	C	June 15 64
2026	Burns Owen	Cav 13 "	C	June 15 64
2046	Bigler M	Cav 4		June 15 61
2127	Brown C	Cav 3 Co	B	June 17 64
2134	Buckhannan W	Art 3 "	B	June 18 64
2180	Ball L	26 "	K	June 19 64
2236	Barr J T	Cav 4 "	K	June 20 64
2323	Baker Henry	Cav 13 "	I	June 22 61
2483	Bisel Jno	Cav 18 "	K	June 25 61
2538	Balsley Wm	Cav 20 "	F	June 25 64
2610	Brown M	Cav 11 "	C	June 28 64

2727	Brenn J	73 Co	K	July 1 64
2733	Bolt J H	Cav 18 "	E	July 1 64
2741	Beam Jno	73 "	E	July 1 64
2816	Burns Jno	Cav 13 "	A	July 3 64
2913	Bish J	103 "	F	July 5 64
2918	Belford Jno	115 "	F	July 5 64
3005	Bryan P	Art 3 "	A	July 7 64
3019	Barr S	103 "	G	July 7 64
3027	Braney J	43 "	E	July 7 64
3051	Barnes W	101 "	H	July 8 64
3097	Butler L J	113 "	E	July 10 64
3109	Brunt A	110 "	G	July 10 64
3216	Beraine A A	101 "	B	July 12 64
3294	Burns Jas	103 "	F	July 14 64
3442	Brinton J	157 "	D	July 17 64
3477	Baker Wm	103 "	F	July 17 64
3535	Burnside J	57 "	H	July 18 64
3600	Black W O	103 "	G	July 19 64
3693	Billig J L	Cav 3 "	H	July 21 64
3716	Brenlinger W R	Cav 4 "	D	July 21 64
3808	Butter C P	143 "	A	July 22 64
3821	Batchell D	55 "	D	July 23 64
3017	Bright E	90 "	I	July 23 64
3088	Bradford L	10 "	I	July 26 64
4002	Berkley M	50 "	I	July 26 64
4084	Backner Adam	116 "	G	July 27 64
4330	Barrett J	6 "	K	July 30 64
4360	Brown J	53 "	G	July 31 64
4402	Butler D	53 "	G	July 31 64
4494	Barton Jas	Cav 4 "	B	Aug 1 64
4500	Burke J	90 "	A	Aug 1 64
4610	Baker E	4 "	K	Aug 3 64
4667	Behreas A	7 "	E	Aug 4 64
4732	Bennett Geo	55 "	D	Aug 5 64
4939	Bowers J	Art 2 "	I	Aug 7 64
5040	Bammratta ——	73 "	D	Aug 8 64
5071	Barber C	6 "	D	Aug 8 64
5084	Buck B F	Cav 2 "	K	Aug 8 64
5113	Brown M	50 "	D	Aug 9 64
5324	Burlingame A J	141 "	K	Aug 11 64
5391	Bear Jno	79 "	D	Aug 12 64
5416	Bruce Jno	101 "	C	Aug 12 64
5526	Bower Benjamin	Cav 6 "	L	Aug 13 64
5587	Burnham H	143 "	F	Aug 14 64
5592	Broadbuck Adam	Cav 11 "	A	Aug 14 64
5662	Buck B F	Cav 2 "	K	Aug 14 64
5877	Browning Thos	103 "	A	Aug 16 64
5918	Bohnaberger A	115 "	G	Aug 17 64
5969	Boyer F	43 "	E	Aug 17 64
6061	Baker Jas	101 "	C	Aug 18 64
6074	Bower G W	103 "	K	Aug 18 64
6099	Baily J F	18 "	D	Aug 18 64
6127	Benhand J A	103 "	D	Aug 19 64
6229	Bear Sam'l	55 "	G	Aug 20 64
6244	Boles M S	Cav 4 "	K	Aug 20 64
6279	Bower C	101 "	C	Aug 20 64
6319	Birney J	Cav 4 "	C	Aug 20 64
6359	Bennett A	67 "	K	Aug 21 64
6542	Blackman W	18 "	D	Aug 23 64

Pennsylvania — (*Continued.*)

6551	Brannon P	7	Co A	Aug 23 64
6554	Baldwin C H	Cav 2	" K	Aug 23 64
6604	Barnett E T	149	" I	Aug 23 64
6621	Bell Thos	11	" E	Aug 23 64
6660	Blair Jno G	46	" F	Aug 24 64
6663	Breckinridge W	73	" K	Aug 24 64
6688	Bowman A	63	" B	Aug 24 64
6701	Boyd J W	101	" C	Aug 24 64
6704	Beemer Wm	145	" K	Aug 24 64
6887	Brown T	Cav 11	" I	Aug 26 64
6928	Bryan L	106	" F	Aug 26 64
7125	Bridaham H W	55	" H	Aug 28 64
7181	Bemer S	104	" E	Aug 29 64
7347	Ball P	49	" H	Aug 31 64
7460	Barnes W	119	" G	Sept 1 64
7477	Bennett J	55	" D	Sept 1 64
7541	Barnett M	145	" K	Sept 2 64
7634	Black J	103	" I	Sept 3 64
7717	Blair J G	49	" E	Sept 3 64
7775	Brink F	Cav 11	" M	Sept 4 64
7910	Browers J A	184	" F	Sept 5 64
7963	Brumley Frederick	54	" K	Sept 6 64
8073	Bright Adam	101	" K	Sept 7 64
8073	Boland	103	" I	Sept 7 64
8256	Barr P	103	" C	Sept 9 64
8286	Brown L	Cav 8	" C	Sept 9 64
8356	Brown A	101	" H	Sept 10 64
8358	Brickenstaff W	101	" I	Sept 10 64
8363	Bruce J B	104	" F	Sept 10 64
8413	Blosser Jonas	Reserve 7	" H	Sept 11 64
8434	Bowsteak T D	103	" H	Sept 11 64
8499	Bicklet E H	57	" K	Sept 11 64
8606	Boots E N	101	" H	Sept 12 64
8719	Beattie Robert	93	" D	Sept 14 64
8769	Boyer J M	Cav 7	" F	Sept 14 64
8793	Bentley T	54	" H	Sept 14 64
8794	Brown P	53	" A	Sept 15 64
8902	Baker J	184	" C	Sept 15 64
8917	Baker Wm	Cav 11		Sept 16 64
9147	Blake E	69	Co K	Sept 18 64
9320	Boyler Jas	7	" E	Sept 22 64
9332	Baldwin A	51	" K	Sept 24 64
9745	Bowers F	Cav 5	" A	Sept 25 64
9809	Bonewell W W	Cav 14	" C	Sept 26 64
9952	Blair Geo	Art 7		Sept 28 64
10201	Burdge H	Cav 3	Co D	Oct 2 64
10226	Byers J	23	" E	Oct 2 64
10260	Burns J	103	" E	Oct 3 64
10292	Brown G M	19	" I	Oct 4 64
10357	Burgess H	27	" C	Oct 5 94
10531	Buck D C	Cav 2	" L	Oct 8 64
10577	Ballinger Geo	87	" D	Oct 9 64
10674	Blackman W	84	" A	Oct 11 64
10753	Beightel J F	51	" G	Oct 12 64
10779	Boice J N	115	" G	Oct 12 64
10783	Bowling J	3	" A	Oct 12 64
10943	Barthart I	116	" H	Oct 14 64
10980	Baney Geo	4	" I	Oct 15 64
10983	Bowyer J S	55	" E	Oct 15 64
11024	Bunker F	55	Co K	Oct 15 64
11087	Bowman G	149	" E	Oct 18 64
11322	Bissel B	142	" F	Oct 22 64
11329	Bruce A	11	" I	Oct 23 64
11434	Berk G	51	" A	Oct 24 64
11445	Ball J	19	" K	Oct 25 64
11504	Bain G	133	" G	Oct 26 64
11528	Baney I	Cav 4	" I	Oct 26 64
11536	Baker B H	143	" B	Oct 27 64
11563	Brock C	46	" A	Oct 27 64
11569	Beighley W	103	" C	Oct 27 64
11597	Blair Jno	103	" H	Oct 28 64
11611	Boyer T	11	" F	Oct 28 64
11635	Burr E	115	" K	Oct 28 64
11674	Bolinger G	87	" D	Oct 30 64
11818	Bayley H	63	" K	Nov 4 64
11894	Burch W	Art 2	" F	Nov 7 64
11929	Burke J D	Cav 22	" D	Nov 9 64
11972	Bupp L	139	" G	Nov 12 64
12039	Bailey J J	Art 2	" F	Nov 16 64
12059	Bogar David	184	" C	Nov 17 64
12079	Bond C C	20	" K	Nov 18 64
12096	Brady N	Cav 5	" M	Nov 19 64
12168	Brubaker B P	79	" D	Nov 26 64
12177	Braddock T	77	" C	Nov 27 64
12418	Barrens J	Cav 5	" G	Jan 9 65
12812	Barnett J	6	" D	Mch 25 65
2917	Brim Jas	56	" I	July 5 64
12665	Bennett J	184	" E	Feb 16 65
45	Carter Wm	139	" H	Mch 14 64
97	Chase Wm B	Cav 15	" C	Mch 22 64
156	Compsey Jas	Cav 14	" H	Mch 25 64
835	Carman F H	54	" F	April 2 64
445	Coyle P	45	" A	April 9 64
466	Crouch Levi	40	" I	April 9 64
479	Croghan Jno	Cav 3	" A	April 9 64
548	Case Daniel	Cav 8	" M	April 14 64
734	Conner Andrus	Cav 4	" L	April 25 64
837	Cravener S P	Cav 14	" K	May 1 64
869	Curry A	119	" E	May 3 64
1015	Campbell Wm	Cav 8	" E	May 10 64
1099	Case Silas	Cav 2	" L	May 14 64
1158	Carmichael Geo	Cav 18	" K	May 16 64
1186	Crisholm J H	150	" H	May 18 64
1206	Caldwell S A	Cav 14	" E	May 19 64
1232	Coburg M C	Cav 6	" L	May 20 64
1490	Coon J H	Cav 13	" K	May 31 64
1493	Campbell H B	103	" E	May 31 64
1530	Clatter F	Cav 13	" C	May 31 64
1703	Calihan Thos	Cav 14	" H	June 7 64
1731	Cephas L	145	" I	June 8 64
1829	Carter Wm	101	" K	June 11 64
1832	Calvert R R	6	" B	June 11 64
1871	Coombs Jno	Art 3		June 12 64
1873	Cox J A	Cav 113		June 12 64
2069	Cooper T	Cav 18	Co K	June 16 64
2319	Curry R	73	" F	June 23 64
2399	Coyle H	Cav 8	" F	June 24 64
2435	Crouse E	141	" A	June 25 64

24

Pennsylvania —(*Continued.*)

2695	Copple F	54	Co H	June 30 64
2713	Chapman J	7	" H	July 1 64
2849	Carron Jas	Cav 4	" C	July 4 64
2884	Calean Sam'l	103	" K	July 4 64
2995	Coleman J	Cav 18	" K	July 7 64
3320	Chase F M	72	" G	July 14 64
3362	Clark N	Cav 8	" D	July 15 64
3417	Caton W T	49	" D	July 16 64
3430	Couch Benj	50	" H	July 17 64
3948	Coyle Ed	58	" E	July 25 64
3993	Curtey L	10	" I	July 25 64
4045	Carpenter L	12	" K	July 27 64
4117	Cantrill M	6	" B	July 28 64
4263	Conklin N	90	" K	July 29 64
4331	Chapman J	Art 3	" B	July 30 64
4353	Crawford M	Cav 14	" G	July 31 64
4357	Cox Jas	103	" A	July 31 64
4369	Claybaugh G W	Art 2	" F	July 31 64
4512	Crock H	45	" A	Aug 1 64
4682	Croup W S	103	" L	Aug 4 64
4729	Cochran C	103	" I	Aug 4 64
4903	Chew Jno	18	" F	Aug 6 64
5177	Cranes E	Cav 4	" M	Aug 9 64
5375	Campbell Jas	Cav 3	" F	Aug 11 64
5417	Cregg J G	54	" I	Aug 12 64
5423	Cumberland Thos	Cav 14	" B	Aug 12 64
5484	Conahan M	115	" B	Aug 13 64
5578	Carpenter W C	145	" G	Aug 14 64
5584	Campbell R D	11	" E	Aug 14 64
5623	Cox H	Cav 7	" B	Aug 14 64
5828	Cummings Benj	3	" A	Aug 16 64
5979	Conor J N	184	" C	Aug 17 64
6237	Corbin W	49	" C	Aug 20 64
6269	Campbell R G	11	" C	Aug 20 64
6320	Coon George	2	" F	Aug 21 64
6336	Cameron Wm	101	" A	Aug 21 64
6395	Connelly Wm	55	" C	Aug 21 64
6430	Conner J	6	" D	Aug 22 64
6502	Cline J	3	" H	Aug 22 64
6615	Crawford J	77	" E	Aug 23 64
6645	Coleman C	19	" E	Aug 23 64
6746	Conly Jno	101	" A	Aug 24 64
6913	Craft A	90	" G	Aug 26 64
7045	Cobert F C	Cav 11	" L	Aug 27 64
7095	Carr J	51	" G	Aug 28 64
7116	Cathcart Robt	103	" H	Aug 29 64
7209	Crain J	Cav 4	" H	Aug 29 64
7456	Craig Wm	103	" D	Sept 1 64
7463	Clay Henry	184	" A	Sept 1 64
7617	Curry S	140	" C	Sept 2 64
7632	Carroll A	Cav 2	" A	Sept 2 64
7669	Campbell Geo T	Art 3	" A	Sept 3 64
7696	Criser M	54	" F	Sept 3 64
8117	Crawford J A	103	" B	Sept 8 64
8121	Collins M	101	" K	Sept 8 64
8169	Cole J C	118	" K	Sept 8 64
8260	Chapman ——	18	" A	Sept 9 64
8512	Coyle M	79	" B	Sept 12 64
8594	Culver J	69		Sept 12 64

8665	Clutler L	11	Co C	Sept 13 64
8700	Cavender J L	119	" E	Sept 14 64
8834	Cysey A	Heavy Art 3		Sept 15 64
9094	Coffman Wm	13	Co F	Sept 18 64
9124	Cramer E	55	" F	Sept 18 64
9141	Church C H	45	" B	Sept 18 64
9169	Clark J	101		Sept 19 64
9396	Coats S R	135	" C	Sept 20 64
9410	Combs S	1	" H	Sept 21 64
9508	Clonay J	145	" F	Sept 22 64
9554	Crum C	149	" G	Sept 23 64
9639	Cline J	118	" A	Sept 24 64
9773	Coulter G	45	" K	Sept 25 64
9823	Cummings R	65	" K	Sept 27 64
9886	Callahan M	52	" D	Sept 27 64
9931	Conrad W	Cav 14	" M	Sept 28 64
10104	Campbell Wm	Cav 13	" D	Sept 30 64
10120	Coats L R	139	" H	Oct 1 64
10271	Crawford Geo	1	" F	Oct 3 64
10276	Cantler J L	13	" A	Oct 3 64
10283	Cromich F	7	" H	Oct 4 64
10286	Cornelius Wm	Cav 7		Oct 5 64
10399	Cullingford P	55	Co C	Oct 6 64
10443	Clark W	Cav 5	" K	Oct 7 64
10462	Canby G C	Cav 2	" E	Oct 7 64
10497	Coperhewer Wm	1	" D	Oct 8 64
10541	Culberton Louis	73	" B	Oct 9 64
10842	Corbin M	184	" D	Oct 13 64
10847	Clark G	Cav 1	" H	Oct 13 64
11005	Coe Geo W	145	" E	Oct 16 64
11025	Clark J	3	" D	Oct 16 64
11250	Clark H	184	" F	Oct 21 64
11309	Clark E B	101	" B	Oct 22 64
11370	Carrol W	145	" B	Oct 23 64
11436	Crawford L	184	" R	Oct 24 64
11438	Cole H O	Cav 2	" L	Oct 24 64
11477	Campbell C A	Cav 11	" C	Oct 26 64
11565	Creagan G	Cav 1	" F	Oct 27 64
11614	Crawford M	14	" K	Oct 28 64
11656	Coyle H	51	" K	Oct 30 64
11659	Craney Geo	Cav 20	" L	Oct 30 64
11800	Cregger W H	Cav 5	" G	Nov 4 64
11815	Chacon A W	103	" B	Nov 4 64
11826	Colebaugh W	60	" K	Nov 5 64
11876	Crandall L	145	" I	Nov 6 64
11922	Cleaveland E	Cav 19	" I	Nov 8 64
11993	Crampton A B	143	" B	Nov 13 64
12120	Cullen T I	31	" I	Nov 22 64
12141	Conway C C	Art 2	" A	Nov 23 64
12255	Crompton F G	71	" F	Dec 10 64
12295	Cone S	115	" E	Dec 16 64
12301	Culp P K	138	" B	Dec 17 64
12368	Connor S	112	" H	Jan 1 65
12424	Clark J	89	" D	Jan 9 65
12487	Collins G	118	" E	Jan 19 65
12599	Cassell D	20	" E	Feb 6 65
12672	Clark F D	7	" C	Feb 20 65
12818	Copeland B	Cav 14	" D	Mch 29 65
1961	Culbertson Jno	Cav 13	" B	June 14 64

Pennsylvania—(*Continued.*)

152	Davidson H	57	Co I	Mch 25 64
866	Dorr Phineas	119	" K	May 3 64
1020	Doran McK	63	" D	May 11 64
1161	Duntler Henry	51	" K	May 16 64
1338	Dooner M	2	" K	May 24 64
1463	Davis Richard	Cav 8	" L	May 29 64
1541	Deamott J K	45	" C	June 1 64
1545	Davis Isaac	Cav 8	" H	June 1 64
2630	Dun R B	101	" B	June 29 64
2657	Donovan J	139	" K	June 29 64
2716	Deily Wm	53	" H	July 1 64
2938	Davis M	Cav 22	" B	July 6 64
3338	Degret N	Cav 15	" M	July 15 64
3363	Davidson Chas	100	" M	July 15 64
3741	Dallin Jas	Cav 8	" H	July 21 64
3795	Davis J	103	" A	July 22 64
3873	Davis M H	103	" E	July 24 64
3985	Dougherty J	7	" E	July 26 64
4087	Deron Robt	149	" B	July 29 64
4202	Drenkle J A	79	" K	July 29 64
5232	Dechman Jno	184	" G	July 29 64
4481	Dodrick Louis	50	" I	Aug 1 64
4491	Denton M	Cav 9	" B	Aug 1 64
4497	Day Wm	97	" A	Aug 1 64
4625	Davis J	101	" E	Aug 3 64
4711	Dort C R	Cav 4	" H	Aug 4 64
4786	Dondle Robt	101	" A	Aug 5 64
4792	Davy H	68	" K	Aug 5 64
4806	Davenbrook J J	101	" G	Aug 5 64
4885	Delaney J	101	" A	Aug 6 64
4897	Dunbar Jno	Cav 14	" M	Aug 6 64
4910	Dean J	148	" F	Aug 6 64
5023	Dawlin	110	" D	Aug 8 64
5256	Ditztell L	73	" I	Aug 10 64
5431	Davidson Geo	57	" C	Aug 12 64
5468	Dougherty	101	" I	Aug 13 64
5664	Decker J	45	" B	Aug 14 64
5740	Day And H	Cav 2	" H	Aug 15 64
5746	Doran P	99	" I	Aug 15 64
6017	Deal F	63	" A	Aug 17 64
6045	Degroot H	Cav 13	" A	Aug 18 64
6176	Defree Jas	15	" G	Aug 19 64
6226	Dodd J	18	" F	Aug 20 64
6316	Davis Wm	153	" A	Aug 20 64
6568	Dawney Geo	148	" B	Aug 23 64
9679	Donavan D	90	" B	Aug 24 64
6678	Dunn Johnes	69	" F	Aug 25 64
6797	Dailey M	7	" I	Aug 25 64
6879	Dunn Jno	184	" A	Aug 26 64
7053	Dakenfelt J	55	" D	Aug 28 64
7077	Deets R	3	" A	Aug 28 64
7282	Day S	13	" A	Aug 30 64
7360	Dively J	110	" C	Aug 31 64
7488	Dilks C	1	" K	Sept 1 64
7651	Dewell Samuel	50	" G	Sept 3 64
7828	Dougherty J	184	" D	Sept 4 64
8211	Dixon J	105	" B	Sept 8 64
8334	Doherty J	73	" F	Sept 10 64
8569	Duff J	Cav 4	" B	Sept 12 64
8579	Dougherty F	90	Co C	Sept 12 64
8718	Durharse B	Cav 11	" G	Sept 14 64
8828	Donnelly J	97	" H	Sept 15 64
8887	Dean R	Cav 2	" M	Sept 15 64
9109	Davidson C	90	" G	Sept 18 64
9146	Driscoll N C	26	" I	Sept 18 64
9191	Duffie J	52	" F	Sept 18 64
9289	Delaney E	7	" G	Sept 19 64
10004	Davidson G	12	" K	Sept 29 64
10193	Dougherty M	Cav 3	" D	Oct 2 64
10436	Durkale Jno	Cav 1	" F	Oct 6 64
10917	Dalzell J G	139	" I	Oct 14 64
11295	Derry Frederick	20	" C	Oct 22 64
11350	Dichell Espy	55	" D	Oct 23 64
11394	Dewitt M	Cav 1	" E	Oct 24 64
11628	Davidson S	184	" A	Oct 28 64
11958	Dickens Chas	Art 2	" A	Oct 13 64
12136	Dairysuffle J E	145	" K	Oct 23 64
12399	Donley P	120	" G	Jan 5 65
12575	Deeds J	Cav 13	" H	Feb 2 65
11181	Dixon B	145	" K	Oct 19 64
972	Ellers Henry	Cav 13	" H	May 9 64
1081	Eisley Jno	Cav 18	" K	May 14 64
1436	Engle Peter	Cav 14	" K	May 28 64
2105	Elliott Jno	Cav 13	" F	June 17 64
2794	Elliott J	69	" D	July 2 64
3038	Erwin C	78	" D	July 8 64
3052	Epsey Jas	145	" H	July 9 64
3295	Elliott J P	103	" D	July 14 64
3823	Ebright Benj	Cav 9	" A	July 23 64
4278	Eaton Nat	Rifle 1	" E	July 30 64
4761	Ellenberger P	145	" D	Aug 5 64
5687	Ennies Andrew	145	" K	Aug 15 64
6424	Ewetts Jas	103	" G	Aug 22 64
6607	Ellis F	53	" G	Aug 23 64
6873	Eckles E	77	" E	Aug 26 64
6839	Ensley C	184	" A	Aug 26 64
7309	Ellis H H	Cav 18	" I	Aug 30 64
7657	Egan Jno	55	" C	Sept 3 64
8066	Exline Jacob	55	" K	Sept 7 64
8543	Eichnor C	143	" F	Sept 12 64
8964	Earlman J	7	" K	Sept 16 64
10009	Elfrey B S	7	" K	Sept 29 64
10694	Elliott Jno H	83	" D	Oct 11 64
10731	Erdibach C	Cav 5	" B	Oct 11 64
10799	Ervingfelts Jacob	187	" D	Oct 12 64
11834	Edgar W H	7	" G	Nov 5 64
11838	Erebedier J	5	" B	Nov 5 64
12001	Etters D	145	" D	Nov 14 64
12673	Ebhart J	87	" E	Feb 18 65
9490	English J C	100	" K	Sept 21 64
200	Fluher Jno	73	" D	Mch 23 64
511	Fich Jno	83	" B	April 12 64
791	Fry L	Cav 4	" D	April 28 64
1010	Fuller H	Cav 13	" H	May 10 64
1098	Fifer Chas	27	" I	May 14 64
1431	Fry Alex	Cav 4	" B	May 28 64
1728	Fink Peter	73	" C	June 8 64
1957	Freeman W M	Art 4	" A	June 14 64

Pennsylvania—(*Continued.*)

2078	Fulton Thos A	103	Co H	June 17 64
2099	Friday S D	101	" H	June 17 64
2147	Fish Chas W	101	" B	June 18 64
2155	Farley Jas	54	" F	June 18 64
2261	Fox Geo	78	" E	June 21 64
2477	Flay L	26	" G	June 25 64
2530	Funkhanna Jas	101	" C	June 26 64
2537	Fatleam A	50	" D	June 26 64
2594	Fagartus T	90	" K	June 28 64
2853	Fancy Geo	Cav 13	" F	July 4 64
3088	Ford M	53	" K	July 19 64
3258	Fisher B M	101	" H	July 13 64
3582	French A	Art 2	" G	July 19 64
3742	Forsyth J	Cav 18	" H	July 21 64
3870	Fingley Jno	Cav 14	" D	July 24 64
4307	Flick L	184	" G	July 30 64
4439	Filey J H	53	" E	July 31 64
4452	Foreman G S	Cav 1	" B	Aug 1 64
4521	Flashorse B	Cav 12	" A	Aug 2 64
4586	Flynn M	Cav 13	" B	Aug 2 64
4642	Fewer E	87	" H	Aug 3 64
4668	File C	145	" D	Aug 4 64
5062	Fish J	85		Aug 8 64
5172	Fleming W	97	Co E	Aug 9 64
5586	Flickinger Jno	50	" B	Aug 14 64
5788	Ferry W	79	" A	Aug 15 64
5873	Fee Geo M	103	" G	Aug 16 64
6092	Faiss A	145	" E	Aug 18 64
6134	Farman E	57	" E	Aug 19 64
6155	Feltharsea	145	" G	Aug 19 64
6180	Fatlenger F	53	" K	Aug 19 64
6365	Fanen Jas F	Reserve 7	" G	Aug 21 64
6396	Finlaugh S	Cav 14	" G	Aug 21 64
6649	Fox R	155	" H	Aug 23 64
6675	Fritzman J W	18	" K	Aug 24 64
6694	Finlin Thos	143	" G	Aug 24 64
6881	Fuller G	Cav 2	" A	Aug 26 64
6884	Frederick L	148	" B	Aug 26 64
6890	French Jas	101	" H	Aug 26 64
6892	Ford Thos	7	" I	Aug 26 64
7041	Fullerton E	99	" E	Aug 27 64
7097	Fester Jno	103	" B	Aug 28 64
7169	Fisher W	54	" I	Aug 29 64
7198	Fry	101	" E	Aug 29 64
7575	Fitzgerald M	145	" K	Sept 2 64
7588	Fahy Jno	Cav 13	" B	Sept 2 64
7776	Fritz D	Cav 18	" K	Sept 4 64
8006	Felter H M	Cav 13	" K	Sept 6 64
8149	Fullerton J	118	" I	Sept 8 64
8175	Fetterman J	48	" H	Sept 8 64
8321	Francis N	69	" G	Sept 10 64
8631	Fagan R	118	" F	Sept 13 64
9062	Fisher C	Cav 4		Sept 17 64
9099	Floyd B	67	Co K	Sept 18 64
9232	F[illegible] r J C	107	" H	Sept 19 64
9869	Faith Alex	183	" C	Sept 27 64
10176	Fessenden N E	149	" F	Oct 1 64
10408	Fingley S	14	" B	Oct 6 64
10639	Fisher W	101	" E	Oct 10 64
10667	Flynn S	76	Co C	Oct 11 64
10688	Free J	145	" H	Oct 11 64
11026	Flemming J	97	" E	Oct 16 64
11112	Flanney J	106	" K	Oct 18 64
11164	Ferguson J R	Cav 11	" D	Oct 19 64
11367	Fox M	Cav 8	" H	Oct 23 64
11378	Frill D	55	" C	Oct 24 64
11601	Ferguson Jno	134	" A	Oct 28 64
11802	Frishi H	115	" E	Nov 4 64
11916	Freed S	53	" B	Nov 8 64
11962	Fairbanks E	140	" A	Nov 11 64
12000	Fagley C	Cav 14	" I	Nov 14 64
12025	Forest S L	149	" I	Nov 15 64
12207	Foster C W	76	" B	Dec 1 64
12244	Falkenstine F	148	" C	Dec 8 64
12336	Fruce J	52	" A	Dec 26 64
12445	Fisk J	67	" H	Jan 13 65
12605	Faile W D	Cav 20	" A	Feb 7 65
71	Goodman Robt	Cav 13	" M	Mch 19 64
131	Gesse Christian	54	" F	Mch 23 64
314	Graffell Wm	73	" B	April 2 64
529	Guley J	145	" G	April 12 64
573	Green Wm	Cav 3	" A	April 16 64
968	Garman B	Cav 18	" E	April 9 64
1001	Greer J A	Cav 3	" E	May 10 64
1008	Graham W J	4	" C	May 10 64
1063	Goodman Henry	27	" I	May 13 64
1302	Gray M	7	" B	May 23 64
1373	Gilbert Jno	29	" G	May 25 64
1399	Gilroy Berney	73	" F	May 26 64
1528	Getts B	84	" G	May 31 64
1649	Griffil G W	Cav 13	" L	June 5 64
1761	G[illegible]st J W	57	" I	June 9 64
1793	Gardner (negro)	8	" F	June 10 64
192[illegible]	Gensle Jno	Cav 19	" F	June 13 64
1939	Goerlt E	73	" H	June 14 64
2060	Galliger F	Cav 13	" B	June 16 64
2084	Gilmore Jas	110	" E	June 17 64
2297	Gunn Alex	Cav 4	" D	June 21 64
2356	Greenwald G	27	" H	June 23 64
2531	Gumbert A	103	" B	June 26 64
2587	Gettings J H	Rifle 1	" C	June 28 64
2944	Gross Sam'l	51	" E	July 6 64
2955	Gotwalt H	55	" D	July 6 64
2988	Griffin J	103	" I	July 7 64
2992	George A	149	" G	July 7 64
2996	Gists H	103	" H	July 7 64
3037	Gilleland Wm	Cav 14	" B	July 8 64
3528	Gorsuch M A	110	" B	July 18 64
3599	Gibbs E	Cav 18	" K	July 19 64
4944	Gost W H	Cav 5	" K	Aug 7 64
5422	Gregg T	139	" K	Aug 12 64
5655	Gross Jno	62	" K	Aug 14 64
5735	Gregg D	142	" A	Aug 15 64
5737	Graham Wm	103	" F	Aug 15 64
5803	Graham D	Cav 4	" K	Aug 16 64
5831	Grouse G	145	" C	Aug 16 64
5838	Gettenher D M	103	" I	Aug 16 64
6006	Geand C	Cav 4	" M	Aug 17 64

Pennsylvania—(*Continued.*)

5288	Gladen A	21	Co C	Aug 11 64
6140	Garrett Jas	51	" K	Aug 19 64
6158	Gunn J W	101	" H	Aug 19 64
6384	Gamble O J	77	" A	Aug 21 64
6389	Gallagher E	48	" A	Aug 21 64
6897	Green J C	Cav 13	" D	Aug 26 64
7223	Gibson D	56	" A	Aug 29 64
7320	Graham J	56	" B	Aug 30 64
7340	Geary D	184	" G	Aug 30 64
7357	Groves A T	45	" A	Aug 31 64
7352	Glass Wm	55	" C	Aug 31 64
7527	Griffith A	54	" F	Sept 1 64
7589	Granger E H	55	" C	Sept 2 64
7679	Geslin E H	4	" G	Sept 3 64
7773	Giles C	7	" K	Sept 4 64
7839	Gross G W	79	" A	Sept 4 64
8109	Galbraith C	11	" K	Sept 6 64
8311	Garrison W	8	" K	Sept 10 64
8448	Gallagher Wm	Cav 5	" F	Sept 11 64
8735	Griffin J C	Cav 5	" D	Sept 14 64
9005	Gearhan S	142	" C	Sept 17 64
9210	Griffin D	11	" E	Sept 19 64
9326	Gilbert H	53	" F	Sept 20 64
9437	Gorbay F J	Cav 19	" M	Sept 21 64
9503	Goodman F	55	" H	Sept 21 64
9764	Grubbs J	103	" F	Sept 25 64
9776	Gibson J	11	" D	Sept 26 64
9792	Glenn Wm	101	" C	Sept 26 64
9811	Grear R	73	" H	Sept 26 64
9966	Gilbert D	138	" B	Sept 28 64
9989	Garrett F	139	" G	Sept 29 64
10051	Gibson D G	Cav 16	" A	Sept 30 64
10127	Gemperling Wm	79	" A	Oct 1 64
10468	Grant M	Cav 18	" I	Oct 7 64
10615	Griffin J	56	" A	Oct 10 64
10706	Gimberling I	184	" F	Oct 11 64
11060	Greathouse E	14	" B	Oct 17 64
11197	Grabb M P	83	" H	Oct 20 64
11299	Gilbert A F	Cav 14	" F	Oct 20 64
11496	Grant J	6	" E	Oct 26 64
11573	Ganse R	22	" B	Oct 27 64
11806	Gordon R	65	" F	Nov 4 64
11901	Green W S	12	" I	Nov 7 64
12181	Giher P	73	" H	Nov 27 64
12237	George F	Cav 18	" D	Dec 6 64
12337	Garrety Thos	106	" C	Jan 2 65
12411	Gates J	Cav 11	" E	Jan 7 65
12432	Grunnell Jno	26	" H	Jan 11 65
5843	Gillespie J	11	" A	Aug 16 64
5118	Gibbons Wm	11	" H	Aug 9 64
6228	Gallagher T	101	" A	Aug 21 64
5971	Gray L	103	" D	Aug 17 64
423	Hanson T R	119	" E	April 7 64
470	Herbert Otto	73	" A	April 9 64
555	Hoffmaster L	16	" H	April 14 64
654	Hamilton J G	Cav 4	" L	April 20 64
711	Hall J. (negro)	8	" E	April 24 64
769	Hessimer P	73	" E	April 27 64
988	Hammons J	Art 3	" A	May 10 64

990	Heager J	2	Co B	May 10 64
1080	Huff Arthur	54	" F	May 14 64
1113	Hates Chas	2	" H	May 15 64
1225	Henderson Rob't	Cav 18	" D	May 20 64
1311	Heckley M	Cav 4	" M	May 23 64
1420	Hill H C	18	" K	May 28 64
1483	Holtenstein G W	Cav 18	" I	May 30 64
1562	Henen Pat	145	" E	June 2 64
1650	Hendricks N	Cav 4	" D	June 5 64
1768	Holmes Rob't	Cav 12	" H	June 9 64
2011	Hannah Thos	Cav 4	" D	June 15 64
2153	Hammer P C	Cav 18	" D	June 13 64
2189	Harts Jno	51	" H	June 19 64
2337	Hooks T	103	" D	June 24 64
2450	Hiler H	50	" C	June 25 64
2551	Hammer Jno	73	" G	June 27 64
2707	Howard Jas	83	" I	June 30 64
2723	Henderson A	58	" F	July 1 64
2736	Hollibaugh W	57	" C	July 2 64
2800	Hastings J	118	" D	July 2 64
2916	Homer D	Cav 13	" F	July 5 64
3020	Holley E F	57	" A	July 7 64
3201	Harrington Jno	55	" C	July 12 64
2	Headley J D	18	" G	Mch 15 64
3379	Height S C	55	" H	July 16 64
3439	Hughes Jno	113	" A	July 17 64
3525	Heenan Jno	Cav 14	" F	July 18 64
3554	Hazlet J	Cav 4	" G	July 18 64
3563	Hester I P	7	" H	July 18 64
3626	Heth R	2	" A	July 20 64
3785	Harrington J W	Cav 3	" A	July 22 64
3792	Haller Peter	139	" K	July 22 64
3836	Harvey P D	57	" B	July 23 64
3853	Hollenbeck J A	55	" B	July 24 64
3920	Hall Henry	53	" H	July 25 64
3953	Haller A	73	" A	July 25 64
4105	Hartlick C	90	" E	July 27 64
4136	Hiffelfinger V	14	" K	July 28 64
4147	Hobbs A	141	" H	July 28 64
4154	Hill P	101	" B	July 28 64
4222	Hoover Jno	Cav 18	" E	July 29 64
4332	Holland J	143	" I	July 31 64
4370	Hilt Jno	73	" I	July 31 64
4379	Hardinger W	147	" B	July 31 64
4431	Hill Thos	18	" L	July 31 64
4474	Hans Jno	116	" K	Aug 1 64
4790	Haffinger J	91	" C	Aug 5 64
4921	Hick G	12	" G	Aug 6 64
5045	Haher C	Cav 14	" B	Aug 8 64
5080	Hall	149	" I	Aug 8 64
5082	Hunter L	63	" C	Aug 8 64
5131	Hardis J L	11	" A	Aug 9 64
5178	Harden M, Res Hme Gds		F	Aug 9 64
5281	Huffman Chas	Cav 7	Co K	Aug 11 64
5284	Hickey D C	Cav 3	" C	Aug 11 64
5289	Hanson J	76	" B	Aug 11 64
5486	Harder ——	184	" C	Aug 13 64
5575	Hoffmaster G	20	" F	Aug 14 64
5688	Heinback S	116	" H	Aug 15 64

Pennsylvania – (*Continued.*)

5954	Holinbeck D	101	Co E	Aug 17 64
6175	Honigan C	55	" C	Aug 19 64
6302	Henry R W	4	" H	Aug 20 64
6367	Hill J E	Cav 2	" L	Aug 21 64
6481	Hollingworth J	(neg) 8	" A	Aug 22 64
6597	Hofmaster L	73	" I	Aug 23 64
6635	Hazenfflucey J	Bat 26		Aug 23 64
6711	Hoch Jno	103	Co K	Aug 24 64
6752	Haden R	119	" A	Aug 24 64
6792	Hogan Thos	103	" K	Aug 25 64
6845	Hurling A	57	" C	Aug 25 64
6910	Hammer Jno	Art 3	" B	Aug 26 64
7000	Hoy J	101	" F	Aug 27 64
7102	Houseman G	118	" I	Aug 28 64
7286	Holloman Wm	102	" G	Aug 30 64
7328	Hopes W	Art 2	" A	Aug 30 64
7422	Havert B	52	" I	Aug 31 64
7491	Halliger C	63	" D	Sept 1 64
7531	Hill E	110		Sept 1 64
7537	Henry A B	103	Co E	Sept 1 64
7568	Hobson B F	7	" G	Sept 2 64
7571	Harman Jno	14	" H	Sept 2 64
7588	Harris A	Cav 2	" K	Sept 2 64
7613	Homiker J	119	" H	Sept 2 64
7661	Hockenbroch J	Art 2	" F	Sept 3 64
7661	Hughes J	Cav 11	" B	Sept 3 64
7682	Hoover S P	7	" H	Sept 3 64
7687	Hunter Chas	3	" A	Sept 3 64
7881	Holmes S	140	" B	Sept 5 64
7965	Hutton Jas	118	" I	Sept 6 64
7990	Hazel Geo	Cav 2	" D	Sept 6 64
8254	Hecker G	Reserves 6	" C	Sept 9 64
8162	Henry O H	Cav 2	" L	Sept 11 64
8526	Heselport J F	68	" G	Sept 12 64
8532	Hopkins ——	50	" K	Sept 12 64
9088	Hansey ——	90	" C	Sept 18 64
9118	Hooker Wm	8	" G	Sept 18 64
9123	Holdhaus C	63	" E	Sept 18 64
9404	Houghbough J	143	" D	Sept 21 64
9434	Hanks J	1	" A	Sept 21 64
9433	Hartzel J	7	" I	Sept 21 64
9532	Houston D	4	" B	Sept 22 64
9579	Harmony J	169	" H	Sept 23 64
9843	Heninshalt W	149	" E	Sept 27 64
9884	Hibbane J	99	" H	Sept 27 64
9904	Hughly Jno	69	" D	Sept 27 64
10022	Hamilton B	183		Sept 29 64
10070	Holden Isaac	7	Co G	Sept 30 54
10109	Harper R	103	" B	Sept 30 64
10239	Hicks J F	Cav 14	" A	Oct 2 64
10319	Hammond J	10	" D	Oct 5 64
10385	Hills S M	14	" D	Oct 5 64
10430	Haldwell P	Cav 7	" E	Oct 6 64
10448	Hiller S	64	" D	Oct 7 64
10474	Howe M A	Cav 12	B	Oct 7 64
10538	Hand H	58		Oct 8 64
10571	Holden P	Cav 12	Co B	Oct 9 64
10574	Hayes J	Cav 15	" G	Oct 9 64
10640	Hands J	106	" A	Oct 10 64
10670	Hull Ed	77	Co G	Oct 11 64
10804	Hennessy P	49	" H	Oct 12 64
10814	Hunbach J	116	" G	Oct 12 64
10862	Hoberg A J	Cav 2	" M	Oct 13 64
10903	Hannesay A	55	" I	Oct 14 64
10906	Hall A	118	" E	Oct 14 64
10952	Hoover S	79	" G	Oct 14 64
10962	Huffman S	64	" C	Oct 15 64
11033	Happy G	101	" K	Oct 16 64
11092	Harty Jas	148	" I	Oct 18 64
11113	Horton S	106	" I	Oct 18 64
11183	Hess G	118	" D	Oct 19 64
11194	Hepsey M	73	" K	Oct 20 64
11383	Hunter T	Cav 5	" M	Oct 21 64
11481	Hart J	7	" I	Oct 26 64
11219	Hunter J	Cav 14	" M	Oct 20 64
11495	Hardinwick J	2	" C	Oct 26 64
11609	Hosaflock H A	Cav 6	" E	Oct 28 64
11643	Hacket J	30	" D	Oct 30 64
11702	Hoover J	90	" A	Oct 31 64
11799	Hagerty W R	7	" G	Nov 4 64
11897	Hart M	11	" K	Nov 7 64
12215	Hyatt J F	118	" F	Dec 3 64
12260	Healy J B	100	" M	Dec 11 64
123 6	Hammond W	20	" K	Dec 18 64
12610	Heneman E L	5	" C	Feb 7 65
12632	Healey J	143	" K	Feb 10 65
12719	Hummell J	87	" B	Mch 2 64
7020	Hazen M J	101	" H	Aug 22 64
3474	Hall B	105	" F	July 17 64
10227	Haman I	118	" E	Oct 1 64
124	Isheart N	Cav 18	" G	Mch 23 64
1401	Illy Tobias	27	" C	May 27 64
10304	Irvin T	Cav 15	" M	Oct 8 64
10616	Ireton S R	138	" I	Oct 10 64
11560	Irwin W	184	" A	Oct 27 64
831	Ingersoll Saml	3	" D	May 1 64
233	Johnson Jno J	45	" I	Mch 29 64
463	Johnson Chas	90	" C	April 9 64
565	Johnson Jno	Cav 2	" G	April 15 64
576	Jacobs Jacob	Cav 2	" M	April 9 64
1303	Jones Wm	145	" A	May 23 64
1595	Jones J	147	" C	June 3 64
1840	Jones Wm	26	" C	June 11 64
2108	Jones O	Cav 4	" D	June 17 64
2312	Johnston Wm	Art 3	" A	June 22 64
2593	Jones R	103	" D	June 28 64
2914	Jordan D W	103	" B	July 5 64
3199	Johnson D	45	" I	July 18 64
3510	Jennings H	45	" G	July 18 64
3835	Jones Wm	55	" C	July 24 64
4057	John Thomas	54	" E	July 27 64
4093	Jones J	79	" A	July 27 64
4540	Johnson J W	50	" G	Aug 2 64
4590	Jameson Wm	103	" H	Aug 3 64
4817	Johns Rob't	101	" I	Aug 5 64
5295	Johnson H	Art 2	" I	Aug 11 64
5516	Jacobs B G	150	" F	Aug 13 64
5871	Jones Rob't	100	" A	Aug 16 64

Pennsylvania—(*Continued.*)

6197	Jones T	101	Co	I	Aug 19 64
6200	Jones W E	27	"	B	Aug 19 64
6317	Jones S	49	"	G	Aug 22 64
6760	Joslin J	145	"	I	Aug 25 64
6817	Jober J	77	"	B	Aug 25 64
6931	Jarmter C	7	"	A	Aug 26 64
7566	Johnson Chas	53	"	G	Sept 2 64
8318	Johnson J	45	"	I	Sept 10 64
8853	Jolly Jas	101	"	H	Sept 15 64
9303	Jones P	63	"	F	Sept 20 64
9351	Jordan J M	149	"	D	Sept 20 64
9378	Jacobs J S	Cav 6	"	F	Sept 20 64
9982	Jeffries C	4	"	B	Sept 29 64
9999	Jones T	101	"	B	Sept 29 64
10735	Jabin Jas	55	"	E	Oct 11 64
10987	Jones A	27	"	D	Oct 16 64
11058	Johnson Wm	184	"	D	Oct 17 64
11430	Jordan Thos	148			Oct 24 64
11539	Jenks J C	115	Co	H	Oct 27 64
12007	Johnson L	118	"	C	Nov 4 64
12331	Jack J P	7	"	E	Dec 24 64
2889	Johnson A G	103	"	I	July 4 64
2	Kelley Chas H	71	"	H	Mch 1 64
238	Kelley H S	Cav 13	"	H	Mch 30 64
266	Kuntzelman J	63	"	E	Mch 31 64
1024	Kenny Wm	12	"	F	May 11 64
1824	Kyle Wm	5	"	H	June 10 64
1875	Kelly Peter	73			June 12 64
2076	Knight Jno	Cav 7	"	K	June 17 64
2335	Kehoe Moses	8	"	H	June 22 64
2639	Kenoan M A	Cav 14	"	L	June 29 64
3048	King C	6	"	C	July 8 64
3187	Kiech N	54	"	A	July 12 64
3265	Klink A	101	"	C	July 13 64
3471	Kemp E	103	"	A	July 17 64
3634	Keeston E	103	"	I	July 20 64
4162	Kagman J T	45	"	B	July 28 64
4293	Kuffman S D	45	"	E	July 30 64
4545	Kauf J	Art 2	"	B	Aug 2 64
4895	Kelley O F	148	"	B	Aug 6 64
5058	Kock H	21	"	H	Aug 8 64
5145	Kawell Jno	Cav 18	"	E	Aug 9 64
5154	Keys Alex C	Cav 16	"	H	Aug 9 64
5208	Kester L	149	"	F	Aug 10 64
5443	Kelley T	Cav 13	"	H	Aug 12 64
5851	Kahn R	96	"	K	Aug 13 64
5718	Keister Jno M	103	"	A	Aug 15 64
5744	Keeley Wm	Cav 13	"	A	Aug 15 64
6028	Kauffman B F	45	"	K	Aug 18 64
6084	Kemper J	73	"	D	Aug 18 64
6459	Kiger Wm	Cav 3	"	C	Aug 22 64
6497	Kenter A W	67	"	B	Aug 2[illegible] 64
6[illegible]14	Kniver S	184	"	F	Aug 2[illegible] 64
6638	Krigle H	11	"	K	Aug 23 64
6965	Krader W O	55	"	H	Aug 27 64
7005	King M	Cav [illegible]	"	A	Aug 27 64
7372	Keller A	9	"	M	Aug 31 64
7553	Keller M	105	"	G	Sept [illegible]
7781	Kyle Wm	116		F	Sept 4 64
8210	Kinsman F P	184	Co	F	Sept 8 64
8734	Kanford Jno C, S m	Cav 5			Sept 14 64
8799	Kaufman J	45	"	E	Sept 17 64
9139	Kipp W	Cav 12	"	D	Sept 18 64
9563	Kinmick T	145	"	K	Sept 23 64
9630	Kearney L	50	"	F	Sept 24 64
10335	Kerr B	149	"	B	Oct 4 64
10367	Kirby J A	101	"	E	Oct 5 64
10439	Kline Ross	184	"	F	Oct 6 64
10502	Kennedy J	152	"	A	Oct 8 64
10698	King M	11	"	K	Oct 11 64
10747	Kirkwood H	101	"	C	Oct 11 64
10926	Kneiper C	89	"	F	Oct 14 64
11238	Kurtz J	55	"	K	Oct 21 64
11332	King J R	55	"	K	Oct 23 64
11384	Kelley E	Cav 7	"	F	Oct 24 64
11463	King R	6	"	E	Oct 26 64
11645	Kramer Geo	116	"	G	Oct 30 64
12695	Knox J	184	"	A	Feb 23 65
8676	Kerer H N	63	"	E	July 20 64
88	Liesen Lewis	Cav 13	"	A	Mch 21 64
243	Lancaster E	Cav 14	"	F	Mch 30 64
297	Luck W	Cav 11	"	H	April 1 64
549	Lynch Adam	Cav 6	"	L	April 14 64
1403	Levy Frank	Cav 3	"	H	May 27 64
1429	Liesine Wm	13	"	E	May 28 64
1579	Lindine J	Art 3	"	A	June 3 64
1588	Little M	106	"	F	June 3 64
1621	Luhaus Melter	145	"	A	June 4 64
2250	Lackey Jas	183	"	D	June 21 64
2379	Leach J	Cav 3	"	D	June 23 64
3091	Larimer J	11	"	E	July 9 64
3734	Ladbeater Jas	7	"	K	July 21 64
3305	Link P	98	"	H	July 14 64
3306	Long A	118	"	H	July 14 64
3369	Lanigan N	Cav 13	"	L	July 15 64
3403	Lewis Ed	101	"	I	July 16 64
3448	Leonard Geo	49	"	G	July 17 64
3489	Logan B	90	"	B	July 17 64
3545	Lee Jas	Cav 13	"	B	July 18 64
4312	Long D F B	101	"	I	July 30 64
4434	Lambert W	Cav 4	"	K	July 31 64
4696	Larrison Wallace	Cav 14	"	C	Aug 4 64
4818	Lewis A	Cav 3	"	D	Aug 5 64
4857	Laughlin J	101	"	E	Aug 6 64
4907	Lahman C	73	"	C	Aug 6 64
4929	Livingston J K	2	"	B	Aug 6 64
5199	Long Augustus	55	"	H	Aug 10 64
5225	Loudin H N	14	"	H	Aug 10 64
5314	Lacock Hugh	116	"	E	Aug 11 64
6252	Lodiss H	90	"	A	Aug 20 64
6636	Leach Jas	49	"	E	Aug 23 64
6783	Light S	143	"	H	Aug 25 64
7145	La Belt J	21	"	F	Aug 29 64
7938	Lemon Jno E	Cav 4	"	I	Sept [illegible] 64
7950	Lockhard J	145	"	B	Sept [illegible] 64
8405	Lepley Chas	103	"	E	Sept 10 64
8754	Layman F	49	"	B	Sept 1[illegible] 64
8833	Laughlin J L	1	"	H	Sept 15 64

Pennsylvania—(*Continued.*)

8895	Lester W H	Cav 7	Co I	Sept 16 64
8904	Lippoth J	5	" E	Sept 16 64
9085	Logne S	26	" A	Sept 18 64
9291	Leary C	83	" K	Sept 19 64
9647	Lolen J	Cav 4	" C	Sept 24 64
10066	Laytin P	110	" D	Sept 30 64
10086	Lutz P M	21	" G	Sept 30 64
10091	Lebos C	116	" D	Sept 30 64
10273	Limar W	140		Oct 3 64
10298	Long W	67	Co G	Oct 4 64
10372	Long P	Cav 11	" C	Oct 5 64
10548	Lancaster C	119	" B	Oct 8 64
10572	Lynch W J	Cav 3	" I	Oct 9 64
10580	Labor R	7	" F	Oct 10 64
10687	Luchford R	143	" F	Oct 11 64
10873	Lang I	110	" C	Oct 13 64
11004	Leuchlier J	5		Oct 16 64
11255	Lanz Wm	7	Co C	Oct 21 64
11465	Lewis J	Cav 4	" L	Oct 26 64
11728	Luther I	Cav 4	" L	Nov 1 64
11869	Lego Geo	12	" A	Nov 6 64
11907	Ladd A	53	" M	Nov 7 64
12192	Lape J	18	" K	Nov 28 64
12210	Lewis D S	53	" K	Dec 2 64
12489	Linsey D	77	" G	Jan 19 65
5699	Ledwick F M	139	" C	Aug 15 64
7084	Latchem David	Cav 4	" K	Aug 28 64
7307	Lochery A	Cav 14	" E	Aug 30 64
5985	Logan W	97	" A	Aug 17 64
6030	Loudon S	101	" A	Aug 18 64
6053	Layton Samuel	181	" A	Aug 18 64
6071	Lamb C	71	" B	Aug 18 64
6082	Lane Amos	Cav 6	" E	Aug 18 64
6152	Lehnich Jno	Art 2	" F	Aug 19 64
753	Lenard M	Cav 13	" D	April 26 64
761	Lord G W	141	" E	April 27 64
871	Loudon Samuel	2	" F	May 4 64
183	Maynard Jno	105	" G	Mch 27 64
208	Missile Val	47	" C	Mch 28 64
225	Miller Daniel	Cav 13	" H	Mch 29 64
361	Martin J F	Cav 14	" K	April 2 64
461	McEntire W	51	" F	April 9 64
538	Mine Josh	51	" F	April 14 64
586	Marple S L	14	" A	April 17 64
605	McKissick Jno	23	" F	April 18 64
667	Myers G	Cav 1	" E	April 22 64
736	McKeever E L	71	" F	April 25 64
773	McDonald R	23	" C	April 28 64
780	McCarthy Jas	Cav 18	" E	April 28 64
969	McQueeny W	79	" B	May 9 64
1006	Meyer Jno	Cav 2	" E	May 10 64
1128	McKey J	Cav 1	" I	May 15 64
1139	McMahon J	73	" F	May 16 64
1147	McKnight J E	57	" B	May 16 64
11[illegible]	McHale J	Cav 14	" D	May 16 64
1185	Moser Jno	Cav 13	" B	May 18 64
1273	McCollen W	Cav 4	" L	May 22 64
1287	Milligan J	61	" F	May 22 64
1308	McCartney M	73	" B	May 23 64
1460	Murray Jno	Cav 13	Co E	May 29 64
1586	Miles Lewis	Cav 4	" I	June 3 64
1643	Myers J R	Cav 13	" M	June 5 64
1722	Marshall M M	58	" E	June 8 64
1748	Moyer Thos	103	" E	June 9 64
1792	Miller M	118	" A	June 10 64
1858	McHose J	Cav 4	" A	June 12 64
1907	Miller Henry	8	" G	June 13 64
1982	Muchollans J	101	" K	June 15 64
2056	Monny W H	Cav 3	" A	June 16 64
2068	Matchell J J	101	" K	June 16 64
2159	Monan J	101	" C	June 19 64
2265	McCutchen J	Cav 4	" C	June 21 64
2278	Milton Wm	Cav 19	" H	June 21 64
2333	Myers F	27	" H	June 22 64
2364	Myers Peter	76	" G	June 23 64
2388	Morton T	79	" I	June 24 64
2409	McCabe J	Cav 3	" L	June 24 64
2411	McKay M J	103	" B	June 24 64
2493	Merry Jas	67	" E	June 26 64
2503	Martin A J	Cav 4	" E	June 26 64
2508	Morris J	Cav 13	" A	June 26 64
2653	McManes ——	77	" B	June 29 64
2684	Mipes J	101	" B	June 30 64
2690	Morris G	77	" G	June 30 64
2798	Marsh D	50	" D	July 2 64
2831	McCane Chas	14	" C	July 3 64
3017	McRath J	48	" C	July 7 64
3065	Morris Calvin	53	" D	July 9 64
3133	McCalasky J E	Cav 4	" K	July 10 64
3151	Mattiser B	57	" F	July 11 64
3172	Madden Daniel	149	" G	July 11 64
3250	Myers M	103	" E	July 13 64
3374	Mink H	Art 3	" A	July 16 64
3467	Meaker E N	155	" H	July 17 64
3481	McKeon Jno	101	" H	July 17 64
3488	Mihan J	133	" D	July 17 64
3939	Maroney Jno	Cav 1	" D	July 20 64
3690	McCarron J	Cav 4	" A	July 21 64
3766	Myers Jno	116	" D	July 22 64
3971	Martin G	45	" I	July 25 64
4016	McDermott J M	70	" F	July 26 64
4123	McGee Jas	103	" I	July 28 64
4197	Moore M G	Art 1	" A	July 29 64
4341	Marquet M	6	" M	July 30 64
4407	McKever Jno	100	" A	July 31 64
4414	McFarland Jas	55	" E	July 31 64
4546	Moan Jas	101	" K	Aug 2 64
4607	Martin Bryant	7	" F	Aug 3 64
4635	McKeral Jas	14	" K	Aug 3 64
4710	Mathews C W	145	" B	Aug 4 64
4734	Moore	71	" I	Aug 4 64
4796	McDevitt J	Art 3	" D	Aug 5 64
4824	Miller H	Cav 14	" I	Aug 5 64
4876	Mills Wm	150	" G	Aug 6 64
4898	Muldany M	96	" K	Aug 6 64
5068	Martain Jno	103	" E	Aug 8 64
5069	Measler Jas	103	" E	Aug 8 64
5139	McCaffrey Jno, h s	Art 3	" A	Aug 9 64

Pennsylvania—(*Continued.*)

5159	Martin C	Cav 8	Co A	Aug 9 64
5266	Marey H F	103	" F	Aug 10 64
5291	Mohr J R	14	" G	Aug 11 64
5415	McCarty Dennis	101	" K	Aug 12 64
5433	McGee J	14	" H	Aug 12 64
5595	Mickelson B	Cav 16	" B	Aug 14 64
5642	McClough L C	18	" C	Aug 14 64
5704	Miller Jno	101	" G	Aug 15 64
5723	McCann Jno	Art 3	" A	Aug 15 64
5781	Miller S	143	" B	Aug 15 64
5809	Montgomery R	62	" A	Aug 16 64
5868	McQuillen A	Art 6	" L	Aug 16 64
5893	McCuller S	Cav 4	" B	Aug 16 64
5926	Mulchey J A	50	" D	Aug 17 64
5983	Mann Jas	119	" G	Aug 17 64
6014	McPherson D	103	" F	Aug 17 64
6038	Moore C	103	" G	Aug 18 64
6148	McCracker J	53	" K	Aug 19 64
6291	McLaughlin Jas	Cav 4	" A	Aug 20 64
6441	McWilliams H	82	" I	Aug 22 64
5480	Martin Jno	103	" D	Aug 22 64
6532	McGan J	Cav 18		Aug 23 64
6664	McKee ——	141	Co C	Aug 24 64
6689	Manner M	73	" K	Aug 24 64
6910	McGlann H	143	" B	Aug 26 64
6925	McGuigan H C	7	" K	Aug 26 64
7026	Marks P	143	" B	Aug 27 64
7061	Moore M J	107		Aug 28 64
7107	Moyer Wm H	55	Co H	Aug 28 64
7119	Miller Jno L	53	" K	Aug 28 64
7127	McAffee Jas	72	" F	Aug 28 64
7175	Moore Thos	69	" D	Aug 29 64
7263	Martin Jno	77	" C	Aug 30 64
7265	Musser Jno	77	" D	Aug 30 64
7305	Moser S	103	" E	Aug 30 64
7333	Morris Jno	183	" G	Aug 30 64
7407	Marchin Wm	50	" E	Aug 31 64
7512	Millinger Jno H	7	" C	Sept 1 64
7602	Moorhead J S	103	" D	Sept 2 64
7719	Myers H	9	" A	Sept 3 64
7875	Mayer W	8	" M	Sept 5 64
7925	Mays N J	103	" H	Sept 5 64
8027	Murphy A	Cav 13	" I	Sept 6 64
8047	McKnight J	Cav 18	" I	Sept 6 64
8122	Miller J	101	" C	Sept 8 64
8123	Mullings W	145	" G	Sept 8 64
8128	Munager W	Cav 13	" L	Sept 8 64
8134	Mehaffey J M	Cav 16	" B	Sept 8 64
8153	McCantley W	Art 2	" A	Sept 8 64
8158	McLane T	12	" E	Sept 8 64
8194	McKink J	119	" D	Sept 8 64
8216	Mansfield J	101	" G	Sept 8 64
8322	Myers A	118	" I	Sept 10 64
8469	Magill H	103	" I	Sept 11 64
8595	Morrison J	146	" E	Sept 12 64
8627	McKinney D	90	" C	Sept 13 64
8691	Moritze A	118	" D	Sept 14 64
8802	McCullogh ——	101	" E	Sept 15 64
9071	Maynard A	Art 3		Sept 17 64
9090	McCall Wm	Cav 22	Co B	Sept 18 64
9128	McCullough S	133	" K	Sept 19 64
9270	Mayhan F	Cav 20		Sept 19 64
9315	Marsh W	149	Co K	Sept 20 64
9339	Meyers J A	138	" C	Sept 20 64
9526	McQuigley Jno	101	" C	Sept 22 64
9583	Mead H J	184	" B	Sept 23 64
9598	Martin J	Cav 17	" C	Sept 23 64
9644	Morris J	54	" I	Sept 24 64
9646	Morgan J E	2	" A	Sept 24 64
9651	McCook B	118	" A	Sept 24 64
9761	McMurray Wm	Cav 1	" I	Sept 25 64
9871	Mason Jno	112	" A	Sept 27 64
4578	McKerner S	73	" E	Aug 2 64
10050	Mesin Jas	90	" F	Sept 30 64
10060	Morgan C	45	" A	Sept 30 64
10119	McClany J	101	" C	Oct 1 64
10154	McElroy Wm	Cav 13	" L	Oct 1 64
10306	Meese J	48	" A	Oct 4 64
10396	McGraw Jno	Art 3	" A	Oct 6 64
10407	Miller H	79	" K	Oct 6 64
10486	Miller Wash'gton	Cav 18	" C	Oct 7 64
10610	McKearney J W	118	" K	Oct 10 64
10620	McClief Wm	7	" A	Oct 10 64
10641	Marker W H	118	" D	Oct 10 64
10678	Martin J P	7	" I	Oct 11 64
10684	Miller Jas	7	" I	Oct 11 64
10803	Mattis Aaron	138		Oct 12 64
10825	Moore C H	Cav 13	" C	Oct 13 64
10929	Martin Geo H	108	" I	Oct 14 64
10981	Maxwell S	Cav 14	" B	Oct 15 64
10991	Moses W	Cav 16	" H	Oct 16 64
10993	McKnight Jas	118	" K	Oct 16 64
11081	Mitchell J O	53	" H	Oct 18 64
11142	Mansfield Geo	101	" I	Oct 19 64
11229	McClay J H	Cav 11	" D	Oct 20 64
11305	McBride ——	Cav 2	" H	Oct 22 64
11326	Marshall L	184	" A	Oct 23 64
11387	Moore S	101	" F	Oct 24 64
11439	Moore J	Cav 13	" B	Oct 25 64
11464	McNelse J H	100	" E	Oct 26 64
11542	Miller F	54	" K	Oct 27 64
11655	Midz J	Cav 20	" A	Oct 30 64
11658	Menk W	Cav 12	" F	Oct 30 64
11683	Morrow J C, Ser Maj	101	" E	Oct 31 64
11684	McCann J	Cav 11	" L	Oct 31 64
11686	Moore W	184	" B	Oct 31 64
11692	Mulligan J	7	" H	Oct 31 64
11909	McCune J	67	" E	Nov 8 64
11913	McClush N	97	" E	Nov 8 64
11982	Manee M	53	" H	Nov 13 64
12008	McCray J	145	" A	Nov 14 64
12088	Maher D	118	" E	Nov 18 64
12103	Miller W	31	" I	Nov 22 64
12218	Murray W	Cav 14	" H	Dec 8 64
12326	McIntire J	55	" C	Dec 24 64
12334	Myers A D	52	" A	Dec 26 64
12554	Matthews J	Cav 6	" F	Jan 30 65
12595	Maloy J M	184	" D	Feb 5 65

Pennsylvania—(*Continued.*)

12625	McGenger —	20	Co C	Feb 9 65
12696	Myers H	87	" E	Feb 23 65
12771	McDonald ——	9	" G	Mch 13 65
12806	McGarrett R W	103	" F	Feb 21 65
1134	Nicholson Jno	Cav 3	" H	May 16 64
1298	Nelson Wm	76	" H	May 23 64
2832	Nolti Wm	6	" F	July 3 64
3653	Newell G S	183	" A	July 20 64
4246	Nicholson W	Cav 1	" H	July 29 64
4489	Nelson Geo	2	" K	Aug 1 64
4936	Naylor G W	Cav 13	" L	Aug 7 64
5109	Nichols D A	125	" D	Aug 9 64
6001	Neal H G	90	" B	Aug 17 64
6011	Nickle C	37	" G	Aug 17 64
6702	Nickem Jas	77	" G	Aug 24 64
8154	Naylor S	Cav 20	" H	Sept 8 64
8907	Noble J	73	" D	Sept 16 64
9424	Nice Isaac	11	" L	Sept 21 64
9468	Neff J	Cav 4	" D	Sept 21 64
10146	Nelson G	55	" A	Oct 1 64
10286	Nelson J A	145	" G	Oct 4 64
10764	Newberry Jno	Cav 20	" A	Oct 12 64
11107	Nelson A	160	" E	Oct 18 64
11254	Noble Thos	Cav 19	" G	Oct 21 64
11776	Nichols G	20	" C	Nov 3 64
414	Osbourne S K	4	" K	April 7 64
622	Oglesby J	Cav 4	" K	April 19 64
1318	O'Brien P	13	" A	May 23 64
1409	Ottinger L	Cav 8	" I	May 27 64
1817	O Neil Jno	69		June 12 64
2589	Oswald Stephen	55	Co G	June 28 64
3161	O Conor ——	83		July 11 64
3199	O'Neil J	63	Co I	July 12 64
3704	Olmar H	Cav 2	" H	July 21 64
3861	O Connor H	49	" E	July 24 64
4161	Owens G H	7	" A	July 28 64
5119	Offlebach Z	90	" K	Aug 9 64
5184	Oliver W	103	" D	Aug 9 64
5939	O Hara M	101	" E	Aug 17 64
6254	O Connell Wm	183	" G	Aug 20 64
6535	O'Hara Jno	150	" E	Aug 23 64
6658	Oiler Sam'l	103	" G	Aug 24 64
6908	O'Rourke Chas	109	" C	Aug 26 64
7105	Otto Jno	Cav 5	" B	Aug 28 64
9330	Owens E	50	" D	Aug 20 74
10805	Osborn E	Cav 11	" A	Oct 13 64
30	Peck Albert	57	" K	Mch 9 64
62	Patterson Rob't	Res 2	" E	Mch 18 64
125	Parker Jas M	76	" B	Mch 23 64
500	Petrisky H	54	" F	April 12 64
1110	Patterson Thos	Cav 3	" A	May 15 64
1119	Patent Thos	73	" G	May 15 64
1258	Powell Wm	Cav 14	" D	May 21 64
1556	Powers Jno	26	" I	June 2 64
1780	Preso Thos	26	" E	June 9 64
1884	Powell Frank	18		June 12 64
2566	Page J	183	Co G	June 27 64
2590	Porter David	101	" H	June 28 64
2903	Parsons J T	103	" D	July 5 64
3197	Painter J G	26	Co F	July 11 64
3445	Painter S	63	" A	July 17 64
4049	Patterson R	101	" H	July 27 64
4157	Pickett J C	Cav 3	" A	July 28 64
4177	Pratt F	Cav 14	" I	July 28 64
4191	Plymeer W	Cav 20	" B	July 28 64
4415	Page Jno	112	" A	July 31 64
4473	Powell H	102	" H	Aug 1 64
5323	Prosser J	63		Aug 11 64
5579	Pyers Isaac	72	Co G	Aug 14 64
5610	Phillips Jas B	101	" I	Aug 14 64
5947	Parish J A	184		Aug 17 64
6341	Preans H	149	Co K	Aug 21 64
6439	Palmer H	140	" D	Aug 22 64
6527	Poole G	52	" B	Aug 22 64
6536	Pifer M	13	" G	Aug 23 64
6574	Phillips J W	Cav 1	" F	Aug 23 64
6813	Peterson G	103	" D	Aug 25 64
6844	Penn Jno	Cav 5	" E	Aug 25 64
6885	Patten H W	Art 2	" F	Aug 26 64
7118	Potts Edw	183	" H	Aug 28 64
7232	Perkins N	103	" D	Aug 29 64
8030	Powell A T	149	" C	Sept 6 64
8160	Pricht F	87	" H	Sept 8 64
8763	Peck C W	145	" H	Sept 14 64
8877	Persil Frederick	101		Sept 15 64
9220	Palmer A	143	Co D	Sept 19 64
9684	Perego W	143	" G	Sept 24 64
9754	Phipps J H	57	" E	Sept 25 64
10074	Price G	106	" H	Sept 30 64
10573	Penstock A	144	" B	Oct 9 64
10858	Powell I	101	" I	Oct 13 64
11168	Price O	109	" C	Oct 19 64
11261	Phay M	69	" C	Oct 21 64
11637	Phillips F	61	" K	Oct 28 64
11737	Pees M T	145	" H	Nov 2 64
11833	Penn J	Cav 18	" I	Nov 6 64
11918	Phelps W	Cav 4	" G	Nov 8 64
11328	Porterfield J K	Cav 5	" M	Oct 23 64
12075	Pencer W	18	" C	Nov 18 64
12191	Pryor Wm	11	" C	Nov 28 64
12359	Poleman H	Cav 1	" F	Dec 30 64
12378	Perry H	121	" C	Jan 2 65
12388	Pritchett J	72	" C	Jan 3 65
12479	Potter B F	148	" I	Jan 17 65
6756	Quinby L C	76	E	Aug 24 64
47	Reed Sam'l	Cav 4	" D	Mch 15 64
126	Robertson J	119	" K	Mch 23 64
132	Rosenburg Henry	49	" G	Mch 24 64
171	Reign Jno	83	" K	Mch 26 64
308	Richpeder A	13	" B	April 2 64
610	Ray Wm	Cav 8	" F	April 18 64
847	Rhinehart J	Cav 3	" D	May 3 64
895	Russell F	4	" D	May 5 64
907	Rhinebolt J	Cav 18	" I	May 5 64
940	Robinson C W	150	" E	May 7 64
1152	Randall H	Cav 4	" H	May 16 64
1218	Rigney Chas	Cav 4	G	May 19 64
1454	Raleigh A	51	" G	May 29 64

Pennsylvania—(*Continued.*)

1485	Rudolph S	Cav 13	Co K	May 30 64
1599	Rhine Geo	63	" I	June 4 64
1624	Rosenburg H	Cav 13	" H	June 4 64
1719	Raymond Jno	Cav 18	" H	June 8 64
1803	Rheems A	73	" I	June 10 64
1833	Ramsay J D	103	" F	June 11 64
1922	Rush S	18	" G	June 14 64
1942	Robinson Wm	77	" D	June 14 64
2235	Roush Peter	101	" E	June 20 64
2528	Rupert F	Cav 2	" H	June 26 64
2602	Roat J	54	" F	June 28 64
2735	Rhoades F	79	" E	July 1 64
2911	Rock J E	5	" M	July 5 64
2979	Regart Jno	Cav 13	" E	July 7 64
2103	Ray A	77	" E	July 17 64
8024	Rugh M J	103	" D	July 7 64
3270	Robins R	69	" B	July 13 64
8468	Ransom H	148	" I	July 17 64
8827	Rinner L	Cav 5	" A	July 23 64
4074	Ringwalk F J	79	" H	July 27 64
4241	Roger L	115	" L	July 29 64
4309	Rogers C	73	" C	July 30 64
4476	Ray Jas R	134	" B	Aug 1 64
4507	Riese S	103	" D	Aug 1 64
4844	Richie Jas	103	" B	Aug 6 64
4940	Ruthfer J	Art 2	" F	Aug 7 64
5319	Rice Sam'l	101	" K	Aug 11 64
5389	Ross David	103	" B	Aug 12 64
5430	Robinson John	99	" D	Aug 12 64
5537	Rose B	13	" I	Aug 13 64
5800	Robins J	Cav 2	" M	Aug 15 64
5879	Rider H	Cav 7	" L	Aug 16 64
5894	Richards E	143	" E	Aug 16 64
5912	Reese Jacob	103	" B	Aug 17 64
5940	Richards Jno	Cav 1	" G	Aug 17 64
6321	Robbins G	106	" G	Aug 21 64
6373	Roger Jno L	110	" H	Aug 21 64
6520	Reynolds J	14	" H	Aug 22 64
6725	Rowe E	103	" A	Aug 24 64
6777	Rangardener J	149	" H	Aug 25 64
6789	Richards G	Cav 13	" A	Aug 25 64
6790	Runcls Jno	Cav 6	" L	Aug 25 64
6322	Rum A	183	" C	Aug 25 64
6838	Reese D	148	" K	Aug 25 64
6896	Raiff T	1	" A	Aug 26 64
6933	Richardson —	61		Aug 26 64
7067	Reese D	143	Co F	Aug 28 64
7202	Ruff J	103	" F	Aug 29 64
7292	Redmire H	98	" B	Aug 30 64
7293	Robins Geo	62	" A	Aug 30 64
7410	Richardson H	103	" K	Aug 31 64
7467	Richard D	Cav 18	" D	Sept 1 64
7716	Rice E	7	" B	Sept 3 64
7738	Roads Frederick	101	" E	Sept 3 64
8139	Rathburn K	2	" F	Sept 8 64
8540	Russell S A	79	" A	Sept 12 64
8545	Ray A	149	" D	Sept 12 64
8602	Richards J	106	" H	Sept 12 64
8635	Rhangmen G	138	" D	Sept 13 64
8742	Root D	48	Co B	Sept 14 64
9019	Rot Geo	18	" A	Sept 17 64
9272	Ramsay J I	149		Sept 19 64
9535	Richie H	11	Co F	Sept 3 64
9590	Renamer W H	87	" H	Sept 23 64
9612	Richards Jno	113	" D	Sept 23 64
9653	Reed R	103	" A	Sept 24 64
9766	Ramsay R	84	" D	Sept 25 64
9832	Richards J	53	" K	Sept 27 64
10174	Reed J	55	" A	Oct 1 64
10363	Ramsay Wm	87	" B	Oct 13 64
10622	Reedy E T	87	" B	Oct 10 64
10915	Roundabush H B	51	" A	Oct 14 64
10947	Rockwell A	Cav 2	" L	Oct 14 64
11071	Raeff J B	72	" E	Oct 17 64
11115	Rinkle Jno A	20	" A	Oct 18 64
11293	Rolston J	18	" F	Oct 22 64
11147	Rudy J	13	" F	Oct 19 64
11414	Riffle S G	189	" C	Oct 25 64
11566	Richardson A	144	" E	Oct 27 64
11868	Rowland N	111	" F	Nov 6 64
12008	Rapp A E	Cav 18	" I	Nov 15 64
12048	Ruth B S	23	" I	Nov 16 64
12236	Rothe C	101	" A	Dec 1 64
12355	Reese D	7	" A	Dec 29 64
12372	Reed W S	128	" H	Jan 1 65
377	Smith M D	18	" B	April 5 64
788	Smith Geo	Cav 5	" H	April 23 64
881	Smith Wm	4	" A	May 4 64
882	Smith T	19	" G	May 4 64
921	Steffler W J	Cav 12	" G	May 6 64
1014	Serend H	Cav 4	" D	May 10 64
1030	Shebert Gotlieb	73	" C	May 11 64
1058	Spilyfiter A	54	" F	May 13 64
1105	Sullivan D	101	" K	May 15 64
1114	Shindle S R	140	" K	May 15 64
1155	Stearnes E K	Cav 14	" A	May 16 64
1169	Sloat D	76	" I	May 16 64
1175	Scott Wm	4	" B	May 16 64
1216	Severn C	139	" A	May 19 64
1236	Sammoris B	Cav 2	" B	May 21 64
1249	Smith Chas	26	" A	May 24 64
1453	Schlenbough C	Cav 4	" G	May 29 64
1503	Smith Martin	Cav 18	" H	May 31 64
1535	Stone Samuel	26	" F	June 1 64
1543	Shoemaker M	Cav 13	" H	June 1 64
1605	Swearer G	13	" H	June 4 64
1620	Schiefeit Jacob	51	" F	June 4 64
1632	Schmar R	45	" F	June 5 64
1933	Smith D	Cav 11	" H	June 14 64
2039	Slough H	53		June 15 64
2070	Stevens A	Cav 13	Co M	June 16 64
2121	Sherwood C H	Cav 4	" M	June 17 64
2123	Stall Sam'l	75	" D	June 17 64
2126	Say J R	Cav 4	" K	June 17 64
2163	Steele J S	Cav 7	" F	June 19 64
2230	Scoles M	27	" K	June 21 64
2231	Sims B	Cav 14	" G	June 22 64
2412	Shoop Jacob	2	" M	June 24 64

Pennsylvania—(*Continued.*)

2622	Springer Jno	101	Co E	June 28 64
2650	Stewart J B	103	" A	June 29 64
2725	Scott Allen	150	" H	July 1 64
2738	Schimgert J	73	" G	July 1 64
2791	Shimer J A	Cav 13	" A	July 2 64
2854	Scott Wm, (Negro)	8	" D	July 4 64
2905	Stump A	11	" I	July 5 64
2941	Smith Jacob	51	" H	July 6 64
2932	Shaw W	149	" B	July 7 64
2999	Smulley Jno	112	" K	July 7 64
3057	Sutton R M	103	" I	July 9 64
3113	Sweet H	57	" K	July 10 64
3136	Shoemaker M	148	" G	July 10 64
3154	Sillers Wm	77	" D	July 11 64
3211	Stone W F	53	" G	July 12 64
3480	Swelser J	103	" D	July 17 64
3567	Smalley L	58	" K	July 19 64
3568	Stevens S G	150	" H	July 19 64
3586	Sickles Daniel	116	" K	July 19 64
3632	Serders J S	112	" K	July 20 64
3670	Stopper Wm	16	" B	July 20 64
3763	Stillenberger F	172	" F	July 22 64
3775	Strance D	11	" H	July 22 64
3855	Smith J	79	" F	July 24 64
3906	Smith O C	77	" G	July 24 64
3936	Seilk A	144	" D	July 25 64
3960	Sullivan T	77	" F	July 25 64
4005	Smith F	64	" K	July 26 64
4009	Shafer J H	84	" E	July 26 64
4012	Shapley Geo	103	" G	July 26 64
4043	Strickley C	53	" H	July 27 64
4064	Shrively E S	Cav 19	" M	July 27 64
4113	Sheppard E	145	" G	July 28 64
4164	Smith S W	101	" B	July 28 64
4213	Shaffer Peter	52	" F	July 29 64
4223	Shister F	Cav 3	" A	July 29 64
4228	Stein J	7	" G	July 29 64
4274	Sloan J	11	" E	July 29 64
4285	Shone P	Cav 4	" D	July 30 64
4345	Stobbs W W	101	" E	July 30 64
4348	Scott A	22	" F	July 31 64
4351	Scundler J	67	" A	July 31 64
4372	Smith P	72	" C	July 31 64
4763	Salo Thos	15	" M	Aug 2 64
4775	Shink Jas	81	" F	Aug 5 64
4791	Sullivan Ed	67	" H	Aug 5 64
4797	Sear C	Cav 14	" L	Aug 5 64
4845	Shember Jno	Cav 11	" D	Aug 6 64
4928	Slicker J	77	" D	Aug 6 64
4931	Sheit P	61	" G	Aug 7 64
4945	Swartz P	27	" I	Aug 7 64
5100	Stiner Jno	Cav 22	" G	Aug 9 64
5180	Striker F	Cav 14	" C	Aug 9 64
5215	Swordland Wm	184	" A	Aug 10 64
5232	Speck A	113	" A	Aug 10 64
5411	Shaffer Daniel	Cav 13	" F	Aug 12 64
5429	Spangrost A	103	" D	Aug 12 64
5437	Shears J S	149	" K	Aug 12 64
5463	Stibbs W	56	" H	Aug 13 64
5494	Shape F	Cav 18	Co A	Aug 13 64
5503	Somerfield W	69	" E	Aug 14 64
5700	Stinebach A	150	" C	Aug 15 64
5750	Spears W M	Cav 2	" K	Aug 15 64
5874	Sheppard N	79	" F	Aug 16 64
5935	Shultz F	Cav 13	" K	Aug 17 64
6205	Shoop G	103	" K	Aug 19 64
6289	Smith H	26	" K	Aug 20 64
6337	Smith W	Cav 18	" B	Aug 21 64
6332	Swager M	101	" F	Aug 21 64
6436	Spain Thos	103	" H	Aug 22 64
6523	Stover J	49	" F	Aug 22 64
6526	Stahler S	149	" G	Aug 22 64
6534	Snyder Jno	113	" C	Aug 23 64
6584	Sloate E	50	" D	Aug 23 64
6595	Shirley Henry	105	" I	Aug 23 64
6639	Sherwood P	84	" I	Aug 24 64
6776	Shellito R	150	" C	Aug 25 64
6823	Spain Richard	118	" H	Aug 25 64
6829	Sturgess W A	79	" G	Aug 25 64
6880	Stuler D	Cav 4	" A	Aug 26 64
7029	Strickler J W	11	" F	Aug 27 64
7106	Smith Jno F	55	" C	Aug 28 64
7137	Sloan J M	Cav 13	" D	Aug 28 64
7141	Springer J	103	" F	Aug 29 64
7202	Shriver B	Cav 18	" K	Aug 30 64
7302	Singer J	Art 2	" A	Aug 30 64
7358	Scoleton J	53	" F	Aug 31 64
7353	Sweeney D	Cav 14	" E	Aug 31 64
7379	Scott W B	Cav 4	" D	Aug 31 64
7631	Streetman J	7	" E	Sept 2 64
7638	Steele J	62	" M	Sept 2 64
7648	Spencer Geo	20	" C	Sept 3 64
7662	Snyder M S	183	" A	Sept 3 64
7765	Swartz Geo	Cav 5	" A	Sept 3 64
7770	Stockhouse D	Cav 13	" I	Sept 4 64
7905	Sellers H	149	" G	Sept 5 64
7929	Shultz Jno	Cav 4	" I	Sept 5 64
7969	Smith A C	7	" F	Sept 6 64
8033	Simpson T	53	" K	Sept 6 64
8103	Stump J	145	" I	Sept 7 64
8112	Slade E	150	" H	Sept 7 64
8414	Shirk M B	142	" A	Sept 11 64
8567	Simons Wm H	76	" K	Sept 12 64
8659	Spould E	90	" E	Sept 13 64
8773	Smith Wm	2	" K	Sept 14 64
8795	Stella J F	1	" B	Sept 15 64
9296	Signall ——	79	" H	Sept 19 64
9012	Steadman W	54	" F	Sept 17 64
9123	Schably J	54	" A	Sept 18 64
9138	Shoup S	Cav 16	" B	Sept 18 64
9310	Smith Chas	7	" H	Sept 20 64
9365	Stebbins Z	7	" H	Sept 20 64
9411	Scott D	149	" G	Sept 21 64
9567	Snyder A	148	" I	Sept 23 64
9593	Sternholt Wm	38		Sept 23 64
9742	Supple C M	63	Co B	Sept 25 64
9780	Surplus W	Cav 13	" L	Sept 26 64
9890	Siherk Christian	145		Sept 27 64

Pennsylvania—(*Continued.*)

9893	Sweeny W P	Cav 13		Sept 27 64
9912	Sanford C	69	Co H	Sept 28 64
9985	Sheppard C	118	" E	Sept 29 64
10088	Sloan P	115	" A	Sept 30 64
10132	Smith J S	Cav 22	" B	Oct 1 64
10299	Strong H	55	" E	Oct 4 64
10323	Smith E	10	" H	Oct 4 64
10516	Snyder Wm	54	" H	Oct 8 64
10525	Stones T	101	" K	Oct 8 64
10530	Smallwood C	7	" F	Oct 8 64
10609	Small H	101	" H	Oct 10 64
10720	Smallman J W	63	" A	Oct 11 64
10808	Steele F F	Cav 20	" A	Oct 12 64
10837	Shank A	184	" C	Oct 13 64
11044	Smith Andrew	Cav 22	" B	Oct 17 64
11069	Stevens C P	11	" A	Oct 17 64
11233	Smith H W	53	" B	Oct 21 64
11246	Smith Jas	57	" E	Oct 21 64
11355	Silvy David	Cav 13	" I	Oct 23 64
11368	Seyoff H	81	" C	Oct 23 64
11488	Sunderland E	11	" D	Oct 26 64
11529	Stevenson Jno	111	" I	Oct 26 64
11661	Speck Olive	67	" H	Oct 30 64
11741	Smith H	103	" D	Nov 2 64
11785	Snodgrass R J	145	" H	Nov 4 64
11792	Sellentine M	145	" C	Nov 4 64
11825	Seltzer D	20	" K	Nov 5 64
11885	Smith W B	Cav 14	" E	Nov 6 64
11890	Shure J P	184	" F	Nov 7 64
11895	Snively G W	Cav 20	" F	Nov 7 64
11926	Scover J H	79	" G	Nov 8 64
11951	Shefiley W	118	" G	Nov 9 64
12057	Stitzer G	2	" E	Nov 16 64
12081	Stensley D	1 4	" A	[illegible]v 18 64
12217	Smith J S	118	" F	Dec 3 64
12218	Skinner S O	77	" A	Dec 4 64
12282	Shafer T	184	" E	Dec 13 64
12308	Stafford W	67	" H	Dec 19 64
12384	Sourbeer J E	20	" A	Jan 3 65
12590	Sipe F	87	" C	Feb 5 65
12598	Stauffer J	1	" K	Feb 6 65
12648	Stain G W	Cav 20	" K	Feb 13 65
12660	Slough E B	Cav 1	" D	Feb 17 65
12670	Scott A J	14	" D	Feb 17 65
12676	Sheridan M	183	" F	Feb 19 65
12817	Sharks J N	14	" D	Mch 27 65
12824	Shultz H H	87	" A	April 5 65
778	Thistlewood J	73	" E	April 28 64
785	Tolland D	Cav 13	" D	April 23 64
1141	Taylor J F	13	" E	May 16 64
1145	Tull D	4	" D	May 16 64
1153	Toner Peter	10	" A	May 16 64
1814	Thompson H	57	" C	June 10 64
2182	Thompson A, Mus	Cav 4	" C	June 19 64
2302	Townsend D	Cav 13	" D	June 22 64
2635	Tyser L	145	" D	June 29 64
2897	Terwilliger E	103	" H	July 5 64
3033	Thompson R	103	" F	July 7 64
47	Taylor C W	84	" D	May 24 64
3329	Titus W	171	Co D	July 14 64
3473	Todd Wm	103	" K	July 17 64
3571	Thompson J S	[illegible]03	" H	July 19 64
3768	Terrell A	Cav 12	" B	July 22 64
3968	Trumbull H	3	" E	July 25 64
4116	Thompson Jas	Cav 18	" G	July 28 64
4160	Tinsdale ——	149	" E	July 28 64
4713	Thompson J	Art 3	" A	Aug 4 64
5179	Thompson W W	101	" E	Aug 9 64
5345	Thomas F	7	" F	Aug 11 64
5966	Thompson J B	100	" H	Aug 17 64
6146	Thompson F A B	69	" I	Aug 19 64
6447	Tubbs E	143	" I	Aug 23 64
6476	Toll Wm	Res 11	" I	Aug 22 64
6791	Turner Jno	118	" H	Aug 25 64
7250	Thomas E	23	" F	Aug 30 64
7409	Thorpe L	61	" E	Aug 31 64
7904	Trash Seth	81	" A	Sept 6 64
8231	Truman E W	9	" G	Sept 9 64
8531	Tilt W	115	" A	Sept 12 64
8619	Tutor C	134	" A	Sept 13 64
9027	Tits P		" C	Sept 17 64
9212	Thorpe D	18	" D	Sept 19 64
9302	Thompson H	Cav 18	" I	Sept 20 64
9726	Tonson J	99	" B	Sept 25 64
9775	Thuck I	7	" C	Sept 26 64
9981	Tones E	145	" F	Sept 26 64
10008	Thompson J	90	" H	Sept 29 64
10725	Tibbels Geo	69	" K	Oct 11 64
11002	Thatcher R	14	" C	Oct 16 64
11407	Thompson J	Cav 12	" E	Oct 24 64
11734	Trespan P	67	" H	Nov 2 64
12080	Townsend C	103	" E	Nov 18 64
971	Ulrick Jno	17	" E	May 9 64
4181	Urndragh W	4	" B	July 28 64
12133	Utter Wm	45	" H	Nov 23 64
1369	Ventler Chas	55	" G	May 25 64
7739	Vogel L	150	" A	June 8 64
2428	Vernon S	7	" K	June 21 64
4265	Vanholt T	13	" A	July 29 64
5392	Vandeby B	7	" A	Aug 12 64
6877	Vanderpool F	57	" B	Aug 26 64
7716	Vancampments Geo	52	" I	Sept 4 64
8270	Vail G B	77	" G	Sept 9 64
8791	Vaughan J	183	" A	Sept 15 64
8948	Varndale J	112	" A	Sept 16 64
9688	Vandier Wm, Phila			Sept 24 64
57	Wilkins A	Cav 12	Co L	Mch 17 64
128	Waterman Jno	83	" B	Mch 23 64
193	Wise Isaac	18	" G	Mch 27 64
496	Wheeler J	150	" I	April 12 64
516	Warren J	73	" A	April 12 64
587	Weed A B	4	" K	April 17 64
657	Wentworth Jas	83	" G	April 21 64
665	Watson F F	2	" B	April 22 64
686	Wahl Jno	73	" C	April 23 64
764	Wilson Jno	Cav 14	" H	April 27 64
852	Williams S	Cav 18	" I	May 3 64
941	Wolf J H	Cav 13	" H	May 7 64

Pennsylvania—(*Continued.*)

1021	Wright J	Cav 12	Co B	May 11 64
1067	Whitton Robt	145	" C	May 13 64
1093	Wright Wm	Cav 16	" A	May 14 64
1386	Wymans Jas	150	" C	May 26 64
1387	Wilson Jas	Cav 13	" D	May 26 64
1443	Williams F	Cav 3	" B	May 28 64
1494	Williams Fred	101	" K	May 30 64
1525	Wallace H	Cav 13	" H	May 31 64
1563	Waltermeyer H	76	" H	June 2 64
1721	Whitney W	83	" A	June 8 64
1749	Woodsides W I	18	" E	June 9 64
1791	Wolf Samuel	77	" A	June 10 64
1903	Woodward G W	Cav 3		June 13 64
1977	Wyant H	103	Co G	June 15 64
2338	Walters C	73	" B	June 22 64
2516	Williams J	83	" F	June 28 64
2699	Wike A	96	" B	June 30 64
2790	Whitaker —— (negro)	8		July 2 64
2937	Winsinger S	96	Co E	July 6 64
3023	Weider L	50	" H	July 7 64
3135	Wallace A	116	" I	July 10 64
3277	Wright W A	Cav 20	" G	July 14 64
3384	Woodruff W D	103	" B	July 16 64
3392	Wait Geo	Cav 1	" G	July 16 64
3605	Walker E	7	" A	July 19 64
3694	White E D	Cav 2	" H	July 21 64
4181	Wisel M	Cav 18	" K	July 28 64
4338	Ward Daniel	138	" E	July 30 64
3880	White M	7	" C	July 24 64
3822	Wilson Andrew	103	" H	July 23 64
4069	Wolf A	146	" D	July 27 64
4046	Winegardner A	73	" G	July 27 64
3921	Wilson Wm	43		July 25 64
4428	Williams Geo	51	Co H	July 31 64
4702	Willebough E	148	" I	Aug 4 64
4828	Ward P	103	" B	Aug 6 64
4966	Wetherholt C	54	" F	Aug 7 64
4931	Waserun G	Cav 4	" I	Aug 7 64
4996	White S	Cav 14	" B	Aug 7 64
5106	Weaver Jas	90	" K	Aug 9 64
5353	Wilks S	77	" G	Aug 11 64
5458	Wilson Wm	7	" K	Aug 12 64
5677	Weeks D	53	" G	Aug 14 64
6050	Williams	7	" A	Aug 18 64
6052	Waterhouse W	Cav 3	" L	Aug 18 64
6133	Workman A	118	" D	Aug 19 64
6305	Whipple H, Corpl	18	" B	Aug 20 64
6427	Wart C	143	" E	Aug 22 64
6530	Winerman Jas	77	" A	Aug 23 64
6563	Wible Paul	57	" A	Aug 23 64
6626	Walker S A	103	" I	Aug 23 64
6808	Wick R C	103	" E	Aug 25 64
6980	Woolslaer W H, Corpl	77	" C	Aug 27 64
6981	White Jas P	149	" D	Aug 27 64
7023	Woodford J A	101	" E	Aug 27 64
7277	White Ed	103	" K	Aug 30 64
7382	Webb J S	69	" K	Aug 31 64
7386	Walton A, Sergt	Cav 4	" A	Aug 31 64
7680	Walwork T	118	" D	Sept 3 64
7714	Warner L	Cav 5	Co C	Sept 3 64
7799	Wynn H	101	" F	Sept 4 64
7809	Wiggins D	Art 2	" D	Sept 5 64
7914	Weekland F	101	" K	Sept 5 64
7933	Wade Geo W	118	" E	Sept 5 64
8081	Weber W	116	" F	Sept 7 64
8330	White D	Art 2	" F	Sept 10 64
8879	Wheeler J	7	" C	Sept 15 64
9091	Wheeler C C	Cav 14	" M	Sept 18 64
9343	Williams W	Cav 20		Sept 20 64
9134	Wilson W H	3	Co I	Sept 21 64
9534	Woolman H	Cav 18	" A	Sept 23 64
9573	Wingert C	111	" I	Sept 23 64
9634	Wismer J	100	" A	Sept 24 64
9657	Wilson G M	Cav 7	" M	Sept 24 64
9825	Walke G	Cav 4	" K	Sept 27 64
9909	Wentley J	115	" G	Sept 28 64
10092	Watson Wm	99	" I	Sept 30 64
10217	Weeks C	76	" F	Oct 2 64
10229	Waltz J	7	" H	Oct 2 64
10236	Weekly John	14	" A	Oct 2 64
10253	Weeks C	76	" F	Oct 3 64
10315	Wolthope J	184	" A	Oct 4 64
10400	Wilson G	55	" C	Oct 6 64
10426	Wilson J	118	" D	Oct 6 64
10521	Williams W	46	" K	Oct 8 64
10568	Walk W	87	" E	Oct 9 64
10632	Welsy Jno M, Corp	116	" E	Oct 10 64
10659	Watts A J	Cav 13	" I	Oct 11 64
10729	White J M	21	" G	Oct 11 64
10797	Walker Wm	148	" B	Oct 12 64
9464	Warner Cyrus W	114	" B	Oct 21 64
10340	Wright Wm	16	" I	Oct 13 64
10902	Wolford D	54	" K	Oct 14 64
10974	Watson C	184	" E	Oct 15 64
11048	Wilderman E	14	" D	Oct 17 64
11108	Walker A	45	" D	Oct 18 64
11129	Wilson G	140	" F	Oct 18 64
11498	Warrington J H	103	" H	Oct 26 64
11503	Walter W	134	" F	Oct 26 64
11557	Wood J, Sergt	19	" C	Oct 27 64
11722	Woodburn D J	7	" G	Nov 1 64
11750	Wyncoop F P	7	" I	Nov 2 64
11899	Webster J, Sergt	Cav 20	" L	Nov 7 64
11978	Wilkinson C, Sergt	104	" I	Nov 12 64
11937	Weaver J	53	" K	Nov 13 64
12095	Walder John	Cav 5	" L	Nov 19 64
12098	Wider N H	134	" F	Nov 19 64
12123	Weatherald H W	7	" H	Nov 22 64
12129	Webb C M, Sgt	101	" H	Nov 23 64
12222	Williams J	145	" A	Dec 4 64
12137	Wood J M	2	" A	Nov 23 64
12380	Watson H	184	" A	Jan 2 65
12485	Williams B	75	" B	Jan 19 65
12493	Walker N C	87	" B	Jan 20 65
10158	Van Dyke D L	103	" A	Oct 1 64
11810	Vanmarkes D	6	" E	Nov 4 64
12154	Vanhatterman I	4	" G	Nov 25 64
3958	Vogle V	73	" D	July 25 64

Pennsylvania — (*Continued.*)

3799	Yocumbs W B	93	Co B	July 22 64
4900	Yocum D	Cav 1	" M	Aug 6 64
6103	Yingling E	78	" E	Aug 18 64
6545	Yeager Samuel	158	" D	Aug 23 64
10204	Young J B	49	" G	Oct 2 64
11040	Young W H	145	" F	Oct 17 64
11872	Yeager J	49	Co C	Nov 6 64
1806	Zerphy J	79	" E	June 10 64
4255	Zimmerman B	148	" B	July 29 64
6573	Zane Wm	19	" K	Aug 23 64
6818	Zerl S	103	" F	Aug 25 64
11327	Zane M	118	" E	Oct 23 64

TOTAL 1808.

RHODE ISLAND.

3266	Austin J A, Sgt	Cav 1	Co H	July 13 64
6231	Allen Chas	Cav 1	" D	Aug 21 64
1744	Boneley Wm	Cav 1	" M	June 8 64
1958	Bidmead Jas	Cav 1	" G	June 14 64
2521	Blake J F	Cav 1	" M	June 26 64
3647	Burk Jas	1	" C	July 20 64
4261	Bether J	2	" C	July 29 64
4576	Baine H	5	" A	Aug 2 64
1339	Carpenter P	Cav 1	" E	May 24 64
1413	Carson B F	Cav 1	" K	May 27 64
3810	Callahan Jas	Bat		July 23 64
7966	Calvin E O, Corp'l	Art 5	Co A	Sept 6 64
12832	Collins J H	Cav 1	" A	April 16 65
651	Delanah E B, Sgt	Cav 1	" G	April 20 64
1217	Dix Geo	Cav 1	" M	May 19 64
1435	Dickinson J, Sgt	Cav 1	" K	May 28 64
3036	Dearborn G	Cav 1		July 8 64
4742	Durden Robert	Cav 1	Co F	Aug 5 64
4927	Doolittle G S	Art 2	" B	Aug 6 64
5670	Doyle Jas	Art 5	" A	Aug 14 64
827	Eustace Geo C	Cav 1	" M	May 1 64
10203	Eaton A	Art 5	" A	Oct 1 64
939	Freelove H	Cav 1	" H	May 7 64
4533	Farrell Jas F	Art 1	" A	Aug 2 64
4672	Fay John	2	" G	Aug 4 64
7356	Fay A	Art 5	" A	Aug 31 64
1866	Goudy John	Art 5	" A	June 12 64
4866	Gallagher C	5	" A	Aug 6 64
5561	Garvey Wm	Art 5	" A	Aug 13 64
8308	Green R	2	" B	Sept 10 64
9978	Green Daniel	2	" H	Sept 29 64
1075	Henry T	Cav 1	" F	May 13 64
2656	Healy A	Cav 1	" D	June 29 64
2746	Hunt C W	Cav 1	" A	July 1 64
3904	Hampstead J	Art 5	" F	July 24 64
7?32	Hooker A	Cav 1	" G	Aug 27 64
?843	Hawkins D F	5	" A	Nov 5 64
12016	Hanley T	Art 5	Co A	Nov 15 64
1962	Ide S R	Cav 1	" H	June 14 64
3049	Johnson A G	Art 5	" A	July 8 64
2968	Kettell Jas	Cav 1	" B	July 6 64
3096	Kiney J	2	" B	July 10 64
4215	Lewis Edward	Art 5	" A	July 29 64
5827	Littlebridge, Corp	Art 5	" A	Aug 16 64
6793	Lee Cornelius	Art 5	" A	Aug 25 64
7849	Leach L D	Cav 1	" F	Sept 5 64
11688	Livingston J, Mus	Art 5	" A	Oct 31 64
1750	Miner S	Cav 1	" D	June 9 64
7393	McKay Thos	2	" F	Aug 31 64
8306	McKenna J	Art 3		Sept 10 64
3192	Northorp E	Cav 1	Co H	July 12 64
7904	Navoo G	5	" K	Sept 5 64
607	Peterson John	1	" D	April 18 64
7219	Rathburn J	Cav 1	" A	Aug 29 64
2382	Sweet M	Cav 1	" D	June 23 64
2563	Spink J	Cav 1	" H	June 27 64
2859	Slocum Geo T, 2 Lt	Cav 1	" A	July 4 64
4158	Smith P	Cav 1	" A	July 28 64
4949	Stalord J	Bat 1	" A	Aug 7 64
6186	Sisson Chas T	Art 5	" A	Aug 19 64
6187	Seymour H	Art 5	" A	Aug 19 64
6351	Sullivan J	Art 5	" A	Aug 21 64
7129	Sander Charles	Art 5	" A	Aug 28 64
7425	Slocum C A, Corpl	Art 5	" A	Aug 31 64
3075	Turner Chas	7	" E	July 9 64
8522	Thomas J	5		Sept 12 64
19	Wright Moses	Cav 2	Co A	Mch 7 64
1788	West H	1	" A	June 10 64
3173	Wallace Wm	Art 5	" A	July 11 64
5908	Wood J B	5	" A	Aug 16 64
6222	West J	Cav 2	" A	Aug 21 64
6766	Wayne S	Cav 1	" A	Aug 25 64
7831	Wilson J	5	" A	Sept 4 64
9273	Witham B, Lieut	Art 1		19 64

TOTAL 74.

TENNESSEE.

883	Allen James W	11	Co B	May 4 64
987	Amos F G	2	" C	May 10 64
2313	Allison B F	Cav 13	" D	June 22 64
2631	Andrewson Joseph	2	" C	June 20 64
3167	Anderson S	Cav 8	" B	July 11 64
3194	Aber A	Cav 7	" A	July 12 64
3334	Anglon Wm	Cav 7	" A	July 15 64
4004	Athens J H	East 2	" C	July 23 64
6411	Aikin Geo W, Corpl	7	" K	Aug 22 64
6474	Ashby J F	Cav 7	Co B	Aug 22 64
6541	Antoine P	Cav 13	" H	Aug 23 64
7572	Aspray Wm, Sergt	13	" B	Sept 2 64
7907	Anderson C S, Sergt	10	" D	Sept 5 64
9151	Achley A	8	" A	Sept 18 64
9910	Atkins L	2	" D	Sept 28 64
1895	Arrowood James	Cav 8		June 13 64
8493	Alexander P S	Cav 13	Co D	Sept 11 64
12710	Allen G W	7	" I	Feb 28 65

Tennessee—(*Continued.*)

539	Bowling Wm	11	Co E	April 14 64
535	Blaton Benjamin	2	" E	April 17 64
663	Bond Jas J T	2	" F	April 21 64
695	Baker T K	Cav 5		April 23 64
705	Batey W H	2	Co B	April 24 64
772	Burton Wm	Art 1	" A	April 23 64
808	Brannin Ellis	2	" F	April 30 64
845	Browden H V	2	" K	May 1 64
839	Byer'y W H	1	" A	May 3 64
920	Brewer M	2	" E	May 6 64
1053	Boyden A L	2	" B	May 13 64
1137	Beatty Thomas	2	" B	M y 16 64
1242	Bryant James A	8	" I	May 20 64
1244	Barnard W H	2	" A	May 20 64
1248	Boyd A D, Corp'l	2	" F	May 20 64
1527	Butler J J, Sgt	7	" B	May 31 64
1538	Bradshaw A G	2	" B	June 1 64
1610	Browning J	2	" F	June 4 64
1635	Brown J	Cav 13	" E	June 5 64
1847	Branon Wm	2	" F	June 11 64
1876	Birket W D, Corp'l	7		June 12 64
1883	Burchfield W R	2		June 12 64
1976	Berger W	2	Co B	June 15 64
2037	Berger W M	2		June 15 64
2555	Bontwright A, Sgt	7	Co A	June 27 64
2744	Brewer W T	Cav 7	" A	June 27 64
2939	Bibbs Alexander	Cav 7	" D	July 6 64
2983	Bright John	8	" G	July 7 64
3176	Blalock H	2	" D	July 11 64
3198	Brown J B, Sgt	2	" F	July 12 64
6	Brandon C	4	" D	April 4 64
16	Burke John	2	" D	April 12 64
52	Brummell A D	2	" H	June 3 64
57	Broits S	4	" F	June 20 64
58	Beeler Daniel	5	" D	June 25 64
3328	Barton F F	Cav 13	" A	July 14 64
3330	Bynom J W	Cav 13	" C	July 14 64
3414	Brennan James	2	" I	July 16 64
3636	Burris D B	13	" B	July 20 64
3643	Brannan J	2	" A	July 20 64
3726	Billings W	6	" I	July 21 64
3786	Bowman J	Cav 7	" C	July 22 64
3934	Boles H	13	" C	July 25 64
4108	Boyd W H	Cav 9	" C	July 27 64
4221	Barnes A C	15	" H	July 29 64
4770	Bryant Wm'	2	" D	Aug 5 64
5017	Butler W W	Cav 7	" B	Aug 8 64
4371	Bradfield E L	7	" C	July 31 64
5049	Brummetti B	11	" C	Aug 8 64
5277	Barnhart D F	7	" B	Aug 11 64
5294	Baker Isaac	13	" B	Aug 11 64
5313	Blackwood G W	11	" B	Aug 11 64
5533	Boles G W	Cav 13	" B	Aug 13 64
5617	Baker M A	Cav 13	" E	Aug 14 64
6003	Boles W G	Cav 13	" B	Aug 17 64
6142	Boyles K	2	" C	Aug 19 64
6194	Burnett S H	6	" H	Aug 1[illegible] 64
6287	Butler W J	7	" B	Aug 20 64
6563	Barnes Wm	Cav 7	" M	Aug 23 64
6372	Bishop W	Cav 7	Co H	Aug 23 64
7130	Brewer J	2	" D	Aug 31 64
7361	Bales Henry	2	" K	Sept 2 64
7943	Boyer D	15	" D	Sept 5 64
8222	Bird S H	Cav 13	" D	Sept 8 64
8393	Blackner Thomas	Cav 7	" L	Sept 17 64
9023	Bill F	5	" I	Sept 17 64
9079	Boyle R C	Cav 7	" I	Sept 17 64
9149	Bean C S	Cav 3	" E	Sept 18 64
9178	Bowlen C F	13	" B	Sept 21 64
9513	Bromley H, Sergt	7		Sept 23 64
4388	Brannon L	2	Co A	Aug 6 64
10093	Byerly James	E C 1	" A	Sept 30 64
10452	Bible W	8	" D	Oct 7 64
10617	Blackney B	7	" E	Oct 10 64
10823	Bartholomew Jno	Cav 7	" H	Oct 13 64
11015	Bosworth W H	Cav 7	" E	Oct 16 64
11208	Brogan John, Corpl	2	" C	Oct 22 64
11372	Brown J B, Corpl	2	" K	Oct 23 64
12171	Bradford H A	7	" E	Oct 26 64
12565	Brown J W	13	" B	Jan 31 65
12613	Barnhart G	7	" C	Feb 8 65
12662	Barnes F B	Cav 7	" D	Feb 16 65
432	Bell E S	4	" C	April 9 64
4783	Barnes G	10	" D	Aug 5 64
139	Cardwell W C	6	" C	Mch 27 64
216	Conaster Philip	2	" D	Mch 28 64
230	Chimney Jesse, Sgt	2	" A	Mch 29 64
375	Colwell J H	2	" C	April 5 64
426	Crosswell Samuel	2	" K	April 8 64
459	Childers J M	2	" D	April 10 64
482	Clark Lewis	Cav 2	" B	April 9 64
615	Covington A	2	" K	April 13 64
717	Chitwood J H	2	" G	April 24 64
811	Carden Robert	2	" C	April 30 64
840	Cardwell W C	6	" G	May 2 64
1050	Cooper C	2	" B	May 12 64
1213	Clark Alexander	2	" C	May 19 64
1425	Cross M C	2	" F	May 28 64
1574	Childers J	13	" A	June 3 64
1636	Clemens J D	Cav 7	" D	June 5 64
1751	Campbell W	2	" A	June 9 64
1839	Carden A K	Cav 7	" E	June 11 64
2031	Covington J B	2	" K	June 15 64
2062	Carwin James	1		June 16 64
2071	Crow J, Sergt	2	Co F	June 16 64
2239	Crawford A	Cav 13	" B	June 21 64
2466	Childers Thomas L	2	" G	June 25 64
2632	Cooper E	1	" A	June 20 64
2739	Cook W P E	2	" A	July 1 64
2858	Cooper G W	7	" B	July 4 64
2886	Collins W	2	" H	July 4 64
2940	Carter H C	Cav 13	" E	July 6 64
3687	Cross N	2	" H	July 21 64
3985	Corwine J,	East Tenn	" G	July 26 64
4691	Cornish A	Cav 13	" C	Aug 4 64
5298	Chase A P	Cav 7	" I	Aug 11 64
5829	Collins R	Cav [illegible]	" K	Aug 16 64
5893	Clyne E T, Sgt	Cav 11	" E	Aug 16 64

Tennessee—(*Continued.*)

6310	Crews G	Cav 7	Co B	Aug 20 64
7523	Childers E	13	" E	Sept 1 64
7525	Clark James	13	" A	Sept 1 64
7601	Cunisc E	Cav 7	" I	Sept 2 64
7702	Childers W E	Cav 7	" E	Sept 3 64
7857	Cothrain S	13	" E	Sept 5 64
7871	Camp W W	7	" K	Sept 5 64
7880	Cotterell G W	7	" C	Sept 5 64
8219	Creery S P	Cav 7	" K	Sept 8 64
9021	Crum A	4	" F	Sept 17 64
9208	Cooley J	Cav 7	" L	Sept 18 64
9693	Chadwick M	16	" I	Sept 24 64
10137	Cole Geo M, Sgt	9	" C	Oct 1 64
10268	Clay H	13	" H	Oct 3 64
10403	Cleaver W	7	" G	Oct 6 64
10654	Churchill E	13	" A	Oct 11 64
11239	Check R	Cav 6	" D	Oct 20 64
11312	Carter W B	11	" E	Oct 23 64
12643	Camway H	6	" K	Feb 13 65
302	Dodd Benjamin	2	" D	April 1 64
399	Doss J W	2	" C	April 6 64
485	Dudley Samuel	Cav 1	" A	April 9 64
645	Dutrow Irdell	2	" G	April 20 64
759	Duncan G W, Corpl	2	" B	April 27 64
876	Doak I V	2	" F	May 3 64
894	Davis Leroy	7	" K	May 5 64
1016	Diggs J G	2	" C	May 9 64
43	Dykes Pleasant	2	" K	May 11 64
1182	Duff I W	16	" B	May 18 64
1581	Davis J W	2	" C	June 3 64
2266	Dabney B	1	" A	June 20 64
2366	Daniel Suttrell	2	" K	June 23 64
2449	Diggs John G	East 2	" C	June 25 64
3513	Deer H	7	" M	July 13 64
3567	Davis J	3	" A	July 20 64
5398	Disney E W Sergt	Cav 11	" C	Aug 12 64
6261	Dunn R	19	" I	Aug 20 64
6991	Dyn Wm	Cav 7	" K	Aug 27 64
4821	Draan R H	10	" I	Aug 5 64
8423	Davis Levi	Cav 7	" K	Sept 11 64
7219	Davis James	7	" C	Aug 30 64
7608	Diel S F, Sergt	Cav 7	" B	Sept 2 64
8329	Dyer W	Cav 7	" K	Sept 10 64
9373	Dodd Chas, Citizen Dec Co			Sept 20 64
9453	Dort R	7	Co G	Sept 21 64
9701	Duke Wm	7	" E	Sept 25 64
10014	Dyer H	Cav 4	" A	Sept 29 64
10244	Davis Wm	7	" D	Oct 3 64
12119	Dodd J A	Cav 1	" M	Nov 22 64
12379	Dykes L	2	" K	Jan 2 65
12498	Delf E	8	" C	Jan 21 65
12794	Doty I, Citizen			Jan 18 65
293	Edwards I	5	Co B	April 1 64
360	Everitt A T	2	" A	April 2 64
510	Evans S D	8	" C	April 12 64
557	Everitte John	2	" G	April 14 64
848	Evans W, Sergt	7	" C	May 3 64
873	Edwards C S	5	" B	May 4 64
970	Evans J M	7	" M	May 9 64
979	Etler Valentine	11	Co D	May 9 64
1836	Emmert J C, Sergt	4		June 14 64
55	Eddes James C	2	Co E	June 16 64
3751	Ellison Isaac, East	2	" F	July 22 64
4735	Ellis C O	Cav 13	" C	Aug 5 64
5904	Ethridge Wm	13	" B	Aug 16 64
7402	Elder P	2	" F	Aug 31 64
9075	Escue H, Corpl	Cav 6		Sept 17 64
10560	Elliott Wm	4	Co A	Oct 9 64
10835	Easton J	Cav 13	" B	Oct 16 64
11630	Ellington J	Cav 13	" B	Oct 30 64
383	Fairchilds Jesse	2	" B	April 2 64
633	Fryer W L, Sergt	2	" H	April 23 64
697	Fagen Parker	8	" I	April 23 64
1145	Fannon G H, Tenn St Gd			April 23 64
2468	Fisher C N	2	Co K	June 24 64
2536	Francisco R	Cav 7	" B	June 26 64
62	Friar John	2	" H	July 9 64
2835	Fox E, Tenn St Gd			July 3 64
5220	Firestone ——	Cav 1	Co M	Aug 11 64
5907	Frazier John	8	" H	Aug 17 64
6299	Flowers W P, Sgt	Cav 13	" B	Aug 20 64
7244	Franks W W	2	" B	Aug 29 64
7732	Fields R G	1		Sept 4 64
8555	Finch A	Cav 7	Co L	Sept 12 64
10183	Finch J B	7	" B	Oct 1 64
12302	Franshier J D	8	" K	Jan 21 65
3036	Fowler I	4	" A	July 7 64
3733	Finch H	Cav 7	" I	July 21 64
578	Goddard John	2	" B	April 16 64
1831	German P	2	" C	June 11 64
2043	Gorman James	6		June 15 64
2571	Graham J D	Cav 7	Co D	June 27 64
2891	Gooding James	2	" D	July 4 64
3	Guild James	11	" B	Mch 18 64
15	Graves Henry	2	" E	April 11 64
59	Gray John W	2	" I	June 29 64
3201	Gorman F	6	" B	July 14 64
3357	Grays L	12	" F	July 15 64
9228	Gamon I A	Cav 7	" A	Sept 19 64
3820	Grundee Alex	4	" D	July 20 64
3719	Grier J O, Corpl	7	" B	July 21 64
3837	Gilson C G	1	" B	July 24 64
4531	Grevett S P	Cav 7	" C	Aug 1 64
5132	Given I A	9	" I	Aug 9 64
5143	Griswell Thos J	Cav 7	" H	Aug 9 64
5374	Garrett M T	Cav 7	" L	Aug 11 64
5388	Green S G	Cav 7	" I	Aug 12 64
6376	Grims Wm	2	" A	Aug 21 64
6400	Graves J C	2	" E	Aug 21 64
6493	Grisson C	8	" B	Aug 22 64
7221	Green J C	7	" I	Aug 29 64
7454	Gunter R C, Sergt	13	" A	Sept 1 64
7903	Griswold W H	Cav 7	" K	Sept 5 64
8012	Gibbs J A	Cav 7	" L	Sept 6 64
8093	Griffin W A	Cav 2	" C	Sept 7 64
8646	Gill G W	Cav 1	" L	Sept 16 64
9271	Gaff R	Cav 1	" C	Sept 19 64
9875	Gibson James	Cav 13		Sept 27 64

Tennessee — (*Continued.*)

10334	Gardner H	Cav 14	Co C	Oct 4 64
10590	Garrison A, Corp'l	7	" E	Oct 10 64
11063	Galbraith G W	Cav 7	" E	Oct 17 64
11632	Grier J	7	" B	Oct 28 64
11925	Giles M C	7	" I	Nov 8 64
12402	Ganon T	Cav 4	" I	Jan 6 65
12428	Gilbert Wm	Cav 7	" C	Jan 12 65
12464	G.lden J H	Cav 7	" C	Jan 18 65
1000	Gray Thomas	11	" E	May 19 64
433	Graves James	2	" E	April 8 64
58	Hampton I A	8	" D	Mch 16 64
85	Henniger Peter	11	" I	Mch 21 64
163	Hoover Samuel	2	" B	Mch 26 64
316	Huff Benjamin	2	" K	April 2 64
357	Huckleby Thomas	2	" C	April 2 64
467	Hickson George	11	" E	April 9 64
616	Hurd William	2	" B	April 18 64
660	Head Daniel	Cav 12	" B	April 21 64
682	Hixton John	2	" F	April 23 64
714	Henderson Robert	2	" B	April 24 64
805	Hayes J	7	" E	April 29 64
844	Hughes E	2	" I	May 2 64
958	Hickley Thomas	2	" K	May 8 64
1036	Hickson Henry	2	" I	May 12 64
1124	Hall John	2	" B	May 15 64
1159	Heatherby John	1	" C	May 19 64
1491	Hickson Daniel	2	" F	May 31 64
1551	Hopkins A	Art 1	" A	June 2 64
1554	Hunt J	2	" B	June 2 64
1766	Harrison Wm	8	" I	June 9 64
1774	Hodges I M	2	" F	June 9 64
1846	Harman A B	4	" A	June 11 64
1925	Hendson J S	2	" K	June 14 64
1950	Hickerman T	Cav 9	" B	June 14 64
2276	Hilton A F, Sgt	2	" H	June 20 64
2375	Hugely C W	Cav 13	" D	June 23 64
2491	Hawa E A	2	" B	June 26 64
2642	Hale R H	3	" F	June 29 64
2851	Hall B A	2	" A	Ju'y 4 64
2949	Hudson J A	Cav 8	" F	July 9 64
3012	Haines J A	13	" E	July 7 64
4855	Hall J J	Cav 13	" E	Aug 6 64
4836	Hermsen Wm	Cav 13	" B	Aug 6 64
4805	Haywood J G	7	" I	Aug 5 64
3098	Hawkins S D	3	" E	July 10 64
3121	Hodgen ——	7	" K	July 10 64
3248	Hopson Thomas	Cav 3	" E	July 13 64
3421	Howard A	2	" F	July 16 64
3672	Heckman Wm, Corp'l	2	" G	July 20 64
3712	Henderson J R	6	" B	July 21 64
3720	Hendlay J	9	" A	July 21 64
3807	Hayes J C	Cav 7	" C	July 22 64
4535	Henry Wm	7	" C	Aug 1 64
5278	Hudson John	55	" I	Aug 11 64
5526	Harvey Morgan	2	" F	Aug 11 64
5535	Hensley James M	3	" E	Aug 13 64
5604	Hicks M	2	" I	Aug 14 64
5607	Hasborough J H	Cav 13	" E	Aug 14 64
6393	Haines G	Cav 13	" A	Aug 21 64
6553	Hughes Wm	2	Co F	Aug 23 64
6581	Hibbrath M H	Cav 7	" I	Aug 27 64
6648	Harris A G	5	" E	Aug 23 64
6681	Horton W C	Cav 7	" H	Aug 24 64
78 8	Hinson John	Cav 7	" H	Sept 4 64
8091	Hallford J A	13	" A	Sept 7 64
8115	Hicks E	9	" F	Sept 7 64
8486	Hale Ira	Cav 7	" C	Sept 11 64
8529	Haywood A J, Sergt	7	" I	Sept 12 64
9044	Henderson A G	13	" C	Sept 13 64
9788	Hodges John	13	" E	Sept 26 64
9797	Herbs D	Cav 1	" D	Sept 26 64
9805	Haney H	Cav 7	" A	Sept 26 64
9892	Hanks A, Sergt	11	" D	Sept 27 64
10003	Hall W R	2	" D	Sept 29 64
10145	Halliwarke ——	7	" E	Oct 10 64
10329	Hooks John L	Cav 7	" A	Oct 4 64
10810	Holler W	Cav 6	" E	Oct 12 64
10956	Holloway H B	2	" G	Oct 14 64
11377	Herman H	4	" K	Oct 23 64
11791	Hickman D	2	" I	Nov 4 64
11801	Howard ——	16		Nov 4 64
11861	Higgs L	7	Co D	Nov 6 64
12028	Hazzle Wm	7	" C	Nov 13 64
12146	Hall J M	1	" A	Nov 24 64
12212	Hanley T	2	" E	Dec 2 64
12423	Hoag B F	7	" E	Jan 9 65
12655	Huffaker J	2	" K	Feb 14 65
12693	Hanbuck J	7	" K	Feb 22 65
1941	Israel S	21	" B	June 14 64
9515	Irwin P P	49	" F	Sept 22 64
52	Jones Rufus	2	" I	Mch 16 64
291	Jones Warren T	11	" C	April 1 64
358	Jeffers J	2	" C	April 2 64
584	Jack Benjamin S	2	" B	April 17 64
668	Jones H D	4	" F	April 22 64
1181	Johnson E A, Sergt	2	" A	May 18 64
1227	Johnson S L	2	" A	May 19 64
1536	Jones John J	Cav 13	" C	June 1 64
3805	Jones H	2	" H	July 22 64
3980	Johnson A	10	" C	July 26 64
4571	Jones D	6	" C	Aug 2 64
5517	Johnson C F	7	" K	Aug 13 64
5921	Jones J M	2	" K	Aug 17 64
7447	Jones Albert, Sgt	Cav 13	" B	Sept 1 64
8013	Joiner J M	Cav 7	" B	Sept 6 64
8503	Jones J	Cav 13	" B	Sept 12 64
8560	Johnson J, Corpl, East	3		Sept 12 64
8761	Johnson C M		Co K	Sept 14 64
9552	Jones D	11	" E	Sept 23 64
9618	Jones Wm T, Corp	Cav 11		Sept 23 64
10479	Johnson M	Cav 13	Co G	Oct 7 64
12319	Johnson E W	Cav 7	" C	Dec 21 64
12702	Johnson W	13	" D	Feb 26 65
32	Kirby James		" M	Mch 11 64
434	Kilpatrick R	2	" E	April 8 64
595	Kelsey John, Sergt	2	" A	April 17 64
600	Kentzler Henry	2	" G	April 17 64
35	King James T	2	" D	April 25 64

Tennessee—(*Continued.*)

8702 Kirk B J Cav 7 Co B July 21 64
8749 Keene Hoza Cav 7 " C July 22 64
7367 Keen J S Cav 7 " C Aug 31 64
7641 Kirk J P 3 " D Sept 2 64
8183 Kingsley S 2 " D Sept 8 64
8714 Kenser Joseph Cav 2 Sept 14 64
9407 Kelley J W, Sergt 2 Co E Sept 21 64
11241 Kissinger F 7 " I Oct 21 64
12570 Kidwell J 4 " C Feb 2 65
1157 Kuner E B 3 " E May 16 64
627 Long Jonathan 2 " H April 19 64
688 Lane L E 2 " I April 23 64
713 Lofty R J 2 " I April 24 64
1223 Lovette W T Cav 13 " A May 19 64
1252 Langley E G 11 " B May 21 64
1352 Long C C 2 " C May 25 64
1597 Long John 2 " C June 3 64
2193 Looper E 2 " D June 19 64
8 Lanen Thomas 2 " H April 5 64
45 Lingo James 2 " C May 17 64
53 Levi J N 2 " I June 3 64
3696 Lamphey J Cav 7 " C July 21 64
3760 Little E D 7 " A July 22 64
3830 Lemmar J E, Sgt Cav 13 " A July 23 64
4114 Lawrence J C Cav 13 " I July 28 64
4292 Lewis R Bat 1 " B July 30 64
4575 Long John 13 " H Aug 2 64
8640 Lawson M 8 " H Sept 13 64
8926 Lawson H G 8 " I Sept 14 64
9591 Lester James Cav 7 " M Sept 23 64
9641 Lewis J 3 " G Sept 24 64
11827 Laprint J 11 " K Nov 5 64
1352 Long C C 2 " C May 25 64
11979 Leonard J 7 " C Nov 12 64
388 McCune Robert 2 " E April 5 64
405 Meyers W J 12 " F April 6 64
558 Miller W H 2 " F April 15 64
562 Macklin John 2 " H April 15 64
583 Malcolm S A 4 " B April 16 64
722 Maines Wm 1 " D April 27 64
801 McCart Wm 2 " B April 29 64
815 McDowell G I 2 " D April 26 64
1051 Mynck Eli 2 " A May 12 64
1176 May W 10 " C May 16 64
1289 Meyers D 2 " H May 22 64
1402 Martin F A 2 " A May 27 64
1451 McLane H C East Tenn 2 " I May 29 64
1561 Massie Eli 2 " C June 1 64
1663 Myers John, Corp'l 2 " H June 6 64
1703 Moulden Wm 2 " A June 7 64
1723 McCart J 2 " B June 8 64
1960 McDonald L M, Sgt 2 " G June 14 64
2050 Meyers Wm, Sgt 2 " H June 16 64
2171 Matheney D C 7 " D June 19 64
2224 Melterberger M 2 " G June 20 64
2277 Morris J, Corp'l Cav 2 " E June 20 64
2475 Mitchiner H 13 " H June 25 64
2500 Mackin W Cav 7 " K June 26 64
2516 Moss J 2 " A June 26 64
3124 McAllister W H Cav 4 Co H July 10 64
24 Mayes William 2 " E April 15 64
38 Mee Thomas 2 " F April 29 64
46 Mergen H S 2 " G May 18 64
3243 McGee Wm Cav 7 " B July 3 64
3642 Maynard W J 13 " A July 20 64
4567 Millar J W Cav 8 " G Aug 2 64
4523 McLean A G 3 " C Aug 1 64
3897 McCoy W C 2 " G July 24 64
4236 McDover H 2 " C July 29 64
4237 Montgomery Wm 4 " C July 29 64
4751 McGwin M Cav 7 " C Aug 5 64
4905 Mussurgo M Cav 9 " H Aug 6 64
4496 Mulanox A C, Corpl 2 " B Aug 1 64
5008 Myers A Cav 13 " C Aug 8 64
5064 Miles Samuel 2 " A Aug 8 64
5282 Morris H S Cav 13 " C Aug 11 64
5594 Mitchell Jas Cav 7 " K Aug 14 64
5782 Miflin Wm 13 " B Aug 15 64
6555 Maddro Jas 2 " C Aug 23 64
7435 Mefford J, Corpl Cav 8 " C Sept 1 64
7574 Moore Jas 13 Sept 2 64
7764 McGee A 13 Co B Sept 4 64
8059 Mayher J W 2 " E Sept 7 64
8174 Martin J S Cav 7 " H Sept 8 64
8954 Mackey S 7 " D Sept 16 64
9140 McKeese Samuel Cav 8 " G Sept 17 64
9542 McDonald W 7 " D Sept 23 64
9559 Montgomery C F Cav 1 " L Sept 29 64
9783 Metheney V V Cav 13 " A Sept 26 64
9861 Macart R 2 " B Sept 27 64
10795 Martin S Cav 7 " G Oct 12 64
10976 Meare J H Cav 7 " I Oct 15 64
11532 May S L Cav 9 " A Oct 26 64
11544 McCaslin M C 7 " D Oct 27 64
11649 Myracle C 7 " C Oct 30 64
11667 Morris Wm Cav 7 " I Oct 30 64
11845 Moore Wm P 11 " D Nov 5 64
12277 McNealy W Cav 7 " C Dec 3 64
12368 Moore T Cav 7 " I Dec 26 64
7497 Norton J 10 " K Sept 1 64
160 Newman Jesse 2 " K Mch 25 64
828 Norris Thomas 2 " D May 1 64
1237 Norman J, Corpl Cav 13 " C May 20 64
3191 Newport H Cav 11 " E July 12 64
50 Nicely A 8 " H June 2 64
6262 Nichols W T Cav 7 " A Aug 20 64
7818 Newman T A, Sergt 4 Sept 4 64
9068 Norwood Wm Cav 7 Co I Sept 17 64
9447 Norris P W Cav 7 " B Sept 21 64
9640 Needham F 13 " C Sept 24 64
9996 Neighbour M 7 " E Sept 29 64
10223 Norris W 2 " D Oct 2 64
12642 Neighbor A 7 " B Feb 13 65
4689 Odorn John, Sergt 8 " B Aug 4 64
1753 Owen A 2 " D June 9 64
10743 Oliver L 13 " C Oct 11 64
923 Ollenger John 2 " I May 6 64
2697 Overton J S 2 " C June 30 64

Tennessee—(*Continued.*)

689	Palmer Wm	2	Co K	April 23 64
806	Perkins G W, Sergt	7	" M	April 29 64
1141	Penix John	5	" G	May 16 64
1363	Perry Jas	Cav 6	" L	May 25 64
1517	Proffett Jas	13	" C	May 31 64
1638	Powers H, Sergt	Cav 7	" A	June 5 64
2146	Parder E H	11	" K	June 18 64
2748	Perry Thomas	13	" B	July 1 64
2767	Pursley W B, Sgt	Cav 13	" C	July 2 64
3170	Pankey A J	13	" B	July 11 64
506	Pilot Joseph	2	" K	April 12 64
4592	Piscall J B	13	" B	Aug 3 64
4572	Powell A N, Sgt	7	" K	Aug 2 64
8605	Pavies S	Cav 7	" C	Sept 12 64
1	Polivar Martin	2	" E	Mch 12 64
10	Phillips N	2	" H	April 5 64
32	Parker Wiley	3	" B	April 25 64
4041	Parmer E	7	" I	July 26 64
4380	Palmer D P	Cav 7	" I	July 31 64
6190	Parks R T	Cav 7	" I	Aug 19 64
6335	Prison E T	7	" B	Aug 21 64
6485	Princes Nelson	15	" B	Aug 22 64
6600	Phillips T	2	" G	Aug 23 64
7290	Park Jas	Cav 7	" E	Aug 30 64
9020	Penn W H	2	" E	Sept 17 64
9121	Paddock D W, Corp	Cav 2	Co I	Sept 17 64
9606	Pennington G W, Corp	11		Sept 23 64
10304	Pegram W	7	Co A	Oct 4 64
10318	Powers H M, Corp'l	7	" A	Oct 4 64
10364	Poster N P, Sgt	13	" E	Oct 4 64
10655	Pomeroy John	7	" K	Oct 11 64
10852	Pierce Wm	8	" A	Oct 13 64
10907	Parham W	7	" K	Oct 14 64
11285	Pickering E	Cav 4	" G	Oct 22 64
11406	Pinkley J	7	" B	Oct 24 64
11501	Powers J	Cav 7	" A	Oct 26 64
11644	Powers R	Cav 7	" H	Feb 13 65
675	Perry Wesley	2	" I	April 22 64
1978	Pope F	Cav 7	" D	June 15 64
2232	Quiller T	Cav 7	" D	June 20 64
271	Ragan J	2	" B	Mch 28 64
380	Ronden Wm	2	" A	April 5 64
382	Reynolds Henry	Cav 11	" L	April 5 64
454	Russell R	2	" K	April 9 64
4644	Roberts John	2	" F	Aug 3 64
5815	Ronser A, Corpl	1	" A	Aug 16 64
2519	Reed John C	7	" A	June 26 64
523	Robinson Jas M	3	" A	April 13 64
646	Robinson Isaac	3	" A	April 20 64
951	Robinson Wm	1	" G	May 8 64
1438	Rayle F	Art 1	" C	May 28 64
1450	Reice James	13	" C	May 29 64
1783	Ralph J F	13	" E	June 10 64
1924	Reed G W	7	" A	June 14 64
2305	Ringoland W H	2	" D	June 15 64
2006	Rabb G W	13	" A	June 15 64
2093	Ryan Wm	3	" K	June 17 64
2219	Robinson J C	2	" B	June 20 64
2314	Roberts T	2	" H	June 22 64
2691	Riley J M	6	Co G	June 30 64
2750	Ryan C P	2	" G	July 1 64
17	Riddle Robert	2	" F	April 12 64
3752	Ritter John	3	" C	July 22 64
3765	Robbins T	2	" D	July 22 64
3772	Reeves Geo W	4	" F	July 22 64
4086	Robinson A	2	" B	July 27 64
4254	Renshaw H G	Cav 7	" C	July 29 64
4368	Rainwater A	7	" F	July 31 64
5974	Riter Henry	Cav 7	" E	Aug 17 64
4516	Roberts Chas	7	" A	Aug 3 64
6267	Reeves A	Cav 11	" B	Aug 20 64
6409	Rider W R, Sergt	12	" C	Aug 22 64
6837	Rogers A G	Cav 7	" B	Aug 25 64
7082	Russell J S	7	" E	Aug 28 64
7090	Ross John	Cav 7	" B	Aug 28 64
7099	Roach J W	Cav 7	" K	Aug 28 64
7190	Riter John	7	" E	Aug 29 64
7774	Reynolds W	3	" G	Sept 4 64
7978	Reagan Geo W	3	" G	Sept 6 64
8137	Rose M L	East 2	" A	Sept 8 64
8523	Ramsay W A			Sept 12 64
9513	Renmeger Jeff	Cav 13	Co E	Sept 22 64
10107	Richardson R	Cav 13	" E	Sept 30 64
10869	Rushing W R	7	" B	Oct 13 64
11995	Roberts J G	7	" I	Nov 18 64
12101	Risley J	6	" E	Nov 20 64
12753	Robins W	7	" B	Mch 12 65
8968	Reeder C, Sutler	51		Sept 16 64
293	Stinger A E	2	Co K	April 1 64
319	Sane Joseph	8	" B	April 2 64
374	Sukirk J F	2	" B	April 5 64
390	Smith John	Cav 2	" I	April 16 64
776	Scott R S	2		April 28 64
985	Smithpater Eli	11	Co K	May 9 64
1140	Seals John	2	" D	May 15 64
1191	Stepp Preston	2	" D	May 18 64
1254	Stafford Wm	Cav 13	" C	May 21 64
1278	Sisson James	2	" E	May 22 64
1284	Smith T A	2	" C	May 22 64
1313	Short L H	Cav 7	" C	May 23 64
1353	Smith C	2	" B	May 25 64
1408	Simpkins Thomas	9	" A	May 27 64
1475	Smith Joel	2	" A	May 30 64
1481	Stansberry A	8	" A	May 30 64
1488	Sutton John	2	" I	May 31 64
1526	Stover A	2	" C	May 31 64
1670	Smith Wm	2	" D	June 6 64
2280	Stevens R	2	" D	June 20 64
2284	Smith J	Cav 13	" E	June 21 64
2958	Smith J B	20	" I	July 6 64
11	Stanton W	4	" E	April 5 64
12	Sutton Thomas	2	" I	April 8 64
39	Sandusky G	2	" B	April 29 64
56	Stout D D	2	" F	June 18 64
3035	Scarbrough S N	13	" E	July 8 64
3276	Shrop J B	East 2	" E	July 14 64
3298	Sells W	East Cav 2	" D	July 14 64
3302	Swappola O B	4	" A	July 15 64

Tennessee—(*Continued.*)

3520 Slaver A Cav 11 Co C July 18 64
3865 Smith John M 12 " M July 24 64
4038 Sapper S 8 " H July 26 64
4170 Snow W Cav 7 " M July 23 64
5462 Smith L 13 " L Aug 13 64
5625 Sutton Andrew Cav 13 " E Aug 11 64
5859 Swan John 2 " D Aug 16 64
5962 Scott John 13 " B Aug 17 64
6643 Sutton D Cav 1 " H Aug 23 64
7056 Smith J 6 " M Aug 28 64
7296 Stewart J W Cav 13 " B Aug 30 64
7314 Smidney E Cav 1 " E Aug 30 64
7787 Scobey L A H Cav 13 " B Sept 2 64
7923 Sarret Jas D Tenn St Gd Sept 5 64
8637 Smith J Cav 3 Co E Sept 13 64
9192 Smith T A 13 " C Sept 18 64
9381 Southerland J Cav 13 " C Sept 20 64
9395 Stewart E Cav 13 " D Sept 20 64
9555 Smith W H 7 " B Sept 23 64
9719 Swatzell W L Cav 8 " E Sept 25 64
9803 Stratten J L Cav 7 " M Sept 25 64
10409 Stafford S 13 " A Oct 6 64
10454 Shonall John 13 " C Oct 7 64
11594 Shay D 11 " E Oct 28 64
12558 Smith H 2 " E Jan 30 65
12749 Stevens J F Cav 2 " E Mch 8 65
12756 Smith J D 4 " C Mch 12 65
12784 Stewart R H 7 " C Mch 15 65
12800 Shook N A 7 " B Mch 19 65
12836 Smith George 2 " B April 18 65
36 Stiner W H 2 " E April 28 64
3995 Slorer A W 2 " C July 26 64
211 Tompkins T B 2 " F Mch 28 64
258 Thompson W D 2 " F Mch 31 64
793 Thompson Charles 2 April 29 64
932 Thomas W H 2 Co K May 7 64
1657 Tomlin A Cav 7 " M June 6 64
1704 Thanton S A Art 1 " H June 7 64
2229 Tice S J 7 " B June 20 64
2718 Tipton W H 2 " I July 1 64
3460 Taylor J 13 " D July 17 64
4122 Tyffle John Cav 1 " A June 28 64
4778 Templeton G W 2 " C Aug 5 64
5646 Tite W S 13 " C Aug 14 64
7052 Thomas W H Cav 7 " A Aug 28 64
9203 Tolley D 8 " H Sept 19 64
9375 Terry D Cav 9 " D Sept 20 64
10780 Thinn R A Cav 7 " B Oct 12 64
12694 Tidwell T 13 " D Feb 22 65
4825 Tidwell J W 13 " C Aug 5 64
2592 Usley T R 2 " A June 28 64
4518 Undergrate A 2 " I Aug 2 64
885 Vaugh I 8 " H May 5 64
1203 Vanhorn J 2 " H May 19 64
2915 Varner T W Cav 11 " E July 5 64
7217 Vanhook J M, Cor Cav 11 " H July 29 64
4530 Vaughry Frederick 2 " D Aug 1 64
60 Wolfe John 11 " E Mch 18 64
259 Woolen I 2 " A Mch 31 64
339 Webb Robert 2 Co B April 2 64
359 Wuas M 2 " I April 2 64
501 Watts C C 3 " A April 12 64
570 Ward Jordan 2 " A April 15 64
810 White John 2 " B April 30 64
902 William C. 7 " B May 5 64
1052 Ward A 3 " I May 12 64
1756 Watts J W 7 " M June 9 64
1794 White I 2 " D June 10 64
1865 Wallace L East 2 " C June 12 64
2057 Ward C 2 " H June 16 64
2066 Watts T, Corpl 2 " I June 16 64
2132 Wray Samuel 13 " C June 18 64
2496 Wilson A Cav 8 June 26 64
2764 Winningham J 2 Co B July 2 64
2810 Wells E 8 " H July 3 64
3021 Watkins J M 4 " I July 7 64
3031 Woodsend T 7 " K July 8 64
3139 Webb D Cav 8 " G July 12 64
21 Winchester J D Cav 1 " E April 15 64
19 Weaver P 2 " D April 13 64
4554 West W F 2 " H Aug 2 64
4869 Ward John, Citizen Aug 6 64
22 Whitby R B 2 Co C April 15 64
33 Weese W 2 " I April 23 64
3297 Weir I Cav 1 " B July 14 64
3304 Wilson H 2 " B July 14 64
3319 Wolf A 10 " C July 14 64
3453 Williams A Cav 3 " E July 17 64
3615 Willis James Tenn St Guards July 20 64
3714 Webbe J 2 Co B July 21 64
3737 Wilson J 12 " F July 21 64
3932 Wilson S L 2 " D July 26 64
4033 Walford W 7 " A July 26 64
4704 Wallace L 2 " C Aug 4 64
5267 Wright J W Cav 7 " B Aug 10 64
5572 Withyde S 1 " A Aug 14 64
6103 Wood P D 3 " B Aug 19 64
6580 Webb Robert 2 " B Aug 23 64
6608 Wortell H H Cav 7 " I Aug 23 64
7618 White R O M 13 " B Sept 2 64
8740 Whicks N 7 " H Sept 14 64
7231 Wood J 7 " C Aug 29 64
9193 Woolsey J 2 " F Sept 18 64
9479 Walker John Cav 13 " C Sept 21 64
9658 Williams C S Cav 9 " B Sept 24 64
9670 Whittle H W Cav 7 " C Sept 24 64
9730 Webb T 6 " G Sept 25 64
9929 White L S Cav 11 " D Sept 28 64
10337 Wiggins G W Cav 11 " C Oct 4 64
10338 White H, Sgt Cav 7 " A Oct 4 64
10739 Warrell J W, Corp Cav 7 Oct 11 64
10605 Webb W 3 Co A Oct 10 64
11386 Warden J W, Serg't 7 " E Oct 24 64
12107 Winelug J 7 " M Nov 21 64
12125 White Wm M 11 " D Nov 22 64
12139 Watson I C Cav 7 " C Nov 23 64
12576 Walker C H 6 " H Feb 3 65
12699 Woodruff J Cav 4 " B Feb 24 65

Tennessee — (*Continued.*)

12779	Woods Thomas	13	Co B	Mch 15 65
8190	White J, Serg't	Cav 7	" A	Sept 8 64
5669	Wilson Wm A	6	" A	Aug 14 64
4717	Westbrook J H	Cav 6	" A	Aug 4 64
4793	Wilson J M	Cav 13	" D	Aug 5 64
383	Yarbor Wiley	5	Co I	April 5 64
878	Young James	2	" D	May 4 64
1142	Young James	2	" F	May 16 64
14	Yeront Samuel	3	" E	April 10 64
5682	Yarnell J E	3	" E	Aug 14 64

TOTAL 736.

VERMONT.

3975	Averill T E	9	Co I	July 25 64
4579	Adams Daniel	Cav 1	" L	Aug 2 64
8301	Albee S, Serg't	11	" G	Sept 9 64
9960	Atwood A	1	" C	Sept 28 64
10664	Aldrich L E, Serg't	11	" A	Oct 11 64
11259	Aldrich H B	Art 1	" A	Oct 21 64
12092	Aiken M A	1	" A	Nov 19 64
12766	Avery B F	3	" C	Mch 13 65
2035	Bloomer J	Bat 2		June 15 64
3166	Bailey James	2	Co A	July 11 64
4036	Brown George	16	" B	July 20 64
4173	Bailey S P	Cav 1	" H	July 28 64
4200	Beadle H H	9	" G	July 29 64
4509	Bucker James	1	" M	Aug 1 64
4637	Boyd A M	Cav 1	" L	Aug 3 64
4954	Bently M W	6	" A	Aug 7 64
5671	Bacom A M	8	" G	Aug 14 64
5728	Bliss J H	Cav 1	" L	Aug 15 64
6334	Burchard C	11	" L	Aug 21 64
6349	Benson A	1	" C	Aug 21 64
6416	Bennvills J	4	" D	Aug 22 64
6594	Barnes W	Cav 1	" F	Aug 23 64
7886	Barton W	11	" K	Sept 5 64
8029	Beady Wm	9	" I	Sept 6 64
8086	Barker F	Art 1	" A	Aug 7 64
8315	Burrows H	11	" F	Sept 10 64
8591	Brainard J B	Cav 1	" L	Aug 12 64
10305	Brown G	9	" D	Oct 4 64
10371	Bowles L H	7	" A	Oct 5 64
10431	Burton C	4	" A	Oct 6 64
10745	Barker C	4	" D	Oct 11 64
11068	Brown J B	1	" A	Oct 17 64
11225	Batch B F	4	" C	Oct 20 64
11375	Bohamar J	9	" I	Oct 24 64
11469	Baker John	11	" E	Oct 26 64
11747	Bonlon A	2	" B	Nov 2 64
11811	Babcock T	1	" K	Nov 5 64
12055	Barber W H	1	" C	Nov 16 64
12185	Burns J	7	" B	Nov 28 64
12239	Butler A F	Art 1	" L	Dec 7 64
12406	Baxter G	4	" A	Jan 6 65
12412	Bishop E	11	" E	Jan 8 65
12585	Bailey E	4	" B	Feb 4 65
1044	Corey C A	Cav 1	" F	May 12 64
1170	Clifford Jas	4	" F	May 17 64
1228	Chatfield Wm, Corp'l	10	" F	May 20 64
1973	Collit Jas	Cav 1	" H	June 15 64
2675	Caswell F	9		June 30 64
2694	Clough B	9	Co A	June 30 64
2811	Chase M	6	" H	July 3 64
3351	Cole A H	9	Co H	July 15 64
3317	Crocker D	5	" D	July 23 64
3918	Clough John D	11	" A	July 24 64
4205	Chamberlain ——	6	" A	July 29 64
4883	Crouse N	5	" C	Aug 6 64
5103	Chester A	11	" K	Aug 9 64
5480	Carey Thomas	Art 1		Aug 13 64
6806	Carmine P	Art 1	Co L	Aug 25 64
6932	Conner W A, Sgt	4	" A	Aug 26 64
7345	Clark M L	11	" F	Aug 31 64
7361	Clark John	Art 11	" M	Aug 31 64
7698	Cunningham J	Cav 1	" F	Sept 3 64
8320	Cook J J, Corp'l	Cav 1	" I	Sept 10 64
8923	Chase E L	Art 1	" C	Sept 16 64
9724	Crowley D	11	" F	Sept 25 64
11738	Cross E F	11	" L	Nov 2 64
11769	Carter J	11	" A	Nov 3 64
10330	Colborn W	Art 1	" M	Oct 4 64
3068	Drew F	Cav 1	" F	July 9 64
5927	Donohoe P	Cav 1	" D	Aug 17 64
6104	Dunn G E, Corpl	1	" G	Aug 18 64
6238	Doying F W	Art 1	" F	Aug 21 64
6840	Darcy F	4	" D	Aug 25 64
7974	Day Geo	11	" H	Sept 6 64
8271	Davis O F	9	" I	Sept 9 64
10430	Dunn W W	Cav 1	" G	Oct 6 64
10458	Day J D	Cav 1	" A	Oct 7 64
12375	Dragoon N	Cav 1	" G	Jan 1 65
6358	Ennison G	11	" A	Aug 21 64
10316	Eliot C	4	" F	Oct 4 64
821	Farmer E L	14	" H	May 1 64
3464	Freeman C R	9	" H	July 17 64
4077	Farnsworth M	1	" B	July 26 64
5851	Farnham L B	Art 1	" A	Aug 16 64
5914	Foster A	17	" K	Aug 17 64
6758	Fuller W	Cav 1	" G	Aug 25 64
7165	Forrest S	3	" I	Aug 29 64
8096	Fox W	11	" K	Sept 7 64
8201	Foster H B	11	" L	Sept 8 64
10784	Feast Geo	Art 1	" K	Oct 12 64
10969	Fisk W P	4	" K	Oct 15 64
11314	Farrell J H	4	" D	Oct 22 64
11351	Flint C B	4	" D	Oct 23 64
11458	Foster H C	Art 1	" D	Oct 25 64
12317	Ferand A	Art 1	" B	Dec 21 64
12322	Ferrett J	1	" K	Dec 23 64
12065	Fairchild G L	Art 1	" A	Nov 17 64
6264	Farnham L D, Sgt	11	" A	Nov 20 64
1730	Gelo A	3	" B	June 8 64
5273	Green E	Bat 2		Aug 10 64

Vermont—(*Continued.*)

8572	Gleason C W	Art 1 Co	H	Sept 12 64
9739	Gillman S A	4 "	G	Sept 26 64
11598	Graves J	11 "	E	Oct 23 64
12531	Gerry E B, Corp'l	4 "	H	Jan 26 65
2176	Hubbard F	Bat 2		June 19 64
3851	Humphrey J	Cav 1 Co	A	July 14 64
5218	Hall Benj	11 "	A	Aug 10 64
6145	Hyde E, Corp'l	11 "	L	Aug 18 64
6657	Havens E W	9 "	H	Aug 24 64
7394	Hazen W	9 "	H	Aug 31 64
10324	Hines L	11 "	A	Oct 13 64
10843	Hart S L	2		Oct 13 64
10910	Hudson J B	11 Co	A	Oct 14 64
10996	Hudson J M	11 "	A	Oct 16 64
11442	Howard J	Cav 1 "	K	Oct 25 64
11730	Holmes Joseph	Art 1 "	K	Nov 2 64
11814	Howard J	11 "	A	Nov 4 64
1206	Hall C A	1 "	A	Nov 17 64
12300	Hodges J	Cav 1 "	H	Dec 17 64
3309	Jones H L	6 "	B	July 14 64
3858	Joslin H	1 "	B	July 24 64
3883	Jordan A E	17 "	A	July 24 64
4690	Johnson D W	11 "	H	Aug 4 64
10183	Johnson John	Art 1 "	K	Oct 1 64
4007	Knapp L	1 "	G	July 25 64
6968	Kelsey L C	Art 1 "	F	Aug 27 64
7762	Kingsley S	1 "	D	Sept 4 64
8901	Knowles C W	4 "	H	Sept 16 64
6239	Knight Chas	Art 1 "	K	Aug 26 64
4597	La Boney H	1 "	M	Aug 3 64
4661	Larraway H	5 "	A	Aug 3 64
7653	Lapcam A	Cav 1		Sept 3 64
7891	Laddenbush J	17 Co	A	Sept 5 64
8355	Leoport C	11 "	L	Sept 10 64
10180	Lungershaw W C	Cav 1 "	F	Oct 1 64
11074	Lacker H	11 "	A	Oct 17 64
12916	Lumsden C	Cav 4 "	D	Feb 8 65
1335	Mitchell Jacob	Bat 2		May 24 64
1544	Mosey A	Cav 1 Co	K	June 1 64
2088	McIntire John	7 "	F	June 17 64
2394	Manian P	9		June 24 64
4617	Morse W	1 Co	F	Aug 3 64
5073	Martin Jas	1 "	M	Aug 8 64
5949	Mills Wm	1 "	E	Aug 17 64
7324	Merrill B J	1 "	B	Aug 30 64
8475	Mayhim J	6 "	C	Sept 11 64
8965	Manchester J M	Cav 1 "	I	Sept 16 64
9252	McGager J	2 "	G	Sept 20 64
9405	Montgomery O A	10 "	A	Sept 21 64
11327	McAllister W B	3 "	I	Oct 20 64
11735	Martin M	Art 1 "	A	Nov 2 64
12631	Monroe A	Art 11 "	L	Feb 10 65
9901	Morgan Chas	Art 11 "	M	Sept 27 64
4478	McCrillis Edw	Cav 1 "	C	Aug 1 64
7289	Milcher Wm	9 "	F	Aug 30 64
6559	Nownes Geo H	Cav 1 "	C	Aug 23 64
11067	Nichols H	Art 1 "	A	Oct 17 64
12283	Nelson S H	Art 4 "	I	Dec 13 64
704	O'Brien Wm	1 "	H	April 23 64
4300	O'Neil J M	10 Co	A	July 30 64
3133	Plude John	Bat 2		July 11 64
3213	Pev Jas	17 Co	D	July 12 64
4081	Preston F	Art 1		Aug 7 64
5135	Phelps H W	9 Co	H	Aug 9 64
5605	Poppins Frank	3 "	I	Aug 14 64
6586	Parmor E	4 "	C	Aug 23 64
7290	Park James	Cav 7 "	E	Aug 30 64
10040	Pillsbury F	Cav 4 "	C	Sept 29 64
10237	Paul John C	Cav 4 "	G	Oct 2 64
11041	Page E	4 "	I	Oct 17 64
11307	Powers A	4 "	H	Oct 22 64
11992	Packard M G, Cor	Art 1 "	A	Nov 13 64
12198	Pike N N	4 "	I	Nov 30 64
12721	Perry A B	4 "	H	Mch 3 65
1888	Reed D W	Cav 1		June 13 64
6699	Ransom Geo W	Art 1 Co	L	Aug 24 64
7697	Roscoe C	11 "	H	Sept 3 64
8138	Roberts J M	11 "	K	Sept 8 64
8173	Richards J	Cav 1 "	L	Sept 8 64
9162	Raynor Louis	Cav 4 "	C	Sept 21 64
9894	Ross H E	Bat 11 "	K	Sept 27 64
11039	Reynolds F	11 "	F	Oct 16 64
11436	Raney A	4 "	A	Oct 24 64
11591	Rice F W	14 "	F	Oct 13 64
12519	Rouncervee E T	9 "	D	Jan 25 65
648	Spoore W O	Cav 1 "	B	April 20 64
2943	Smith J C	1 "	H	July 6 64
3382	St John A	11 "	A	July 17 64
4380	Seward O	5 "	C	Aug 2 64
5707	Skinner F A	4 "	H	Aug 15 64
5963	Stone Jas A	Art 1 "	H	Aug 17 64
6640	Simons L	1 "	G	Aug 23 64
7309	Seaton T B	4 "	F	Sept 1 64
7310	Sweeney Henry	11 "	C	Sept 4 64
7813	Sprout A	17 "	F	Sept 4 64
8444	Stockwell A	11 "	H	Sept 11 64
10696	Sanburn H	4 "	G	Sept 11 64
10811	Styles A B, Corp'l	4 "	K	Sept 12 64
10897	Sheldon H	Cav 1 "	M	Sept 14 64
11282	Sarlett L	1 "	M	Oct 22 64
11476	Swaddle W	4 "	G	Oct 26 64
11966	Sanborn M L	Art 1 "	A	Nov 11 64
12266	Scott R O	4 "	F	Dec 12 64
12514	Shay J	Cav 1 "	K	Jan 23 65
12552	Sheldon G	1 "	K	Jan 29 65
12567	Stewart E W	11 "	A	Feb 1 65
5911	Scott Geo W	Cav 1 "	C	Aug 17 64
8436	Suppes T E	Cav 1 "	K	Sept 11 64
3784	Tuttle C S	Cav 1 "	F	July 22 64
5833	Tatro Alfred	9 "	F	Aug 16 64
6587	Taylor H C	Art 1 "	L	Aug 23 64
6659	Trow H	17 "	D	Aug 24 64
9374	Tanner H, Corp'l	11 "	I	Sept 20 64
9774	Tolman W C, Sgt	11 "	F	Sept 23 64
11171	Taylor J W	Art 1 "	A	Oct 19 64
11220	Thompson W A	Art 1 "	I	Oct 20 64
5603	Varnum E G J	11 "	F	Aug 15 64
3177	Weller D	9 "	B	July 11 64

Vermont—(*Continued.*)

4376	Whitehall Geo	6	Co B	July 31 64
4475	Wilson A	6	" B	July 31 64
4585	Wilder L F	11	" H	Aug 2 64
5075	Whitney A	9	" D	Aug 8 64
5307	Warner Geo O	10	" E	Aug 11 64
5751	Woodward S P	Art 1	" H	Aug 15 64
7003	Wells Geo A	4	" F	Aug 23 64
7222	Wright E S	Art 11	" A	Aug 30 64
7689	Witt T	Cav 1	" F	Sept 3 64
7910	Ward Alfred	11	" A	Sept 5 64
8239	Watkins G C	1	" C	Sept 9 64
9254	Woodmance G	11	Co F	Sept 9 64
9178	Welles C	11	" H	Sept 13 64
10310	White A	11	" A	Oct 8 64
10711	Webster W A, Serg't	4	" A	Oct 11 64
11239	Wakefield J W	4	" H	Oct 22 64
11398	Woods J M	1	" F	Oct 24 64
11783	Wheeler B	11	" K	Nov 3 64
11840	Warden G	3	" B	Nov 5 64
11865	Worthers S T	Cav 1	" D	Nov 6 64
12156	Willey J S	Art 1	" A	Nov 25 64
4533	Washburn Tru	Cav 1	" D	Aug 2 64

TOTAL 240.

VIRGINIA.

824	Anderson A	2	Co H	May 1 64
873	Armstrong —, St Mil	8	" C	May 4 64
942	Ayers S V	11	" C	May 7 64
1968	Armstrong G B	8	" C	June 14 64
2760	Armhalt W H, Corp'l	10	" I	July 1 64
5011	Armstrong J	3	" C	Aug 8 64
5341	Arbogast C W	Art 1	" C	Aug 11 64
8865	Abercrombie W H	12	" C	Sept 15 64
11525	Allison G.	1	" F	Oct 23 64
221	Burns S A, Sergt	8	" C	Mch 29 64
255	Brooks Samuel F	10	" I	Mch 30 64
448	Boone Jas	Cav 1	" L	April 9 64
756	Bennett L J	11	" C	April 27 64
943	Brake J, Sergt	6	" C	May 7 64
980	Blackburn Geo	10	" I	May 9 64
1705	Bates T E	11	" F	June 7 64
2318	Brown M	14	" E	June 26 64
2627	Bowermaster S R	Cav 3	" D	June 23 64
3407	Bateman D P	2	" B	July 16 64
4427	Barber Jas	Cav 1	" F	July 31 64
5495	Bishop J C	3	" C	Aug 12 64
6706	Bearer P	10	" I	Aug 24 64
10297	Boutwell O	4	" F	Oct 3 64
7123	Beasley P	9	" G	Aug 28 64
7909	Bogard Jno R, Corpl	14	" A	Sept 5 64
8539	Batt M	18	" E	Sept 12 64
9796	Butcher Peter	14	" F	Sept 26 64
10198	Broom J	Cav 1	" B	Oct 2 64
11090	Blessing P	15	" K	Oct 18 64
11337	Bush H H	14	" B	Oct 23 64
11411	Burton W B	Cav 6	" A	Oct 24 64
11609	Barnett J	Cav 6	" K	Oct 30 64
11924	Beach J F	14	" K	Nov 8 64
12045	Boggs H C, Corpl	Cav 6	" E	Nov 16 64
12414	Burton N	Cav 3	" B	Jan 8 65
110	Corbett L B W, Va Mil		C	Mch 23 64
403	Carr Wm	8	" B	April 6 64
835	Clendeman C L	Cav 4	" D	May 1 64
1032	Caste Jesse	8	" E	May 11 64
1100	Coon Nathan	14	" K	May 14 64
2013	Carrington Jas	2	" A	June 15 64
2235	Coffman F	Cav 3	" A	June 20 64
2569	Cunderson —	8	" D	June 27 64
2651	Carnes H	10	" E	June 29 64
2817	Conrad H	3	Co F	July 3 64
2930	Cunningham J	8	" E	July 5 64
3315	Cox T A, Sergt	Cav 3	" A	July 14 64
4363	Cool J B, Corpl	Cav 3	" H	July 31 64
4741	Crook E H, Sergt	7	" I	Aug 5 64
5174	Cuppett J	3	" H	Aug 9 64
5384	Covil Wm	3	" I	Aug 12 64
6674	Clements L	Cav 3	" A	Aug 24 64
6809	Curtin B	Cav 4	" B	Aug 25 64
7091	Clark —	9	" E	Aug 28 64
7179	Cremones D	9	" D	Aug 29 64
8990	Cook J	Cav 7	" I	Sept 17 64
9106	Campbell O H	14	" F	Sept 21 64
9755	Christian J	15	" C	Sept 25 64
9762	Catnill L	9	" B	Sept 25 64
9967	Cobin J M	14	" B	Sept 28 64
10598	Childs S P	Cav 1	" C	Oct 10 64
11561	Castle C H	1	" A	Oct 27 64
11830	Cooper A H, Corp'l	Cav 7	" I	Nov 5 64
12174	Campbell B	12	" I	Nov 26 64
24	Deboard H A	5	" G	Mch 8 64
202	Douglas Geo	8	" C	Mch 23 64
347	Dean Samuel	5	" H	April 2 64
632	Deflbaugh W R, Crp'l	Art 1	" G	April 19 64
647	Davis S	3	" D	April 20 64
843	Duncan J M	5	" D	May 2 64
2081	Daly Jas	Cav 3	" A	June 17 64
3105	Duckworth W B	14	" A	July 10 64
3246	Dyer James	10	" I	July 13 64
5507	Drake Samuel	9	" B	Aug 13 64
5588	Dorsey A L	15	" K	Aug 23 64
6745	Daner J	10	" I	Aug 24 64
6936	Darsey M	9	" L	Aug 26 64
6949	Dodd S, Sgt	9	" F	Aug 26 64
7092	Dunberger Geo	9	" C	Aug 28 64
8248	Divers G	15	" D	Sept 9 64
8467	Dant Jno M	Cav 7	" H	Sept 10 64
8582	Dason N	Cav 8	" L	Sept 12 64
9159	Dunn I	2	" K	Sept 18 64
12235	Duncan Wm	Cav 6	" C	Dec 6 64
12307	Donohue S	9	" C	Mch 21 65
12508	Doty John	Cav 6	" A	Jan 23 65
10975	Estuff Jno	Cav 1	" L	Oct 12 64
117	Fuller Irwin	Militia		Mch 23 64

Virginia — (*Continued.*)

613	Foster Charles K	9 Co H	April 18 64
935	Fox H C, Corp'l	1 " D	May 8 64
5765	Fawkes Wm	14 " D	Aug 15 64
7203	Foster S	8 " A	Aug 29 64
7941	Feather J B	14 " B	Sept 5 64
8698	Feasley Leu	Art 1	Sept 14 64
8723	Fusner J E	Cav 6 Co D	Sept 14 64
10206	Freeborn R L, Sgt	14 " B	Oct 2 64
10709	Furr E	10 " K	Oct 11 64
11022	Fleming W W	Cav 6 " A	Oct 16 64
10314	Forth R	8 " D	Sept 3 64
2485	Grey P	Va 3 " A	June 25 64
2649	Greshoe M	11 " C	June 29 64
2712	Golden J	Cav 2 " G	July 1 64
4733	Gordon S	2 " G	Aug 4 64
6348	Guenant A	2 " I	Aug 21 64
10381	Garton Wm, Corpl	2 " I	Oct 10 64
11574	Gluck A E	10 " D	Oct 28 64
11864	Gibson A	1 " A	Nov 6 64
84	Hollingshead S	1 " G	Mch 8 64
294	Harrison D	10 " I	April 1 64
305	Henry Robert O	8 " C	April 2 64
398	Hunter G W	8 " A	April 6 64
563	Heller Wm, Corpl	3 " D	April 15 64
839	Halpin Jno	2 " D	May 2 64
997	Hoffman G W	8 " E	May 10 64
1013	Hess J	11 " C	May 10 64
1421	Hatfield J	1 " B	May 28 64
1554	Harkins H	2 " F	June 11 64
2702	Hoover W H	3 " A	June 30 64
2902	Howell A	14 " E	July 5 64
2957	Howe S	2 " I	July 5 64
3930	Horant E A	3 " C	July 25 64
4739	Hine Wm	2 " A	Aug 5 64
5061	Hammer S	Cav 3 " G	Aug 8 64
5412	Hartley Isaac	3 " I	Aug 12 64
5649	Hall Henry	10 " F	Aug 14 64
6538	Harper W	8 " H	Aug 23 64
8061	Hushman W	10 " I	Sept 7 64
8268	Hardway D B	9 " G	Sept 9 64
8341	Harden G W	Cav 6 " A	Sept 10 64
8344	Hutson J	14 " A	Sept 10 64
9166	Hanslan B	Cav 6	Sept 18 64
9537	Hudgins J	14 Co B	Sept 22 64
9794	Handland H	1 " H	Sept 26 64
10990	HollinbeckWH,Crp	Cav 1 " B	Oct 14 64
11316	Hubert W C	12 " G	Oct 23 64
11396	Hendershot F F	7 " E	Oct 24 64
11739	Hurn R	8 " E	Nov 2 64
12014	Hartzel S	1 " D	Nov 15 64
12153	Hickman E	11 " B	Nov 24 64
312	Johns E K	Mil 8 " C	April 2 64
3045	Jake A R	8 " I	July 8 64
3969	Jackson S E	2 " E	July 25 64
6098	Jones G	Cav 2 " D	Aug 18 64
7631	Johnston I A	Cav 1 " D	Sept 3 64
8371	Jenkins W	Art 1 " D	Sept 10 64
323	Kane J	Cav 4 " L	April 2 64
5322	Kimball Jno	14 " K	Aug 16 64

589	Ludihing W	2 Co A	April 17 64
1565	Langstan N H	Cav 1 " A	June 2 64
1592	Lanham Henry	8 " C	June 3 64
1949	Logger J	Cav 3 " B	June 14 64
2734	Lyshon Wm	2 " I	July 1 64
2739	Loud Geo	9 " D	July 1 64
6924	Lansbury W, Serg't	15 " E	Aug 26 64
7237	Lough H	Cav 1 " L	Aug 29 64
10564	Liston David	Cav 6 " C	Oct 9 64
10569	Lowe J	9 " C	Oct 9 64
11021	Lowe W G	13 " G	Oct 16 64
11325	Layman W F	14 " C	Oct 23 64
11624	Laughlin D, Corp'l	9 " E	Oct 28 64
11989	Lucas J	9 " D	Nov 13 64
12262	Loring J	Art 1 " D	Dec 12 64
41	Maddons W L	Cav 4 " K	May 3 64
280	Mason Peter	10 " G	April 1 64
337	Magaher J	Cav 3 " A	April 5 64
422	McNelly Jas	Cav 3 " A	April 7 64
582	McCormick R	" F	April 16 64
786	McConnaughy D	11 " F	April 28 64
820	McGitton J	6 " G	May 1 64
1068	Morris J M	Cav 3 " E	May 13 64
1419	Murphy J	8 " D	May 28 64
1675	Moore M	14 " K	June 6 64
2932	Millum Jas	8 " I	July 5 64
3955	Mokie R	Cav 7	July 20 64
6950	Miller C W	2 Co C	Aug 27 64
7018	Meiner H	12 " I	Aug 27 64
9699	Mencar L B	14 " B	Sept 24 64
9767	Morris G	14 " A	Sept 25 64
9955	Miller D	14 " C	Sept 28 64
10567	Moody R W	Cav 6 " E	Oct 9 64
10578	McKinney Wm	Cav 1 " L	Oct 9 64
10934	McConkey A, Cor	Cav 6 " B	Oct 14 64
10970	McLaughlin R	Art 1 " D	Oct 15 64
11546	Monsen J F	14 " C	Oct 27 64
12099	Matt Henry	12 " E	Nov 19 64
12272	McCausland R	1 " G	Dec 12 64
9488	McGregor P	1 " E	Sept 21 64
12068	McWilson J	14 " F	Nov 17 64
2857	Norman H	2 " I	July 4 64
3395	Newman A	Cav 1 " B	July 16 64
6442	Nichols L D	9 " F	Aug 22 64
12472	Nicholson J	Cav 3 " B	Jan 17 65
241	Oxley Robert	14 " C	Mch 30 64
1767	Osborne Thos	5 " H	June 9 64
39	Packard Myron C	Cav 2 " I	Mch 13 64
1707	Peterfield Jno	4 " F	June 7 64
2433	Porrellson C D	10 " I	June 24 64
2345	Patney J	8 " G	June 29 64
2737	Painter C, Sgt	9 " F	July 1 64
3053	Petit J, Corp'l	Cav 1 " L	July 9 64
4707	Paine M, Corp'l	8 " F	Aug 3 64
5004	Pugh L	3 " I	Aug 8 64
5213	Polland Jno	10 " I	Aug 10 64
6004	Polley J	8 " C	Aug 17 64
6196	Perkins James A	12 " K	Aug 19 64
11267	Palmer Jno, Sgt	Cav 1 " L	Oct 21 64

Virginia—(*Continued.*)

849	Reakes Wm	Militia 8 Co	C	April 2 64
521	Rice A	Cav "	G	April 13 64
560	Randall, Jas A	9 "	K	April 15 64
959	Rinker F A	Cav 3 "	A	May 8 64
1040	Robb M	2 "	A	May 12 64
1916	Richards G L	14 "	D	June 14 64
3459	Rummer L	5 "	A	July 17 64
3465	Read J	12 "	B	July 17 64
3641	Redden J	9 "	F	July 20 64
4163	Ronsey Wm	9 "	C	July 29 64
7257	Rutroff Jacob	7 "	H	July 30 64
8032	Reush Jas	7 "	B	Sept 7 64
10527	Reed J M, Corpl	12 "	B	Oct 7 64
11518	Rock J H	12 "	C	Oct 26 64
11794	Raleigh S	Cav 1 "	I	Nov 4 64
7005	Richardson W	14 "	K	Aug 27 64
273	Sayre Michael	14 "	I	Mch 31 64
680	Sprague Geo	11 "	F	April 23 64
927	Stacklcford S	Cav 3 "	A	May 7 64
1510	Scott Z, Sergt	8 "	D	May 31 64
2226	Steward C	Cav 2 "	I	June 20 64
2359	Stagg Wm	10 "	I	June 23 64
2437	Stutter J N	Cav 3 "	B	June 25 64
2931	Skillington G	Cav 4 "	D	July 5 64
3321	Stephenson A	Cav 1 "	B	July 16 64
3588	Shilber C A	3 "	A	July 19 64
3747	Shaub F	2 "	E	July 22 64
3895	Simons C E	8 "	C	July 24 64
3865	Stewart Wm A	14 "	I	July 25 64
4163	Steele A	Cav 2 "	C	Aug 1 64
4812	Snider S	3 "	K	Aug 5 64
4935	Sturn E E	12 "	F	Aug 7 64
5130	Smith ——	2 "	F	Aug 8 64
5237	Simmons E	8 "	C	Aug 10 64
5727	Sprouse A	11 "	F	Aug 15 64
5975	Smith J W	8 "	G	Aug 17 64
6473	Sprouse W	11 "	F	Aug 22 64
6510	Squares Samuel	Cav 6 "	D	Aug 23 64
7091	Stratton B B	Art 1 "	F	Aug 28 64
7944	Stoker S	Cav 3 "	C	Sept 5 64
8011	Sands Wm	10 "	F	Sept 6 64
8104	Scritchfield W	6 Co	F	Sept 18 64
8390	Stuck H M	14 "	B	Sept 10 64
8516	Smith B	9 "	H	Sept 2 64
8616	Sturgiss W T, Drum	14 "	B	Sept 12 64
9217	Smith G H	Cav 7 "	G	Sept 19 64
9714	Sullivan E	2 "	A	Sept 25 64
9786	Snyder J V, Serg't	3 "	D	Sept 26 64
9372	Semcir G S	Cav 4		Sept 27 64
9306	Sands G W	1		Sept 28 64
10151	Smith J	14 Co	B	Oct 1 64
11576	Smith J A	9 "	B	Oct 22 64
11625	Slee R, Serg't	Cav 1 "	D	Oct 25 64
11824	Spaulding F	Cav 1 "	A	Nov 5 64
11836	Stockwell C H	3 "	B	Nov 5 64
7221	Saylor C M	9 "	B	Aug 30 64
1108	Thatcher J P	2 "	A	April 15 64
3404	Trobridge S	6 "	B	July 16 64
5136	Tyom T	8 "	H	Aug 8 64
6379	Thurston C C	1 "	I	Aug 21 64
8663	Taylor J	8 "	G	Sept 13 64
12332	Thorpe S S	3 "	I	Dec 26 64
3846	Tomlinson S, Serg't	3 "	I	July 24 64
8119	Tatro L	11 "	B	Sept 8 64
244	Vincent Jas	8 "	C	Mch 30 64
814	Very W	Cav 1 "	C	April 30 64
1149	Vanscoy A, Corp	Cav 3 "	E	May 16 64
1322	Virts R	Cav 3 "	A	May 23 64
945	Wilson Walter	11 "	F	May 7 64
1757	Weaver M	Cav 1 "	C	June 7 64
2854	Warp J	3 "	F	July 6 64
3723	Wich J	Cav 1 "	L	July 21 64
3925	Whitney W A	8 "	F	July 25 64
3996	Whit A	5 "	F	July 25 64
7542	Wilson J	3 "	B	Sept 2 64
7832	Warwicke E	2 "	D	Sept 4 64
8598	Wells E	7 "	F	Sept 12 64
9626	Wolfe C	14 "	B	Sept 24 64
10854	White J N	Cav 6 "	C	Oct 13 64
148	Young A	8 "	C	Mch 25 64
456	Young A B	8 "	C	April 9 64
694	Young Ed	8 "	C	April 23 64

TOTAL 288.

WISCONSIN.

2113	Allwise J R	24 Co	E	June 17 64
4477	Austin Isaac	25 "	G	Aug 1 64
5241	Abbott A, Sgt	21 "	D	Aug 10 64
5453	Allen C P	2 "	G	Aug 12 64
8693	Adams A F	36 "	F	Sept 14 64
10830	Adams P	10 "	A	Oct 13 64
11492	Aultin E V, Corp'l	13 "	E	Oct 26 64
12728	Antone C	31 "	D	Mch 4 65
1341	Bower H	1 "	A	May 24 64
1838	Burk O	15 "	B	June 11 64
2009	Bawgarder B	2 "	K	June 15 64
2055	Ball A	7 "	A	June 16 64
2128	Bowhan H A, Sgt	10 "	F	June 18 64
2334	Brooks E	Cav 1 "	H	June 22 64
2451	Broomer B F, Corp'l	10 Co	I	June 25 64
2081	Brown O	15 "	G	June 30 64
3233	Brown J	4 "	H	July 13 64
3673	Bruce H	24 "	H	July 20 64
4870	Brumsted G, Sergt	15 "	A	Aug 6 64
5026	Briggs H	Cav 1 "	L	Aug 8 64
5109	Budson John	Cav 1 "	L	Aug 9 64
5164	Bemis H	10 "	C	Aug 9 64
5322	Briggs E	Cav 1		Aug 11 64
5564	Bailey W, Corpl	25 Co	E	Aug 13 64
6234	Banick S	17 "	I	Aug 19 64
7295	Bailey J	36 "	I	Aug 30 64
7323	Burk J	Cav 10 "	E	Aug 30 64
7755	Borden E, Corpl	21 "	K	Sept 3 64

Wisconsin—(*Continued.*)

7759	Boyle P	25	Co	D	Sept 4 64
8576	Batchelder J	1	"	I	Sept 12 64
8641	Bushell C C	2	"	B	Sept 13 64
9607	Brinkman J	2	"	A	Sept 23 64
10686	Britton H, Sergt	15	"	I	Oct 11 64
10919	Bohnsen N	15	"	I	Oct 14 64
11754	Butler M	10	"	K	Nov 2 64
12032	Blakeley R	7	"	F	Nov 15 64
11610	Batterson L	10	"	K	Oct 28 64
2360	Church A	7	"	H	June 23 64
2663	Chapman J	2	"	G	June 29 64
2969	Cowles D	10	"	B	July 6 64
3192	Cummings S	21	"	A	July 14 64
3828	Crane R, Drummer	7	"	D	July 23 64
4390	Chapel C	1	"	E	July 31 64
5102	Cavanaugh John	Cav 1	"	H	Aug 9 64
8105	Chase F M, Corpl	1	"	A	Sept 7 64
9418	Currier C C	21	"	F	Aug 22 64
9169	Carlintyre G	23			Sept 18 64
10752	Castle C	Cav 1	Co	C	Oct 12 64
11020	Cofam W	10	"	A	Oct 16 64
11088	Chusterson F	15	"	E	Oct 18 64
11535	Chamberlain J	21	"	I	Oct 27 64
11744	Clark W C	10	"	E	Nov 2 64
10346	Crommings H	7	"	C	Oct 5 64
1591	Duffey E	1	"	L	June 3 64
2522	Damhocker E	26	"	I	June 26 64
3244	Daggo John	Cav 1	"	L	July 13 64
5830	Destler Fred	26	"	G	July 16 64
6967	Dick Benjamin	36	"	G	Aug 27 64
7455	Davis J	36	"	B	Sept 1 64
8530	Decker G, Sergt	Bat	"	F	Sept 12 64
8587	Depas A	21	"	A	Sept 12 64
8900	Doryson W	7	"	C	Sept 15 64
9739	Dacy G	12	"	I	Sept 25 64
10771	Davis John	1	"	B	Oct 12 64
12750	David D P	25	"	B	Mch 8 65
2419	Enger J	15	"	K	June 24 64
5247	Egan John	7	"	A	
6160	Erickson C	15	"	B	Aug 19 64
8601	Ellwood S, Sergt	10	"	C	Aug 13 64
9337	Erricson S	50	"	D	Sept 20 64
11687	Ellenger P	21	"	K	Oct 31 64
12286	Enkhart H	36	"	G	Dec 14 64
36	Fordway G W	7	"	E	Mch 12 64
1250	Fuller C W, Corpl	7	"	E	May 21 64
2283	Fountain W F	10	"	A	June 20 64
5007	Forslay W K	8	"	K	Aug 8 64
5759	Flenis Oscar	Cav 1	"	H	Aug 15 64
5811	Fisk J B, Sgt	Cav 1	"	H	Aug 16 64
6097	Fischnor D, Sgt	36	"	H	Aug 13 64
6236	Fanon Wm	1	"	A	Aug 20 64
8460	Farnham M B	4	"	K	Sept 11 64
9664	Ferguson I	15	"	G	Sept 21 64
10234	Fagan M	15	"	G	Oct 2 64
12618	Frost A	7	"	B	Feb 2 65
12653	Ferguson W R	24	"	D	Feb 14 65
1529	Gilbert I	16	"	K	May 31 64
2392	Grush Fred	15	"	I	June 24 64
3164	Guth H	1	Co	D	July 11 64
3390	Greenman D	21	"	K	July 16 64
5557	Greenwall M	Cav 1	"	C	Aug 16 64
7355	Grunds L	15	"	I	Aug 31 64
8226	Groupe D	4	"	F	Sept 10 64
10601	Gunduson H	15	"	I	Oct 11 64
6614	Goon Jno E	36			Aug 23 64
303	Helt Carl	26	Co	E	April 1 64
710	Hale A C	21	"	I	April 24 64
1022	Haskins J	1	"	E	May 10 64
1655	Hoffland ——, 1 Sgt	15	"	K	June 5 64
1673	Harvey D M	1	"	I	June 6 64
2384	Hanson J	15	"	K	June 23 64
2536	Hough B J	10	"	K	June 27 64
3720	Henderson O	15	"	F	July 24 64
4542	Hewick Nelson	10	"	B	Aug 2 64
4570	Halts S	26	"	C	Aug 2 64
5312	Howard F B	10	"	K	Aug 11 64
5623	Holenback A	25	"	D	Aug 14 64
6463	Hall A W	21	"	I	Aug 22 64
7081	Hanley T	Art 3	"	D	Aug 28 64
7149	Hutchings B	Cav 1	"	E	Aug 29 64
7649	Hanson L	15	"	B	Sept 3 64
7791	Harding W F	21	"	C	Sept 4 64
8584	High M	25	"	E	Sept 12 64
9333	Halter D	22	"	D	Sept 20 64
10427	Hans P	10	"	D	Oct 6 64
11443	Holenbeck C	13	"	A	Oct 25 64
11927	Hanson ——	1	"	B	Nov 8 64
12167	Harris N	12	"	D	Nov 26 64
12586	Hardy E L	6	"	E	Jan 4 65
12848	Hanson R L	1	"	F	April 28 65
12468	Hand G	10	"	D	Jan 16 65
8314	Ingham J	10	"	K	Sept 13 64
9803	Irwin A	25	"	C	Sept 26 64
2003	Jacobson O	15	"	D	June 15 64
3281	Jackson T	4	"	H	July 13 64
3478	Jillett J	7	"	H	July 17 64
5388	Jennings J R	45	"	G	Aug 5 64
11284	Johnson W H	6	"	H	Oct 22 64
1165	Kemmett J	1	"	H	May 17 64
2498	Kundson J	15	"	E	June 26 64
4133	Kellett Jno B	21	"	B	July 27 64
4105	Kull L	24	"	C	July 31 64
4614	Klepps C H	Cav 1	"	E	Aug 3 64
8592	Kendall W	32			Sept 12 64
9063	Keeroger Wm	36	Co	G	Sept 17 64
10536	Kane F	26	"	E	Oct 8 64
10692	Knowles H	21	"	D	Oct 11 64
8299	Kinds M O	21	"	A	Sept 9 64
3009	Lack Peter	7	"	A	July 7 64
5397	Livingston J H	Art 3	"	E	Aug 12 64
6642	Lansing G	10	"	A	Aug 23 64
7235	Lowe F	16	"	G	Aug 29 64
7522	Lawson M	15	"	B	Sept 1 64
8944	Laich F	26	"	K	Sept 16 64
9397	Latgen E	15	"	A	Sept 29 64
8977	Laich F	26	"	K	Sept 17 64
1752	Manger Jas	24	"	H	June 9 64

Wisconsin—(*Continued.*)

1896	Mulligan J	1 Co	I	June 13 64
2732	McMann W	Bat 3		July 1 64
2951	McCormick E	Cav 1 Co	L	July 6 64
2981	McKenzie J	1 "	F	July 7 64
3625	McLanlin C	36 "	I	July 20 64
4925	Mathison E N	2 "	E	Aug 6 64
5043	Many J	24 "	D	Aug 8 64
5163	McFadden H	Cav 1 "	F	Aug 9 64
5683	Mortes B	10 "	D	Aug 15 64
5739	Main Henry	30 "	F	Aug 15 64
6231	McClury A	10 "	I	Aug 20 64
6377	Messer F	5 "	B	Aug 21 64
10289	Myers S	15 "	G	Oct 4 64
11936	Mulasky E	21 "	B	Nov 9 64
4289	Nelson R	15 "	K	July 30 64
4980	Northam S R	10 "	C	Aug 7 64
6090	Nichols Wm	10 "	I	Aug 18 64
10369	Neff Wm	33 "	I	Oct 6 64
3162	Olson O	15 "	B	July 11 64
11545	Ochle F	26 "	E	Oct 27 64
11931	Olston M	15 "	B	Nov 7 64
604	Palmer Jno	7 "	C	April 18 64
2535	Plum A	Cav 4 "	K	June 26 64
2847	Peterson A	15 "	K	July 4 64
3511	Picket T B	1 "	F	July 18 64
4340	Purdy M	10 "	E	July 30 64
6406	Pirisis J	17 "	F	Aug 22 64
7530	Purdee J	10 "	I	Sept 1 64
7893	Peterson S	15 "	K	Sept 5 64
8515	Pillsbury A J	Cav 1 "	H	Sept 12 64
8654	Patterson J	21 "	A	Sept 13 64
9014	Painter H	10 "	F	Sept 17 64
9902	Patterson S	15 "	I	Sept 27 64
9461	Peterson C	15 "	I	Sept 21 64
2028	Roach A	21 "	F	June 15 64
3624	Renseler H	2 "	G	July 20 64
3665	Reynolers F S	10 "	K	July 20 64
4997	Reed G	1 "	K	Aug 7 64
5792	Rasmusson A	Cav 1 "	L	Aug 15 64
6088	Robinson Will	10 "	C	Aug 18 64
9860	Rice J	7 "	C	Aug 27 64
11812	Randles J	25 "	D	Nov 4 64
12233	Richmond B	Cav 1 "	L	Dec 6 64
12242	Randell P D	Cav 1 "	K	Dec 7 64
68	Schleassen J J	7 "	F	Mch 19 64
440	Shrigley H	10 "	G	April 8 64
2814	Stiffus R	15 "	F	July 3 64
3078	Sirbirth F	24 "	E	July 9 64
3503	Shoop W	1 "	G	July 18 64
3583	Sutton J	10 Co	B	July 19 64
4313	Sharp J W	2 "	G	July 30 64
4378	Smith W F	10 "	B	July 31 64
4436	Shun J	24 "	H	July 31 64
47[illegible]8	Scott E G	21 "	D	Aug 5 64
4382	Slingerland Jno	Cav 1 "	B	Aug 6 64
6943	Starr E	16 "	F	Aug 26 64
7614	Seaman M	21 "	D	Sept 2 64
8168	Smith L	Cav 4 "	K	Sept 8 64
9693	Snyder M	26 "	E	Sept 24 64
11037	Smith S M	21 "	F	Oct 17 64
11047	Sales A D	4 "	K	Oct 17 64
2148	Tung S W	21 "	D	June 18 64
2385	Tay S	1 "	K	June 24 64
2588	Tomlinson Robert	6 "	B	June 28 64
3120	Thompson D D	26 "	B	June 10 64
3375	Tyler J	10 "	A	July 16 64
3661	Tucker C P	1 "	I	July 20 64
4467	Taylor A L	25 "	E	Aug 1 64
6358	Taylor I	6 "	E	Aug 26 64
7160	Thorn P C	Cav 1 "	L	Aug 29 64
8500	Troutman A	2		Sept 12 64
11236	Thurber D	36 Co	G	Oct 21 64
11420	Tyler E P	10 "	F	Oct 24 64
11475	Thorson P	24 "	G	Oct 26 64
12374	Thompson O	15 "	K	Jan 1 65
2309	Updell J S	15 "	B	June 22 64
2954	Vohoss O H	1 "	L	July 6 64
3076	Vitter J	6 "	F	July 9 64
8359	Vancoster H	Cav 1 "	C	Sept 10 64
8427	Vanderbilt J	36 "	D	Sept 11 64
11390	Voclee F	10 "	E	Oct 24 64
929	Webster A C	7 "	E	May 7 64
884	Winleis P	1 "	M	May 5 64
1007	Wilder Jno	Cav 1 "	F	May 10 64
1520	Welcome E D	Cav 1 "	L	May 31 64
1693	Walter S P	21 "	G	June 7 64
1909	Welton M S	Cav 1 "	L	June 13 64
2591	Winchester Geo	21 "	I	June 28 64
2894	Weaver H	10 "	F	July 4 64
3378	Wens Chas	7 "	B	July 16 64
4706	Wakefield D	25 "	K	Aug 4 64
9484	Woodward W B	1		Sept 21 64
9938	Wick J	Cav 1 Co	H	Sept 28 64
10213	Willis E	7 "	E	Oct 2 64
10395	Winchell S	1 "	D	Oct 6 64
12111	Whalen W	12 "	B	Oct 21 64
12363	Ward A	Cav 1 "	C	Dec 31 64
12626	Yessen A	24 "	A	Feb 10 65

TOTAL 244.

UNITED STATES ARMY.

1798	Anderson A	16 Co	C	June 10 64
3666	Atweil Thos	Cav 6 "	M	July 20 64
4349	Allen Chas	18 "	H	July 31 64
4537	Aschley D B	16 "	C	Aug 2 64
6077	Arnold H	18 "	H	Aug 18 64
6089	Adams G	14 "	C	Aug 18 64
8069	Austin Jas	Cav 4 "	K	Sept 7 64
11523	Annis Chas, (colored)	8 Co	I	Oct 26 64
9250	Alfka A H	Cav 2 "	D	Sept 19 64
102	Blossom Chas	Cav 6 "	E	Mch 22 64
1122	Boughton M	15 "	E	May 15 64
1158	Bailey Andrew	16 "	K	May 16 64
1199	Britner A	16 "	K	May 18 64
1201	Banks E E	17 "	C	May 19 64

United States Army—(*Continued.*)

1266	Burton Geo, Col'd	8 Co I	May 21 64
1397	Bardon Chas S	15 " E	May 26 64
1442	Beal H	15 " C	May 28 64
1461	Becker L	2 " B	May 29 64
1762	Brown C	16 " D	June 9 64
2122	Bates E L	Cav 5 " E	June 17 64
2434	Brannagan J	18 " D	June 24 64
2436	Bigler N M	Cav 2 " B	June 25 64
2749	Bradshaw H	Marine Corps	July 1 64
3370	Bush W	15 Co E	July 15 64
4861	Baldwin G	19 " A	Aug 6 64
4969	Baker F, Signal Corps		Aug 7 64
5657	Boyd S	4 Co C	Aug 14 64
5774	Breen A	2 " F	Aug 15 64
6126	Boyd John B	4 " K	Aug 19 64
6628	Bradman A M	Cav 6 " M	Aug 23 64
6652	Burd W H	6 " E	Aug 23 64
6937	Bowers J	4 " K	Aug 26 64
7717	Burk Jas	1 " K	Sept 3 64
7921	Brossessault M	Art 2 " M	Sept 5 64
8909	Banvall J	4 " F	Sept 16 64
9477	Bartlett E K	S S 2 " D	Sept 21 64
9631	Barstow J	18 " D	Sept 24 64
9848	Barrett J	18 " D	Sept 27 64
10621	Britzer L B	15 " C	Oct 10 64
11577	Brown J	12 " H	Oct 28 64
11706	Brickley H	1 " K	Nov 1 64
12077	Ball W	12 " C	Nov 18 64
12112	Boyer J	Cav 1 " K	Nov 21 64
12564	Bromley J	18 " G	Jan 31 65
760	Chisholm J M	M Corps	April 27 64
1947	Clemens D	6 Co L	June 14 64
2174	Clemburg J	16 " D	June 19 64
2316	Cassman A	M Corps	June 20 64
2726	Carter Thos	15 Co H	July 1 64
3126	Cavanaugh P	16 " A	July 10 64
3500	Conden H	12 " A	July 18 64
3911	Crookey S	15 " H	July 24 64
4346	Chase V	16 " C	July 30 64
4930	Campbell S L	15 " C	Aug 7 64
5107	Croy J	18 " B	Aug 9 64
5156	Cussey Jas	15 " A	Aug 9 64
5234	Casey J	15 " A	Aug 10 64
5436	Champney P A	Sig Corps	Aug 12 64
6420	Cammell J	12 Co H	Aug 22 64
7532	Coolidge M	17 " B	Sept 1 64
7722	Connor H	15 " H	Sept 3 64
7906	Corst Jas	14 " D	Sept 5 64
8161	Connell J	14 " D	Sept 8 64
8243	Chamberlain C	17 " B	Sept 9 64
8570	Collins M	Cav 4 " H	Sept 12 64
8767	Carter C A	1 " B	Sept 14 64
9031	Clifford J	Cav 6 " B	Sept 17 64
9113	Chase L	10 " C	Sept 18 64
9186	Carroll L	Cav 2 " G	Sept 18 64
9295	Congreve E	5 " A	Sept 19 64
9482	Cuyler W	16 " B	Sept 21 64
9814	Crocker Chas	2 " A	Sept 26 64
10210	Corgill C	12 " F	Oct 2 64

10557	Clark R W	S S 2	Oct 9 64
11176	Casey Jno	19 Co A	Oct 19 64
11201	Childs G	16 " B	Oct 20 64
11633	Cramer A	19 " C	Oct 28 64
914	Dunn Jno	6 " A	May 6 64
910	Dangler W G	5 " M	May 5 64
1255	Doney J W	Cav 6 " D	May 21 64
1653	Dunn Wm	19 " F	June 5 64
2274	Dunn Jno	18 " H	June 20 64
2495	Donalan M	Cav 2 " L	June 26 64
3325	Deyer H	18 " D	July 7 64
4377	Darwin W W	S S 2 " B	July 31 64
4490	Dinslow B F	12 " G	Aug 1 64
4623	Delaney Jacob	Art 5 " F	Aug 3 64
5348	Doll R	14 " C	Aug 11 64
5459	Dolan P	19 " F	Aug 12 64
5756	Davis G	19 " A	Aug 15 64
6025	Decker Jas	10	Aug 18 64
6210	Davis J W	15 Co E	Aug 19 64
6297	Doran J M	19 " E	Aug 20 64
6770	Doughty D B	Art 3 " C	Aug 25 64
6805	Davidson J H	15 " C	Aug 25 64
6955	Delaney E	19 " F	Aug 26 64
7049	Davis G	15 " F	Aug 27 64
7241	Delaney J	2 " F	Aug 29 64
7792	Dean Samuel	Cav 4 " B	Sept 3 64
8214	Downing M	10 " D	Sept 8 64
8332	Donle J	10 " D	Sept 15 64
10235	Davis Clarke	Bat 1 " K	Oct 2 64
10883	Draper L	14 " F	Oct 14 64
11554	Davy H	18 " G	Oct 27 64
11613	Diller O M	Cav 5 " I	Oct 28 64
12140	Drummond J	18 " F	Nov 23 64
12591	Dunn C	15 " C	Feb 4 65
5648	Evans T	14 " F	Aug 14 64
6813	Edwards Wm, (negro)	8 " A	Aug 25 64
7576	Erick J	2 " K	Sept 2 64
7616	Ellerton N	16 " D	Sept 2 64
12689	Emmich S S	5 " C	Feb 22 65
42	Ferguson J	Cav 6 " E	Mch 15 64
1213	Fitzgibbons Thos	2 " C	May 20 64
1509	Ferrell J	13 " A	May 31 64
2355	Fifley H	18 " E	May 23 64
2888	French Geo, 1st Lieut	37	July 3 64
3007	Feed G	Cav 6 Co D	July 7 64
3256	Frenchy D	2 " F	July 13 64
3543	Fielding A	13 " E	July 18 64
5487	Filestine S	16 " C	Aug 13 64
6804	Felps Daniel, negro	8 " H	Aug 25 64
7167	Flanigan M	2 " I	Aug 29 64
8536	Faunton H	14 " F	Sept 12 64
9154	Flanery M	Cav 1 " H	Sept 18 64
9725	Frum E	Cav 3 " C	Sept 25 64
9983	Flarety O	16	Sept 29 64
10655	Fenall J	14 Co G	Oct 11 64
10839	Flanagan P	Cav 14 " D	Oct 13 64
11402	Fritz A	19 " A	Oct 24 64
12312	Foster J	" H	Dec 19 64
272	Gilligan Mat	1 " I	Mch 31 64

United States Army — (*Continued.*)

1639	Gardener C	Sig Corps	June 5 64
2801	Gutterman S	16 Co D	July 2 64
4977	Gray Wm	18 " C	Aug 7 64
6182	Gale Walter	11 " F	Aug 19 64
7220	Gulvere David	4 " C	Aug 29 64
8057	Griffith S	11 " F	Sept 7 64
8671	Gunter Jno	Cav 4	Sept 13 64
8857	Grace Thos	1 Co B	Sept 15 64
9851	Gilbert A	5 " K	Sept 27 64
12066	Getts F	19 " E	Nov 16 64
7335	Golton R	76 " B	Aug 30 64
397	Hatch T C	11 " A	April 6 64
533	Halbert F	2 " H	April 13 64
1547	Halpin P	Art 5 " H	June 1 64
1585	Haney H	16 " D	June 3 64
1608	Hurman J H	Cav 4 " E	June 4 64
2096	Hendricks J	16 " D	June 17 64
2209	Hogan M	16 " A	June 20 64
2706	Henry Wm	2 " B	June 30 64
2730	Hurley D, Marine Corps		July 1 64
2987	Hulit Wm	16 Co D	July 7 64
3753	Hill Geo	17 " H	July 22 64
3893	Hopkins W, (negro)	17 " C	July 24 64
4429	Hill D S, (negro)	16 " C	July 31 64
7238	Heddington W	15 " F	Aug 29 64
7405	Horsham J R	15 " G	Aug 31 64
8004	Halley J	13 " B	Sept 6 64
9104	Hook H	19 " F	Sept 18 64
9155	Heir J	14 " A	Sept 18 64
9665	Hildreth Jas	12	Sept 24 64
9918	Haney J	12 Co C	Sept 28 64
10054	Hasler C	13 " M	Sept 30 64
10439	Hirchfield G	M Corps	Oct 7 64
10857	Harman J	15 Co E	Oct 14 64
11136	Hamilton S	S S 2 " D	Oct 19 64
12369	Hill M A	2 " G	Jan 1 65
12601	Hoit E (negro)	35 " H	Feb 6 65
10332	Hamman W H	15 " F	Oct 8 64
5532	Imhoff I	15 " E	Aug 13 64
7647	Ireland Geo	14 " E	Sept 3 64
10742	Ireson I	Cav 4 " A	Oct 11 64
8125	Johnson P	Bat 2	Sept 8 64
8366	Jones W	Art 1 Co K	Sept 10 64
10319	Jones C B	Cav 1 " H	Oct 3 64
11923	Jerald W H	18 " F	Nov 8 64
495	Kingeny J	1 " K	April 12 64
912	Kelly Jno	16 " C	May 5 64
1662	Kain P F	15 " A	June 6 64
3256	Kenley D	2 " F	July 13 64
3341	Kerkney F	18 " F	July 15 64
3685	Kilbride J	15 " F	July 21 64
4245	Kane Wm	18 " H	July 29 64
4266	Kalkrath C	8 " I	July 29 64
4271	Kelly D	4 " H	July 29 64
4694	Kester J	15 " F	Aug 4 64
5640	Kay Robert	4 " F	Aug 14 64
5643	Kelly J	M Corps	Aug 14 64
6271	Kochel J	19 Co G	Aug 20 64
6577	Kelly Wm	9 " I	Aug 23 64
6764	King I	7 Co K	Aug 25 64
7465	Kinney G W	Bat 1 " D	Sept 1 64
8261	Klinty H	Art 1 " K	Sept 9 64
8490	Kricks F	14 " C	Sept 11 64
8527	Kripp J	16 " D	Sept 12 64
9082	Knapp C	11 " A	Sept 18 64
11268	Kain Pat	15 " A	Oct 21 64
11767	Kelly J S	2 " D	Nov 3 64
11919	Kennedy J	12 " A	Nov 10 64
12205	Kahl Chas	Art 2 " M	Dec 1 64
12532	Kemp J W	2 " K	Jan 27 65
55	Lore Wm	6 " F	Mch 17 64
2282	Larreby G	16 " D	June 20 64
2774	Little J	19 " E	July 21 64
3999	Lackey J	16 " B	July 26 64
4453	Langstaff R	10 " F	Aug 1 64
5711	Lake Horace	Cav 4 " K	Aug 15 64
5891	Lynch B	18 " E	Aug 16 64
6116	Lattin E	12 " A	Aug 19 64
6300	Lawrence C	11 " E	Aug 20 64
6352	Lyons E, Signal Corps		Aug 21 64
6561	Little R	19 Co F	Aug 23 64
9732	Larqdell Wm	14 " A	Sept 25 64
10317	Louby O	Cav 4 " H	Oct 3 64
10379	Lockewood H, negro	8 " D	Oct 5 64
11038	Lyons R	Cav 1 " E	Oct 17 64
11543	Lyman O S	18 " A	Oct 27 64
11973	Lewis Wm P	8 " B	Nov 12 64
180	McCoy Augustus	6 " M	Mch 26 64
267	McClellan J	Cav 6 " D	Mch 31 64
828	Mason C H	12 " I	May 1 64
948	Murphy D	12 " B	May 8 64
1012	McEvers T L	13 " C	May 10 64
1043	McGuire J	3 " C	May 12 64
1332	Murray Thos	Art 1 " I	May 24 64
1471	Mulhall Peter	M Corps	May 30 64
1823	Marze Jas	12 Co D	June 10 64
1946	McLaughlin J	2 " H	June 14 64
1965	McConaghy P, M Corps		June 14 64
2444	Meadow Jno	Cav 6 Co K	June 25 64
3054	Muller J	M Corps	June 30 64
2920	Miller C H	Cav 6 Co K	July 5 64
3054	McKinney J	M Corps	July 9 64
3083	Maloney B	19 " B	July 9 64
3950	Merkill Peter	14 " H	July 25 64
4712	Murch Wm	11 " C	Aug 4 64
4823	McClintock J S	18 " H	Aug 5 64
4863	Martin M	Mar Corps	Aug 6 64
5303	Martin J	Cav 1 Co K	Aug 11 64
5364	McCann B	12 " B	Aug 11 64
5456	Michols R	Cav 1 " K	Aug 12 64
5581	McLean P	17 " C	Aug 14 64
5769	McCoslin Robt	Art 1 " B	Aug 15 64
6073	McDonald	Cav 4 " E	Aug 18 64
6081	McClair R	11 " G	Aug 18 64
6313	Munson C	12 " D	Aug 20 64
6407	Mulhern C	Cav 4 " C	Aug 22 64
6515	Mantle J M	15 " F	Aug 22 64
6851	Marston B	S S 51 " G	Aug 25 64

United States Army — (*Continued.*)

6973	McKinley E W, Mar Cor			Aug 27 64
7341	McGuire J	12	Co D	Aug 30 64
8293	Munn W	18	" H	Sept 9 64
8473	McGinnis A	Art 4	" E	Sept 11 64
9110	Montgomery C	13	" G	Sept 18 64
9231	McCoy J M, M Brigade			Sept 19 64
9363	Miller H	Art 2		Sept 20 64
9472	Morris G J	18	Co I	Sept 21 64
9830	McDermott H	18	" E	Sept 23 64
10135	Manning J	15	" A	Oct 1 64
10321	McCoy J	4	" F	Oct 3 64
10457	Mills A	15	" G	Oct 7 64
10554	McCord G	14	" E	Oct 9 64
10853	McGee P	2		Oct 13 64
11008	Murray Jas	17	Co G	Oct 16 64
12148	Mizner W	1 Sig Cor	" K	Nov 24 64
12151	Moran J	4	" F	Nov 24 64
7341	McGuire J	12	" D	Aug 31 64
12364	McGorren J	17	" C	Dec 31 64
2876	Northrup H E	4	" H	July 3 64
6803	Newcombe Jno	18	" G	Aug 20 64
6954	Nichols H	12	" A	Aug 26 64
10240	North Jacob	15	" A	Oct 3 64
12386	Neise J	6	" F	Jan 2 65
12833	Naff ——, Bugler,	Art 1	" B	April 16 65
12790	Newel L	18	" G	Mch 17 65
2368	O'Reilly Theodore	3	" K	June 23 64
7036	Ott Jno	10	" A	Aug 27 64
11846	Osrans J	Cav 4	" I	Nov 5 64
492	Partridge J W	Signal Corps		April 12 64
1607	Pace J F	18	Co C	June 4 64
1393	Pulliam Wm	Cav 1		June 13 64
3219	Pigot J	M Corps		July 12 64
3669	Ponter ——	Art 1	Co I	July 18 64
4631	Pearson S C	40	" C	Aug 3 64
5309	Pratt C E	Art 1	" M	Aug 11 64
5729	Pike Wm	Cav 5	" G	Aug 15 64
5731	Poulton Henry	19	" A	Aug 15 64
6392	Page J E	18	" B	Aug 21 64
7008	Phillips C	14	" D	Aug 27 64
7267	Pruet Jas M	19	" A	Aug 30 64
7311	Plummer G	S S 2	" D	Aug 30 64
2611	Preston Jno, Marine Cor			June 23 64
7752	Pratt J	3	Co B	Sept 8 64
9571	Post A	Art 1	" F	Sept 23 64
10951	Palmer Wm E	15	" F	Oct 14 64
11170	Pattit J S	11	" F	Oct 19 64
12142	Puck C	15	" G	Nov 24 64
4022	Quinback J	18	" G	July 23 64
11	Ross ——	19	" A	Mch 5 64
194	Rooney Mark	14	" F	Mch 27 64
404	Reardon D	13	" G	April 6 64
702	Reynolds Edwd	M Cor		April 23 64
3353	Roney F J	18	Co E	July 15 64
3820	Ritzer Geo A	Cav 5	" H	July 23 64
4276	Robison W R	Cav 6	" H	July 30 64
4957	Rhodes A	18	" B	Aug 7 64
5210	Rinkle Geo	Cav 2	" G	Aug 10 64
5904	Ronke J	10	" D	Aug 17 64
7151	Richards Theo	Cav 2	Co D	Aug 23 64
8408	Rogers Wm	18	" G	Sept 11 64
9203	Reynolds D	Cav 4	" C	Sept 19 64
10792	Reilly J	3	" B	Oct 2 64
2701	Rawson J	16	" K	June 20 64
333	Striff Jno	2	" F	April 2 64
1235	Shelton C	8	" F	May 20 64
1233	Spalding Wm	Cav 3	" B	May 21 64
1295	Scripter C E	Cav 5	" D	May 23 64
1647	Sweitzer M	19	" H	June 5 64
1714	Smith H W	15	" C	June 7 64
2073	Stoltz ——	16	" C	June 17 64
2383	Smith Jas	16	" D	June 17 64
2208	Styles J N	13	" A	June 22 64
2550	Sumser J	19	" G	June 27 64
3110	Spaulding Jas	13	" B	July 10 64
3114	Skinner L	13	" C	July 10 64
3308	Smartkash C	15	" C	July 23 64
3978	Somers P	Cav 4	" C	July 26 64
4238	Seybert J S	S S1	" H	July 29 64
4310	Smith Allen	4	" H	July 30 64
4636	Striper M	18	" D	Aug 4 64
5022	Sutgen F	15	" C	Aug 8 64
5305	Sorg A	Art 1	" M	Aug 11 64
5323	Swagger H	Cav 4	" D	Aug 12 64
5801	Sisson J	4	" D	Aug 15 64
6620	Slaughterback B	15	" H	Aug 23 64
6603	Sutgen F	16	" C	Aug 25 64
7377	Smith F	14	" E	Aug 31 64
7606	Starr Darius	S S 2	" F	Sept 2 64
7874	Snider J	11	" B	Sept 5 64
8339	Scott Jas H	Cav 2	" B	Sept 15 64
9215	Stansbury E, Mar Corps			Sept 19 64
9514	Souls J H	15	Co F	Sept 22 64
10214	Sullivan T	11	" C	Oct 2 64
11144	Schroder F	15	" C	Oct 19 64
11201	Smith J	8	" D	Oct 22 64
11223	Stanton R	14	" K	Oct 23 64
11624	Spencer J H	2	" D	Oct 30 64
11620	Shortman J	14	" E	Oct 31 64
12206	Streeter J	16	" B	Nov 28 64
12211	Stanton C	2	" I	Dec 2 64
92	Tooley Michael	18	" G	Mch 21 64
430	Taylor Amos	17	" H	April 12 64
2603	Thompson Wm	18	" G	June 23 64
2833	Truman J	Cav 5	" D	June 29 64
3163	Tyson E S	14	" B	July 17 64
4715	Tredridge A, Musician 13			Aug 4 64
7003	Taylor M D	18	Co E	Aug 31 64
7391	Turk H	18	" H	Sept 4 64
8223	Thomas J	Cav 1	" D	Sept 9 64
8229	Trainer M	6	" F	Sept 9 64
8279	Thomas L, negro	8	" D	Sept 9 64
9115	Taylor E	18	" I	Sept 18 64
11593	Topper J	11	" B	Oct 21 64
7209	Unmuch C	Art 1	" K	Sept 4 64
3357	Volmore J	3	" K	July 13 64
7022	Vancotten Wm	16	" D	Aug 27 64
7135	Vickery Wm	1	" H	Aug 28 64

United States Army—(*Continued.*)

12041	Van Buren W H	16 Co B	Nov 16 64
1259	Walker Wm	6 " D	May 21 64
1299	Worster Chas B	Cav 5	May 23 64
2732	White Thos	1 Co D	July 1 64
4023	Williams D	18 " D	July 26 64
4248	Warner S	16 " E	July 29 64
4306	Williams Jno	4 " D	July 30 64
5425	Walmor ——	10 " D	Aug 12 64
6125	Wickham G H	16 " B	Aug 19 64
6637	Wills S	15 " E	Aug 23 64
7048	Wright C S	12 " C	Aug 27 64
7109	Wadsworth B H	12 " C	Aug 23 64
7254	Warner H	2 " D	Aug 30 64
9105	Whitney J W	Cav 4 " K	Sept 13 64
9181	White Samuel	8 " F	Sept 18 64
9677	Walker John, negro	8 " F	Sept 24 64
9834	Walter I	17 Co B	Sept 27 64
10055	Wigley E	17 " C	Oct 5 64
10074	Waters ——	8 " C	Oct 5 64
10736	Waldo J M	Art 1 " K	Oct 12 64
11137	Williams C	Art 1 " K	Oct 19 64
11395	Wizmaker G	2 " M	Oct 24 64
12009	Wilson C W	15 " A	Nov 14 64
12027	Wise G B	6 " F	Nov 15 64
6436	Yarger A	18	Aug 22 64
7191	Young Robt	Cav 1 Co K	Aug 28 64
10754	Young F B	Art 2 " M	Oct 12 64
11173	Young J C	19 " A	Oct 23 64
7703	Zimmerman J	17 " D	Sept 4 64
10423	Zing P	10 " C	Oct 6 64
10450	Zimmerman M	14 " I	Oct 7 64

TOTAL 399.

UNITED STATES NAVY.

2619	Atkinson A, Nepsia,	June 27 64
4698	Anker Geo, Norman,	Aug 4 64
8071	Anderson Chas, Southfield,	Sept 7 64
2919	Bradley Jno, Southfield,	July 3 64
3475	Broderick W,	July 17 64
5072	Bowers W H, Water Witch,	Aug 8 64
12047	Boucher W, Shawsheen,	Nov 16 64
1914	Carnes Wm,	June 13 64
2149	Conant G S, Southfield,	June 18 64
2580	Carter W J, Montgomery,	June 27 64
6201	Collins Thos, Southfield,	Aug 19 64
7144	Corbet E,	Aug 29 64
7508	Connor J,	Sept 1 64
9544	Culbert J,	Sept 23 64
164	Dillingham J N, Housatonic,	Mch 23 64
6187	Duffney J,	Aug 22 64
8086	Ellis J H, Columbine,	July 9 64
4134	Evans Jno, Shawsheen,	July 23 64
4462	Earl Jas H, Paymaster Steward,	Aug 1 64
5419	Foley Daniel, Southfield,	Aug 12 64
4605	Green G C, Southfield,	Aug 3 64
8871	Goundy Thos,	Sept 15 64
1087	Heald W, Canandaigua,	April 14 64
1469	Hunter Jno, Seaman,	May 30 64
2215	Hilton Jno, Johana,	June 29 64
3448	Hodges L, Norman,	July 17 64
3793	Hughes Benj, Wabash,	July 22 64
5875	Heald H H, Merchantman,	Aug 16 64
9284	Holas Thos, Water Witch,	Sept 19 64
1432	Jones Wm, Underwriter,	May 28 64
2178	Jones Theo, Underwriter,	June 19 64
2206	Journeay Jno, Fireman,	June 19 64
6417	Jackson J, Shawsheen	Aug 22 64
8291	Johnson G P,	Sept 9 64
8858	James F A,	Sept 15 64
9392	Johnson M,	Sept 20 64
10218	Joseph F,	Oct 2 64
602	Keefe Jno, Housatonic,	April 18 64
698	Kultz A T, Ward,	April 23 64
1546	Kelley Jas, Underwriter,	June 1 64
3850	Kinney J, Water Witch,	July 24 64
7375	Lodi Jno,	Aug 31 64
2323	Lindersmith E, Montgomery,	July 3 64
4291	Lawton Jas, Ladona,	July 20 64
225	Mays A H, Mate, Norman,	Mch 29 64
2452	McDonald Jno,	June 25 64
2531	Moore A, Anna,	June 27 64
3118	Malaby P, Montgomery,	July 10 64
3343	Murphy M J,	July 15 64
3529	McDonald Jno,	July 17 64
3834	Matthews J, Underwriter,	July 22 64
4308	McHenry Daniel, Southfield,	July 29 64
4331	McCarty T, Housatonic,	July 30 64
4336	McVey K,	July 31 64
4679	McTier J,	Aug 4 64
4800	McLaughlin E,	Aug 5 64
5405	Meldon J,	Aug 13 64
6355	Marshall N B, Leipzig,	Aug 21 64
6571	McDermott P, Montgomery,	Aug 23 64
6625	Mathews W C,	Aug 25 64
6917	McLaughlin B,	Aug 26 64
7251	McGowan J, Powhattan,	Aug 30 64
11863	Maston J, Ratler,	Nov 6 64
7924	Noe M,	Sept 4 64
2237	O'Brien Wm,	June 20 64
3208	Ottinger M, Water Witch,	July 12 64
3153	Page Lyman,	July 11 64
5825	Parkham Jas C, Shawsheen,	Aug 11 64
9024	Peterson J,	Sept 17 64
2460	Quinlan N,	June 25 64
7837	Quade M,	Sept 5 64
2247	Ragan John, T Ward,	June 20 64
4631	Raymond W, T Ward,	Aug 3 64
5108	Roland Jno, Underwriter,	Aug 9 64
7003	Reynolds T J,	Aug 27 64
169	Stark John,	Mch 26 64
2010	Sullivan J, Underwriter,	June 15 64
2333	Smith Jno W, Southfield	July 3 64
3231	Sampson J R, Nav Battalion	July 13 64
4611	Smith B N, Mendota,	Aug 3 64
6592	Stanley Wm, Southfield,	Aug 23 64
11299	Smith Wm, Water Witch,	Oct 22 64

United States Navy — (*Continued.*)

1713 Thomas Samuel, Southfield, June 7 64
1851 Thomas John, Southfield, June 11 64
3757 Turner Wm, July 1 64
4159 Trymer James, Southfield, July 28 64
7445 Tobin Michael, Sept 1 64
8302 Ta B F, Southfield, Sept 10 64
1646 Willis J P, June 5 64
3004 Wilson A, Southfield, July 7 64
3878 Williams M W, July 24 64
4118 Willis M, Southfield, July 28 64
4198 Williams C, Aries July 29 64
5820 Wordell G K, Aug 16 64
5990 Warren W H, Aug 17 64
6458 Wooley M, Aug 22 64
7503 Walsh Jas, Sept 1 64
8104 Welch V, Southfield, Sept 7 64
10565 West Jno, Southfield, Oct 9 64

TOTAL 99.

MISCELLANEOUS.

1460 Addley A, Citizen, Oct 25 64
887 Amos J, Ringold Bat F, May 4 64
2977 Augar A, July 7 64
282 Bane S, Ringold Bat A, April 1 64
2072 Beatty D, Ringold Bat F, June 17 64
4327 Baker Jno, Teamster, July 30 64
4904 Beimmar L, Aug 6 64
5747 Butterfield Jas, Citizen, Aug 15 64
6100 Blair H, Citizen, Aug 18 64
6366 Bidwell C, Citizen Teamster, Aug 21 64
8102 Burkhead W, Prunell's Legion, Sept 7 64
9344 Blood G P, Sept 20 64
9591 Brogdin D C, Sept 23 64
10500 Burk C, Citizen, Oct 8 64
10602 Bishop J, Citizen Teamster, Oct 10 64
10963 Brown Geo, Bridge's Bat Oct 15 64
12342 Boland Jas, Prunell's Cavalry Dec 26 64
177 Cannon Wm, Teamster, Mch 26 64
389 Campbell D, Ringold Bat E, April 6 64
431 Childers C H, April 8 64
1195 Cobb J, Citizen Teamster, May 13 64
1881 Clark M, Citizen Teamster, June 12 64
3399 Cable C, Citizen, July 16 64
3972 Cregger J F, Musician, July 25 64
6315 Crowley Pat, Aug 20 64
9245 Carroll C, Teamster, 19 Art Cor, Sept 19 64
10485 Corbit J, Oct 7 64
10872 Carey Thos, Oct 13 64
11726 Collins, Cit Teamster, Nov 1 64
12449 Carroll J, Cit Teamster, Jan 13 65
752 Deems P, Ringold Bat E April 26 64
2620 Delp Geo, Cit Teamster, June 28 64
4334 Davis J, Citizen, July 30 64
5866 Danfirth Geo A, Aug 16 64
8202 Delmore W, Cit, Sept 8 64
11084 Dubin M, Cit Teamster, Oct 18 64
11248 Delhanta Wm, Cit, Oct 21 64
182 England E, Mch 27 64
8923 Evans M, Cit, July 25 64
Everett T S, Cit, Md, Aug 30 64
157 Freeman Jno, Mch 25 64
453 Fenley R, Cit, April 9 64
1116 Fannon A, Cit, May 15 64
2332 Faster W, Tel Operator June 22 64
2435 Farrell M, Cit, June 25 64
10478 Flickison J, Oct 7 64
4808 Fitzgerald — Aug 5 64
5078 Frank F M, Wilder's Bat, Aug 8 64
5609 Fox Henry, Cit Teamster, Aug 14 64
7643 Ford P, Teamster, Sept 3 64
9084 Foucks H C, Keyes' Ind't Cav, Sept 18 64
11315 Ferrall M C, Teamster, Oct 22 64
2329 Gildea D, Cit, July 1 64
4115 Grogran D, July 28 64
4747 Gishart J, Aug 5 64
6109 Graham E, Citizen, Aug 19 64
7854 Gorb S, Sept 5 64
9747 Goodman J O, Sept 25 64
10672 Gillman John, Oct 11 64
11862 Goodyear F, Citizen, Nov 6 64
10717 Graves Wm E, Oct 11 64
219 Heartless S, Mch 29 64
264 Hammond S, Teamster, Mch 31 64
606 Hoffman Chas, Cit Teamster, April 13 64
1274 Harkins John, Teamster, May 22 64
2370 Hammond J, Cit Teamster, June 23 64
3322 Hudson G W, Cit Teamster July 12 64
4244 Hughes P, July 29 64
6670 Hanmay D, Cit Teamster, Aug 18 64
8055 Herriage J, Teamster, Sept 7 64
8756 Harkins D S, M M B, Sept 14 64
9006 Hyatt J, Sept 17 64
9051 Hulbert J H S, Sept 17 64
9297 Hall M, A A S, Sept 19 64
9425 Hart Isaac, Cit Teamster, Sept 21 64
10262 Hines Daniel, Oct 3 64
10331 Hopkins John, Oct 4 64
11934 Heckinbridge — Nov 9 64
12456 Harrington J, Jan 15 65
8722 Imhagg — Sept 14 64
4794 Jones Chas, Citizen Teamster, Aug 5 64
6854 Jacobs W C, Citizen, Aug 25 64
12714 Johnson J, Cit, Canada, Mch 1 65
2203 Kingland W H, Cit, June 20 64
3515 Kerr E, Cit Teamster, June 18 64
6273 Kins W H, Cit Teamster, Aug 20 64
7864 Knight J B, Cit Teamster, Sept 5 64
9467 Kellogg E L, Cit, S'g fl'ld Sept 21 64
546 Lee Jas, Cit Teamster, April 14 64
1772 Lafferty Wm, Ring Bat, June 5 64
3689 Lummo Rob't, Citizen, July 21 64
10353 Linton E, Ringold Bat, Oct 5 64
76 Morton J B, Ringold Cav A, Mch 20 64
203 McMahon Pat, Mch 28 64
220 Morrison F, Cit Teamster, Mch 29 64
865 Mower W, Cit, May 3 64

Miscellaneous — (*Continued.*)

2285	McAtie M, Teamster,	June 21 64
2432	Manning B F, Cit Teamster,	June 21 64
2373	McEnshon Peter,	June 23 64
3450	Moyer J,	July 17 64
4017	Messenger H M, Cit,	July 26 64
5387	Morland J S, Cit Teamster,	Aug 12 64
5996	McGee J,	Aug 17 64
6380	McKenna F,	Aug 21 64
8039	McGuire J, Cit,	Sept 6 64
9135	Myers Jno,	Sept 18 64
9247	McDonald J,	Sept 19 64
9616	Munch Christian, Top Eng,	Sept 23 64
12535	McDonald H H, Cit, Ohio,	Jan 27 65
6666	Monteith M, Cit Teamster,	Aug 24 64
184	Newton Wm, Teamster,	Mch 27 64
7074	Norton E, Citizen,	Aug 28 64
8510	Nichols J, Teamster, 15 Art C,	Sept 12 64
4190	Osborne J, Citizen,	July 23 64
5414	Oliver W W,	Aug 12 64
719	Pringle Wm, Cit Teamster	April 25 64
1855	Podzas L, Cit Teamster,	June 12 64
5920	Poole C,	Aug 17 64
8893	Powers G, Citizen,	Sept 16 64
9010	Potter S D,	Sept 17 64
9366	Phillips B B, Teamster,	Sept 20 64
12354	Parker Jas, Cit Teamster,	Dec 29 64
10100	Parkhurst W L, 1 M M B,	Sept 30 64
853	Quinn Jas, Citizen,	May 3 64
5394	Quinlan P, Cit Teamster,	Aug 12 64
5768	Quinn ——, Citizen,	Aug 15 64
3542	Reed A R, Independent,	July 18 64
3779	Rand J, Cit Teamster,	July 22 64
5986	Ronley J,	Aug 17 64
10111	Rendig C H, Citizen,	Oct 1 64
10453	Ryan John, Citizen,	Oct 7 64
11131	Relen R, Citizen,	Oct 18 64
11703	Richardson J C, 1 M M B,	Oct 30 64
449	Scott Blair, Citizen	April 9 64
2431	Smith P, M M B,	June 24 64
2440	St Clair Benj, Cit Teamster,	June 25 64
2532	Slater Chas, Cit Teamster,	June 27 64
2959	Spicer W, Cit Teamster,	July 6 64
3000	Stout Chas, Citizen,	July 7 64
3532	Shunk J, Citizen,	July 20 64
4008	Smith H, Bridge's Bat,	July 26 64
4343	Sawyer J D,	Aug 6 64
9729	Stanton J, Citizen,	Sept 25 64
10315	Smays David,	Oct 12 64
136	Thompson Jno, Teamster,	Mch 24 64
1531	Tullis L B G, Citizen,	June 1 64
2593	Thompson Geo,	June 30 64
3409	Thomas J H, Cit Teamster,	July 16 64
3396	Taylor J W, Citizen,	July 24 64
12337	Tucer B, Citizen, Indiana,	Dec 26 64
9397	Ulmgender G, M M B, C,	Sept 21 64
9497	Vankirk W, Ringold Bat,	Sept 21 64
9683	Vandier W M, Cit, Phila, Pa,	Sept 24 64
739	Wilkins A, Ringold Bat,	April 29 64
1092	Welsh G L, Citizen Teamster,	May 14 64
1121	White George, Citizen,	May 15 64
2784	Wilson D E, Ringold Bat,	July 2 64
10053	Weir ——, Cit Teamster,	Oct 14 64
11606	Woods R C, Knapp's Bat,	Oct 28 64
4730	Wright Chas, Cit Teamster,	Aug 4 64
4839	Ward John, Cit Teamster,	Aug 6 64
9043	Williams F G,	Sept 17 64
10073	Wentgel Thos,	Sept 30 64
4127	Young Henry, Cit Teamster,	July 28 64
12246	Young D, Citizen Teamster,	Nov 8 64

TOTAL 165.

Men that were Hung.

1	Sarsfield Jno, 144 N Y,	July 11 64
2	Collins Wm, 88 Pa D	July 11 64
3	Curtis Chas, 5 R I Art A,	July 11 64
4	Delaney Pat, 83 Pa E,	July 11 64
5	Mun A, U S Navy,	July 11 64
6	Rickson W R, U S Navy,	July 11 64

Colonel Moore, of the U. S. Quartermaster's Department, in his report to the Quartermaster-general, says of the graveyard at Andersonville:—

"United States soldiers while prisoners at Andersonville had been detailed to inter their companions; and by a simple stake at the head of each grave, which bore a number corresponding with a similarly numbered name upon the Andersonville Hospital Record, I was enabled to identify and mark with a neat tablet, similar to those in the cemeteries at Washington, the number, name, rank, regiment, company, and date of death of twelve thousand, four hundred and sixty-one (12,461) graves, there being but four hundred and fifty-one (451) that bore the sad inscription 'Unknown U. S. Soldier.'"

RECAPITULATION OF DEATHS BY STATES.

ALABAMA	15	NEW JERSEY . . .	170
CONNECTICUT	315	NEW YORK . . .	2572
DELAWARE	45	NORTH CAROLINA .	17
DIST. OF COLUMBIA .	14	OHIO	1030
ILLINOIS	850	PENNSYLVANIA . .	1811
INDIANA	594	RHODE ISLAND . . .	74
IOWA	174	TENNESSEE . . .	738
KANSAS	5	VERMONT	212
KENTUCKY	436	VIRGINIA . . .	288
LOUISIANA	1	WISCONSIN	244
MAINE	233	U. S. ARMY . . .	399
MARYLAND	194	U. S. NAVY	100
MASSACHUSETTS . .	768	Citizens, Teamsters, &c. .	166
MINNESOTA	79	Men that were Hung by the Prisoners . . .	6
MICHIGAN	630	Unknown U. S. Soldiers . .	443
MISSOURI	97	Died in Small Pox Hospital .	68
NEW HAMPSHIRE . . .	124		
TOTAL			12,912.

The following exhibit, as collated from the Hospital Register and Prison Records, will be found to be as correct as any yet published:

Total number of Prisoners on hand at end of

APRIL, 1864	10,427	NOVEMBER, 1864	1,359
MAY, 1864	18,454	DECEMBER, 1864 . . .	4,706
JUNE, 1864	26,367	JANUARY, 1865	5,046
JULY, 1864	31,678	FEBRUARY, 1865 . . .	5,851
AUGUST, 1864	31,693	MARCH, 1865	3,319
SEPTEMBER, 1864 . . .	8,218	APRIL, 1865	51
OCTOBER, 1864	4,208		

Deaths in Stockade and Hospital during the Existence of the Prison.

MARCH, 1864	283	OCTOBER, 1864	4590
APRIL, 1864	576	NOVEMBER, 1864	492
MAY, 1864	708	DECEMBER, 1864	160
JUNE, 1864	1201	JANUARY, 1865	190
JULY, 1864	1817	FEBRUARY, 1865 . . .	139
AUGUST, 1864	3076	MARCH, 1865	192
SEPTEMBER, 1864* . . .	2794	APRIL, 1865	32
TOTAL			12,912.

* The greater number of deaths in September and October, in proportion to the number in prison, will be explained by the fact that all the well men were removed from Andersonville in these months, and none were left except the sick and wounded.

Day and date of greatest number of Prisoners at Andersonville—33,114—August 8th, 1864.

Day and date of greatest number of deaths, August 23d, 1864, 127.

Number of Prisoners received during its occupation, 45,613.

Daily average of deaths during its occupation, 29¾.

Ratio of mortality per 1000 of mean strength, 24 per cent.

Mortality of 18,000 registered patients, 75 per cent.

The Diseases of which the Prisoners died will be found in the following classification:

Anasarca	377	Hydrocele	1
Asphyxia	7	Hemorrhoids	1
Ascites	24	Jaundice	9
Asthma	3	Laryngitis	4
Bronchitis	93	Nostalgia	7
Catarrh	55	Nephritis	4
Constipation	5	Phthisis	137
Diarrhœa, Chronic	4000	Pleuritis	54
" Acute	817	Pneumonia	321
Debilitas	198	Paralysis	1
Diphtheria	3	Rheumatism	83
Dyspepsia	2	Scurvy	3574
Diabetes	1	Syphilis	7
Dysenteria	1384	Scrofula	3
Erysipelas	11	Stricture	1
Febris Typhoides	229	Sunstroke	52
Fistula	2	Small Pox	68
Fracture	1	Vaccine Ulcers	4
Febris Remittens	177	Gunshot Wounds	155
Gonorrhœa	3	Unknown	443
Gangrene	678	Hung in Stockade	6

TOTAL . . . . 12,912.

B

I would not consider my work complete, without a list of the names of the Federal officers that were confined at Camp Asylum, Columbia, S. C., and who were more or less the recipients of the kind consideration of General John H. Winder, in his efforts, through Mr. J. G. Gibbes, to alleviate their sufferings whilst in prison at that place. The generosity displayed by him to those men, in permitting them to buy Confederate currency with which to procure extra rations, ought forever to silence all clamors that have been made against him of inhumanity to Federal prisoners of war. That there were men amongst these Federal officers possessed with the instincts of gratitude, and those better feelings that tend to ennoble our race, I do not deny. Notwithstanding all this, none of them, it seems, have had the kindness to come forward and denounce those wicked slanders and revengeful anathemas that have been from time to time heaped upon those who had charge of the captives.

A List of Officers Imprisoned at Camp Asylum, Columbia, S. C.

Name.	Rank.	Command.	Residence.
Aldrich C S	Cap	85th N Y Vol	Canandaigua N Y
Austin J W	Lieut	5th Iowa Cav	Lansing Iowa
Alters J B	Cap	75th O Vol	Spring Dale O
Albaugh Wm	"	51st Pa Vol	Morristown Pa
Alger A B	Lieut	22d O Bat	Mansfield O
Avery W B	Cap	132d N Y Vol	
Allender W F	Lieut	7th Tenn Cav	Memphis Tenn
Adair W A	"	51st Ind Vol	North Salem Ind
Albro S A	"	80th Ill Vol	Upper Alton Ill
Adams J	"	" "	Nashville Ill
Allstaedt C L	Adjt	54th N Y Vol	Newark N J

NAME.	RANK.	COMMAND.	RESIDENCE.
Ahern M	Lieut	10th W Va Vol	
Ahlert T H	"	45th N Y Vol	New York City
Adams C A	Cap	1st Vt Cav	Wallingford Vt
Alban H H	"	21st O Vol	
Andrews H B	"	17th Mich Vol	
Apple H	Lieut	1st Md Cav	
Anderson C S	"	3d Iowa Vol	
Allee A	"	16th Ill Cav	Lincoln Ill
Abernathy H C	A Adjt	" "	Paris Mo
Acker G D	Lieut	123d O Vol	Fostoria O
Adkins P	"	2d Tenn Vol	
Aigan John	Cap	5th R I Art	Pawtucket R I
Adams J G B	Lieut	19th Mass Vol	Groveland Mass
Alexander E P	"	26th Mich Vol	Detroit Mich
Anderson H M	"	3d Me Vol	
Anderson J F	"	2d Pa Art	Philadelphia Pa
Anderson R W	"	122d O Vol	Columbus O
Andrus W R	"	16th Conn Vol	East Berlin Conn
Abbey A L	"	8th Mich Cav	Armada Mich
Arthur J A	Cap	8th Ky Cav	
Arthurs S C	"	67th Pa Vol	Brookville Pa
Allen S	"	85th N Y Vet Vol	Black Creek N Y
Adams S B	"	" " "	Lenox O
Andrews S T	Lieut	" " "	Black Creek N Y
Albright J	Cap	87th Pa Vol	York Pa
Abbott A O	Lieut	1st N Y Drag	Portageville N Y
Armstrong T S	"	122d O Vol	Gratiot O
Airey W	Cap	15th Pa Cav	Philadelphia Pa
Appleget A S	Lieut	2d N J Cav	Hightstown N J
Allen Robert	"	2d N J Drag	
Auer M	Cap	15th N Y Cav	Syracuse N Y
Anshutz H T	Lieut	12th W Va Vol	Moundville W Va
Adams H W	"	89th O Vol	Frankfort Ill
Austin G A	R Q M	14 & 15 Ill V Bat	Woodstock Ill
Albin H S	Lieut	79th Ill Vol	Tuscola Ill
Andrews E E	"	22d Mich Vol	Milford Mich
Alden G C	R Q M	112th Ill Vol	Annawan Ill
Ashworth J H	Col	1st Ga U Vol	
Adams W C	Lieut	2d Ky Cav	Star Furnace Ky
Amory C B	Cap	A A Gen	Jamaica Plains Mass
Affleck E T	Adjt	170th O Nat Gds	Bridgeport O
Alexander A H	Cap	103d Pa Vol	Callensburg Pa
Abbott E A	Lieut	23d O Vet Vol	Olmsted Falls O
Belger James	Cap	1st R I Art	
Baker S S	Lieut	6th Mo Vol	
Butler C P	"	29th Ind Vol	Peru Ill
Baird, J F	"	1st W Va Vol	Wheeling W V
Bricker W H	"	3d Pa Vol	Newville Pa
Bick W C	Cap	62d Pa Vol	
Braiday Count S	Lieut	2d N J Cav	Vienna, Austria
Bulon A	"	3d N J Cav	
Burdick C H	Cap	1st Tenn Cav	

NAME.	RANK.	COMMAND.	RESIDENCE.
Bartram D S	Lieut	17th Conn Vol	Redding Conn
Brown J A	Cap	85th N Y Vet Vol	Wellsville N Y
Bradley A B	R Q M	" " "	Friendship N Y
Butts L A	Lieut	" " "	Cuba N Y
Bowers G W	Cap	101st Pa Vol	Pittsburg Pa
Benner H S	"	" "	Gettysburg Pa
Bowers G A	Lieut	16th Conn Vol	Hartford Conn
Blakeslee B F	"	" "	New Britain Conn
Bruns H	"	" "	Bridgeport Conn
Bryson R R	"	103d Pa Vol	Butler Pa
Burns S D	"	" "	Circlesville Pa
Bierbower W	"	87th Pa Vol	York Pa
Beegle D F	"	101st Pa Vol	Ramsburg Pa
Bryan J H	"	184th Pa Vol	Harrisburg Pa
Berry A	Cap	3d Md Cav	Baltimore Md
Bunting G	Lieut	5th Md Cav	Baltimore Md
Bascomb R	"	50th N Y Vol	Rome N Y
Baldwin M R	Cap	2d Wis Vol	
Blake	Lieut	3d Me Vol	
Brown W H	"	93d O Vol	Dayton O
Beard J V	"	89th O Vol	
Byron C	Cap	3d O Vol	
Banks B V	"	13th Ky Cav	New England O
Burch J	"	42d Ind Vol	Winslow Ind
Bailey G W	Lieut	3d O Vol	Columbus O
Brownell F G	"	51st Ind Vol	Dayton O
Booker A H	"	73d Ind Vol	Westville Ind
Brown J L	"	" "	
Barlow J W	"	51st Ind Vol	London Ind
Bath W	"	132d N Y Vol	
Bending H R	Cap	61st O Vol	Circleville O
Bush J G	"	16th Ill Cav	
Blinn L B	"	100th O Vol	
Baldwin C W	Lieut	2d N J Vol	New York City
Bartley R	"	U S A Sig Corps	
Bradley G	Cap	2d N J Vol	
Brandt C W	Lieut	1st N Y Vet Cav	Belmont N Y
Bontin C W	Cap	4th Vt Vol	Chester Vt
Barrett D W	"	89th O Vol	Ramesboro O
Brandt O B	Lieut	17th O Vol	Lancaster O
Byers S H M	Adjt	5th Iowa Vol	Newton Iowa
Barker H P	Lieut	1st R I Cav	
Boone S G	"	88th Pa Vol	Reading Pa
Bisbee L C	"	16th Me Vol	Canton Mills Me
Bisbee G D	"	" "	" "
Button G W	"	22d Mich Vol	Farmington Micl
Barker H E	"	22d N Y Cav	
Butler T H	Col	5th Ind Cav	Clifty Ind
Bowen C D	Cap	18th Conn Vol	
Bennett B	"	22d N Y Cav	Hammondsport N Y
Brush Z T	Lieut	100th O Vol	Clyde O
Bigley C H	"	82d N Y Vol	

NAME.	RANK.	COMMAND.	RESIDENCE.
Burns M	Lieut	13th N Y Cav	New York City
Bassett M M	"	53d Ill Vol	
Bortwick N	Cap	20th O Vol	
Brown C A	Lieut	1st N Y Art	
Benson J F	Cap	120th Ill Vol	Vienna Ill
Bosport W R	Lieut	1st N Y Vol	
Burns J	"	57th Pa Vol	Clark's Port Pa
Barton J L	"	49th Pa Vol	
Beebee B C	Cap	13th Ind Vol	Seneca Falls N Y
Buchanan W	Lieut	76th N Y Vol	Cohoes N Y
Benson A N	Cap	1st D C Cav	
Barkley C	Lieut	149th Pa Vol	
Blane W	"	43d N Y Vol	Albany N Y
Bristol J H	"	1st Conn Cav	Derby Conn
Burpee E A	Cap	19th Me Vol	Rockland Me
Bryant J W	"	5th N Y Cav	
Biebel H	"	6th Conn Vol	Bridgeport Conn
Bixby H L	Lieut	9th Me Vol	Norridgewock Me
Byrns J M	Cap	2d Pa R C Vol	Philadelphia Pa
Barrett J A	"	7th Pa R C Vol	" "
Burkholder D W	Lieut	" " "	Shippensburg Pa
Beal E	Cap	8th Tenn Vol	
Bayard G A	"	148th Pa Vol	
Brun S	Lieut	81st Ill Vol	
Brady W H	"	2d Del Vol	Wilmington Del
Breon J	"	148th Pa Vol	Potter's Mills Pa
Bischoff P	"	6th U S Art	St Louis Mo
Burnett G M	"	4th Ind Cav	Terre Haute Ind
Blair B F	Adjt	123d O Vol	Norwalk O
Boyce T W	Lieut	" "	
Breckenridge F A	"	" "	Monroeville O
Boyd W J	"	5th Mich Cav	
Brown W L	"	17th Tenn Vol	
Burrows S W	"	1st N Y Vet Cav	
Brown S	A M Mte	U S Navy	
Beman W M	Cap	1st Vt Cav	
Boaz E P	"	20th Ill Vol	Lockport Ill
Bryan G	Adjt	18th Pa Cav	Vincenttown N Y
Bath H	Lieut	45th N Y Vol	New York City
Beadle M	"	123d N Y Vol	South Easton N Y
Bigelow A J	Cap	79th Ill Vol	Kansas Ill
Borchess L T	"	67th Pa Vol	Dyberry Pa
Brown G L	Lieut	101st Pa Vol	Milton Pa
Blanchard Geo A	Cap	85th Ill Vol	Havana Ill
Bradford John	Lieut	4th N J Vol	Hoboken N J
Borchess T F	"	67th Pa Vol	Honesdale Pa
Barnes O P	"	3d O Vol	Barnesville O
Bremen S	Cap	3d Mich Vol	Georgetown Mich
Brickenhoff M	Lieut	42d N Y Vol	New York City
Barse J R	"	5th Mich Cav	
Bliss A T	Cap	10th N Y Cav	Peterboro N Y
Buckley H	Lieut	4th N H Vol	New York City

NAME.	RANK.	COMMAND.	RESIDENCE.
Bader H	Lieut	29th Mo Vol	Cape Girardeau Mo
Blae J G	"	3d O Vol	Cardington O
Boughton S H	"	71st Pa Vol	
Barnes A T	"	14th Ill Vet Batt	
Beasley J L	"	81st Ill Vol	Fredonia Ill
Baker H D	Capt	120th Ill Vol	Golconda Ill
Burke T F	"	16th Conn Vol	Hartford Conn
Barnes W J	"		
Bennett W F	"	39th Iowa Vol	Osceola Iowa
Bassett W H	Lieut	79th Ill Vol	Arcola Ill
Botts W O	"	10th Wis Vol	
Biggs J	"	123d Ill Vol	
Bennett F J	"	18th U S Inf	
Brown J C	"	15th " "	Dayton O
Bryant M C	"	42d Ill Vol	Kankakee City Ill
Butler W O	"	10th Wis Vol	
Brooks E P	Adjt		
Barringer A	Lieut	44th N Y Vol	Nassau N Y
Ballard S H	"	6th Mich Cav	Grand Rapids Mich
Brown J H	Cap	17th Iowa Vol	Des Moines Iowa
Byron S	Lieut	2d U S Inf	
Blaire Geo E	"	17th O Vol	Lancaster O
Bishop F P	"	4th Tenn Cav	
Bowen C T	"	4th R I Vol	Wickford R I
Bateman Wm	"	9th Mich Cav	Ypsilanti Mich
Baird Wm	"	23d U S C T	China Mich
Barnum S D	Cap	" "	North Rome Pa
Biller J N	Lieut	2d Pa Art	Martinsburg W Va
Baker W F	Cap	87th Pa Vol	Gettysburg Pa
Bowley F S	Lieut	30th U S C T	Worcester Mass
Boettger C	"	2d Md Vol	Baltimore Md
Bogle A	Major	35th U S C T	Boston Mass
Barnard W A	Lieut	20th Mich Vol	Lansing Mich
Blasse Wm	"	43d N Y Vol	Albany N Y
Buffum M P	Lt Col	4th R I Vol	Providence R I
Brown C O	Lieut	31st Me Vol	Moro Me
Beecham R K	"	23d U S C T	Sun Prairie Mo
Briscoe A M	"	Cole's Md Cav	Baltimore Md
Burbank H H	Cap	32d Me Vol	Limerick Me
Bearce H M	Lieut	" " "	West Minot Me
Bittenger C L	"	76th Pa Vol	
Bartlett O E	Cap	31st Me Vol	Skowhegan Me
Braidey A J	Lieut	54th Pa Vol	
Bell C A	L&ADC		
Burton R	"	9th N Y Art	
Beebe H E	"	22d N Y Cav	
Coleman S S	Lieut	12th Ky Cav	
Chalfant J T	Cap	11th Pa Vol	Pittsburg Pa
Call C H	"	29th Ill Vol	Inkster Mich
Caswell H	Lieut	95th Ill Vol	
Carpenter E D	"	18th Conn Vol	Putnam Conn
Caldwell C	"	1st Wis Cav	Lind Wis

Name.	Rank.	Command.	Residence.
Cook A A	Lieut	9th O Cav	Springfield O
Casdorph C H	"	7th W Va Cav	Kanawha W Va
Casler B G	Cap	154th N Y Vol	East Randolph N Y
Cook A L	Lieut	2d Pa Vol	
Cusac J	Cap	21st O Vol	McComb Ohio
Canfield S S	"	" "	
Catin M	"	" "	
Coffin V L	Lieut	31st Me Vol	Harrington Me
Chandler G A	"	5th Me Vol	
Coren J H	"	1st W Va Cav	
Culver F B	"	123d O Vol	
Carothers J J	"	" "	
Claghorn A C	"	21st O Vol	
Carey S E	"	13th Mass Vol	Boston Mass
Campbell L A	"	152d N Y Vol	Cherry Valley N Y
Carnes W C	Cap	2d Tenn Vol	
Center A P	"	" " "	
Carroll E	Lieut	11th Tenn Vol	
Carr C W	"	4th Vt Vol	
Cunningham J	"	7th Pa R C Vol	Leesport Pa
Coslett C	"	115th Pa Vol	Philadelphia Pa
Cooper R	"	7th N J Vol	Jersey City N J
Crawford C H	"	183d Pa Vol	Philadelphia Pa
Cromack S O	"	77th N Y Vol	Bennington Vt
Correll H	"	2d Vt Vol	New Haven Vt
Cornell C H	"	95th N Y Vol	New York City
Cutter C H	"	" " "	Boston Mass
Creasey G W	"	35th Mass Vol	Newburyport Mass
Chute R H	"	59th " "	Chelsea Mass
Cross H M	"	" " "	Newburyport Mass
Chapin H A	"	95th N Y Vol	
Clyde J D	Cap	76th " "	Cherry Valley N Y
Cahill W	Lieut	" " "	Solon N Y
Casler J L	"	" " "	Otsego N Y
Chisman H	"	7th Ind Vol	Cincinnati O
Cooper A	"	12th N Y Cav	Oswego N Y
Cribben H	"	140th N Y Vol	Rochester N Y
Curtis G M	"	" " "	" "
Caldwell J S	"	16th Ill Cav	Chicago Ill
Caslin C S	"	151st N Y Vol	
Crossley S	"	118th Pa Vol	Philadelphia Pa
Chauncey C R	Cap	34th Mass Vol	Westfield Mass
Carlisle S B	Lieut	145th Pa Vol	Luthersburg Pa
Conover S D	Cap	125th Ill Vol	Squaw Villgae N J
Cole O L	Lieut	50th Ill Vol	Elgin Ill
Cain J H	"	104th N Y Vol	Albany N Y
Cassell E F	"	11th Iowa Vol	Illinois City Ill
Chambers J H	"	103d Pa Vol	Apollo Pa
Cottingham E	"	35th Pa Vol	
Coddington J P	Vet Sur	8th Iowa Cav	Dubuque Iowa
Cole A F	Cap	59th N Y Vol	Lowville N Y
Curtiss W H	Adjt	19th Mass Vol	Randolph Mass

Name.	Rank.	Command.	Residence.
Clark J W	Lieut	59th N Y Vol	Butler O
Clark J H	"	1st Mass Art	Boston Mass
Case D L Jr	Adjt	102d N Y Vol	Lansing Mich
Cope J D	Lieut	116th Pa Vol	Uniontown Pa
Cove J W	"	6th W Va Cav	
Coulter W J	"	15th Mass Vol	Clinton Mass
Cubbetson W M	"	30th Ind Vol	
Casey J	"	45th N Y Vol	Tuckahoe N Y
Carter W H	"	5th Pa R C Vol	Elmsport Pa
Chittenden J L	"	5th Ind Cav	Knoxville Ill
Conney W H	"	69th N Y Vol	New York City
Cameron P	"	16th N Y Cav	
Campbell W F	"	51st Pa Vol	Slifer Pa
Cameron J F	"	5th Pa Cav	Philadelphia Pa
Carr J P	Cap	93d Ind Vol	Austin Ind
Clegg M	Lieut	5th Ind Cav	
Curtice H A	"	157th N Y Vol	Courtland N Y
Coffin J A	"	" "	
Collins W A	Cap	10th Wis Vol	Milwaukee Wis
Carlisle J B	Lieut	2d W Va Cav	Ironton O
Christopher W	"	" "	Willow Grove Pa
Chandler G W	"	1st W Va Cav	Birmingham O
Chatburn J	"	150th Pa Vol	Germantown Pa
Childs J W	"	16th Me Vol	Farmington Me
Chase H R	"	1st Vt H Art	Guilford Centre Vt
Conover W H	"	22d N Y Cav	Norwich N Y
Clark J A	Cap	7th Mich Cav	
Cook W B	Lieut	140th Pa Vol	Candor Pa
Califf B F	"	2d W S S S	Salem Mass
Cook E F	Major	2d N Y Cav	
Cooke H P	A A G		Deckerstown N J
Crocker H	Lieut	1st N J Cav	Port Jervis N Y
Camp T B C	Cap	52d Pa Vol	Camptown Pa
Clark L S	"	62d N Y Vol	Saratoga Springs N Y
Chapin H C	"	4th Vt Vol	Elmira N Y
Conyngham J B	Lt Col	52d Pa Vol	
Christopher J	Cap	16th U S Inf	
Cochrane M A	"	" "	Oswego N Y
Causten M C	Lieut	19th U S Inf	Washington D C
Chubbuck D B	"	19th Mass Vol	
Carpenter S D	"	3d O Vol	Springfield O
Carley A A	Cap	73d Ind Vol	
Connelly R J	Lieut	73d Ill Vol	
Cartwright A G	Cap	85th N Y Vet Vol	Philip's Creek N Y
Clark M L	"	101st Pa Vol	Mansfield Pa
Compher A	"	" "	Rainsburg Pa
Clapp J B	Adjt	16th Conn Vol	Weathersfield Conn
Case A G	Lieut	" "	Simsburg Conn
Cratty E G	Cap	103d Pa Vol	Butler Pa
Coats H A	"	85th N Y Vet Vol	Wellsville N Y
Crooks S J	Col	22d N Y Cav	Rochester N Y
Case S F	Cap	2d O Cav	Wellington O

NAME.	RANK.	COMMAND.	RESIDENCE.
Cutler J	Cap	34th O Vol	
Coglin T	"	14th N Y H Art	
Cord T A	Lieut	19th U S Inf	Danville Ind
Cloadt J	Cap	119th N Y Vol	
Calkins W W	Lieut	104th Ill Vol	Ottawa Ill
Craig J	Cap	1st W Va Vol	Wheeling W Va
Colville J W	"	5th Mich Vol	E Saginaw Mich
Crosby T J	"	157th Pa Vol	Titusville Pa
Cohen M	"	4th Ky Vol	Louisville Ky
Copeland J R	"	7th O Vol	Locust Grove O
Creps F A M	Lieut	77th Pa Vol	
Curtis R	"	4th Ky Vol	Louisville Ky
Clements J	"	15th Ky Vol	Hewalton Ind
Caldwell D B	"	75th O Vol	
Cubbison J C	"	101st Pa Vol	Irish Ripple Pa
Crawford H P	Cap	2d Ill Cav	
Chase E E	"	1st R I Cav	
Coffin G A	Adjt	29th Ind Vol	
Cockran T G	Lieut	77th Pa Vol	Chambersburg Pa
Conrad W F	Cap	25th Iowa Vol	
Carperts L M	"	18th Wis Vol	
Cox J L	Lieut	21st Ill Vol	Hutsonville Ill
Cunningham M	"	42d N Y Vol	Norwich Conn
Charters A M	"	17th Iowa Vol	Leavenworth Kan
Carpenter J Q	"	150th Pa Vol	Germantown Pa
Campbell B F	Cap		
Clark H L	Lieut	2d Mass Art	Springfield Mass
Copeland W A	"	10th Mich Vol	
Cuniffe H	"	13th Ill Vol	
Carpenter E N	Cap	6th Pa Cav	Germantown Pa
Clemmons T	Lieut	13th Ill Vol	
Crocker Geo A	A A G		New York City
Cook W C	Adjt	9th Mich Cav	Tecumseh Mich
Cowles H F	Lieut	18th Conn Vol	Norwich Conn
Cramer C P	"	21st N Y Cav	West Troy N Y
Clancey C W	Lt Col	52d O Vol	Smithfield O
Coram Geo	R Q M	2d Ky Cav	Greenupsburg Ky
Case M B	Lieut	23d U S C T	Owattona Minn
Cline D G	"	75th O V M I	Logan Hocking O
Conn C G	"	1st M S S	Elkhart Mich
Cook J L	"	6th Iowa Vol	St Louis Mo
Cunningham M	"	1st Vt H Art	
Copeland C D	"	58th Mass Vol	Fall River Mass
Chamberlain V B	Cap	7th Conn Vol	
Catlin J E	Lieut	45th Pa Vol	Wellsboro' Pa
Cashell C P	"	12th Pa Cav	
Clark M W	Cap	11th Iowa Cav	Columbus City Iowa
Channel J R	Lieut	1st Ill Art	Ottawa Ill
Day J W	"	17th Mass Vol	Arevill Mass
Damrell W S	"	13th Mass Vol	Boston Mass
Dearing G A	"	16th Me Vol	
Duferr T J	"	5th Mich Cav	

NAME.	RANK.	COMMAND.	RESIDENCE.
Dickerson A A	Lieut	16th Conn Vol	Hartford Conn
Donaghy J	Cap	103d Pa Vol	Allegany City Pa
Davis W G	Lieut	27th Mass Vol	
Day A P	"	15th Conn Vol	New Haven Conn
Dewees J H	Major	13th Pa Cav	Philadelphia Pa
Daniels E S	Cap	35th U S C T	Old Cambridge Mass
Dietz Henry	"	45th N Y Vol	New York City
Dodge C C	"	20th Mich Vol	Marshall Mich
Dieffenbach A C	Lieut	73d Pa Vol	Philadelphia Pa
Dewees T B	"	2d U S Cav	
Dooley A T	"	51st Ind Vol	New Winchester Ind
Downing O J	Cap	2d N Y Cav	Rochester N Y
Denny W N	"	57th Ind Vol	Vincennes Ind
Delano J A	Lieut	51st Ind Vol	Marietta Ind
Davis Q R	"	123d O Vol	Marcellus O
Derrickson J G	Cap	66th N Y Vol	New York City
Dean S V	Lieut	145th Pa Vol	West Springfield Pa
Daily W A	Cap	8th Pa Cav	Philadelphia Pa
Davis C G	Lieut	1st Mass Cav	
Doruschke B	Cap	26th Wis Vol	
Dennis J B	"	7th Conn Vol	
Davis L R	"	7th O Vol	
Drake L	Lieut	22d Mich Vol	Pontiac Mich
Dutton W G	"	67th Pa Vol	Philadelphia Pa
Dillon C D	"	7th Iowa Cav	Marengo Iowa
Drennan J S	"	1st Vt H Art	Morrisville Vt
Deane T J	"	5th Mich Cav	Wayne Mich
Dunn J	"	64th N Y Vol	New York City
Dunning A J	"	7th N Y Art	
Davenport T F	Cap	75th O Vol	
Davis H C	"	18th Conn Vol	Canterbury Conn
Davis T C	Lieut	38th Ill Vol	
Dirlan C L	Cap	72d O Vol	Clyde O
Doughton O G	Lieut	111th O Vol	Stryker O
Day J R	Cap	3d Me Vol	Waterville Me
Donovan J	Lieut	2d N J Vol	Elizabeth N J
Durbrow W	Cap	40th N Y Vol	New York City
Dyre E B	Lieut	1st Conn Cav	Derby Conn
Dinsmore A	Cap	5th Pa Cav	
Duzenburgh A	"	35th N Y Vol	
Dorris W C	Lieut	111th Ill Vol	
Dodge H G	"	2d Pa Cav	Philadelphia Pa
Dixon A	Cap	104th N Y Vol	
Dunn M	Major	19th Mass Vol	
Doane E B	Cap	8th Iowa Cav	Salem Iowa
Davidson J	Lieut	6th N Y Art	Haverstraw N Y
Drake J W	"	136th N Y Vol	Dansville N Y
Downs C	"	33d N J Vol	Pa terson N J
Davis J W	"	115th N Y Vol	
Duven J	"	5th N H Vol	Keene N H
Dushane J M	Cap	142d Pa Vol	Connellsville Pa
Davis W H	"	4th Md Vol	Baltimore Md

NAME.	RANK.	COMMAND.	RESIDENCE.
Dircks C S F	Cap	1s Md Tenn Vol	
Devine J S	Lieut	71st Pa Vol	Philadelphia Pa
Diemer M	"	10th Mo Vol	Palmyra Mo
Dingley F	"	7th R I Vol	
Durfee W H	"	5th R I Vol	Newport R I
Durboyne G	"	66th N Y Vol	
Donohey G B	Cap	7th Pa Res	
Dieffenbach W H	Lieut	" " "	Huntingdon Pa
De Lay R	"	3d Iowa Cav	Centreville Iowa
Demmick O W	"	11th N H Vol	Strafford Vt
Drake C H	"	142d Pa Vol	Stroudsburg Pa
Dygest K S	Cap	16th Mich Vol	
Dick L	Lieut	72d O Vol	Fremont O
Davis L B	Cap	93d Ind Vol	Patriot Ind
Dillon F W	"	1st Ky Cav	
Dahl O R	Lieut	15th Wis Vol	Chippewa Falls Wis
Dickey M V	"	94th O Vol	Franklin O
Davis Byron	"	71st Pa Vol	
Day E	Cap	89th O Vol	Bainbridge O
Dalton G A	Lieut	22d Mich Vol	
Dickerson E	"	44th Wis Vol	
Durnam T J	"	16th U S Inf	
Dunn H C	"	10th Ky Vol	
Driscoll D	"	24th Mo Vol	Cannonsburg Mich
Davis E J	"	44th Ill Vol	Rocktown Ill
Dugan J	"	35th Ind Vol	Richmond Ind
Dorr H G	A Q M	4th Mass Cav	Boston Mass
Drake J M	Lieut	9th N J Vol	Trenton N J
Dicey E C	Cap	1st Mich S S	Detroit Mich
Downing H A	Lieut	31st U S C T	Poughkeepsie N Y
Dibeler J B	Cap	45th Pa Vol	Bainbridge Pa
Davidson J W	Lieut	95th O Vol	Big Plains O
Denny W N	Major	51st Ind Vol	Vincennes Ind
Drew G H	Lieut	9th N H Vol	Milford N H
Everett Chas	"	70th O Vol	Cleveland O
Eastman F R	"	2d Pa Cav	Mount Clemens Mich
Elkin J L F	Adjt	1st N J Vol	New Brunswick N J
Eastmond O	Cap	1st N C U Vol	New York City
Evans T E	Lieut	52d Pa Vol	Hyde Park Pa
Egertone J W	"	13th Ind Vol	Washington Iowa
Ellinwood W B	"	10th Wis Vol	Oshkosh Wis
Edwards D C	"	2d Md Vol	
English D	Major	11th Ky Cav	Owenton Ky
Elder S S	Cap	1st U S Art	
Eckings T K	Lieut	3d N J Vol	
Evans B W	Cap	4th O Cav	Kirkersville O
Errickson J H	Lieut	57th N Y Vol	Brooklyn N Y
Eberheart H H	Cap	120th O Vol	Wooster O
Eagan M	"	15th W Va Vol	
Evans N C	"	184th Pa Vol	Rainsburg Pa
Eglin A R	"	45th O Vol	Kenton O
Ewen M	"	21st Wis Vol	Fond du Lac Wis

NAME.	RANK.	COMMAND.	RESIDENCE.
Eagan John	Lieut	1st U S Art	
Elder John	"	8th Ind Vol	
Edwards T D	AsstEng	U S Navy	
Edminston S	Lieut	89th O Vol	
Evans H F			
Eans M	Cap	15th N Y Cav	
Elheny J L F	Adjt	1st N J Vol	New Brunswick N J
Flick M	Lieut	67th Pa Vol	Rainsburg Pa
Fritz J	"	11th Tenn Vol	
Fay S A	"	85th N Y Vet Vol	Olean N Y
Frost C W	"	" " "	Rochester N Y
Freeman D W D	Cap	101st Pa Vol	Irish Ripple Pa
Fiske J E	"	2d Mass Art	Grantville Mass
Fish O M	Lieut	" "	Boston Mass
Fluke A L	"	103d Pa Vol	Kittanning Pa
Fahs J	Cap	87th Pa Vol	York Pa
Foot M C	Lieut	92d N Y Vol	Cooperstown N Y
Fontaine J	"	73d Pa Vol	Washington D C
Fairbanks J	"	72d O Vol	Rollersville O
Follett W H	"	2d Mass Art	Quincy Mass
Fry Alfred	"	73d Ind Vol	Crown Point Ind
Fish G W		3d O Cav	Hamilton O
Frasier J	Col	140th Pa Vol	
Fleming C K	Major	11th Vt Vol	Bellows Falls Vt
Foster J W	Cap	42d Ill Vol	Belvidere Ill
Fales J M	Lieut	1st R I Cav	
Finney G E	Adjt	19th Ind Vol	Elizabethtown Ind
Fowler J H	Lieut	100th O Vol	
Fox G B	Major	75th O Vol	Cincinnati O
Farr W V	Cap	106th Pa Vol	
Forbes W H	Major	2d Mass Cav	
Ford E W	Cap	9th Minn Vol	Austin Minn
Ferris J M	Lieut	3d Mich Vol	
Fairchild H	"	10th Wis Vol	Platteville Wis
Funk J W	Cap	39th N Y Vol	New York City
Faye E M	Lieut	42d N Y Vol	" "
Furgerson J	"	1st N J Vol	Philadelphia Pa
Flannery D	"	4th N J Vol	Trenton N J
Fowler H M	"	15th N J Vol	Newark N J
Fisk W M	Cap	73d N Y Vol	New York City
Fleeger G W	Lieut	11th Pa R C Vol	Butler Pa
Fagan C A	"	" " "	Ebensburg Pa
French H	"	3d Vt Vol	Hartford Vt
Francis J L	Cap	135th O Vol	
Field A	Lieut	94th N Y Vol	Weedsport N Y
Fritchy A W	"	26th Mo Vol	St Louis Mo
Fortescue L R	"	Signal C U S A	Middleborne W Va
Fellows M	"	149th Pa Vol	
Fisher R	"	17th Mo Vol	St Louis Mo
Fenner W	"	2d R I Vol	Providence R I
Fox J D	"	16th Ill Cav	Aurora Ill
Fritze C	"	24th Ill Vol	Chicago Ill

Name.	Rank.	Command	Residence.
Fisher L W	Lieut	4th Vt Vol	Danville Vt
Fatzer S	"	108th N Y Vol	Rochester N Y
Fontaine E	"	7th Pa R C Vol	
Flamsburgh D	Cap	4th Ind Bat	
Forney D	Lieut	30th O Vol	Coshocton O
Fisher S	"	93d Ind Vol	
Fiedler J	Cap	Eng C U S A	
Finney D S	Lieut	14&15 Ill Vet Bat	Beardstown Ill
Fairfield O B	"	89th O Vol	
Fitzpatrick L	"	146th N Y Vol	Brooklyn N Y
Fales L D C	"		
Freeman H B	"	18th U S Inf	
Foster H C	"	23d Ind Vol	Jeffersonville Ind
Foley John	"	59th Mass Vol	Boston Mass
Faass Louis	"	14th N Y Art	Utica N Y
Frost R J	"	9th Mich Cav	Albion Mich
Fall J P	Cap	32d Me Vol	South Berwick Me
Filler J H	Major	55th Pa Vol	Bedford Pa
Fay W W	Cap	56th Mass Vol	
George G J	Lieut	40th Ill Vol	
Gillespie J B	Cap	120th Ill Vol	Vienna Ill
Gunn T M	Lieut	21st Ky Vol	Shelbyville Ky
Gilbert E C	Cap	152d N Y Vol	Butternut N Y
Gill A W H	"	14th N Y Vol	Brooklyn N Y
Greble C E	"	8th Mich Cav	Battle Creek Mich
Green J H	Lieut	100th O Vol	Fremont O
Gotshall J	Adjt	55th Pa Vol	
Godwin J M	Lieut	12th Ind Vol	Fort Wayne Ind
Grover J E	"	6th Ind Cav	
Gayer H	"	133d W Va Mil	Rock Case W Va
Gatch O C	Cap	89th O Vol	Milford O
Gross J M	"	18th Ky Vol	
Galbraith H E	"	22d Mich Vol	Lexington Mich
Goetz J	"	" "	Mount Clemens Mich
Gray W L	"	151st Pa Vol	
Gross C M	Lieut	110th O Vol	Covington O
Grant G W	"	88th Pa Vol	Reading Pa
Grant H D	"	117th N Y Vol	
Gray R H	"	15th U S Inf	Cleveland O
Gariss A J	Adjt	1st Md Cav	Baltimore Md
Gates A L	Lieut	10th Wis Vol	Hustisford Wis
Goodwin J A	"	1st Mass Cav	Medford Mass
Gamble G H	Adjt	8th Ill Cav	
Gates R C	Lieut	18th U S Inf	
Gilmore J A	"	79th N Y Vol	
Gamble H	"	73d Ind Vol	Monroeville O
Grant E	Cap	1st Vt Cav	
Granger C M	Lieut	88th N Y Vol	
Goodrich J O	Adjt	85th N Y Vet Vol	Scottsville N Y
Glazeer W W	Lieut	2d N Y Cav	Fowler N Y
Goodin A	"	82d O Vol	
Gordon C O	"	1st Me Cav	Phillips Me

NAME.	RANK.	COMMAND.	RESIDENCE.
Green E H	Cap	107th Pa Vol	Maytown Pa
Gimber H W	“	150th Pa Vol	Philadelphia Pa
Gilman ——	Lieut	3d Me Vol	
Gottland C	“	134th N Y Vol	
Getman D	Cap	10th N Y Cav	Mayfield N Y
Griffin H G	Lieut	112th Ill Vol	Cambridge Ill
Gordon E	“	81st Ind Vol	
Geasland S A	“	11th Tenn Cav	Kingston Tenn
Grey F C	“	11th Pa Vol	Donegal Pa
Green C W	“	44th Ind Vol	
Goss J W	“	1st Mass Art	Ipswich Mass
Grafton B	Cap	64th O Vol	Marion O
Gates J	“	33d O Vol	
Grant A	“	19th Wis Vol	
Green G W	“	19th Ind Vol	Muncie Ind
Goodrich A L	“	8th N Y Cav	Churchville N Y
Gamble N P	Lieut	63d Pa Vol	Pittsburg Pa
Garbet D	“	77th Pa Vol	Hyde Park Pa
Good T G	“	1st Md Cav	
Gordon H M	“	143d Pa Vol	Shickshinny Pa
Gray P	“	77th Pa Vol	Philadelphia Pa
Gallagher J	“	4th O Vt Vol	Brookfield Vt
Galloway J L	C'pAAG		Pensacola Fla
Green E A	Lieut	81st Ill Vol	
Green J L	A A G	U S A	Monroe Mich
Gove W A	Lieut	3d Mass Cav	East Boston Mass
Grant S	“	6th Mich Art	Schoolcraft Mich
Griffin T	Adjt	55th U S C T	Pulaski Ill
Gore J B	Lieut	115th Ill Vol	Taylorsville Ill
Gross T	“	21st Ill Vol	Bement Ill
Gordon G C	Cap	24th Mich Vol	Detroit Mich
Gerhardt H	Lieut	24th Ill Vol	
Gageby J H	“	19th U S Inf	Johnstown Pa
Gutjahr C	Cap	16th Ill Vol	
Galloway ——	Lieut	15th U S Inf	
Grayham P	Cap	54th Pa Vol	Johnstown Pa
Godley M L	Lieut	17th Iowa Vol	Ashland Iowa
Gould D	Cap	33d W Va Vol	
Grey W H	Lieut	14th Ill Cav	Vandalia Ill
Gude A	Cap	51st Ind Vol	Bruceville Ind
Glenn S A	“	89th O Vol	Hillsboro O
Grey Philip	Lieut	72d Pa Vol	
Huey Pennock	Col	8th Pa Cav	Westchester Pa
Hetsler J W	Cap	9th O Cav	Culina O
Hicks D W	Lieut		
Halsey T J	Major	11th N J Vol	Dover N J
Hutchinson J	Lieut	2d W Va Mt Inf	Pittsburg Pa
Huffman J W	“	5th Iowa Vol	Birmingham Iowa
Hinds H H	“	57th Pa Vol	Montrose Pa
Hagler J S	Cap	5th Tenn Vol	
Helms M B	Lieut	1st W Va Vol	Rossby's Rock W Va
Hall C B	Cap	“ “ “	

NAME.	RANK.	COMMAND.	RESIDENCE.
Hallenburg G	Lieut	1st O Vol	Louisville Ky
Hall A M	"	9th Minn Vol	
Haveley T	Cap	79th Ill Vol	Marshall Ill
Hubbard H R	Lieut	119th Ill Vol	
Heffley A	Cap	142d Pa Vol	Berlin Pa
Hays A H	"	7th Tenn Cav	Lovington Tenn
Hare T H	Lieut	5th O Cav	
Helm J B	"	101st Pa Vol	Shellsburg Pa
Heffley C P	"	142d Pa Vol	Berlin Pa
Hubbell F A	"	67th Pa Cav	Honesdale Pa
Heffner W	"	" "	Pottsville Pa
Harrington B F	"	18th Pa Cav	Waynesburg Pa
Hart E R	"	1st Vt Art	Hartford Vt
Hanson J B	"	1st Mass Art	Danvers Mass
Hodge W E	"	5th Md Vol	Baltimore Md
Hawkins S W	"	7th Tenn Cav	Huntingdon Tenn
Henry C D	"	4th O Cav	Tiffin City O
Hays W W	"	34th O Vol	
Hodge J F	"	55th Pa Vol	
Hall R F	"	75th O Vol	Cincinnati O
Haight J T	"	8th Iowa Cav	Tipton Iowa
Hastings T J	"	15th Mass Vol	Wooster Mass
Hock A	Cap	63d N Y Vol	
Hill G W	Lieut	7th Mich Cav	Detroit Mich
Heslit J	"	3d Pa Cav	Philadelphia Pa
Hazel E J	"	6th Pa Cav	Baltimore Md
Hanon J	"	115th Ill Vol	Taylorsville Ill
Herrick L C	"	1st N Y Cav	Syracuse N Y
Hine J J	"	100th O Vol	
Herbert R	"	50th Pa Vol	Lebanon Pa
Harris S	"	5th Mich Cav	
Heppard T H	"	101st Pa Vol	Philadelphia Pa
Hamilton W	"	2d Mass Art	West Amesbury Mass
Hastings G L	"	24th N Y Bat	Oswego N Y
Horton S H	"	101st Pa Vol	
Huff H B	Cap	184th Pa Vol	Altoona Pa
Hampton C G	Lieut	15th N Y Cav	Brockport N Y
Hard W B	"	17th Mich Cav	Jackson Mich
Heil J	Cap	45th N Y Cav	New York City
Hauf N	Lieut	" "	" "
Hitt W R	Cap	113th Ill Cav	Urbana O
Harris W	"	24th Mo Cav	Mt Vernon Mo
Hobbie C A	"	17th Conn Cav	Stamford Conn
Holden E	Lieut	1st Vt Cav	Barre Vt
Hedges S P	Adjt	112th N Y Vol	Jamestown N Y
Hinds H C	Lieut	102d N Y Vol	Richfield Springs N Y
Hall W P	Major	6th N Y Cav	Brooklyn L I
Hart R K	Cap	19th U S Inf	
Hodge A	"	80th Ill Vol	Fosterburg Ill
Harvey W H	Lieut	51st Ind Vol	
Hay D	Cap	80th Ill Vol	
Harmer R J	Lieut	" "	

NAME.	RANK.	COMMAND.	RESIDENCE.
Hart C M	Lieut	45th Pa Vol	Wellsboro Pa
Hopper J	"	2d N Y Cav	
Hand G T	"	51st Pa Vol	Shelbyville Ind
Hartzog R H O	Cap	1st N Y Cav	New York City
Hagler J S	"	5th Tenn Vol	
Hintz H	"	16th Conn Vol	Hartford Conn
Hunt C O	Lieut	5th Me Bat	
Halpin G	"	116th Pa Vol	Philadelphia Pa
Hagenback J C	"	67th Pa Vol	
Hagan P A	"	7th Md Vol	
Holland W R	"	5th Md Cav	
Hawkins H E	Cap	78th Ill Vol	Coastburg Ill
Heer T A	"	28th O Vol	Tell City Ind
Hart G D	"	5th Pa Cav	
Hull G W	Lieut	135th O Vol	
Hoyt H B	Cap	40th N Y Vol	Rochester N Y
Hamilton H E	Lieut	" "	" "
Hezelton D W	"	22d N Y Cav	Peterboro N Y
Hovey H	"	78th Ill Vol	
Hame D J	Cap	19th Mass Vol	Boston Mass
Holahan C P	Lieut	19th Pa Cav	Philadelphia Pa
Hamilton H N	"	59th N Y Vol	Belleville O
Hoppin H P	"	2d Mass Art	Cambridge Mass
Huntington E S	"	11th U S Inf	
Hutchison R C	Cap	8th Mich Vol	
Hoyt W H	Lieut	16th Iowa Vol	Comanche Iowa
Hart P H	"	19th Ind Vol	Edensburg Ind
Hughes R M	"	14th Ill Cav	Vandalia Ill
Henckly L D	"	10th Wis Vol	Wanpan Wis
Harkness R	Major	" "	Elkhorn Wis
Hewitt J	Lieut	105th Pa Vol	
Hastings C W	Cap	12th Mass Vol	
Heston J	Lieut	4th N J Vol	Taylorsville Pa
Hayes E	Cap	95th N Y Vol	Sing Sing N Y
Heffelfinger J	Lieut	7th P R V Corps	Mechanicsburg Pa
Harvey J L	"	2d Pa Art	Philadelphia Pa
Hobart M C	Cap	7th Wis Vol	Fall River Wis
Hock R B	"	12th N Y Cav	New York City
Holman W C	Lieut	9th Vt Vol	West Braintree Vt
Hadley H V	"	7th Ind Vol	Indianapolis Ind
Hall C	"	13th Wis Cav	
Hayden J A	Cap	11th P R V Corps	Uniontown Pa
Hill J B	Lieut	17th Mass Vol	Averill Mass
Hallett M V B	"	2d Pa Cav	Osceola Pa
Hodge W L	Cap	120th Ill Vol	Golconda Ill
Henry A J	Lieut	" "	
Hamlin S G	Cap	134 N Y Vol	Glennville N Y
Holladay V G	Lieut	2d Ind Cav	Wintersett Ind
Havens D	"	85th Ill Vol	Manito Ill
Hays C A	"	111th Pa Vol	Eagle Pa
Hastings J L	Adjt	7th Pa R V Corps	Salona Pa
Haines H A	Cap	184th Pa Vol	

NAME.	RANK.	COMMAND.	RESIDENCE.
Hunter A W	Lieut	2d U S (C'd) Art	New Hudson Mich
Harris J W	"	2d Ind Cav	Terre Haute Ind
Heltemus J B	Cap	18th Ky Vol	
Herzberg F	Lieut	66th N Y Vol	New York City
Henry J M	"	154th N Y Vol	Olean N Y
Harris G	"	79th Ind Vol	
Holt W C	Cap	6th Tenn Vol	Trenton Tenn
Harrison C E	Lieut	89th O Vol	Higginsport O
Huey R	"	2d E Tenn Vol	
Henderson J H	"	14 & 15 Ill Vt Bat	Greenfield Ill
Higley E H	"	1st Vt Cav	Castleton Vt
Hendryks W H	"	11th Mich Bat'n	
Hull G W	"	135th O Vol	Brownsville O
Hamilton W B	"	22d Mich Vol	Romeo Mich
Hendrick F	Cap	1st N Y Cav	New York City
Huston J	Lieut	95th O Vol	Clayhick O
Henderson R	"	1st Mass Art	Lawrence Mass
Howe C H	"	21st Ill Vol	
Haldeman J	"	129th Ill Vol	
Hymer S	Cap	115th Ill Vol	Rushville Ill
Hieurod P	"	105th O Vol	Waterford Pa
Hackett A N	Lieut	110th O Vol	Massillon O
Huntley C C	"	16th Ill Cav	Huntley Ill
Hand S P	"	43d U S C T	Binghampton N Y
Hurst T B	"	7th Pa Res V C	Dillsburg Pa
Hale G W	"	101st O Vol	Upper Sandusky O
Hopf Geo	"	2d Md Vol	Baltimore Md
Hescock H	Cap	1st Mo Art	St Louis Mo
Hill O M	Lieut	23d U S C T	Orleans Co N Y
Hall C T	"	13th Mich Vol	Battle Creek Mich
Heck F W	Cap	2d Md Vol	Baltimore Md
Hill V H	A Q M		
Hogeland D B	Cap	76th Pa Vol	Mercer Pa
Hood John	Lieut	80th Ill Vol	
Hogue J B	"	4th Pa Cav	
Holmes A J	Cap	37th Wis Vol	
Haywood L E	Lieut	58th Mass Vol	
Irwin C L	"	78th Ill Vol	Columbus Ill
Irwin S E	"	3d Iowa Vol	
Irwin W H	Adjt	103d Pa Vol	Alleghany City Pa
Imbric J M	Cap	3d O Vol	Wellsville O
Isett J H	Major	8th Ind Cav	Wappello Iowa
Irsch F	Cap	45th N Y Vol	New York City
Isham A B	Lieut	7th Mich Cav	Detroit Mich
Ingleden L	Cap		Janesville Wis
Jackson R W	Lieut	21st Wis Vol	Oshkosh Wis
Jenkins J H	Adjt	" "	" "
Johnson H A	Lieut	3d Me Vol	
James H H	"	6th Ind Vol	Montezuma Ind
Jones S F	Cap	80th Ill Vol	Jones Creek Ill
Johnson G	Lieut	16th Conn Vol	Hartford Conn
Judd J H	"	27th Mass Vol	East Hampton Mass

NAME.	RANK.	COMMAND.	RESIDENCE.
Jacobs J W	Cap	4th Ky Vol	
John E P	Lieut	135th O Vol	
Johnson J C	Cap	149th Pa Vol	Conder's Point Pa
Jobe B A	"	11th Pa R V C	Salem Cross Roads Pa
Johnson V W	Lieut	10th N Y Cav	Wolcott N Y
Jones J A	"	21st Ill Vol	Olney Ill
Johnson C K	"	1st Me Cav	Carmel Me
Jennings J T	Cap	75th O Vol	Kenton O
Jones D	"	14th N Y Art	Utica N Y
Judson S C	"	106th N Y Vol	Ogdensburg N Y
Jenkins H	"	40th Mass Vol	
Jackson C G	"	84th Pa Vol	Berwick Pa
Jones J P	Lieut	55th O Vol	Norwalk O
Jenkins G W	"	9th W Va Vol	Portland O
Jones C W	"	16th Pa Cav	Duncannon Pa
Justus J C	"	2d Pa R V C	Philadelphia Pa
Jackson J	"	4th Ind Cav	Oshkosh Wis
Jackson J S	"	22d Ill Vol	Salem Ill
Jones S E	"	7th N Y Art	
Jones H	"	5th U S Cav	
Jones W	"	38th O Vol	Charles O
Jones M J	Cap	115th Ill Vol	Rushville Ill
Johnson R	"	6th N Y Cav	Ogdensburg N Y
Johnson J W	Lieut	1st Mass Art	Methuen Mass
Johnson W N	Correspt		
Jones Alfred	R Q M	50th Pa Vet Vol	Reading Pa
Johnson J D	Cap	10th N J Vol	Hainesport N J
Jordan E C	Lieut	7th Conn Vol	Bridgeport Conn
Jacks J	"	15th W Va Vol	
Kelley D O	"	100th O Vol	Kelly's Island O
Krohn P	"	5th N Y Cav	Oswego N Y
Keeler A M	Cap	22d Mich Vol	Disco Mich
Kendal T	Lieut	15th U S Inf	Brooklyn N Y
Keniston J	"	100th Ill Vol	Joliet Ill
Keith C E	"	19th Ill Vol	Chicago Ill
Knowles E M	"	42d Ind Vol	
Kreuger W	"	2d Mo Vol	
Kreps F A M	"	77th Pa Vol	
Kane S	"	38th Ind Vol	
Kelly D A	Cap	1st Ky Vol	
Kendrick E	Adjt	10th N J Vol	New York City
Kerr S C	Lieut	126th O Vol	Salineville O
Kendall H T	Adjt	50th Pa Vol	Reading Pa
Kelly A	Lieut	126th O Vol	Barnesville O
Keen J	"	7th Pa V R C	Bart Pa
Kuchin A	"	5th Md Vol	
Kees G W	"	18th Conn Vol	
Kreiger A	"	67th Pa Vol	Broadheadville Pa
Knowles R A	"	116th O Vol	
Knapp F H	"	9th O Cav	
Kennaly J D	"	8th O Cav	Piqua O
Kempton J F	"	75th O Vol	Trimble Athens O

NAME.	RANK.	COMMAND.	RESIDENCE.
Kline D J	Lieut	75th O Vol	
Kennedy J W	"	134th N Y Vol	
Kankel E	"	45th N Y Vol	New York City
Kandler H	"	" " "	Baltimore Md
Kidd J H	"	1st Md Art	Port Deposit Md
Kendrick R H	"	25th Wis Vol	Potosi Wis
Kenyon G C	"	17th Ill Vol	Danton Ill
Kidder G C	"	113th Pa Vol	
Kelly H K	Cap	118th Pa Vol	
Knox G	Lieut	109th Pa Vol	Philadelphia Pa
Kelly J M	"	4th Tenn Vol	Athens Tenn
Kessler J G	Cap	2d Ind Cav	
Kirby W M	Lieut	3d N Y Art	
King T	R Q M	101st Pa Vol	Bradford Pa
Keister W H H	Lieut	103d Pa Vol	Hillsville Pa
Kirk J B	"	101st Pa Vol	" "
Krause J	Cap	3d Pa Art	Fort Monroe Va
Kempton F H	Lieut	58th Mass Art	
Kennits H	"	2d Mass Vol	
Kauts J D	"	1st Ky Cav	Dent O
Kellogg H	"	6th Mich Cav	
Kronemeyer C	Cap	52d N Y Vol	Williamsburg N Y
King M D	Lieut	3d O Vol	Barnesville O
Kendal J	Cap	43d Ind Vol	
King G E	"	103d Ill Vol	Middleport Ill
Knight H B	Lieut	20th Mich Vol	
Kelly J B	"	1st Pa Cav	Patterson Pa
Kirkpatrick G W	"	15th Iowa Vol	Smyrna Iowa
Knox J C	"	4th Ind Cav	Ladoga Ind
Kepheart J S	"	5th Ind Vol	Franklin Ind
Kerin J	"	6th U S Cav	Washington D C
Kenyon P D	Cap	14 and 15 Ill V Bat	Mt Carroll Ind
King Abe	Lieut	12th O V Inf	Xenia O
King John	"	15th Ill Cav	Geneva Ill
Kissam Edgar	Cap	9th N J Vol	Jersey City N J
Kepheart J	Lieut	13th O Vol	Russell Station O
Kelton J	"	2d Pa Art	Honesdale Pa
Kibby G L	"	4th R I Vol	Providence R I
Kendale W M	Major	73d Ind Vol	Plymouth Ind
Kost R	Lieut	6th Conn Vol	Bridgeport Conn
Kenfield F	Cap	17th Vt Vol	Morristown Vt
King John	Lieut	6th Conn Vol	New Haven Conn
Kings S B	Cap	12th Pa Cav	
Lindemeyer L	"	45th N Y Vol	New York City
Lemson A T	Lieut	104th N Y Vol	Genesee N Y
Litchfield J B	Cap	4th Me Vol	
Lombard H G	Adjt	4th Mich Vol	
Logan W S	Cap	17th Mich Vol	Richland Mich
Love J E	"	8th Kan Vol	St Louis Mo
Lucas John	"	5th Ky Vol	
Lovett L T	"	" " "	
Lodge G R	Lieut	53d Ill Vol	Ottawa Ill

NAME.	RANK.	COMMAND.	RESIDENCE.
Lucas W D	Cap	5th N Y Cav	East Gainesville N Y
Little J S	"	143d Pa Vol	Nicholson Pa
Lewis C E	Lieut	1st N Y Drag	Nunda N Y
Laycock J B	"	7th Pa R V C	
Lyman H H	"	147th N Y Vol	Pulaski N Y
Larrabee W H	"	7th Me Vol	Portland Me
Lanning A	Serg'nt	24th Mich Vol	Nankin Mich
Leigh S J	A D C		
Lee A	Lieut	152d N Y Vol	Utica N Y
Lynch C M	Major	145th Pa Vol	Erie Pa
Lynn J L	Lieut	" "	West Greenville Pa
Lyttle C W	Cap	" "	Nicholson Pa
Loud E J C	Lieut	2d Pa Art	Philadelphia Pa
Ludney M S	"	53d Pa Vol	
Lewry D W	"	2d Pa Art	Philadelphia Pa
Longnecker J H	Adjt	101st Pa Vol	Woodbury Pa
Landen H	Lieut	16th Conn Vol	
Laughlin J M	"	103d Pa Vol	Callensburg Pa
Langworthy D A	Cap	85th N Y Vol	New York City
Lafler J A	Lieut	" "	Penn Yan N Y
Lyman J	"	27th Mass Vol	East Hampton Mass
Laird J O	"	35th U S Inf	
Litchfield A C	Lt Col	7th Mich Cav	Grand Rapids Mich
Lym W C	Lieut	23d O Vol	Leeville O
Lintz W J	"	8th Tenn Vol	
Leslee J L	"	18th Pa Cav	Titusville Pa
Leonard A	"	71st N Y Vol	
Laird M	"	16th Iowa Vol	Desmoine Town Iowa
Luther J C	"	1st Pa V R C	Ridgeway Pa
Lemon M W	"	14th N Y Art	Canton N Y
Lane L M	"	9th Minn Vol	
Lamson T D	"	3d Ind Cav	Venny Ind
Loomis A W	"	18th Conn Vol	Tolland Conn
Locke W H	"	" "	Willimantic Conn
Lindsy A H	"	" "	Greenville Conn
Leith S	"	132d N Y Vol	
Long C H	"	1st Md Vol	Frederick City Md
Lewis D B	"	12th Pa Cav	Waterbury Vt
Livingston C H	"	1st W Va Cav	Union Town Pa
Law G	Cap	6th W Va Cav	Ellenboro W Va
Loyd J K	"	17th Mass Vol	Boston Mass
Leeds M A	Lt Col	153d O Vol	Bantam O
Lock D R	Lieut	8th Ky Cav	Newport Ky
Limbard A	"	M'Laughlin's Sqn	Delphos O
Lloyd T S C	"	6th Ind Cav	Terre Haute Ind
Lawrence G H	"	2d N Y M'd Rifles	Buffalo N Y
Laud J R	Cap	66th Ind Vol	Leavenworth Ind
Lee E N	"	5th Mich Cav	
Larkin F A	Lieut	13th Ind Vol	
Locklin A W	"	94th N Y Vol	Great Bend N Y
Lang C H	"	59th Mass Vol	Reading Mass
Latimer E C	Cap	27th U S C T	Canton O

Name.	Rank.	Command.	Residence.
Lenter A P	Cap	2d Tenn Inf	
Myers T	Lieut	107th Pa Vol	Chambersburg Pa
Mooney J	"	"	Dushore Pa
Mussel O	Cap	68th N Y Vol	
Millis V	Lieut	" "	
Mosely H H	"	25th O Vol	Summerfield O
Makepeace A J	Cap	19th Ind Vol	Anderson Ind
McDade A	Lieut	154th N Y Vol	Westfield N Y
Murphy F	Cap	97th N Y Vol	Salisbury Centre N Y
Moran F	Lieut	73d N Y Vol	New York City
Mendenhall J A	"	75th N Y Vol	Ringgold O
Mell J R	"	61st N Y Vol	Deerfield O
Morres W J	"	5th Md Vol	Baltimore Md
Metta J S	"	" "	
Merwin S T C	"	18th Conn Vol	Norwich Conn
Madera W B	"	6th W Va Vol	Morgantown W Va
Meany D B	Cap	13th Pa Cav	Philadelphia Pa
Matherson E J	Lieut	18th Conn Vol	Dison Conn
McKeag F	"	" "	Norwich Conn
Morningstar H	"	87th Pa Vol	Hanover Pa
Manning J S	"	116th O Vol	
Mash P	Cap	67th Pa Vol	Scranton Pa
McNeal D	Lieut	13th Pa Cav	
Matson C C	Lt Col	6th Ind Cav	Greencastle Ind
McCarty W W	Cap	18th O Cav	McConnellsville O
Morgan C H	Lieut	21st Wis Cav	Oshkosh Wis
McGruder W H	"	" "	
McDowal J S	Cap	77th Pa Cav	Fort Little Pa
Moses H	Lieut	4th Ky Cav	
Morrison M V B	"	33d O Cav	Chilicothe O
McKinison A H	"	10th Wis Cav	Pine Hill Wis
Mead L C	"	22d Mich Cav	Ann Arbor Mich
McKercher D	Col	10th Wis Cav	New Lisbon Wis
Mathews A S	Adjt	22d Mich Vol	Pontiac Mich
McGowan E	Lieut	29th Ind Vol	
Murphy J	"	16th U S Inf	Newark N J
Mitchell J	"	79th Ill Vol	
McCune A W	"	2d O Vet Vol	
Muhlemon J R	Maj &c		Woodburn Ill
McNeil S	Lieut	51st O Vol	Spring Mountain O
Metcalf C W	Cap	42d Ind Vol	Dale Ind
Messick J M	Lieut	42d Ind Vol	Evansville Ind
Mackey J T	"	16th U S Inf	Dallas City Ill
Mahoney J S	"	21st O Vol	Prairie Depot O
Mead W H	"	6th Ky Cav	
Moore M	Cap	29th Ind Vol	
Moore G W	"	7th Tenn Vol	Lovington Tenn
McConalee W J	Lieut	14th Iowa Cav	Wintersett Iowa
Morton J W	Cap	4th Mass Cav	
Malambre J M	Lieut	75th O Vol	Dayton O
Morse E	"	78th Ill Vol	Macomb Ill
Marshall W S	Major	5th Iowa Vol	

NAME.	RANK.	COMMAND.	RESIDENCE.
McGovern J	Lieut	75th Pa Vol	
McKinley J	"	98th O Vol	
McNiece A	"	73d Pa Vol	
Mann G	"	80th O Vol	
Moore F	"	73d Pa Vol	
Mooney A H	Cap	16th N Y Cav	Plattsburg N Y
McHugh J	"	69th Pa Vol	Philadelphia Pa
McFadden W M	"	59th N Y Vol	
Monaghan J	Lieut	62d Pa Vol	
McIntosh J C	"	145th Pa Vol	Erie Pa
Mather F W	"	7th N Y Art	Albany N Y
McCray H	Cap	115th Pa Vol	
Mockrie P B	Lieut	7th N Y Art	Albany N Y
May J	Cap	15th Mass Vol	
Moore N H	"	7th N Y Art	Albany N Y
McCutcheon E F	Lieut	64th N Y Vol	Gowanda N Y
McWain E J	"	1st N Y V Art	Rochester Vt
McCreary D B	Lt Col	145th Pa Vol	Erie Pa
Murry S F	Cap	2d U S S S	Candia N H
McKage J	"	184th Pa Vol	Hollidaysburg Pa
Muffley S F	Adjt	" "	Howard Pa
Mangus H F	Lieut	53d Pa Vol	Winfield Pa
McLaughlin J	"	" "	James's Creek Pa
McGinnes W A	"	19th Mass Vol	Boston Mass
Mathews A R	"	1st Vt Art	Bennington Vt
Morse A	"	" "	Fayetteville Vt
Maish L	Cap	87th Pa Vol	York Pa
McQuiddy ——	"	5th Tenn Cav	
Marshall W S	Adjt	51st Ind Vol	Indianapolis Ind
McDill H	Lieut	80th Ill Vol	
Maxwell C A	"	3d O Vol	Springfield O
Mall D H	Cap	73d Ind Vol	
Munday J W	Lieut	" "	Laporte Ind
Murdock H S	"	" "	Logansport Ind
McHolland D A	Cap	" "	Adriance Ind
Morey H	Lieut	10th N Y Cav	
McColgin J	"	7th O Cav	Georgetown O
Morris J H	"	4th Ky Vol	
McLernan P	Major	22d N Y Cav	Memphis N Y
Mattock C P	"	17th Me Vol	
Myers W H	Lieut	76th N Y Vol	Cortland N Y
McGeehan J	"	146th N Y Vol	Brooklyn N Y
Miller F C	Col	147th N Y Vol	Oswego N Y
Mitchell H W	Lieut	14th N Y Vol	
Maltison A C	Cap	12th N J Vol	
Morrisy G H	A Q M	12th Iowa	
McKay D S	Lieut	18th Pa Cav	Meadville Pa
Mayer L	"	12th Pa Cav	Philadelphia Pa
Merritt H A D	"	5th N Y Cav	Hoboken N J
Metzger J	Cap	55th Pa Vol	
Moore Le Roy	"	72d O Vol	Fremont O
McCain J C	Lieut	9th Minn Vol	Logansport Ind

NAME.	RANK.	COMMAND.	RESIDENCE.
McKee T H	Cap	1st W Va Vol	Logansport Ind
McGuire T	"	7th Ill Vol	St Charles Ill
Miller J W	Lieut	14th Ill Cav	Lincoln Ill
Murphy J	"	69th N Y Vol	Newark N J
Mallison J	"	94th N Y Vol	Brandon Wis
Moulton O	LieutCol	25th Mass Vol	
Morgan S M	Cap		Lindy N Y
McGraylis M	"	93d Ind Vol	
Morgan Ben B	LieutCol	75th O Vol	Franklin O
Mulligan J A	Lieut	4th Mass Cav	Biddeford Me
Mead S	Cap	111th N Y Vol	Moravia N Y
McCall O	Lieut	103d Pa Vol	Remersburg Pa
Mullin D W	Cap	101st Pa Vol	Bedford Pa
Morrow J M	Lieut	" "	
McHenry C	"	85th N Y Vet Vol	East Bloomfield N Y
Miller W G	"	16th Conn Vol	
Mackey J F	Cap	103d Pa Vol	Clarion Pa
Morrow J J	"	" "	Plumville Pa
Mathews W F	Lieut	1st Md Vol	Martinsburg W Va
Merrill H P	Cap	4th Ky Vol	
Menier N J	Lieut	93d Ind Vol	Leopold Ind
McDonald H J	Cap	11th Conn Vol	Kingston N J
Moodey J E	Lieut	59th Mass Vol	Newburyport Mass
Martin J C	Cap	1st Tenn Cav	
Melkorn M	"	135th O Vol	Ada O
Moon R A	Lieut	6th Mich Cav	B' Rapids Mich
Moore M M	"	" "	
Manley J A	Cap	64th N Y Vol	
Miller H	Lieut	17th Mich Vol	Detroit Mich
McMannus P W	Adjt	27th Mass Vol	Davenport Iowa
Moses C C	Cap	58th Pa Vol	Alleghany Bridge Pa
Mudgett A G	"	11th Me Vol	Newburgh Me
McMahon E	Lieut	72d O Vol	
McKinstry J	"	16th Ill Cav	Mattoon Ill
McEvoy W	Adjt	3d Ill Vol	
McBeth N	Lieut	45th O Vol	Zanesfield O
Merry W A	"	106th N Y Vol	Ogdensburg N Y
Marney A	Cap	2d Tenn Vol	Kingston Tenn
Moore D T	Lieut	" "	Clinton Tenn
Morton G C	"	4th Pa Cav	
McKay R G	"	5th Mich Cav	
Molton H	"	1st U S Cav	
Montgomery R H	"	5th U S Cav	
Marrow H C	Ass Egr	U S N	Baltimore Md
Morgan J T	Cap	17th Mich Vol	Ypsilanti Mich
Manning G A	"	2d Mass Cav	Oldtown Me
Mather E	Lieut	1st Vt Cav	Fair Haven Vt
McDonald C	"	2d Ill Art	Tamaroa Ill
Moore W Q	"	2d Md Cav	Wilmington Del
McCafferty N J	"	4th U S Art	Pittsburg Pa
Millis J	"	66th Ind Vol	Paoli Ind
McClure T W	"	6th U S Art	Wabash Ind

NAME.	RANK.	COMMAND.	RESIDENCE.
McNitt R J	Cap	1st Pa Cav	Milroy Pa
Mason J	Lieut	13th Pa Cav	
Main C A	Cap	5th Ill Cav	
McDonald J	Lieut	2d E Tenn Vol	
Morse C W	"	16th Conn Vol	New Hartford Conn
Miller C	Adjt	14th Ill Cav	Chicago Ill
McAdams J	Lieut	10th W Va Vol	
Mayer G W	"	37th Ind Vol	Lawrenceburg Ind
Mure C	"	15th Mo Vol	St Louis Mo
McIntyre ——	Cap	15th Wis Vol	
McCormick J	Lieut	21st N Y Cav	Troy N Y
Moore L	Cap	72d O Vol	Fremont O
McKay R G	Lieut	1st Mich Cav	Detroit Mich
Marshland A J	"	2d Pa Art	Nicetown Pa
Millard R J	Cap	" "	Fowlersville Pa
Mix W H	Lieut	19th U S Cav	Warsaw N Y
Munger T J	"	37th Wis Vol	Madison Wis
McNure A	"	73d Pa Vol	Philadelphia Pa
Mitchell H G	"	32d Me Vol	Portland Me
Marshall J D	"	57th O Vol	Wapakonetta O
McLane ——	"	9th Minn Vol	
Morris W M	"	93d Ill Vol	Rock Island Ill
Norris A W	"	107th Pa Vol	
Norcross J C	"	2d Mass Cav	Farmington Me
Niedenhoffen C	"	9th Minn Vol	Winona Minn
Nyce W	"	2d N Y Cav	Hainesville N J
Nelson W H	"	13th U S Inf	
Nutting J H	Cap	27th Mass Vol	
Norris O P	Lieut	111th O Vol	
Nelson P	Major	66th N Y Vol	Westchester N Y
Nelson A	Lieut	" "	Westchester N Y
Nolan L	Cap	2d Del Vol	
Needham J B	Lieut	4th Vt Vol	Shrewsbury Vt
Noggle C L	"	2d U S Inf	Janesville Wis
Nichols C H	Cap	6th Conn Vol	
Newbrant J F	Lieut	4th Mo Cav	Cincinnati O
Norwood J	"	76th N Y Vol	Slatersville N Y
Norton E E	Cap	24th Mich Vol	Detroit Mich
Nealy O H	Lieut	11th U S Inf	Ft Ind Boston Mass
Netlerville W McM	"	12th U S Inf	Albany N Y
Nash W H	Cap	1st U S S S	New York City
Neher W	Lieut	7th Pa R V Cav	Philadelphia Pa
Newsome E	Cap	81st Ill Vol	Carbondale Ill
Neal A	Lieut	5th Ind Cav	
Nuhfer A	Cap	72d O Vol	Woodville O
Nolan H J	"	14th N Y Cav	
Niswander D M	Lieut	2d Pa Art	Welch Run Pa
Niemayer B H	"	11th Ky Cav	
Newlin C	Cap	7th Pa Cav	
Nyman H J	Lieut	19th Mich Vol	
Nulland W R	"	5th Ind Cav	Lafayette Ind
Norris J	Cap	2d Pa Art	Washington D C

Name.	Rank.	Command.	Residence.
Noyes C S	Cap	31st Me Vol	Mt Desert Me
Outcolt R V	Lieut	135th O Vol	
O'Harre J	"	7th N Y Art	Cohoes N Y
Osborne F	"	19th Mass Vol	Byfield Mass
Ong O C	"	2d Va Cav	Meigsville O
Ottinger W	Cap	8th Tenn Vol	
Oliphant D	Lieut	35th N J Vol	
O'Connor W	"	13th Pa Cav	Philadelphia Pa
O'Brien E	Cap	29th Mo Vol	Cape Girardeau Mo
O'Shea E	Lieut	13th Pa Cav	Philadelphia Pa
Olcott D W	Cap	134th N Y Vol	New York City
O'Kain J	Lieut	7th Ill Cav	Polo Ind
Oats J G	"	3d O Vol	Greenwich O
O'Connel P	"	55th Pa Vol	Johnstown Pa
Owens W N	Major	1st Ky Cav	Somerset Ky
Ogden J	Lieut	1st Wis Cav	Winona Minn
Ogan H W	Cap	14th O Vol	
O'Sullivan F J	Lieut	67th O Vol	Toledo O
Olden G C	"	112th Ill Vol	
Pickenpaugh A C	"	6th W Va Vol	Morgantown W Va
Picquet H	"	32d Ill Vol	Olney Ill
Parker J T	"	13th Iowa Vol	Sigourney Iowa
Phinney A	"	90th Ill Vol	Rockford Ill
Provine W M	"	84th Ill Vol	Vermont Ill
Purcell T	"	16th Iowa Vol	Muscatine Iowa
Powell W H	"	2d Ill L Art	
Parker G M	"	45th Ill Vol	Carmi Ill
Purveance J S	"	130th Ind Vol	Huntington Ind
Pratt J E	"	4th Vt Vol	Bennington Vt
Pemberton H V	Cap	14th N Y Art	New York City
Piffard D H	Lieut	" "	New York City
Price C A	"	5th Mich Vol	Maple Rapids Mich
Parker E B	"	1st Vt Art	
Pumphry J B	"	123d O Vol	Marseilles O
Paxton W N	"	140th Pa Vol	
Porter E	Cap	154th N Y Vol	Olean N Y
Poole S V	"	" "	Springville N Y
Potts G P	Lieut	151st Pa Vol	Pottsville Pa
Potts J H	"	75th O Vol	
Powers J L	"	157th N Y Vol	Hamilton N Y
Pettijohn	"	2d U S S S	Fort Snelling Minn
Parsons W L	Major	2d Wis Vol	
Parker J	Cap	1st N J Vol	Trenton N J
Powell J P	"	146th N Y Vol	Clinton N Y
Paine L B	"	121st N Y Vol	Garrottsville N Y
Partridge W H	Lieut	67th N Y Vol	Brooklyn N Y
Pierce H H	"	7th Conn Vol	Unionville Conn
Pasco H S	Major	16th Conn Vol	Hartford Conn
Pitt G W	Lieut	85th N Y Vet	Short Tract N Y
Peake L S	"	" "	Hinsdale N Y
Pierson E C	"	" "	Waterloo N Y
Piggott J T Jr	Cap	8th Pa Cav	Philadelphia Pa

Name.	Rank.	Command.	Residence.
Phelps L D	Lieut	8th Pa Cav	Colchester Conn
Plase W B	Cap	87th U S Inf	Dayton O.
Pentzell D	Lieut	4th N Y Cav	
Peetrey J G	"	95th O Vol	London O
Powers D H	Cap	6th Mich Cav	
Parmalee J A	"	7th Ind Vol	Valparaiso Ind
Penfield J A	Major	5th N Y Cav	Crown Point N Y
Potter E D	Lieut	6th Mich Cav	Jeddo
Purlier H	"	2d O Vol	
Powell O	"	42d Ill Vol	
Patterson J B	"	21st O Vol	
Perley J P	"	13th Mich Vol	New York City
Pierce G S	Cap	19th U S Inf	Dubuque Iowa
Perry F W	"	10th Wis Vol	Menasha Wis
Pulliam M D	Lieut	11th Ky Cav	
Prather Z R	"	116th Ill Vol	
Pierson M P	"	100th N Y Vol	LeRoy N Y
Pilsbury S H	Cap	5th Me Vol	Biddeford Me
Phares W	Lieut	46th W Va Vol	Seneca W Va
Paul A C	A A G		Newport Ky
Pettit G	Cap	120th N Y Vol	Lexington N Y
Preston A L	Lieut	8th Mich Cav	Mount Clemens Mich
Pendleton D B	Cap	5th Mich Cav	Detroit Mich
Porter D M	"	120th Ill Vol	
Pennybacker E J	"	18th Pa Cav	Philadelphia Pa
Patterson F A	"	3d W Va Cav	Washington D C
Potter H C	Lieut	18th Pa Cav	Philadelphia Pa
Paul J S	"	122d O Vol	
Phillipp F	"	5th Pa Cav	Philadelphia Pa
Pierce S C	Cap	3d N Y Cav	Rochester N Y
Protsman C N	Lieut	7th Wis Vol	Plainfield Wis
Potter G A	"	2d Ky Vol	Cincinnati O
Peters G	"	9th N J Vol	Elizabeth N J
Pitt J H	"	118th N Y Vol	Canton N Y
Post James	"	149th Pa Vol	Shickshinny Pa
Page J E	Cap	5th Iowa Vol	Iowa City Iowa
Pace N C	"	80th Ill Vol	Mt Vernon Ill
Piper S B	Adjt	3d O Vol	Barnesville O
Phelps J D	Cap	73d Ind Vol	Michigan City Ind
Palmer E L	Lieut	57th N Y Vol	Martville Conn
Poston J L	Cap	13th Tenn Vol	Cageville Tenn
Patree L B	Lieut	126th O Vol	
Poole J F	"	1st W Va Cav	Martinsburg W Va
Peterson C J A	"	1st R I Cav	
Peck M D	"	2d N Y Cav	Syracuse N Y
Pelton E W	"	2d Md Vol	Cumberland Md
Patterson G W	"	135th O Vol	Alexandria O
Price J C	"	75th O Vol	
Pain H C	"	20th Ill Vol	
Porter B B	Cap	10th N Y Art	Taylor N Y
Perrin Z	Lieut	72d O Vol	Clyde O
Platt L H	"	34th Mass Vol	Pittsfield Mass

NAME	RANK.	COMMAND.	RESIDENCE.
Porter L G	Lieut	87th Ill	Tamaroa Ill
Paine J A	Cap	2d Ind Cav	Bridgetown Ind
Phelps L A	Major	5th W Va Vol	Ceredo W Va
Palmer J H	Lieut	12th O Vol	Ripley O
Peckeville W F	Cap	5th Iowa Vol	
Pope W A	Lieut	18th Wis Vol	
Pyne D B	"	3d Mo Vol	Alden Iowa
Ping T	Cap	17th Iowa Vol	Ashland Iowa
Park A	Lieut	" "	Germainville Iowa
Perrin J	Adjt	6th U S Cav	
Pierce W	Lieut	17th Vt Vol	Woodstock Vt
Phillips W B	"	2d Pa Art	Hyde Park Pa
Poindexter C O	"	31st Me Vol	Bridgeton Me
Pierson A P	"	9th Mich Cav	Lapier Mich
Phillips W E	"	7th Conn Vol	Woodstock Conn
Payne L S	Cap	100th N Y Vol	Tonawanda N Y
Price Chas A	Lieut	3d Mich Vol	Maple Rapids Mich
Quigg D	Major	14th Ill Cav	Bloomington Ill
Rees M	Lieut	72d O Vol	Rollersville O
Robinson J L	"	7th Tenn Cav	Huntington Pa
Robbins H	Cap	2d Wis Vol	
Rockwell W O	Lieut	134th N Y Vol	Esperance N Y
Robbins N A	"	4th Me Vol	Union Me
Russell J H	"	12th Mass Vol	Boston Mass
Rockwell J O	"	97th N Y Vol	Booneville N Y
Richardson H	"	19th Ind Vol	
Robinson G L	"	80th O Vol	
Robertson G W	"	22d Mich Vol	Mount Clemens Mich
Roach S	"	100th Ill Vol	
Riggs B T	Cap	18th Ky Vol	
Rice J A	"	73d Ill Vol	Harrisburg Ill
Retilley W L	Lieut	51st O Vol	Roscoe O
Ray T J	"	49th O Vol	
Reynolds H	"	42d Ill Vol	
Rose W B	"	106th Pa Cav	
Rourke J	Cap	1st Ill Art	Milwaukee Wis
Reynolds W H	Major	14th N Y Art	Utica N Y
Ruger J M	Lieut	57th Pa Vol	
Richards L S	"	1st Vt Art	West Concord Vt
Ronnels J R	"	145th Pa Vol	
Rieneckar G	"	5th Pa Cav	
Rahn O	"	184th Pa Vol	Duncannon Pa
Ritter H	Cap	52d N Y Vol	Philadelphia Pa
Reynolds W J	"	75th O Vol	
Reynolds E P	Lieut	5th Tenn Cav	McMinnville Tenn
Robbinson J F	"	67th Pa Vol	Scott Pa
Ruff J	"	" "	Philadelphia Pa
Randolph J F	Cap	123d O Vol	
Robbins A	"	" "	Upper Sandusky O
Rosenbaum O H	"	" "	Sandusky City O
Rossman W C	"	3d O Vol	Hamilton O
Russel M	"	51st Ind Vol	

NAME.	RANK.	COMMAND.	RESIDENCE.
Randall W	Lieut	80th Ill Vol	
Richley J A	Cap	73d Ind Vol	
Roach A C	Lieut	51st Ind Vol	Indianapolis Ind
Rosencranz A C	Cap	4th Ind Cav	Evansville Ind
Rowley G A	Lieut	2d U S Inf	
Reid J A	"	2d N C Vol	Whitestown Pa
Robinson B E	"	95th O Vol	Reynoldsburg O
Ryder S B	Cap	5th N Y Cav	Arbane N Y
Robinson W A	"	77th Pa Vol	Pittsburg Pa
Roach W E	Lieut	49th N Y Vol	Rochester N Y
Rogers A	Cap	4th Ky Cav	Louisville Ky
Raymond H W	Lieut	8th N Y Art	Elba N Y
Ross C W	"	1st Ky Vol	
Rose J E	"	120th Ill Vol	Vienna Ill
Roberts E R	"	7th Ill Vol	
Reed J H	"	120th Ill Vol	
Richard J M	"	1st W Va Vol	Wheeling W Va
Rings G	Adjt	100th O Vol	
Rothe H	Lieut	15th N Y Art	Alexandria Va
Robb W J	Cap	1st W Va Vol	Wheeling W Va
Ramsey E K	Lieut	1st N J Vol	Phoenixville Pa
Riley L H	"	7th Pa R V Cps	
Ruby S V	"	" "	
Ross C H	Adjt	13th Ind Vol	Zanesville O
Risedon I	Lieut	11th Tenn Vol	Huntsville Tenn
Robs E W	"	1st Tenn Vol	
Ring A	"	12th O Vol	
Richardson J A	"	2d N Y Cav	Stoneham Mass
Romaine L	"	2d N J Vol	
Roberts G	"	7th N H Vol	Dover N H
Ross G	"	7th Vt Vol	Vergennes Vt
Rathbone T W	"	153d O Vol	
Rugg C L	"	6th Ind Cav	Newport Ky
Roger J R	"	157th Pa Vol	Lancaster Pa
Reed ——	Cap	107th N Y Vol	
Roney J C	Lieut	3d O Vol	Newark O
Robinson T B	Cap	16th Conn Vol	Bristol Conn
Richards J S	Lieut		
Russell J A	Cap	93d Ill Vol	Neponsett Ill
Rice J S	Lieut	13th Ind Vol	Washington Iowa
Reade J	"	57th Mass Vol	Milford Mass
Richards R C	Cap	45th Pa Vol	Cherry Flats Pa
Raynor A J	Lieut	19th U S Cav	Ontario N Y
Rainear L	"	2d N J Cav	Freehold N J
Reynolds W J	Cap	4th R I Vol	Wickford R I
Robeson J S	Lieut	7th Tenn Cav	Huntington Tenn
Riley W S	"	21st N Y Cav	Brighton N Y
Randall W H	"	1st Mich S S	Ypsilanti Mich
Reir Geo W	Cap	107th N Y Vol	Staten Island N Y
Robinson C	"	31st U S Cav	
Rorick D	A D C	31st Iowa Vol	London Iowa
Reynolds B J	Cap	143d N Y Vol	Neversink N Y

NAME.	RANK.	COMMAND.	RESIDENCE.
Sturgeon W B	Lieut	107th Pa Vol	Shippensburg Pa
Stover M H	"	184th "	
Sweetland A A	"	2d Pa Cav	
Snyder J	Cap	14th N Y Vol	Havelton N Y
Smith E B	Lieut	1st Vt Art	Newport Vt
Stoughton H R	LieutCol	2d U S S S	
Steele J	Major	2d Pa Cav	Pittsburg Pa
Smart G F C	Cap	145th Pa Vol	West Greenville Pa
Schurr C	Lieut	7th N Y Art	
Shafer W H	"	5th Pa Cav	
Standeford S A	"	42d N Y Vol	Trenton N J
Smith H I	Cap	53d Pa Vol	Huntington Pa
Sargeant M G	Lieut	1st Vt Art	Newport Vt
Schooley D	Cap	2d Pa "	Pittston Pa
Stallman C H	Lieut	87th Pa Vol	York Pa
Socks J	"	5th Md Art	
Sweadner J	"	"	Liberty Md
Stewart T H	"	"	Philadelphia Pa
Stroman C P	"	87th Pa Art	York Pa
Sibley H L	"	116th O "	Racine O
Smith M H	"	123d " "	Monroeville O
Schuyler J F	"	" " "	Attica O
Simpson G W	"	67th Pa "	Mauch Chunk Pa
Schroeder E	"	5th Md "	York "
Smith J	"	67th Pa "	Latrobe "
Schortz D	Cap	12th Pa Cav	Easton "
Sheppard E A	"	110th O Vol	Arcanum O
Smith O J	Major	6th Ind Cav	Terre Haute Ind
Sanders A H	LieutCol	16th Iowa Vol	Davenport Iowa
Shedd W	Col	30th Ill Vol	Aledo Ill
Strang H W	Cap	"	Collins Station Ill
Smith J H	"	16th Iowa Vol	Lyons Iowa
Skilton A S	"	57th O Vol	
Shuttz W	"	37th O Vol	Toledo O
Smythe S S	Lieut	1st Ill Art	Elkhorn Ill
Smith A B	Cap	48th Ill Vol	
Scott Geo	Lieut	10th Ind Vol	Lebanon Ind
Swift E	"	74th Ill Vol	Pecatonica Ill
Sutherland G W	Adjt	126th O Vol	Smithfield O
Starkweather W L	Cap	85th N Y Vol	Olean N Y
Shaefer James	"	101st Pa Vol	Carlisle Pa
Strong E E	Lieut	16th Conn Vol	N Manchester Conn
Sampson I B	Cap	2d Mass H Art	Springfield Mass
Sinclair R B	Lieut	" "	Worcester "
Spence D M	"	103d Pa Vol	Pittsburg Pa
Stoke G W	"	"	Orrsville "
Smullin F	Cap	"	Oakland "
Stewart A Jr	"		Uniontown "
Sweeny J	Ass Egr	U S N	
Starr G H	Cap	104th N Y Vol	Rochester N Y
Schell G L	"	88th Pa Vol	Philadelphia Pa
Seely H B	Adjt	86th N Y Vol	S Troupsburg N Y

NAME.	RANK.	COMMAND.	RESIDENCE.
Schroeders E	Lieut	74th Pa Vol	
Sears D C	"	94th N Y Vol	Somerville N Y
Smith J A	"	154th N Y Vol	
Schuld G	"	45th N Y Vol	
Sampson J B	"	12th Mass Vol	N Bridgewater Mass
Spring W	Cap	45th N Y Vol	
Schroeder C H	Lieut	12th Ill Vol	Chicago Ill
Stevens C G	"	154th Ill Vol	Machias N Y
Swift R R	Cap	12th Mass Vol	Springfield Mass
Skinner J L	Lieut	" "	Amherst Mass
Stone D	Cap	118th N Y Vol	Warrensburg N Y
Spindler J	Lieut	73d Ill Vol	
Spencer S A	Cap	82d Ind Vol	
Spafford A C	Lieut	41st O Vol	
Schwade J C	Cap	77th Pa Vol	Lancaster Pa
Singer G P	"	33d O Vol	
Spaulding E G	Lieut	22d Mich Vol	Port Huron Mich
Smythe W H	"	16th U S Inf	
Schummerhone J	Cap	42d Ind Vol	
Schwainforth F	Lieut	24th Ill Vol	Chicago Ill
Sanger A W	"	21st Ill Vol	Xenia Ill
Spencer F	"	17th O Vol	Wilmington O
Simpson J D	"	10th Ind Vol	
Stover J C	Cap	3d Tenn Vol	
Stevens J H	Lieut	5th Me Vol	North Lebanon Me
Stevens F	"	190th Pa Vol	
Stuart C	"	24th N Y Vol	Newburg N Y
Shanan M	"	140th N Y Vol	
Stevens J R	Cap	40th N Y Vol	Brooklyn N Y
Speece L B	Major	7th Pa R V C	Wilkesbarre Pa
Shelton W H	Lieut	1st N Y Art	Bloomfield N Y
Smith M S	"	16th Me Vol	E Livermore Me
Snowwhite E	"	7th Pa R V C	Palmyra Pa
Swann E J	Cap	76th N Y Vol	Cherry Valley N Y
Sweet W H S	Lieut	146th N Y Vol	Utica N Y
Schofield E	Cap	11th Pa R V C	Brookville Pa
Steel J M	Lieut	1st W Va Vol	Wellsville O
Sitler J R	"	2d Pa Cav	Harmonsburg Pa
Shaw J C	"	7th O Vol	
Sheerd D G	"	5th Ky Cav	Jamestown Ky
Shannon A L	"	3d Ind Cav	Hanover Ind
Smith C B	"	4th N Y Cav	New York City
Smith A M	"	1st Tenn Cav	
Sutter C	"	39th N Y Vol	New York City
Spaulding E J	"	2d U S Cav	Galesburg Mich
Shaffer H C	"	2d N Y Cav	
Swayzie W A	Cap	3d O Vol	Columbus O
Sharp E	Lieut	51st Ind Vol	Kokoma Ind
Smith D D	Cap	1st Tenn Vol	
Segar T W	Lieut	81st Ill Vol	Chester Ill
Smith J C	"	24th Ind Bat	Burlington Ind
Saber G E	"	2d R I Cav	

Name.	Rank.	Command	Residence.
Sullivan J	Adjt	7th R I Vol	
Smith J B	Lieut	5th W Va Cav	
Sandon W	"	1st Wis Cav	Ontario Wis
Sutcher C B	Cap	16th Ill Vol	
Sharp G A	Lieut	19th Pa Cav	Philadelphia Pa
Stone L L	R Q M	2d Vt Vol	McIndoe's Falls Vt
Smith L S	Lieut	14th N Y Cav	Littleton N H
Sanford O L	Major	7th Conn Vol	
Smith J P	Lieut	49th Pa "	Spring Mills Pa
Stevens J G	"	52d Pa "	
Smith T A	Major	7th Tenn Cav	Lexington Tenn
Swope C T	Lieut	4th Ky Vol	
Stewart A S	"	" "	
Strickland E P	"	114th Ill Vol	
Smith P	"	4th Tenn Cav	Mornstown Tenn
Stanton J W	"	5th Ind "	Carmel Ind
Soper M H	Major	" "	Sheldon Ill
St John W H	Lieut	" "	Greensburg Ind
Shepard E	"	6th O "	Newburgh O
Scripture F E	R Q M	7th N Y Art	
Simmons A B	Lieut	5th Ind Cav	Union City Ind
Starr H P	"	22d N Y "	Rochester N Y
Spring B	"	75th O Vol	
Shurtz E	Cap	8th Iowa Cav	
Stover A C	Lieut	95th O Vol	Urbana O
Stansbury M L	Cap	" "	
Schofield R	"	1st Vt Cav	Brattleboro Vt
Stone C P	Lieut	" "	" "
Scudder A A	R Q M	35th Pa Vol	
Scoville H C	Lieut	92d Ill "	Rockford Ill
Stebbins J	"	77th N Y Vol	
Schwartz C S	"	2d N J Cav	Philadelphia Pa
Sailor J	"	13th Pa "	Newport "
Smyser H C	"	2d Md Vol	Ashland Furnace Pa
Scott R F	"	11th Ky Cav	Kirksville Ky
String T B	Cap	" "	Louisville Ky
Stewart R R	Lieut	2d N Y Cav	N Y City
Stribling M W	"	61st O Vol	Circleville O
Shoemaker F M	Cap	100th O Vol	Waterville O
Smith J	Lieut	5th Pa Cav	
Stout J O	"	McL's S O Cav	Wooster O
Shepstrong M N	"	60th O Vol	
Snodgrass J G	Cap	110th O Vol	New Madison O
Sargent H R	"	32d Me "	Portland Me
Stanton J W	Lieut	5th Ind Cav	Carmel Ham'n co Ind
Sheehan J P	"	31st Me Vol	Dennysville Me
Shull J F	"	28th U S C T	Bloomington Ind
Smith S B	"	30th " "	Woodbury N J
Stauber B F	"	20th Pa Cav	Lewistown Pa
Schulter H	"	43d N Y Vol	Albany N Y
Sherman S U	Cap	4th R I "	Providence R I
Seely L D	Lieut	45th Pa "	Knoxville Pa

Name.	Rank.	Command.	Residence.
Stewart R T	Cap	138th Pa Vol	Norristown Pa
Stevens Frank	Lieut	12th Pa V R Cps	Meadow Gap Pa
Scott D W	Cap	23d U S Cav	Pottsville Pa
Schroeder H	Lieut	82d Ill Vol	
Septon A F	"	8th Iowa Cav	
Senter A P	Cap	2d E Tenn Cav	
Scofield T D	Lieut	27th Mich Vol	
Sanders C B	"	30th U S Cav	
Simondson P A	"	23d U S Cav	
Shaefer N W	"	24th Ind Cav	
Tuthill P A	"	104th N Y Vol	Nunda N Y
Templeton O F	Cap	107th Pa Vol	Laceyville Pa
Thonsen B E	Lieut	9th O Vol	Cincinnati O
Teter A J	"	2d O Vol	Steubenville O
Teneyck S	Cap	18th U S Inf	
Tainter H S	Lieut	82d N Y Vol	
Tanner D	"	118th Ill Vol	
Tompkins H V	"	59th N Y Vol	
Trent B W	"	106 Pa Vol	Canton Pa
Tyler L D C	Cap	" "	Philadelphia Pa
Thomas D	Major	135 O Vol	Newark O
Thornbury J M	Lieut	39th Ky Vol	
Thompson C H	Major	5th Ind Cav	Lafayette Ind
Tillottson H H	Lieut	73d Ind Vol	Calumet Ind
Thomas A V	"	" "	
Thompson J S	"	10th Vt Vol	
Thorp T J	LieutCol	1st N Y Drag	Almond N Y
Terwilliger J E	Lieut	85th N Y Vol	" "
Turner M C	Cap	16th Conn Vol	Hartford Conn
Tyler L E	Lieut	1st Conn Cav	Preston City Conn
Timpson S C	Cap	95th N Y Vol	New York City
Thayer H O	Lieut	67th Pa Vol	
Taylor A A	"	122d O Vol	Cambridge O
Thompson R	"	67 Pa Vol	Stoddardsville Pa
Tilbrand H	Cap	4th N H Vol	
Thorn R F	Lieut	5th Ky Vol	Gardner Kan
Tinn A	"	16th Iowa Vol	Davenport Iowa
Turner J H	Cap	" "	Muscatine Iowa
Todd O	Lieut	18th Wis Vol	Adrian Mich
Tiffany A W	"	9th Minn Vol	Carver Minn
Taylor H	"	55th Ind Vol	
Temple H	"	2d N Y Cav	Brooklyn N Y
True W M	"	16th Ill Cav	Chicago Ill
Thompson J J T	Ass Surg	12th O Vol	Maysville Ky
Tibbles H G	Cap	" "	Dayton O
Taylor J	Lieut	2d Pa V R Cps	
Tubbs A			
Tower D W	Lieut	17th Iowa Vol	Farmington Iowa
Towson F	"	" "	Oskaloosa Iowa
Tipton A F	"	8th Iowa Cav	Elkader Iowa
Tourtillotte J	Cap	7th Conn Vol	Putnam Conn
Turner D	Lieut	118th Ill Vol	Warsaw Ill

Name.	Rank.	Command.	Residence.
Tobel C	Lieut	15th N Y Art	New York City
Thomson J	Cap	4th O Cav	
Toby J P F	Lieut	31st Me Vol	Machiasport Me
Tinker S H	"	93d Ind Vol	Allensville Ind
Unthank C L	Cap	11th Ky Cav	
Ullenbaugh G	Lieut	1st O Vol	
Urwiler S C	Cap	67th Pa Vol	Philadelphia Pa
Ulem J	Lieut	3d O Vol	Wooster O
Uptigrove J R	"	73d Ind Vol	
Underdown J D	Cap	2d Tenn Vol	
Ulffar H A	A A G		
Underwood J W	Cap	57th O Vol	
Von Keiser A	"	30th N Y Bat	
Van Netter R N	Lieut	1st Mich Cav	Watervliet Mich
Von Valack D D	"	12th U S Inf	
Vanderhiff J W	Cap	45th N Y Vol	E Brooklyn N Y
Velfort G	Lieut	54th N Y Vol	New York City
Vickers D	Major	4th N J Vol	Philadelphia Pa
Von Rottenburg H N	Lieut	103d N Y Vol	Dykeman's Sta N Y
Von Helmrich G	Lt Col	4th Mo Cav	St Louis Mo
Vinay F	Lieut	85th N Y Vol	New York City
Van Doren D	"	72d O Vol	Fremont O
Van Ness G A	"	73d Ind Vol	Logansport Ind
Van Rensalaer C	"	148th N Y Vol	Seneca Falls N Y
Vaughn Z	Cap	1st Me Cav	Freeman Me
Van Buren G M	Cap	6th N Y Cav	Stuyvesant Falls N Y
Van Alin W C	Lieut	45th Pa Vol	Fleming Pa
Von Bulow A	"	3d N J Cav	New York City
Von Haack A	Cap	68th N Y Vol	
West O W	Lieut	1st N Y Drag	Dansville N Y
Warner J B	"	8th Mich Cav	Marshall Mich
Williams G	"	" "	
Whitney M G	Cap	29th Mo Vol	St Louis Mo
Winters J	Lieut	72d O Vol	Townsend O
Warner J	"	33d N J Vol	Newark N J
Wheeler J F	"	149th N Y Vol	Salina N Y
West J H	Cap	11th Ky Vol	Big Hill Ky
Waidmann F	Lieut	16th Iowa Vol	Davenport Iowa
Walker J	"	8th Tenn Vol	Bull's Gap Tenn
Western C S	"	21st Wis Vol	Chelton Wis
Willcts W	"	22d Mich Vol	Birmingham Mich
Wands H P	Cap	" "	St Clair Mich
Welker W H	Lieut	21st O Vol	Neoga Ill
Welshimer P	Cap	21st Ill Vol	"
Weatherby J	Lieut	51st O Vol	Port Washington O
Weesner T A	"	14 & 15 Ill V Bat	Greenfield Ill
Wyman E F	C S		Augusta Me
West D J	Lieut	6th Conn Vol	Bridgeport Conn
Ware E W	"	9th Me Vol	Bangor Me
White Dan	Col	31st Me Vol	" "
Washburne W	Cap	35th Mass Vol	Boston Mass
Wing G H	Lieut	14th N Y Art	Glenn's Falls N Y

NAME.	RANK.	COMMAND.	RESIDENCE.
Wilder G O	Adjt	15th Mass Vol	Holliston Mass
Willis A R	Cap	8th Me Vol	Biddeford Me
Wilcox C W	Lieut	9th N H Vol	
Westbrook U S	Cap	135th O Vol	Zanesville O
Weeks E J	Lieut	67th Pa Vol	Phœnixville Pa
Woodard J E	"	18th Conn Vol	Norwich Conn
Weakly T J	"	100th O Vol	New Carlisle O
Wright B F	Cap	146th N Y Vol	Utica N Y
Wilson W M Jr	"	122d O Vol	Zanesville O
Watson J C	Lieut	126th O Vol	New Salem O
Woodruff F M	"	76th N Y Vol	Oswego Falls N Y
Wright D L	"	51st Ind Vol	Indianapolis Ind
Whiting J D	"	3d O Vol	New York City
Wright W R	Cap	80th Ill Vol	Upper Alton Ill
Wilson A	"	" "	
Wolbach A R	Lieut	3d O Vol	Wooster O
Woodrow J C	"	73d Ind Vol	
Williamson J B	"	14th W Va Vol	Middlebourne W Va
Weaver J R	"	18th Pa Cav	Latrobe Pa
Wilson H	"	" "	Houston Pa
Worthen T A	"	118th Ill Vol	Warsaw Ill
Wakefield H B	Cap	55th Ind Vol	Azalia Ind
Whitman W S	Lieut	66th Ind Vol	New Albany Iowa
Wiltshire J W	"	45th O Vol	Cincinnati O
Weddle Geo	"	144th O Vol	Perrysburg O
Woodrow C W	"	19th Iowa Vol	Mt Pleasant Iowa
Webb G W	Cap	2d Pa Art	Murcy Pa
White A B	Lieut	4th Pa Cav	Alleghany City Pa
Warwick Jos F	"	101st Pa Vol	Beaver Pa
Willis H H	"	40th N Y Vol	Aurora Ill
Winship J	"	88th Ill Vol	Chicago Ill
Whitney J N	"	2d R I Cav	Raymond Me
Wilson R	"	113th Ill Vol	Chicago Ill
Whitten B F	"	9th Me Vol	
Whiteside J C	Cap	94th N Y Vol	Wyoming N Y
Warren J W	Lieut	1st Wis Cav	Beaver Dam Wis
Wanzer G G	Major	24th N Y Cav	Rochester N Y
Wadsworth M C	Lieut	16th Me Vol	Pittston Me
Warchaw F	"	54th N Y Vol	New York City
Wilson W C	Cap	104th N Y Vol	Spencer Mass
White H G	"	94th N Y Vol	Lysander N Y
Widdess C C	"	150th Pa Vol	Germantown Pa
Whiston D	Lieut	13th Mass Vol	
Welsh W H H	"	87th Pa Vol	York Pa
White C W	Cap	5th W Va Cav	Baltimore Md
Wilson J	"	57th O Vol	
Williams W H	"	41st N Y Vol	
Watson W L	Lieut	21st Wis Vol	Waupaca Wis
Winner C N	"	1st O Vol	
Wasson J M	"	40th O Vol	
Webb G W	Cap	2d Pa Art	
Williams R	"	12th O Vol	Dayton O

Name.	Rank.	Command.	Residence.
Welch J C	Lieut	85th N Y Vol	Angelica N Y
Wheeler J D	Cap	15th Conn Vol	New Haven Conn
Wenrick J E		19th Pa Cav	Philadelphia Pa
Williams W	Lieut	8th Mich Cav	
Willis W	"	51st Ind Vol	
Williams M F	"	15th Ky Vol	
Wiley M	Cap	1st Tenn Vol	
Whittaker E B	Cap	72d Pa Vol	
Wallace J	Lt Col	47th O Vol	Morning Sun O
Ward T H	Lieut	59th U S Cav	Westerville O
Wheaton J	"	" "	
Wright R J	Cap	6th O Vol	Springfield O
Wilcox W H H	Lieut	10th N Y Cav	New York City
Wallace R P	"	120th O Vol	Loudonville O
Walpole H H	Cap	122d N Y Vol	
Wright J W	Lieut	10th Iowa Vol	Des Moines City Ia
Whittemore B W	"	5th N Y Vol	
Wallace J J	"	7th Tenn Cav	Dowagiac Mich
Wentworth H A	"	14th N Y H Art	Randolph N Y
Wall M W	Cap	69th N Y Vol	
Walker W H	Lieut	4th O Vol	Arcadia O
Wilson E S	"	1st Mass Cav	Havana Cuba
Warren D H	Ass Surg	8th Iowa Cav	Glencoe O
Wilson R P	Lieut	5th U S Cav	Philadelphia Pa
Willets W	"	22d Mich Vol	Birmingham Mich
White H	Major		Indiana Pa
White G M	Cap	1st W Va	Wellsburg W Va
Whitney J de W		O Vet Inf	New York City
Yaw E C	Lieut	67th N Y Vol	Naples N Y
York J H	"	63d Ind Vol	
Youtz H C	Cap	126th O Vol	New Salem O
Young D G	"	81st Ill Vol	De Soto Ill
Young W J	Lieut	111th Ill Vol	Xenia Ill
York E D	"	2d N C U Vol	Friendship N Y
Young J W	Major	76th N Y Vol	Cherry Valley N Y
Yates C H	Lieut	96th Ill Vol	
Young A	"	4th Pa Cav	Newark N J
Young T P	"	4th Ky Vol	
Zarracher F K	Cap	18th Pa Cav	Philadelphia Pa
Zeigler Aaron	Lieut	7th Pa V R C	Myerstown Pa
Zeis H	Cap	80th Ill Vol	
Zimm A	Lieut	15th Iowa Vol	
Zobel C	"	15th N Y Art	
Zeigler J D	"	114th Ill Vol	

DEATHS.

Eckings, T. R , Lieut. 3d N. J. Vol.
Henderson, J. H., Lieut. 14th Ill. Vet. Battalion.
Jackson, R. W., Lieut. 21st Wis. Vol.
Spafford, A. C., Lieut. 41st O Vol.
Wenrick, J. E., Capt. 19th Penn. Cav.
Young, A., Lieut. 4th Penn. Cav.

C

I append a list of the Federal officers who applied to me for aid when prisoners in Columbia, S. C.; also a sample of the "bills of exchange" which they gave me. I advanced them over $1,500,000 in *Confederate currency*, equal to something over $50,000 in gold, not one dollar of which was ever paid; and many of the drafts were drawn on fictitious parties.

JAS. G. GIBBES.

August, 1875.

INDIANA REGIMENTS.

Lt. W. Adair	51st	Lt. — Marshall	51st
Capt. B. L. Beebe	13th	Lt. W. M. Betts	45th
Capt. W. N. Denney	51st	Capt. J. D. Phelps	73d
Lt. J. H. Delano	51st	Lt. A. B. Simmons	5th Cav.
Lt. H. Harvey	51st	Lt. J. W. Stanton	5th Cav.
Lt. — Long	1st	Lt. D. L. Wright	51st

OHIO REGIMENTS.

Lt. R. W. Anderson	122d	Capt. Gatch	89th
Lt. G. W. Bailey	3d	Lt. Harrison	89th
Lt. F. A. Brackenridge	123d	Lt. Hull	135th
Lt. G. E. Blair	17th	Lt. J. E. Johns	155th
Capt. D. M. Barnatt	89th	Lt. J. P. Jones	55th
Lt. O. B. Brandt	17th	Lt. King	3d
Lt. Barnes	3d	Lt. Col. Leed's	153d
Capt. J. Cusac	21st	Lt. H. H. Moseley	20th
Lt. E. Cottingham	35th	Lt. McColgen	7th
Capt. Mike Caton	21st	Capt. Melhorn	135th
Capt. E. Day	89th	Lt. Mahoney	21st
Capt. Byron A. Evans	4th	Lt. G. W. Patterson	135th
Lt. Edmonton	89th	Lt. Purveyance	134th
Capt. A. R. Eglan	45th	Lt. F. Spencer	17th
Lt. G. W. Fish	3d	Lt. F. H. Weakley	110th
Capt. Glenn	89th	Lt. W. H. Welker	21st
Capt. Green	100th	Lt. Joy Winter	72d

ILLINOIS REGIMENTS.

Capt. Boas	20th	Capt. Hagler	5 Tenn.
Capt. C. H. Call	29th	Lt. Hawkins	7 Tenn. Cav.
Lt J. L. Cox	27th	Capt. Hescock	1 Mo. Art.
Lt E. T. Davis	44th	Capt. Harris	24 Mo.
Lt T E Gross	21st	Lt. Hamilton	2 Mass. Art.
Lt. Geshardt	24th	Lt. Harrison	1 Mass. Art.
Lt H. G Griffin	112th	Lt. J. Histon	4 N. J.
Lt J. A Jones	21st	Lt. D. R. Moore	2 Tenn.
Capt. J. Rouhe	1st	Capt. McQuiddy	5 Tenn. Cav.
Lt H C Scovil	92d	Lt. H. G. Mitchell	32 Me.
Lt J. Winship	88th	Lt. Thos. Purcell	16 Iowa
Capt. P. Welsheimer	21st	Lt. E. W. Petton	2 Md.
Lt. G. E Saber	2 R. I. Cav.	Capt. Robeson	7 Tenn.
Lt. J. W. Austin	5 Iowa	Lt. Rinden	11 Tenn.
Lt. Flannery	4 N. J.	Capt. A. P. Senter	2d Tenn.
Lt. Fisher	4 Vt.	Lt. H. C. Smyser	2d Md.
Lt. Garcio	1 Md. Cav.		

NEW YORK REGIMENTS.

Lt. Cutter	95th	Lt. H. M. Mitchell	14th
Lt. Campbell	152d	Lt. Matteson	94th
Lt. C. Cramer	21st	Capt. H. J. Howlan	14th
Capt. G. A. Crocker	1st Cav.	Lt. J. L. Powers	157th
Capt. Gilbert	152d	Lt. W. H. Partridge	67th
Capt. A. H. Gill	4th	Lt. M. P. Pierson	100th
Lt. Hamilton	59th	Capt. L. B. Raine	121st
Lt. H. C. Hind	102d	Capt. Rockwell	134th
Capt. J. D. Johnson	10th	Lt. E. C. Yaw	67th
Capt. R. Johnson	6th	Lt. W. S. Riley	21st
Lt. J. W. Johnson	10th	Lt. L. S. Smith	14th
Lt. A. Lee	152d	Lt. W. H. S. Sweat	146th

PENNSYLVANIA REGIMENTS.

Capt. Borcher	67th	Lt. Hewitt	165th
Capt. J. Byrne	2d	Lt. Halpin	116th
Lt C H. Crawford	183d	Lt. Hunt	7th
Lt. Flute	103d	Lt. Hollaham	19th
Lt. Forgin	11th	Lt. Hanzelton	27th
Lt. Grant	88th	Lt. Luther	1st
Lt. Grey	72d	Lt. A. McNiece	73d
Capt. Gimber	150th	Lt. McHugh	69th
Lt. Hazel	6th	Adjt. S. T. Muffley	184th

EXTRACTS FROM LETTERS, DOCUMENTS, &c.,

In Relation to the Treatment of the Federal Prisoners at Andersonville.

LETTER FROM EX-PRESIDENT DAVIS TO HON. JAMES LYONS.

NEW ORLEANS, *January* 27, 1876.

HON. JAMES LYONS:

My Dear Friend.—Your very kind letter of the 14th instant was forwarded from Memphis, and has been received at this place.

I have been so long the object of malignant slander and the subject of unscrupulous falsehood by partisans of the class of Mr. Blaine, that, though I cannot say it has become to me matter of indifference, it has ceased to excite my surprise, even in this instance, when it reaches the extremity of accusing me of cruelty to prisoners. What matters it to one whose object is personal and party advantage, that the records, both Federal and Confederate, disprove the charge; that the country is full of witnesses who bear oral testimony against it, and that the effort to revive the bitter animosities of the war obstructs the progress toward the reconciliation of the sections? It is enough for him if his self-seeking purpose be promoted.

It would, however, seem probable that such expectations must be disappointed, for only those who are wilfully blind can fail to see in the circumstances of the case the fallacy of Mr. Blaine's statements. The published fact of an attempt to suborn Wirz, when under sentence of death, by promising him a pardon if he would criminate me in regard to the Andersonville prisoners, is conclusive as to the wish of the Government to make such charge against me, and the failure to do so shows that nothing could be found to sustain it. May we not say the evidence of my innocence was such that Holt and Conover, with their trained band of suborned witnesses, dared not make against me this charge—the same which Wirz, for his life, would not make, but which Blaine, for the Presidential nomination, has made?

Now let us review the leading facts of this case. The report of the Confederate commissioner for exchange of prisoners shows how persistent and liberal were our efforts to secure the relief of captives. Failing in those attempts, I instructed General R. E. Lee to go under flag of truce and seek an interview with General Grant, to represent to him the suffering and death of Federal prisoners held by us, to explain the causes which were beyond our control, and to urge in the name of humanity the observance of the cartel for the exchange of prisoners. To this, as to all previous appeals, a deaf ear was turned. The interview was not granted. I will not attempt, from memory, to write the details of the correspondence. Lee no longer lives to defend the cause and country he loved so well and served so efficiently; but General Grant cannot fail to remember so extraordinary a proposition, and his objections to executing the cartel are well known to the public. But whoever else may choose to forget my efforts in this regard, the prisoners at Andersonville, and the delegates I permitted them to send to President Lincoln to plead for the resumption of exchange of prisoners, cannot fail to remember how willing I was to restore them to their homes and to the comforts of which they were in need, provided the imprisoned soldiers of the Confederacy should be in like manner released and returned to us.

This foul accusation, though directed specially against me, was no doubt intended as, and naturally must be, the arraignment of the South, by whose authority and in whose behalf my deeds were done. It may be presumed that the feelings and the habits of the Southern soldiers were understood by me, and in that connection any fair mind would perceive in my congratulatory orders to the army after a victory, in which the troops were most commended for their tenderness and generosity to the wounded and other captives, as well the instincts of the person who issued the order as the knightly temper of the soldiers to whom it was addressed. It is admitted that the prisoners in our hands were not as well provided for as we would, but it is claimed that we did as well for them as we could. Can the other side say as much?

To the bold allegations of ill treatment of prisoners by our side, and humane treatment and adequate supplies by our opponents, it is only necessary to offer two facts — first, it appears from the reports of the United States War Department that, though we had sixty thousand more Federal prisoners than they had of Confederates, six thousand more of Confederates died in Northern prisons than died of Federals in

Southern prisons; second, the want and suffering of men in Northern prisons caused me to ask for permission to send out cotton and buy supplies for them. The request was granted, but only on condition that the cotton should be sent to New York and the supplies be bought there. General Beale, now of St. Louis, was authorized to purchase and distribute the needful supplies.

Our sympathy rose with the occasion and responded to its demands — not waiting for ten years, then to vaunt itself when it could serve no good purpose to the sufferers.

Under the mellowing influence of time and occasional demonstrations at the North of a desire for the restoration of peace and good will, the Southern people have forgotten much — have forgiven much, of the wrongs they bore. If it be less so among their invaders, it is but another example of the rule that the wrong-doer is less able to forgive than he who has suffered causeless wrong. It is not, however, generally among those who braved the hazards of battle that unrelenting vindictiveness is to be found. The brave are generous and gentle. It is the skulkers of the fight — the Blaines — who display their flags on an untented field. They made no sacrifice to prevent the separation of the States. Why should they be expected to promote the confidence and good-will essential to their union?

When closely confined at Fortress Monroe, I was solicited to add my name to those of many esteemed gentlemen who had signed a petition for my pardon, and an assurance was given that on my doing so the President would order my liberation. Confident of the justice of our cause and the rectitude of my own conduct, I declined to sign the petition, and remained subject to the inexcusable privations and tortures which Dr. Craven has but faintly described. When after two years of close confinement, I was admitted to bail, as often as required I appeared for trial under the indictment found against me, but in which Mr. Blaine's fictions do not appear. The indictment was finally quashed on no application of mine, nor have I ever evaded or avoided a trial upon any charge the General Government might choose to bring against me, and have no view of the future which makes it desirable to me to be included in an amnesty bill.

Viewed in the abstract or as a general question, I would be glad to see the repeal of all laws inflicting the penalty of political disabilities on classes of the people, that it might, as prescribed by the Constitution, be left to the courts to hear and decide causes, and to affix penalties according to pre-existing legislation. The discrimination made against our people is unjust and impolitic, if the fact be equality and the purpose be fraternity among the citizens of the United States. Conviction and sentence without a hearing, without jurisdiction, and affixing penalties by *ex post facto* legislation, are part of the proceeding which had its appropriate end in the assumption by Congress of the executive function of granting pardons. To remove political disabilities which there was not legal power to impose, was not an act of so much grace as to form a plausible pretext for the reckless diatribe of Mr. Blaine.

The papers preserved by Dr. Stevenson happily furnish full proof of the causes of disease and death at Andersonville. They are now, I believe, in Richmond, and it is to be hoped their publication will not be much longer delayed. I have no taste for recrimination, though the sad recitals made by our soldiers returned from Northern prisons can never be forgotten. And you will remember the excitement those produced, and the censorious publications which were uttered against me because I would not visit on the helpless prisoners in our hands such barbarities as, according to reports, had been inflicted upon our men.

Imprisonment is a hard lot at the best, and prisoners are prone to exaggerate their sufferings, and such was probably the case on both sides. But we did not seek by reports of committees, with photographic illustrations, to inflame the passions of our people. How was it with our enemy? Let one example suffice. You may remember a published report of a committee of the United States Congress which was sent to Annapolis to visit some exchanged prisoners, and which had appended to it the photographs of some emaciated subjects, which were offered as samples of prisoners returned from the South.

When a copy of that report was received, I sent it to Colonel Ould, commissioner for the exchange of prisoners, and learned, as I anticipated, that the photographs, as far as they could be identified, had been taken from men who were in our hospital when they were liberated for exchange, and whom the hospital surgeon regarded as convalescent, but too weak to be removed with safety to themselves. The anxiety of the prisoners to be sent to their homes had prevailed over the objections of the surgeon. But this is not all, for I have recently learned from a priest who was then at Annapolis, that the most wretched-looking of these photographs was taken from a man who had never been a prisoner, but who had been left on the "sick list" at Annapolis when the command to which he was attached had passed that place on its southward march.

Whatever may be said in extenuation of such imposture because of the exigencies of war, there can be no such excuse now for the attempts of Mr. Blaine, by gross misrepresentation and slanderous accusation, to revive the worst passions of the war; and it is to be hoped that, much as the event is to be regretted, it will have the good effect of evoking truthful statements in regard to this little-understood subject, from men who would have preferred to leave their sorrowful story untold if the subject could have been allowed peacefully to sink into oblivion.

Mutual respect is needful for the common interest, is essential to a friendly union; and when slander is promulgated from high places, the public welfare demands that truth should strip falsehood of its power for evil.

I am, respectfully and truly, your friend,

JEFFERSON DAVIS.

COMMENT OF MR. DANA (FORMERLY U. S. ASSISTANT SECRETARY OF WAR) ON MR. DAVIS'S LETTER.

In an editorial in his paper, the New York *Sun*, Mr. Dana, after speaking of the bitterness of feeling towards Mr. Davis at the North, thus comments on his recent letter to Mr. Lyons:

This letter shows clearly, we think, that the Confederate authorities, and especially Mr. Davis, ought not to be held responsible for the terrible privations, sufferings and injuries which our men had to endure while they were kept in the Confederate military prisons. The fact is unquestionable, that while the Confederates desired to exchange prisoners, to send our men home and to get back their own, General Grant steadily and strenuously resisted such an exchange. While, in his opinion, the prisoners in our hands were well fed, and were in better condition than when they were captured, our prisoners in the South were ill-fed, and would be restored to us too much exhausted by famine and disease to form a fair set-off against the comparative vigorous men who would be given in exchange. "It is hard on our men held in Southern prisons," said Grant, in an official communication, "not to exchange them; but it is humane to those left in the ranks to fight our battles. If we commence a system of exchanges which liberates all prisoners taken, we will have to fight on until the whole South is exterminated. If we hold those caught, they count for no more than dead men." "I did not," he said, on another occasion, "deem it justifiable or just to reinforce the enemy; and an immediate resumption of exchanges would have had that effect, without any corresponding benefit."

This evidence must be taken as conclusive. It proves that it was not the Confederate authorities who insisted on keeping our prisoners in distress, want and disease, but the commander of our own armies. We do not say that his reason for this course was not valid; but it was not Jefferson Davis, or any subordinate or associate of his, who should now be condemned for it. We were responsible ourselves for the continued detention of our captives in misery, starvation and sickness in the South.

Moreover, there is no evidence whatever that it was practicable for the Confederate authorities to feed our prisoners any better than they were fed, or to give them better care and attention than they received. The food was insufficient; the care and attention were insufficient, no doubt; and yet the condition of our prisoners was not worse than that of the Confederate soldiers in the field, except in so far as the condition of those in prison must of necessity be worse than that of men who are free and active outside.

Again, in reference to those cases of extreme suffering and disease, the photographs of whose victims were so extensively circulated among us toward the end of the war, Mr. Davis makes, it seems to us, a good answer. Those very unfortunate men were not taken from prisons, but from Confederate hospitals, where they had received the same medical treatment as was given to sick and wounded Confederate soldiers. The fact mentioned by Mr. Davis, that while they had 60,000 more prisoners of ours than we had of theirs, the number of Confederates who died in our prisons exceeded by 6000 the whole number of Union soldiers who died in Southern prisons, though not entirely conclusive, since our men were generally better fed and in better health than theirs, still furnishes a strong support to the position that, upon the whole, our men were not used with greater severity or subjected to greater privations than were inevitable in the nature of the case. Of this charge, therefore, of cruelty to prisoners, so often brought against Mr. Davis, and reiterated by Mr. Blaine in his speech, we think he must be held altogether acquitted.

There are other things in his letter not essential to this question, expressions of political opinion and intimations of views upon larger subjects, which it is not necessary that we should discuss. We are bound, however, to say, that in elevation of spirit, in a sincere desire for the total restoration of fraternal feeling and unity between the once warring parts of the Republic, Mr. Davis's letter is infinitely superior and infinitely more creditable to him, both as a statesman and a man, than anything that has recently fallen from such antagonists and critics of his as Mr. Blaine.

STATEMENT OF MR. L. M. PARK, OF LA GRANGE, GEORGIA

(Originally published in the *Southern Magazine.*)

THE "REBEL PRISON PEN" AT ANDERSONVILLE, GEORGIA.

It is the duty of every lover of justice, when he sees a gross and injurious calumny put into circulation which he is able to refute from direct knowledge, to challenge it at once, and more especially if it is aimed at his own people, and meant to be used to their injury. It is true that in those regions for which these calumnies are prepared they are too generally preferred to the truth, even when the truth is offered; but the duty of affirming the truth is no less obligatory on those who are able to affirm it. It is with this view that the following paper is written, to correct certain statements which recently appeared in *Appletons' Journal,** professing to relate facts gleaned during a trip to Andersonville, Georgia, concerning the Confederate military prison there and the treatment of Federal prisoners. Instead of reviewing the article in detail, I will merely take up, one by one, the principal false statements.

THE WATER THE PRISONERS DRANK.

It was my fortune to be stationed at Andersonville almost from the first establishment of the prison until the removal to Millen, Georgia, or Camp Lawton, and I unhesitatingly pronounce the statement that "the prisoners had to drink the water which conveyed the offal of three camps and two large bakeries or kitchens off before it reached them," utterly

* See September monthly part "A Jaunt in the South." These corrections were offered to that journal, but declined on the ground of personal regard for the author of "A Jaunt in the South," who is a regular contributor.

false. The guards drank of the same water that quenched the prisoners' thirst, cooked their food with the same water, the same large stream or creek flowing through the encampment of guards and stockade, or prison pen, as Northern writers sneeringly call it. The camps of the guards all faced the stream, while their sinks were far off in the rear, and orders were most strict not to muddy the water, much less defile it in any way. As to the offal of the bakeries, these being presided over by prisoners on parole, and who did the cooking for the entire prison, I cannot believe they would pollute the water their brother prisoners had to drink. As rapidly as they could, the prisoners dug wells; in all, some two hundred were dug, and purer, sweeter, colder water I never drank. Being on the staff of Captain Wirz, I had free access to the prison at all times day or night, and whenever I wished to quench my thirst I went inside the prison and drank from one of these wells.

REASONS WHY THERE WERE NO BARRACKS.

The Confederate Government has always been harshly assailed for its want of humanity in not having barracks to house the prisoners from the sun and rains. A more senseless hue and cry was never heard. How was it possible to saw timber into planks without saw-mills? There were two water-power mills distant three and six miles respectively, but such rude, primitive affairs undeserving the name. The nearest steam saw-mill was twenty-three miles distant (near Smithville), the next at Reynolds, about fifty miles distant; but the great bulk of the lumber used, fully two-thirds, was brought from Gordon, a distance of eighty miles. Even if these mills had had the capacity to supply the necessary amount of lumber, it would still have been impossible to have provided barracks for the prisoners, as all the available engines of all the railroads in the Confederacy were taxed to their utmost capacity in transporting supplies for the army in the field and to the prisons. But few even of the officers of the guard had shanties, and these few were built of slabs and sheeting, which every one knows is the refuse of the mills. And even though there were no lack of lumber, when we remember that there was but one solitary manufactory of cut nails in the limits of the Confederacy, certainly no blame could be attached to the authorities for not furnishing more comfortable quarters for them. Nearly every building in the encampment was built of rough logs and covered with clap-boards split from the tree and held to their places by poles. The force of these statements is readily appreciated by every intelligent, unprejudiced mind. Besides, is it customary for any nation in time of war to treat their prisoners in a more humane manner than their own soldiers in the field? The inquiry becomes pertinent when we reflect, that during the last two years of the war there was not a tent of any description to be found in any of the armies of the Confederacy, save such as were captured from the Federals.

HOW THE STOCKADE WAS BUILT.

The stockade was built by the negroes belonging to the neighboring farms, either hired or pressed into service by the Confederate authorities to cut down the immense pine-trees growing on the ground intended for the stockade; and these same trees were then cut into proper lengths and hewn upon the spot, and then planted in a ditch dug four feet deep to receive them. In this manner was the stockade made. Before it was completed the prisoners were forwarded in great numbers; and it being impossible to keep them in the cars, we had to put them in the completed end of the stockade and double the guards, and our whole force kept ever ready day and night for the slightest alarm; for at first we had only the shattered remnants of two regiments — the Twenty-sixth Alabama and the Fifty-fifth Georgia — numbering in all some three hundred and fifty men. This constituted the guard. In about ten days thereafter my regiment — the First Georgia Reserves, composed of young boys and old men (I was not sixteen), just organized — were sent to take the place of the Twenty-sixth Alabama and Twenty-sixth Georgia, so they could be sent to the front for duty. In a few days after our arrival the 2d, 3d and 4th Georgia Reserves, all composed of lads and hoary-headed men (for we were reduced to the strait of "robbing the cradle and the grave for men to make soldiers of"), joined us as rapidly as they could be organised. The author of "A Jaunt in the South" says: "When the stockade was occupied in 1864 there was not a tree or blade of grass within it. Its reddish sand was entirely barren, and not the smallest particle of green showed itself. But now the surface is covered completely with underbrush; a rich growth of bushes, trees and plants has covered the entire area, and where before was a dreary desert there is now a wild and luxurious garden." I have before said the ground was covered with a pine forest, and the trees were utilised to build the stockade. Any one who has travelled south of Macon, Georgia, knows the pine is abundant, and in fact almost the only tree.

In these forests the ground is covered by wire grass or other grass peculiar to them.

WHY ANDERSONVILLE WAS SELECTED.

The main reasons for locating the prison at Andersonville, after its first being thought the most secure place in the Confederacy from Yankee cavalry raids, was the abundance of the water, and the timber wherewith to construct the prison rapidly, and its being in the very heart of the grain-growing region of the South, which would make it less inconvenient to supply with provisions such a vast multitude.

RATIONS TO GUARDS AND PRISONERS THE SAME.

I was for three months a clerk in the Commissary Department at Andersonville, and it was my business to weigh out rations for the guards and prisoners alike; and I solemnly assert, that the prisoners got ounce for ounce and pound for pound of just the same quality and quantity of food as did the guards. The State authorities of Ohio ought to blush at thus traducing and slandering a fallen foe, and never in the first instance to have placed on exhibition for preservation as truth this fabrication of partisan hate. No Andersonville prisoner, unless he were lost to all sense of honor and shame, could make such a statement as that the rations were no more than the specimens shown.

WHY THE PRISONERS WERE FED ON CORN BREAD.

It has been charged as a crying shame upon the Confederacy by ignorant humanitarians, that the South might at least have given the prisoners wheat bread occasionally; that they rarely ate corn bread in their own land, and that the bread we issued was made of meal so coarse and unsifted that it caused dysentery, thereby largely increasing the mortality. It is well known now that the South depends very largely, and with shame I confess it, on the West for her bread and bacon, and the cotton belt proper makes but little pretension of raising wheat, for the climate, it is said, is unsuited; so that the region round about Andersonville, being in the very heart of the cotton-growing section of Georgia, such a thing as feeding prisoners on flour was simply impossible, and the little flour that was obtained as tithes (one-tenth of all the crops raised was required by our Government) was devoted entirely to the use of the hospitals. Not only was this true of the territory immediately surrounding Andersonville, but of the whole South. Our own armies were unsupplied with flour, and perhaps not one family in fifty throughout the whole land enjoyed that luxury. The guards ate the same bread or rather meal; the bread eaten by the prisoners being baked by regular bakers (prisoners detailed for that purpose), while the guards did their own cooking. The meal, however, was the same, and both were unsifted, and in truth very coarse. I ate the unsifted meal always.

THE DEAD LINE.

Another cry of holy horror is raised every time the "Dead Line" is mentioned, as if this dead line was *prima facie* evidence that the Southerners were as barbarous and cruel a race as ever blotted the face of earth. The civilised North, however, had the same barbarous dead line in their prisons, and in fact originated the device. It was a necessity with us, for we had never at one time more than 1200 to 1500 guards in the four regiments fit for duty, and we had the keeping at one time of very nearly 40,000 prisoners. By a concerted plan of onslaught they could at any time have scaled the walls, captured guards, and with the weapons of their keepers overrun the entire country, which, all south of Dalton, Georgia (100 miles north of Atlanta), was left wholly unprotected, save by gray-haired old men and young boys; and the women, children, and negroes, who were the only hope for the making of crops for our armies, would have been helplessly at their mercy. This dead line was clearly defined, and consisted of stakes driven into the ground twenty feet from the stockade walls, and on these stakes was a three-inch strip of plank nailed all around the inside of the prison. They were all notified that a step beyond this line was not prudent, and they were not so unwise as to venture beyond that limit.

BURIAL OF DEAD PRISONERS.

Speaking of the number and burial of the dead, the writer of the aforesaid "Jaunt" says: "The authorities at the stockade who had charge of the interment of the Federal dead did their work rudely, . . . digging pits and burying them in." Then he goes on: "It is hard to comprehend the true value of the number, 14,000; its magnitude eludes you. Fourteen thousand men would form a great mob, or a great army, or a great town. Here you have 14,000 men lying silently in a few acres. Within these bounds men have suffered as greatly as have any since the world began." In reply to this, I would merely say the burial was the work of prisoners paroled especially for the purpose; both the hauling of the bodies to the ground, the digging of the graves, and even the records of the names were all done by paroled prisoners. Books and a tent were provided solely for the latter purpose. Owing to the weakness of the guard, paroled prisoners were employed for this duty, as we could spare no men for the purpose; and if the work was rudely or carelessly done, the blame rests with them. As compensation they were given double rations and almost entire freedom. As to the number of the dead, we admit that it is great, but statistics show that more Southern soldiers died in Northern prisons than Northern soldiers in Southern prisons. In vain have Northern writers tried to disprove this fact.

MORTALITY NO GREATER AMONG PRISONERS THAN GUARD.

Great as was the mortality among the prisoners, it was no greater in proportion to numbers than that of the guard, which is fully attested by the reports of the surgeon in charge. Besides, it is well known to every soul that can or does read, that the Confederacy, through their agent, Judge Ould, made frequent and tireless efforts to get the United States Government, through their agent, General Butler, to exchange. But no, the Federal authorities would not hear of it; but acting on the avowed and promulgated idea that the South, being blockaded, could not recruit her armies from foreign lands, while to the North the whole of Europe was opened, they cruelly determined not to exchange, so as to detain our soldiers from again fighting them, well knowing that even then we had made our last conscription (17 to 50 years), and when those we had were killed up or in prison we would of course be overpowered. This was their cold-blooded, brutal policy; and closely did they stick to it, even till we were almost literally wiped out; while the men they had fighting us were in most part hired substitutes, drafted men, and foreign hirelings.

PRINCIPAL CAUSE OF MORTALITY.

Farther, as to the mortality among the prisoners, let it be remembered that a majority of the deaths caused in our prisons was for want of proper medicines, which we did not have and could not get, except by blockade-running. Had the Federal Government any of the milk of human kindness in its composition, it would have acceded to our earnest request to take cotton in exchange for drugs to administer to their own dying soldiers. Their immense manufactories were lying idle for want of cotton, while we had it but could not use it. But as these self-same drugs and medicines would also be applied to the relief of our own sick soldiers, they determined it would be to their advantage to let all die alike, knowing the South could get no more men to supply the places of the sick, the dying, and those they had imprisoned; so refused all overtures. After using every effort and exhausting every argument to get an exchange, we proposed—as we had no medicines, and could get none, except what we accidentally ran in through the blockade from Europe (they being declared contraband, and always confiscated whenever captured by the blockading fleet)—we proposed to turn over to them all their sick, without requiring man for man, but giving them absolutely up, if the United States would only send vessels for transporting them. This was done at Camp Lawton (Millen, Georgia), after the prison was removed from Andersonville for greater security.

EXTRACTS FROM AN OFFICER'S DIARY.

From the private journal of a Confederate officer high in command both at Andersonville and other Southern prisons, I glean the annexed facts, the first bearing directly upon the foregoing:—"At one time an order came to Camp Lawton to prepare 2000 men for exchange. The order from Richmond was to select first the wounded, next the oldest prisoners and the sickly, filling up with healthy men according to date. This party went first to Savannah, as arranged; but by some mistake the ships were at Charleston, and the poor wretches had to be taken there; and every one who knew the Southern railroads in those days, and the difficulty, or rather impossibility to procure food for such a crowd along the road, will know what those poor fellows suffered. At Charleston they were refused, the commissioner declaring that 'he was not going to exchange able-bodied men for such miserable specimens of humanity.' (The term used was more brutal). Finding him obdurate, Colonel Ould requested him to take them without exchange. This he refused with a sneering laugh, and the crowd was ordered back. Never did the writer of this witness such woe-begone countenances, in which misery and hopelessness were more strongly painted, than shown by those poor fellows on their return. And the curses leveled against the rulers who thus treated the defenders of their country were fearful, although certainly well deserved. As the stockade-gate closed upon them, the surgeon in charge said to the writer: 'Poor fellows! the world has closed upon more than half of them; this disappointment will be their death-knell.' His words proved true. Who murdered those men? Let history answer the question."

CLOTHING FOR PRISONERS.

Again I extract from the aforesaid journal:—"The Northerners talk so much of the cruelty of the South to the Federal prisoners. At one time the unfortunate prisoners were almost without clothing, indeed some had hardly as much as common decency required. The South could not provide them, not being able to clothe their own men. An application was made to Seward. The reply was that 'the Federal Government did not supply clothing to prisoners of war.' Luckily for the poor fellows, a society in New York took the matter in hand, and several bales of clothing and cases of shoes were forwarded to Richmond, and divided, in proportion to numbers, among the prisons."

CRUELTY TO PRISONERS.

A great deal has been said of the cruelty to the prisoners inside the stockade. This so-called cruelty was inflicted by their own men. In every prison, a police with a chief, all from the prisoners, was appointed to keep order, see to the enforcement of the regulations, and inquire into all offences, reporting through their chief to the Commandant. The punishments, such as were used in the Federal army, were ordered to be inflicted by these men, and some were of such a barbarous nature that they were prohibited with disgust by the Confederate officers, who substituted milder and more humane ones; and yet the former were in common practice in the Federal armies, as testified by all the prisoners.

BLOODHOUNDS.

Among the numerous lies invented by Northerners, and actually still believed by some parties to this day, was the story that the Confederates used to hunt and worry prisoners with bloodhounds. Now it is well known that the breed of bloodhounds is nearly extinct in the South, and the large packs of those dogs alluded to by writers on this subject existed only in their imaginations, the prolific brains of penny-a-liners, whose vile and lying compositions even now abound in many so-called respectable New York papers. No public man is safe from their atrocious attacks. Among the various speciments of this dog alluded to by the above-named gentry, was the famous bloodhound of the Libby Prison. The writer has often seen this formidable animal, which certainly in his youth must have been as fine a specimen of the kind as could be met anywhere ; but, unfortunately for the thrilling portion of the account of his doings at the time of the war, the poor beast, worn out from old age, and with hardly a tooth in his head, wandered about, a harmless, inoffensive creature. He was the property of the Commandant of Libby, who kept him because he was a pet dog of his father's, and there the brute lived, a pensioner in his old age. As to his worrying men, he could not, had he even tried, have worried a child. The other prisons had none, not even as pensioners. Among the records history gives us of using those dogs to hunt men, it is stated that during the Florida war a number of bloodhounds were imported by the Federal Government from Cuba to hunt the Indians out of the Everglades, and that numbers of the natives were worried to death by the ferocious beasts. The writer does not deny that when a prisoner got out of the stockade trying to escape, if no clue could be obtained of his whereabouts, a few mongrel or half-breed fox-hounds were used to *track* him, but the worrying was all done in the correspondent's own brain. However, it suited the times and made the article sell. The only complaint made is, that this vile and malicious lie is still, if not believed, repeated by some who use it for party purposes, and thus help to keep up the bad feeling between North and South.

LETTER OF GEN. IMBODEN TO GEN. MAURY.

RICHMOND, VA., *January* 12, 1876.

GENERAL D. H. MAURY,

Chairman of the Executive Committee of the Southern Historical Society:

GENERAL—At your request, I cheerfully reduce to writing the facts stated by me in our conversation this morning, for preservation in the archives of your society, and as bearing upon a historical question—the treatment of prisoners during our late civil war, which it seems certain politicians of the vindictive type in the North, led by a Presidential aspirant, have deemed it essential to their party success to thrust upon the country again, in the beginning of this our centennial year.

It is to be hoped that, after a lapse of ten years since we of the South grounded our arms, passion has so far yielded to patriotism, reason, and sentiments of a common humanity in the minds and hearts of the great mass of intelligent people at the North, that all the facts relating to the great struggle between the States of the North and South may be calmly presented, if not for final decision by this generation, at least to aid impartial mankind in the future to judge correctly between the conquering and the vanquished parties to the contest; and to fix the responsibility where it attaches, to the one side or the other, or to both, for sufferings inflicted that were not necessarily incident to a state of war between contending Christian powers.

I now proceed to give you a simple historical narrative of facts within my personal knowledge, that I believe have never been published, although at the request of Judge Robert Ould, of this city, who was the Confederate Commissioner for the Exchange of Prisoners, I wrote them out in 1866, and furnished the MS. to a reporter of the New York *Herald*. But the statement never appeared in that journal, for the reason assigned by the reporter, that the conductors of the *Herald* deemed the time inopportune for such a publication. My MS. was retained by them, and I have never heard of it since.

It is perhaps proper to state how I came to be connected with the prison service of the Confederate States. An almost fatal attack of typhoid fever, in the summer and fall of 1864, so impaired my physical condition that I was incapable of performing efficiently the arduous duties of my position as a cavalry officer on active service in the mountains of Virginia, and therefore I applied to the Confederate War Office for assignment to some light duty farther south, till the milder weather of the ensuing spring would enable me to take my place at the head of the brave and hardy mountaineers of the Valley and western counties of Virginia I had the honor to command. General R. E. Lee kindly urged my application in person, and procured an order directing me to report to Brigadier-general J. H. Winder, then Commissary of Prisoners, whose headquarters were at Columbia, South Carolina. I left my camp in the Shenandoah Valley late in December 1864, and reached Columbia, I think, on the 6th of January 1865. General Winder immediately ordered me to the command of all the prisons west of the Savannah river, with leave to establish my temporary headquarters at Aiken, South Carolina, on account of the salubrity of its climate. I cannot fix dates after this with absolute precision, because all my official papers fell into the hands of the United States military authorities after the surrender of General Joseph E. Johnston to General Sherman; but for all essential purposes my memory enables me to detail events in consecutive order, and approximately to assign each to its proper date.

A few days after receiving my orders from General Winder, I reached Aiken, and visited Augusta, Georgia, and established an office there in charge of a staff-officer, Lieutenant George W. McPhail, for prompt and convenient communication with the prisons of the department.

About my first official act was to dispatch Lieutenant-Colonel Bondurant on a tour of inspection of the prisons in my department, with instructions to report fully on their condition and management. Whilst Colonel Bondurant was on this service, I was forced to quit Aiken by the approach of Kilpatrick's cavalry, moving on the flank of Sherman's army. A detachment of this cavalry reached Aiken within four hours after I left it. I then made Augusta my permanent headquarters, residing, however, a few miles out on the Georgia railroad at Berzelia. Colonel Bondurant promptly discharged the duty assigned to him, and on the state of facts presented in his reports, I resolved to keep up but two prisons, the one at Andersonville and the other at Eufaula. I did this for economical reasons, and because it was easier to supply two posts than four or five so widely scattered; and besides, the whole number of prisoners in the department then did not exceed 8000 or 9000—the great majority, about 7500, being at Andersonville.

Before I received Colonel Bondurant's report, General Winder died, when, having no superior in command, I reported directly to the Secretary of War at Richmond. Communication with the War Office was at that period very slow and difficult. Great military operations were in progress. General Sherman was moving through the Carolinas. The Federal cavalry under Kilpatrick with Sherman, and Stoneman co-operating from Tennessee, almost suspended mail facilities between Georgia and Virginia, and the telegraph was almost impracticable, because the line was taxed almost to its capacity, in connection with active military operations. After the death of General Winder, I made repeated efforts to establish communication with the Secretary of War, and with Commissioner Ould, and obtain some instructions in regard to the prisons and prisoners under my charge. All these efforts failed, at least I received no reply by wire, mail or messenger to any of my inquiries. A newspaper fell into my hands, in which, as an item of news, I saw it stated that Brigadier-general Gideon J. Pillow had been appointed General Winder's successor. General Pillow was then at Macon, but had received no official notification of his appointment, and I having none, could not, and did not, recognise him as entitled to command me, but cheerfully, as will appear further on, consulted him in regard to all important matters of administration.

Colonel Bondurant's report on the Andersonville prison, taken in connection with written applications from Captain Wirz which I had received, suggesting measures for the amelioration of the condition of the prisoners, strongly endorsed and approved by Colonel Gibbs, an old United States army officer, a cultivated, urbane and humane gentleman, commanding the post, made it apparent to my mind that I ought to make a personal examination into its condition. This was no easy undertaking, as I had to travel over almost impassable country roads, through the desolated belt of country traversed by Sherman's army in its march through Georgia, for a distance of over seventy miles, before I could reach a railroad to take me to Andersonville. I made the journey, however, in February.

On my arrival at Andersonville, unannounced and unexpected, I made an immediate and personal inspection of everything—not only as then existing, but with the aid of the post and prison record, I went back several months, to the period when the mortality was so great, to ascertain, if possible, its cause.

The guard then on duty consisted of a brigade of Georgia State troops, under command of Brigadier-general Gartrell. The post was commanded by Colonel Gibbs, who, as before stated, was an old army officer; and the prison proper was under the immediate command of Captain Wirz, who was tried and executed at Washington, in 1865, most unjustly, as the verdict of impartial history will establish; just as will be the case in regard to Mrs. Surratt's horrible murder.

The officers first named, and all others on duty there, afforded me every facility to prosecute my investigations to the fullest extent, and were prompt to point out to me measures of relief that were practicable. I went within the stockade and conversed with many of the prisoners. I found the prison and its inmates in a bad condition; not as bad as our enemies have represented, yet unfortunately bad. The location of the stockade was good, and had been judiciously chosen for healthfulness. It occupied two gently sloping hillsides, with a clear flowing brook dividing them; and being in the sandy portion of the pine-woods of Georgia, it was free from local malaria, and had the benefit of a genial and healthy climate. It was of sufficient capacity for from 8000 to 9000 prisoners, without uncomfortable crowding. The great mortality of the previous year, I have no doubt, resulted in part from an excess of prisoners over the fair capacity of the stockade, and from the lack of sufficient shelter from the sun and rain. Before my arrival at Andersonville, Captain Wirz had, by a communication forwarded through Colonel Gibbs, and approved by him, called my attention to the great deficiency of shelter in the stockade, and asked authority to supply it. He had made a similar application, I was informed, to General Winder some time before, but it had not been acted on before the General's death. In consequence of this want of buildings and shedding within the stockade, the prisoners had excavated a great many subterranean vaults and chambers in the hillsides, which many of them occupied, to the injury of their health, as these places were not sufficiently ventilated.

The prisoners were very badly off for clothing, shoes and hats, and complained of this destitution, and of the quantity and kind of rations — corn bread and bacon chiefly — issued to them. I found, what I anticipated, that we had no clothing to give them. Many of the men on duty as guards were in rags, and either barefooted, or had their feet protected with worn-out shoes, held together with strings and thongs, and in lieu of overcoats many had to protect themselves against inclement weather with a tattered blanket drawn over the shoulders. Our own men being in this destitute condition, it can be well understood that we could not supply a large demand for clothing prisoners.

They also suffered greatly, and there had been great mortality, for want of suitable medicines to treat the diseases incident to their condition with any considerable success. From this cause, and this alone, I have no doubt thousands died at Andersonville in 1864, who would be living to-day if the United States Government had not declared medicines contraband of war, and by their close blockade of our coasts deprived us of an adequate supply of those remedial agents that therapeutical science and modern chemistry have produced for the amelioration of suffering humanity. The object of this barbarous decree against the Confederacy, it is now well understood, was to expose our soldiers, as well as our wives, children and families, without protection or relief, to the diseases common in our climate, and to make us an easy prey to death, approach us in what form he might; not foreseeing, perhaps, that when the grim monster stalked through our prisons, he would find not alone *Confederates* for his victims, but the stalwart soldiers of the Government which had invoked his aid against us. At the time of my inspection, there was a good deal of sickness amongst the prisoners, but not a large percentage of mortality. Our medical officers, even with their scanty pharmacopœia, gave equal attention to sick friends and enemies, to guard and to prisoners alike.

I investigated particularly the food question, and found that no discrimination was made in the issue of rations to guards and prisoners. In quantity, quality and kind, the daily supply was exactly the same, man for man. It is true it was very scanty, consisting of a third or half a pound of meat a day, and usually a pint or pint and a half of corn-meal, with salt. Occasionally there were small supplies of wheat flour, and sometimes a very few potatoes, but they were rarely to be had. Other vegetables we had none. General Lee's army in Virginia lived but little, if any better. The food was sound and wholesome, but meagre in quantity, and not such in kind and variety as Federal soldiers had been accustomed to draw from their abundant commissariat. Our soldiers did very well on "hog and hominy," and rarely complained. The Federals thought it horrible to have nothing else, and but a scanty supply of this simple food. Great scoundrelism was detected among the prisoners in cheating each other. They were organised in companies of a hundred each in the stockade, and certain men of their own selection were permitted to come outside the stockade and draw the rations for their fellows, and cook them. Many of these rascals would steal and secrete a part of the food, and as opportunity offered, sell it at an exorbitant rate to their famished comrades. Shortly before I went to Andersonville, six of these villains were detected, and by permission of the prison authorities, the prisoners themselves organised a court of their own, tried them for the offence, found them guilty, and hung them inside the stockade. This event led to a change in the mode of issuing rations, which precluded the possibility of such a diabolical traffic in stolen food.

Bad as was the physical condition of the prisoners, their mental depression was worse, and perhaps more fatal. Thousands of them collected around me in the prison, and begged me to tell them whether there was any hope of release by an exchange of prisoners. Some time before that, President

Davis had permitted three of the Andersonville prisoners to go to Washington to try and change the determination of their Government and procure a resumption of exchanges. The prisoners knew of the failure of this mission when I was at Andersonville, and the effect was to plunge the great majority of them into the deepest melancholy, home-sickness and despondency. They believed their confinement would continue to the end of the war, and many of them looked upon that as a period so indefinite and remote that they believed that they would die of their sufferings before the day of release came. I explained to them the efforts we had made and were still making to effect an exchange. A Federal captain at Andersonville, learning that I had a brother of the same rank (Captain F. M. Imboden, of the Eighteenth Virginia Cavalry) incarcerated at Johnson's Island, in Lake Erie, where he was in a fair way to die from harsh treatment and a lack of food, represented to me that he had powerful connections at Washington, and thought that if I would parole him he could effect his exchange for my brother, and perhaps influence a decision on the general question of exchanges. He agreed to return in thirty days if he failed. I accepted his terms, and with some difficulty got him through the lines. He failed, and returned within our lines, but just in time to be set at liberty again, as will appear further on. I regret that I have forgotten his name, and have no record of it.

I have already alluded to Captain Wirz's recommendation to put up more shelter. I ordered it, and thereafter daily a hundred or more prisoners were paroled and set to work in the neighboring forest. In the course of a fortnight, comfortable log-houses, with floors and good chimneys—for which the prisoners made and burnt the brick — were erected for twelve or fifteen hundred men, and were occupied by those in feeble health, who were withdrawn from the large stockade and separated from the mass of prisoners. This same man (Captain Wirz), who was tried and hung as a murderer, warmly urged the establishment of a tannery and shoemaker's shop, informing me that there were many men amongst the prisoners skilled in these trades, and that some of them knew a process of very rapidly converting hides into tolerably good leather. There were thousands of hides at Andersonville, from the young cattle butchered during the previous summer and fall, whilst the country yet contained such animals. I ordered this, too; and a few weeks later many of the barefooted prisoners were supplied with rough, but comfortable shoes; one of them made and sent to me a pair that surprised me, both by the quality of the leather and the style of the shoes. Another suggestion came from the medical staff of the post that I ordered to be at once put into practice: it was to brew corn beer for those suffering from scorbutic taint. The corn-meal — or even whole corn — being scalded in hot water and a mash made of it, a little yeast was added to promote fermentation, and in a few days a sharp acid beverage was produced, by no means unpalatable, and very wholesome. Captain Wirz entered warmly into this enterprise. I mention these facts to show that he was not the monster he was afterwards represented to be, when his blood was called for by infuriate fanaticism. I would have proved these facts if I had been permitted to testify on his trial after I was summoned before the court by the United States, and have substantiated them by the records of the prison and of my own headquarters, if these records were not destroyed, suppressed or mutilated at the time. But after being kept an hour in the court-room, during an earnest and whispered consultation between the President of the court and the Judge-advocate, and their examination of a great mass of papers, the contents of which I could not see, I was politely dismissed without examination, and told I would be called at another time; but I never was, and thus Wirz was deprived of the benefit of my evidence. My personal acquaintance with Captain Wirz was very slight, but the facts I have alluded to satisfied me that he was a humane man, and was selected as a victim to the bloody Moloch of 1865, because he was a foreigner and comparatively friendless. I put these facts on record now, to vindicate, as far as they go, his memory from the monstrous crimes falsely charged against him. No such charges ever reached me, whilst I was in a position to have made it a duty to investigate them, as those upon which he was tried and executed. He may have committed grave offences, but if so, I never knew it, and do not believe it.

After having given my sanction and orders to carry out every suggestion of others, or that occurred to my own mind, for the amelioration of the condition of the prisoners as far as we possessed the means, and having issued stringent orders to preserve discipline amongst the guarding troops, and subordination, quiet and good order amongst the prisoners, I went to Macon to confer with General Howell Cobb and General Gideon J. Pillow as to the proper course for me to pursue in the event of our situation in Georgia becoming more precarious, or the chance of communication with the Government at Richmond being entirely cut off, which appeared to be an almost certain event in the very near future. After a full discussion of the situation, there was perfect accord in our views. General Pillow was expecting to receive official notice of his appointment as Commissary of Prisons, in which event he would become my commanding officer. General Cobb commanded the State troops of Georgia, and I was dependent on him for a sufficient force to discharge my duties and hold the prisoners in custody. There was eminent propriety, therefore, in our conferring with each other, and acting harmoniously in whatever course might be adopted. General Pillow took a leading part in the discussion, and in shaping the conclusions to which we came. In the absence of official information or instructions from Richmond, we acted upon what the newspapers announced as a recently established arrangement with General Grant, which was, in effect, that either side might deliver to the other on parole, but without exchange, any prisoners they chose, taking simply a receipt for them. We had no official information of any such agreement from our Government, but it was regarded by us as very probably true, and we decided to act upon it. The difficulty of supplying the prisoners with even a scanty ration of corn-meal and bacon was increasing daily. The Cotton States had never been a grazing country, and therefore we had few or no animals left there for food, except hogs. These States were not a large wheat-producing region, and for that reason we had to depend mainly on corn for bread. Salt was scarce and hard to obtain. Vegetables we had none for army purposes. We were destitute of clothing, and of the materials and machinery to manufacture it in sufficient quantities for our own soldiers and people. And the Federal Government, remaining deaf to all appeals for exchange of prisoners, it was manifest that the incarceration of their captured soldiers could no longer be of any possible advantage to us, since to relieve their sufferings that Government would take no step, if it involved a similar release of our men in their hands. Indeed, it was manifest that they looked upon it as an advantage to them, and an injury to us, to leave their prisoners in our hands to eat out our little remaining substance. In view of all these facts and considerations, Generals Cobb and Pillow and I were of one mind, that the best thing that could be done was, without further efforts to get instructions from Richmond, to make arrangements to send off all the prisoners we had at Eufaula and Andersonville to the nearest accessible Federal post, and having paroled them not to bear arms till regularly exchanged, to deliver them unconditionally, simply taking a receipt on descriptive rolls of the men thus turned over.

In pursuance of this determination, and as soon as the necessary arrangements could be made, a detachment of about 1500 men, made up from the two prisons, was sent to Jackson, Mississippi, by rail, and delivered to their friends. General "Dick" Taylor at that time commanded the department through which these prisoners were sent to Jackson, and objected to any more being sent that way, on the ground that they would pick up information on the route detrimental to our military interests. The only remaining available outlet was at Saint Augustine, Florida, Sherman having destroyed railway communication with Savannah. Finding that the prisoners could be sent from Andersonville by rail to the Chattahoochie, thence down that river to Florida, near Quincy, and from Quincy by rail to Jacksonville, within a day's march of Saint Augustine, it was resolved to open communication with the Federal commander at the latter place. With that view, somewhere about the middle of March, Captain Rutherford, an intelligent and energetic officer, was sent to Saint Augustine. A few days after his departure for Florida, he telegraphed from Jacksonville, "Send on the prisoners." He had, as he subsequently reported, arranged with the Federal authorities to receive them. At once all were ordered to be sent forward who were able to bear the journey. Three days' cooked rations were prepared, and so beneficial to health was the revival of the spirits of these men by the prospect of once more being at liberty, that I believe all but twelve or fifteen reported themselves able to go, and did go. The number sent was over 6000. Only enough officers and men of the guard went along to keep the prisoners together, preserve order, and facilitate their transportation. To my amazement, the officer commanding the escort telegraphed back from Jacksonville that the Federal commandant at Saint Augustine refused to receive and receipt for the prisoners till he could hear from General Grant, who was then in front of Petersburg, Virginia, and with whom he could only communicate by sea along the coast, and asking my instructions under the circumstances. Acting without the known sanction of the Government at Richmond, I was afraid to let go the prisoners without some official acknowledgment of their delivery to the United States; and knowing that two or three weeks must elapse before General Grant's will in the premises could be made known, and it being impossible to subsist our men and the prisoners at Jacksonville, I could pursue but one course. I ordered their return to Andersonville, directing that the reason for this unexpected result should be fully explained to them. Provisions were hastily collected and sent to meet them, and in a few days all were back in their old quarters. I was not there on their return, but it was reported to me that their indignation against their Government was intense, many declaring their readiness to renounce allegiance to it and take up arms with us. The old routine was resumed at Andersonville, but it was not destined to continue long.

Before any further communication reached me from Saint Augustine, General Wilson, with a large body of cavalry, approached Georgia from the West. It was evident that his first objective point was Andersonville. Again conferring with Generals Cobb and Pillow, and finding we were powerless to prevent Wilson's reaching Andersonville, where he would release the prisoners and capture all our officers and troops there, it was decided, without hesitation, again to send the prisoners to Jacksonville, and turn them loose to make the best of their way to their friends at Saint Augustine. This was accomplished in a few days, the post at Andersonville was broken up, the Georgia State troops were sent to General Cobb at Macon, and in a short time the surrender of General Johnston to Sherman, embracing all that section of country, the Confederate prisons ceased to exist, and on the 3d of May, 1865, I was myself a prisoner of war, on parole at Augusta, Georgia. A few days later I was sent with other paroled Confederates to Hilton Head, South Carolina, where I met about 2000 of the Andersonville prisoners, who had been sent up from Saint Augustine, to be thence shipped North. Their condition was much improved. Many of them were glad to see me, and four days later I embarked with several hundred of them on the steam transport "Thetis" for Fortress Monroe, and have reason to believe that every man of them felt himself my friend rather than an enemy.

It has been charged that Mr. Davis, as President of the Confederate States, was responsible for the sufferings of prisoners held in the South. During my four months' connection with this disagreeable branch of Confederate military service, no communication, direct or indirect, was ever received by me from Mr. Davis, and, so far as I remember, the records of the prison contained nothing to implicate him in any way with its management or administration. I have briefly alluded to the causes of complaint on the part of prisoners; and even were these well founded, I am at a loss to see how Mr. Davis is to be held responsible before the world for their existence, till it is proved that he knew of them and failed to remove delinquent officers.

The real cause of all the protracted sufferings of prisoners, North and South, is directly due to the inhuman refusal of the Federal Government to exchange prisoners of war; a policy that we see, from the facts herein stated, was carried so far as to induce a commanding officer, at Saint Augustine, to refuse even to receive, and acknowledge that he had received, over 6000 men of his own side, tendered to him unconditionally, from that prison in the South which, above all others, they charged to have been the scene of unusual suffering. The inference is irresistible, that this officer felt that it would be dangerous to his official character to relieve the Confederacy of the burthen of supporting these prisoners, although he and his countrymen affected to believe that we were slowly starving them to death. The policy at Washington was to let Federal prisoners starve, if the process involved the Confederates in a similar catastrophe—and "fired the Northern heart."

I have introduced more of my personal movements and actions into this recital than is agreeable, or apparently in good taste; but it has been unavoidable, in making the narrative consecutive and intelligible, and, I trust, will be pardoned, even if appearing to transcend the bounds of becoming modesty. In the absence of all my official papers relating to these subjects (which I presume were taken to Washington after I surrendered them, and are still there, unless it was deemed policy to destroy them when Captain Wirz was on trial), I have not been able to go into many minute details that might add interest to the statement; but nothing, I think, to the leading fact — that the United States refused an unconditional delivery of so many of its own men, inmates of that prison (Andersonville) which they professed then to regard as a Confederate slaughter-pen, and place of intentional diabolical cruelties inflicted on the sick and helpless. Was this course not a part of a policy of deception for "firing the Northern heart"? Impartial history will one day investigate and answer this question. And there we may safely leave it, with a simple record of the facts.

Very truly, your friend,

J. D. Imboden.

LETTER OF HON. R. G. H. KEAN, CHIEF CLERK OF THE CONFEDERATE WAR DEPARTMENT.

LYNCHBURG, VA., *March* 22, 1876.

REV. J. WILLIAM JONES,

Secretary Southern Historical Society:

My Dear Sir:—Yours of the 20th is received this A. M., and I snatch the time from the heart of a busy day to reply immediately, because I feel that there is no more imperious call on a Confederate than to do what he may to hurl back the vile official slanders of the Federal Government at Washington in 1865, when Holt, Conover & Co., with a pack of since convicted perjurers, were doing all in their power to blacken the fame of a people whose presence they have since found and acknowledged to be indispensable to any semblance of purity in their administration of affairs.

In September, 1865, I was required by the then commandant at Charlottesville to report immediately to him. The summons was brought to me in the field, where, in my shirt sleeves, I was assisting in the farming operations of my father-in-law, Colonel T. J. Randolph, and his eldest son, Major T. J. Randolph. I obeyed, and was sent by the next train to report to General Terry, then in command in Richmond. He informed me that I was wanted, and had long been sought for, to testify before the Commission engaged in trying Wirz, and I was sent to Washington by the next train. I attended promptly, but it was two or three days before I was examined as a witness When I was, a paper taken from the records of our War Office was shown me — the report of Lieutenant-Colonel Chandler of his inspection of the post at Andersonville. I remembered the paper well. This writer in the *Sauk Rapids Sentinel* is in error when he says this report was "delivered in person to the Confederate Assistant Secretary of War." It had been sent through the usual channels, and reaching the hands of Colonel R. H. Chilton, Assistant Inspector-General, in charge of the inspection branch of the Adjutant and Inspector-General's bureau, was brought into the War Office by Colonel Chilton and placed in my hands, with the endorsement quoted by this writer, or something to that effect. Colonel Chilton explained to me that the report disclosed such a state of things at Andersonville, that he had brought it to me, in order that it might receive prompt attention, instead of sending it through the usual routine channel. I read it immediately, and was shocked at its contents. I do not remember the passage quoted by this writer, but I do remember that it showed that the 32,000 men herded in the stockade at Andersonville were dying of scurvy and other diseases, engendered by their crowded condition and insufficient supplies of medicines, suitable food, and medical attendance, at the rate of ten per cent., or about 3000 a month. Shocked at such a waste of human life, produced by the fraudulent refusal to observe the cartel for exchange of prisoners, whom we had neither the force to guard in a large enclosure, nor proper food for when sick, nor medicines, save such as we could smuggle into our ports or manufacture from the plants of Southern growth, I took the report to Judge Campbell, Assistant Secretary of War, and told him of the horrors it disclosed. He read it, and made on it an endorsement substantially the same quoted, and carried it to Mr. Seddon, then Secretary of War. My office was between that of the Assistant Secretary and the Secretary, and the latter passed through mine with the paper in his hand. I testified to these facts before the Wirz Commission, and also to this further. As well as I remember, it was early in August that these endorsements were made. In October, Colonel Chandler, who was, I think, a Mississippian, and with whom I had no previous acquaintance, presented himself in my office, and stated to me that he had been officially informed that General Winder, on being called on, in August, for a response to the parts of his report which reflected on or blamed him (Winder), had responded by making an issue of veracity with him (Chandler); that he (C.) had promptly demanded a court of inquiry, but that none had ever been ordered. He expressed himself as very unwilling to lie under such an imputation, and urgently desirous to have the subject investigated. His appearance and manner were very good — those of a gentleman and a man of honor; and, in sympathy with his feelings (though I told him that it was extremely improbable that officers of suitable rank could be spared from the service to conduct such an investigation at that time), I told him I would call the attention of the Secretary to the matter. Accordingly, I got the report, and placing around it a slip of paper in the usual official manner, I endorsed to this effect: "Lieutenant-Colonel Chandler is here in person, urging that a court of inquiry be named to investigate the issues between him and General Winder touching this report. He seems to feel his position painfully"— addressed to the Secretary of War. Mr. Seddon told me afterwards that in the then state of things it was impossible to spare officers of suitable rank — so many were prisoners that the supply in the field was insufficient, or to that effect—and Colonel Chandler was so informed, either by me in person or by letter. This endorsement of mine, dated in October, 1864, was the thing which connected me with the report, and caused me to be summoned to Washington to trace it into the hands of the Secretary of War. The effort was assiduously made by Colonel L. R. Chipman, the Judge-advocate of the Wirz Commission, to show by me that this report was seen by President Davis; but that effort failed, because I knew nothing on that subject. This was substantially all that I knew of my own knowledge, and so was competent to prove as a witness, in respect to the report. But very much more came to my knowledge as hearsay, not competent legally, yet as credible as what I knew directly.

My observations, during the several days I was in attendance and watching the proceedings of the Commission, convinced me — whether rightly or wrongly, subsequent events have in some degree developed — that the destruction of Wirz was a very subordinate object of his so-called trial; that the main objects were to blacken the character of the Southern Government, and, as I thought, to compass the death of Mr. Davis and Mr. Seddon, who were not technically on trial, but were alleged to have "conspired" with Wirz and others to kill and murder the Federal prisoners, &c. One was immured in irons in a casemate of Fortress Monroe, the other was in a casemate in Fort Pulaski. Believing that their lives were in danger, I sought Mr. L. Q. Washington, who was then in Washington, and communicated to him the apprehensions I felt, and urged him to communicate them to Mr. Seddon's friends, with whom I knew him to be intimate. I learned that he did so; and Mrs. Seddon sent Captain Philip Welford, a gentleman of great intelligence, to Washington, to see what was best to be done to protect her helpless husband, who was being prosecuted while a prisoner six hundred miles away. The result of Captain Welford's investigations and conferences with friends in Washington, was that it was not deemed judicious for Mr. Seddon to be represented directly by counsel, but that he should place his materials of defence and explanation touching the Chandler report in the hands of Wirz's counsel; and this was done. The Government had gone into all this matter, and the response, therefore, on every principle of fair dealing or of law, was legitimate *in that cause.* Colonel Robert Ould and General J. E. Mulford, therefore, were summoned to show what the action of the Confederate Government on Colonel Chandler's report was. Judge Ould attended, and General Mulford was prepared to do so and to corroborate him. Judge Ould, as Mr. Welford informed me, unless my memory is at fault, was prepared to state that as soon as Colonel Chandler's report was presented to Mr. Seddon, the latter sent for him and showed the terrible mortality prevailing at Andersonville, instructed him to go down James river at once with his flag-of-truce boat, see General Mulford, inform him of the state of things there; that its causes, by reason of the blockade, were beyond our resources to prevent, but that we were unwilling that the breach of the cartel should entail such suffering; and to propose that the Federals might send as many medical officers to Andersonville and other prisons as they pleased, with such supplies, and funds, medicine, clothing, and whatever else would conduce to health and comfort, with power to organise their own methods of distribution, and without other restriction than a personal parole of honor not to convey information prejudicial to us, on condition that we, too, should be allowed to relieve the sufferings of our men in Northern prisons by sending medical officers with like powers, who should take cotton (the only exchange we possessed) to buy supplies necessary for our people; that this was immediately communicated early in August, 1864, to General Mulford, who was informed of the state of things at Andersonville; that he communicated this proposition to his immediate superiors, and had no answer for some two or three weeks, and when the answer came it was a simple refusal; that General Mulford promptly communicated this to Judge Ould, and he to Mr. Seddon; that immediately thereon Mr. Seddon directed Colonel Ould to return down the river (James), see General Mulford, and say that in three days from the time we were notified that transportation would be at Savannah to receive them, the Federals should have delivered them ten thousand of the sick from Andersonville, *whether we were allowed any equivalent in exchange for them or not*, as a mere measure of humanity; that this was promptly done; and General Mulford, as I was informed, would have stated that, so impressed was he with the enormous suffering, which it was the desire of our Government to spare, that not content with an official letter through the usual channels, he went in person to Washington, into the office of Secretary Stanton, told him the whole story, and urged prompt action, but got no reply. Nor was a reply vouchsafed to this offer until the latter part of December, 1864; meanwhile, some fifteen thousand men had died. If these be the facts, who is responsible?

My deliberate conviction at the time, and ever since, has been, that the authorities at Washington considered thirty thousand men just in the rear of General Johnston's army in Georgia, drawing their rations from the same stores from which his army had to be fed, would be better used up there than in the Federal ranks, in view of the fact that they could recruit their armies, while we had exhausted our material; that the refusal to exchange prisoners, and the denial of our offers in regard to the sick at Andersonville, was part of the plan of *attrition*. It will be remembered that the friends of Federal soldiers in prison at the South had become clamorous about the stoppage of exchanges. The Northern press had taken the matter up, and the authorities had been arraigned as responsible. I have never doubted that one collateral object of the Wirz trial was, by a perfectly unilateral trial (?), in which the prosecutor had everything his own way, to manufacture an answer to these just complaints. And I feel a conviction that the truth will one day be vindicated; that, having reference to relative resources, Federal prisoners were more humanely dealt with in Confederate hands than Confederate prisoners were in Federal hands. It was their interest, on a cold-blooded calculation, to stop exchanges when they did it; and as soon as it was their interest, they did it without scruple or mercy. The responsibility of the lives lost at Andersonville rests, since July, 1864, on General Meredith, Commissary-General of Prisoners, and (chiefly) on Edwin M. Stanton, Secretary of War. No one of sound head or heart would now hold the Northern people responsible for these things. The blood is on the skirts of their then rulers; and neither Mr. Garfield nor Mr. Blaine can change the record.

I never heard that there was any particular "suffering" at Libby or Belle Isle, and do not believe there was. Crowded prisons are not comfortable places, as our poor fellows found at Fort Delaware, Johnson's Island, &c.

I have at this late day no means of refreshing my memory in regard to the general orders on the subject of prison treatment; but this as a general fact I do know, that Mr. Davis's humanity was considered to be a stronger sentiment with him than public justice, and it was a common remark, that no soldier capitally convicted was ever executed if the President reviewed the record of his conviction. He was always slow to adopt the policy of retaliation for the barbarities inflicted by local commanders on the other side. The controversy between General Winder and Colonel Chandler was never brought to an investigation, for the reasons mentioned above. What the result of that investigation would have been, no one can now tell; but I will say in reference to this true old patriot and soldier—a genial man, whose zeal was sometimes ahead of his discretion—that if he was, at Andersonville, the fiend pretended by the "Bloody Shirt" shriekers, he had in his old age changed his nature very suddenly. I never saw any reason to consider Colonel Chandler's report wilfully injurious to General Winder, and supposed that it was the result of those misunderstandings which not unfrequently spring up between an inspecting officer and a post commander, when the former begins to find fault.

I have written hastily. In minor details, the lapse of twelve years may render my memory inaccurate; but of the general accuracy of the narrative I have given, as lying in my own knowledge or reported to me by those whose names I have mentioned, I vouch without hesitation.

Respectfully, yours truly,

R. G. H. Kean.

EXTRACT FROM A LETTER FROM SECRETARY SEDDON, OF MARCH 27, 1876.

"Unfortunately, during my imprisonment after the war, nearly all the papers and memoranda I had connected with the administration of the War Department were destroyed; and I have had so little satisfaction in dwelling upon the sad sacrifices and sufferings that attended and resulted from the futile though glorious efforts of our people in their lost cause, that I have sought rather to allow my memories of events to be dimmed or obliterated, than to brighten or cherish them. I have not a copy of any of my own reports, nor of that of Colonel Chandler, to which you specially refer, and have of that by no means a lively recollection. I do remember, however, generally, that it severely reflected on General Winder; and while it induced calls for explanation and defence from General Winder, it at the same time, from its terms, inspired an impression of controversy, and perhaps angry and incautious expressions between them, which warned to caution in receiving them as accurate representations of the facts. The Department was aware of the strict instructions which had been given, both verbally and by written orders, for the selection and preparation of the military prisons, especially that of Andersonville, with special view to the health and comfort of the prisoners, and for their humane treatment and supply on the same footing with our own troops, and could not hastily accept an account of such orders being wantonly disregarded by an old, regularly trained officer, rather noted as a rigid disciplinarian, or of cruel and unofficerlike treatment of prisoners on his part. The authorities, too, knew only too well the grave and growing deficiencies of all supplies, and the sad necessities the war was by its ruthless conduct imposing on all affected by its course. They also knew that unexpected events had forced the assemblage of a far greater number of prisoners than had been anticipated and provided for in the few safer points of confinement, before others had or could be provided for them, and we were daily looking and counting on a large number being removed by the liberal offer of some 10,000 of those suffering from sickness to be returned (without equivalent) to the Federals; and on the completion of new, safe prisons for the accommodation of others. The Department, under such circumstances, could not so hastily receive and act on the representations of this report, or condemn General Winder without investigation and response from him. His reports and explanations were of a very different character, and, as far as I now recollect, deemed exonerating. I cannot recall exactly the time or circumstances of his promotion as General, but certainly no advance was ever accorded under any conviction of inhumanity or undue severity to prisoners by him, much less as a support to him therein, or a reward for such conduct."

LETTER OF SECRETARY SEDDON TO W. S. WINDER.

SABOT HILL, *December* 29, 1875.

MR. W. S. WINDER, *Baltimore:*

Dear Sir:— Your letter reached me some two weeks since, and I have been prevented by serious indisposition from giving it an early reply.

I take pleasure in rendering my emphatic testimony to relieve the character and reputation of your father, the late General John H. Winder, from the unjust aspersions that have been cast upon them in connection with the treatment of the Federal prisoners under his charge during our late civil war.

I had, privately and officially, the fullest opportunity of

knowing his character, and judging his disposition and conduct towards the Federal prisoners: for those in Richmond, where he was almost daily in official communication with me, often in respect to them, had been some time under his command before. In large measure from the care and kindness he was believed to have shown to them, he was sent South to have the supervision and control of the large number there being aggregated.

His manner and mode of speech were perhaps naturally somewhat abrupt and sharp, and his military bearing may have added more of sternness and imperiousness; but these were mere superficial traits, perhaps, as I sometimes thought, assumed in a manner to disguise the real gentleness and kindness of his nature.

I thought him marked by real humanity towards the weak and helpless — such as women and children, for instance — by that spirit of protection and defence which distinguished the really gallant soldier.

To me he always expressed sympathy, and manifested a strong desire to provide for the wants and comforts of the prisoners under his charge. Very frequently, from the urgency of his claims in behalf of the prisoners while in Richmond, controversies would arise between him and the Commissary-General, which were submitted to me by them in person for my decision, and I was struck by his earnestness and zeal in claiming the fullest supplies the law of the Confederacy allowed or gave color or claim to. This law required prisoners to have the allowance provided for our own soldiers in the field, and constituted the guide to the settlement of such questions. Strict injunctions were invariably given from the Department for the observance of this law, both then and afterwards, in the South, and no departure was to be tolerated from it except under the direst straits of self-defence. Your father was ever resolved, as far as his authority allowed, to act upon and enforce the rule in behalf of the prisoners.

When sent South, I know he was most solicitous in regard to all arrangements for salubrity and convenience of location for the military prisons, and for all means that could facilitate the supplies and comforts of the prisoners, and promote their health and preservation. That afterwards great sufferings were endured by the prisoners in the South was among the saddest necessities of the war; but they were due, in a large measure, to the cessation of exchange, which forced the crowding of numbers, never contemplated, in the limited prison bounds which could be considered safe in the South, to the increasing danger of attack on such places, which made Southern authorities and commanders hostile to the establishment of additional prisons in convenient localities, and to the daily increasing straits and deficiencies of supplies of the Confederate Government, and not to the want of sympathy or humanity on the part of your father, or his most earnest efforts to obviate and relieve the inevitable evils that oppressed the unfortunate prisoners. I know their sad case, and his impotency to remedy it caused him keen anguish and distress.

Amid the passions and outraged feelings yet surviving our terrible struggle, it may be hard still to have justice awarded to the true merits and noble qualities of your father; but in future and happier times I doubt not all mists of error obscuring his name and fame will be swept away under the light of impartial investigation, and he will be honored and revered, as he ought to be, among the most faithful patriots and gallant soldiers of the Southern Confederacy.

Very truly yours,

JAMES A. SEDDON.

*** The letters succeeding the Report of Col. Moore have been taken from the Southern Historical Society's *Papers*, Vol. 1, No. 3.

LETTER OF GENERAL LEE TO GENERAL COMMANDING U. S. ARMY, AND COPY OF GENERAL ORDERS.

HEADQUARTERS ARMY OF THE CONFEDERATE STATES,
Near Richmond, Virginia, August 2, 1862.

To the General Commanding United States Army, Washington:

General — In obedience to the order of his Excellency, the President of the Confederate States, I have the honor to make to you the following communication:

On the 22d of July last a cartel for a general exchange of prisoners of war was signed by Major-General John A. Dix, on behalf of the United States, and by Major-General D. H. Hill, on the part of this Government. By the terms of that cartel it is stipulated that all prisoners of war hereafter taken shall be discharged on parole until exchanged.

Scarcely had the cartel been signed when the military authorities of the United States commenced a practice changing the character of the war from such as becomes civilised nations, into a campaign of indiscriminate robbery and murder.

A general order, issued by the Secretary of War of the United States, in the city of Washington, on the very day that the cartel was signed in Virginia, directs the military commander of the United States to take the property of our people, for the convenience and use of the army, without compensation.

A general order, issued by Major-General Pope, on the 23d of July last, the day after the date of the cartel, directs the murder of our peaceful citizens as spies, if found quietly tilling their farms in his rear, *even outside of his lines.*

And one of his Brigadier-Generals, Steinwehr, has seized innocent and peaceful inhabitants to be held as hostages, to the end that they may be murdered in cold blood if any of his soldiers are killed by some unknown persons, whom he designated as "bushwhackers."

Some of the military authorities of the United States seem to suppose that their end will be better attained by a savage war, in which no quarter is to be given, and no age or sex to be spared, than by such hostilities as are alone recognised to be lawful in modern times. We find ourselves driven by our enemies, by steady progress, towards a practice which we abhor, and which we are vainly struggling to avoid.

Under these circumstances this Government has issued the accompanying general order, which I am directed by the President to transmit to you, recognising Major-General Pope and his commissioned officers to be in a position which they have chosen for themselves — that of robbers and murderers, and not that of public enemies, entitled, if captured, to be treated as prisoners of war.

The President also instructs me to inform you that we renounce our right of retaliation on the innocent, and will continue to treat the private enlisted soldiers of General Pope's army as prisoners of war; but if, after notice to your Government that we confine repressive measures to the punishment of commissioned officers, who are willing participants in these crimes, the savage practices threatened in the orders alluded to, be persisted in, we shall reluctantly be forced to the last resort of accepting the war on the terms chosen by our enemies, until the voice of an outraged humanity shall compel a respect for the recognised usages of war.

While the President considers that the facts referred to would justify a refusal on our part to execute the cartel, by which we have agreed to liberate an excess of prisoners of war in our hands, a sacred regard for plighted faith, which shrinks from the semblance of breaking a promise, precludes a resort to such an extremity. Nor is it his desire to extend to any other forces of the United States the punishment merited by General Pope and such commissioned officers as choose to participate in the execution of his infamous orders.

I have the honor to be, very respectfully, your obedient servant,

R. E. LEE, *General Commanding.*

ADJUTANT AND INSPECTOR-GENERAL'S OFFICE,
Richmond, August 1, 1862.

General Orders, No. 54.

I. The following orders are published for the information and observance of all concerned:

II. Whereas, by a general order, dated the 22d July, 1862, issued by the Secretary of War of the United States, under the order of the President of the United States, the military commanders of that Government within the States of Virginia, South Carolina, Georgia, Florida, Alabama, Mississippi, Louisiana, Texas and Arkansas, are directed to seize and use any property, real or personal, belonging to the inhabitants of this Confederacy, which may be necessary or convenient for their several commands, and no provision is made for any compensation to the owners of private property thus seized and appropriated by the military commanders of the enemy:

III. And whereas, by General Order, No. 11, issued on the 23d July, 1862, by Major-General Pope, commanding the forces of the enemy in Northern Virginia, it is ordered that all "commanders of army corps, divisions, brigades and detached commands, will proceed immediately to arrest all disloyal male citizens within their lines or within their reach, in rear of their respective commands. Such as are willing to take the oath of allegiance to the United States, and will furnish sufficient security for its observance, shall be permitted to remain at their homes and pursue in good faith their accustomed avocations. Those who refuse shall be conducted South, beyond the extreme pickets of this army, and be notified that if found again anywhere within our lines, or at any point in rear, they will be considered spies, and subjected to the extreme rigor of military law. If any person, having taken the oath of allegiance, as above specified, be found to have violated it, he shall be shot, and his property seized and applied to the public use":

IV. And whereas, by an order issued on the 13th July, 1862,

by Brigadier-General A. Steinwehr, Major William Steadman, a cavalry officer of his brigade, has been ordered to arrest five of the most prominent citizens of Page county, Virginia, to be held as hostages, and to suffer death in the event of any of the soldiers of said Steinwehr being shot by "bushwhackers," by which term are meant the citizens of this Confederacy who have taken up arms to defend their homes and families:

V. And whereas it results from the above orders that some of the military authorities of the United States, not content with the unjust and aggressive warfare hitherto waged with savage cruelty against an unoffending people, and exasperated by the failure of their effort to subjugate them, have now determined to violate all the rules and usages of war, and to convert the hostilities hitherto waged against armed forces into a campaign of robbery and murder against unarmed citizens and peaceful tillers of the soil:

VI. And whereas this Government, bound by the highest obligations of duty to its citizens, is thus driven to the necessity of adopting just such measures of retribution and retaliation as shall seem adequate to repress and punish these barbarities; and whereas the orders above recited have only been published and made known to this Government since the signature of a cartel for exchange of prisoners of war, which cartel, in so far as it provides for an exchange of prisoners hereafter captured, would never have been signed or agreed to by this Government if the intention to change the war into a system of indiscriminate murder and robbery had been known to it; and whereas a just regard to humanity forbids that the repression of crime which this Government is thus compelled to enforce should be unnecessarily extended to retaliation on the enlisted men in the army of the United States, who may be the unwilling instruments of the savage cruelty of their commanders, so long as there is hope that the excesses of the enemy may be checked or prevented by retribution on the commissioned officers, who have the power to avoid guilty action, by refusing service under a Government which seeks their aid in the perpetration of such infamous barbarities.

VII. Therefore, it is ordered that Major-general Pope, Brigadier-general Steinwehr, and all commissioned officers serving under their respective commands, be and they are hereby expressly and specially declared to be not entitled to be considered as soldiers, and therefore not entitled to the benefit of the cartel for the parole of future prisoners of war. Ordered, further, that in the event of the capture of

Major-general Pope or Brigadier-general Steinwehr, or of any commissioned officer serving under them, the captive so taken shall be held in close confinement so long as the orders aforesaid shall continue in force and unrepealed by the competent military authorities of the United States; and that in the event of the murder of any unarmed citizen or inhabitant of this Confederacy, by virtue or under pretext of any of the orders hereinbefore recited, whether with or without trial, whether under pretence of such citizen being a spy or hostage, or any other pretence, it shall be the duty of the Commanding General of the forces of this Confederacy to cause immediately to be hung, out of the commissioned officers, prisoners as aforesaid, a number equal to the number of our own citizens thus murdered by the enemy.

By order. S. COOPER,
Adjutant and Inspector General.

DESPATCH FROM GEN. GRANT TO GEN. BUTLER.

CITY POINT, *August* 18*th*, 1864.

"*To General Butler:*—I am satisfied that the chief object of your interview, besides having the proper sanction, meets with my entire approval. I have seen, from Southern papers, that a system of retaliation is going on in the South, which they keep from us, and which we should stop in some way. On the subject of exchange, however, I differ from General Hitchcock; it is hard on our men held in Southern prisons not to exchange them, but it is humanity to those left in the ranks to fight our battles. Every man released on parole, or otherwise, becomes an active soldier against us at once, either directly or indirectly. If we commence a system of exchange which liberates all prisoners taken, we will have to fight on until the whole South is exterminated. If we hold those caught, they amount to no more than dead men. At this particular time, to release all Rebel prisoners North would insure Sherman's defeat, and would compromise our safety here.

"U. S. GRANT, *Lieutenant-general.*"

TESTIMONY OF GEN. GRANT BEFORE THE COMMITTEE ON THE CONDUCT OF THE WAR, FEBRUARY 11, 1865.

Question. It has been said that we refused to exchange prisoners because we found ours starved, diseased, unserviceable when we received them, and did not like to exchange sound men for such men ?

Answer. There never has been any such reason as that. That has been a reason for making exchanges. *I will confess that if our men who are prisoners in the South were really well taken care of, suffering nothing except a little privation of liberty, then, in a military point of view, it would not be good policy for us to exchange, because every man they get back is forced right into the army at once, while that is not the case with our prisoners when we receive them.* In fact, the half of our returned prisoners will never go into the army again, and none of them will until after they have had a furlough of thirty or sixty days. Still, the fact of their suffering as they do is a reason for making this exchange as rapidly as possible.

Question. And never has been a reason for not making the exchange?

Answer. It never has. Exchanges having been suspended by reason of disagreements on the part of agents of exchange on both sides before I came in command of the armies of the United States, and it then being near the opening of the spring campaign, *I did not deem it advisable or just to the men who had to fight our battles, to reinforce the enemy with thirty or forty thousand disciplined troops at that time.* An immediate resumption of exchanges would have had that effect without giving us corresponding benefits. The suffering said to exist among our prisoners South was a powerful argument against the course pursued, and I so felt it.

LETTER OF CHIEF JUSTICE SHEA TO THE NEW YORK TRIBUNE.

The New York *Tribune* of the 24th January, 1876, publishes the following letter from Judge Shea, which was called forth by Mr. Blaine's accusations on the floor of the House of Representatives. The *Tribune* introduces the letter, with the following additional comments :

Chief Justice George Shea, of the Marine Court, who sends us an interesting letter about Jefferson Davis, was, as is well known, the principal agent in securing the signatures of Mr. Greeley, Gerrit Smith, and others to Mr. Davis's bail bond. The essential point of his present statement is, that Mr. Greeley and the other gentlemen whom he approached on that subject were unwilling to move in the matter until entirely satisfied as to Mr. Davis's freedom from the guilt of intentional cruelty to Northern prisoners at Andersonville; that Judge Shea at the instance of Mr. Greeley and Vice-President Wilson, went to Canada to inspect the journals of the secret sessions of the Confederate Senate—documents which up to this time have never passed into the hands of our Government, or been accessible to Northern readers; that from these secret records, including numerous messages from Davis on the subject, it conclusively appeared that the Rebel Senate believed the Southern prisoners were mistreated at the North; that they were eager for retaliation, and that Davis strenuously and to the end resisted these efforts; and that he attempted to send Vice-President Stephens North to consult with President Lincoln on the subject. No more important statements than these concerning that phase of the civil war have been given to the public. They shed light upon the course of Mr. Greeley and other eminent citizens of the North; and it seems to us clear that, on many accounts, the Rebel authorities owe it to themselves and to history to give to the public the documents which Judge Shea was permitted to see. It is not likely that they will have any material effect upon the fate of Mr. Davis, or upon political questions now pending. But they are of vital consequence to any correct history of the rebellion, and their revelations, if sustaining throughout the portions submitted to Judge Shea, might do as much to promote as the late Andersonville debate did to retard the reconciliation of the sections.

To the Editor of the Tribune:

SIR—I apprehend no one will accuse me with having ever harbored disunion proclivities, or of any inclination toward secession heresies. But truth is truth, justice is justice, and an act of proposed magnanimity should not be impaired by both an untruth and an injustice. The statement in the House of Representatives on Thursday last, made by General Banks, during the debate on the proposed amnesty bill, was more entirely correct than, perhaps, he had reason to credit.

What I now relate are facts: Mr. Horace Greeley received a letter dated June 22d, 1865, from Mrs. Jefferson Davis. It was written at Savannah, Georgia, where Mrs. Davis and her family were then detained under a sort of military restraint. Mr. Davis himself, recently taken prisoner, was at Fortress Monroe; and the most conspicuous special charge threatened against him by the "Bureau of Military Justice" was of guilty knowledge relating to the assassination of President Lincoln. The principal purpose of the letter was imploring Mr. Greeley to bring about a speedy trial of her husband upon that charge, and upon all other supposed cruelties that were inferred against him. A public trial was prayed, that the accusations might be as publicly met, and her husband, as she insisted

31

could be done, readily vindicated. To this letter Mr. Greeley at once forwarded an answer for Mrs. Davis, directed to the care of General Burge, commanding our military forces at Savannah. The morning of the next day Mr. Greeley came to my residence in this city, placed the letter from Mrs. Davis in my hand, saying that he could not believe the charge to be true; that aside from the enormity and want of object, it would have been impolitic in Mr. Davis, or any other leader in the Southern States, as they could not but be aware of Mr. Lincoln's naturally kind heart and his good intentions toward them all; and Mr. Greeley asked me to become professionally interested in behalf of Mr. Davis. I called to Mr. Greeley's attention that, although I was like-minded with himself as to this one view of the case, yet there was the other pending charge of cruel treatment of our Union soldiers while prisoners at Andersonville and other places, and that, unless our Government was willing to have it imputed that Wirz was convicted and his sentence of death inflicted unjustly, it could not now overlook the superior who was, at least popularly, regarded as the moving cause of those wrongs; and that if Mr. Davis had been guilty of such breach of the rules for the conduct of war in modern civilisation, he was not entitled to the right of, nor to be manumitted as a mere prisoner of war. I expressed the thought that my services before a military tribunal would be of little benefit. I hesitated; but finally told Mr. Greeley that I would consult with some of our common friends, whose countenance would give strength to such an undertaking, if it was discovered to be right, and that none but Republicans, and some of the radical kind, were likely to be of positive aid; indeed, any other would have been injurious. It occurred to me, from recollecting conversations with Mr. Henry Wilson, the previous April, while we were together at Hilton Head, South Carolina, that if Mr. Davis were guiltless of this latter offence, an avenue might be opened for a speedy trial, or for his manumission as any other prisoner of war. I did consult with such friends, and Mr. Henry Wilson, Governor John A. Andrew, Mr. Thaddeus Stevens, and Mr. Gerrit Smith were among them. The result was that I thereupon undertook to do whatever became feasible. Although not in strictness required to elucidate our present intent, it is, nevertheless, becoming the history of the case simply to mention that Mr. Charles O'Conor was, from the first, esteemed the most valuable man to lead for the defence by Mr. Greeley and Mr. Gerrit Smith. A Democrat of pronounced repute, still his appearance would impart no partisan aspect to the great argument, and would excite no feelings but those of admiration and respect among even extreme men of opposite opinion. Public expectation looked to him, and soon after it was made known that he had already volunteered his services to Mr. Davis. Mr. O'Conor's course during the war was decided, understood, and consistent, but never offensive nor intrusive; his personal honor without reproach; his courage without fear; his learning, erudition, propriety of professional judgment conceded as most eminent.

There was a general agreement among the gentlemen of the Republican party whom I have mentioned that Mr. Davis did not, by thought or act, participate in a conspiracy against Mr. Lincoln; and none of those expressed that conviction more emphatically than Mr. Thaddeus Stevens. The single subject on which light was desired by them was concerning the treatment of our soldiers while in the hands of the enemy. The *Tribune* of May 17th, 1865, tells the real condition of feeling at that moment, and unequivocally shows that it was not favorable to Mr. Davis on this matter. At the instance of Mr. Greeley, Mr. Wilson and, as I was given to understand, of Mr. Stevens, I went to Canada the first week in January, 1866, taking Boston on my route, there to consult with Governor Andrew and others. While at Montreal, General John C. Breckinridge came from Toronto, at my request, for the purpose of giving me information. There I had placed in my possession the official archives of the Government of the Confederate States, which I read and considered — especially all those messages and other acts of the Executive with the Senate in its secret sessions concerning the care and exchange of prisoners. I found that the supposed inhuman and unwarlike treatment of their own captured soldiers by agents of our Government was a most prominent and frequent topic. That those reports current then — perhaps even to this hour — in the South were substantially incorrect is little to the practical purpose. From those documents — not made to meet the public eye, but used in secret session, and from inquiries by me of those thoroughly conversant with the state of Southern opinion at the time — it was manifest that the people of the South believed those reports to be trustworthy, and they individually, and through their representatives at Richmond, pressed upon Mr. Davis, as the Executive and as the Commander-in-Chief of the army and navy, instant recourse to active measures of retaliation, to the end that the supposed cruelties might be stayed. Mr. Davis's conduct under such urgency and, indeed, expostulation, was a circumstance all-important in determining the probability of this charge as to himself. It was equally and decisively manifest, by the same sources of information, that Mr. Davis steadily and unflinchingly set himself in opposition to the indulgence of such demands, and declined to resort to any measure of violent retaliation. It impaired his personal influence, and brought much censure upon him from many in the South, who sincerely believed the reports spread among the people to be really true. The desire that something should be attempted from which a better care of prisoners could be secured seems to have grown so strong and prevalent that, on July 2d, 1863, Mr. Davis accepted the proffered service of Mr. Alexander H. Stephens, the Vice-President, to proceed as a military commissioner to Washington. The sole purpose of Mr. Davis in allowing that commission appears, from the said documents, which I read, to have been to place the war on the footing of such as are waged by civilised people in modern times, and to divest it of a savage character, which, it was claimed, had been impressed on it in spite of all effort and protest; and alleged instances of such savage conduct were named and averred. This project was prevented, as Mr. Stephens was denied permission by our Administration to approach Washington, and intercourse with him prohibited. On his return, after this rejected effort to produce a mutual kindness in the treatment of prisoners, Southern feeling became more unquiet on the matter than ever; yet it clearly appears that Mr. Davis would not yield to the demand for retaliation.

The evidence tending to show this to be the true condition of the case as to Mr. Davis himself was brought by me and submitted to Mr. Greeley, and in part to Mr. Wilson. The result was, these gentlemen, and those others in sympathy with them, changed their former suspicion to a favorable opinion and a friendly disposition. They were from this time kept informed of each movement as made to liberate Mr. Davis, or to compel the Government to bring the prisoner to trial. All this took place before counsel, indeed before any one acting on his behalf, was allowed to communicate with or see him.

The *Tribune* now, at once, began a series of leading editorials demanding that our Government proceed with the trial; and on January 16, 1866, incited by those editorials, Senator Howard, of Michigan, offered a joint resolution, aided by Mr. Sumner, "recommending the trial of Jefferson Davis and Clement C. Clay before a military tribunal or court-martial, for charges mentioned in the report of the Secretary of War, of March 4, 1866." It will be interesting to mention now that if a trial proceeded in this manner, I was then creditably informed, Mr. Thaddeus Stevens had volunteered as counsel for Mr. Clay.

After it had become evident that there was no immediate prospect of any trial, if any prospect at all, the counsel for Mr. Davis became anxious that their client be liberated on bail, and one of them consulted with Mr. Greeley as to the feasibility of procuring some names as bondsmen of persons who had conspicuously opposed the war of secession. This was found quite easy; and Mr. Gerrit Smith and Commodore Vanderbilt were selected, and Mr. Greeley, in case his name should be found necessary. All this could not have been accomplished had not those gentlemen, and others in sympathy with them, been already convinced that those charges against Mr. Davis were unfounded in fact. So an application was made on June 11, 1866, to Mr. Justice Underwood, at Alexandria, Virginia, for a writ of *habeas corpus*, which, after argument, was denied, upon the ground that "Jefferson Davis was arrested under a proclamation of the President charging him with complicity in the assassination of the late President Lincoln. He has been held," says the decision, "ever since, and is now held, as a military prisoner." The Washington *Chronicle* of that date insisted that "the case is one well entitled to a trial before a military tribunal; the testimony before the Judiciary Committee of the House, all of it bearing directly, *if not conclusively*, on a certain intention to take the life of Mr. Lincoln, is a most important element in the case." This was reported as from the pen of Mr. John W. Forney, then clerk of the Senate, and is cited by me as an expression of a general tone of the press on that occasion. Then, the House of Representatives, on the motion of Mr. Boutwell, of Massachusetts, the following day passed a resolution "that it was the opinion of the House that Jefferson Davis should be held in custody as a prisoner and subject to trial according to the laws of the land." It was adopted by a vote of 105 to 19.

It is very suggestive to reflect just here that, in the intermediate time, Mr. Clement C. Clay had been discharged from imprisonment without being brought to trial on either of these charges, upon which he had been arrested, and for which arrest the $100,000 reward had been paid.

This failure to liberate Mr. Davis would have been very discouraging to most of men; but Mr. Greeley, and those friends who were acting with him, determined to meet the issue made, promptly and sharply, and to push the Government to a trial of its prisoner, or to withdraw the charge made by its board of military justice. The point was soon sent home, and was felt. Mr. Greeley hastened back to New York, and the *Tribune* of June 12, 1866, contained, in a leader from his pen, this unmistakable demand and protest:

"How and when did Davis become a prisoner of war? He was not arrested as a public enemy, but as a felon, officially charged, in the face of the civilised world, with the foulest, most execrable guilt—that of having suborned assassins to murder President Lincoln—a crime the basest and most cowardly known to mankind. It was for this that $100,000 was offered and paid for his arrest. And the proclamation of Andrew Johnson and William H. Seward offering this reward says his complicity with Wilkes Booth & Co. is established 'by evidence now in the Bureau of Military Justice.' So there was no need of time to hunt it up.

"It has been asserted that Davis is responsible for the death by exposure and famine of our captured soldiers; and his official position gives plausibility to the charge. Yet while Henry Wirz—a miserable wretch—a mere tool of tools—was long ago arraigned, tried, convicted, sentenced, and hanged for this crime—no charge has been officially preferred against Davis. So we presume none is to be."

The *Tribune* kept up repeating this demand during the following part of that year, and admonished the Government of the increasing absurdity of its position, not daring, seemingly, to prosecute a great criminal against whom it had officially declared it was possessed of evidence to prove that crime. On November 9th, 1866, the *Tribune* again thus emphasised this thought:

"Eighteen months have nearly elapsed since Jefferson Davis was made a State prisoner. He had previously been publicly charged by the President of the United States with conspiring to assassinate President Lincoln, and $100,000 offered for his capture thereupon. The capture was promptly made and the money duly paid; yet, up to this hour, there has not been even an attempt made by the Government to procure an indictment on that charge. He has also been popularly, if not officially, accused of complicity in the virtual murder of Union soldiers while prisoners of war, by subjecting them to needless, inhuman exposure, privation and abuse; but no official attempt has been made to indict him on that charge. . . . A great government may deal sternly with offenders, but not meanly; it cannot afford to seem unwilling to repair an obvious wrong."

The Government, however, continued to express its inability to proceed with the trial. Another year had passed since the capture of Mr. Davis, and now another attempt to liberate him by bail was to be made. The Government, by its conduct, having tacitly abandoned those special charges of inhumanity, a petition for a writ was to be presented, by which the prisoner might be handed over to the civil authority to answer the indictment for treason. In aid of this project, Mr. Wilson, chairman of the Committee of Military Affairs, offered in the Senate, on the 18th of March, 1867, a resolution urging the Government to proceed with the trial. The remarkable thoughts and language of that resolution were observed at the time, and necessarily caused people to infer that Mr. Wilson, at least, was not under the too common delusion that the Government really had a case on either of those two particular charges against Mr. Davis individually; and a short time after this Mr. Wilson went to Fortress Monroe and saw Mr. Davis. The visit was simply friendly, and not for any purpose relating to his liberation.

On May 14th, 1867, Mr. Davis was delivered to the civil authority; was at once admitted to bail, Mr. Greeley and Mr. Gerrit Smith going personally to Richmond, in attestation of their belief that wrong had been done to Mr. Davis in holding him so long accused upon those charges, now abandoned, and as an expression of magnanimity toward the South. Commodore Vanderbilt, then but recently the recipient of the thanks of Congress for his superb aid to the Government during the war, was also represented there, and signed the bond through Mr. Horace F. Clark, his son-in-law, and Mr. Augustus Schell, his friend.

The apparent unwillingness of the Government to prosecute, under every incentive of pride and honor to the contrary, was accepted by those gentlemen and the others whom I have mentioned as a confirmation of the information given to me at Montreal, and of its entire accuracy.

These men—Andrew, Greeley, Smith and Wilson—have each passed from this life. The history of their efforts to bring all parts of our common country once more and abidingly into unity, peace, and concord, and of Mr. Greeley's enormous sacrifice to compel justice to be done to one man, and he an enemy, should be written.

I will add a single incident tending the same way. In a consultation with Mr. Thaddeus Stevens, at his residence on Capitol Hill, at Washington, in May, 1866, he related to me how the chief of this "Military Bureau" showed him "the evidence" upon which the proclamation was issued charging Davis and Clay with complicity in the assassination of Mr. Lincoln. He said that he refused to give the thing any support, and that he told that gentleman the evidence was insufficient in itself, and incredible. I am not likely ever to forget the earnest manner in which Mr. Stevens then said to me: "Those men are no friends of mine. They are public enemies; and I would treat the South as a conquered country and settle it politically upon the policy best suited for ourselves. But I know these men, sir. They are gentlemen, and incapable of being assassins."

Yours, faithfully, GEORGE SHEA.

NO. 205 WEST 46TH STREET, NEW YORK, January 15, 1876.